TRANSFORMATIONS IN CRIMINAL JURISDICTION

The digital era presents fundamental challenges for the application and enforcement of state criminal laws. Questions of jurisdiction are becoming increasingly important to the investigation, prosecution, and punishment of crime, as with the growth of technology and the internet many crimes no longer take place within neat national boundaries.

This is unfamiliar ground for criminal practitioners, and it begs the question of whether traditional approaches to criminal jurisdiction can adapt to the new global reality. In this innovative book, leading experts in criminal, international and internet law unite to address this fundamental question. They consider how jurisdictional regimes are orientated around concepts of territoriality and extraterritoriality, how these categories are increasingly blurred in the digital era, and how a range of jurisdictional transformations are occurring in the process.

Part I presents novel doctrinal, empirical and theoretical perspectives on criminal jurisdiction, exploring how states are shaping and reimagining jurisdictional concepts in the crafting and interpretation of criminal offences, and the ramifications of increasing jurisdictional concurrency in state practice. Part II focuses on the investigative and enforcement powers of the state to assess how these issues are transforming traditional understandings of jurisdictional rules and boundaries, the challenges and opportunities that these present for law enforcement authorities, and the sorts of constraints and safeguards that may be necessary as a result. The picture that emerges is a world of jurisdictional rules in a state of flux, which demands the diversity of legal perspectives presented in this book for documenting, rationalising and moving beyond the transformations that are taking shape in modern statecraft.

Transformations in Criminal Jurisdiction

Extraterritoriality and Enforcement

Edited by
Micheál Ó Floinn
Lindsay Farmer
Julia Hörnle
and
David Ormerod CBE, KC

• HART •
OXFORD • LONDON • NEW YORK • NEW DELHI • SYDNEY

HART PUBLISHING
Bloomsbury Publishing Plc
Kemp House, Chawley Park, Cumnor Hill, Oxford, OX2 9PH, UK
1385 Broadway, New York, NY 10018, USA
29 Earlsfort Terrace, Dublin 2, Ireland

First published in Great Britain 2023

A catalogue record for this book is available from the British Library.

Library of Congress Cataloging-in-Publication data

Names: W.G. Hart Workshop (2021 : Online) | Floinn, Micheál Ó, editor. | Farmer, Lindsay, 1963- editor. | Hörnle, Julia, 1970- editor. | Ormerod, David, 1966- editor.

Title: Transformations in criminal jurisdiction : extraterritoriality and enforcement / edited by Micheál Ó Floinn, Lindsay Farmer, Julia Hörnle and David Ormerod CBE, KC.

Description: Oxford ; New York : Hart, 2023. | "The essays in this book are the result of papers delivered at the WG Hart Workshop 2021, which was held in April 2021 as an online event"—ECIP acknowledgements. | Includes bibliographical references and index. | Summary: "The digital era presents fundamental challenges for the application and enforcement of state criminal laws. Questions of jurisdiction are becoming increasingly important to the investigation, prosecution, and punishment of crime, as with the growth of technology and the internet many crimes no longer take place within neat national boundaries. This is unfamiliar ground for criminal practitioners, and it begs the question of whether traditional approaches to criminal jurisdiction can adapt to the new global reality. In this innovative book, leading experts in criminal, international and internet law unite to address this fundamental question. They consider how jurisdictional regimes are orientated around concepts of territoriality and extraterritoriality, how these categories are increasingly blurred in the digital era, and how a range of jurisdictional transformations are occurring in the process. Part I presents novel doctrinal, empirical and theoretical perspectives on criminal jurisdiction, exploring how states are shaping and reimagining jurisdictional concepts in the crafting and interpretation of criminal offences, and the ramifications of increasing jurisdictional concurrency in state practice. Part II focuses on the investigative and enforcement powers of the state to assess how these issues are transforming traditional understandings of jurisdictional rules and boundaries, the challenges and opportunities that these present for law enforcement authorities, and the sorts of constraints and safeguards that may be necessary as a result. The picture that emerges is a world of jurisdictional rules in a state of flux, which demands the diversity of legal perspectives presented in this book for documenting, rationalising and moving beyond the transformations that are taking shape in modern statecraft."—Provided by publisher.

Identifiers: LCCN 2023010856 | ISBN 9781509954223 (hardback) | ISBN 9781509954261 (paperback) | ISBN 9781509954247 (pdf) | ISBN 9781509954230 (Epub)

Subjects: LCSH: Criminal jurisdiction—Congresses. | Jurisdiction (International law)—Congresses.

Classification: LCC K5036.A6 W44 2021 | DDC 345/.0122—dc23/eng/20230517

LC record available at https://lccn.loc.gov/2023010856

ISBN: HB: 978-1-50995-422-3
ePDF: 978-1-50995-424-7
ePub: 978-1-50995-423-0

Typeset by Compuscript Ltd, Shannon

PREFACE

The papers published in this important and timely volume were first delivered in April 2021 at a WG Hart Workshop organised under the auspices of the Institute of Advanced Legal Studies. It had originally been intended to hold the workshop in London but, in the event, the pandemic necessitated that it be held online. I was privileged to be invited to welcome the speakers on that occasion. The Workshop addressed, at both a theoretical and a practical level, many profound problems concerning prescriptive jurisdiction and enforcement jurisdiction in the criminal law. It is particularly pleasing that many of the distinguished contributions to the Workshop are now available in a permanent form to a wider audience.

Approaching the subject from the angle of international law, I have long had an interest in the ambit of national criminal laws and the scope of national criminal jurisdiction. From my early days as a lawyer, I was intrigued by the problems thrown up by cross-border crimes – by situations in which people shot at each other across frontiers or blackmailed each other or tried to defraud each other across international boundaries. There were questions about the extent of the realm and the ambit of criminal law (*R v Keyn* (1876) 2 Exch Div 63), the low water mark, the Territorial Waters Jurisdiction Act 1878, closing lines of bays and estuaries, pirate radio stations, offences committed on board British registered vessels on the high seas or in foreign ports, and offences on board foreign registered vessels in ports in the UK affecting the peace and good order of the port. Quite early on in practice, I came across *R v Martin* [1956] 2 QB 272, a decision of Devlin J in 1956, in which the defendants had been charged with possession of opium on board a British-registered aircraft flying from Bahrain to Singapore. Although there was jurisdiction under the Civil Aviation Act 1949 over offences on board a British aircraft, the ambit of the substantive offences with which they were charged did not extend to the location in which the conduct took place. More recently, technological advances have thrown up more and more novel possible locations for the commission of crime, for example on or within 500 metres of an oil platform in a designated area of the UK continental shelf (Criminal Jurisdiction (Offshore Activities) Order 1987; Petroleum Act 1998, section 10) or on board the Eurostar as it crosses the midpoint of the Channel Tunnel (Channel Tunnel Act 1987, section 10).

The fascination of such situations is readily understandable, even if some of the examples might seem a bit quaint. But there is nothing quaint about the grave threat posed by international criminal activities on an increasingly broad plane. Drug trafficking, money laundering, online fraud, people trafficking and terrorism, among other fields of criminal endeavour, present very real challenges to vital national and international interests. Nor is there anything quaint about piracy, which has seen a resurgence in modern times and has become a scourge of shipping in many parts of the world, including the shipping lanes off East Africa. Nations and their populations need the effective protection of the criminal law against international crime more than ever.

In particular, the invention of the Internet and the World Wide Web has opened a new dimension for criminal activities, and cyberspace is a new frontier posing wholly new challenges for regulation by the criminal law. Crimes could be said to be committed everywhere or nowhere – in the ether. It may be entirely fortuitous where a server is located. It may be impossible to fix with any confidence the precise geographical location of an offence or an element of an offence, and the relevance of its location may be greatly diminished. The effective investigation and prosecution of international criminal activities have never faced greater challenges.

In this jurisdiction – England and Wales – attempts have been made to keep abreast of these developments. Notably, an earlier approach adopted in judicial decisions whereby a crime was regarded as committed only where it was completed (*Harden* [1963] 1 QB 8; *DPP v Stonehouse* [1978] AC 55) – a terminatory approach to jurisdiction – has fallen out of favour. This was clearly inadequate to meet the changing situation. In particular, it meant that many cases where the conduct had a strong connection with this jurisdiction could not be tried here. It has been superseded by a more inclusive approach which accepts that a crime may be regarded as committed within the jurisdiction if a substantial part of the offence was committed in England and Wales (*Smith (Wallace Duncan) (No 4)* [2004] QB 1418; *R (Purdy) v DPP* [2010] 1 AC 345). In a parallel development, the Criminal Justice Act 1993 introduced special rules in respect of designated offences – principally theft, blackmail, handling, fraud and forgery – and made separate provision for inchoate offences. This is not a straightforward matter (see, eg *Pogmore* [2017] EWCA Crim 925). To determine the appropriateness of any extensions in the ambit of a state's criminal law and the jurisdiction of its courts will require consideration of factors such as the nature of the offence and the interests which are sought to be protected.

One important development in recent decades has been the acknowledgement by international law that some criminal activities are so heinous or present such a threat to all nations that they require co-ordination of national criminal law and jurisdiction by agreement. Thus, for example, the UN Convention against Torture provides that each state party shall ensure that all acts of torture as defined in the Convention are offences under its criminal law (Article 4), and shall establish its jurisdiction over such offences in widely defined circumstances, including where the alleged offender is present in any territory under its jurisdiction and it does not extradite him to another state (Article 5). Further, a state party in whose territory an alleged offender is found is required either to extradite him or to submit the case to its authorities for the purpose of prosecution (Article 7). A similar approach is adopted by the Hague Convention for Suppression of Unlawful Seizure of Aircraft (Articles 4 and 7). Widespread participation in such conventions has led to the creation of what comes close to a consensual universal jurisdiction in specific fields. These are areas where a consistency of purpose, embodied in international agreements, has resulted in a near-uniform approach to certain of the most serious offences, although these new conventional regimes are not without their difficulties. That was apparent when the Appellate Committee of the House of Lords considered the UN Convention against Torture in the *Pinochet* litigation (*R v Bow Street Metropolitan Stipendiary Magistrate ex parte Pinochet Ugarte (No 3)* [2000] 1 AC 147) and, once again, in 2019, when the Supreme Court considered the scope of the offence of torture in international law in the context of the civil war in Liberia in *Reeves-Taylor* [2019] UKSC 51, [2019] 3 WLR 1073.

In the case of other criminal activities – those not subject to such international agreements – other difficulties are apparent. There are undoubtedly limitations and restrictions imposed by international law on the conduct of states in proscribing, investigating and prosecuting crimes with an extraterritorial element. It is a characteristic of the criminal law and of criminal jurisdiction that they can give rise to intense controversy between states as to their proper limits. In particular, views may differ profoundly from state to state as to what standards should be applied and by whom. The problem here is that international law has never developed clear rules as to the limits of national criminal jurisdiction. Undoubtedly, some limits are set by the principle of the sovereignty and independence of states. Legislation of one state requiring conduct in a foreign state could be in breach of the laws of that foreign state, or otherwise inconsistent with its sovereign right to regulate activities within its own territory, in violation of principles of international law. But short of such extreme situations lies a grey area of uncertainty. For example, in *Serious Organised Crime Agency v Perry* [2013] 1 AC 182, the issue was whether section 357 of the Proceeds of Crime Act 2002 authorised the imposition of a disclosure order on foreign persons out of the jurisdiction. So, the case was concerned with the exercise of investigatory powers in criminal cases as opposed to curial jurisdiction over crime. The Supreme Court concluded that the legislation did not authorise the making of an order against persons out of the jurisdiction. Lord Phillips observed:

> Subject to limited exceptions, it is contrary to international law for country A to purport to make criminal conduct in country B committed by persons who are not citizens of country A. Section 357 … does not simply make proscribed conduct a criminal offence. It confers on a United Kingdom public authority the power to impose on persons positive obligations to provide information subject to criminal sanction in the event of non-compliance. To confer such authority in respect of persons outside the jurisdiction would be a particularly startling breach of international law. (paragraph 94)

More recently, in another case before the Supreme Court, *R (KBR, Inc) v Director of the Serious Fraud Office* [2021] UKSC 2, it was submitted by counsel for the appellant, KBR Inc, that this reference to a breach of international law should be read as referring, rather, to a breach of comity in the sense of a non-binding usage (paragraph 51).

Comity between states is a concept which has been much criticised – although perhaps mainly when used as a claimed basis for declining jurisdiction in civil cases. However, it may have an important role to play when seeking to delimit the appropriate scope of application of national systems of criminal law. That role is all the more important because of the lack of clear, binding rules of customary international law. The Supreme Court touched on this in its judgment in *KBR*, where it cited Judge James Crawford's explanation of comity as something less than a rule of international law whereby certain usages are carried on out of courtesy and are not articulated or claimed as legal requirements. It is a species of accommodation involving neighbourliness, mutual respect and the friendly waiver of technicalities. As a concept it is far from a binding norm, but it is more than mere courtesy exercised between state courts (J Crawford, *Brownlie's Principles of Public International Law*, 9th edn (Oxford, Oxford University Press, 2019) 21, 468). In *KBR*, the Supreme Court suggested that the presumption in our legal system against the extraterritorial application of legislation was founded, in part, on such a principle of comity (paragraph 63). Comity possesses the great advantage that it is capable of providing a degree of lubrication to machinery which lacks clear hierarchical rules in customary international law. It does, however, have the disadvantage that its content is not clearly defined. It may be that there is valuable work to be done in defining principles for determining the appropriateness of exercising extraterritorial jurisdiction, whether in proscribing, investigating or prosecuting criminal activity.

The publication of this volume is, therefore, most welcome. Jurisdiction in the criminal law is not only a rich field for scholarship, but also an area in which the law faces greater challenges than ever before on so many different fronts. The timing is thus particularly opportune for such a distinguished group of scholars and practitioners to have assembled to debate these pressing issues. Their deliberations, as represented by the papers in this volume, are likely to be highly influential in the future development of the law.

Lord Lloyd-Jones

ACKNOWLEDGEMENTS

The essays in this book are the result of papers delivered at the WG Hart Workshop 2021, which was held in April 2021 as an online event due to the pandemic. This was, at first, a daunting task given the size of the Workshop, and the fact that we had all, at that point, developed some experience of online events with broken links or access and screensharing difficulties. However, our concerns were quickly allayed by the organisation and efficiency of the team at the Institute of Advanced Legal Studies. We would particularly like to thank Professor Carl Stychin, Daly Sarcos and Alex Bussey for all their support in organising and hosting the event, and for ensuring that it ran so smoothly and seamlessly. We also thank all of the presenters, chairs and attendees at the Workshop. While it was unfortunately not possible to include all the papers from the Workshop, the discussions at the event greatly assisted in the development of the ideas and arguments to be found in this collection. We are also grateful for the financial support from the WG Hart Bequest, and from the law departments at University of Glasgow, Queen Mary University of London and UCL. Lindsay Farmer would like to extend special thanks to the Leverhulme Trust (MRF 2018-075) for supporting his research throughout the period during which we have been working on this book.

We thank all the staff at Hart Publishing for their production and marketing of the book, and for their patience and understanding with deadlines! Thanks, in particular, are due to Kate Whetter, Sarah Skinner, Rosie Mearns, Linda Goss and Verity Stuart. Thanks also to Chris Myers at Forewords for his excellent editorial work on the book.

We are extremely grateful to Nicholas Burgess for his editorial assistance before we handed over the copy to the publishers. He has a keen attention to detail and every chapter in this book benefited hugely from his meticulous reviews.

Finally, we thank Lord Lloyd-Jones, both for opening the WG Hart Workshop and for his generous preface.

Micheál Ó Floinn, Lindsay Farmer,
Julia Hörnle and David Ormerod
December 2022

TABLE OF CONTENTS

APPENDICES TO CHAPTER 5

LIST OF CONTRIBUTORS

Darryl Brown, Professor of Law, University of Virginia

Alejandro Chehtman, Professor of Law, Universidad Torcuato Di Tella

Áine Clancy, Lecturer in Law, University of Sheffield

Tim Cochrane, PhD Candidate in Law, University of Cambridge

Matthew Garrod, Senior Lecturer, University of Sussex

Mireille Hildebrandt, Research Professor on 'Interfacing Law and Technology', Vrije Universiteit Brussels

Julia Hörnle, Professor of Internet Law, Queen Mary University of London

Uta Kohl, Professor of Commercial Law, University of Southampton

Vincenzo Mongillo, Professor of Criminal Law, Unitelma Sapienza University of Rome

Mattia Pinto, Lecturer, University of York

Cedric Ryngaert, Professor of Public International Law, Utrecht University

Jessica Shurson, Lecturer in Law, University of Sussex

Introduction

MICHEÁL Ó FLOINN, LINDSAY FARMER, JULIA HÖRNLE AND DAVID ORMEROD

I. Background

The question of jurisdiction is of fundamental practical and theoretical significance for the criminal law, but has rarely been the subject of sustained academic discussion and analysis. In practical terms, questions of jurisdiction are immanent to the investigation, prosecution and punishment of crime, and an elaborate system of rules has developed to regulate these questions. However, these rules have often been regarded as primarily technical in nature and of little jurisprudential interest or significance. This picture, though, has begun to change over the last 20 or 30 years as both the practical significance and theoretical understanding of jurisdiction have been transformed in different ways. One reason for this, as will be discussed later in this Introduction, is the increase in what has come to be known as transnational crime – broadly speaking, where different elements of a course of criminal conduct take place in two or more separate jurisdictions – giving rise to questions of which jurisdictions have the legal authority to investigate and prosecute those offences. While transborder criminal conduct is hardly novel, it has become a matter of increasing concern recently because of factors such as the greater facility and affordability of international travel, the creation of international markets and, latterly, the rise of the Internet. These developments allow actors who are physically located in different jurisdictions to co-ordinate their conduct, potentially using computer servers or markets located in a third jurisdiction, so as to commit a crime in one of those places – or even in a different location altogether. In the case of crimes committed by means of the Internet, it may even be unclear where a crime has been 'committed' according to traditional rules of jurisdiction. This gives rise to numerous problems, ranging from the questions about which law is to be applied, to the authority of particular government agencies to investigate and enforce that law, and to questions about where such criminal conduct should be tried and punished. Some of the transformations of criminal jurisdiction are thus being driven by practical concerns about law enforcement.

These developments have been accompanied by a renewed interest in the theoretical foundation of criminal jurisdiction. Much of the literature in this area is responding to the growth of international criminal law, and notably the creation of the International Criminal Court in 2002. The emergence of this new body of criminal law, and its accompanying institutions, has posed the fundamental question of the basis of authority for the assertion of jurisdiction. From where does a law enforcement authority derive its standing to prosecute and punish offenders for committing international crimes (and in whose name do they act)? What is the ambit of international (and national) criminal law? And how should it interact with existing forms of national and transnational law? The answer to these questions has been sought in the concept of universal jurisdiction – a concept which is novel, but which draws on the language and structures of already-existing forms of criminal jurisdiction. And importantly, for our purposes, the lively debate around the bases and scope of universal jurisdiction has prompted a renewed interest in theories of criminal jurisdiction more broadly.

The essays in this book address some of these transformations of criminal jurisdiction, combining theoretical and practical questions so as to develop new perspectives on jurisdiction and the criminal law. They are based on papers delivered at the WG Hart Workshop 2021, the first major conference in the UK for a number of years to be dedicated to the theme of criminal jurisdiction, with contributions from legal theorists, criminal lawyers, Internet lawyers and international lawyers, and with participants attending from around the globe.[1] And while it has not proved possible to include all the papers delivered or all the areas discussed at the Workshop, the papers included here discuss some of the most pressing issues around the contemporary transformations of criminal jurisdiction.

II. The Meaning of Jurisdiction

Jurisdiction is a term of art with different meanings in different contexts, and it is thus frequently used in an opaque manner.[2] Classically, it refers to the power of a state to make and enforce its law.[3] It thus raises fundamental questions about the nature of legal authority and the scope and limits of the law. In criminal law, this is normally analysed in terms of a distinction between prescriptive and enforcement jurisdiction. Prescriptive jurisdiction refers to questions about the scope or ambit of the criminal law of a particular state. It relates to the authority of a state to 'make law applicable to persons, property or conduct'.[4] These are therefore questions about where the law applies and who it applies to – as well as questions about the

[1] The Conference was originally to have been held in person in 2020 but was postponed as a result of the pandemic. It was eventually held in April 2021 as an online event.

[2] For discussion, see J Hörnle, *Internet Jurisdiction: Law and Practice* (Oxford, Oxford University Press, 2021) ch 1.

[3] See, eg A Chehtman, 'Jurisdiction' in M Dubber and T Hörnle (eds), *The Oxford Handbook of Criminal Law* (Oxford, Oxford University Press, 2014) for a useful survey of the literature.

[4] American Law Institute, *Restatement of the Law Fourth: The Foreign Relations Law of the United States* (Philadelphia, American Law Institute, 2018) § 401.

competence or authority of particular courts to judge certain disputes (sometimes referred to as adjudicative jurisdiction).[5] Thus, the UK Parliament might enact extraterritorial legislation which criminalises conduct that takes place outside the UK, or which applies to UK nationals wherever they are in the world. Questions of prescriptive jurisdiction thus determine where the conduct has taken place and connects this to the authority of the relevant UK court. The second dimension of jurisdiction is referred to as enforcement jurisdiction – namely the question of whether a state is able to investigate or prosecute an offence. It 'concerns the authority of a state to exercise its power to compel compliance with law'.[6] In the example above, it might concern questions such as whether or not police forces from the UK possess the authority to investigate, arrest or prosecute a particular suspect. A further analytical separation is now sometimes also made in the literature sub-dividing 'investigative' and 'enforcement' jurisdiction.[7] The former is said to be concerned with a state's power to carry out investigative activities (such as law enforcement's access to data in the cloud), including outside its territory. Before the Internet, absent international co-operation, investigations normally required the physical presence of law enforcement authorities on the territory where the investigative measure was taken (such as in the execution of a warrant for search and seizure). However, with the advent of the Internet, states can with relative ease engage in remote access to data not physically stored (or even controlled) on that state's territory.

It is also important to note that while many of these jurisdictional questions relate to the scope or ambit of certain laws – whether or not a particular state can 'reach' conduct taking place around the globe – they are also fundamentally concerned with limits of state powers. As we will see, as technology has potentially expanded the reach of certain states' jurisdiction, the question of how the law might impose limits on the exercise of that power becomes increasingly urgent.

We have organised this volume in terms of this distinction – moving broadly from discussions of issues of prescriptive jurisdiction in Part I to those of enforcement jurisdiction in Part II. However, before we move on, we want to note that this superficially simple distinction also masks a considerable degree of complexity. This is, in part, because issues of the scope and enforcement of the law continually bleed into each other, such that the distinction is of greater use as an analytical tool than as a guide to practice. It is also because in this rapidly changing area –

[5] 'Adjudicative' jurisdiction is normally distinguished as a distinct category of jurisdiction in an international law sense, though some international lawyers have questioned the need for this further sub-division. For analysis of different perspectives, see A Mills, 'Rethinking Jurisdiction in International Law' (2014) 84 *British Yearbook of International Law* 187, 194–95. In the civil sphere, distinguishing between jurisdiction to prescribe and jurisdiction to adjudicate can be important, as they do not coincide in situations where eg a court applies foreign law. However, in the criminal sphere, they have been said to be 'one and the same'. See M Akehurst, 'Jurisdiction in International Law' (1972–73) 46 *British Yearbook of International Law* 145, 179.

[6] American Law Institute (n 4) § 432 comment.

[7] Hörnle (n 2) 7.

the transformations that we refer to in our title – many of the traditional distinctions that have organised this field are breaking down under the pressure of social, economic and technological change. We will discuss these transformations, and the way that they cut across the categories of prescriptive and enforcement jurisdiction, in the next two sections.

III. Transformations

A. Expansive Territoriality

Both prescriptive and enforcement jurisdiction use the concept of 'territory' as their primary organising concept, but this concept has different meanings. On the one hand, it can refer to land, and lawyers have a tendency to think about territory and states in this way – as a geographical, physical fact. Discussions of the limits of enforcement jurisdiction centre on this physical framework, as enforcement jurisdiction in international law is almost exclusively territorial. The police of one state cannot, for example, enter the territory of another state to effect an arrest or execute a search warrant in the absence of authorisation from the other state. On the other hand, territory is a legal construct denoting control and authority over land.[8] As Elden notes, 'territory is not simply an object: the outcome of actions conducted toward it or some previously supposedly neutral area. Territory is itself a process, made and remade, shaped and shaping, active and reactive.'[9] Its concomitant 'territoriality principle', as understood in the international law of prescriptive jurisdiction, is thus inherently elastic and malleable. As a source of authority under international law, it can facilitate the regulation of conduct that relates to the 'territory' of a state (including territorial airspace and coastal waters), whether because it occurs there in whole or in part,[10] or because of any actual or potential effects within the state. It can, therefore, be a matter of some contention as to what types of connecting factors to territory are required before a state can assert jurisdiction under international law.

Nevertheless, in the literature, the territoriality principle is sometimes cast as an insufficient and limited jurisdictional basis for criminalising – and regulating more broadly – the transnational harms that states and their citizens face in today's globalised world.[11] Relatedly, the domestic interpretation of the

[8] See, eg H Buxbaum, 'Territory, Territoriality, and the Resolution of Jurisdictional Conflict' (2009) 57 *American Journal of Comparative Law* 631, 635.

[9] S Elden, *The Birth of Territory* (Chicago, University of Chicago Press, 2013) 17.

[10] It has long been recognised that a state can exercise jurisdiction over acts which constitute domestic crimes and have been committed 'in whole or in part' within its territory. See ED Dickinson, 'Jurisdiction with Respect to Crime' (1935) 29(Suppl S1) *American Journal of International Law* 435, 480.

[11] Szigeti, for example, notes how some 'commentators have argued that widespread extraterritorial jurisdiction results in over-regulation, but widespread territorial jurisdiction results in under-regulation'. See P Szigeti, 'In the Middle of Nowhere: The Futile Quest to Distinguish Territoriality from

territoriality principle in the substantive criminal jurisdiction of certain common law countries is singled out as particularly conservative, at least when compared to the approaches of states employing the 'constituent elements' approach[12] or the 'ubiquity principle'.[13] Traditionally, for example, the 'terminatory theory', as applied by the courts of England and Wales, required that the 'last act' in a course of criminal conduct must take place domestically in order for these courts to assume territorial jurisdiction over an offence.[14]

As a matter of doctrine, these critiques sometimes overlook significant domestic developments. For example, courts in the UK have recently begun to move away from the territorial strictures of the 'terminatory theory' towards a more enabling criterion which looks at whether a 'substantial measure' of the criminality occurred within the state.[15] Moreover, with respect to certain common law and statutory offences, a more expansive approach to territorial jurisdiction has long been adopted.[16] But more generally, any framing of territoriality as *restrictive* of state competence, at least with respect to criminal jurisdiction, is likely to have underestimated the ease of accommodating transnationality through this legal construct, particularly in the globalised and interconnected world within which transnational crime operates today. It will not come as a surprise that the opportunities for – and challenges to – state regulation via territoriality come in large part from technology, which enables increasing mobility of persons, capital and goods, as well as the remote provision of services. Technological change has accelerated in recent years, due to the Internet and the increased connectivity, interaction and transactions between people around the globe and across cultural, linguistic and religious divides. The Internet has led to a continuing, incremental innovation, from search to user-to-user services and social media, cloud computing, peer-to-peer file-sharing networks, blockchain technologies, digitisation of everything (eg digital assets), the 3D Internet (eg metaverse) and artificial intelligence. While delocalised activities with fewer connecting factors to any particular territory may provide less scope for regulation by public and criminal law, territoriality exerts remarkable staying power.

A number of chapters in this volume take stock of these modern transformations by charting the operation and role of the territoriality principle and the profound challenges presented for the framework of law, which is largely composed

Extraterritoriality' in DS Margolies et al (eds), *The Extraterritoriality of Law: History, Theory, Politics* (Abingdon, Routledge, 2019) 44.

[12] On this, see C Ryngaert, 'Territorial Jurisdiction Over Cross-Frontier Offences: Revisiting a Classic Problem of International Criminal Law' (2009) 9 *International Criminal Law Review* 187.

[13] Hörnle (n 2) 118.

[14] On the terminatory theory, see generally M Hirst, *Jurisdiction and the Ambit of the Criminal Law* (Oxford, Oxford University Press, 2003).

[15] See, eg *Smith (Wallace Duncan) (No 4)* [2004] QB 1418; *R v Sheppard and Whittle* [2010] EWCA Crim 65; *Laskowski v R* [2023] EWCA Crim 494. For discussion of this development, see Hörnle (n 2) 139–40.

[16] See, eg the jurisdictional regime in the Criminal Justice Act 1993. For a recent judicial interpretation in the context of transnational blackmail offences, see *R v Pogmore* [2017] EWCA Crim 925.

of territorial legal systems (national law). Chehtman sets the scene for this in chapter one, providing an understanding of territoriality and jurisdiction based not on land or territory, but on political community. Through the presumption against extraterritorial jurisdiction in international law, he proposes an understanding of jurisdiction as being rooted in the interests of particular political communities to self-government, based on the authority of states. On his account, jurisdiction is understood not only as a matter of relations between states, but also of the relationship between a state and its citizens. This allows him to rethink jurisdiction as a normative power and explain why and when extraterritorial jurisdiction is objectionable and why it cannot provide the same type of public good as territorial jurisdiction. In chapter two, Hildebrandt moves on to situate the link between technology and jurisdiction, and provides a rich account of how an exclusive, monopolistic territorial jurisdiction was enabled by the technologies of cartography and the printing press. She argues that modern positive law arose out of printing and cartography, the ability to read and print being directly linked to rule-making and the rule of law, but that the cyberspatial context, which can lack clear geographical boundaries, raises complex issues of jurisdiction where territoriality can create rather than solve problems. In particular, Hildebrandt interrogates whether and how long-standing legal protections, like the legality principle, can hold in the modern technological environment where delocalised transactions and events can undermine a rule-based system linked to territory. In chapter three, Brown further elucidates the role that territoriality is playing, by examining several strategies adopted by the USA to enable domestic law to reach criminal conduct committed outside US territory. The USA has, in particular, been able to leverage the transnational nature of Internet infrastructure, due to the concentration of much of this infrastructure in the USA, as well as maximising the advantages of a large domestic economy. This segues well into the topic of chapter four, where Mongillo outlines how states have responded to the rise of the transnational enterprise, and the ease through which such enterprises can evade local or national legal constraints. A number of strategies for regulation are identified, including the introduction of criminal/punitive sanctions for corporations, and expansive jurisdictional regimes. While the latter include a range of extraterritorial bases of jurisdiction designed specifically for corporate liability, enabling states to 'delocalise' the application of national criminal law, Mongillo also outlines the more subtle means through which states can capture extraterritorial conduct by maximising the territorial application of criminal law.

What these analyses demonstrate is that while territoriality is, and always has been, inherently malleable and capacious, the financial, social and technological frameworks to which it is attached increasingly enable states to assert a jurisdictional connection over transnational events even where there may only be a thin territorial nexus. They develop and support a wider body of literature demonstrating how territoriality has become 'unbound',[17] and how the 'problem of ambiguous territoriality has hardly been realised'.[18]

B. Expansive Extraterritoriality

Even though, as we have seen, the line between the territorial and the extraterritorial has been blurred, and the sense has developed that 'territory' is not (if it ever was) a stable basis for delineating jurisdiction, forms of jurisdiction have developed that we might characterise as 'extraterritorial' – that is to say, states might exercise a prescriptive jurisdiction over criminal conduct even where there is no territorial nexus. These include the principle of nationality (that states exercise jurisdiction over their nationals), the principle of passive personality (where the victim is the national of the state seeking to prosecute), the protective principle (that a state is justified in prosecuting conduct which affects its interests) and the principle of universal jurisdiction.[19] While some of these forms might more properly be described as non-territorial, in the sense that there never was a link with territory, others are extraterritorial precisely because they were developed to escape some of the limitations of territorial bases of jurisdiction. We will not discuss these in full here, but will focus on universal jurisdiction and ideas around nationality and national interest as examples of 'expansive extraterritoriality'.

As with other developments in this area, universal jurisdiction is not necessarily new. It has long been claimed that certain forms of conduct (such as piracy) are wrong by the laws of all 'civilised' nations and thus that those nations might prosecute such conduct wherever it took place. Historically, this supported claims that pirates, for example, were *hostis humani generis* (enemies of the human race) and might be tried and punished by the authorities of any nation, irrespective of whether their ships or nationals had been actual victims of piracy. Claims to universal jurisdiction have underpinned the development of an international criminal law based around crimes against humanity (including genocide and war crimes) in the post-World War II period. This was given an institutional structure with the creation in 2002 of the International Criminal Court, with jurisdiction over 'the most serious crimes of concern to the international community'.[20] However, this jurisdiction is intended to be complementary to the jurisdiction of national courts over the same crimes, to be exercised only when national courts

[17] N Krisch, 'Jurisdiction Unbound: (Extra)territorial Regulation as Global Governance' (2022) 33 *European Journal of International Law* 482, 501.

[18] Szigeti, 'In the Middle of Nowhere' (n 11) 31.

[19] For discussion of these, see Chehtman (n 3).

[20] As defined in the Rome Statute of the International Criminal Court (Rome, 17 July 1998) 2187 UNTS 3.

are unwilling or unable to exercise their jurisdiction. This, in effect, recognises that states might exercise a prescriptive jurisdiction over certain crimes, and that they might exercise it on behalf of other states (where those states have failed to act) or in the name of a common good or cosmopolitanism.[21]

This, however, can give rise to complex doctrinal and practical issues, and these questions are taken up in the chapters by Garrod and Pinto. Garrod, in chapter five, traces how state practice is evolving (suggesting some new heads of jurisdiction and how others may be falling away or better understood in different terms). In chapter six, Pinto, by contrast, looking at the scale of new developments, argues that the development of different forms of universal jurisdiction has actually led in practice to an expansion of criminal law.

Jurisdiction has also been asserted over people on the basis of their nationality (or residence) or national interests: countries asserted the power to punish their nationals for crimes wherever these were committed, or over conduct which threatened their interests. Historically, as a matter of English law, this typically applied only to serious criminal wrongs, such as homicide, or to conduct which offered a direct threat to the legal authority of the home jurisdiction (eg planning an insurrection from a base in a foreign country). The nexus of jurisdiction was seen either in the responsibility assumed by one state for the conduct of its nationals abroad or in the threat posed by those persons to the institutions of their 'home' jurisdiction. The active personality principle, by contrast, has been regularly applied by states in continental Europe, subject to the dual criminality principle.[22]

However, as interdependence between states has grown as a result of globalisation, some states have increasingly asserted jurisdiction over conduct even where these traditional grounds appear weak. States appear to be increasingly turning to bases of extraterritorial jurisdiction with respect to a wide variety of crimes, as demonstrated by Garrod in chapter five; and, as Mongillo argues, traditional connecting factors like nationality and residence are being developed to apply to corporate entities.

C. Expansive Enforcement

While Part I of the book demonstrates how states are increasingly expanding the jurisdictional ambit of their domestic criminal laws by availing themselves of the malleability of the concept of territoriality and expanding extraterritorial bases of jurisdiction, these efforts to tackle international and transnational crime can fall flat where there is no enforcement machinery in place to investigate and prosecute underlying conduct. The intensification of transnational activities and the delocalised or extraterritorial nature of the data required for investigations are examples of fundamental obstacles which can result in impunity. The enduring hurdle for

[21] C Ryngaert, *Selfless Intervention: The Exercise of Jurisdiction in the Common Interest* (Oxford, Oxford University Press, 2020).
[22] Hörnle (n 2) 131.

law enforcement will often be enforcement jurisdiction. While customary international law is said to be relatively permissive with respect to the jurisdiction to prescribe,[23] allowing states to assert their laws to address situations which take place partly or wholly outside of the prescribing state, enforcement jurisdiction is, as noted, generally accepted to be strictly territorial.[24] A state cannot exercise enforcement jurisdiction to compel compliance with its laws outside its own territory in the absence of prescriptive authority,[25] but even with this authority, the act may not be internationally lawful.[26] As Mann notes, 'There can be no question of the two jurisdictions [prescriptive and enforcement] necessarily coinciding'.[27] Without consent for any foreign enforcement action, 'the rights and privileges of the territorial sovereign prevail'.[28]

However, while there are obstacles for law enforcement in the digital age, there are also opportunities, and Part II of this volume surveys recent state practice and raises fundamental questions for whether and how the classical separation between the jurisdiction to prescribe and the jurisdiction to enforce can be sustained in light of modern developments. In chapter seven, Ryngaert considers state enforcement practices in 'a-territorial' spaces like the high seas and cyberspace, and argues that states are pushing for a relaxation of the traditional limitations of extraterritorial enforcement jurisdiction. Often drawing on permissive principles of prescriptive jurisdiction, they are extending their enforcement activities to stateless vessels on the high seas, and pulling data, regardless of location, from local or foreign service providers by purporting to frame these activities as regulatory claims made by the state within its jurisdiction, rather than state acts in the territory of another state. Domestic examples abound of judicial and legislative efforts to extend production powers to foreign service providers,[29] to order local providers to produce data under their control regardless of location[30] or to engage

[23] See American Law Institute (n 4) § 407, claiming that customary international law 'permits exercises of prescriptive jurisdiction if there is a genuine connection between the subject of the regulation and the state seeking to regulate'.

[24] C Ryngaert, *Jurisdiction in International Law*, 2nd edn (Oxford, Oxford University Press, 2015) 9. See further American Law Institute (n 4) § 432(b): 'a state may not exercise jurisdiction to enforce in the territory of another state without the consent of the other state'. It was noted in the now infamous *Lotus* case to be 'the first and foremost restriction imposed by international law', stipulating that a state 'may not exercise its power in any form in the territory of another State' failing the existence of a permissive rule to the contrary. See *The Case of the SS Lotus (France v Turkey)* PCIJ Rep Series A No 10 [45].

[25] See American Law Institute (n 4) § 432 comment: 'A state may exercise jurisdiction to enforce its own law only when it has jurisdiction to prescribe.'

[26] FA Mann, *The Doctrine of International Jurisdiction Revisited after Twenty Years*, Recueil des cours vol 186 (The Hague, Martinus Nijhoff, 1984) 34.

[27] ibid 35. See further FA Mann, *Further Studies in International Law* (Oxford, Clarendon Press, 1990) 19: 'The mere existence of legislative jurisdiction is insufficient to justify the State to exercise enforcement jurisdiction in another State's territory.'

[28] Mann, *The Doctrine* (n 26) 37.

[29] See, eg the extraterritoriality of the UK's Investigatory Powers Act 2016.

[30] See, eg the US Microsoft Warrant case, *In re Warrant to Search a Certain E-Mail Account Controlled and Maintained by Microsoft Corp* 829 F3d 197 (2d Cir 2016); *United States v Microsoft Corp* 138 S Ct 356 (2017) which is discussed in several chapters of this volume.

in extraterritorial searches of data servers where they are implicated in criminal offences.[31] And according to Ryngaert, this state practice appears to be increasingly blurring the distinction between prescriptive and enforcement jurisdiction as a result. In chapter eight, Kohl further explores these cross-border law enforcement activities and situates them squarely within the territoriality principle. The challenge – and in some instances futility – of trying to distinguish and delineate the territorial and extraterritorial is revealed to be particularly acute in this realm, and both Kohl and Ryngaert demonstrate that states are clearly availing themselves of the relative uncertainty as to 'where' enforcement activities should be understood to take place. As the authors outline in their respective contributions, this raises fundamental questions for international law of when exactly the international law prohibition against extraterritorial enforcement actually bites with respect to cross-border data activities. Kohl intervenes on this topic with a fresh perspective, arguing that enforcement jurisdiction is preoccupied with physical displays of state authority in another state. The consequence, she argues, is that international law may be more permissive than is commonly assumed with respect to cross-border data interventions, again leaving the strong impression that territoriality is an unstable and unsatisfactory basis for delineating jurisdiction even in the realm of enforcement jurisdiction.

Nevertheless, there is a difference between laws *applying* extraterritorially and those laws being effective and enforceable. States may purport to bind foreign entities as a matter of domestic law, and argue that they are complying with international law in the process. This, however, may not carry a domestic investigation or prosecution very far if the order is ignored or comes up against a conflict of laws in a foreign country which effectively mandates non-compliance. This is why some states are increasingly turning to further bilateral and multilateral data access instruments alongside any domestic initiatives. The Council of Europe's Second Additional Protocol to the Cybercrime Convention[32] is the most recent multilateral instrument providing explicitly for 'direct access' to foreign intermediaries with respect to certain categories of data, while a number of bilateral agreements have also emerged following the passing of the US CLOUD Act (2018 Clarifying Lawful Overseas Use of Data Act),[33] with the correspondent US–UK Agreement entering into force in October 2022.[34] These developments suggest that a new and important generation of 'direct access' is upon us, and two chapters in the volume analyse these instruments from different perspectives. Cochrane, in chapter ten,

[31] For discussion, see D Brown, 'Extraterritorial Ambit through Offence Definitions, Technology and Economic Power', ch 3 in the present volume; A Lubin, 'The Prohibition of Extraterritorial Enforcement Jurisdiction in the Datasphere' in A Parrish and C Ryngaert (eds), *Research Handbook on Extraterritoriality in International Law* (Cheltenham, Edward Elgar, forthcoming) ch 20.

[32] Second Additional Protocol to the Convention on Cybercrime on enhanced co-operation and disclosure of electronic evidence (Strasbourg, 12 May 2022) (European Treaty Series No 224).

[33] Clarifying Lawful Overseas Use of Data (CLOUD) Act, Pub L 115–141, 132 Stat 1213.

[34] US Department of Justice, 'Landmark US–UK Data Access Agreement Enters into Force' (*Justice*, 3 October 2022) www.justice.gov/opa/pr/landmark-us-uk-data-access-agreement-enters-force.

considers how CLOUD Act agreements interact with enforcement jurisdiction from a public international law perspective. While there may be uncertainty as to how to frame extraterritorial data requests within the architecture of enforcement jurisdiction, CLOUD Act agreements serve to resolve this issue for parties by allowing states to enforce their domestic laws extraterritorially against foreign service providers. Nevertheless, as Cochrane outlines, whether the public international law benefits of such direct access mechanisms can be realised in practice turns on evolving legal issues at the level of both international and domestic law. One such issue concerns encrypted data, a hugely important factor which can stymie many criminal investigations before they even get off the ground. In chapter eleven, Shurson addresses this topic by exploring the extraterritoriality of domestic encryption orders and how they may interact with this emerging paradigm of CLOUD Act agreements. She elucidates the factors which may lie behind the failure of the states involved from taking a clear position on the jurisdictional reach of such orders within these bilateral instruments and the consequences that may flow from this for global cybersecurity.

In the final chapter of this part, we move to a context where questions of enforcement jurisdiction may be expected to be less opaque. Enforcement jurisdiction is most clearly concerned with state powers to arrest and punish offenders or seize their assets, which is largely a territorial exercise, absent international co-operation through, for example, extradition treaties. However, in chapter twelve, Clancy considers the problem of dealing with assets obtained through illegal means and removed from foreign jurisdictions to the UK and the civil investigative tool, the Unexplained Wealth Order (UWO), which was recently introduced by the UK to overcome the jurisdictional and enforcement challenges faced by receiving states. Clancy's discussion shows that even here, the assertion of enforcement jurisdiction in the UK could be seen as a form of jurisdictional overreach for crimes committed on foreign territory, but the chapter concludes that, notwithstanding the jurisdictional concerns, the civil recovery process has been a necessary tool to tackle impunity for criminal activity. This discussion can also be situated within a broader and recent UK strategy of facilitating extraterritorial enforcement by clothing these powers in civil law, as also revealed by, for example, the civil enforcement powers in the Online Safety Bill.

D. New Bases of Jurisdiction

One of the transformations in criminal law jurisdiction is potentially the emergence of new bases of jurisdiction and new interpretations of existing bases of jurisdiction. Given the cross-border challenges caused by cybercrime and Internet communications generally, and the 'un-territoriality of data',[35] it is probably

[35] J Daskal, 'The Un-territoriality of Data' (2015) 125 *Yale Law Journal* 326.

surprising that international scholarship and state practice have not led to the recognition of new bases of jurisdiction. The reason for this lies probably in the aforementioned malleability and flexibility inherent in the territoriality principle, which has allowed states to find sufficient connecting factors for domestic jurisdictional purposes, even if it requires a reformulation of criminal offences under national law. But chapters in this volume are now suggesting that state practice is beginning to reveal new categories and understandings of jurisdiction, as discussed by Mongillo and Garrod, in chapters four and five, respectively. At the very least, these contributions reveal new and expansive interpretations of existing bases of jurisdiction.

In the realm of enforcement jurisdiction, a number of contributions to this volume also reveal the uncertainties and limitations of the language of 'enforcement' and 'territoriality' in the digital era. Where customary international law stands with respect to extraterritorial enforcement jurisdiction appears to be in a state of flux, and in some quarters, as noted, it is being argued that new jurisdictional concepts may be emerging, or may at least be needed, in order to fill some of the gaps. The ability of law enforcement agencies to remotely access data in the cloud through various techniques such as network exploitation or through coercive production orders directed at communication service providers means that they can act with extraterritorial effect without physically acting on foreign territory for the purpose of investigating crime. As noted above, in some scholarship, these activities are being analysed and understood through a new concept of investigative jurisdiction which could be extraterritorial in nature and subject to the principles of comity and non-interference with the affairs of other states. It raises troubling issues about a state's powers and sovereignty over the privacy and security of its citizens and state responsibility for international human rights obligations.

IV. Conflicts and Challenges

Criminal jurisdiction is firmly connected to the sovereign power of states governed by national law and internal executive and judicial powers of the state. This connection gives rise to the problem of concurrency: there is no institution or mechanism to co-ordinate the exercise of these powers at an international level, which leads to jurisdictional conflicts. Jurisdictional principles at the international law level only provide a very loose and general framework for the national assertion of jurisdiction in criminal cases, and arguably do little to solve jurisdictional conflicts between states.

Jurisdictional conflicts in criminal law can occur at three different levels: at the level of substantive law (jurisdictional scope and ambit of criminal offences); at the level of investigative powers connected to the investigation of offences; and finally, at the level of enforcement jurisdiction, eg connected to the prosecution and punishment of offenders. Jurisdictional conflicts can further be divided into negative and positive conflicts: positive conflicts lead to two or more states prosecuting the same crime (concurrency); negative conflicts lead to no state prosecuting a crime (for example, because the evidence is in another state, inadequate legal provisions or the crime being spread over several states, leading to uncertainty as to which state should take the lead).

From a theoretical standpoint, national criminal justice systems attempt to triangulate three important aims, namely the integrity of their criminal justice system, the efficiency of criminal prosecutions and the defendant's civil liberties. However, achieving these aims is made infinitely more complex by the positive and negative criminal jurisdiction conflicts. Jurisdictional conflicts can arise because of the criminal conduct or result occurring in more than one state, with each state prosecuting the offender, leading to concurrency. This concurrency is poorly addressed under international law, as effective international co-ordination is largely absent (other than co-operation initiatives such as Eurojust and frameworks for such co-operation, like the Eurojust Guidelines). However jurisdictional conflicts can also arise because of significant differences in criminal laws and constitutional rights standards (such as those relating to free speech, privacy and freedom of religion), which can mean that the same conduct is a criminal offence in one state but legal in another. This raises the concern of territorial 'overspill' of criminal law of the former state in the territory of the latter state. This second type of jurisdictional conflict cannot be solved through international co-ordination measures, given the cultural, religious and legal differences, absent harmonisation, but can only be addressed by states limiting the reach of their criminal laws. One way of addressing this overspill problem is the concept of targeting, which broadly concerns an examination of whether the defendant's conduct was directed at the particular state that is prosecuting. As noted previously, with respect to the criminal law of England and Wales, the courts have now established the 'substantial measure' test, which requires that a substantial measure of the criminality must have occurred domestically before the courts can assume jurisdiction (unless legislation provides otherwise). However, conduct may be targeted at more than one state, or alternatively it may not be targeted at any particular state. Thus, while targeting may sometimes help to reduce conflicts deriving from jurisdictional overspill, it can never completely eliminate them.

Jurisdictional conflicts additionally cause difficult issues with respect to double jeopardy law and the *ne bis in idem* principle which, while well established in the context of national law, has limited application across borders. As Mongillo outlines in chapter four, many states, including the USA, do not always recognise a criminal judgment or sentence handed down by the courts of a foreign state as binding and final. While there are regional inter-state protections against double jeopardy in the form of Article 50 of the EU Charter of Fundamental Rights and Article 54 of the 1990 Convention implementing the Schengen Agreement of 14 June 1985, international human rights treaties do not extend the principle across borders. Cultural and legal differences between criminal justice systems as to the just punishment for a crime committed, the length of sentences, or the balance between deterrence, retribution and rehabilitation, as well as potential mutual mistrust in each other's criminal justice systems, means that many states are not willing to accept a foreign criminal court's judgment as binding and final. Further problems are caused by the divisibility of criminal conduct. Is a single act (such as spreading computer malware or a phishing attack) which leads to criminal results across several states one single crime or several separate crimes which can be prosecuted and punished in all these jurisdictions? As Hildebrandt notes in chapter two, it is these sorts of cyberspatial challenges which raise profound difficulties for the application of principles like *ne bis in idem*. Therefore, the jurisdictional challenge generated by technology is clearly not only concerned with questions of law enforcement, but is also directly linked to the rule of law as a guarantor of civil liberties. This connection is further discussed in chapter nine by Hörnle, who looks at the extraterritorial application of human rights norms where state acts are not limited to one territory because of the modern affordances of technology (such as remote surveillance of foreign citizens). Cochrane also calls for further analysis of the extent to which domestic human rights law can regulate the extraterritorial extensions of jurisdiction brought about by bilateral CLOUD Act agreements. In addressing the question of how human rights might be applied effectively in situations of extraterritorial state enforcement, Hörnle argues for a version of 'state act theory', based on the jurisprudence of the German Constitutional Court, where human rights protection would attach to the specific state *act* which is interfering with fundamental rights, rather than being based on territory. She thus argues that the challenge of protecting individual rights is best met with an approach that recognises the transformations of criminal jurisdiction and responds to them in new and imaginative ways.

* * *

These, then, are the transformations of criminal jurisdiction, and the essays in this volume are an attempt to explore both the practical and theoretical challenges that they present. Our aim in organising the conference and in bringing the papers together in this edited collection was both to draw new attention to this important and neglected field and to stimulate new discussion of how to preserve rule of law values and protections in the face of these challenges.

PART I

Prescriptive Jurisdiction

1

The Presumption against Extraterritorial Criminal Jurisdiction

ALEJANDRO CHEHTMAN*

> Tampoco puedo entregar mis informes a la policía gringa … al fin y al cabo, le pese a quien le pese (empezando por mí) soy mexicana … Esto lo resolvemos nosotros a chingadazos, como siempre, o nos hundimos juntos.
>
> Roberto Bolaño, *2666*†

I. Introduction

There is significant consensus that the fact that a given criminal wrong has been perpetrated on the territory of a particular state is a fundamental, even a decisive, reason why that state has the right to prosecute and punish the perpetrator. This basic insight has been captured by what is called the principle of territoriality – the core and most widely accepted rule on criminal jurisdiction under both domestic and international law. There is some normative work on this principle, albeit far less than its centrality would lead one to assume.[1] By contrast, much less attention has been paid to whether there is – and whether there should be – a presumption

* This contribution was originally prepared for the WG Hart Legal Workshop 2021, 'New Perspectives on Jurisdiction and the Criminal Law', conducted online because of the global pandemic. I have subsequently presented this piece at the 'Citizenship and Criminal Law' workshop at Universidad Pompeu Fabra (Barcelona). I am grateful to audiences at both events for comments and suggestions, especially Antony Duff, Sandra Marshall, José Luis Martí, Mari Takeuchi, Milena Tripkovic and Lucia Zedner. Juan Pappier provided very useful suggestions. I am indebted to Lindsay Farmer and Micheál Ó Floinn, two of the editors of this volume, for detailed and insightful comments on a previous draft. All errors and omissions are, of course, my own.

[1] FA Mann, *The Doctrine of Jurisdiction in International Law*, Recueil des cours vol 111 (The Hague, Martinus Nijhoff, 1964); C Ryngaert, *Jurisdiction in International Law*, 2nd edn (Oxford, Oxford University Press, 2015); RA Duff, *The Realm of Criminal Law* (Oxford, Oxford University Press, 2018), L Farmer, 'Territorial Jurisdiction and Criminalization' (2013) 63 *University of Toronto Law Journal* 225; A Chehtman, *The Philosophical Foundations of Extraterritorial Punishment* (Oxford, Oxford University Press, 2010).

against extraterritorial criminal jurisdiction. That is, whether or when it would be *pro tanto* unlawful under international law for a state to prosecute and punish an offence perpetrated extraterritorially.

This issue was examined at significant length in one of the first, and arguably seminal, decisions by a permanent international tribunal. The *Lotus* case famously involved a collision on the high seas between a Turkish ship (the *Boz-Kourt*) and a French steamer (the SS *Lotus*) in which eight sailors and passengers in the Turkish ship died.[2] When both ships arrived at Constantinople, the Turkish authorities detained Lieutenant Demons, the SS *Lotus*'s officer on watch, who was subsequently convicted of manslaughter. He was sentenced to 80 days in prison and a fine of 22 pounds. But France claimed that Turkish courts had no jurisdiction to try Demons, a French national, for acts that occurred on the high seas, on board a ship flying the French flag. In doing so, France claimed, Turkey had infringed the laws on jurisdiction under international law. France and Turkey agreed to bring the case before the recently created Permanent Court of International Justice (PCIJ). By the slimmest majority (the President breaking a tie), and over deep disagreement, a majority of the PCIJ sided with Turkey. But most importantly for our purposes here, the majority concluded that no presumption against extraterritorial jurisdiction existed under international law. The reasoning of the Court in *Lotus* caused a 'doctrinal storm';[3] as Hertogen recently put it, 'Generations of international lawyers have had a love–hate relationship with the *Lotus* principle'.[4]

Notably, few legal scholars currently think that there is such a presumption of freedom to extend the scope of the criminal law extraterritorially.[5] Contra the majority in *Lotus*, most opinions now advocate a more restrictive framework under which extraterritorial jurisdiction cannot be exercised without some specific nexus recognised by international law.[6] This function is performed by certain bases of extraterritorial criminal jurisdiction, such as the principles of nationality, passive personality, protection or universality.[7] In fact, many influential scholars in this area have criticised the Court's reasoning in *Lotus*. Mann considered it 'retrograde'.[8] Higgins rejected it as simply 'outdated'.[9] Ryngaert

[2] *The Case of the SS Lotus (France v Turkey)* PCIJ Rep Series A No 10 (hereinafter *Lotus*).

[3] P Weil, 'International Law Limitations on State Jurisdiction' in CJ Olmstead (ed), *Extra-territorial Application of Laws and Responses Thereto* (Oxford, ESC Publishing, 1984) 32.

[4] A Hertogen, 'Letting *Lotus* Bloom' (2016) 26 *European Journal of International Law* 902.

[5] Some do think, though, that criminals are liable to punishment for their wrongdoing by anyone who is placed to do so effectively. See, eg M Moore, *Placing Blame: A Theory of the Criminal Law* (Oxford, Oxford University Press, 2010).

[6] J Crawford, *Brownlie's Principles of Public International Law* (Oxford, Oxford University Press, 2012) 456. Ryngaert, *Jurisdiction* (n 1) 21 similarly suggests that the presumption against extraterritorial criminal jurisdiction is currently customary international law.

[7] See, eg A Chehtman, 'Jurisdiction' in M Dubber and T Hörnle (eds), *The Oxford Handbook of Criminal Law* (Oxford, Oxford University Press, 2014).

[8] Mann (n 1) 35.

[9] R Higgins, *International Trade Law and the Avoidance, Containment and Resolution of Disputes: General Course on Public International Law*, Recueil des cours vol 230 (The Hague, Martinus Nijhoff, 1991) 114. For further criticisms, see JL Brierly, *Règles générales du droit de la paix*, Collected Courses

similarly found it 'obsolete'.[10] At the International Court of Justice (ICJ), Judge Simma called it an 'anachronistic, extremely consensualist vision of international law'.[11] More recently, Mills opined that this decision is a great illustration of the enormous (pernicious) influence of legal positivism in international law.[12] Lowe and Staker, in turn, have claimed that the *Lotus* principle favouring a presumption of freedom in the exercise of extraterritorial criminal jurisdiction is 'fallacious'.[13] Nevertheless, many still argue that the reasoning in *Lotus* 'has long represented the prevailing approach to jurisdictional issues in international law'.[14] Most contemporary textbooks open their discussion on jurisdiction by reference to the *Lotus* and the reasoning of the Court.[15] Not one of them explains what is wrong with it.

To defend the presumption against extraterritoriality, I will first argue that the Court in *Lotus* made two conceptual mistakes. This will dispel some of the controversies around this decision and will provide the discussion concerning the presumption against extraterritorial criminal jurisdiction with a fresh analytical start. Second, I will defend the presumption on normative grounds and evaluate its strength and limitations. Ultimately, and perhaps unsurprisingly, I will argue that this presumption stands on a patchwork of arguments which have varying normative force and which apply differently in different contexts. Some of them are admittedly contingent, but others are not. This means that the presumption applies across the board. At the same time, I will acknowledge that this presumption is not absolute, and may ultimately be overridden in certain cases.

Before I start, let me make four brief clarificatory points delimiting some basic terms and the scope of this contribution. First, extraterritorial criminal jurisdiction is of course not concerned with territory per se, that is, physical spaces, rocks and other forms of landscape. Territory in the sense relevant for us here is a political construction. In Elden's terms, it constitutes a 'political technology' that connects a particular form of political organisation – a state – with a certain space/terrain.[16] Territory, for our purposes here, is therefore the outcome of a political process

of the Hague Academy of International Law vol 58 (Brill, 1936) 146–48; H Lauterpacht, *International Law* (Cambridge, Cambridge University Press, 1970) 488.

[10] Ryngaert, *Jurisdiction* (n 1) 55.

[11] *Accordance with International Law of the Unilateral Declaration of Independence in Respect of Kosovo, Advisory Opinion* [2010] ICJ Rep 403, Declaration of Judge Simma, [3].

[12] A Mills, 'Rethinking Jurisdiction in International Law' (2014) 84 *British Yearbook of International Law* 191.

[13] See V Lowe and C Staker, 'Jurisdiction' in MD Evans (ed), *International Law*, 3rd edn (Oxford, Oxford University Press, 2010) 319.

[14] A Bianchi, 'Jurisdictional Rules in Customary International Law' in K Meessen (ed), *Extraterritorial Jurisdiction in Theory and Practice* (The Hague, Kluwer Law International, 1996) 84.

[15] See, eg MN Shaw, *International Law*, 8th edn (Cambridge, Cambridge University Press, 2017) 60; J Klabbers, *International Law* (Cambridge, Cambridge University Press, 2013) 46; R Higgins, *Problems and Process: International Law and How We Use It* (Oxford, Oxford University Press, 1995) 65.

[16] S Elden, 'Land, Terrain, Territory' (2010) 34 *Progress in Human Geography* 799. See, similarly Duff (n 1) 104.

of demarcation and domination.[17] Lisa Ford has persuasively documented how the global consolidation of this form of territorial governance is a product of empire. That is, by organising power in defined territorial units, imperial powers created the conditions under which sovereignty, and thereby jurisdiction, became territorially bound.[18] Nevertheless, as Yahaya has recognised, once this form of sovereignty was consolidated, new power structures establishing public authority emerged.[19] It is within this political architecture – that of territorially bound states – that this inquiry is situated.

Second, my argument here focuses on so-called prescriptive jurisdiction (both legislative and adjudicative), but not on the so-called executive and/or enforcement jurisdiction. Even the majority in *Lotus* acknowledged that under international law executive jurisdiction is 'certainly territorial', namely, that 'it cannot be exercised by a State outside its territory except by virtue of a permissive rule derived from international custom or from a convention'.[20] Put differently, it is only with regard to prescriptive jurisdiction that the presumption against extraterritoriality has been put into question.[21]

Third, I shall not assess here when a particular conduct, or act, may be deemed to be perpetrated on a given territory, or what constitutes a sufficiently strong or too tangential a territorial connection to a particular state. This is a very complicated matter that warrants careful analysis in its own terms. I will thereby concentrate on clear cases of extraterritoriality.

Finally, I will address here the presumption against extraterritorial criminal jurisdiction as a matter of public international law, not of domestic law. Some states have established a similar presumption vis-à-vis the interpretation of their own domestic provisions, and other states have steadily been reluctant to exercise this type of jurisdiction more broadly.[22] This is a matter for domestic legislatures to regulate (ie it may entail a self-imposed limitation or form of restraint), and this article is rather concerned with the limitations that international law should impose over those legislatures, if any.

This is the plan for the chapter. Section II critically engages with the reasoning in the *Lotus* decision. Section III provides a normative defence of the presumption

[17] N Krisch, 'Jurisdiction Unbound: (Extra)territorial Regulation as Global Governance' (2022) 33 *European Journal of International Law* 481.

[18] L Ford, *Settler Sovereignty: Jurisdiction and Indigenous People in America and Australia, 1788–1836* (Cambridge, Harvard University Press, 2010) 13. But see also the insights on this issue in M Hildebrandt, 'Text-Driven Jurisdiction in Cyberspace', ch 2 in the present volume.

[19] N Yahaya, *Fluid Jurisdictions: Colonial Law and Arabs in Southeast Asia* (Ithaca, NY, Cornell University Press, 2020) 2.

[20] *Lotus* (n 2) 18–19.

[21] On enforcement jurisdiction, see further C Ryngaert, 'Enforcement Jurisdiction in A-territorial Spaces: Addressing Crime on the High Seas and in Cyberspace', ch 7 in the present volume. He interestingly suggests that permissive principles of extraterritorial prescriptive jurisdiction may favour broader assertions of extraterritorial enforcement jurisdiction, thereby blurring the distinction between the two. Although his argument is not incompatible with the claims I advocate here, this further issue is beyond the scope of this chapter.

[22] For the situation in the USA, see, eg WS Dodge, 'The New Presumption Against Extraterritoriality' (2020) 133 *Harvard Law Review* 1582.

against extraterritorial criminal jurisdiction and identifies some of its limitations. Section IV addresses two possible challenges to this presumption. Section V briefly concludes.

II. Two Conceptual Mistakes in *Lotus*

As indicated, on 7 September 1927, the PCIJ concluded that the Turkish courts had jurisdiction to try and punish Demons for the death of the people on board the *Boz-Kourt*. The specific rule on which the case was decided – namely, that the ship flying the Turkish flag was relevantly analogous to Turkish territory – has been subsequently derogated.[23] However, the approach adopted by both the majority and the dissenting judges has had a far larger and more persistent influence on the law of jurisdiction (and ultimately on how we see the underlying architecture of the international legal system).

In the proceedings, France had argued that in order to have the right to try Demons, Turkish courts must point to 'some title to jurisdiction recognised by international law in favour of Turkey'.[24] The majority of the court disagreed. It claimed that the issue in contention was not 'a question of stating principles which would permit Turkey to take criminal proceedings, but of formulating the principles, if any, which might have been violated by such proceedings'.[25] The reasoning of the majority is worth quoting in full:

> It does not … follow that international law prohibits a State from exercising jurisdiction in its own territory, in respect of any case which relates to acts which have taken place abroad, and in which it cannot rely on some permissive rule of international law. Such a view would only be tenable if international law contained a general prohibition to States to extend the application of their laws and the jurisdiction of their courts to persons, property and acts outside their territory … But this is certainly not the case under international law as it stands at present.[26]

The structure of this argument is simple. States are 'free' to extend the application of their laws and the jurisdiction of their courts to acts outside their territory; this discretion is only limited by certain prohibitive rules.[27] As Judge Loder put

[23] See International Convention for the Unification of Certain Rules Relating to Penal Jurisdiction in Matters of Collision or other Incidents of Navigation (Brussels, 10 May 1952) 439 UNTS 233, Arts 1–3; Convention on the High Seas (Geneva, 29 April 1958) 450 UNTS 11, Art 11; and more recently, UN Convention on the Law of the Sea (Montego Bay, 10 December 1982) 1833 UNTS 3, Art 97.

[24] *Lotus* (n 2) 18.

[25] ibid.

[26] ibid 19.

[27] In fairness, the majority argued that there is no such presumption, only to subsequently argue that in any case Turkey had exercised a form of territorial jurisdiction insofar as the deaths had been produced on board the Turkish ship, which could be assimilated to Turkish territory for all relevant purposes. This means that the critical finding was obiter dictum. The majority in *Lotus* recognised that whichever of the two approaches 'be adopted, the same result will be arrived at in this particular case', *Lotus* (n 2) 21.

it in his dissent, this proposition is based on the claim that 'under international law everything which is not prohibited is permitted'.[28] Accordingly – the majority continued – treaties and customary rules pursue the tasks of limiting the discretion left to states by international law.[29] This approach was allegedly based on 'the very nature and existing conditions of international law'.[30] More than half a century later, ICJ Judges Higgins, Kooijmans and Buergenthal famously characterised the majority's position as the 'high water mark of laissez-faire in international relations'.[31]

The majority in *Lotus* opposed their reasoning to a different 'standpoint' resting on the 'exclusively territorial character of law', prohibiting extraterritorial criminal jurisdiction except when it rests on 'special permissive rules'.[32] This was the approach adopted by the judges in the minority, who argued that state sovereignty established both jurisdiction over territory *and* a prohibition on any exercise of extraterritorial jurisdiction unless a permissive rule applied.[33] Writing as part of the minority, Judge Loder claimed that this *pro tanto* prohibition 'can be overridden by some convention to the contrary effect'.[34] Judge Altamira, in turn, added that exceptions to the principles of territoriality and nationality had 'been recognised in extreme cases where it has been absolutely necessary or inevitable'.[35]

I believe that there are two conceptual mistakes at the basis of the *Lotus* reasoning, incurred by both the majority and the minority. The first one is about the conceptual understanding of criminal jurisdiction. Jurisdiction is standardly construed as a right (it was traditionally termed *ius puniendi*): the right to criminalise a certain conduct and punish those who violate this prohibition. There is, however, some disagreement about how to understand any such right. In the classical – now canonical – analysis of Wesley Hohfeld, rights are characterised by four different types of jural relations, namely, liberties, claims, powers and immunities. Each of them correlates with a different legal consequence. Liberties correlate with the absence of a duty. Claim rights correlate with duties. Powers correlate with liabilities, and immunities with disabilities.[36] Furthermore, these jural relations belong to two different levels. The first level comprises claims and liberties, which capture deontic modalities. That is, they determine whether a particular action is permissible, impermissible or obligatory. By contrast, second-level rights –

[28] *Lotus* (n 2) Dissenting Opinion by Loder J, 34.

[29] *Lotus* (n 2) 20.

[30] ibid 18.

[31] *Arrest Warrant of 11 April 2000 (Democratic Republic of the Congo v Belgium)* [2002] ICJ Rep 3, Joint Separate Opinion of Judges Higgins, Kooijmans and Burgenthal, [51]. They added that such era had 'been significantly overtaken by other tendencies'.

[32] *Lotus* (n 2) 21.

[33] Judges Nyholm, Altamira and Moore stated that the rule is the territorial principle, to which some exceptions can be construed (see their opinions (ibid) 62, 95 and 68, respectively).

[34] ibid Dissenting Opinion by Loder J, 35.

[35] ibid Dissenting Opinion by Altamira J, 96.

[36] W Hohfeld, *Fundamental Legal Conceptions* (New Haven, CT, Yale University Press, 1919).

ie powers and immunities – capture alethic modalities. They establish the possibility or impossibility of changing legal positions, such as the power to marry, to make contracts or to vote; or the immunity against prosecution held by diplomats. This classification, I suggest, helps us capture the first conflation in *Lotus*.

To illustrate, in his dissent, Judge Finlay extensively quoted Lassa Oppenheim in conceptualising jurisdiction as a claim right. That is, he correlated a state's jurisdiction with other countries' duty to acquiesce in the defendant's punishment.[37] But, of course, this misrepresents the way in which jurisdiction operates. To claim that a state has jurisdiction over a given act or individual centrally concerns the authority of that state over that individual. Furthermore, it is not necessarily the case that other states are duty bound to accept a defendant's prosecution, let alone her conviction. They may refuse to give access to evidence, or to extradite the convicted defendant.

By contrast, Mari Takeuchi rightly notes that this is not what the majority in *Lotus* meant; they only claimed that states are free to exercise their extraterritorial criminal jurisdiction unless there is a prohibitive rule (that is, unless they have a duty not to do so).[38] Namely, she suggests that freedom in this context should be conceptualised only as a Hohfeldian liberty. Liberties entail that states would merely lack a duty not to prosecute crimes perpetrated beyond their territory. In Hart's famous example, under English law, he was at liberty to look over his garden fence at his neighbour, meaning only that he had no legal duty not to do that.[39] But this proposition does not, of course, entail that his neighbour was under a duty to be looked at. He could certainly plant a tree or build a taller fence. Analogously, Turkey having the liberty to try Demons meant that it was not under a duty not to do so. This further meant that France lacked a claim right that Turkey did not prosecute and punish Demons.[40]

This general conceptualisation of jurisdiction as mainly involving first-order normative Hohfeldian incidents – namely, liberties, rights and duties – has become the standard view in international law.[41] Weil, a firm defender of the *Lotus* model, characterised international law as an aggregate of legal norms that dictate what its subjects must do, must not do or may do.[42] Ryngaert portrays the discussion as one between permissibility except when there is a prohibitive rule, and prohibition unless there is a permissive rule to the contrary.[43] Mills similarly holds that

[37] *Lotus* (n 2) Dissenting Opinion by Finlay J, 56–57.

[38] M Takeuchi, 'General Framework of Jurisdiction' 9 (unpublished typescript on file with author).

[39] HLA Hart, *Essays on Bentham* (Oxford, Clarendon Press, 1982) 188.

[40] Writing more than 70 years after *Lotus*, ICJ Judges Higgins, Kooijmans and Buergenthal further clarified that this is not a liberty states are under a duty to exercise, when they argued that a 'State is not required to legislate up to the full scope of the jurisdiction allowed by international law'. See *Arrest Warrant* (n 31) [45].

[41] Crawford (n 6) 447; Weil, 'International Law' (n 3) 36. See also *Application of the Convention on the Prevention and Punishment of the Crime of Genocide (Bosnia and Herzegovina v Serbia and Montenegro)* [2007] ICJ Rep 43, [442].

[42] P Weil, 'Towards Relative Normativity in International Law?' (1983) 77 *American Journal of International Law* 413.

[43] Ryngaert, *Jurisdiction* (n 1) 21.

the idea of jurisdiction in international law should not be construed merely as a matter of state discretion, but rather replaced by a 'mixture of discretionary, mandatory and prohibitive elements'.[44] But if we accept that jurisdiction can only be either permitted or prohibited, that is, if we characterise it only in terms of liberties and claim rights, and we accept that under international law 'everything that is not prohibited is permissible', we seem to be committed to the claim that in the absence of a legal rule extraterritorial criminal jurisdiction must be considered permitted.

Given that I think that as a matter of international law there is such a presumption *against* extraterritorial criminal jurisdiction, and that I do not think it is plausible to reject the legal maxim that everything that is not prohibited under international law is permitted, I suggest that we have reason to put our initial assumption – that legal rules on criminal jurisdiction function exclusively at the deontic level – under closer scrutiny. Elsewhere I have argued that the right to punish does not merely involve first-order Hohfeldian relations (a liberty, a claim right), but rather it is centrally characterised by a second-order normative power. In Hohfeldian parlance, legal powers correlate with liabilities.[45] They entail the legal authority to modify the rights of a given person. To illustrate, when a defendant is convicted and sentenced by a court, her normative position is modified. She enters the courtroom with a certain number of rights, liberties and powers, and these normative positions are changed. Her liberty to move around or to travel could be severely constrained, her privacy is restricted, she may lose rights to some of her property, in many countries she loses her power to vote, etc. This means, among many other things, that it would now be impermissible for her not to be in prison or to try to escape, that her ballot would be invalid, etc. Which rights it is normatively justified to curtail as a response to criminal wrongdoing is not the issue here, even if we agree that states usually go (well) beyond what they are justified to inflict.[46]

To further support this understanding of criminal jurisdiction as a second-order power, we may note that in the Hohfeldian analysis powers are opposed to immunities, which in turn correlate with disabilities. In international law, it is generally accepted as a matter of course that the type of right that constitutes an obstacle to adjudicative criminal jurisdiction is not a claim right, ie a right that correlates or grounds a duty of a state not to punish a particular individual, but the enjoyment of a jurisdictional immunity by the defendant. In the words of the majority of the ICJ in the *Arrest Warrant* case, immunities 'protect the individual concerned against any act of authority of another State'.[47] The normative basis of sovereign immunities is precisely that no state can have authority over another

[44] Mills (n 12) 213.
[45] Hohfeld (n 36).
[46] For a recent theory of the 'punitive power' in these terms, see G Yaffe, 'Norm Shift Theory of Punishment' (2022) 22 *Ethics* 503.
[47] *Arrest Warrant* (n 31) [54].

(*par in parem non habet imperium*).[48] The ICJ, in its *Jurisdictional Immunities* judgment, acknowledged the exclusionary effect of immunity in respect of jurisdiction irrespective of the state's own admission of responsibility, the jus cogens nature of the violated norm and the existence of alternative legal remedies.[49]

More importantly for our purposes, I submit that the fact that jurisdiction is essentially a normative power rather than merely a liberty or a claim right accounts precisely for where the *Lotus* reasoning went wrong.[50] Unlike liberties, which are to be presumed under most (all?) legal systems in the absence of a concrete rule, powers are not presumed in the absence of explicit authorisation. Consider, for instance, powers of attorney, the power to dictate binding decisions by justices in domestic legal systems, powers to pass binding resolutions in international organisations and the power to marry or to vote.[51] As a descriptive matter, in the absence of a power-conferring norm, any decision attempting to modify the rights of another person would be invalid, and would thus simply fail to modify any of the pre-existing legal positions. Even when a body or individual has a particular power conferred upon them, if her decision goes beyond the scope of such power it is considered ultra vires, and therefore incapable of any legal effects. Accordingly, as soon as we conceive of criminal jurisdiction as a normative power, it follows that it cannot be presumed, but that it must be expressly conferred by international law.

The ICJ has silently endorsed this difference between liberties and powers in its subsequent case law. Namely, it is often suggested that the *Lotus* reasoning was echoed by the Court in the *Nuclear Weapons* and *Independence of Kosovo* advisory opinions.[52] In the former, the majority could not find a prohibitive rule banning categorically the use of nuclear weapons. This is clearly a question of whether states were at liberty to use them. Similarly, in the *Kosovo* advisory opinion, the Court controversially claimed that unilateral declarations of independence were not impermissible under international law, again citing the absence of a prohibitive rule. This, again, meant sustaining the maxim that everything that is not expressly prohibited is permitted under international law. Yet note that, in doing so, the Court avoided addressing the elephant in the room, that is, whether

[48] See, generally H Fox and P Webb, *The Law of State Immunity*, 3rd edn (Oxford, Oxford University Press, 2013).

[49] *Jurisdictional Immunities of the State (Germany v Italy), Counter-Claim, Order of 6 July 2010* [2010] ICJ Rep 310. See also Fox and Webb (n 48) ch 4.

[50] Note that rights can be 'molecular' creatures, in that they can be composed of different jural relations. States would normally have the Hohfeldian liberty to exercise their powers, in that it is permissible for them to do so. But states may sometimes have the power to do something which is impermissible (a right to do wrong). I discuss this issue at greater length in Chehtman, *The Philosophical Foundations* (n 1) ch 2. The fact that we cannot understand the right to prescribe and adjudicate criminal rules except as constituted centrally by a normative power accounts for why it cannot be presumed.

[51] See, eg Argentine Constitution, Art 116; Rome Statute of the International Criminal Court (Rome, 17 July 1998) 2187 UNTS 3 pt 2; Statute of the International Criminal Tribunal for the Former Yugoslavia UNSC Res 827 (1993), Arts 1ff; Charter of the United Nations (San Francisco, 26 June 1945), cc IV, V and VII (esp Art 42).

[52] *Legality of the Threat or Use of Nuclear Weapons, Advisory Opinion* [1996] ICJ Rep 226; *Kosovo* (n 11).

seceding groups have the authority (the Hohfeldian normative power) to create a state, thereby changing a significant number of jural relations.

By contrast, the ICJ refused to apply the *Lotus* reasoning to the normative power ('regulatory competences') to determine legal boundaries in the *Anglo-Norwegian Fisheries* case or to the power to confer upon someone citizenship in the *Nottebohm* case.[53] In these cases, legally valid decisions (with their changes in normative positions) could not be issued without the express conferral of powers by international law. These powers are explicitly conferred by international law as the accepted bases of criminal jurisdiction (the principles of nationality, passive personality, protection, universality and so on).

The shift from first-order liberty to second-order power has broader implications for how jurisdictional powers fit into the architecture of international law. Hertogen, like many other commentators, defends the view that *Lotus* was centrally concerned with regulating the horizontal relations between coexisting, independent communities. She cites Huber, President of the Court at the time of the *Lotus* decision, who a few years after the decision argued that international law rested on the notion of the coexistence of wills of the same weight.[54] Horizontality has been used as the 'key imagery' to capture jurisdictional relations between states.[55] Liberties indeed capture horizontal relationships between equals.[56]

By contrast, normative powers establish vertical relations between subjects. In Nico Krisch's analysis, 'states use their regulatory and judicial institutions … to govern activities of companies abroad, and this establishes hierarchies not only over those companies but also over other states whose ability to define their own policy is thereby curtailed'.[57] To clarify, although states exercise their normative power over defendants, by doing so unilaterally, they ultimately superimpose their own legal framework (authority) to the detriment of the territorial political community. As Thorburn has indicated, when a political authority sets and enforces certain terms of interaction between persons, this excludes the possibility of others setting different terms.[58] This is precisely why states often complain or resist instances of extraterritorial criminal jurisdiction as unwarranted interferences in their domestic affairs.

This type of hierarchical relationship is all the clearer if we look at the history of extraterritoriality. Extraterritorial jurisdiction formally shaped vertical relationships of authority between the core and the periphery for most of the nineteenth century. These arrangements were based on capitulation treaties under which

[53] Crawford (n 6) 458.
[54] Cited in Hertogen (n 4) 911 (my translation from the French original).
[55] Krisch (n 17) 503.
[56] Admittedly, some scholars have acknowledged that jurisdiction entails primarily the exercise of certain powers, but they characteristically fail to identify the precise implications of this conceptual difference. See, eg Mann (n 1) 3; Crawford (n 6) 458.
[57] Krisch (n 17) 504.
[58] M Thorburn, 'Soldiers as Public Officials: A Moral Justification for Combatant Immunity' (2019) *Ratio Juris* 405.

European powers exercised exclusive jurisdiction over affairs concerning their nationals abroad, which in turn meant regulating domestic trade and establishing Western legal rules and practices.[59] Kevin Davis aptly recalls when Burke attempted to impeach Warren Hastings for corruption in India 'without calling a single witness from the subcontinent'.[60] Such a regime was based on the view that 'civilised' states had rights of control and administration over 'uncivilised others'. This is why there is ultimately some irony involved in the fact that the PCIJ approved of Turkey's exercise of jurisdiction over a French national for acts he committed on board a French vessel by reference to the Treaty of Lausanne, the treaty which had put an end to the capitulations regime between France and Turkey. That is, it was precisely the treaty that ended a regime by which France was entitled to vertically impose its own authority over Turkish nationals on Turkish territory.

Fortunately, the second conceptual problem in the *Lotus* reasoning is much easier to grasp. The majority and the minority both agreed that the scope of criminal jurisdiction of the state is connected with (or is 'an attribute of', or even 'constitute[s]') its sovereignty,[61] and they treat sovereignty and jurisdiction as concepts emanating from the interests of states themselves. This approach is echoed in much of the relevant literature.[62] Nevertheless, even if we accept that jurisdiction concerns rights that are typically held by sovereign states, ie legal persons, this hardly means that they are based on their own interests *qua states*. If anything, I submit, the relevant interests are ultimately those of the political community, and only derivatively the interests of their organs (legislatures and courts). Put differently, they are group rights held by legal persons.[63]

There are two main conceptions of group rights in the literature which have significantly different implications for our discussion, namely the 'collective' and the 'corporate' conception. The corporate conception entails attributing value to the interests of the group as an entity separate from, and not wholly reducible to, the interests of its members. This type of approach has been resisted precisely because it is not sufficiently sensitive to the interests of individuals and minorities within the group, giving significant leeway to majorities to exercise an abusive rule over them.[64] By contrast, the collective conception of group rights assumes that the rights attributed to the group are entirely based on the interests of its

[59] The literature on this is vast and compelling. See, eg M Craven, 'What Happened to Unequal Treaties? The Continuities of Informal Empire' (2005) *Nordic Journal of International Law* 335; T Kayaoglu, *Legal Imperialism: Sovereignty and Extraterritoriality in Japan, the Ottoman Empire, and China* (Cambridge, Cambridge University Press, 2010), DS Margolies et al (eds), *The Extraterritoriality of Law: History, Theory, Politics* (Abingdon, Routledge, 2019); U Özsu, 'Ottoman Empire' in B Fassbender and A Peters (eds), *The Oxford Handbook of the History of International Law* (Oxford, Oxford University Press, 2012).

[60] K Davis, *Between Impunity and Imperialism* (Oxford, Oxford University Press, 2019) 196.

[61] B Fassbender, 'Sovereignty and Constitutionalism in International Law' in N Walker (ed), *Sovereignty in Transition* (Oxford, Hart Publishing, 2003) 129.

[62] See, eg Crawford (n 6) 447.

[63] Chehtman, *The Philosophical Foundations* (n 1) ch 1.

[64] P Jones, 'Group Rights and Group Oppression' (1999) 7 *Journal of Political Philosophy* 362.

members, and is thereby sensitive to the claim that individuals are the ultimate unit of normative value.[65] In fact, under this analysis, groups' interests have value only insofar as they reflect the interests of their members. This lack of autonomous value entails that collective rights, unlike corporate rights, are not liable to the charge of allowing the interests of the state to displace or superimpose over those of individuals and sub-groups who fall within the state's authority.[66] As a result, this conception of group rights does not pose a serious threat to the rights of individuals belonging to the state.

In making reference to the interests of states as the decisive consideration, the judges in *Lotus*, perhaps unwittingly, adopted the corporate conception of group rights.[67] Yet, as soon as we abandon such an understanding for the collective conception, we get a clearer sense of the considerations underpinning the presumption against extraterritorial criminal jurisdiction. Any such presumption will need to be justified by reference to the interests of members of the territorial political community. But insofar as international law cannot give greater weight to the interests of certain individuals over the interests of others, any such presumption will need to be compatible both with the interests of minorities within the territorial state and with the interests of members and minorities in other states. Mégret recently captured this insight nicely when he suggested that any defensible normative account of extraterritorial criminal jurisdiction would need to take into account the interests of individuals in the territorial state where the offence took place, the interests of individuals in the forum state that seeks to exercise its extraterritorial criminal jurisdiction and the interests of individuals elsewhere, insofar as certain criminal rules may contribute to the provision of public goods beyond the borders of any given state or group of states.[68] Put differently, this more promising notion of group rights will have important implications not only to account for the normative weight of the presumption against extraterritorial criminal jurisdiction, but also for its limitations.

III. The Presumption against Extraterritorial Criminal Jurisdiction: A Defence

The previous section suggests that the legal architecture of international law as a legal system is clearly compatible with – in fact, presupposes – the existence of a presumption against extraterritorial jurisdiction. This proposition is entailed by the fact that criminal jurisdiction centrally embodies a Hohfeldian power, and

[65] J Raz, *The Morality of Freedom* (Oxford, Oxford University Press, 1988) 208.

[66] Jones (n 64) 377.

[67] See, eg *Lotus* (n 2) 27 and 30.

[68] F Mégret, '"Do Not Do Abroad What You Would Not Do at Home?": An Exploration of the Rationales for Extraterritorial Criminal Jurisdiction over a State's Nationals' (2020) 57 *Canadian Yearbook of International Law* 1.

normative powers are typically not presumed under any plausible legal system, but rather must be explicitly conferred upon their holder. It also suggests that this presumption, if anything, must be based on the interests of members of each state qua political community. This section provides a normative justification of this presumption, which, in turn, will help me account for both its scope and its normative weight. That is, a plausible account of the presumption against extraterritorial criminal jurisdiction must explain whether and under what conditions, if any, that presumption can be overridden or defeated.

Writing in the seventeenth century, Ulrik Huber argued that sovereignty of states over their territory is absolute and exclusive. His position can be articulated through two maxims: (i) the laws of each country bind every individual within its territory, whether they are there permanently or temporarily; and (ii) those laws only bind these individuals, but not individuals beyond the boundaries of the state.[69] Judge Marshall in the US Supreme Court replicated this reasoning when he wrote that the 'jurisdiction of the nation within its own territory is necessarily exclusive and absolute … All exceptions, therefore, must be traced up to the consent of the nation itself'.[70] Francis Wharton similarly claimed in 1887 that 'the authority of a nation within its own territory is absolute and exclusive'.[71] Hazel Fox and Philippa Webb trace this understanding of absolute jurisdiction to the writings of Grotius and the external aspects of the concept of a state, as well as Bodin and Austin's views of the sovereign legislative power.[72]

This approach, however, is highly unpersuasive. It not only sits uncomfortably with the practice of a significant number of states which have long claimed certain bases of extraterritorial criminal jurisdiction, but more importantly, it seems to be based on two mistaken assumptions: (i) that the interests of individuals in state A always require that only the laws of A apply to them; and (ii) that the interests of individuals outside state A are never sufficiently important to warrant interference with the authority of state A in the form of extending their own criminal prohibitions on the territory of A. The situation of millions of German nationals under Nazi rule and of hundreds of thousands of Tutsis living in Rwanda in 1994, to name but two of the most striking examples, would suffice to show that (i) does not always hold. The interests of individuals in state V who act directly to affect the good governance of their state (such as an attack on their prime minister) or the massive counterfeiting of V's currency on the territory of state A indicate that (ii) is not necessarily true either. In his classic work on jurisdiction, FA Mann conceded that the principle of territoriality as an exclusive basis of jurisdiction was 'no longer adequate'.[73] In short, this suffices to indicate that the presumption is

[69] Cited in Mills (n 12) 202.
[70] *The Schooner Exchange v McFaddon* (1812) 7 Cranch 116.
[71] Cited in S Kassan, 'Extraterritorial Jurisdiction in the Ancient World' (1935) 29 *American Journal of International Law* 238.
[72] Fox and Webb (n 48) 165.
[73] Mann (n 1).

not absolute. It thereby must be conceptualised as a presumption of the rebuttable type. Namely, it entails that the burden of proof as to the legitimacy of any claim of extraterritorial jurisdiction is asymmetrically distributed between the authority claiming it and that resisting it.[74]

Nevertheless, there are a significant number of reasons that have been articulated against the exercise of extraterritorial criminal jurisdiction. For example, several scholars have argued that there are pragmatic reasons to conduct an investigation and trial in the state on whose territory the offence was committed, given that the perpetrator, the evidence, etc are located there. This argument follows a logic similar to that of the doctrine of *forum non-conveniens* in private international law.[75] More broadly, it is suggested that a system allowing for multiple, independent authorities claiming jurisdiction over the same facts would face steep coordination/collective action challenges, such as competition, blocking and disagreement on how best to conduct an investigation and prosecution, and even about the appropriate sanctions. This, in turn, would undermine the efficiency of law enforcement.[76]

A second type of defence of the presumption against extraterritorial prosecutions relies on defendants' rights. It is often feared that extraterritorial criminal jurisdiction can entail violations of the human rights of defendants.[77] In his dissent in *Lotus*, Judge Altamira argued that the rights of individuals would be affected when an extraterritorial state imposes upon her 'the effects of laws which are not those of the community to which' she belongs, of laws she does not know and which are applied by entirely foreign judges to whom she cannot make herself understood, because she 'does not know their language, their legal mentality, the forms of procedure they employ, etc'.[78] At the very least, in many cases, defendants will lack fair notice that their conduct is subject to the laws of the extraterritorial state, let alone the possibility of being convicted twice for the same conduct.[79]

A third significant worry is that extraterritorial criminal jurisdiction would lead to the unwarranted exercise of domination of weaker states by more powerful ones. As pointed out in the previous section, extraterritorial criminal jurisdiction is usually associated with a colonial or neocolonial political agenda through which central powers impose their economic and/or political interests on peripheral or

[74] See D Walton, *Burden of Proof, Presumption and Argumentation* (Cambridge, Cambridge University Press, 2014) 113.

[75] Crawford (n 6) 474–75.

[76] Davis (n 60) 225ff. He suggests that both the overdeterrence (agencies piling up) and the underenforcement (agencies holding back) resulting from this type of scenario would lead to suboptimal results.

[77] For concerns regarding US extraterritorial prosecutions, see, eg M Farbiarz, 'Accuracy and Adjudication: The Promise of Extraterritorial Due Process' (2016) 116 *Columbia Law Review* 625.

[78] *Lotus* (n 2) Dissenting Opinion by J Altamira, 104.

[79] Davis (n 60) 207 and 229, respectively.

semi-peripheral states.[80] As Krisch suggests, the expansive use of extraterritorial jurisdiction may well lead to an 'oligarchical structure in which a few powerful countries wield the capacity to set and implement their rules'.[81] The USA and certain EU states are likely to be the most active users of this form of global governance, but they will hardly be the only ones.[82] A broad regime of extraterritorial criminal jurisdiction will essentially bring instances of political or economic interference by big powers over developing or peripheral countries as a central outcome.

Each of these arguments is persuasive and, with variations, has substantial normative force. Yet all of them are clearly contingent. Indeed, in some instances, the offender, the victim and much of the evidence would be in the forum state, rather than in the territorial state. This fact has been crucial to the recent growth of prosecutions based on universal jurisdiction.[83] Furthermore, not every instance of extraterritorial criminal jurisdiction would negatively affect the individual rights of defendants. It is not inconceivable that a Belgian foreign fighter in Syria would receive a fairer trial and greater respect for her rights before a Belgian court than before the courts in Syria; or that a person connected to the 9/11 attacks may receive a fairer trial before the courts of Uruguay than before a military commission in the USA.[84] Finally, not every instance of extraterritorial jurisdiction is liable to the neocolonial charge, as the *Lotus* saga nicely illustrates. Virtuous instances of extraterritorial criminal jurisdiction include the trial of Hisenne Habré in the courts of Senegal and the prosecution of Spanish officials before Argentine courts.[85]

The fact that each of these arguments is contingent does not deprive them of their normative force. Together, they can help us provide a fairly robust defence of the presumption against extraterritorial criminal jurisdiction which works largely as a patchwork of independent, partially overlapping considerations. Nevertheless, even if they do provide this presumption with significant normative traction, my sense is that they ultimately fail to capture a substantial, non-contingent reason why extraterritorial criminal jurisdiction is in principle objectionable. Even if not

[80] See, eg H van der Wilt, 'Universal Jurisdiction under Attack: An Assessment of African Misgivings towards International Criminal Justice as Administered by Western States' (2011) 9 *Journal of International Criminal Justice* 1043.

[81] Krisch (n 17) 483.

[82] eg on China, see D Ireland-Piper, *Extraterritoriality in East Asia: Extraterritorial Criminal Jurisdiction in China, Japan, and South Korea* (Cheltenham, Edward Elgar, 2021) ch 3 (with Sanzhuan Guo).

[83] On *fraude à la loi*, see Chehtman, 'Jurisdiction' (n 7). On the relationship between migration and universal jurisdiction, see L Johns, M Langer and ME Peters, 'Migration and the Demand for Transnational Justice' (2022) 116 *American Political Science Review* 1184.

[84] On US Military Commissions, see, eg N Katyal, 'Equality in the War on Terror' (2007) 59 *Stanford Law Review* 1365.

[85] See, eg S Weill, KT Seelinger and KB Carlson, *The President on Trial: Prosecuting Hissène Habré* (Oxford, Oxford University Press, 2020); LÍ Álvarez and AM Tejón, 'Ten Years of the Argentine Inquiry into Franco-Era Crimes: What Has Been Achieved?' (*Oxford Human Rights Hub*, 27 October 2020) ohrh.law.ox.ac.uk/ten-years-of-the-argentine-inquiry-into-franco-era-crimes-what-has-been-achieved/.

always the weightiest one, it is a reason that would explain why it seems problematic for a Bolivian court to try a random case of homicide in Nepal. Namely, extraterritorial jurisdiction is *pro tanto* objectionable because it is incompatible with the principle of self-government (or sovereignty) that members of each political community collectively enjoy. This principle, or right of each political community to determine its fundamental rules on its own, is arguably at the basis of the legal prohibition to intervene in the domestic affairs of any state, as articulated under international law.[86]

This is a non-contingent reason as to why state authorities in principle lack the right to prosecute and convict offences committed extraterritorially. Although this is not a particularly novel claim,[87] I think it is worth unpacking it in a bit more detail. Self-government essentially involves the right of a particular community to set the rules that will regulate its shared life as well as the interactions among its members. Criminal rules are an important, and indeed very sensitive, area of norm-making in every political community. A lot of political energy by different constituencies and stakeholders goes into defending or criticising the criminalisation (or decriminalisation) of certain conduct. This often involves mobilisations, public deliberation/debates and voting strategies in congress and beyond. The recent decriminalisation of abortion in Argentina and the fight for criminalising femicides in Latin America are notable examples of this.[88] In other words, penal policy is deeply connected with the moral and political values of each political community, and with complex legislative and broader epistemic processes which often include commissions of experts, wide debate in the press and on the streets, and ultimately their processing by the political system. These processes cover not only substantive law, but also the laws concerning sentencing, criminal procedure and evidentiary standards. Thus, when 'legal institutions from other states attempt to impose their views through coercion, they are likely to make mistakes about where the affected people's interests lie'.[89] As a result, having the will of an extraterritorial (foreign) political community superimposed over that of the one governing a particular territory requires very substantial reasons as to why such authority is warranted.

Finally, it is important not to overestimate the weight of the reasons in favour of establishing extraterritorial criminal jurisdiction. In the words of Judge Loder, in his dissent in *Lotus*, 'the criminal law of a State loses its compelling force and its applicability in relation to offences committed by a foreigner in foreign territory'.[90] The criminal law, it is often emphasised, is constitutive of civil order.[91]

[86] See further, ICJ, *Nicaragua*, ICJ Reports (1986) 108.
[87] See, eg Duff (n 1) 110.
[88] See, eg B Sutton and NL Vacarezza, *Abortion and Democracy: Contentious Body Politics in Argentina, Chile, and Uruguay* (New York, Routledge, 2021).
[89] Davis (n 60) 230.
[90] *Lotus* (n 2) Dissenting Opinion by Loder J, 38.
[91] L Farmer, *Making the Modern Criminal Law: Criminalization and Civil Order* (Oxford, Oxford University Press, 2016) 43.

In effect, I have argued elsewhere that extraterritorial jurisdiction cannot provide the same type of public good as territorial jurisdiction.[92] The reason for this is partly connected with its diminished political legitimacy (as per above), but also with the fact that extraterritorial authorities are typically unable to enforce individuals' compliance with their laws – they can only exercise police powers within their borders. Vincent Chiao, together with those advocating the 'political turn' in criminal law theory, has plausibly suggested that the criminal law 'stabilizes a public sense of justice by providing assurance that cooperation with legal rules will not leave one open to victimization or exploitation'.[93] This type of assurance can only be adequately provided where a state can enforce any such rules, namely, on its territory.[94]

This consideration helps us better understand where the interests of members of a political community lie. To illustrate, individuals in Kenya generally lack an interest in Kenya's criminal laws applying to individuals in Mexico, just as Mexicans typically lack an interest in Kenyan criminal law applying to individuals in Sinaloa. Even if, as Guyora Binder rightly noted, this consideration does not lead to a non-rebuttable presumption against extraterritoriality,[95] it significantly weakens the weight of the reasons states can invoke to justify the extension of their laws, and the power of their courts to entertain and adjudicate prosecutions concerning conduct on the territory of another sovereign state.

IV. Two Challenges

There are at least two potential challenges to the presumption against extraterritorial criminal jurisdiction, as hereby defended, that I need to consider. The first one embodies a version of legal moralism that connects extraterritorial criminal jurisdiction with violations of human rights. Cécile Fabre has argued that any single act of murder, rape, enslavement or abuse ought to be considered subject to

[92] See A Chehtman, 'A Theory of International Crimes' in K Heller et al (eds), *The Oxford Handbook of International Criminal Law* (Oxford, Oxford University Press, 2020). US Supreme Court Justice Joseph Story most likely exaggerated when he argued that 'the laws of one country can have no intrinsic force … except within the territorial limits of that country': J Story, *Commentary on the Conflicts of Laws* (Boston, Hilliard, Gray and Company, 1834) 7. Extraterritorial criminal prosecutions can provide some force to the laws of a foreign country. Admittedly, he believed that this intrinsic force would travel with nationals of a country extraterritorially.

[93] V Chiao, *Criminal Law in the Age of the Administrative State* (Oxford, Oxford University Press, 2018) 37.

[94] Notably this would include other places where a state exercises jurisdiction, such as vessels, aircrafts and embassies.

[95] G Binder, 'Authority to Proscribe and Punish International Crimes' (2013) 63 *University of Toronto Law Journal* 278. Admittedly, certain criminal laws can have some binding force on individuals on the basis of the jurisdiction of an extraterritorial body. See H Jo and B Simmons, 'Can the International Criminal Court Deter Atrocity?' (2016) 70 *International Organization* 443.

the extraterritorial criminal jurisdiction of any state and/or international criminal tribunal. The reason for this is that these

> are crimes which shock the conscience of all human beings (for short, humankind) because they destroy, or at any rate seek to destroy, that which is specifically and nobly human in their victims (notably, their self-respect and dignity) and are committed in defiance of that which is or at any rate ought to be specifically human in their perpetrators.[96]

Massimo Renzo has similarly characterised this type of wrong as showing a lack of respect and concern that we individuals owe to our fellow human beings qua human beings, and not simply as fellow citizens. Violations of their human rights deny that victims have the status of human beings. This makes every serious violation of a basic human right an offence answerable not only to our fellow citizens, but also to all human beings *qua human beings*.[97] After all, human rights are the kind of moral rights human beings have 'as such', that is, irrespective of 'where they live, … what their social or economic condition is, and … whether these rights are included in the constitution of their state'.[98] As a result, such wrongs would fall under the jurisdiction of every state, regardless of where the offences took place.

This view carves a substantial, expansive exception to the presumption against extraterritorial criminal jurisdiction.[99] Although it does not deny its operation completely, it seems to make it rather marginal. Human rights, at least under international human rights law, include rights other than the right to life and against bodily harm, such as, inter alia, the right to healthcare, to education and to housing.[100] This would entail that different varieties of theft, fraud and offences linked to corruption would also be left out of the presumption against extraterritoriality.[101] Once we see these implications, it seems that whatever intuitive pull the proposal could initially have becomes much weaker.

As indicated, to assess the strength of this argument, we need to consider the different interests at play. This means we need to look centrally to the interests of individuals in the territorial state, in the forum state and possibly in other

[96] C Fabre, *Cosmopolitan Peace* (Oxford, Oxford University Press, 2016) 181.

[97] M Renzo, 'Crimes against Humanity and the Limits of International Criminal Law' (2012) 31 *Law and Philosophy* 449.

[98] ibid 450.

[99] For a critical and largely persuasive account, see M Pinto, 'Historical Trends of Human Rights Gone Criminal' (2020) 42 *Human Rights Quarterly* 729; M Pinto, 'Human Rights as Penal Drivers across the World', ch 6 in the present volume.

[100] See, eg Universal Declaration of Human Rights (Paris, 10 December 1948) UNGA Res 217 A(III), Art 17; Protocol to the Convention for the Protection of Human Rights and Fundamental Freedoms (Paris, 20 March 1952) European Treaty Series No 9, Art 1; American Convention on Human Rights (San José, 22 November 1969), Art 21; African Charter on Human and Peoples' Rights (Nairobi, 27 June 1981), Art 14. See also, more broadly, the International Covenant on Economic, Social and Cultural Rights (New York, 16 December 1966) 993 UNTS 3.

[101] Although Renzo (n 97) seeks to resist this claim, I fear that this is a necessary implication of his view.

places where similar types of offences may be perpetrated. Admittedly, this type of analysis may need to be conducted, if not on a case-by-case basis, at least on an offence-by-offence one. It may be that murder and acts of corruption need not be treated similarly.

Such an individualised analysis is clearly beyond the scope of this chapter. Nevertheless, a few considerations may help us better grasp how this issue should be analysed. The most straightforward seems to be the situation of individuals in the forum state. Do individuals in Thailand have an interest that an act of murder, rape, theft or corruption not be conducted in, say, Peru? Or better, do they have an interest that is sufficiently weighty to override the arguments against Thailand having authority over matters in Peru to the exclusion of Peruvian authorities? Similarly, are we to suggest that individuals in Peru have an interest in Thailand having authority over acts perpetrated in Peru? And finally, do individuals in South Africa, Iran or Belgium have an interest that is sufficiently important to confer upon Thailand authority in Peru? I think all four questions would be generally answered in the negative. This reaction seems all the more persuasive once we acknowledge that this type of authority will typically be exercised by powerful states over weaker ones, would risk human rights abuses for defendants when exercised by states with poor due process safeguards and would disrespect the rules enacted by the relevant domestic political community. These rules include not only what type of conduct should be criminalised, but also what the appropriate penalties and relevant procedures are (including rights for both defendants and victims).

Furthermore, my preferred approach need not deny that violations of human rights warrant some sort of external interference by foreign authorities, including domestic and international tribunals. It only denies that criminal prosecutions via domestic, extraterritorial authorities are the appropriate way to address them. After all, many theorists have identified external interference as one of the defining conceptual features of the notion of human rights.[102] Under international human rights law, this interference does not generally amount to the allocation of extraterritorial criminal jurisdiction to the detriment of local authorities, except for the most acute situations, such as instances of genocide, war crimes or crimes against humanity. States (non-governmental organisations and inter-governmental organisations) have the right, to use Judge Finlay's words in his dissent in *Lotus*, 'to bring pressure to bear upon the government of the offender to have him brought to justice', but they lack the 'right to assert for this purpose in its own courts a jurisdiction which they do not possess'.[103] Ultimately, international human rights law is articulated as a mechanism, or at least a language, for international actors urging, sometimes through legally binding decisions, domestic territorial authorities to

[102] For two classic examples, see J Rawls, *The Law of Peoples* (Cambridge, MA, Harvard University Press, 2001); J Raz, 'Human Rights without Foundations' in S Besson and J Tasioulas (eds), *The Philosophy of International Law* (Oxford, Oxford University Press, 2010).

[103] *Lotus* (n 2) Dissenting Opinion by Finlay J, 56.

exercise their criminal jurisdiction over certain types of wrongs.[104] Even if this type of institutional setting contains significant flaws, it seems to strike a much better balance between the interest in punishment being meted out to offenders and respect for self-government and other collective and individual rights. Most importantly for our purposes, this type of mechanism maintains the presumption against extraterritorial criminal jurisdiction largely unscathed.

The second and final challenge I want to address is well articulated in the recent work of Nico Krisch. He notes that technological developments, together with social and economic changes, have put increasing pressure on the legal framework allocating jurisdiction, which is still largely construed along territorial lines. He identifies five concrete, partially overlapping challenges: (i) unlocalisable acts as illustrated by those taking place in or through 'cyberspace'; (ii) ubiquitous actors, such as global corporations, global value chains and transboundary networks; (iii) unbound markets, which make territorial regulation largely ineffective; (iv) borderless effects, such as those produced by greenhouse gas emissions; and (v) global values, such as those captured by human rights discourse. To address them, Krisch advocates abandoning the existing territorially centred understanding of criminal jurisdiction in favour of an analytically superior picture of assemblage of jurisdictional spheres.[105]

He acknowledges that we must construe the regulation of jurisdiction under international law as an issue of vertical governance rather than as a horizontal device used to distribute authority between states. In line with this proposition, he is sensitive to the perils of expansive jurisdictional claims by powerful actors, and to the possibility that this may lead to an oligarchy of regulatory powers, with central states legislating over peripheral ones. In his words, the 'exercise of unbound jurisdiction to tackle transboundary problems does not merely affect other countries incidentally – it seeks to supersede their own policies and thus engages self-government claims directly'.[106] His solution is thereby to subject extraterritorial jurisdiction to accountability mechanisms.

Notwithstanding several notes of caution, Krisch seems largely supportive of an expansive jurisdictional regime as a technical way to tackle some of the underlying issues he identifies. Although he acknowledges that proper public accountability is unlikely to prosper, he insists that jurisdiction be approached as a governance technique, sensitive mainly to the difficulties of regulating certain

[104] The case law of the Inter-American Court of Human Rights is particularly notable for this. In particular, the Court has equated a violation of a fundamental human right with a duty to prosecute the perpetrators irrespective of statutes of limitations or other domestic obstacles. See, among many others, *Velásquez-Rodrríguez v Honduras (Merits)* IACHR Series C No 4 (29 July 1988); *Bulacio v Argentina (Merits, Reparations and Costs)* IACHR Series C No 100 (18 September 2003); *Bueno-Aves v Argentina (Merits, Reparations, and Costs)* IACHR Series C No 164 (11 May 2007). For a thorough assessment, see A Huneeus, 'International Criminal Law by Other Means: The Quasi-Criminal Jurisdiction of the Human Rights Courts' (2013) 107 *American Journal of International Law* 1.

[105] Krisch (n 17) 495.

[106] ibid 26.

economic activities and technologies. Jurisdiction 'unbound', as he calls it, can ultimately help resolve collective action problems and provide certain public goods which political communities cannot achieve by themselves. In fact, he notes that strong objections to expansive criminal jurisdiction have been raised by the business community, precisely the actors that he wants to restrain. At the same time, this expansive framework would be sensitive to the lack of capacity of states in the Global South to enforce relevant regulations (such as human rights standards) on multinational corporations, many of which are more powerful than states. As a result, allowing for unilateral criminal jurisdiction 'can help close the governance gap and subject large companies to a certain discipline'.[107]

Nevertheless, this proposal likely throws the baby out with the bath water. Unilateral exercises of criminal or regulatory jurisdiction hardly offer a particularly promising solution to these technological and economic challenges. If history can offer any insights, it is more likely that they will be used to pursue the forum state's interests, rather than to further the interests of individuals in the territorial state. Collective action problems require agreed solutions by all states concerned, possibly in the form of a multilateral framework, not impositions from the Global North. Furthermore, in negotiating such a framework, the presumption against extraterritorial jurisdiction can provide weaker states with some leverage to obtain certain guarantees vis-à-vis the expanded jurisdiction of more powerful states. That is, insofar as big powers are required to provide normatively acceptable grounds that would suffice to override a robust presumption against extraterritorial jurisdiction, this presumption can keep their 'unbound' jurisdiction slightly more restrained.

V. Conclusion

This contribution provides a principled defence of the presumption against extraterritorial criminal jurisdiction. It does so by challenging two largely neglected features of the seminal decision by the PCIJ in the *Lotus* case, namely that jurisdiction must be understood as a Hohfeldian liberty and that it is a right that belongs to states qua states, rather than as agents of their political communities. By contrast, I argue that conceptualising jurisdiction as a second-order normative power allows us both to understand why its extraterritorial reach cannot be presumed as a matter of international law (ie normative powers, under any legal system, must be explicitly conferred) and why extraterritorial jurisdiction is *pro tanto* objectionable (it superimposes the authority of an extraterritorial political community over that of the territorial one). Moreover, by arguing that jurisdiction is a collective right held by states but one that is ultimately based on the interests of individual members of each political community, this contribution shows that

[107] ibid 30.

this presumption is rebuttable. Namely, it may and should be overridden under certain circumstances, such as when a political community is unlikely to prosecute crimes that affect important interests of individuals abroad (eg principles of nationality, passive personality and protection)[108] or when it is unlikely to prosecute crimes that affect fundamental interests of certain individuals or groups at home (universal jurisdiction).

[108] I follow international law here as a heuristic device. However, I am still to be persuaded that the nationality of the offender or that of the victim suffices to confer upon an extraterritorial state criminal jurisdiction. See Chehtman, *The Philosophical Foundations* (n 1) ch 3.

2

Text-Driven Jurisdiction in Cyberspace

MIREILLE HILDEBRANDT*

I. Introduction

In this chapter I further develop a philosophy of technology for law and the rule of law, more specifically for the role of territorial jurisdiction in the protection against crime and against arbitrary use of the *ius puniendi* (right to punish). In the face of the code- and data-driven nature of cyberspace, I discuss modern positive law as based on a text-driven jurisdiction, and the main argument of the chapter is that we cannot take for granted that the kind of legal protection that is offered by a text-driven criminal jurisdiction will hold in the context of cyberspatial challenges. In section II, I investigate how modern positive law-as-we-know-it was triggered by the technologies of cartography and the printing press, arguing that both modern democracy and the rule of law are affordances of these technologies, as they enabled the rise of an exclusive, monopolistic territorial jurisdiction. In section III, I explore the scope of written legal speech acts, integrating some key insights from the philosophy of technology in speech act theory. This allows me to explain how the substantive and procedural principles of criminal law legality depend on the performative effect of written legal speech acts, highlighting their connection with the rise of territorial jurisdiction and the creation of an artificial, modern *demos*. In section IV, I discuss the new challenges of competing territorial jurisdictions that claim legal powers outside their territory, as well as challenges posed by new types of 'brute jurisdictions' that are based on the force of technological infrastructures that may overrule the performative effect of written legal speech acts.

In the conclusions, I call for keen attention to the specific affordances of cartography and the printing press that must be preserved if we want to uphold criminal law principles such as the presumption of innocence, the right to a fair trial and the legality principle, taking note that preservation will require reinvention and imagination rather than taking for granted the mode of existence of text-driven jurisdiction.

* The research for this chapter was funded by the European Research Council (ERC) under the HORIZON2020 Excellence of Science program ERC-2017-ADG No 788734, for the project on 'Counting as a Human Being in the Era of Computational Law', see www.cohubicol.com.

II. Modern Positive Law and Territorial Jurisdiction

Lawyers must get their act together as the rise of computational infrastructures and the ubiquity of the Internet challenge much of what we take for granted, notably the way that 'jurisdiction' exists (or what some call its 'mode of existence').[1] Since both international and national law depend on the idea of jurisdiction as a foundational concept, if not as their joint vanishing point, this is not cheap alarmism over difficulties to enforce the criminal law outside one's territory or yet another appeal to Internet exceptionalism, but a sober call to action. This call is based on the findings of a dedicated *philosophy of technology for law* that I have been developing in my research into the implications of data-driven environments for the law,[2] and more specifically for the integration of artificial intelligence into legal practice and legal research.[3] Legal theory and philosophy of law have been children of their time, recounting narratives about the nature of law and the rule of law that assume a text-driven infrastructure. This assumption has, however, been a hidden presumption that may no longer fly. Whereas there was no need to even mention positive law's reliance on the technologies of the word in an era where text was like the air we – lawyers – breathe (invisible, like water for fish), the primacy of the written word and its proliferation by way of the printing press can no longer be taken for granted.

In this chapter, I will defend the crucial importance of positive law as a historical artefact that offers a specific type of double instrumentality. On the one hand, it offers protection against criminal offences by way of the *ius puniendi*, while, on the other hand, it offers protection against arbitrary use of the *ius puniendi* by the state. Unlike morality or politics, this double instrumentality offers more than the moral preferences of whoever holds office on behalf of the state and less than the exercise of mere brute force by whoever manages to claim the monopoly of violence. The nature of positive law entails the attribution of legal effect when specified legal conditions apply, noting that such legal consequence is the performative effect of a dedicated set of speech acts that have been consolidated in a dynamic corpus of legal texts. My emphasis on the double instrumentality of positive law does *not* imply a positivist understanding of law. On the contrary, it highlights the purposive, justice-oriented and positive nature of law,[4] weaving the *fil rouge* of legal certainty through both types of protection, rejecting the separation between law, morality

[1] On the concept of 'the mode of existence', as used here, see M Hildebrandt, 'Three Framing Concepts' (2021) COHUBICOL Working Paper 1 on Text-Driven Normativity, ch 2, s 2.1, www.publications.cohubicol.com/working-papers/text-driven-normativity/chapter-2/.

[2] M Hildebrandt, *Smart Technologies and the End(s) of Law: Novel Entanglements of Law and Technology* (Cheltenham, Edward Elgar, 2015).

[3] M Hildebrandt, 'A Philosophy of Technology for Computational Law' (*LawArXiv*, 2020) www.osf.io/preprints/lawarxiv/7eykj.

[4] G Radbruch, 'Legal Philosophy' in K Wilk (trans), *The Legal Philosophies of Lask, Radbruch, and Dabin* (Cambridge, MA, Harvard University Press, 1950); M Hildebrandt, 'Radbruch's *Rechtsstaat* and Schmitt's Legal Order: Legalism, Legality, and the Institution of Law' (2015) 2 *Critical Analysis of Law* 42.

and politics, while nevertheless highlighting the distinctive performative role of law in 'modern' society, as well as the system of institutional checks and balances that distinguishes law from both morality and politics. Without legal effect, fundamental rights, including property and human dignity, become moral imperatives dependent on personal inclinations or privileges granted by those in power. Legal effect is neither a matter of brute force nor one of mechanical application. This is where a hermeneutical understanding of positive law differs from both formal and sociological positivism,[5] which also clarifies why acknowledging the emphasis on positive law does not imply legal positivism. A hermeneutical approach is focused on the key role played by interpretation when establishing the meaning of both legal text and human action, based on their multi-interpretability – which requires a decision on how the text is read in light of the facts and how the facts are to be read in light of the applicable law. This decision is not defined or determined by either logic (as legal formalism may suggest) or causality (as sociological positivism would have it). Instead, it requires situated human judgement, practical knowledge and keen awareness of the discretion that is inherent in all acts of interpretation. As Dworkin has argued, such discretion is not equivalent with arbitrary judgement based on a judge's contingent moral or political inclinations.[6] Deciding on interpretation, instead, implies a normative commitment to the integrity of the law, taking into account the bandwidth provided by legislation, prior case law and an anticipation of what a dedicated interpretation implies for future decision-making. By defining the decision on interpretation in terms of the attribution of legal effect as performative effect, we may avoid simplistic accounts based on logical or causal inference. Thus, highlighting 'legal effect' as the vanishing point of positive law and of effective legal protection does not assume that one buys into Kelsen, Schmitt, Carré de Marlberg, Hart or Raz, noting that Radbruch, Duguit, Hariou, Dworkin and Waldron developed a keen understanding of the centrality of positive law without falling prey to legal positivism.

A. The Affordances of the Technology of the Printing Press: Rule by Law

In this chapter, I will address the hermeneutical nature of positive law as a historical artifact, grounded in a specific information and communication infrastructure (ICI) – that is, in the technologies of text, or *manuscript (hand written) and*

[5] R Dworkin, *Law's Empire* (London, Fontana, 1991); J Waldron, 'The Rule of Law', *The Stanford Encyclopedia of Philosophy* (Summer edn, 2020) www.plato.stanford.edu/archives/sum2020/entries/rule-of-law; HLA Hart, *The Concept of Law* (Oxford, Clarendon Press, 1994); H Kelsen, *Pure Theory of Law* (Clark, Lawbook Exchange, 2005); J Austin, *The Province of Jurisprudence Determined* (WE Rumble ed, Cambridge, Cambridge University Press, 1995).

[6] R Dworkin, *Taking Rights Seriously*, 5th print edn (Cambridge, MA, Harvard University Press, 1978).

printing-press speech acts (hereinafter called 'written speech acts').[7] As Eisenstein and others have demonstrated, the affordances of printing press ICIs differ from those of an oral ICI, but also from those of handwritten ICIs, in particular with regard to the need for systematicity and abstraction.[8] Scholarship on the history of information confirms that writing and printing gave rise to abstract thought,[9] rather than this being a feature of the human mind in splendid isolation. Writing affords 'distantiation': between author and text, between text and reader, and between meaning and text – both in time and in space. This is how text enabled societies to organise themselves into larger communities (distantiation in space) while planning ahead for a larger timespan (distantiation in time).[10] The relationship with the shift from nomadic to sedentary societies is telling; to move from hunting and gathering (very small groups) to cultivating land and cattle (larger groupings) required storing food, drink and seeds, which, in turn, required counting and planning to make sure that the delay between harvesting and sowing did not leave people starving.[11] Writing affords the externalisation of collective memory that can also serve as a repository of the rules a society lives by, while the proliferation of identical printed copies of text afforded the enactment of statutory laws meant to bind all subjects.[12] The rise of modern positive law over the course of five or six centuries is thus tied up with the possibility of enacting written legal statutes that have legal effect for all those who share the relevant jurisdiction, or with the possibility to write treatises or restatements of law (in common law jurisdictions) and with the ability of courts to stay within a line of reasoning traced from past written decisions while simultaneously anticipating the implications for future case law.

B. The Affordances of the Technology of Cartography: The Spatiality of the Modern State

Modern positive law, however, is not only the fruit of the ICI of the printing press; it is also closely aligned with the emergence of jurisdiction and territory, and their

[7] See s III below for further elaboration of speech act theory.

[8] EL Eisenstein, *The Printing Revolution in Early Modern Europe*, 2nd edn (Cambridge, Cambridge University Press, 2012); SA Baron, EN Lindquist and EF Shevlin *Agent of Change: Print Culture Studies after Elizabeth L Eisenstein* (Amherst, University of Massachusetts Press, 2007); C O'Donnell, 'An Analysis of the History and Development of the Printing Press as Critique of Technological Determinism' (2022) 1 *Communications Undergraduate Journal* 8, http://cujournal.ie/article/id/11/; D Bawden and L Robinson, 'A Distant Mirror?; The Internet and the Printing Press' (2000) 52 *Aslib Proceedings* 51.

[9] J Gleick, *The Information: A History, a Theory, a Flood* (London, Fourth Estate, 2011).

[10] P Ricoeur, 'The Model of the Text: Meaningful Action Considered as a Text' (1973) 5 *New Literary History* 91.

[11] P Lévy, *Les Technologies de l'intelligence: L'avenir de La Pensée à l'ère Informatique* (Paris, La Découverte, 1990).

[12] Hildebrandt, *Smart Technologies and the End(s) of Law* (n 2).

culmination in the concept of sovereignty. To grasp the rise of positive law, we need to invoke the affordances of yet another technology that explains the emergence of internal and external sovereignty.[13] First, it is interesting to note that the concept of jurisdiction preceded the concept of territory. Whereas jurisdiction appeared in the early fourteenth century, referring to the scope of administrative power, territory appeared a century later, referring to land under a specific jurisdiction (of a town or state).[14] Jurisdiction determined the reach of governmental power, which could be based on *ratione personae* (clergy fell under the powers of the pope), *ratione materiae* (marriage fell within the powers of the Catholic church) or *ratione territoriae* (whoever lived on a particular stretch of land fell under the powers of a particular lord). Second, we must note how jurisdictions initially overlapped and competed, and did not depend on the idea of a sovereign state. Berman and Glenn both saliently described the rise of the state's monopolistic claims of territorial jurisdiction versus all other kinds of jurisdiction,[15] culminating in the birth of the sovereign state as an entity that combines protection against external interventions with complete and highest internal power, thus allowing the idea of external and internal sovereignty to crystallise as two sides of the same coin. This raises the salient question of why the reach and scope of jurisdiction shifted towards territory as an exclusive way to 'ground' the exercise of governmental power. Instead of looking for answers in the political, economic or even ecological domain, I will dig a bit deeper by asking what technology may have afforded this shift. In his seminal work, Ford highlighted how the technology of cartography introduced a new type of spatiality, as it enabled mapping of the surface of the earth by drawing lines and thus dividing it in mutually exclusive enclosed spaces.[16] The latter facilitated (i) a shift from authority based on family to one based on land; (ii) providing unambiguous boundaries for the exercise of such authority; (iii) creating an abstract spatiality that does not depend on the specific texture or habitation of the land that is demarcated; and thus (iv) basically mapping a series of bounded empty spaces that cover the entire surface of the earth (with the exception of the high seas). Cartography thus afforded the kind of abstraction that is characteristic of modern statehood, where the sovereign is an office, an empty place,[17] rather than a person, as famously

[13] M Hildebrandt, 'Extraterritorial Jurisdiction to Enforce in Cyberspace? Bodin, Schmitt, Grotius in Cyberspace' (2013) 63 *University of Toronto Law Journal* 196.

[14] 'Jurisdiction' (*Chambers 21st Century Dictionary*) www.chambers.co.uk/search/?query=jurisdictio n&title=21st; 'Territory' (*Chambers 21st Century Dictionary*) www.chambers.co.uk/search/?query=terr itory&title=21st. See also the relevant literature referred to in Hildebrandt, 'Extraterritorial Jurisdiction to Enforce in Cyberspace?' (n 13).

[15] H Berman, *Law and Revolution: The Formation of the Western Legal Tradition* (Cambridge, MA, Harvard University Press, 1983); HP Glenn, *Legal Traditions of the World* (Oxford, Oxford University Press, 2007).

[16] RT Ford, 'A History of Jurisdiction' (1999) 97 *Michigan Law Review* 843.

[17] C Lefort, *Democracy and Political Theory* (New York, Wiley, 1991).

described by Kantorowicz in *The King's Two Bodies*.[18] Here, again, we see that abstraction is not a human invention, based on the genius of a single person or a superior civilisation, but an affordance of a specific technology. Just as writing enabled mathematics and abstract thought, cartography enabled an abstract notion of jurisdiction that is tied to a territory but simultaneously open to any political programme or mandate. This is not to suggest technological determinism; an affordance enables and constrains. Depending on how it does this, it induces or inhibits, enforces or precludes.

C. Democracy and the Rule of Law as Technological Affordances

If cartography enabled the rise of territorial jurisdiction as we know it, and if the printing press enabled the rise of a rule *by* law within the abstract space of territorial jurisdiction, we may wonder which technologies enabled democracy and the rule *of* law. Clearly, the system of international law that emerged from the rise of the contiguous mapping of sovereign states builds on the principle of non-intervention as core to external sovereignty, thus also instituting quasi-absolute powers for internal sovereignty.[19] It is up to the sovereign to decide how its population is governed, even though the proliferation of printed text privileges rule by way of written rules as this affords reaching a larger population or a population that is distributed throughout a large territory. The non-intervention principle implies that those subject to territorial jurisdiction come to depend on the whims of their sovereign, but, due to the abstract nature of sovereignty, this, in turn, generates theoretical reflection upon the nature of government – giving rise to the idea of the social contract in its various modulations (Hobbes, Locke, Rousseau),[20] as well as new ideas about the nature of democracy, aristocracy, monarchy and tyranny (Montesquieu).[21] So, the same abstraction that shaped the sovereign state also allowed for the idea of an internal division of sovereignty, shaping the institution of the state as a system of countervailing powers. Rule *by* law is a rule by a person who holds the office of the sovereign, using legal rules to govern the people without, however, being bound by those rules, thus making the subjects of the sovereign dependent upon the abilities and intent of an actual person. Rule *of* law is the reign of *the office of* sovereignty, based on a system of rules and relationships that operate at different levels, with meta-rules that constrain which rules can be enacted and enforced.[22] Rule *of* law provides for a written or unwritten

[18] EH Kantorowicz, *The King's Two Bodies: A Study in Mediaeval Political Theology* (Princeton, Princeton University Press, 1957).

[19] J Bodin, *Bodin: On Sovereignty* (JH Franklin ed, Cambridge, Cambridge University Press, 1992).

[20] C Friend, 'Social Contract Theory', *Internet Encyclopedia of Philosophy*, www.iep.utm.edu/soc-cont/.

[21] Waldron (n 5).

[22] Hart (n 5), distinguishing between primary and secondary rules.

constitution that restricts the powers of the sovereign, even if the person that holds the office of the sovereign is democratically chosen by a majority. Under the rule of law, the office of the sovereign and whoever holds that office are bound by the law.

Returning to the notion of the empty place of the sovereign, Lefort says:[23]

> This model reveals the revolutionary and unprecedented feature of democracy. The locus of power becomes an empty place. There is no need to dwell on the details of the institutional apparatus. The important point is that this apparatus prevents governments from appropriating power for their own ends, from incorporating it into themselves. The exercise of power is subject to the procedures of periodical redistributions. It represents the outcome of a controlled contest with permanent rules. This phenomenon implies an institutionalization of conflict. The locus of power is an empty place, it cannot be occupied – it is such that no individual and no group can be consubstantial with it – and it cannot be represented.

In a sense, modern types of democracy and the rule of law are affordances of both cartography (which provides the empty space to rule a population, marking clear borders between who is and who is not within a particular jurisdiction) and the printing press (which results in a corpus of written legal norms that require interpretation and systemisation) – thus constituting a *demos* (based on territorial jurisdiction rather than kinship or other loyalties) and a text-driven jurisdiction that invites the contestation of written legal norms due to the distantiation between those who enact the law and those who are subjected to its imperatives.

III. Criminal Law Legality and the Reach of Written Speech Acts

A. The Missing Link between Speech Act Theory and Modern Positive Law

Speech act theory has focused on the act of speaking and taken little notice of the fundamentally different affordances of oral and written speech acts. The theory builds on the idea that *speaking* is a form of *acting*. As such it was first developed by Austin in *How to Do Things with Words*.[24] Austin spoke of performative speech acts (or performatives) whenever an 'utterance' *does what it says*, such as when a civil servant declares a couple husband and wife. The nature of such 'performatives' is not *causal for* but *constitutive of* its effect; the civil servant does not cause the marriage, but nevertheless brings it about. Note that – at least in civil law jurisdictions – this is not even correct, because marriage is only validly

[23] Lefort (n 17) 17.

[24] JL Austin, *How to Do Things with Words*, 2nd edn (Cambridge, MA, Harvard University Press, 1975).

constituted once it has been registered in the civil registry; it requires a written rather than 'merely' an oral speech act. Searle further developed speech act theory by introducing the concepts of institutional and brute facts. Where a table or a stone are considered brute facts, 'marriage' or 'contract' are considered institutional facts, being the result of performative speech acts.[25] This is not to say that if one intends one's words to have a certain effect they will therefore do so. Speech act theory is closely connected with a pragmatist understanding of the meaning of language, emphasising Wittgenstein's point that meaning is constituted in use and depends on a shared background consisting of hidden assumptions, mutual beliefs and a joint practice that grounds the use and thereby the meaning of words and more generally of human action.[26] Whether a speech act has performative effect depends on such a shared background. Taking Wittgenstein seriously, we should understand speech act theory as a theory on *language usage* rather than *speech* (including both written and spoken language use), and, taking philosophy of technology seriously, it seems important to trace the impact of the technologies of the word on the nature and the reach of *written speech* acts.[27] For the sake of simplicity, I will, as indicated, continue to refer to speech acts also when they entail language usage other than speech in the narrow sense of oral utterances, bringing together both written and spoken language use under the heading of speech acts.

Defining written language usage as a written speech act is especially relevant for modern positive law, which can be framed as fundamentally text-driven. Even Austin, though most of his examples concern oral performatives, used the example of a written will to explain the idea of a speech act that must be written down to 'count as' a performative act – that is, to have the intended legal effect. Despite his friendship with Herbert Hart,[28] who seems to have had a major influence on his *How to Do Things with Words*, Austin refrained from a more in-depth analysis of written performatives and how they differ from oral ones. This also goes for the incorporation of speech act theory into legal theory by MacCormick, who was more concerned with the shift from informal to formal norms than with

[25] JR Searle, *Speech Acts: An Essay in the Philosophy of Language* (Cambridge, Cambridge University Press, 1969); JR Searle, *The Construction of Social Reality* (New York, The Free Press, 1995). Searle built on GEM Anscombe, 'On Brute Facts' (1958) 18 *Analysis* 69, and I would side with Anscombe rather than with Searle in highlighting the relative nature of brute facts; whether a fact is qualified as brute or institutional depends on how it relates to other 'facts' and to the context of the 'utterance'.

[26] L Wittgenstein, *Philosophical Investigations: The German Text, with a Revised English Translation*, 3rd edn (GEM Anscombe trans, Malden, Blackwell, 2003); Ricoeur (n 10); C Taylor, *The Language Animal: The Full Shape of the Human Linguistic Capacity* (Cambridge, MA, Belknap Press, 2016); EA Di Paolo, EC Cuffari and H de Jaegher, *Linguistic Bodies: The Continuity between Life and Language* (Cambridge, MA, MIT Press, 2018); CS Peirce, *Pragmatism as a Principle and Method of Right Thinking: The 1903 Harvard Lectures on Pragmatism* (PA Turrisi ed, Albany, State University of New York Press, 1997).

[27] On the nature of written as opposed to oral speech acts, see notably B Fraenkel, 'Actes écrits, actes oraux: la performativité à l'épreuve de l'écriture' [2006] *Études de communication* 69; P Henttonen, *Records, Rules and Speech Acts: Archival Principles and Preservation of Speech Acts* (Tampere, Tampere University Press, 2007).

[28] Fraenkel (n 27) 7.

the underlying technological infrastructure that induced the externalisation of implicit norms, and thus made possible the formalisation of legal norms we now take for granted. As Henttonen notes, in his work on the cusp of archival theory and speech act theory:[29]

> [A] clear shortcoming in the speech act theory is that it does not say much about the contextual information needed for understanding a speech act. This is perhaps a consequence of the largely oral focus of Austin and Searle: in oral communication the speaker and the hearer usually share the same context, which partially hides the context's significance. When it comes to writing, the opposite is often true.

Both Anscombe and MacCormick paid detailed attention to the background knowledge that is implied in speech acts. They did so in terms of the context that is assumed when navigating institutional facts, highlighting the fact that in normal circumstances such tacit knowledge need not be specified. Curiously, however, in law, this knowledge is made explicit. For instance, when describing legal powers, MacCormick describes the background information that must be in place for a specific legal speech act to actually have the intended performative effect:[30]

> (a) Which person or persons, having (b) What general capacity or particular position (c) Subject to what required circumstances, and (d) In the absence of what vitiating circumstances (e) By what special procedures or formalities, and (f) By what act (g) In respect of what if any other persons (h) Having what general capacity (i) In respect of what thing or activity, Can bring about the designed legal outcome.

These kinds of questions demonstrate that legal systems are highly complex animals and depend on intricate stipulations of legal powers that ultimately depend on a meta-rule of recognition that is constitutive of such order, sealing the political order to its legal institution. As a legal positivist, MacCormick was very much aware of the role of the state in instituting, executing and terminating legal institutional facts, but he somehow overlooks the most obvious question: why modern law is a written law, and how that relates to the rise of the sovereign state. This question is pivotal for the development of the state's *ius puniendi*.

Modern positive law has both written and unwritten performatives, that is, utterances that have legal effect. These performatives are intimately connected with *institutional facts*, such as a criminal offence, criminal intent, justification and excuse, and with the *sources of law*, such as the Constitution, the criminal code, the powers of the public prosecutor and police officers, case law, the criminal law legality principle and the presumption of innocence. As Fraenkel explains,[31] other than with oral performatives, written legal performatives have two dimensions that coincide in oral speech acts: (i) the moment of their

[29] Henttonen (n 27) 31.

[30] Anscombe (n 25); N MacCormick, 'Norms, Institutions, and Institutional Facts' (1998) 17 *Law and Philosophy* 301, 341.

[31] Fraenkel (n 27).

utterance (their inscription and enactment); and (ii) the moment of reading (being addressed by a legal norm). The distinction between these moments is enabled by the enduring availability of what was uttered in the form of identical textual embodiment (whether a written judgment or statute). Precisely because the normative force of written legal performatives endures long beyond the moment of enactment, based on an external memory, or on tertiary retention as Stiegler would have it,[32] the context of interpretation will shift over the course of time and space, thus requiring explicit attention to underlying assumptions and tacit background knowledge. It is the written nature of legal speech acts that explains – in part – the nature of modern positive law as a complex system of interacting legal norms. It explains why the background knowledge that defines the scope of a legal power must be made explicit in fine-grained detail, and also clarifies how modern positive law affords so much complexity, as this is required to bridge the distantiation in time and space that is typical for written legal performatives and enabled by means of the granular specification of written legal performatives. Fraenkel indeed argues that modern positive law is necessarily contingent upon the specific performativity of *written* speech acts, highlighting that: (i) the disentanglement between the (legal) person who performs a legal speech act and its sedimentation in text provides for a richer and more adaptive resource for those under its jurisdiction;[33] (ii) the exposition of the provenance of an utterance by tracing it to the relevant sovereign power asserts its binding character and thus provides for modern law's complex, hierarchical and systematic character (eg distinguishing between primary and secondary norms);[34] and (iii) the continuity of the interpretation of legal performatives requires hard work when the context of utterance is distant and different from the context of 'reading', which, in turn, requires courts to insert themselves in a practice of respecting legitimate expectations based on past decisions while anticipating the impact of their judgement on future determinations.[35]

It is thus the written nature of legal speech acts that accounts for the sophistication and complexity of internal sovereignty and the concomitant powers of the

[32] B Stiegler, 'Die Aufklaerung in the Age of Philosophical Engineering' in M Hildebrandt, K O'Hara and M Waidner (eds), *Digital Enlightenment Forum Yearbook 2013: The Value of Personal Data* (Amsterdam, IOS Press, 2013).

[33] Fraenkel (n 27) 9–10, basing her analysis on Reinach's phenomenology: see J DuBois and B Smith, 'Adolf Reinach', *The Stanford Encyclopedia of Philosophy* (Fall edn, 2018) www.plato.stanford.edu/archives/fall2018/entries/reinach/.

[34] Fraenkel does not refer to primary and secondary norms, though she claims to base the aspect of what she calls 'exposition' on Hart's positivism and the need for binding legal text to trace its provenance to the sovereign; she actually refers to Hobbes, which seems more convincing: Fraenkel (n 27) 10. To the extent that her point is about the kind of complexity and systematicity that written performatives generate and require, I believe that the distinction between Hart's primary and secondary rules is pivotal.

[35] Fraenkel refers to Dworkin's famous image of the chain novel that ties the author of a judgment to both previous and subsequent judgments, taking into account the intent of previous authors, the legitimate expectations of the parties and the need to generalise the ratio decidendi to potentially unforeseeable future decisions: Fraenkel (n 27) 11.

state, including the institution and configuration of the *ius puniendi*, which, in turn, includes the intricate organisation of legal protection against a state's potentially arbitrary deployment of that same *ius puniendi*. The brute power to punish is not necessarily constrained in a foreseeable manner. However, once this power becomes a legal power, based on written legal speech acts that define and thereby limit its material and territorial scope, those subject to it can contest the interventions of criminal justice authorities by contesting the interpretation of the law that is implied in those interventions. The double instrumentality of the rule of law referred to above (conferring powers while limiting them, and protecting against the unlawful action of one's fellows in a way that also protects against the state overstepping its lawfully attributed powers) thus depends on the contestability that is enabled by written legal performatives. The latter can then be developed and sustained in the stable context of internal sovereignty (in turn enabled by the specific spatiality afforded by cartography). This stable context of internal sovereignty, which grounds territorial jurisdiction, positive law and effective legal protection, is now challenged by the novel spatiality of cyberspace.

B. Criminal Law Legality, *Demos* and Jurisdiction

The novel spatiality of cyberspace is directly related to the difference between the kind of cybernetics (steering capacity) that defines cyberspace on the one hand and that of the printing press and cartography on the other hand. Whereas printed text induces sequential, diachronic processing of information, the Internet and the World Wide Web induce random, synchronic processing; and whereas cartography induced stable geographical boundaries that instituted mutually exclusive physical spaces, the Internet and the World Wide Web induce flexible and dynamic boundaries that institute a simultaneity of overlapping spaces, where neither the boundaries nor the spaces are limited to geographical, physical space. Before the emergence of cyberspace, context was dependent on one's actual place in a given three-dimensional space (school, home, hospital, shop); in cyberspace, such location no longer defines context because one can easily move from one context to another while remaining in the same physical place (working from home, remote health monitoring, shopping online). By default, cyberspatial context is not geographically defined and thus not contained within national boundaries, raising complex issues of jurisdiction where principles of territory, personality and effects doctrine do not solve problems, but rather create them. If context is what enables the performative effect of written legal speech acts, then the loss of an identifiable context may disable the kind of legal protection offered by modern positive law.

As discussed extensively in previous work,[36] the cross-border nature of cybercrime implies a double challenge. First, cybercrimes can be committed by a

[36] Hildebrandt, 'Extraterritorial Jurisdiction to Enforce in Cyberspace?' (n 13); M Hildebrandt, 'The Virtuality of Territorial Borders' (2017) 13(2) *Utrecht Law Review* 13.

person physically located in one territory with major effects in one or more other territories. Second, this has resulted in many attempts to establish extraterritorial jurisdiction at the material, investigative and enforcement level. Both types of cross-border effects challenge the monopolistic nature of national jurisdiction in the realm of criminal law.

Above, I have argued that speech act theory must be further developed to face the particular characteristics of written legal speech acts. Only after acknowledging their reach as constitutive of a specific type of legal protection and thus their relationship with Beccaria's legality principle (*nullum crimen, nulla poena sine lege*) can we begin to understand the challenges of consolidating legal effect and thus legal protection in cyberspace. This goes especially for the legality requirements that inform criminal investigation and criminal procedure, including the presumption of innocence and the right to a fair trial, which offer legal protection against arbitrary or disproportional use of criminal investigation by states. Here again, it is the double instrumentality of the rule of law that must be preserved and possibly reinvented; both the protection against cyber-related crime and the protection against illegitimate use of the state's legal powers largely depend on a territorial jurisdiction that constitutes the *demos* that hosts the context for law's performative effect. In the next section, on competing jurisdictions, I will pay more detailed attention to the issues of *ne bis in idem* and overlapping investigative powers.

Beccaria's advocacy of substantive and procedural criminal law legality principles is often hailed as part of a utilitarian criminal law theory. Instead, I would like to explore the relevance of his social contract theory for the notion of territorial jurisdiction and the protection it offers by way of the rule of law. As David Young has argued,[37] there are good arguments to ignore attempts to put Beccaria in a box of either retributivism (based on a strict interpretation of Kant's categorical imperative) or utilitarian calculus (even if Bentham lauded Beccaria as one of his own). According to Young, Beccaria grounded his seminal work on criminal law and criminal procedure in a type of contract theory that understands individual human beings and human society as interdependent, explaining punishment as being based on a 'social contract' that is based on an irrevocable respect for both the law and individual agency – even if the agent is considered a criminal: 'There is no liberty whenever the law in some cases permits a man to cease to be a person and to become a thing.'[38] According to Young:

> [Beccaria] thought of people not as units of pleasurable and painful sensations whose purpose is simply to maximize social happiness, but rather as responsible bearers of rights, as beings who, by virtue of being human, can make certain claims which no consideration of utility can override.[39]

[37] DB Young, 'Cesare Beccaria: Utilitarian or Retributivist?' (1983) 11 *Journal of Criminal Justice* 317.

[38] ibid 321, quoting C Beccaria, *An Essay on Crimes and Punishments. By the Marquis Beccaria of Milan. With a Commentary by M de Voltaire. A New Edition Corrected* (Farmington Hills, Gale ECCO Print Editions, 2010) ch 20, p 79.

[39] Young (n 37) 321.

This is particularly interesting as Beccaria also noted that individuals may be forced to serve under a social contract that diminishes them as a person while allowing others to profit from their misery. In this case, Beccaria suggests that if a social contract is not such that it can be understood as being in the interest of each and every citizen, its violation by those on the downside might not justify punishment. In terms of written legal speech act theory, this is a seminal argument; one could reframe it as stating that the unwritten social contract that informs the law of a sovereign state should always be *reconstructable* in such a way that it can claim adherence by each and every person who is subject to its jurisdiction.[40] Social contract theory actually emerged when written law started proliferating, demanding an implied philosophy to make sense of the myriad detailed written speech acts (legislation, administrative decisions, judgments). Contract theory in point of fact emerged around the same time as Montesquieu's plea for a system of countervailing powers, long before representative, deliberative and participatory democracy-as-we-know-it came into its own. Though Montesquieu did not adhere to social contract theory, his argument was based on keen attention to the implied philosophy of different types of government and how they can or cannot protect against arbitrary punishment. Criminal law and criminal procedure are constituted by a plethora of written legal speech acts that must be understood against a background of shared assumptions and mutual beliefs. Both criminal law legality principles demand that written legal speech acts be comprehensible as articulations of the integrity of the law, achieving both coherence for the totality of criminal law performatives and equal concern and respect for each and every citizen. If either coherence or respect for individual agency dissolves, the social contract becomes brittle – precisely because ultimately it does not depend on brute force or mechanical application, but on the shared world of institutional facts we need to navigate.

Written legal performatives create a vast and complex web, invoking authority while consolidating meaning based on adversarial debate. This web is contained within the boundaries of a territorial jurisdiction that restricts the scope of such performatives to a population within reasonably clear national borders. Thus, the ICIs of the printing press and cartography afforded a specific type of criminal law legality, both in the sense of generating the kind of contestation that is inherent in a system that requires iterant interpretation and in the sense of providing for closure in a way that is foreseeable and sufficiently robust, within the context of a *demos* that is constituted by territorial jurisdiction. Though the idea of closure should not be reduced to sovereign imperatives, to be 'practical and effective', written performatives require the support of a sovereign state. It is important to acknowledge that if the reach of written speech acts were global or undefined, this could not have been achieved, precisely because the vastly different background

[40] On reconstructive theory, see, eg F Vandenberghe, *What's Critical about Critical Realism? Essays in Reconstructive Social Theory* (Abingdon, Routledge, 2014).

knowledge, assumptions and mutual beliefs would create *anomia* rather than justice, legal certainty and purposiveness.

IV. Competing Jurisdictions

A. Jurisdictions of Choice?

In their important work on *Rethinking the Jurisprudence of Cyberspace*,[41] Reed and Murray speak of 'competing normativities' as a core challenge to the rule of law in cyberspace. The cross-border 'nature' of cyberspace enables a continued 'workflow' of deterritorialisation and reterritorialisation,[42] based on the material affordances of the Internet's global pipeline, its Transmission Control and Internet Protocols (TCP/IP), the World Wide Web's Hypertext Transfer Protocol (HTTP),[43] topped by cloud servers, virtual platforms, application programming interfaces (APIs) and a whole range of applications, including those of the Internet of Things. By enabling both natural and legal persons to trade, steal and target seamlessly across national borders without them actually crossing any physical border, cyberspace generates a diversity of claims for extraterritorial jurisdiction that in turn generate a new type of pluralism as to applicable law and competent courts. As states grasp cross-border jurisdiction based on a variety of legally relevant leads (subject matter, effects, personality, territory), cyberspace results in legal and natural persons facing a potentially contradictory set of legal obligations which they cannot possibly all comply with. I believe Reed and Murray are right in arguing that this seems to overrule many of the assumptions that underly the monopolistic claims of territorial jurisdiction, which grounds both positive law and the rule of law. I would not agree that this creates a new kind of freedom to choose one's jurisdiction depending on individual preferences, or an individualised law based on an on-the-spot and temporary 'community' of those who decide to comply with the same legal norm. Though I have no doubt that some of the big players at the global level are capable of cherry picking the rules they abide

[41] C Reed and A Murray, *Rethinking the Jurisprudence of Cyberspace* (Cheltenham, Edward Elgar, 2018); M Hildebrandt, 'Book Review: Chris Reed and Andrew Murray, Rethinking the Jurisprudence of Cyberspace' (2020) 83 *MLR* 690.

[42] W de Been, P Arora and M Hildebrandt (eds), *Crossroads in New Media, Identity and Law: The Shape of Diversity to Come* (Basingstoke, Palgrave MacMillan, 2015); J Goldsmith and T Wu, *Who Controls the Internet? Illusions of a Borderless World* (New York, Oxford University Press, 2006); ML Mueller, 'The New Cyber-Conservatism: Goldsmith/Wu and the Premature Triumphalism of the Territorial Nation-State: A Review of Goldsmith and Wu's "Who Controls the Internet? Illusions of a Borderless World"' (Internet Governance Project, 16 June 2006) www.internetgovernance.org/pdf/MM-goldsmithWu.pdf; JE Cohen, 'Cyberspace As/And Space' (2007) 107 *Columbia Law Review* 210.

[43] ML Mueller, *Networks and States: The Global Politics of Internet Governance* (Cambridge, MA, MIT Press, 2010); ML Mueller, *Ruling the Root: Internet Governance and the Taming of Cyberspace*, 2nd edn (Cambridge, MA, MIT Press, 2004).

by, most of us cannot afford such a luxury. More to the point, switching from one social contract to another based on their perceived benefits ignores the nature of a social contract as an implied philosophy that secures the integrity and robustness of a legal system.[44] Hopping from one jurisdiction to another to avoid sharing the costs that create the benefits will result in the anomia referred to at the end of the previous section; it will taint the performative effect of written legal norms and disrupt both legal certainty and justice. This is not only because it comes across as unjust to reap benefits everywhere without sharing cost anywhere (think tax havens), but also because justice and legal certainty are about the foreseeability inherent in equal treatment which requires a stable understanding of whose treatment we should compare with. The latter defines and is defined by the *demos*.

B. *Ne bis in idem* and Overlapping Investigatory Powers

Reed and Murray largely focus on private law jurisdiction. In the case of criminal law, competing jurisdictions may jeopardise the principle of *ne bis in idem* insofar as states do not recognise one another's convictions as relevant for their *ius puniendi*. They may also jeopardise the legality principle insofar as both the articulation and the interpretation of specific criminal offences often differ between states, making it hard to foresee whether the consequences of one's actions will trigger criminal liability in another – competing – jurisdiction. In the case of criminal law, the big players that engage in criminalised conduct may be other states or hacker communities aligned with them, as well as powerful actors that operate in global darknets. In both cases, the ICIs that enable those rogue actors call for supraterritorial or transnational legal powers for justice authorities. This can easily undermine the content, the boundaries and the constitutive context of the social contract, even though precisely in the case of criminalisation the tacit dimensions of the social contract are key. In civil law jurisdictions, the legality principle entails that criminalisation requires written legal speech acts of the legislature to ensure legal certainty and to restrict the potential scope of criminal offences (prohibition of analogous reasoning and limited use of extensive interpretation). For the same reason, criminal law is deemed to be a critical part of the two sides of the sovereignty coin: the *ius puniendi* is seen as more closely connected with the ethos of those sharing jurisdiction (internal sovereignty determines what action is qualified as criminal) and criminalisation is seen as an attribute of sovereign states (external sovereignty rejects criminal justice interventions from other states as to material, procedural or enforcement jurisdiction). The moral blame that is often inherent in criminalisation requires a shared acuity as to what is morally acceptable and what is not, as well as a shared sense of what kinds of investigative powers or sanctions may be expected when the social contract

[44] Dworkin, *Law's Empire* (n 5); C Taylor, *Philosophical Arguments* (Cambridge, MA, Harvard University Press, 1995).

is violated. Imposing punishment where such moral sensitivity is absent would create uncertainty, fear and cynicism. For criminal law to be legitimate and effective, those subject to the criminal law need to share a context that sensitises them to relevant expectations. For instance, the Cybercrime Convention imposes a catalogue of legal obligations on the contracting states to criminalise specific types of cybercrime, to attribute relevant investigative powers and to enforce the law by way of dedicated sanctions.[45] Although it does not impose extraterritorial jurisdiction to enforce,[46] it does call for mutual collaboration between criminal justice authorities, and some states have given themselves the legal power to engage in cross-border hacking whenever it is unclear where the relevant servers are actually located. Some have even argued that the territoriality principle is respected as long as hacking is done from a computing system in the investigating state.[47] These kinds of developments may disrupt the strong connection between sovereignty, *demos* and the legitimacy of criminal law interventions – even more so than in the case of a private law disconnect. Though the Cybercrime Convention requires respect for *ne bis in idem* and legality,[48] written legal speech acts only 'work' if they are embedded in the situated expectations of an identifiable *demos*.

C. Jurisdiction, *Demos* and Community

As we have seen above, cartography and the printing press afforded the constitution of a new type of *demos*, that is, the population that inhabits a defined territory. This *demos* should be seen not as a given community, but as a historical artefact that combines Tönnies's *Gemeinschaft* and *Gesellschaft* as dimensions of a

[45] Budapest Convention on Cybercrime (European Treaty Series No 185).

[46] Some may argue that the Cybercrime Convention, Art 18 (on production orders) may be interpreted as encouraging states to assume extraterritorial jurisdiction to enforce. However, as the Cybercrime Convention Committee's (T-CY) Ad-hoc Sub-group on Jurisdiction and Transborder Access to Data stated, 'Private sector entities may also be formally requested to comply with search, seizure and production orders under the laws of the States in which they operate'; and '[s]uch formal requests are not covered by Article 32 Budapest Convention but provisions on domestic powers, such as search and seizure (Article 19) or production orders (Article 18) – if the request is related to a criminal investigation': T-CY, 'Transborder Access and Jurisdiction: What are the Options?' (Council of Europe, 2012) 44, fn 91. This confirms that there is no imposition on Member States to assume extraterritorial jurisdiction to enforce, even if some parties may grasp such jurisdiction, and even if the T-CY's Guidance Notes on Arts 32 and 18 may be read as encouraging the Parties to 'grasp' such enforcement jurisdiction. See Cybercrime Convention Committee, 'T-CY Guidance Note #3: Transborder Access to Data (Article 32)' (Council of Europe, 2014); Cybercrime Convention Committee, 'T-CY Guidance Note #10: Production Orders for Subscriber Information (Article 18 Budapest Convention)' (Council of Europe, 2017).

[47] J Goldsmith, 'The Internet and the Legitimacy of Remote Cross-Border Searches' (2001) *University of Chicago Legal Forum* 103, 108.

[48] The Cybercrime Convention, Art 15 requires that parties provide for adequate protection of rights and liberties, 'including rights arising pursuant to obligations it has undertaken under the 1950 Council of Europe Convention for the Protection of Human Rights and Fundamental Freedoms [and] the 1966 United Nations International Covenant on Civil and Political Rights'. See also the Explanatory Report to the Convention on Cybercrime, paras 145–48. Art 4 of Protocol 7 to the ECHR provides the right not to be tried or punished twice for the same offence.

partly 'organically grown' (*gemeinschaftlich*) and a partly deliberately constructed (*gesellschaftlich*) artificial society.[49] Neither justice nor legal certainty 'works' if the equality relates to some today and others tomorrow, depending on what offers the greater advantage. The notion of a *demos* is not about romantic communitarianism, but about the conditions of possibility of a shared institutional world that integrates continuity and discontinuity, stability and dynamics, analogy and disanalogy, *Gemeinschaft* and *Gesellschaft*. Such a shared institutional world depends on the artificial construction of a population based not on kinship or local proximity, but on the exclusive territorial jurisdiction of the state, which creates an interpretive community based on the multi-interpretability of text, taking into account the spatial and temporal distantiation between a written legal speech act and its performative effect. Based on such distantiation, I would argue that the difference between *Gemeinschaft* (usually translated as community) and *Gesellschaft* (usually translated as society) is aligned with that between orality and text; the kind of community that is afforded by oral interaction differs from that afforded by text, due to the difference in scope and scale afforded by face-to-face communication on the one hand and text on the other. However, modern states afford and depend on a plethora of communities (based on, amongst others, location, family, education, employment and profession), while simultaneously creating and sustaining the institutional backbone that supports legitimate expectations between citizens who may never meet. In that sense, *Gemeinschaft* and *Gesellschaft* are dimensions of the *demos* rather than separate entities. What is key here is the role of the state as a means to achieve justice and legal certainty within an artificially created, heterogeneous *demos*[50] that instantiates a dedicated configuration of *Gemeinschaft* and *Gesellschaft*, countering on the one hand a moralisation of criminalisation based on one community imposing its moral beliefs on all others and on the other hand an instrumentalisation of the criminal law that mistakes a utilitarian calculus for legitimate criminalisation. If cyberspaces disrupt the notion of a *demos* as a point of reference for both justice and legal certainty, some will cynically reap the benefits by escaping the reach of relevant jurisdictions while others with no such refuge will pay the price.

D. The Force of Law and the Force of Technology

There is another issue when discussing competing jurisdictions. One could argue that positive law's monopolistic claims are now countered from an altogether

[49] J Harris (ed), *Tönnies: Community and Civil Society* (Cambridge, Cambridge University Press, 2010); E Hobsbawm and T Ranger (eds), *The Invention of Tradition*, Canto edn (Cambridge, Cambridge University Press, 1992).

[50] On the key role of criminal law in the construction of a *demos*, highlighting the artificial and projective nature of law, see M Hildebrandt, 'European Criminal Law and European Identity' (2007) 1 *Criminal Law and Philosophy* 57; M Hildebrandt, 'The Artificial Intelligence of European Union Law' (2020) 21 *German Law Journal* 74.

different angle.[51] A new type of competition comes from the *performative effect* of cross-border, code-driven infrastructures, such as social media, tech platforms, decentralised autonomous organisations (DAOs) anchored in crypto-anarchism, and other iterations of Internet exceptionalisms. This may concern the dark net, where child pornography flourishes, challenging the non-intervention principle that grounds territorial jurisdiction, because justice authorities will seek ways to hack into remote data servers. It may concern the use of autonomous weapons in cross-border conflicts where war has not been declared, challenging the Geneva Conventions by way of targeted killings on foreign territory.[52] It could also refer to industrial espionage and the undermining of elections by way of sophisticated malware capable of disrupting critical infrastructure, inviting further erosion of the principle of non-intervention. Note, though, that the performative effect of these infrastructures, or 'the force of technology', is not a matter of speech acts but rather a new type of 'brute facts'. These brute facts compete with the legal written speech acts of national jurisdiction and international law, or 'the force of law'. What matters is that this force of technology has both a performative and a *normative* effect in the sense of inducing, enforcing, inhibiting or precluding specific behavioural patterns – not in the sense of regularity, but in the sense of these patterns gradually becoming points of reference for mutual expectations, thus developing something like a 'normative force of the factual'.

In the context of law and jurisdiction, this should remind us of public law scholar Jellinek's discussion of the normative force of the factual in his seminal work on the dual nature of the state as both a factual and a legal entity.[53] Jellinek explored what we would now qualify as the performative effect of 'the factual', that is, of habits and customs that generate mutual expectations based on the gravitational force of current states of affairs. He based this 'normative force of the factual' on the psychology of individual minds, and rightly guessed that the performative effect of human interaction can both reinforce and negate the performative effect of legal written norms. His goal was not to play the performative effect of the legal constitution of the state against the factual character of its power and authority, but to highlight the interplay between them. In the same work, Jellinek introduced the 'three elements of statehood' (territory, population and government) that have long since defined statehood in the context of international law,[54] complemented by the recognition of the state as a state by other states and the ability to conduct

[51] Reed and Murray (n 41) make this point in ch 5, where they discuss legal, social and design norms.

[52] On the complexities involved, see A Callamard, 'Use of Armed Drones for Targeted Killings: Report of the Special Rapporteur on Extrajudicial, Summary or Arbitrary Executions' (2020) UN Doc A/HRC/44/38.

[53] G Jellinek, *Allgemeine Staatslehre* (Berlin, O Häring, 1905); NB Ladavac, C Bezemek and F Schauer (eds), *The Normative Force of the Factual: Legal Philosophy between Is and Ought* (Cham, Springer, 2019); A Anter (ed), *Die normative Kraft Des Faktischen: Das Staatsverstandnis Georg Jellineks*, 2nd edn (Baden-Baden, Nomos, 2020).

[54] Jellinek (n 53) 381–420.

external relations.[55] It is interesting to see that Jellinek's statehood was focused on internal sovereignty, which, however, critically depends on external sovereignty, notably from the perspective of 'the normative force of the factual'. If a state is not effective in protecting its territory, its population and its monopoly of violence within that territory against interventions by other states, it cannot be qualified as a state – just like a government that fails to enforce its monopoly of violence against militia within its territory cannot be qualified as a state (this is what we would call a failed state). Internal and external sovereignty are mutually constitutive; you cannot have one without the other. The *ius puniendi* itself depends on the monopoly of violence, and thus on the combined force of internal and external sovereignty, because without that it would collapse into private revenge and/or war. Clearly, both the *ius puniendi* and the rule of law itself depend on the combined force of written legal speech acts and the normative force of actual relations of power and authority, sustained by the technological affordances of mutually exclusive territorial jurisdiction.

With the rise of cyberspaces, however, all this seems up for grabs. This is not to deny or ignore that states are becoming more effective and efficient in grasping legal powers within and beyond their borders; rather, it is to acknowledge that big tech companies and global tech platforms are simultaneously grasping powers to regulate human behaviour with little care for territorial jurisdiction, let alone the rule of law. Perhaps the best example here is the 'exposure notification' developed by Apple and Google during the COVID-19 pandemic, enabled by their control over the global market in mobile devices. The notification system allowed public health authorities to develop a national application that allows the combination of proximity tracing via Bluetooth with the matching of those who tested positive. The idea was to contribute to tracing potential infections, helping to at least contain the spread of the disease. What matters here is that Apple and Google wrote the code and held the infrastructure that enabled the notifications; they thus regulated the behaviour of states, defining what data they could and could not access.[56] This was not based on a social contract, international law or democratic legitimation, but on the actual powers of big tech companies to rule by way of their technological platforms and infrastructure. Governments that objected against the limits imposed upon them by the restrictions inherent in the notification system found they had no way to exercise their authority in the realm of public health, as they were dependent on a global infrastructure outside their reach.

[55] Convention on the Rights and Duties of States adopted by the Seventh International Conference of American States (Montevideo, 26 December 1933) 165 LNTS 19, Art 1.

[56] T Sharon, 'Blind-Sided by Privacy? Digital Contact Tracing, the Apple/Google API and Big Tech's Newfound Role as Global Health Policy Makers' (2021) 23 *Ethics and Information Technology* 45; C Newton, 'How Big Tech Is Dictating the Terms of the Coronavirus Response to National Governments' (*The Verge*, 28 April 2020) www.theverge.com/interface/2020/4/28/21238633/apple-germany-contact-tracing-exposure-notification-nhs-shin-bet-australia.

Though it does not make any sense to claim that big tech companies have developed something like sovereignty, which is a very specific legal and factual construct based on exclusive territorial jurisdiction, they do seem to have developed a new type of 'brute jurisdiction' based on the normative force that derives from their control over the new ICI. The prime example in the criminal law realm concerns content moderation, which is based on violations of private companies' terms of service and involves outsourced, low-paid labour that determines what content is actually removed.[57] Though content removal is obviously not punishment in any formal sense, many of the violations constitute criminal offences in many jurisdictions; simultaneously, many criminal offences may be enabled and allowed because they do not violate the terms of service. Whereas the ICI of printed text was deployed by the state to enact written legal speech acts, whose performative effect depends on a shared background and an implied social contract as discussed above, the ICIs of global code- and data-driven infrastructures are not easily brought under the control of states. The content moderation practices referred to above are based on rules that have no democratic legitimation (no *demos* even), due process that is contingent upon whatever suits private corporations and no enforceable presumption of innocence. This is mainly due to the fact that this is not about criminal jurisdiction in the first place; the removal of content and the closing of accounts are private 'punishments' outside the realm of public law, thereby lacking the protection required by constitutional or international human rights in the domain of criminal law. Sometimes not being charged with a criminal offence, though seemingly a good thing, actually restricts the protection that would otherwise be available, whereas the consequences may be similar to those of punishment. Terminology such as 'digital sovereignty' and 'data sovereignty' signals states' keen awareness of the competing 'jurisdiction' of those who develop the code of the new ICIs, but there is no clear road towards gaining such sovereignty. This is not to return to claims of exceptionalism, suggesting that cyberspace is unregulatable, but is an acknowledgement of a new struggle between economic and technological power on the one hand and the public authority of states on the other.

V. Conclusions

Today, much of our critical infrastructure is both computational and interconnected; more precisely, our information and communication infrastructure is progressively cyberspatial and as such drives traditional critical infrastructure such as utilities (water, gas, electricity, public transport, financial institutions and supply chains), but also determines our access to information (search) and

[57] B Perrigo, 'Inside Facebook's African Sweatshop' (*Time*, 14 February 2022) www.time.com/6147458/facebook-africa-content-moderation-employee-treatment/.

mediates both our local and global communication. The increasing dependence on interconnected, computational ICIs creates potentially catastrophic vulnerabilities while simultaneously enabling mass surveillance and pervasive invisible nudging. This, in turn, triggers cyber-related crimes and cross-border cyber investigations, generating overlapping jurisdictional claims of substantive as well as procedural criminal law, while private companies, individual persons and states develop and deploy computational systems capable of cross-border espionage, distribution of fake news and personalised targeting that may directly 'regulate' the behaviour of citizens of multiple jurisdictions in ways that are at odds with the applicable legal framework.

Having traced how the technologies of cartography and the printing press enabled the Westphalian regime of international law that instituted a system of contiguous, mutually exclusive states firmly grounded in territorial jurisdiction, I have investigated the missing link of speech act theory, namely the different affordances of oral and written speech acts. This has allowed me to trace the crucial importance of written legal speech acts for the constitution of text-driven jurisdiction and the implied philosophy it requires, thus explaining the need for a social contract that forms the unwritten context of a written law that brings together a diverse and artificially constructed *demos* of legal subjects that share jurisdiction. The ambiguity of natural language that is greatly enhanced by the distantiation in time and space of text generates the need for interpretation and the concomitant contestability of written legal speech acts, both of which ground the rule of law as a system of checks and balances around the closure that complements the inherent contestability. It is the artificial nature of the *demos*, which is bounded and bound by the territorial jurisdiction it shares, that prevents the contestation from demolishing the social contract, while nevertheless sustaining both contestation and closure.

The carefully crafted, highly dynamic and never-to-be-taken-for-granted social contract that grounds the rule of law in territorial jurisdiction is now faced with two kinds of foundational challenges: first, the challenge of competing written legal speech acts that result from attempts to grasp material and investigative criminal jurisdiction when dealing with cyber-related crime; and second, the challenge of 'brute jurisdictions' whose performative effect may overrule written legal speech acts, even to the extent of evoking 'the normative force of the factual'.

The performative effect that informs these new 'brute jurisdictions' is fundamentally different from that of written legal speech acts. It is first and foremost a brute fact compared to the institutional facts that result from written legal performatives.[58] Increasingly, computational systems determine our choice of architecture, by restricting the kind of choices we have when communicating,

[58] *cf* Anscombe's original article, which inspired Searle's distinction between brute and institutional facts: Anscombe (n 25). Anscombe rightly understood the distinction as relative. In my own words: whether something is an institutional or a brute fact is the result of the performative effect of how we use language.

searching, reading, being recruited or admitted to educational facilities, being monitored due to fraud detection software, being deprived of unemployment benefits by automated decision systems, or simply when buying things or getting a mortgage. These systems induce or even force us to behave in certain ways that are not agreed as part of a social contract; they may also inhibit or overrule our action potential, often without us even noticing how we are being constrained and nudged. The normative force of the factual here is not only a matter of new kinds of habits and expectations due to the proliferation of the smart phone and video conferencing, search engines and e-commerce, but in the first place a result of *brute technological force* that automates the behaviour of machines that are largely hidden beneath the surface of everyday life.

In this chapter, I have argued that this has major consequences for criminal law jurisdiction. One of the reasons why the EU has limited power (jurisdiction) in the domain of criminal law is due to criminal law's close alignment with sovereignty, as the *ius puniendi* is tied up with the monopoly of violence that prohibits taking the law into one's own hands.[59] Another reason is that criminal law is not merely about compensation of harm caused, but is also about the imposition of a fine or detention meant to censure actions considered wrongful.[60] In a sense, criminal law is closer to the moral backbone of a *demos* than private and public law; it is part of the constitution of the *demos* and the social contract that defines the *demos*, while being defined by the *demos* as criminal law signals indignation about the violation of legal norms that define and sustain the implied philosophy of the law. Thus, punishment aims to negate the negation of such norms to assert and reinforce them. In other work, I have argued that a European criminal law would require and could simultaneously institute a distinct European identity and thus a European *demos*, noting that one can identify with more than one *demos*, and that a *demos* integrates difference rather than necessarily imposing homogeneity.[61] The plurality that enables a person to identify with *more than one demos* and the plurality that is inherent in *one and the same demos* do not, however, mean that anything goes. We cannot go around and cherry pick the jurisdiction that condones our actions, and the plurality of opinion within a *demos* assumes enforceable standards based on shared values. Law is not equivalent with morality; we can disagree on what should be done from our different moral perspectives, but we need closure when it comes down to enforceable law. That is a good reason to (i) be sparse with criminalisation and (ii) be cautious about imposing legal obligations to criminalise. Cyberspatial 'jurisdiction', however, may 'punish and prosecute' by way of the brute force of technology, that is, the performative effects of the code it deploys. This is not grounded in any

[59] Though clearly the EU's *sui generis* distribution of sovereignty between the Union and its Member States is a moving target, with the EU imposing further collaboration and mutual recognition in the context of criminal jurisdiction. On the preconditions and implications, see Hildebrandt, 'European Criminal Law and European Identity' (n 50).

[60] RA Duff, *Punishment, Communication, and Community* (Oxford, Oxford University Press, 2001).

[61] Hildebrandt, 'European Criminal Law and European Identity' (n 50).

social contract but is imposed by, for instance, big tech companies that control the global infrastructure of mobile applications.

As lawyers, we should get our act together. The rule of law is a historical artifact, afforded by specific technologies. To sustain the rule of law, we must figure out what affordances are crucial here and how they fare in code- and data-driven 'jurisdictions'. If we do not get to that point sooner rather than later, the normative force of 'brute jurisdictions' may take over and we may not even remember why countervailing powers slow down innovation and diminish efficiency, but will nevertheless prove resilient and robust in the face of unwarranted and unaccountable brute facts and brute force.

3

Extraterritorial Ambit through Offence Definitions, Technology and Economic Power

DARRYL BROWN

I. Introduction

Territoriality is widely recognised as a problematic premise for jurisdiction. International law is permissive because states have legitimate interests in exercising jurisdiction over criminal conduct (and in obtaining evidence) outside their territories; wrongdoing that grows in accord with global trade, travel, communication and digital data distribution.[1] Strict territorial constraints on national jurisdiction would mean impunity for grave criminal conduct, and it would hinder investigations of even domestic crimes for which evidence moves beyond national boundaries.[2] But permissive principles that approve 'extraterritorial' criminal law prescription[3] and data access allow multiple states to make claims over the same people, events or property. This leads to conflicts among states,[4] but also helps to reduce 'impunity gaps' that could otherwise allow transnational bad actors to escape justice.[5]

With those motivations and perils in mind, this chapter examines several ways that the USA takes advantage of international law's permissiveness and ambiguity

[1] eg C Ryngaert, 'Enforcement Jurisdiction in A-territorial Spaces: Addressing Crime on the High Seas and in Cyberspace', ch 7 in the present volume.

[2] See, eg Commission, 'Recommendation for a Council Decision authorising the opening of negotiations in view of an agreement between the European Union and the United States of America on cross-border access to electronic evidence for judicial cooperation in criminal matters' COM (2019) 70 final, 1: 'More than half of all criminal investigations today require access to cross-border electronic evidence. Electronic evidence is needed in around 85% of criminal investigations, and in two-thirds of these investigations there is a need to obtain evidence from online service providers based in another jurisdiction.'

[3] American Law Institute, *Restatement of the Law Fourth: The Foreign Relations Law of the United States* (Philadelphia, American Law Institute, 2018) §§ 402, 408, 409 and 412.

[4] C Ryngaert, *Jurisdiction in International Law*, 2nd edn (Oxford, Oxford University Press, 2015) 143; American Law Institute (n 3) § 407, reporters' note 3.

[5] SA Koh, 'Foreign Affairs Prosecutions' (2019) 94 *New York University Law Review* 340, 342.

to extend its criminal law and digitally based investigations beyond US borders. Following this introduction, the next section considers several US strategies for defining offences, in accordance with the law of jurisdiction, to reach extraterritorial wrongdoing. The third section examines strategies for extraterritorial investigation and enforcement. The aim is twofold. One is to identify with some precision how the USA (and, by extension, other states) can do this in light of international law's territorial premises. I emphasise three ways of doing so: manipulation of statutory offence elements; leveraging the transnational nature of digital infrastructure; and maximising the advantages of a large domestic economy. The second aim is to consider some effects and implications of these policies for other states and for criminal actors. Conclusions on this point are decidedly mixed. An overarching claim is that deciding whether a policy serves only one state's parochial interests, as opposed to common interests or cosmopolitan norms shared by many, depends greatly on contextual details, contested assessments of efficacy and trade-offs among competing values.[6] Sometimes US policies likely serve widely shared interests; in other instances, they can be counterproductive or show insufficient regard for other states' interests.

II. Defining Offences for Global Reach

Transnational crimes[7] are fragmented across territories, a reality that contemporary technologies facilitate (and that sophisticated bad actors exploit by operating from relatively safe havens to cause harm elsewhere). To meet that challenge, jurisdictional principles permit criminal offences with extraterritorial ambit when part of the offence – conduct or effects – occurs within a state's territory, or when conduct occurs wholly outside states but threatens key national interests within it. Their parameters, however, are sometimes ambiguous and contested, because their scope depends in part on domestic law. As Ryngaert observes:

> In international criminal law it is necessary and sufficient that one constituent element of the act or situation has been consummated in the territory of the State that claims jurisdiction … [Yet] it is not international law, but municipal law which defines the constituent elements of a particular offence.[8]

[6] See generally C Ryngaert, *Selfless Intervention: The Exercise of Jurisdiction in the Common Interest* (Oxford, Oxford University Press, 2020) 1–15, discussing 'cosmopolitan' theories and common-interest jurisdiction. Commentators often emphasise US advantages as a wealthy, geopolitically influential state with a central role in an integrated global economy, which provide leverage in multilateral agreements, induce other states' 'consent' to cooperative arrangements or enable insufficient US regard for other states' interests. Because that story is well covered elsewhere, I leave it in the background here. See, eg P Andreas and E Nadelmann, *Policing the Globe* (Oxford, Oxford University Press, 2006); K Raustiala, *Does the Constitution Follow the Flag? The Evolution of Territoriality in American Law* (New York, Oxford University Press, 2011).

[7] See N Boister, 'Transnational Criminal Law?' (2003) 14 *European Journal of International Law* 953, 955.

[8] Ryngaert, *Jurisdiction* (n 4) 78.

Control of offence elements gives states opportunities to define crimes in ways that lawfully maximise extraterritorial ambit. Sometimes this is accomplished by defining an offence so that its focus, or key elements, take place within the state's territory and yet it readily applies to extraterritorial actors. The USA can exercise 'territorial' jurisdiction over transnational activity based on, for example, the territorial presence of multinational banks, large Internet service providers and data-storage firms, and global companies of all sorts operating in US markets. The advantage extends beyond prescriptive jurisdiction to adjudicative and enforcement jurisdiction as well. Large states enjoy advantages in utilising this strategy. The more transnational firms with a domestic presence – or the more transnational transactions flowing through its territory – the more bases there are for territorial offences with extraterritorial reach. Finally, in what follows, one should keep in mind that extraterritorial ambit can be expanded through conspiracy charges,[9] which often accompany substantive charges; drug distribution, bribery, preparations for terrorism, copyright infringement, money laundering and much else virtually always involve multiple actors. Conspiracy law permits prosecutors to assert jurisdiction 'over all members of the conspiracy so long at least one member committed an act in furtherance of the conspiracy whilst on US territory or by using the instrumentalities of US commerce'.[10] And conspiracies can provide more ways for prosecutors to meet the burden of proof. The elements of conspiracy offences are usually easier to prove as, for example, evidence law permits one conspirator's statements to be used against others.[11]

A. Offence Definitions Linked to Enforcement – Drug Trafficking

US criminal law addressed at illicit narcotics trafficking provides ready examples of offences that explicitly target criminal activity beyond US borders, often within other states' territory, regardless of whether US nationals or vessels are involved.

[9] See 18 USC § 371 (punishing conspiracy to commit any federal offence); 18 USC § 1349 (criminalising conspiracy to commit or abetting mail or wire fraud offences); 18 USC § 1956(h) (punishing conspiracy to commit money laundering); 18 USC §§ 2339A and 2339B (both punishing conspiracy to provide material support to terrorism); 21 USC § 963 (punishing conspiracy to commit various drug crimes, including § 959); 46 USC § 70503(a) (punishing conspiracy to destroy property or conceal currency related to illicit drug trade). This is not unique to US law. See Ryngaert, *Jurisdiction* (n 4) 83 (describing EU law); M Hirst, *Jurisdiction and the Ambit of Criminal Law* (Oxford, Oxford University Press, 2003) 142–43, 246 (English law); L Farmer, 'Territorial Jurisdiction and Criminalization' (2013) 63 *University of Toronto Law Journal* 225, 238 (English law).

[10] Organisation for Economic Co-operation and Development, 'Implementing the OECD Anti-Bribery Convention: Phase 4 Report: United States' (OECD, 2020) 38, 60–65, describing conspiracy prosecutions and jurisdiction based on emails in US territory or money transfers through New York banks. See, eg *United States v Technip SA* No H-10-439 (SD Tex 2010), charging a French firm with 18 USC § 371 (conspiracy to pay bribes to Nigerian officials).

[11] See, eg Federal Rules of Evidence, r 801(d)(1)(E) (one conspirator's statements admissible against all members of conspiracy).

The 'workhorse' statute in this context is the Maritime Drug Law Enforcement Act (MDLEA), which prohibits illicit drug trafficking (among other things) by anyone anywhere who is aboard 'a vessel subject to the jurisdiction of the United States'.[12] The statute defines such vessels to include those 'registered in a foreign nation if that nation has consented or waived objection to the enforcement of United States law by the United States' or those 'in the territorial waters of a foreign nation if the nation consents to the enforcement of United States law by the United States'.[13]

As a matter of international law, the MDLEA rests on the protective principle.[14] What is interesting is the integration of bilateral enforcement agreements into the offence definition to expand the statute's scope. In general, enforcement jurisdiction constrains prescriptive jurisdiction, because the former remains much more tightly bound by territorial boundaries. But the MDLEA anticipates bilateral agreements that permit US law enforcement to act in other states' territory (including ships flagged to other states). The statute's prescriptive ambit grows with co-operative arrangements that expand US enforcement authority.

A separate offence targets extraterritorial drug trade in circumstances the MDLEA does not reach. As recently amended by the Transnational Drug Trafficking Act (TDTA),[15] US law forbids 'any person to manufacture or distribute a controlled substance … intending, knowing, or having reasonable cause to believe that such substance … will be unlawfully imported into the United States' or into waters within 12 miles of the US coast.[16] Unlike the MDLEA, this statute is not limited to conduct on certain 'vessels', nor to the territory of other states that consent to US enforcement.[17] The *mens rea* element defines the domestic effects on which jurisdiction rests.[18] The negligence standard added by the TDTA ('having reasonable cause to believe') expands the ambit of the offence to negligent actors. It also helps to offset constraints on extraterritorial evidence gathering by reducing the prosecution's evidentiary burden.[19]

[12] 46 USC § 70503(a) and (e).

[13] 46 USC § 70502(c)(1)(C) and (E).

[14] 46 USC § 70501 (noting Congress found that 'trafficking in controlled substances aboard vessels is a serious international problem, is universally condemned, and presents a specific threat to the security and societal well-being of the United States'); *United States v Cardales* 168 F3d 548, 553 (1st Cir 1999): 'the MDLEA … is consistent with the protective principle of international law because Congress has determined that all drug trafficking aboard vessels threatens our nation's security'. Under US law, prescriptive jurisdiction may be authorised by the consent of other states. See American Law Institute (n 3) § 402, reporters' note 11.

[15] 21 USC § 959(a) (amended by Pub L 114-154 (16 May 2016)).

[16] 21 USC § 959.

[17] The MDLEA, on the other hand, is not confined to drug shipments intended for the USA.

[18] Other statutes do the same, sometimes without the negligence standard. See, eg 21 USC § 331(a) (prohibiting 'introduction or delivery for introduction into interstate commerce of any food, drug, device, tobacco product, or cosmetic that is adulterated or misbranded'); 21 USC § 337a ('There is extraterritorial jurisdiction over any violation of this chapter … if such article was intended for import into the United States').

[19] Legislative history makes clear that, at the suggestion of the Department of Justice, the 2015 amendment was intended to make extraterritorial trafficking prosecutions easier. US officials became aware that international drug dealers sought to avoid harsh US drug sentences and enforcement efforts by

From one perspective, these 'extraterritorial' offences – meaning those that apply to extraterritorial conduct, even though jurisdiction rests on a nominal territorial connection[20] – appear straightforwardly to serve widely shared interests in suppressing illicit drug trafficking, and to do so with other states' endorsement, since MDLEA jurisdiction is defined by the consent of other states. On this view, the scheme is one in which the USA provides enforcement capacity to smaller, sometimes more fragile states that lack resources to investigate drug trafficking and face greater risks of violence in response to prosecutions.[21] On the other hand, 'consent' is heavily incentivised, or coerced, by policies that make consent a prerequisite to US economic and military aid, market access, intelligence sharing and other benefits.[22] To the extent that this reduces partner states' input into operations in their own jurisdictions, it seems a version of the 'democratic deficit' Ryngaert has identified when states engage in extraterritorial intervention even in the service of common interests.[23] Beyond that, the efficacy of US 'drug war' policy itself is hotly debated. One analysis, for example, suggests that suppressing Caribbean drug trafficking led to more trafficking through Mexico, with a consequent increase in domestic violence, in part because prosecuting drug cartel leadership led to trafficking by smaller, more violently competitive groups.[24]

B. Offence Definitions Built on Communications Infrastructure

Outside of drug trafficking, the drafters of offence definitions employ other strategies to extend their ambit beyond national borders while retaining a jurisdictional basis that is nominally territorial. Very often, statutes do this by focusing on use of the emails, phones, electronic communications, bank transfers or digital distribution of videos, writings or other data. Even for actors outside the USA, use of any distribution or communication infrastructure often means that one element

directing large-scale shipments to buyers in other countries, particularly Mexico. See S Sola, P Laymon and T Johnson, 'Transnational Drug Trafficking Act of 2015' (January 2018) 66 *US Attorneys' Office Bulletin* 179, discussing *United States v Borda*, in which a Columbian national who shipped cocaine to Mexico explicitly refused to ship to the USA.

[20] Ryngaert, *Jurisdiction* (n 4) 6–7, noting confusion in uses of 'extraterritorial jurisdiction', which 'ought to imply that a State exercises its jurisdiction without any territorial link … although the expression is typically used in a context of States asserting jurisdiction on the basis of some, admittedly non-exclusive, territorial link'.

[21] See M Farbiarz, 'Extraterritorial Criminal Jurisdiction' (2016) 114 *Michigan Law Review* 507, 513; Koh, 'Foreign Affairs Prosecutions' (n 5) 361.

[22] See 22 USC § 2291h (requiring the President to report annually on whether countries receiving US aid met objectives defined in various agreements aimed at drug trafficking); J Kramek, 'Bilateral Maritime Counter-Drug and Immigrant Interdiction Agreements: Is This the World of the Future?' (2000) 31 *Miami Inter-American Law Review* 121, 145–46.

[23] Ryngaert, *Selfless Intervention* (n 6) 109–25.

[24] P Andreas, *Killer High: A History of War in Six Drugs* (Oxford, Oxford University Press, 2020) 233–56.

of an offence nominally occurs within US territory. Sometimes the nexus is relatively meaningful, such as communication with US-based individuals or transfers of money or digital goods to or from US accounts. In other cases, it is thinner, such as when use of 'wires' consists of posting videos accessible to US web users or data stored in US servers.

(i) Fraud and Copyright Offences

Federal fraud statutes are prime examples that have proven exceptionally effective at reaching fraud-based wrongdoing outside the USA. The primary federal wire fraud statute punishes any person who 'having devised … any scheme … to defraud … transmits … by means of wire … in interstate or foreign commerce, any writings … for the purpose of executing such scheme'.[25] The 'commerce' element is required as a matter of US constitutional law,[26] but it also ensures some degree of US nexus (perhaps minimal) when the offence is applied to extraterritorial conduct. The recent prosecution in New York of FIFA (Fédération Internationale de Football Association) officials for a vast bribery scheme, committed almost wholly outside the USA, illustrates the point.[27]

Napout and Marin were the presidents of the Brazilian and Paraguayan football federations, respectively. Each accepted millions of dollars in bribes in connection with their roles in FIFA's sale of broadcasting and marketing rights for various football (soccer) tournaments. Both lived and worked in South America; both attended FIFA meetings in Switzerland, where they were eventually arrested and then extradited to the USA. The US nexus to the case consisted almost entirely of bank transfers. Marin's bribery payments were sent to the New York bank account of his shell company, which he occasionally drew from to buy US goods. The cash payments Napout received (usually in Brazil, often in US currency) originated from the payee's New York account.[28]

Both defendants argued that the wire fraud statute did not extend to their conduct outside US territory. In *United States v Napout*, the Court of Appeals for

[25] 18 USC § 1343. The mail fraud statute, 18 USC § 1341, prohibits the same range of fraudulent schemes when they involve use of 'the Postal Service, or … any private or commercial interstate carrier' rather than wire communications; 18 USC § 1346 extends the reach of both §§ 1341 and 1343 by defining '"scheme or artifice to defraud" [to] include a scheme or artifice to deprive another of the intangible right of honest services'. Conspiring to commit or abetting any of these offences is criminalised by 18 USC § 1349.

[26] See US Constitution, Art I, § 8, cl 3. Many federal statutes that reach extraterritorial conduct also include a 'mail' or 'commerce' element. See 18 USC § 2332b (punishing various crimes of personal injury or endangerment 'involving conduct transcending national boundaries' if 'the mail or any facility of interstate or foreign commerce is used in furtherance of the offense'); 18 USC § 2339B(d)(1)(E) (extending the offence of providing material support to terrorist organisations to extraterritorial conduct if 'the offense occurs in or affects interstate or foreign commerce'); 18 USC § 2339D(b)(5) (same, for the offence of receiving military training from terrorist groups).

[27] See *United States v Napout* 963 F3d 163, 178 (2d Cir 2020), describing interaction of §§ 1343, 1346 and 1349.

[28] ibid 174–75, 180–81.

the Second Circuit disagreed – not by holding that the statute applies extraterritorially, but instead by concluding that the criminal conduct was domestic. Under the now-standard analysis, to 'determine whether the case involves a domestic application of the statute', federal courts first identify the statute's 'focus', meaning the conduct it seeks to regulate.[29] *Napout* quoted the US Supreme Court's decision in *RJR Nabisco* on this point:

> If the conduct relevant to the statute's focus occurred in the United States, then the case involves a permissible domestic application even if other conduct occurred abroad; but if the conduct relevant to the focus occurred in a foreign country, then the case involves an impermissible extraterritorial application regardless of any other conduct that occurred in U.S. territory.[30]

Applying this analysis, the Second Circuit concluded that it was the use of the wires, rather than the defendants' corrupt actions, that was the 'focus' of the wire fraud offence, and that wire transfers to and from New York banks were 'central' and 'essential' to the defendant's scheme to defraud,[31] making the statute's application domestic, not extraterritorial. *Napout* is not unusual. Other federal court decisions take the same view and characterise prosecutions as domestic based on emails, phone calls or electronic transmission of documents, even though defendants acted primarily whilst outside US territory.[32]

The same reliance on global digital infrastructure is the basis for copyright infringement, an offence that does not apply extraterritorially,[33] to reach those whose conduct is wholly beyond US borders. The prosecution of Kim DotCom and his associates in MegaUpload Limited, which distributed digital goods worldwide, provides a well-known example. All defendants lived outside the USA, primarily in New Zealand, but the US indictment relied on components of their distribution infrastructure to treat the case as domestic. The defendants had leased data storage from Internet-hosting providers that stored copyrighted property on servers located in Virginia.[34] They also used a US-based e-commerce

[29] ibid 178.

[30] *RJR Nabisco, Inc v European Community* 579 US 325, 337 (2016), quoted in *Napout* (n 27).

[31] *Napout* (n 27) 178, 180–81.

[32] *United States v Hussain* 972 F3d 1138, 1141–44 (9th Cir 2020). Hussain was convicted of wire fraud committed whilst being the chief financial officer of a UK tech firm. He and others misrepresented information about their firm's finances to a US firm. Evidence included emails and telephone calls between US and UK participants. See also *United States v McLellan* 959 F3d 442, 467–71 (1st Cir 2020), affirming that a conviction based on communications about a financial fraud scheme between US and UK executives was a domestic application of § 1343. Although his conviction was overturned on other grounds, London-based trader Gavin Black did not even challenge his US prosecution for wire fraud and conspiracy on jurisdictional grounds. See *United States v Connolly* 24 F4th 821 (2d Cir 2022) (noting evidence of Black's emails and of transactions through US banks).

[33] See *Update Art, Inc v Modiin Publishing, Ltd* 843 F2d 67, 73 (2d Cir 1988): 'It is well established that copyright laws generally do not have extraterritorial application'; *Palmer v Braun* 376 F3d 1254, 1258 (11th Cir 2004).

[34] *United States v DotCom* Crim No 1:12CR3 (ED Va 2012) paras 25, 38–41, 88–89 (also charging money laundering).

firm, PayPal, to accept subscription payments and pay business expenses, which 'affect[ed] interstate and foreign commerce', and some bank transfers involved US accounts.[35]

Like the drug statutes, nominally domestic crimes of wire fraud and copyright achieve extraterritorial ambit by the design of offence definitions in conjunction with modern communications infrastructure. This strategy is available to all states, not only powerful ones (unlike the MDLEA, which depends on winning other states' consent and funding far-reaching enforcement operations). The domestic infrastructure connection ensures at least a modest nexus with the USA, although in the FIFA cases and other wire fraud prosecutions, other states have concurrent jurisdiction and often stronger jurisdictional claims over the wrongful conduct. How willingly those states consent to US enforcement is not always clear; protests between states, and pressure tactics to win consent, are not always public. Public evidence of co-operation, such as arresting and extraditing defendants or providing other assistance to US officials – especially by European states, which are somewhat less vulnerable to US coercion[36] – might suggest that they see some common benefits from US enforcement in many cases. On the other hand, backlash against extraditions to the USA (and elsewhere) prompted the UK to amend its extradition legislation with a 'forum bar', pursuant to which courts may block an extradition based on a multi-factor 'interests of justice' analysis.[37]

(ii) Material Support Offences

Thin claims of US nexus are also a feature of some extraterritorial terrorism-related prosecutions. The statutes used most aggressively in this context are those that prohibit providing 'material support or resources' for terrorist activity or to designated terrorist organisations.[38] In several cases, US courts have found minimal US connections to extraterritorial conduct to be sufficient for due process and fair notice requirements. The case of Abid Naseer is illustrative.

[35] ibid paras 79–82.

[36] Switzerland extradited the FIFA defendants: *Napout* (n 27) 176–77. UK authorities assisted in the investigation of its national convicted of wire fraud in *Hussain* (n 32) 1141. New Zealand courts eventually approved extradition of several MegaUpload defendants. See *Ortmann v United States* [2021] NZSC 187; *Ortmann v the United States* [2017] NZHC 189; J Anthony, 'Final Supreme Court Ruling Clears Path for Decision on Kim Dotcom Extradition' (*Stuff*, 22 December 2021) www.stuff.co.nz/business/industries/127354588/final-supreme-court-ruling-clears-path-for-decision-on-kim-dotcom-extradition.

[37] See Extradition Act 2003, ss 19B–F, 83A–E. Extraditions to the USA have been blocked by the forum bar, eg *Love v US* [2018] EWHC 172 (Admin), but some have questioned the provision's effectiveness. See P Arnell and G Davies, 'The Forum Bar in UK Extradition Law: An Unnecessary Failure' (2020) 84 *Journal of Criminal Law* 142.

[38] 18 USC §§ 2339A and 2339B. See also 18 USC § 2339D (punishing one who 'knowingly receives military-type training from or on behalf of' a terrorist organization). Different sub-sections rely on distinct jurisdictional bases. See American Law Institute (n 3) § 402, reporters' note 5, describing § 2339B(d)(1)(D) as an exercise of territorial jurisdiction); reporters' note 7, noting that § 2339C(b)(2)(A) exercises active-personality jurisdiction; and reporters' note 10, describing § 2339B(d)(1)(C) and § 2339D(b)(3) as asserting universal jurisdiction.

Naseer, a Pakistani citizen, was one of several defendants prosecuted for participating in an al-Qaeda plot that planned a bombing in Manchester, England.[39] All of Naseer's conduct occurred whilst in the UK, where he was arrested. After being extradited to New York, he was convicted by a federal jury in 2015 of providing material support to al-Qaeda and conspiracy to do the same.[40] The primary statute under which he was convicted, 18 USC section 2339B, provided for jurisdiction 'if … after the conduct required for the offence occurs an offender is *brought into* or found in the United States, even if the conduct required for the offence occurs outside the United States' (emphasis added).[41] Naseer's extradition satisfied the 'brought into' requirement, and the trial judge concluded that applying section 2339B to Naseer's extraterritorial conduct met the constitutional due process fairness standard because there was 'sufficient nexus between the defendant and the United States'. Even 'For non-citizens acting entirely abroad, a [sufficient] jurisdictional nexus exists when the aim of that activity is to cause harm … to US citizens or interests', which providing support to terrorist groups does.[42] Still, with regard to international law (which the court did not directly address), Naseer's link to US interests are minimal and indirect, especially compared to the UK's. Naseer planned an attack in Great Britain; his US connection was 'merely' involvement in a transnational network of al-Qaeda operatives, some of whom intended a New York bombing without Naseer's assistance.[43] Under US due process doctrine, that is enough: 'fair warning' does not require that defendants abroad foresee the possibility of US prosecution 'so long as they would reasonably understand that their conduct was criminal and would subject them to prosecution somewhere'.[44] Whether the modest nexus with the USA that existed in the case is sufficient under international law is more debatable. It hardly provides the strongest claim among the states with concurrent jurisdiction, but the UK opted not to prosecute Naseer, so in the event no conflict arose.[45]

In other cases, US connections are arguably even thinner. Consider the three Somali-born men with European citizenships – Madhi Hashi, Ali Yasin Ahmed and Mohamed Yusuf – who returned to Somalia to fight for the terrorist group al-Shabaab. They were arrested in Djibouti en route to Yemen and transferred to

[39] US Department of Justice, 'Al-Qaeda Operative Sentenced to 40 Years in Prison for Role in International Terrorism Plot that Targeted the United States and Europe' (*Justice*, 4 November 2015) www.justice.gov/opa/pr/al-qaeda-operative-sentenced-40-years-prison-role-international-terrorism-plot-targeted, also noting other US-based members of the conspiracy were convicted of planning to bomb the New York City subway.

[40] ibid.

[41] 18 USC § 2339B(d)(1)(c).

[42] *United States v Naseer* 38 F Supp 3d 269, 272 (EDNY 2014), quoting *United States v Al Kassar* 660 F3d 108, 118 (2d Cir 2011).

[43] US Department of Justice, 'Al Qaeda Operative Convicted by Jury in One of the Most Serious Terrorist Plots against America since 9/11' (*Justice*, 1 May 2012) www.justice.gov/opa/pr/al-qaeda-operative-convicted-jury-one-most-serious-terrorist-plots-against-america-911.

[44] *Naseer* (n 42) 273, quoting *Al Kassar* (n 42) 119.

[45] S Swann, 'Abid Naseer: How 2009 UK Terror Case Ended in US Court' (*BBC News*, 4 March 2015) www.bbc.co.uk/news/uk-31697290.

US custody. Once in New York, they were charged with material support offences, to which they eventually pled guilty.[46] The nexus to US interests was attenuated: the defendants sought to fight for al-Shabaab in Africa and Yemen, but al-Shabaab's leaders had publicly threatened eventually to attack American targets.[47] At the guilty plea hearing, prosecutors also asserted that they could prove one defendant had appeared in recruitment videos that were accessible in the USA via the Internet, which 'had an impact on US commerce'.[48] In other cases, the US nexus depends wholly on US availability of terrorism-related videos. Lawal Babafemi is a Nigerian citizen who, after travelling to Chad, Sudan and Yemen on behalf of al-Qaeda in the Arabian Peninsula, was arrested in Nigeria and extradited to New York. Prosecutors pointed to Babafemi's assistance with al-Qaeda's English-language recruitment and media operations.[49] Other extraterritorial prosecutions likewise rest largely or wholly on contributions to Internet videos or web publications by foreign nationals acting abroad with little or no specific targeting of US interests.[50]

Here, too, it is difficult to assess cosmopolitan benefits from US prosecutions without attention to the details. Other states have concurrent jurisdiction and often a much stronger nexus, yet they accede to US enforcement, extradite suspects and provide other assistance.[51] Perhaps the weaker capacity to prosecute these cases domestically explains Nigeria's and Djibouti's assent to US control. Yet they also are susceptible to US leverage. That is less true of the UK,[52] so perhaps

[46] S Clifford, '3 Somali Natives Who "Went Home to Fight" Plead Guilty to Terror Charges in Brooklyn' *New York Times* (12 May 2015) www.nytimes.com/2015/05/13/nyregion/3-somali-natives-who-went-home-to-fight-plead-guilty-to-terror-charges-in-brooklyn.html; US Department of Justice, 'Three Members of al-Shabaab Plead Guilty to Conspiring to Provide Material Support to the Terrorist Organization' (*Justice*, 12 May 2015) www.justice.gov/opa/pr/three-members-al-shabaab-plead-guilty-conspiring-provide-material-support-terrorist (defendants charged under 18 USC §§ 2339B and 2339D).

[47] *United States v Ahmed* 94 F Supp 3d 394, 409–10 (EDNY 2015).

[48] See Clifford (n 46).

[49] US Department of Justice, 'Terrorist Sentenced to 22 Years for Providing Material Support to al-Qaeda in the Arabian Peninsula' (*Justice*, 12 August 2015) www.justice.gov/opa/pr/terrorist-sentenced-22-years-providing-material-support-al-qaeda-arabian-peninsula.

[50] US Department of Justice, 'The District of Connecticut's National Security Program' (*Justice*) www.justice.gov/usao-ct/district-connecticuts-national-security-program, describing prosecutions of UK nationals Babar Ahmad and Syed Talha Ahsan extradited to the USA; S Sinnar, 'Separate and Unequal: The Law of "Domestic" and "International" Terrorism' (2019) 117 *Michigan Law Review* 1333, 1351–54, describing prosecutions under 18 USC § 2332b with the element of 'conduct transcending national boundaries' being met by digital communications.

[51] See US Department of Justice, 'Al-Qaeda Operative Sentenced' (n 39), describing 'significant assistance' from 'law enforcement authorities in the United Kingdom and Norway'.

[52] Britain has denied some US extradition requests. See O Bowcott, 'Alleged Hacker Who Avoided Extradition to US Seeks Return of Computers' *The Guardian* (11 February 2019) www.theguardian.com/uk-news/2019/feb/11/lauri-love-computer-activist-seeks-return-computers-extradition-us-nca. UK officials have criticised the treaty as favouring US over UK requests. See M Aitchison and B Carlin, 'One Law for Them: UK–US Extradition Treaty is Labelled "Not Fit for Purpose"' (*Mail Online*, 30 January 2022) www.dailymail.co.uk/news/article-10456167/UK-extradition-treaty-branded-not-fit-purpose-deportation-Britains-Bill-Gates.html.

more consultation and less coercion lies behind cases such as *Naseer*. Nonetheless, justifications for US enforcement are unclear. The impact of videos on 'commerce' is merely a technical claim to satisfy constitutional doctrine that defines limits on federal legislation; it does not speak to the interests recognised by the protective principle. Links to genuine US interests are comparatively attenuated. The charged offences address preparatory conduct several steps removed from acts that would cause real harm; in several cases, defendants' acts posed direct threats to *other* states, whilst threats to US security came from defendants' *associates*. That does not wholly undermine justifications for US jurisdiction, but it does leave unexplained why US prosecutions have superseded enforcement by other states. One answer may be simply greater US enforcement resources coupled with an uncompromising 'tough on terrorism' policy. Little suggests the USA stepped in as a 'forum of necessity' to prevent impunity for bad actors.[53] It is not clear whether defendants enjoyed more due process in US courts.[54] And other states lost opportunities for communities directly threatened to hold offenders accountable, with consequent loss in the normative and expressive value of liability.[55]

C. Offence Definitions Built on Economic Infrastructure – Corruption

Communications or transactions through emails, wires or 'any instrumentality of interstate commerce' is an element of many US offences, not least the Foreign Corrupt Practices Act (FCPA) and the Money Laundering Control Act (MLCA).[56] But both of those statutes achieve their extraterritorial reach primarily through a different structure than drug or wire fraud crimes. The FCPA is in one sense more limited. It applies only to US persons and firms, or to foreign firms (and their employees) listed on US securities exchanges,[57] whereas money laundering laws apply to foreign persons and firms if part of the conduct occurs in the USA or if the firm has a US bank account.[58] This enables the MLCA to support the FCPA

[53] See D Ireland-Piper, 'Extraterritorial Criminal Jurisdiction and the Cosmopolitan' in R Beardsworth, GW Brown and R Shapcott (eds), *The State and Cosmopolitan Responsibilities* (Oxford, Oxford University Press, 2019) 147, 149.

[54] For an argument about due process deficiencies in US extraterritorial prosecutions, see M Farbiarz, 'Accuracy and Adjudication: The Promise of Extraterritorial Due Process' (2016) *Columbia Law Review* 625.

[55] Ireland-Piper (n 53) 155; Farmer (n 9) 233, 241; A Chehtman, 'The Extraterritorial Scope of the Right to Punish' (2010) 29 *Law and Philosophy* 127.

[56] See, eg Foreign Corrupt Practices Act, 15 USC §§ 78dd-1(a) and 78dd-2(a); Money Laundering Control Act, 18 USC § 1956(b)(2), defining 'financial transaction' to mean '(A) a transaction which in any way or degree affects interstate or foreign commerce (i) involving the movement of funds by wire or other means … or (B) a transaction involving the use of a financial institution which is engaged in, or the activities of which affect, interstate or foreign commerce in any way or degree'.

[57] 15 USC §§ 78dd-1(a) and 78dd-2(a).

[58] 18 USC § 1856(b)(2) (adjudicative jurisdiction over foreign firms); 18 USC § 1956(f) (applies extraterritorially if 'the conduct occurs in part in the United States'). For money laundering counts

by punishing foreign officials' acceptance of bribes (if illegal under the law of the official's country) whenever proceeds are deposited in US banks.[59]

Both sets of offences have been repeatedly – many would say aggressively – applied to crimes committed by non-US persons and entities where most of the conduct occurred outside the USA.[60] They achieve this broad ambit not by links to US communications infrastructure, but by taking advantage of the global importance of: (i) US markets, which leads transnational firms to have a US presence; (ii) US capital markets, which many foreign firms utilise; and (iii) the centrality of US banks and currency in global financial networks, which results in foreign transactions flowing through US banks.[61] All this economic activity provides territorial nexuses for otherwise-extraterritorial conduct. Critically, these territorial links also facilitate adjudicative jurisdiction.[62] US subpoenas, in conjunction with monitoring and reporting requirements, enlist private firms as investigators and help overcome barriers to extraterritorial evidence gathering. Nonetheless, many bribery and money laundering cases still require international co-operation among law enforcement and regulatory agencies, for which networks are now well established.[63]

against the MegaUpload defendants that involved bank transfers outside the USA, the copyright violations facilitated by US servers and the generated illicit profits constituted the US conduct. See *DotCom* (n 34).

[59] See 18 USC § 1956(c)(7)(B)(iv): 'the term "specified unlawful activity" means– … (B) with respect to a financial transaction occurring in whole or in part in the United States, an offence against a foreign nation involving– … (iv) bribery of a public official, or the misappropriation, theft, or embezzlement of public funds by or for the benefit of a public official'. See, eg *United States v Chi* 936 F3d 888 (9th Cir 2019), affirming conviction for wire transfers to the defendant's bank account involving proceeds from the violation of the South Korean bribery statute; *United States v Lazarenko* 564 F3d 1026 (9th Cir 2009), affirming the conviction of a former Ukrainian official based on bank deposits of extortion conduct in Ukraine. See also *Technip* (n 10); OECD (n 10) 60–65.

[60] See, eg *United States v JGC Corp* No 11 CR 260 (SD Tex 2011) (deferred prosecution agreement – jurisdiction based on New York bank transfers for a Japanese national who bribed Nigerians); *United States v Magyar Telekom, Plc* No 1:11CR00597 (ED Va, 29 December 2011) (asserting jurisdiction based on storage of two emails on US server for Hungarian firm's bribery of Macedonian officials); Ryngaert, *Jurisdiction* (n 4) 86–88.

[61] Federal prosecutors use the FCPA in cases of extraterritorial transactions by foreign firms if some part of the activity, such as emails or fund transfers through New York banks, occurs within the USA, or if transactions are denominated in US dollars. See US Department of Justice and US Securities and Exchange Commission, 'FCPA: A Resource Guide to the US Foreign Corrupt Practices Act, 2nd edn' (Department of Justice, 2020) 10–11; S Koh, 'The Criminalization of Foreign Relations' (2021) 90 *Fordham Law Review* 737, 766; J Bae, KA Cooper and M Driscoll, 'Client Memorandum: VimpelCom Agrees to Landmark $795 Million FCPA Resolution' (*Paul Weiss*, 26 February 2016) https://www.paulweiss.com/media/3367479/26feb16fcpaalert.pdf 2: 'The DOJ asserted jurisdiction over Unitel on the basis that Unitel … furthered the corruption scheme by using US-based email accounts and making numerous corrupt payments that were executed through bank accounts at financial institutions in the US.'

[62] 18 USC § 1856(b)(2).

[63] See generally Financial Action Task Force and Egmont Group, 'Trade-Based Money Laundering: Trends and Developments' (FATF/OECD, 2020), describing the need for and challenges to transnational cooperation among law enforcement agencies to address multi-national money laundering operations.

US enforcement against foreign bribery conduct is comparatively aggressive.[64] While motivated by national interest rather than altruism,[65] prospects for common interests flowing from extraterritorial enforcement help explain international co-operation and multilateral agreements against corruption.[66] A key problem is that the factors that define a strong nexus to crimes of corruption – officials who demand bribes or large firms that pay them – can undermine states' domestic political capacity to fight corrupt conduct. That reality, in turn, points to a benefit of concurrent jurisdiction through which 'bystander' states can play a valuable enforcement role.[67]

III. Extraterritorial Information Gathering

International law restricts enforcement jurisdiction much more than prescriptive jurisdiction. Where the law clearly bars extraterritorial actions such as police searches, states rely on multinational co-operation to facilitate information sharing, evidence gathering and arrests through co-operative institutions and formal agreements.[68] But international law in this domain is also permissive in a critical respect, because it is unclear how territorial limits on enforcement apply to remotely conducted digital searches.[69] Remote searches challenge jurisdictional limits for the same reason that transnational crimes do: officials' conduct in one state has effects in another. Without an international law of 'investigative jurisdiction',[70]

[64] G Dell, 'Exporting Corruption: Progress Report 2020: Assessing Enforcement of the OECD Anti-Bribery Convention' (Transparency International, 2020) 11–14: 'Only four of the 47 countries surveyed actively enforce against foreign bribery', with the USA the most active.

[65] Ryngaert, *Jurisdiction* (n 4) 81–82; C Ryngaert, 'Cosmopolitan Jurisdiction and the National Interest' in S Allen et al (eds), *Oxford Handbook on Jurisdiction in International Law* (Oxford, Oxford University Press, 2019) 209.

[66] See, eg UN Convention against Corruption (New York, 31 October 2003) 2349 UNTS 41. Cooperative institutions include Interpol, Europol and the Financial Crimes Enforcement Network. See OECD (n 10) 14; Andreas and Nadelmann (n 6) 211–14; K Raustiala, 'The Architecture of International Cooperation: Transgovernmental Networks and the Future of International Law' (2002) 43 *Virginia Journal of International Law* 1, 24: 'powerful States play leading roles in networks and it is the weak nations of the world that are adopting many of the regulatory policies of the more powerful'. Sharing offenders' fines among affected states also facilitates cooperation. See, eg OECD (n 10) 45: 'US authorities ... structured their foreign bribery resolutions in certain multi-jurisdictional cases [so that] ... the bulk of monetary penalties imposed went to the country most affected by the corruption.'

[67] *cf* Ryngaert, 'Cosmopolitan Jurisdiction' (n 65) 215–16; W Dodge, 'Jurisdictional Reasonableness under Customary International Law' (2019) 62 *Questions of International Law* 5, 17–18.

[68] See, eg Budapest Convention on Cybercrime (European Treaty Series No 185), Arts 16–18 (obligations to enact domestic laws for data preservation and production from persons within territory).

[69] J Hörnle, *Internet Jurisdiction: Law and Practice* (Oxford, Oxford University Press, 2021) 146–49; D Svantesson, *Solving the Internet Jurisdiction Puzzle* (Oxford, Oxford University Press, 2017) 51–52; Ryngaert, *Jurisdiction* (n 4) 81–82, 92; J Daskal, 'Transnational Government Hacking' (2020) 10 *Journal of National Security Law and Policy* 677.

[70] See Ryngaert, 'Enforcement Jurisdiction' (n 1); Svantesson (n 69) 165; S Allen, 'Enforcing Criminal Jurisdiction in the Clouds and International Law's Enduring Commitment to Territoriality' in Allen et al (n 65) 381, 389–402; Hörnle (n 69).

extraterritorial digital searches by various means are regulated largely by domestic law and ad hoc state interactions.[71] And states have good reasons for seeking extraterritorial data. It is often stored in territory unrelated to data owners' locations or the crimes to which it relates, in states with perhaps little reason, or jurisdiction, to prosecute.[72]

Unsurprisingly, the same factors that permit domestic offences with extraterritorial reach are at play in state strategies to gather evidence beyond their national boundaries. For the USA (and the European Union), that includes the advantages which come with a large domestic economy and geopolitical leverage.[73] As noted above, the USA claims personal (adjudicative) jurisdiction over most major Internet service and data-hosting providers, international banks and large transnational firms, because all have some presence in US territory. Those firms are subject to US warrants, subpoenas, production orders and reporting requirements,[74] which provide access to the globally distributed information assets that those firms own, manage or control. Other advantages flow from geopolitical influence and capacity to fund extraterritorial enforcement operations, not unlike what we see in the MDLEA's enforcement infrastructure. US law enforcement agencies (LEAs) station hundreds of agents in dozens of countries pursuant to various agreements.[75] Intelligence surveillance by US security agencies – which sometimes supplements traditional law enforcement investigations – has distinct (occasionally notorious)[76] extraterritorial capacity that builds on digital technologies and information sharing with other states.

The most hotly debated practices involve digital searches and data retrieval, for much-noted reasons: countries regulate data within their territories, but data is often distributed in locations that bear little relation to its owners or the crimes to which it is linked. A pair of distinctions are useful to understand US policy in this domain. The first is between direct versus indirect government access to extraterritorial digital data – that is, whether LEAs access data themselves or compel a private third party to disclose the data. The second is whether investigators know the location where data is stored; when the location is unknown, officials obviously

[71] See, eg Hörnle (n 69) 202, 207–09, discussing Belgian, Danish and US examples of court-authorised remote searches.

[72] Allen (n 70) 388–90.

[73] See, eg Andreas and Nadelmann (n 6) 196–97, 220–21, 241–43: 'US strategy to secure greater law enforcement cooperation … could best be described as coercive co-optation involving a mix of sticks and carrots'; Sinnar (n 50) 1372, describing US pressure on other states to adopt anti-terrorism policies.

[74] See American Law Institute (n 3) § 431, reporters' note 2; Ryngaert, *Jurisdiction* (n 4) 90–91.

[75] The US Drug Enforcement Agency has 90 offices abroad in 60 countries. See US DEA, 'Foreign Offices', www.dea.gov/foreign-office-locations. The Federal Bureau of Investigation (FBI) has international operations in 93 offices abroad. See FBI, 'International Operations', www.fbi.gov/about/leadership-and-structure/international-operations. More than 70 federal prosecutors are stationed outside the USA, often under the Office of Overseas Prosecutorial Development, Assistance and Training (OPDAT). See OPDAT, 'Office of Overseas Prosecutorial Development, Assistance and Training' (*Justice*) www.justice.gov/criminal-opdat.

[76] See, eg TB Lee, 'Here's Everything We Know about PRISM to Date' *Washington Post* (12 June 2013) www.washingtonpost.com/news/wonk/wp/2013/06/12/heres-everything-we-know-about-prism-to-date/.

cannot seek permission or help from the hosting state.[77] US law is more permissive for indirect than direct searches, and for direct searches of data when its location is unknown to LEAs.

A. Indirect Access to Extraterritorial Information

Two important devices – national security letters and database search warrants – authorise US investigators to compel private firms to search and retrieve information stored in other states. Both rely on US personal jurisdiction over transnational firms,[78] which in practical effect operates as investigative jurisdiction over firms' extraterritorial conduct and information.[79] Such orders can conflict with laws in other states. Arguably, they violate no clearly established international law,[80] although that view is sharply disputed by some commentators and states, which view the practice as an impermissible exercise of indirect enforcement jurisdiction.[81]

Warrants are authorised by the Stored Communications Act (SCA), as amended by the 2018 US CLOUD Act, which has drawn much commentary.[82] The latter Act clarified that SCA warrants require firms providing remote data storage and communication services to preserve and disclose data stored outside as well as within the USA.[83] The much-noted problem is that compliance with SCA warrants might conflict with firms' obligations under other states' regulation of data stored in their territory. The CLOUD Act provides two ways to avoid those conflicts. First, it encourages bilateral agreements to resolve such conflicts, set common standards for privacy and human rights, and create a speedy alternative to mutual legal assistance treaty requests for other states seeking data controlled

[77] See Daskal (n 69) 678.

[78] Other states do much the same. See, eg *Yahoo! Inc v Belgium* Hof van Cassatie (Supreme Court of Belgium, 1 December 2015), No P.13.2082.N, translated in J Vandendreissche, 'Case Translation: Belgium' (2016) 13 *Digital Evidence and Electronic Signature Law Review* 156, paras 8–9. See also Hörnle (n 69) 199–200, criticising this basis for jurisdiction alone as inadequate.

[79] Ryngaert, *Jurisdiction* (n 4) 13–27, 91, describing US discovery orders as 'indirect enforcement jurisdiction'.

[80] eg Daskal (n 69) 697: 'cross-border accessing and copying of data for law enforcement purposes, without more, does not violate clearly established international law'.

[81] Ryngaert, *Jurisdiction* (n 4) 89–93; Allen (n 70) 408–09; FA Mann, *The Doctrine of International Jurisdiction Revisited after Twenty Years* (The Hague, Martinus Nijhoff, 1985) 47.

[82] eg Hörnle (n 69) 201, 212–15.

[83] 18 USC § 2713 (duty to preserve data applies 'regardless of whether such communication, record, or other information is located within or outside of the United States'); 18 USC § 2703 (warrants can require disclosure of contents of communications); 18 USC § 2711 (defining 'remote computing service'); 18 USC § 2510 (defining 'electronic communication service' as one 'which provides to users … the ability to send or receive wire or electronic communications'). Warrants must be time-limited relatively specifically as to the targeted person, the suspected crime and the data sought. Federal Rules of Criminal Procedure, r 41(c)–(e).

by US firms.[84] Second, it empowers US courts to employ comity analysis to deny warrants if 'the required disclosure would cause the provider to violate the laws of a qualifying foreign government' – that is, a government that entered a bilateral agreement with the USA.[85] Hörnle correctly describes the coercive nature of this scheme. She suggests that, in negotiating compacts, the USA likely will be able to 'achieve concessions from other States', given its greater 'data power' from the large share of the world's data that is stored in the USA or controlled by US ISPs.[86]

National security letters (NSLs) provide an alternate means to compel data disclosures from communication service providers, credit reporting agencies and banks. Several statutes authorise the FBI to issue NSLs, which are effectively subpoenas issued directly by investigators rather than courts, although recipients can seek judicial review of certain requests.[87] The most frequently used type of NSL is also part of the SCA and is directed at metadata on specific individuals' phone and email accounts.[88] Other NSL statutes address financial data.[89]

To enforcement agencies, NSLs offer the advantage of not requiring court preapproval. But they are limited in two important respects: they can be used to obtain only communications metadata (not email contents) and they can be issued only as part of an 'investigation to protect against international terrorism or clandestine intelligence activities'.[90] Information obtained through NSLs is often shared with criminal prosecutors, mostly for terrorism-related cases. How often is unknown. The FBI claims that NSL responses have played a critical role in specific counter-terrorism convictions, and an independent review found that the FBI 'routinely shared' information from NSLs with prosecutors, who also sometimes ask the FBI to issue NSLs. But no records exist of which or how many criminal cases benefited from NSL-obtained evidence, although the number is likely substantial.[91] In the years 2003–05, the FBI issued at least 143,074 NSL requests, almost three-quarters of which were for counter-terrorism (rather than counter-intelligence)

[84] See 18 USC § 2523; E Lostri, 'The CLOUD Act' (*CSIS Strategic Technologies*, 2 October 2020) www.csis.org/blogs/technology-policy-blog/cloud-act: 'bilateral agreements contemplated by the CLOUD Act intend to … ensur[e] both jurisdictions share similar privacy and civil-liberties protections'. Lostri also notes the 'complaints by foreign governments over the lengthy process to access electronic evidence from providers based in the United States'. The Act codifies some US policy preferences as substantive requirements for agreements on such topics as speech regulation and privacy. See 18 USC § 2523. Thus, such agreements become vehicles for generating US-favoured transnational legal norms.

[85] 18 USC § 2703(h)(2)(B).

[86] Hörnle (n 69) 201, 214–15, 224–29.

[87] 18 USC §§ 2709(d) and 3511.

[88] See 18 USC § 2709 (requests limited to 'subscriber information and toll billing records information, or electronic communication transactional records' and similar metadata); Office of the Inspector General (OIG), 'A Review of the Federal Bureau of Investigation's Use of National Security Letters' (US Department of Justice, 2007) xviii–xix.

[89] Fair Credit Reporting Act, 15 USC § 1681u (authorising limited data disclosures from credit reporting agencies); Patriot Act § 358(g) (authorising greater data disclosure from credit agencies); Right to Financial Privacy Act, 12 USC § 3414 (financial data).

[90] ECPA, 18 USC § 2709(b)(2); 15 USC § 1681u(a)–(b); 12 USC § 3414(a)(5)(A).

[91] OIG, 'A Review' (n 88) xxvii–xxviii, xlvi, 49, 62.

investigations.[92] Nor is there data on how often NSL requests require disclosure of extraterritorial data, but here too the number is likely substantial, given that requests must focus on international terrorism and counter-intelligence.[93]

B. Direct Access of Extraterritorial Information

Not all remotely stored information can be obtained by compelling private entities to disclose it. The US Justice Department uses the term 'network investigative techniques' to describe ways that LEAs directly access websites and stored data, especially when the server location or user identities of those targets are concealed through 'dark web' technologies such as Tor networks.[94] For example, to identify the location of a server hosting child pornography, officials may surreptitiously deploy computer code designed to identify users and administrators by causing computers to send the IP and MAC addresses and other information to a government computer[95] – techniques fairly characterised as government hacking. Like the digital data and networks they target, these techniques can disregard territorial boundaries; the location of data, and of administrators or users, can be widespread. The FBI's investigation of the 'Playpen' child porn and exploitation site identified 8000 IP addresses that visited the site, many outside the USA.[96]

As a matter of federal law, search warrants may be issued for electronic or digital searches only for devices located within the USA – or at least *not known to be outside* the USA, if the search is otherwise lawful.[97] The distinction between these direct searches and the indirect searches via SCA warrants is subtle but important. No statute authorises law enforcement officials to knowingly and directly

[92] ibid xx–xxi.

[93] Few, if any, court decisions resolving NSL challenges address data stored abroad. Most seem to focus on whether the recipient can be compelled not to disclose the fact that it received and complied with an NSL. See, eg *In re National Security Letter* 863 F3d 1110 (9th Cir 2017); *Twitter, Inc v Sessions* 2017 WL 5751299, *3 (ND Cal 2017).

[94] Through layers of encryption and routing, Tor networks conceal the identity and location of hidden or 'onion' services, such as the website, the server hosting a website and the users of the website. OIG, 'Audit of the Federal Bureau of Investigation's Strategy and Efforts to Disrupt Illegal Dark Web Activities' (Department of Justice, 2020) 2 perma.cc/2GM4-9NNR.

[95] P Kakkar and J Wheatley, 'Overcoming Technical Obfuscation: NITs and Remote Search Warrants' (May 2021) 69 *DOJ Journal of Federal Law and Practice* 3, 8–9, 13 (describing a warrant authorising delivery of NIT code embedded in an email that retrieved the user's operating system type, browser type and time zone).

[96] OIG, 'Audit' (n 94) 13; J Cox, 'Dozens of Lawyers across the US Fight the FBI's Mass Hacking Campaign' (*Vice*, 27 July 2016) www.vice.com/en/article/aek4ak/dozens-of-lawyers-across-the-us-fight-the-fbis-mass-hacking-campaign-playpen. US officials shared that information to foreign counterparts, leading to several hundred arrests in other countries: Kakkar and Wheatley (n 95) 9.

[97] Federal Rules of Criminal Procedure, rr 41(a)–(b) and Adv Cmte Note 1990. *cf* US Department of Justice, *Justice Manual*, § 9-13.525: 'Where the location of the computer is uncertain, but possibly within the United States, judicial approval will assure that Constitutional requirements have been met'. Likewise, courts may authorise wiretaps only for 'interception of … communications within the territorial jurisdiction of the court': 18 USC § 2518(3).

search a server in another state's territory. Justice Department policy reinforces that constraint by directing prosecutors to limit warrants to searches within the USA unless conducted in co-operation with foreign counterparts.[98] These limits implicitly recognise direct searches by officials as extraterritorial exercises of enforcement jurisdiction even though conducted remotely. But because SCA warrants are understood as exercises of adjudicative jurisdiction over domestic firms, and the duty to preserve and disclose applies regardless of the location of data, US law makes extraterritorial reach explicit.

The line grows greyer when the location of servers is unknown. A partial answer is provided in Federal Rule of Criminal Procedure 41(b)(6). As amended in 2016, that rule authorises a judge:

> [I]n any district where activities related to a crime may have occurred … to issue a warrant to use remote access to search electronic storage media and to seize or copy electronically stored information located within *or outside* that district if … the district where the media or information is located has been concealed through technological means' (emphasis added).

Thus, the rule permits direct NIT (Network Investigative Technique) searches of extraterritorial data, but only when (i) the data or server location is unknown and (ii) it is unknown because it was deliberately concealed.[99] In these circumstances, seeking assistance from states in which the data resides is not possible. And ordinary warrant requirements are unchanged by the amendment. Warrants must identify the person or property to be searched with 'reasonable particularity'.[100] US courts give those requirements some teeth; a few have rejected NIT warrant requests that did not sufficiently specify the target computer and when the prospect of searching innocent users was too great.[101]

In sum, US law and Justice Department policy disapprove of officials *knowingly* and *directly* searching devices outside US territory. However, when a 'significant purpose' of the search – but not the sole or even primary one – is 'to obtain foreign

[98] US Department of Justice, *Justice Manual* (n 97) § 9-13.525 (also observing that treaties 'require that the United States attempt to obtain records using the mutual legal assistance process prior to resorting to unilateral compulsory measures'). One example of an investigation with substantial international LEA cooperation targeted child exploitation sites on 39 Tor services and identified nearly 2.4 million users worldwide, which led to 16 arrests by US or foreign LEAs. See OIG, 'Audit' (n 94) 14–15; Federal Bureau of Investigation, 'Violent Crimes against Children International Task Force (VCACITF)', www.fbi.gov/investigate/violent-crime/cac/international-task-force, describing 'real-time transfer of information between the FBI and task force members from other countries'.

[99] Federal prosecutors are instructed to make 'reasonable efforts … to identify whether the computer to be searched is located inside or outside the United States' before seeking a warrant under 41(b)(6): US Department of Justice, *Justice Manual* (n 97) § 9-13.525.

[100] *United States v Karo* 468 US 705, 713–14 (1984); *Maryland v Garrison* 480 US 79, 84 (1987); Federal Rules of Criminal Procedure, r 41(e)(2)(A). Warrants for NITs can describe the thing to be searched without knowing its location. See R Bercovitz, 'Law Enforcement Hacking: Defining Jurisdiction' (2021) 121 *Columbia Law Review* 1251, 1267–68 (citing examples); Kakkar and Wheatley (n 95) 16, 19 (noting warrants need not identify a specific computer).

[101] *In re Warrant to Search a Target Computer at Premises Unknown* 958 F Supp 2d 753, 756–59 (SD Tex 2013).

intelligence information' rather than to investigate crime,[102] section 702 of the Foreign Intelligence Surveillance Act Amendments Act of 2008 (FISA) provides greater authority to monitor and gather electronic communications data of non-citizens outside the USA[103] – via US infrastructure – than is permissible when non-citizens are within US territory. Instead of a search warrant, officials can get preapproval of their surveillance tactics and plans for analysing data from the Foreign Intelligence Surveillance Court (FISC).[104] The FISC ensures that surveillance targets are people outside the USA, and that techniques minimise data collection from (and analysis of) people within US borders.[105]

Section 702 searches have gathered massive amounts of data, particularly during the PRISM programme, through which the National Security Agency accessed vast amounts of users' data – more than 250 million Internet communications annually.[106] And despite its constraints, section 702 collections can include data of US persons if gathered 'incidentally' whilst targeting non-citizens outside US territory.[107] Such data have proven useful in several criminal prosecutions (usually for terrorism-related offences) to justify domestic intelligence surveillance under FISA, to obtain domestic search warrants or as trial evidence.[108]

The focus of section 702 operations is explicitly on extraterritorial actors and data (when accessible via US-based communications service providers).[109] Its justification rests in part on a distinction between foreign intelligence and

[102] 50 USC § 1881a(h)(2)(A)(v).

[103] See 50 USC §§ 1881a(a) and (b)(1)–(3) (surveillance 'may not intentionally target any person known … to be located in the United States' nor 'a United States person reasonably believed to be located outside the United States'); 50 USC § 1801(i) ('United States persons' includes citizens and lawful non-citizen residents).

[104] 50 USC § 1881a(d)(2), (e)(2), (f)(1)(C) and (j).

[105] 50 USC § 1881a(a), (d)–(f) and (j). See also *In re DNI/AG* 702(h) Certifications 2018, 941 F3d 547, 552 (FISA Ct Rev 2019) (*per curiam*): 'the Attorney General and the Director of National Intelligence can execute a Section 702 authorisation only after the FISC enters an order approving the proposed acquisition'.

[106] L Donohue, 'Section 702 and the Collection of International Telephone and Internet Content' (2015) 38 *Harvard Journal of Law and Public Policy* 117, 120; Lee (n 76).

[107] 50 USC § 1881a(a) and (b)(2); *United States v Muhtorov* 20 F4th 558, 604–05 (10th Cir 2021); *United States v Hasbajrami* 945 F3d 641, 654 (2d Cir 2019). It appears that the government maximises this domestic surveillance by asserting that minimal acts by domestic actors, such as posting YouTube videos, satisfy the international-nexus requirement. See Sinnar (n 50) 1347. The constitutional warrant requirement does not apply to extraterritorial searches: *United States v Verdugo-Urquidez* 494 US 259 (1990). Federal courts have extended that holding to domestic communications obtained incidentally to extraterritorial surveillance, although such searches still must be 'reasonable'. *Hasbajrami* 662, 666; *Muhtorov* 593–94.

[108] See, eg *Muhtorov* (n 107) 590–92 (§ 2339B conviction for conspiracy to provide material support); *Hasbajrami* (n 107) 645–46 (§ 2339A conviction for attempting to provide material support).

[109] Wiretaps can work the same way to intercept calls between mobile phones outside the USA that, in border areas, are routed through US-based cellular towers. Courts define the 'interception' location as the tower rather than where phone users are located. See *United States v Cano-Flores* 796 F3d 83, 86–87 (DC Cir 2015) (phone conversation in Mexico lawfully interpreted in Texas); *United States v Henley* 766 F3d 893, 911–12 (8th Cir 2014); *United States v Luong* 471 F3d 1107, 1109–10 (9th Cir 2006); 18 USC § 2518(3) (authorising wiretaps only for 'interception of … communications within the territorial jurisdiction of the court').

law enforcement activities. Espionage – especially by remote surveillance – is often said not to violate international law (although it usually violates domestic law).[110] Section 702 surveillance is designed to serve national security interests, but is not classic espionage; it targets not state secrets, but non-state actors – the kind of intelligence that states often share. But international law ambiguity, and the fact that all states seek foreign intelligence by various means, helps to explain section 702's comparatively expansive surveillance authority. When surveillance is primarily for law enforcement purposes, US law is more restrictive of extraterritorial searches, whether conducted both directly via ordinary warrants or indirectly via CLOUD Act warrants. An additional political explanation would point in part to the US global footprint – notably, but not solely, via its military – as creating more targets for (and animosity from) international bad actors. And here as in other contexts, US financial resources provide the capacity for expansive infrastructure and operations.

IV. Conclusion

Because the international law of jurisdiction rests on criminal offence elements defined in domestic law, states can maximise the ambit of offences by designing elements that provide a territorial connection to extraterritorial conduct. The transnational nature of large corporations, financial networks and communications technology make this easy because states regulate domestic firms and infrastructure that extend far beyond national boundaries. The USA and other large, wealthy states have advantages here: the more transnational firms operate in, digital data is stored in and financial transactions flow through their territory, the greater their opportunities for criminalising extraterritorial activity. These advantages extend beyond prescriptive to enforcement jurisdiction for multiple reasons: international law is unclear on digital investigation practices; adjudicative jurisdiction can be used to enlist domestic entities for extraterritorial information disclosures; economic power translates to bargaining power when seeking other states' co-operation; and more wealth funds more investigative capacity.

US criminal law and enforcement agencies use all these opportunities. And in this context, because the government controls the levels and targets of enforcement, US courts have been largely receptive.[111] Reactions from other states, and scholars, are a mix of praise, grudging assent and critique. Some disputes, such as those about policies on data privacy, reflect competing normative preferences. In some contexts, there are good arguments that aggressive extraterritorial application

[110] Daskal (n 69) 680–81.

[111] In private civil litigation, by contrast, US courts have significantly restricted extraterritorial application. See, eg *Kiobel v Royal Dutch Petroleum Co* 569 US 108 (2013); *F Hoffmann-LaRoche Ltd v Empagran SA* 542 US 155 (2004).

of US law fills in for other states' failures to act and serves widely shared interests. Some prosecutions of transnational corruption provide plausible examples. In other circumstances, benefits of US enforcement are hotly contested, dubious or reflect parochial rather than common interests. Cases in point include copyright prosecutions and the fraught complications of anti-drug trafficking policies. Even when the case for broad-based benefits is strong, extraterritorial enforcement risks diminishing democratic input from parties with a strong nexus to targeted conduct,[112] while giving outsized roles to states with economic and technological advantages. Customary international law seems an unpromising vehicle either for restraining the transnational reach of US criminal law or, more generally, for allocating priority when states share concurrent jurisdiction.[113] If that is so, then the best hopes lie in domestic law, bilateral and multilateral instruments, and policy reforms in both domestic and international institutions.[114]

[112] Ryngaert, 'Cosmopolitan Jurisdiction' (n 65) 216.
[113] For different views, see Ryngaert, *Jurisdiction* (n 4), urging a stronger role for the reasonableness standard in international law; Svantesson (n 69), urging primary roles for reasonableness and nexus in jurisdiction law.
[114] eg Eurojust, *Guidelines for Deciding 'Which Jurisdiction Should Prosecute?'*, revised edn (The Hague, Eurojust, 2016).

4

The Jurisdictional Reach of Corporate Criminal Offences in a Globalised Economy: Effectiveness and Guarantees 'Taken Seriously'

VINCENZO MONGILLO

I. The Unstoppable Rise of Multinational Corporations and the Extension of States' Jurisdiction Over Transnational Crimes

Since the mid-1970s there has been a radical shift from an international market economy to a global economy. This transformation has increased in speed and range since the fall of the Berlin Wall in 1989, the end of the Cold War and the consequent bipolar division of the world. In these new circumstances, multinationals (or 'transnational corporations', in UN terminology)[1] have become 'the biggest players in world trade'.[2] By the late 1990s, 60,000 transnational corporations with over 500,000 foreign affiliates accounted for approximately 25 per cent of global output.[3] As noted 25 years ago in a UN report, 'of the 100 biggest concentrations of wealth in the world, 51 per cent are owned by transnational corporations and 49 per cent by States'.[4] The sales of some multinational corporations are for values

[1] According to ECOSOC/UNCHR, 'Norms on the Responsibilities of Transnational Corporations and Other Business Enterprises with Regard to Human Rights' (2003) UN Doc E/CN.4/Sub.2/2003/12/Rev.2, para 20, 'the term "transnational corporation" refers to an economic entity operating in more than one country or a cluster of economic entities operating in two or more countries – whatever their legal form, whether in their home country or country of activity, and whether taken individually or collectively'.

[2] See M Delmas-Marty, 'Globalisation et sociétés transnationales' (*GoodPlanet*, 16 September 2008) www.goodplanet.info/2008/09/16/globalisation-et-societes-transnationales/; D Litvin, *Empires of Profit: Commerce, Conquest and Corporate Responsibility* (Mason, Thomson, 2004).

[3] UNCTAD, *World Investment Report 1999: Foreign Direct Investment and the Challenge of Development* (New York, United Nations, 1999).

[4] ECOSOC/UNCHR and EH Guissé, 'The Realization of Economic, Social and Cultural Rights: The Question of Transnational Corporations' (1998) UN Doc E/CN.4/Sub.2/1998/6.

greater than the gross domestic product of many states (including some developed Western countries),[5] so their resources and ability to influence world – including geopolitical – events tends to overwhelm nation states themselves.

However, what currently makes the role and activities of transnational enterprises so problematic from a legal viewpoint is not so much (or only) their enormous economic power, which does not exceed that of the largest national companies of a few decades ago, both in Europe and elsewhere,[6] as their the capacity to pursue their own best interests by evading local or national constraints. The removal of barriers to trade and the movement of capital and labour, the rise of digitalisation and contemporary technologies, and the role of lawyers and legal coding in transforming wealth into an asset that automatically creates further wealth[7] have given transnational corporations 'enormous flexibility in the organisation of production and has made them "footloose", able to exploit economic opportunities around the world',[8] with the consequence that the (global) economy has been decoupled from political control.[9]

It is also worth mentioning that a boundless market economy is not only characterised by the globalisation of trade: the same phenomenon was widespread in the years just preceding World War I. Another distinctive trait is the worldwide expansion of the organisation of production:[10] local branches, foreign subsidiaries, international joint ventures and global supply chains.[11] It is difficult to predict the future impact on globalisation of the recent COVID-19 outbreak and, more lately, the international crisis caused by the Russian–Ukrainian war. In any event, according to many observers, globalisation appears to be an irreversible process, since a tendency towards economic autarky would create higher costs, unforeseen harm and vulnerabilities, considering that 'domestic supply chains are even less resilient than global ones'.[12]

[5] See D Grayson and A Hodges, *Everybody's Business: Managing Risks and Opportunities in Today's Global Society* (London, DK, 2001) 29.

[6] See RB Reich, *Supercapitalism: The Transformation of Business, Democracy, and Everyday Life* (New York, Alfred A Knopf, 2007) ch 1.

[7] K Pistor, *The Code of Capital: How the Law Creates Wealth and Inequality* (Princeton, Princeton University Press, 2019).

[8] Y Ghai, 'Rights, Social Justice, and Globalization in East Asia' in JR Bauer and DA Bell (eds), *The East Asian Challenge for Human Rights* (Cambridge, Cambridge University Press, 1999) 251; DP Forsythe, *Human Rights in International Relations*, 3rd edn (Cambridge, Cambridge University Press, 212) 277ff. Other scholars advocate an unusual distinction between 'multinational corporations' and 'transnational corporations', arguing that 'MNCs are those international companies that are still tethered to a national economy, despite the fact that they may operate in a supranational regional context', as opposed to TNCs, which represent genuine and relatively rare 'footloose stateless companies', having severed their contact to any particular national economy: P Hirst, G Thompson and S Browley, *Globalization in Question*, 3rd edn (Cambridge, Polity Press, 2009) 50, 130, 149, 331 and fn 2.

[9] See C Boggs, 'Economic Globalization and Political Atrophy' (2001) 7 *Democracy and Nature* 303.

[10] F Galgano, 'L'impresa transnazionale e i diritti nazionali' (2005) *Rivista trimestrale di diritto e procedura civile* 39, 51.

[11] As noted by T Bartley, 'Transnational Corporations and Global Governance' (2018) 44 *Annual Review of Sociology* 145, esp 148: 'global firms have taken the form of networked TNCs … TNCs such as Nike, Apple, Wal-Mart, IKEA, and H&M built their fortunes by nimbly managing networks of independent contract manufacturers'.

[12] 'Global Supply Chains are Still a Source of Strength, Not Weakness' *The Economist* (31 March 2021) 9.

Due to the unstoppable rise of corporations in the contemporary era,[13] new critical criminology denounces an unprecedented 'corporate totalitarianism',[14] the more malignant side of which is precisely the spread of transnational corporate crime. An influential Australian scholar noted nearly 40 years ago that, 'as more of world trade becomes concentrated in the hands of fewer transnational corporations, the corporate crime problem increasingly assumes a transnational character'.[15] 'Unbound' production, corporations, and financial transactions in themselves encourage undesirable forms of forum or law shopping,[16] and produce growing opportunities for corporate crime: toxic waste spills in foreign countries; transfer pricing; fraudulently obtaining EU grants or subsidies; international bribery; money laundering; insider trading and securities fraud; dumping of products on transboundary markets (eg low-quality or unsafe foodstuffs); formation of illegal cartels or monopolies on an international scale; infringement of intellectual property rights; and dangerous working conditions and labour exploitation, up to and including forms of slavery or forced labour, especially in the poorest and undemocratic nations.

Against this background, 'pure' or 'free' self-regulation,[17] market reputational sanctions (informed by a neoliberal vision) and soft law instruments – including those of the most authoritative international organisations, such as the UN and OECD – are insufficient to effectively counter transnational corporate crime. The role of criminal law remains essential and, in the continuing absence of global enforcement mechanisms against transnational corporate crimes, national enforcement is the only option available. Accordingly, in the last two decades, nation states have sought to react to the loss of influence over corporate activities and transnational corporate offences through a dual strategy, including through reliance on EU law and various regional and international conventions.

The first strategy is based on the introduction of criminal/punitive sanctions for corporations.[18] Between the second half of the nineteenth century and the first

[13] J Bakan, *The Corporation: The Pathological Pursuit of Profit and Power* (London, Constable, 2004).

[14] ER Zaffaroni, 'La crítica en tiempos de totalitarismo corporativo' (2019) *Revista Nueva Crítica Penal* 1, 4ff.

[15] J Braithwaite, *Corporate Crime in the Pharmaceutical Industry* (London, Routledge, 1984) 369; M Delmas-Marty and K Tiedemann, 'La criminalité, le droit pénal et les multinationales' (1979) 1 *La Semaine juridique* 2935; J Gobert and M Punch, *Rethinking Corporate Crime* (London, Butterworths, 2003) 146ff.

[16] RJ Michalowski and RC Kramer, 'The Space between Laws: The Problem of Corporate Crime in a Transnational Context' (1987) 34 *Social Problems* 1, 34ff; A Bernardi, 'Il diritto penale tra globalizzazione e multiculturalismo' (2002) 2 *Rivista italiana di diritto pubblico comunitario* 485.

[17] On the different types of self-regulation, see C Coglianese and E Mendelson, 'Meta-Regulation and Self-Regulation' in R Baldwin, M Cave and M Lodge (eds), *The Oxford Handbook of Regulation* (Oxford, Oxford University Press, 2010) 152.

[18] See M Pieth and R Ivory (eds), *Corporate Criminal Liability: Emergence, Convergence, and Risk* (Dordrecht, Springer, 2011); A Fiorella (ed), *Corporate Criminal Liability and Compliance Programs, vol 1: Liability 'Ex Crimine' of Legal Entities in Member States; vol 2: Towards a Common Model in the European Union* (Naples, Jovene, 2012); G Vermeulen, W De Bondt and C Ryckman, *Liability of Legal Persons for Offences in the EU* (Antwerp, Maklu, 2012); OECD, 'The Liability of Legal Persons: A Stocktaking Report' (2016); T Hoppe et al, 'Liability of Legal Persons for Corruption Offences'

decades of the twentieth century, the new organisational complexity and the huge economic power of railway companies led the UK courts, and then the US courts, to countenance direct punishment of corporations.[19] In the last two decades, it was once again the debate on the enormous power of multinationals that prompted national legislatures – including in all civil law countries – to overcome the axiom *societas delinquere non potest.*

The second strategy to react to the erosion of state sovereignty over transnational corporations is the adoption of an expansive jurisdictional approach that enables one to 'delocalise' the application of national criminal law, also thanks to multilateral investigative and judicial co-operation.

This chapter will analyse the second issue from two perspectives: the effectiveness of enforcement against corporate crime, on the one hand, and the protection of defendants' rights, on the other. From the first perspective, I will first focus on the different rules on extraterritorial jurisdiction (section II), commonly considered by international organisations and many experts to be an essential tool for improving the accountability of transnational corporations in relation to human rights abuses and for countering the crimes they can commit or contribute to in their operations outside the country of origin.[20] In this context, I will also deal with the perennially debated question of double criminality as a potential condition of extraterritorial jurisdiction (section III).

Moreover, in the course of my examination, I intend to emphasise that the aim of expanding state jurisdiction, which is directly pursued by employing various principles of extraterritorial jurisdiction, such as the active personality principle and the protective principle, can also be achieved by a more subtle method – namely, by maximising the territorial application of criminal law. In this view, on closer inspection, we can observe two forms of extraterritorial jurisdiction: a formal, genuine one and another 'camouflaged' under the notion of territoriality extended to the extreme. This second path could also be described as a process of 'territorialising the extraterritorial'[21] or, in other words, as a form of 'unbound

(Strasbourg, Council of Europe, 2020); V Mongillo, *La responsabilità penale tra individuo ed ente collettivo* (Turin, Giappichelli, 2018) 96ff.

[19] For more on that issue, see V Mongillo, 'Necessità e caso nell'allocazione della responsabilità da reato tra individui ed enti collettivi. Considerazioni alla luce dell'"incontro" tra società ferroviaria e giudice penale nell'Europa del XIX secolo' (2014) 3 *Rivista italiana di diritto e procedura penale* 1291.

[20] O de Schutter, 'Extraterritorial Jurisdiction as a Tool for Improving the Human Rights Accountability of Transnational Corporations' (Business and Human Rights Resource Centre, 2006) www.business-humanrights.org/en/latest-news/pdf-extraterritorial-jurisdiction-as-a-tool-for-improving-the-human-rights-accountability-of-transnational-corporations/; Amnesty International, 'Comments in Response to the UN Special Representative of the Secretary General on Transnational Corporations and other Business Enterprises' *Guiding Principles – Proposed Outline*' (Amnesty International, October 2010) www.amnesty.org/es/documents/ior50/001/2010/en/.

[21] See M Ó Floinn, 'Territorialising the Extraterritorial: The Role of "Suppression Conventions"' in V Militello and A Spena (eds) *The Challenges of Illegal Trafficking in the Mediterranean Area* (Cham, Springer, forthcoming). See further C Ryngaert, 'Enforcement Jurisdiction in A-territorial Spaces: Addressing Crime on the High Seas and in Cyberspace', ch 7 in the present volume.

territoriality'[22] (section IV). Finally, and from the second of the two perspectives outlined above, I will address the issue of the violation of the *ne bis in idem* principle in transnational criminal cases (section V).

II. Extraterritorial Jurisdiction: Four Paths to 'Capture' Transnational Corporations

In the contemporary era, human rights abuses and business crimes are often committed in foreign countries by transnational corporations. In view of this background, in June 2011, the UN Human Rights Council, within the Guiding Principles on Business and Human Rights, declared that 'States should set out clearly the expectation that all business enterprises domiciled in their territory and/or jurisdiction respect human rights throughout their operations' ('foundational principle' No 2 concerning 'the State duty to protect human rights'), suggesting a range of approaches with extraterritorial implications.[23]

As regards corporate crime, a typical illegal method used by multinationals to conquer cross-border markets and win business abroad is foreign bribery; hence, it is normally committed outside the home country. In this specific field, Article 42(2) of the United Nations Convention against Corruption of 2003 (UNCAC) indicates extraterritorial jurisdiction is a necessary instrument to prosecute corruption where it is committed across borders, starting from the remark that corruption 'is no longer a local matter but a transnational phenomenon that affects all societies and economies'.[24]

State extraterritorial jurisdiction is traditionally subject to stringent requirements. However, in order to combat more effectively transnational corporate crime, the tendency of national legal systems worldwide is to make them increasingly flexible.[25] There are – or, at least, it is ordinarily assumed that there are – different bases of extraterritorial jurisdiction:[26] (i) *personal jurisdiction*

[22] I borrow this expression from N Krisch, 'Jurisdiction Unbound: (Extra)territorial Regulation as Global Governance' (2022) 33 *European Journal of International Law* 482, 501.

[23] UN Human Rights Office of the High Commissioner, 'Guiding Principles on Business and Human Rights: Implementing the United Nations "Protect, Respect and Remedy" Framework', HR/PUB/11/04 (New York, United Nations, 2011) 4. The Human Rights Council endorsed the Guiding Principles developed by the Special Representative of the Secretary-General in its Resolution 17/4 of 16 June 2011.

[24] United Nations Convention against Corruption (New York, 31 October 2003) 2349 UNTS 41 (UNCAC) preamble.

[25] See M Garrod, 'Extraterritorial Criminal Jurisdiction in International Law: Time for an Empirical Examination' ch 5 in the present volume, and his empirical work showing how enabling these bases are in state practice.

[26] European Committee on Crime Problems, *Extraterritorial Criminal Jurisdiction* (Strasbourg, Council of Europe, 1990) distinguishes, in a more detailed manner, between seven forms of extraterritorial criminal jurisdiction: (1) the principle of the nationality of the offender (or active personality principle); (2) the principle of the flag; (3) the principle of the nationality of the victim (or passive

(the active personality principle or passive personality principle); (ii) *protective jurisdiction*, which 'permits States to establish jurisdiction over specific categories of offences which though committed entirely extraterritorially, have an impact on or threaten that State's sovereignty, security, integrity, or some other important governmental function';[27] and (iii) *universal jurisdiction*, permitting a court in any state to try someone for a crime committed in another state regardless of the aforementioned more restrictive criteria.[28]

Normally, states' extraterritorial jurisdiction for corporate crimes is not based on the universality principle, but on some variant of the principle of *active personality*. In fact, companies are subject to extraterritoriality rules if they meet certain *personality characteristics* specified by law. Nonetheless, the features that a corporation must have for a state legitimately to exercise jurisdiction for extraterritorial wrongdoing differ significantly in various legal systems.

Currently, we can identify at least four models for the application of the active personality principle to corporations, which in some jurisdictions are wholly or partially combined with one another. Obviously, the question of jurisdiction over a corporation precedes and – if it is held to exist – does not absorb the other issue of the rules according to which a corporation (and its members) can be held criminally liable for corporate crimes.[29]

A. The (Active) Nationality Model

Pursuant to the 'nationality model', state jurisdiction for corporate crimes committed abroad depends on the legal person's incorporation in the national territory (*place of incorporation*), with which the entity's *registered office* or *statutory seat* (which, hypothetically and in certain circumstances, could be shifted from one state to another) tends to be equated in some legal systems. Traditionally, state jurisdiction over citizens for crimes committed abroad was based on the idea that

personality principle); (4) the principle of protection; (5) the 'representation' principle; (6) the principle of universality; and (7) forms of extraterritorial jurisdiction which do not fall under the aforementioned categories. See also C Ryngaert, *Jurisdiction in International Law*, 2nd edn (Oxford, Oxford University Press, 2015).

[27] N Boister, *An Introduction to Transnational Criminal Law*, 2nd edn (Oxford, Oxford University Press, 2018). Regarding the protective principle, see also I Cameron, *The Protective Principle of International Criminal Jurisdiction* (Aldershot, Dartmouth, 1994).

[28] It is common ground that the universality principle expresses an idea of moral and legal solidarity among states. See, eg L Reydams, *Universal Jurisdiction: International and Municipal Legal Perspectives* (Oxford, Oxford University Press, 2004) 30.

[29] On the different criteria for attributing corporate responsibility in EU Member States, see V Mongillo, 'The Nature of Corporate Liability for Criminal Offences: Theoretical Models and European Union Member States' Laws' in Fiorella, *Corporate Criminal Liability*, vol 1 (n 18) 55–120; V Mongillo, 'The Allocation of Responsibility for Criminal Offences between Individuals and Legal Entities in Europe' in Fiorella, *Corporate Criminal Liability*, vol 2 (n 18) 121–69. Currently, the rules by which English law holds companies criminally liable for serious economic and financial misconducts are attracting strong criticism. See, eg Law Commission, 'Corporate Criminal Liability: An Options Paper' (10 June 2022).

they owed their country allegiance.[30] In the case of corporations, the rationale may be quite different and roughly based on the duty of a nation state to level the playing field by establishing the lawfulness of the operations carried out abroad by domestic multinationals.

At the outset, it is also worth highlighting that the nationality principle as a basis for extraterritorial jurisdiction is traditionally one of the most disputed in the general international law or transnational criminal law literature. As far back as the 1930s, the nationality criterion was criticised as a bad policy on which to base state jurisdiction, as 'the government has no interest in the conduct of its citizens abroad except when that conduct results in injury to it, because the peace and good order of its territory is not disturbed'.[31] Again, more recently, some scholars have provided a fairly robust critique of this ground of jurisdiction,[32] which in ancient times was the basic jurisdictional principle as only the advent of the modern territorial state gave rise to the right to subject foreigners to the *lex loci*.[33] In relation to cybercrime – a form of crime attracting much attention in the current digital age – one author contends that in cases of concurrent jurisdiction the perpetrator's nationality 'seems to be a factor that militates against, rather than for, the assertion of jurisdiction', and has proposed that 'injured sovereigns should be given priority over the non-injured sovereign'.[34]

Nevertheless, in recent decades, the international trend has gone in the opposite direction, especially in the fight against business crime and organised crime. Consequently, although the usual literature on active personality does not mention corporate nationality, this criterion tends to be extended to corporate actors as a ground for state jurisdiction.

Transnational crime conventions also deal with this subject, and some related official guides include companies in promoting nationality jurisdiction. For instance, in the Technical Guide to the United Nations Convention Against Corruption, active personality jurisdiction is recommended as a necessary tool to combat corrupt practices more effectively, regardless of whether the offender is an individual or a company.[35] In particular, the Guide points out that this

[30] CL Blakesley, 'Extra-Territorial Jurisdiction' in MC Bassiouni, *International Criminal Law*, 2nd edn (New York, Ardsley, 1999) 61.

[31] See EE Stimson, *Conflict of Criminal Laws* (Chicago, The Foundation Press, 1936), who added that the principle of active personality also risked violating the *ne bis in idem* principle (on which see s V below): 'It would subject its citizens to the possibility of double punishment for the same act, because in most cases the citizen's foreign act or omission would be a violation of the criminal law of the sovereignty in whose territory he was at the time, and a conviction of violating the foreign law would not bar proceedings for a violation of the domestic law.'

[32] See, eg A Chehtman, *The Philosophical Foundations of Extraterritorial Punishment* (Oxford, Oxford University Press, 2010) 59–66.

[33] JL Brierly, 'The *Lotus* Case' (1928) 44 *Law Quarterly Review* 154, 155–56.

[34] SW Brenner, 'The Next Step: Prioritizing Jurisdiction' in BJ Koops and SW Brenner (eds), *Cybercrime and Jurisdiction: A Global Survey* (The Hague, TMC Asser Press, 2006) 341, 343.

[35] UNODC and UNICRI, 'Technical Guide to the United Nations Convention Against Corruption' (United Nations, 2009) 134–35.

approach could be essential in dealing with contemporary corruption, in particular in order to promote comparable standards of behaviour at home and abroad, providing for the possibility of states parties exerting jurisdiction over their citizens or a stateless person who has their habitual residence in their territory and hence cannot be extradited, irrespective of the place where they might commit a corruption offence.

As far as corporations are concerned, the Guide points out a number of issues: 'First of all, States Parties may consider implementing the term "national" in a manner which would encompass national legal persons. Second, States Parties may take note of two models of implementation in relation to the nationality principle.' In fact, 'most States Parties exert jurisdiction according to the principle of nationality when a national legal person is liable of a corruption offence', and 'a corporation may be regarded as national, if it has been founded according to the national law or if the corporation resides in the territory'.[36]

With regard to those states parties that answer the question of jurisdiction with reference to the nationality of the acting *natural* person, and not (also) to the nationality of the *legal* person for whose benefit a cross-border crime is committed, the Guide critically observes that this approach 'may cause serious legal loopholes since in the crucial cases of corporate liability investigative agencies may not be able to identify the individual instigator or perpetrator'.[37] Consequently, the principle of liability of legal persons should require linking the consequent sanction to the legal person itself, irrespective of the nationality of the individual perpetrator.

Currently, most states follow this approach. In many countries, such as the Netherlands,[38] it is undisputed that a legal person incorporated under the relevant national law is subject to nationality jurisdiction therein, despite the lack of special regulations on jurisdiction in cases of liability of legal persons. In other jurisdictions, like the Czech Republic,[39] it is expressly stated that the scope of corporate criminal liability extends to crimes committed abroad by a legal person with its registered office (in Czech, *sídlo*) in the state.

Starting from a 1998 reform, the US law against international corruption – the Foreign Corrupt Practices Act 1977 (FCPA) – envisages the principle of nationality as a basis for US jurisdiction in relation to any act committed in furtherance of unlawful payments to foreign officials that take place wholly outside the USA (so-called 'alternative jurisdiction').[40] In fact, the subjective reach of the FCPA includes any 'US person', namely any national of the USA (as defined in section 101

[36] ibid 135. See also Hoppe et al (n 18) 64, para 7.1.1, according to which, because the UN Convention against Corruption, the OECD Convention and the Council of Europe Criminal Law Convention on Corruption all require liability of legal persons, 'it seems logical to treat legal persons analogously to natural persons for matters of jurisdiction'.

[37] UNODC and UNICRI (n 35) 135.

[38] *cf* Hoppe et al (n 18) 64, para 7.1.1.

[39] eg s 3 of Act No 418/2011 on Criminal Liability of Legal Persons and the Proceedings against Them.

[40] USC 15 § 78dd-2(i).

of the Immigration and Nationality Act[41]) or 'any corporation, partnership, association, joint-stock company, business trust, unincorporated organisation, or sole proprietorship *organised under the laws* of the United States or any State, territory, possession, or commonwealth of the United States, or any political subdivision thereof' (emphasis added). In amending the FCPA, the US government introduced this alternative basis for jurisdiction in 1998 in order to fully implement the 1997 OECD Convention on Combating Bribery of Foreign Public Officials in International Business Transactions.[42]

Another recent example comes from the UK Bribery Act 2010, where there is extraterritorial jurisdiction for the offences in sections 1 (offences of bribing another person), 2 (offences relating to being bribed) and 6 (bribery of foreign public officials), provided that the person's extraterritorial acts or omissions 'would form part of [a section 1, 2 or 6] offence if done or made in the United Kingdom' and the person has 'a close connection with the United Kingdom'.[43] The concept of 'close connection' includes British citizens and other British nationals; individuals ordinarily resident in the UK; bodies incorporated under the law of any part of the UK; and Scottish partnerships.[44] Clearly, this rule represents an extended version of the classic nationality criterion.

B. The Actual Residence or (Real) Head Office Model

Pursuant to the 'residence model' applied to corporations, the jurisdictional link is the location of the *head office* (or *principal office*) in the territory of the state. This criterion is similar to that of the habitual or permanent residence in a state used for natural persons, and can be considered an extensive evolution of the principle of active personality based on nationality.[45] As regards legal persons, many national laws adopt this connecting factor as a permissible ground of extraterritorial jurisdiction over corporations. This is the case, amongst others, in the Italian legal system and under the US FCPA, but with some significant differences.

[41] 8 USC § 1101.

[42] United States Senate, 'Senate Report: The International Bribery Act of 1998' (30 July 1998) Sen Rep No 105-277, 3. By contrast, outside the circle of domestic natural and legal persons, US courts do not allow US law enforcement agencies to apply the FCPA to foreign nationals acting exclusively outside US territory: *United States v Hoskins* No 16-1010-cr (2d Cir 2018).

[43] UK Bribery Act 2010, ss 12(2) and (3).

[44] The list does not include foreign subsidiaries of UK parent companies, a facet criticised by GR Sullivan, 'The Bribery Act 2010: An Overview' [2011] *Crim LR* 87, 97–98.

[45] *cf* J Crawford, *Brownlie's Principles of Public International Law*, 8th edn (Oxford, Oxford University Press, 2012) 459–60. Somewhat differently, other authors frame the habitual residence criterion as a form of territorial jurisdiction. See, eg J Bourguignon, 'France's New Approach towards Extraterritoriality in Anti-Corruption Law: Paving the Way for a Protective Principle in Economic Matters?' in R Bismuth, J Dunin-Wasowicz and PM Nichols (eds), *The Transnationalization of Anti-Corruption Law* (Abindgon, Routledge, 2021) 159. However, it is clear that in the case under consideration the territoriality criterion refers not to the offence, but to the residence of its perpetrator.

Under Article 4 of Italian Legislative Decree No 231 of 8 June 2001[46] concerning the liability of legal entities (*enti collettivi*) for criminal offences (a nominally 'administrative' but essentially 'criminal' corporate responsibility), only organisations having their head office (*sede principale*) in Italy – regardless of the fact that they are incorporated therein[47] – may be held liable for crimes committed abroad. To avoid circumvention of the legislation and the risk of forum shopping, Italian case law and legal literature hold that the concept of 'head office' has to be understood as the centre of the administrative, managerial and organisational activities of the company[48] ('real head office', akin to the notion of 'headquarters' or 'main headquarters'). Therefore, it can be different from the place of incorporation or the registered office of the corporation, namely the latter's official address.

Despite some semantic imprecision or ambiguity, the concept of '(real) head office' tends to coincide with the US expression of 'principal place of business', which, according to US courts,[49] refers to the place from which the company's officials direct, control and coordinate all activities in the furtherance of the corporate objective, so that it can be considered to be the 'nerve centre' of the organisation. This place is not to be confused with the business locales in which the board meetings are held.[50]

It should be pointed out, however, that in the Italian legal system, jurisdiction *contra societates* for offences committed abroad depends also on conditions related to jurisdiction *contra homines*. In particular, the requirements prescribed in Articles 7–10 of the Italian Criminal Code for prosecuting natural persons

[46] Legislative Decree 8 June 2001, No 231, 'Regulation on administrative responsibility of legal entities, companies and associations, including those not having legal personality, according to Article 11, Law 29 September 2000, No 300'.

[47] See OECD, 'Italy: Phase 2: Report on the Application of the Convention on Combatting Bribery of Foreign Public Officials in International Business Transactions and the 1997 Recommendation on Combatting Bribery in International Business Transactions' (29 November 2004) para 169.

[48] L Pistorelli, 'Profili problematici della "responsabilità internazionale" degli enti per i reati commessi nel loro interesse o vantaggio' [2011] *Responsabilità amministrativa delle società e degli enti* 15; AF Tripodi, 'Il diritto penale degli enti nello spazio: deantropomorfizzazione e globalizzazione a confronto' (2019) 1 *Archivio penale* 3: the author defines *sede principale* as the 'center of prevalent and effective performance of the administrative management and organization of the entity'; C Piergallini, 'Globalizzazione dell'economia, rischio-reato e responsabilità *ex crimine* delle multinazionali' (2020) 33 *Rivista trimestrale di diritto penale dell'economia* 157, 159; V Mongillo, 'Imprese multinazionali, criminalità transfrontaliera ed estensione della giurisdizione penale nazionale: efficienza e garanzie "prese sul serio"' (2021) 170 *Giornale di diritto del lavoro e di relazioni industriali* 179, 190.

[49] See, in particular, *Hertz Corp v Amico*, 559 US 77, 130 S Ct 1181.

[50] It is worth noting that the expression 'principal place of business' is also used in the US FCPA in defining 'domestic concern', one of the three categories of individuals and entities covered by the FCPA anti-bribery provisions, in addition to issuers and foreign actors engaging in any act in furtherance of a corrupt payment while in US territory. The expression 'domestic concern' is defined as '(A) any individual who is a citizen, national, or resident of the United States; and (B) any corporation, partnership, association, joint-stock company, business trust, unincorporated organization, or sole proprietorship which has its principal place of business in the United States, or which is organized under the laws of a State of the United States or a territory, possession, or commonwealth of the United States': 15 USC § 78dd-2(h)(1).

for offences committed entirely abroad must be followed.[51] In addition, Article 4 of Legislative Decree No 231/2001 provides two further jurisdictional requirements for prosecuting corporations. First, in all cases in which the request of the Minister of Justice is necessary for prosecution on the basis of the rules of transnational criminal law, that request must be 'formulated also in relation to the entity'. Second, the prosecution of the corporation for crimes committed abroad is only possible provided that the state in which the criminal offence has been committed does not take action. This is an innovative resolution clause addressing a potential conflict of jurisdiction, based on simple *lis pendens*, in accordance to which it is the beginning of proceedings and not the adoption of a final judicial decision that precludes the exercise of jurisdiction.[52]

Regardless of the specific features of the legal system, the condition of residence (real head office) in the state denotes a greater space–time dynamism compared to the nationality criterion in the strict sense, which attaches decisive importance to the place of incorporation and consequently to the national law under which the legal person was incorporated. In fact, the real head office model is based on the management activity of the entity, and evokes at least in part the requirement of the presence of the individual offender in the territory of the state as a condition for prosecution in some forms of extraterritorial jurisdiction.[53] In any event, the operation and offices of an entity, unlike a physical perpetrator, may well be ubiquitous, so the idea of 'corporate presence' related to the head office has a more decision-making/organisational connotation.

It should also be noted that the criterion at issue is not to be understood as a constitutive element of the corporate liability offence in cases of transnational or cross-border crimes, but as a rule limiting a state's extraterritorial jurisdiction for those offences. In other words, it has to be understood as a rule of transnational punitive/criminal law laid down for crimes in which a precise element of (spatial) 'extraneousness' occurs, ie the commission of the crime entirely abroad.

[51] The Criminal Code criteria for Italian extraterritorial jurisdiction are – like in many other legal systems – the following: (a) the principles of active personality (Art 9) and passive personality (Art 10, para 1), concerning, respectively, the citizenship status of the offender or the victim; (b) the principle of defence, relating to the political nature of the crime committed (Art 8), the impact of the crime on essential interests of the Italian State (Art 7, para 1, sub-paras 1–4) or in any case the commission of a crime against the Italian State (Art 10, para 1); and (c) the principle of universality with reference to 'crimes to which the application of Italian criminal law is established by special Italian law or international convention provisions' (Art 7, para 1, sub-para 5) or crimes committed abroad by a foreigner against a foreign state or a foreigner (Art 10, para 2, which sets many conditions). On these rules, see F Palazzo, *Corso di diritto penale: Parte generale*, 8th edn (Turin, Giappichelli, 2021) 161ff; D Pulitanò, *Diritto penale*, 9th edn (Turin, Gappichelli, 2021) 530ff; A Pagliaro, *Principi di diritto penale: Parte generale* (Milan, Giuffrè, 2020) 159ff.

[52] See S Manacorda, 'Limiti spaziali della responsabilità degli enti e criteri di imputazione' (2012) 55 *Rivista italiana di diritto e procedura penale* 91, 110; V Mongillo, *La corruzione tra sfera interna e dimensione internazionale* (Naples, Esi, 2012) 344ff.

[53] A di Martino, 'Reati commessi all'estero e responsabilità degli enti' in D Piva (ed), *La responsabilità degli enti* ex *d.lgs. n 231/2001: tra diritto e processo* (Turin, Giappichelli, 2021) defines the head office criterion as 'functional territoriality'.

C. The Stock Market Model

According to a third mechanism of extraterritorial jurisdiction over corporate offenders, the personal link between a company and state jurisdiction may be the issuance of corporate securities on the national stock market, even regardless of the state of incorporation or where the corporation's head office or principal business is located.

This corresponds to the US FCPA regime and to securities regulations generally. First, the FCPA prohibits issuers of US securities from falsifying their books and records (the accounting provisions of the Act).[54] Second, the anti-bribery FCPA provisions also apply to any 'issuer' who has securities registered under § 12 of the Securities Exchange Act of 1934 or files periodic reports under § 15(d) of the Securities Exchange Act of 1934.[55] The point is that the corporation need not be a US company to be an issuer.

It is not easy to discern the principle underlying the extension of US jurisdiction to foreign issuers in international bribery cases. The most plausible rationale is the legislative will to protect national economic interests, given the actual or potential effects of FCPA bribery offences on domestic securities markets. Such a regulatory model therefore seems to reflect a rather broad conception of the protective principle as a possible basis for extraterritorial jurisdiction.

However, a further clarification is necessary. Under the FCPA, in order to prosecute an issuer – as well as their officers, directors, employees, agents or stockholders – it is also essential that use be made of US mails or any means or instrumentality of interstate commerce in the furtherance of a corrupt payment to a foreign official,[56] unless the issuer is organised under the laws of the USA.[57] The Act defines 'interstate commerce' as 'trade, commerce, transportation, or communication among the several States, or between any foreign country and any State or between any State and any place or ship outside thereof'.[58] The term also includes 'the intrastate use of: (A) a telephone or other interstate means of communication, or (B) any other interstate instrumentality'.[59]

However, in published guidance and enforcement actions, the US government has adopted a broad view of the interstate commerce requirement, which

[54] 15 USC § 78m.
[55] 15 USC § 78dd-1.
[56] 15 USC § 78dd-1(a).
[57] 15 USC § 78dd-1(g): 'Alternative Jurisdiction'.
[58] 15 USC §§ 78dd-2(h)(5); § 78dd-3(f)(5).
[59] Communications or transactions through any instrumentality of interstate commerce is also an element of many other US offences, such as those provided for by the Money Laundering Control Act, 18 USC § 1956(b)(2), which apply to foreign persons and firms if part of the conduct occurs in the US or if the firm has a US bank account. See D Brown, 'Extraterritorial Ambit through Offence Definitions, Technology and Economic Power', ch 3 in this volume, s IIC.

can thus also make a largely foreign scheme subject to US jurisdiction. As the US Department of Justice (DOJ) Guide to the FCPA clarifies:

> [P]lacing a telephone call or sending an e-mail, text message, or fax from, to, or through the United States involves interstate commerce – as does sending a wire transfer from or to a US banking system, or traveling across state borders or internationally to or from the United States.[60]

In conclusion, the interstate commerce element does represent a territorial nexus,[61] but an extremely tenuous one.

D. The 'Carrying On a Business' Model

The last model of extraterritorial application of criminal rules against commercial entities is based on an autonomous and even more extensive factor of 'personal connection' between a legal person and national jurisdiction, which arguably ends up encompassing an unprecedented conception of the *protective principle*,[62] not referring – as usual – to the vital interests of a state, such as defence and national security, but to a state's economic interests at large.

This jurisdictional mechanism was most famously coined by the UK Bribery Act 2010, which has considerably expanded the jurisdictional ambit of UK law in the anti-bribery sector.[63] Besides the already mentioned criterion of 'close

[60] Criminal Division, US Department of Justice and Enforcement Division, US Securities and Exchange Commission, 'A Resource Guide to the US Foreign Corrupt Practices Act: Second Edition' (US Government, July 2020) 10. An enforcement action in which the government has followed this view is *United States v JGC Corp*, in which a Japanese defendant was charged with FCPA violations concerning a scheme to bribe Nigerian officials on the assumption that 'certain alleged bribe payments … flowed through US bank accounts and that co-conspirators faxed or e-mailed information into the United States in furtherance of the bribery scheme'. Similarly to the large majority of FCPA enforcement actions, the case was resolved through a Deferred Prosecution Agreement (DPA): *United States v JGC Corp* No 11-cr-260 (SD Tex 6 April 2011); M Koehler, *The Foreign Corrupt Practices Act in a New Era* (Cheltenham, Edward Elgar, 2014) 110. In *SEC v Straub* 921 F Supp 2d 244 (SDNY 2013), the use of interstate commerce by the officers of an issuer to further their bribery scheme was deemed proved by the court since the defendants had sent emails that were 'routed through and/or stored' on US servers.

[61] Perhaps this is the reason why Ryngaert, *Jurisdiction* (n 26) 87, classifies this connecting factor under territorial jurisdiction.

[62] Among the multilateral instruments against corruption, on the protective principle, see UNCAC (n 24) Art 42(2)(d), in accordance with which a state party may establish its jurisdiction when 'the offence is committed against the State Party'; COE, 'Explanatory Report to the Criminal Law Convention on Corruption (European Treaty Series No 173)' (27 January 1999) para 83, which declares that territorial and national principles 'may … not always suffice to exercise jurisdiction, for example over cases occurring outside the territory of a Party, not involving its nationals, but still affecting its interests'.

[63] Sullivan (n 44) 96–98. On the Bribery Act 2010 and its jurisdictional issues, see N Cropp, 'The Bribery Act 2010: Part 4: A Comparison with the Foreign Corrupt Practices Act: Nuance v Nous' [2011] *Crim LR* 122; C Rose, 'The UK Bribery Act 2010 and Accompanying Guidance: Belated Implementation of the OECD Anti-Bribery Convention' (2012) 61 *International and Comparative Law Quarterly* 484; C Wells, 'Who's Afraid of the Bribery Act 2010?' (2012) 5 *Journal of Business Law* 420; DJ Dickson, 'Cross Border Investigation and Prosecution of Bribery and Corruption Offences' (2014) 15 *ERA Forum* 51; P Arnell and N Evans, 'The Effect of the Bribery Act 2010' [2015] *Juridical Review* 167.

connection' (section 2A above), which represents an extended version of the classic nationality criterion, the main novelty – as far as the subject matter addressed herein is concerned – is with regard to the jurisdictional regime of the new offence of a failure of a commercial organisation to prevent persons associated with it[64] from committing bribery.[65] The jurisdictional scope of the novel corporate offence is even wider than the ordinary regime just described. It can be committed 'irrespective of whether the acts or omissions which form part of the offence take place in the United Kingdom or elsewhere',[66] and the organisation may even fail to have a close connection with the UK, so as to make the place of incorporation or formation irrelevant. In fact, the notion of 'relevant commercial organisation' also includes 'any body corporate (wherever incorporated) which *carries on* a business, or part of a business, in any part of the United Kingdom' (emphasis added).[67]

The Bribery Act 2010 does not specify the meaning of carrying on a business in the UK. Is an even minimal operation of the corporation in the UK enough in order to establish UK jurisdiction? According to the non-binding government guidance, only organisations that have a *demonstrable business presence* in the UK would be caught by this special jurisdictional nexus. In any event, the government:

> [W]ould not expect, for example, the mere fact that a company's securities have been admitted to the UK Listing Authority's Official List and therefore admitted to trading on the London Stock Exchange, in itself, to qualify that company as carrying on a business or part of a business in the UK ... Likewise, having a UK subsidiary will not, in itself, mean that a parent company is carrying on a business in the UK, since a subsidiary may act independently of its parent or other group companies.[68]

This jurisdictional scheme was then adopted in other UK legislation, eg the tax evasion facilitation offences provided for by the Criminal Finances Act 2017, further to which it is immaterial whether the relevant criminal conduct takes place in the UK or not:

> By way of example, a court sitting in London would have jurisdiction to try a Brazilian company, that carries on part of its business in the UK, for failing to prevent one of its employees from facilitating the commission of a Brazilian tax evasion facilitation offence in relation to tax owed in Brazil.[69]

State jurisdiction thus acquires, through this legislative technique, an almost sprawling force of attraction. Its transplantation into other legal systems reveals the global dynamism of state anti-corruption measures towards a progressive

[64] An 'associated person' can expressly be a subsidiary company too. See Bribery Act 2010, s 8(3).
[65] ibid s 7.
[66] ibid s 12(5).
[67] ibid s 7(5)(b). The same provisions are extended to partnerships: s 7(5)(d).
[68] Ministry of Justice, 'The Bribery Act 2010: Guidance' (2011) 9 (ss 15–16), 15 (s 36).
[69] K Laird, 'The Criminal Finances Act 2017 – An Introduction' [2017] *Crim LR* 915.

legislative alignment,[70] also fuelled by the concern of nation states to ensure that domestic businesses are not at a competitive disadvantage vis-à-vis their foreign competitors in the global economic arena.[71]

A very significant example is France's recent shift towards extraterritoriality in the field of anti-corruption law, which followed in the footsteps of the UK Bribery Act 2010 and the US FCPA. In response to many successful FCPA enforcement actions against French global companies[72] in complex international corruption cases and the long-standing OECD (and other international bodies, such as the Council of Europe's anti-corruption monitoring body, GRECO) criticism of French authorities for their poor results in the fight against transnational bribery, on 9 December 2016, the French Parliament adopted the Loi Sapin II,[73] named after the Minister for the Economy and Finance, Michel Sapin, who presented the Bill. The law followed an extensive parliamentary report on the extraterritoriality of US legislation, which labelled it as a 'form of legal *imperium*'.[74] Article 21 of the new law considerably extends France's extraterritorial jurisdiction as regards corruption offences. In addition to abandoning the traditional procedural constraints for the prosecution of extraterritorial offences (active personality jurisdiction), including dual criminality and the need for a formal complaint filed by the victim or their successor or an official accusation made by the foreign authority,[75] the reform extends 'in any circumstances' (*en toutes circonstances*) French criminal law to foreign bribery and influence peddling directed towards foreign public officials entirely 'committed abroad by a French national, or by a person having habitual residency in France or carrying out his/her economic activity, either in whole or in part, on French territory'.[76]

If the reference to French nationals reflects the traditional principle of active personality based on nationality, and the second element (habitual residence in France) seems to express a more common extensive variation of the principle of personality, the real novelty lies in the third element, namely the phrase *exerçant tout ou partie de son activité économique sur le territoire français*.[77]

[70] See R Brewster, 'Enforcing the FCPA: International Resonance and Domestic Strategy' (2017) 103 *Virginia Law Review* 1611.

[71] Another significant aspect of the transnationalisation process of anti-corruption law is represented by the global spread of DPAs, originally trialled in the US context. See the cross-country examination reported in OECD, 'Resolving Foreign Bribery Cases with Non-Trial Resolutions: Settlements and Non-Trial Agreements by Parties to the Anti-Bribery Convention' (2020).

[72] Including Technip, Alcatel-Lucent, Alstom and Société Générale.

[73] *Loi n° 2016-1691 du 9 décembre 2016 relative à la transparence, à la lutte contre la corruption et à la modernisation de la vie économique.*

[74] K Berger and P Lellouche, *Rapport d'information sur l'extraterritorialité de la législation américaine* (5 October 2016) Assemblée Nationale Rep No 4082.

[75] In this regard, the new Arts 435-6-2 and 435-11-2 establish an exception to the French Criminal Code, Art 113-6, para 2 (dual criminality in cases of misdemeanours (*délits*) committed by French nationals outside the territory of the French Republic) and to Art 113-8 (victim's complaint or official accusation made by the authority of the country where the offence was committed). *cf* L d'Ambrosio, 'L'implication des acteurs privés dans la lutte contre la corruption: un bilan en demi-teinte de la loi Sapin 2' (2019) 1 *Revue de science criminelle et de droit pénal comparé* 15.

[76] New Arts 435-6-2 and 435-11-2 of the French Criminal Code.

[77] '[C]arrying out an economic activity, either in whole or in part, on French territory.'

In this respect, the Loi Sapin II appears to be inspired by section 7 of the UK Bribery Act 2010. In any event, in extending the exercise of extraterritorial jurisdiction over corruption, the French legislation seems to have gone beyond even UK law – and even more so than the US FCPA – in two directions: (i) section 7 of the Bribery Act 2010 refers to a specific offence of a failure to prevent bribery that can only be committed by 'relevant commercial organisations', whereas the new French jurisdictional rule applies to a wide range of active and passive corruption and trading-in-influence offences having a manifest transnational or international character, which both natural and legal persons can commit; and (ii) the 'business in the UK' criterion is slightly narrower than the notion of 'economic activities' (*activités économiques*), since the latter is not limited to business activities (*activités commerciales*).[78] Moreover, unlike in the UK Guide mentioned before, the French Ministry of Justice's Circular of 2 June 2020 on the criminal policy on combating international corruption, known as the Belloubet Circular, has advocated the notion that a person carrying out all or part of their economic activity in France covers at least foreign legal persons who have a subsidiary, branches, commercial offices or other establishments in France, even if they do not have their own separate legal personality.[79]

Where does the justification for this extensive and vague jurisdictional nexus lie? As already noted above, it seems to rely on an extensive form of the protective principle – where the conduct may carry significant consequences for the authority and international relations of the states involved – and in particular:

> [O]n the (bold) presumption that the behaviour of a person which carries out an 'economic activity' on the territory of a State has the potential to affect that state's essential economic interests – even when the said conduct is adopted by a foreign person abroad.[80]

The possibilities afforded by this broad form of extraterritorial jurisdiction make it likely that many other states worldwide will follow suit in the future. Nevertheless, on the one hand, it can foment an unreasonable and undesirable multiplication

[78] Bourguignon (n 45) 160.

[79] Ministère de la Justice, *Circulaire du 2 juin 2020 de politique pénale en matière de lutte contre la corruption internationale* (2020) (*Belloubet Circular*) 9.

[80] Bourguignon (n 45) 155ff, 160ff, who adds that 'from a legal perspective, [the Loi Sapin II] challenges existing categories of criminal jurisdiction in international law and reopens the debate on the core principles applying to extraterritorial jurisdiction'. Obviously, although the criterion in question can be considered a reflection of the protective principle, great uncertainty remains about the precise jurisdictional basis. Just consider that it applies to any business/economic activities which could be relatively small scale and not impinge on 'essential' economic interests of a state in any credible sense. Alternatively, it could also be argued that such a flexible jurisdictional regime reflects an amalgamation of protective/territorial principles, considering the actual or potential territorial impact of the extraterritorial conduct. However, the fact remains that in the new French legislation corruption crimes could be committed entirely abroad by a foreigner and – in the case of the UK offence of a failure to prevent bribery – the management centre of the corporation could also be located outside the UK. Therefore, the principle of territoriality can only be evoked in these cases in a very different sense from the traditional one.

of states with potential jurisdiction,[81] while, on the other, it raises doubts about compliance with the principles of predictability and legal certainty.

III. The Question of Double Criminality

With regard to both individual and corporate liability, in Italy and elsewhere, it is still a subject of debate as to whether or not it is appropriate to require *double criminality* as a condition of extraterritorial jurisdiction, in the sense that the alleged criminal conduct must also constitute a criminal offence in the foreign state (*lex loci*). Traditionally, this requirement is not uncommon where extraterritorial jurisdiction is based on nationality/active personality. Nonetheless, the issue is still strongly debated.

International conventions tend not to include binding provisions in this regard. For example, the 1997 OECD Convention on combating international bribery merely states that each party may establish nationality jurisdiction in respect of the bribery of a foreign public official, in accordance with the general principles and conditions in its legal system.[82] As clarified by the OECD Commentaries on the Convention, these principles can include a dual criminality requirement. If so, this condition 'should be deemed to be met if the act is unlawful where it occurred, even if under a different criminal statute'.[83]

According to one current of opinion, the double criminality principle must be recognised.[84] In line with this assumption, in certain legal systems, dual criminality is expressly stated in respect of nationals, eg by section 5 of the Dutch Criminal Code, further to which:

> The criminal law of the Netherlands shall apply to any Dutch national who commits outside the territory of the Netherlands … an offence that is regarded as a serious offence under the criminal law of the Netherlands and is punishable under the law of the country where it was committed.[85]

[81] ibid 170: for these reasons, Bourguignon suggests amending the relevant French provision, 'by replacing "economic" with "business" interests and by adding the word "substantial" to characterise the "(business) activity in the country"'.

[82] Art 4(2).

[83] OECD, 'Commentaries on the Convention on Combating Bribery of Foreign Public Officials in International Business Transactions' (adopted by the Negotiating Conference on 21 November 1997) s 26.

[84] In Italian literature, for an affirmative answer in relation to individual criminal liability, see G Marinucci, E Dolcini and GL Gatta, *Manuale di diritto penale: Parte generale*, 11th edn (Milan, Giuffrè, 2022), 'albeit in the absence of an express legislative indication'; F Mantovani, *Manuale di diritto penale*, 5th edn (Padua, Cedam, 2009) 861. For case law, see Corte di Cassazione (Italian Supreme Court), First Criminal Section, Judgment No 38401 of 15 November 2002. For an opposing view, see Pagliaro (n 51) 168. The Italian Criminal Code, Art 13(2) expressly requires this condition for extradition; see also Arts 7(1) and 8(1) of the Italian Law No 69/2005 on the European arrest warrant.

[85] The outer limits of that provision were explored in the *Asean Explorer* case in 2002 (Netherlands Supreme Court, Case No HR 00555/01, LJN: AD9557, 21 May 2002). On this matter, see Boister (n 27) 250; C van den Wyngaert, 'Double Criminality as a Requirement for Jurisdiction' in J Dugard and C van den Wyngaert (eds), *International Criminal Law and Procedure* (Aldershot, Dartmouth, 1996) 131; European Committee on Crime Problems (n 26).

Similarly, the French Criminal Code – which by virtue of the principle of active personality also applies to a wide range of criminal offences committed by French citizens or legal persons outside the national territory – explicitly requires double criminality with respect to offences classified as *délits*.[86] As I have already pointed out, the only exceptions are those introduced by the Loi Sapin II in the anti-corruption field, since it is possible to prosecute foreign bribery even in countries where it is not an offence. An example in the opposite direction, ie expressly rejecting dual criminality, is section 35(2) of South Africa's Prevention and Combating of Corrupt Activities Act 12 of 2004.

There are strong arguments in favour of dual criminality when it comes to individual criminal responsibility, in particular the accessibility and foreseeability of the criminal law's provisions and sanctions, inherent in the principle of legality (*nulla poena sine lege*). Even the principle of culpability (*nulla poena sine culpa*),[87] with reference to the possibility for individual offenders to know the criminal law rules of their own state of origin, could lead to an exclusion of criminal responsibility in respect of offences committed abroad and not punished as a crime in the foreign state. In fact, citizens could invoke as a defence unavoidable ignorance of the (national) criminal law, especially when, beyond citizenship, no relationship has ever linked offenders with their own legal system of origin. Obviously, the opinions in favour of double criminality acquire greater weight in the face of *mala quia prohibita*[88] (especially regulatory offences) rather than *mala in se*.

We must ask ourselves whether these arguments based on fundamental principles of criminal law could be reconsidered when it comes to corporations. The case against double criminality in the sphere of corporate criminal liability is supported by socio-criminological evidence, since 'the mobility of multinational corporations enables them to take advantage of differences in the laws of various countries (eg by selling dangerous products where it is not prohibited)'.[89] Consequently, the application of extraterritorial jurisdiction in the state of origin, regardless of double criminality, could be – also from an international solidarity point of view – a means to avoid a situation of impunity where multinational corporations are involved in serious crimes and/or human

[86] Art 113-6 of the Criminal Code. *cf* H Ascensio, 'Extraterritoriality as an Instrument' (Contribution to the Work of the UN Secretary-General's Special Representative on Human Rights and Transnational Corporations and Other Businesses, 2010) para 14ff.

[87] Commencing from its Judgment Nos 364 and 1085 (1988), the Italian Constitutional Court has linked the principle of culpability to the principles of legality and non-retroactivity in criminal law, pointing out that all the principles in question aim to guarantee that those subject to the criminal law have the freedom to choose their own course of action through the calculability of the legal consequences of their conduct.

[88] On this concept, see SP Green, 'The Conceptual Utility of Malum Prohibitum' (2016) 55 *Dialogue* 33.

[89] See M Delmas-Marty, 'Globalisation and Transnational Corporations' (February 2008 Contribution) in Y Queinnec, 'The OECD Guidelines for Multinational Enterprises: An Evolving Legal Status' (Sherpa, June 2007) 40.

rights violations, which could otherwise allow bad economic players to escape justice.[90]

But apart from the 'impunity gaps' argument, a corporation's plea as to the impossibility of knowing specific criminal law rules is much less persuasive than in the case of individual offenders. In fact, one has to also consider that usually corporations, and especially large multinationals, have better opportunities to inform themselves of conflicting legal commitments through their legal advisors. Better still, they can (and so they must) inform themselves through their legal departments and outside counsel.

IV. 'Unbound' Territoriality

The above-mentioned new jurisdictional connection factors based on 'business activity' (UK) or 'economic activity' (France) have so far had an extremely small prosecutorial impact. In many states, in terms of practical effects on corporate criminal liability for crimes committed abroad, another trend appears more significant: an extensive territoriality concept as a basis for domestic jurisdiction, a sort of 'unbound territoriality'.[91] This jurisdictional path – the second that I mentioned before (in section I) – clearly is not altogether novel, particularly in civil law countries. However, it has intensified in times of economic globalisation as a means to counter transnational business crimes more effectively. Two aspects are worth underlining.

First, the classic conception of the territoriality principle in criminal law has little difficulty in allowing for the prosecution of foreign corporations who commit a crime in domestic territory. In fact, that happens in almost all legal systems worldwide. For example, foreign companies may be held responsible for offences committed in Italy[92] or France[93] pursuant to their respective domestic laws. Across the Atlantic, since 1998, the anti-bribery provisions of the US FCPA also apply to foreign non-issuer companies that, either directly or through an agent, engage in any act in furtherance of a corrupt payment 'while in the territory of the United States'. Likewise, under section 12(1) of the UK Bribery Act 2010, the bribery offences provided for by sections 1, 2 and 6 apply under the principle of territoriality to any person (individual or corporation) 'if any act or omission which is part of

[90] OK Fauchald and J Stigen, 'Corporate Responsibility before International Institutions' (2009) 40 *George Washington International Law Review* 1028. In connection with corporate liability under the above-mentioned Italian Legislative Decree No 231/2001, Art 4, see, as regards excluding the double criminality principle, LD Cerqua, 'L'applicabilità del d.lgs. 231/2001 alle società estere' [2009] *La responsabilità amministrativa delle società e degli enti* 122.

[91] Krisch (n 22) 482, 501ff.

[92] See, inter alia, Corte di Cassazione, Sixth Criminal Section, Judgment No 11626 of 7 April 2020.

[93] *cf* Bourguignon (n 45) 170.

the offence takes place in that part of the United Kingdom'.[94] Similarly, the recent Argentinian Law No 27401/2017 imposes criminal liability for certain crimes[95] on private legal persons, whose corporate capital is either national or foreign, whether or not under state ownership (Article 1).[96]

The second aspect is the tendency for 'territorialising the extraterritorial'. Since the birth of the modern state, the territoriality principle has been the primary basis for jurisdiction.[97] In the traditional sense, it refers to the commission of a crime in the territory of a state. However, the contours of the territoriality principle are not as self-evident as they might seem at first sight: 'Indeed, the question arises as to what territorial connections are decisive when a legal situation has a nexus with several States.'[98]

The conception of the territoriality principle based on the 'ubiquity theory' or 'constituent elements approach'[99] recognises the possibility for an offence to occur in more than one place.[100] In fact, a state can claim jurisdiction over an offence when at least one of its constituent elements, either the criminal conduct or the result, occurred within its territory. But nowadays, many states are inclined to maximise the reach of territorial jurisdiction even beyond the traditional theory of ubiquity. Assuming a really extended notion of territoriality, the effects can be similar to explicit and genuine forms of extraterritorial jurisdiction, but without having to resort to uncertain and more problematic (in terms of legitimacy) criteria such as those examined above (section II).[101]

[94] Bribery Act 2010, s 12(1). For an in-depth analysis of territorial jurisdiction in the context of the Bribery Act 2010, see A Moiseienko, 'Territorial Criminal Jurisdiction over Bribery in the UK: The Limits of the Bribery Act 2010' [2016] *Crim LR* 405.

[95] Domestic or international bribery and influence peddling; illegal payments made to public officials under the appearance of charges or fees owed to the relevant government agency upon undue request by the official (*concusión*); illegal enrichment by public officers and employees; and falsification of financial statements and reports.

[96] Art 1 of Argentinian Criminal Code – as replaced by Art 29 of Law No 27401/2017 – states that 'This Code will apply: 1) For crimes committed or whose effects must be produced in the territory of the Argentine Nation, or in places subject to its jurisdiction. 2) For crimes committed abroad by agents or employees of Argentine authorities in the performance of their duties. 3) For the crime provided for in article 258 *bis* [foreign bribery offence] committed abroad, by Argentine citizens or legal persons domiciled in the Argentine Republic, either that established in its statutes or that corresponding to the establishments or branches that it owns in Argentine territory.'

[97] In English-language literature, a useful starting point for a correct understanding of the issue is ED Dickinson, 'Jurisdiction with Respect to Crime' (1935) 29 (suppl 1) *American Journal of International Law* 435, 494.

[98] Ryngaert, *Jurisdiction* (n 26) 49.

[99] G Gilbert, 'Crimes Sans Frontières: Jurisdictional Problems in English Law' (1992) 63 *British Yearbook of International Law* 415, 430, has defined the modern theory of ubiquity as 'the widest application of the qualified territoriality principle'.

[100] C Ryngaert, 'Territorial Jurisdiction over Cross-Frontier Offences: Revisiting a Classic Problem of International Criminal Law' (2009) 9 *International Criminam Law Review* 187. On the ubiquity theory/constitutive elements approach to territoriality, see Ryngaert, *Jurisdiction* (n 26) 77–79.

[101] As noted by M Pieth, 'Article 4: Jurisdiction' in M Pieth, LA Low and N Bonucci (eds), *The OECD Convention on Bribery: A Commentary*, 2nd edn (Cambridge, Cambridge University Press, 2013) 322ff: 'to a certain extent these developments may seem interchangeable; sometimes the concepts are also

The starting point for such an extensive territoriality concept is that an offence can be deemed to have been committed in the state's territory even when it occurred there 'in part' (and not in whole). The point of arrival is that the relevant 'part' tends to become more and more evanescent in enforcement practices. The 'part' could be not solely an element of the offence (conduct or event), but also a single preparatory act, a fraction of the conduct, aiding and abetting, etc, in cases where most of the criminal conduct occurred outside the national territory. For instance, in the field of bribery, in order to trigger jurisdiction on a territorial basis in State A, it could be enough that there is a bank wire transfer from State A sent to bribe a foreign public official in State B, or a conference call from State A whereby a senior manager of a domestic company instructs a director of a foreign branch to bribe a public official in State B.

In principle, many international or regional anti-corruption instruments adopt this approach. Among others, Article 4(1) of the OECD Convention on Combating Bribery of Foreign Public Officials in International Business Transactions states as follows: 'Each Party shall take such measures as may be necessary to establish its jurisdiction over the bribery of a foreign public official when the offence is committed in whole *or in part* in its territory' (emphasis added). Commentary 25 to the Convention clarifies that 'the territorial basis for jurisdiction should be interpreted broadly, so that an extensive physical connection to the bribery act is not required'. A similar provision can be found in Article 7(1) of the Convention on the Fight against Corruption involving Officials of the European Communities or Officials of Member States of the European Union of 26 May 1997, or in Article 11(1) of the Directive 2017/1371 of 5 July 2017 on the fight against fraud to the Union's financial interests by means of criminal law.

With respect to national jurisdictions, in UK law, an example of an expansive version of territorial jurisdiction is section 2(1) of the Criminal Justice Act 1993.[102] The Italian legal system provides one of the most relevant and older examples of an extensive territoriality approach. Article 6 of the 1930 Italian Criminal Code provides as follows:

> Whoever commits an offence in the territory of the State shall be punished according to Italian law. An offence shall be deemed to be committed in the territory of the State when the act or omission which constitutes it occurred therein *in whole or in part*, or when an event which is a consequence of the act or omission took place therein (emphasis added).

muddled. These extensions of traditional concepts are not, however, necessarily equal in all respects, since "territoriality" is adopted absolutely, whereas "extra-territoriality" is frequently subject to conditions, such as "dual criminality".'

[102] On English law, see generally M Hirst, *Jurisdiction and the Ambit of Criminal Law* (Oxford, Oxford University Press, 2003); L Farmer, 'Territorial Jurisdiction and Criminalization' (2013) 63 *University of Toronto Law Journal* 225; M Hirst, 'Country Report: "England and Wales"' in M Böse, F Meyer and A Schneider (eds), *Conflicts of Jurisdiction in Criminal Matters in the European Union, vol 1: National Reports and Comparative Analysis* (Baden-Baden, Nomos, 2013) 27ff.

Therefore, current Italian law does not even require that a 'substantial' part of the conduct must occur in Italy. As a consequence, Italian courts have regularly held that territorial jurisdiction is also to be applied when just a segment of the conduct, namely any fragment of the *iter criminis* or preparatory act, occurred in Italy,[103] or when an offence is wholly committed abroad with the complicity (aiding and abetting) of another person in Italy.[104]

Italian courts hold that this broad form of territorial jurisdiction also applies to legal persons under Legislative Decree No 231/2001, because what is relevant is the place of commission of the crime by an individual agent operating on a corporation's behalf and not the place of the organisational fault and hence where the corporation is managed from. Moreover, in the case that marked the first final conviction of a corporation after a trial for international bribery in Italy (*Saipem*), it was held that it was 'sufficient that the mere conception (or ideation) of the crime occurred in Italy' in order to trigger Italian territorial jurisdiction.[105] It is not entirely clear whether under this approach Italian jurisdiction may rest on a mere *mens rea* element; if so, a mere intention to commit an offence could serve as a jurisdictional basis. Probably, in the view of the Italian Supreme Court (Corte di Cassazione), a conspiracy in Italy to commit a crime abroad is sufficient to establish territorial jurisdiction without even the need for actual preparation (namely, carrying out any material act) on national territory in furtherance of the criminal design.[106] This is an extremely weak territorial link that permits the aggressive prosecution of the *actus reus* wholly committed abroad, far from the traditional conception of the territoriality principle as a connecting factor capable of ensuring a genuine contact with the relevant state.

To give another EU Member State example, in French criminal law, under the territorial principle, an offence is deemed to be committed in France where one of its basic elements, whether action or event, is located in France (the theory of ubiquity[107]).[108] As reaffirmed by the French Court of Cassation

[103] See Corte di Cassazione, Sixth Criminal Section, Judgment No 47922 of 9 December 2009. However, pursuant to Corte di Cassazione, Sixth Criminal Section, Judgment No 56953 of 20 December 2017, a merely general intent to commit crimes abroad is not sufficient insofar as that intent lacks concreteness and specificity.

[104] See, eg the expansive notion of territoriality adopted for crimes on the High Seas in Corte di Cassazione, First Criminal Section, Judgment No 14510 of 27 March 2014, *Haji Hassan*; Corte di Cassazione, First Criminal Section, Judgment No 36052 of 20 August 2014, *Arabi*; Corte di Cassazione, First Criminal Section, Judgment No 15556 of 7 December 2021, *Essaush Shaouk*.

[105] Corte di Cassazione, Sixth Criminal Section, Judgment No 11442 of 17 March 2016.

[106] As a general principle (Criminal Code, Art 115), the Italian legal system does not envisage the criminalisation of a mere agreement (*accordo*) with one or more persons to commit a crime (the 'conspiracy' of English tradition), save in the exceptional cases expressly provided for. Moreover, pursuant to the Criminal Code, Art 56, a punishable attempt requires acts that are more than merely preparatory to the commission of the offence, in particular, suitable acts unequivocally directed at committing a felony (*delitto*).

[107] Art 113-2 of the Criminal Code.

[108] In addition, French territorial jurisdiction applies subsidiarily when a primary offence (*crime* or *délit*) committed in another country is aided and abetted (*complicité*) in France, subject to two conditions (French Criminal Code, Art 113-5): double criminality and final judgment of the foreign court

(Cour de cassation) in a case of international bribery, an offence is deemed to have been committed in France when only one of its 'constitutive facts' is carried out on the territory.[109] This rule is consistently interpreted broadly. As a consequence, French criminal courts have asserted their jurisdiction where, inter alia, the funds intended for bribery were remitted in France[110] or the signature of contracts that allowed payments to corrupt agents was decided at board meetings held in Paris.[111] Moreover, in a foreign bribery case, the Court of Cassation espoused a particularly wide understanding of domestic jurisdiction, deeming sufficient for its application that the acts, even if committed entirely abroad, are indivisible from those carried out in part in France, ie that they are 'linked in such a way that the existence of the one would not be understood without the existence of the other'.[112] Beyond corruption cases, French jurisdiction has been exercised in relation to an insider trading offence involving the securities of a foreign company listed on a foreign market when the stock market order was placed in France, or in relation to the pollution of a watercourse with repercussions in France caused by a firm located in Belgium.[113]

Likewise, the FCPA expression 'acting while in the territory'[114] has been interpreted widely by US courts to include tenuous connections with domestic territory. For instance, according to US case law, a foreign national who attends a meeting in the USA that furthers a foreign bribery scheme may be prosecuted, even apart from the use of US mail or a means or instrumentality of interstate commerce.[115] Trends in US FCPA enforcement also reveal that an expanded notion of the territoriality principle (or genuine forms of extraterritorial jurisdiction) can even become a tool for engaging in protectionist economic policies rather than promoting the fair competition of all multinational enterprises in international markets. If it is irrefutable that in the last few decades the most active enforcement jurisdiction has been the USA,[116] it is probably not a mere coincidence that so far many of the most expensive settlements for violations of the US FCPA have involved

convicting the perpetrator of the primary offence (following the Loi Sapin II, the second condition need no longer be fulfilled for foreign bribery or influence peddling committed abroad).

[109] Cour de cassation, Criminal Division, Judgment No 16-82.117 of 14 March 2018, *Total and Vitol*.

[110] Cour de cassation, Criminal Division, Judgment No 12-84.220 of 31 October 2012.

[111] Cour de cassation, Criminal Division, Judgment No 19-83.969 of 1 April 2020, *TSKJ (Nigeria)*.

[112] *Arms Materials (Cameroon and Mali)* Case No 101 (2012), cited in OECD, 'Implementing the OECD Anti-Bribery Convention: Phase 4 Report: France' (9 December 2021) 79.

[113] Ascensio (n 86) 4.

[114] 15 USC § 78dd-3.

[115] See Superseding Indictment, *United States v Nervis G Villalobos-Cardenas, et al* No 17-cr-514 (SD Tex 24 April 2019), establishing jurisdiction under 15 USC § 78dd-3 based on meetings in the USA; Criminal Information, *United States v Steven Hunter* No 18-cr-415 (SD Tex 17 September 2018); *United States v Ramiro Andres Luque Flores* No 17-cr-537 (EDNY 6 October 2017). All these cases are cited in Criminal Division, US Department of Justice (n 60) fn 59. In general, the broad scope of the territorial principle as conceived by US enforcement authorities emerges clearly where transnational financial crime and global economic relations are concerned. It is illustrated well by the recent corruption scandal surrounding FIFA, about which see Krisch (n 22) 488–89.

[116] G Dell and A McDevitt, 'Exporting Corruption 2022: Assessing Enforcement of the OECD Anti-Bribery Convention' (Transparency International, 2022) 10, 87.

foreign multinationals. Consequently, some scholars maintain that enforcement of FCPA has become a new 'international business tax' on non-US companies,[117] supported by the fact that the payments are ordinarily the result of non-trial resolutions rather than court judgments. That gives US companies an unfair competitive advantage in the global marketplace and induces other states to enact laws with a similar extensive reach.

V. 'The Other Side of the Moon': The Risk of *bis in idem* as a Consequence of Expanded State Jurisdiction

Against this background, on the one hand, the extension of grounds for jurisdiction appears to be a justifiable option, above all in order to avoid situations of impunity for serious corporate offences, especially in developing countries whose authorities may be unlawfully subjugated or influenced by big multinationals. On the other hand, in the absence of an international framework of rules to prevent positive jurisdictional conflicts, without legally recognised hierarchies between several valid jurisdictional claims, extraterritorial or wide-ranging territorial forms of state jurisdiction to prosecute corporations or individuals may easily lead to parallel criminal proceedings and multiple convictions in different states for the same crime and against the same defendant – all to the detriment of the principles of *ne bis in idem* ('double jeopardy'), legal certainty[118] and proportionate punishment. Not surprisingly, then, 'from the start the multinational corporation was defined in terms of jurisdiction and potential jurisdictional conflict'.[119]

Many criminal cases in different countries demonstrate the above, for example those involving the Italian company Saipem, the German Siemens AG, the Norwegian Statoil and the French Alstom SA.

The *Siemens* case had far-reaching repercussions. In 2008, Siemens AG, along with three subsidiaries, settled bribery investigations by paying $450 million in fines to the US DOJ and $350 million in disgorgement of 'ill-gotten gains' to the US Securities and Exchange Commission. In the same year, Siemens paid an additional $569 million to settle bribery charges by German regulators, and then resolved additional actions brought by the World Bank ($100 million), the Nigerian Economic and Financial Crimes Commission (EFCC) ($46.5 million), Greek authorities (€270 million) and the Swiss Federal Prosecutor's Office ($75.6 million).

[117] See A Leibold, 'Extraterritorial Application of the FCPA under International Law' (2015) 51 *Willamette Law Review* 225, 259–60.

[118] J Lelieur, '"Transnationalising" *Ne Bis In Idem*: How the Rule of *Ne Bis In Idem* Reveals the Principle of Personal Legal Certainty' (2013) 9 *Utrecht Law Review* 198.

[119] SJ Kobrin, 'Soverignty@Bay: Globalization, Multinational Enterprise and the International Political System' in AM Rugman (ed), *The Oxford Handbook of International Business*, 2nd edn (Oxford, Oxford University Press, 2009) 183.

The *TSKJ (Nigeria)* case is also very instructive. Since 2009, the DOJ and the SEC have settled FCPA charges against three partners in a TSKJ joint venture – KBR, Inc, Technip SA and Snamprogetti Netherlands BV (a subsidiary of Italian company Eni SpA, incorporated in 2008 by Saipem SpA) – that allegedly bribed Nigerian government officials over a 10-year period to win more than $6 billion in contracts for drilling concessions in Nigeria. The Italian Snamprogetti entered into a two-year deferred prosecution agreement with the DOJ and agreed to pay a $240 million fine.[120] The SEC also filed a complaint against Snamprogetti Netherlands BV and ENI, and both agreed to be jointly and severally liable to pay $125 million in disgorgement and pre-judgment interest.[121] After the FCPA prosecutions, the Nigerian EFCC reached several settlements, including with Snamprogetti ($32.5 million). Then the Italian authorities proceeded against Saipem in relation to the same facts on the basis of the territorial principle, since it had been alleged that some persons involved in the corruption scheme conspired during a meeting in Italy to commit bribery abroad. In 2016, a final judgment was issued against Saipem ordering it to pay a €600,000 fine and confiscating €24.53 million of illegal profits.[122] Thus, the crucial dilemma is: do legal persons (or individuals) have any legal safeguard(s) to avoid multiple prosecutions and duplicative penalties in different jurisdictions?

Outside the legal literature, the transnational dimension of *ne bis in idem* is uncertain and raises many technical difficulties when applied in practice.[123] Let us examine the issue from a threefold perspective: European, international and national.

At the *European level*, within the EU's area of freedom, security and justice, individuals and legal persons are protected from the risk of multiple proceedings or convictions for the same cases in different EU countries under Article 50 of the EU Charter of Fundamental Rights and Article 54 of the 1990 Convention implementing the Schengen Agreement of 14 June 1985, both expressly including the principle of *ne bis in idem*. In particular, Article 50 of the Nice Charter of Fundamental Rights states: 'No one shall be liable to be tried or punished again in criminal proceedings for an offence for which he or she has already been finally acquitted or convicted within the Union in accordance with the law.'[124]

[120] *US v Snamprogetti Netherlands BV* No 10-cr-460 (SD Tex 2010).

[121] *SEC v ENI, SpA e Snamprogetti Netherlands BV* No 10-cv-2414 (SD Tex 2010).

[122] Corte di Cassazione, Judgment No 11442 (n 105).

[123] Lelieur (n 118) 199.

[124] On the concept of *idem* in European Courts' case law, see M Ó Floinn, 'The Concept of *Idem* in the European Courts: Extricating the Inextricable Link in European Double Jeopardy Law' (2017) 24 *Columbia Journal of European Law* 75, who notes that 'the *ne bis in idem* principle as defined in European law and human rights instruments, has proven to be a veritable legal quagmire'. The thorny question of whether duplication of criminal and administrative proceedings and penalties in the same country breach the *ne bis in idem* principle is outside the scope of this chapter, since it concerns national *ne bis in idem*. On this latter issue, see M Vetzo, 'The Past, Present and Future of the *Ne Bis In Idem* Dialogue between the Court of Justice of the European Union and the European Court of Human Rights: The Cases of *Menci*, *Garlsson* and *Di Puma*' (2018) 2 *Review of European Administrative*

However, it should be specified that the transactional protection guaranteed by these supranational provisions applies only to situations governed by EU law, so the Court of Justice of the European Union (CJEU) 'has no power to examine the compatibility with the Charter of national legislation lying outside the scope' of supranational law.[125] Moreover, nothing in the EU framework bars the beginning of parallel criminal proceedings in several Member States at the same time, each of which can continue until a *final* decision (acquittal, conviction or other resolution) about the same matter is reached in one of the EU Member States. In fact, the CJEU (and the European Court of Human Rights (ECtHR) from an intra-state perspective[126]) has clarified that only such a decision in a Member State prevents the initiation of new criminal proceedings in another jurisdiction or requires their termination if they have already begun.

In this regard, Council Framework Decision 2009/948/JHA of 30 November 2009 on prevention and settlement of conflicts of exercise of jurisdiction in criminal proceedings only requires direct consultations between the competent authorities of the Member States. Nevertheless, the outcome of the national consultations is not binding: Recital 11 clarifies that 'No Member State should be obliged to waive or to exercise jurisdiction unless it wishes to do so'. As a consequence, the matter is still shrouded by legal uncertainty and unpredictability.

Outside the EU, no transnational double jeopardy protection exists under customary international law.[127] As a consequence, there can be multiple prosecutions and convictions *in idem factum* in many jurisdictions against the same individual or corporation for the same misconduct.

Among the multinational instruments against corruption, the OECD Anti-Bribery Convention (Article 4.3) does not bar multiple prosecutions or conviction for the same conduct in different nations that are subject to the Convention. It only attempts to prevent such a situation by providing that, in cases of concurrent jurisdiction, the parties shall consult each other, at the request of one of them. Similarly, the UNCAC only requires state parties to consult with other interested state parties in appropriate circumstances in order to avoid, as much as possible, the risk of improper overlapping of exercised jurisdictions (Article 42.5).

At the *national level*, recognition of a transnational *ne bis in idem* principle differs significantly from country to country and tends to evolve in many states, principally through case law.

Law 55; G Lasagni and S Mirandola, 'The European *Ne Bis In Idem* at the Crossroads of Administrative and Criminal Law' (2019) 2 *eucrim* 126. Regarding recent CJEU case law concerning the increasing convergence with ECtHR case law from *A and B v Norway*, see V Davio and I Gambardella, 'Greater Coherence for the *Ne Bis in Idem* Principle, at Last: The Bpost Judgment (C–117/20)' (*EU Law Analysis*, 5 June 2022) eulawanalysis.blogspot.com/2022/06/greater-coherence-for-ne-bis-in-idem.html.

[125] Case C-617/10 *Åklagaren v Hans Åkerberg Fransson* ECLI:EU:C:2013:105, [16]ff.

[126] eg *Mihalache v Romania* App No 54012/10 (8 July 2019).

[127] *cf* AJ Colangelo, 'Double Jeopardy and Multiple Sovereigns: A Jurisdictional Theory' (2009) 86 *Washington University Law Review* 769.

In some jurisdictions, such as France, cross-border *ne bis in idem* is recognised provided that the acts judged by a foreign court were not committed, in whole or part, within the domestic territory.[128] On this issue, the view of the French courts has varied greatly over time. In a decision of 14 March 2018, the Court of Cassation held that 'if the prosecution is based on French territorial jurisdiction, then the *non bis in idem* principle does not prevent prosecution in France in cases that have already resulted in convictions or other resolution abroad'.[129] In light of the analysis in the previous section, this limit is not much of a safeguard, given the expansive interpretation of territoriality.

In a different vein, some legal systems recognise the transnational dimension of *ne bis in idem* even if the crime took place within domestic territory (eg section 68 of the Dutch Criminal Code;[130] section 5(4) of the Canadian Corruption of Foreign Public Officials Act, as amended in 2013), while, pursuant to the Article 3(3) of the Swiss Criminal Code, the same principle is applicable provided that the prosecution abroad took place at the request of the Swiss authorities.

In direct contrast, in Italy, a transnational *ne bis in idem* principle is expressly excluded by Article 11 of the Criminal Code, which establishes the principle of renewal of proceedings subject to the request of the Minister of Justice only in the case of extraterritoriality. The severity of this regime is mitigated by Article 138 of the Criminal Code, which requires that a sentence served abroad be counted, in line with consolidated international practice. In 2016, the Supreme Court expressly stated that international double jeopardy does not constitute a principle or custom of international law, so it can only be rooted in a treaty or multilateral agreement obligation.[131]

This assumption is also undisputed in the USA. According to the US courts, the double jeopardy clause of the Fifth Amendment of the US Constitution 'only bars successive prosecutions by the same sovereign'.[132] In fact, 'the Constitution of the United States has not adopted the doctrine of international double jeopardy'.[133]

[128] Art 113-9 of the French Criminal Code and Art 692 of the French Criminal Procedure Code.

[129] OECD, 'Phase 4 Report' (n 112) 81. Also, the *Belloubet Circular* (n 79) has advocated this solution in multi-jurisdictional cases.

[130] *cf* JAE Vervaele, 'The Transnational *Ne Bis In Idem* Principle in the EU: Mutual Recognition and Equivalent Protection of Human Rights' (2005) 1 *Utrecht Law Review* 100, 104. On the transnational *ne bis in idem* in the EU, see also A Eser, 'Konkurrierende nationale und transnationale Strafverfolgung: Zur Sicherung von "ne bis in idem" und zur Vermeidung von positiven Kompetenzkonflikten' in U Sieber et al (eds), *Europäisches Strafrecht* (Baden-Baden, Nomos, 2011) 557ff; H Satzger, *International and European Criminal Law*, 2nd edn (Oxford, Hart Publishing, 2018) 149ff; M Böse, 'The Transnational Dimension of the *Ne Bis In Idem* Principle and the Notion of *Res Iudicata* in the European Union' in M Böse et al (eds), *Justice without Borders: Essays in Honour of Wolfgang Schomburg* (Leiden, Brill Nijhoff, 2018) 49ff.

[131] Corte di Cassazione, Judgment No 11442 (n 105).

[132] *United States v Villanueva* 408 F3d 193, 201 (5th Cir 2005).

[133] *United States v Martin* 574 F2d 1359, 1360 (5th Cir 1978), citing *Bartkus v Illinois* 359 US 121, 128, No 9 (1959); *United States v Jeong* 624 F3d 706 (5th Cir 2010), in a case concerning whether a South Korean national could be prosecuted under US criminal laws (bribery and wire fraud) for conduct which he had already been prosecuted for by South Korean authorities under South Korea's equivalent of the FCPA.

This approach is consistent with the *dual-sovereignty doctrine*, concerning double convictions by a state court and a federal court, the separate sovereigns being here the federal and state governments. Recently, this doctrine was reaffirmed by the Supreme Court in the *Gamble* case,[134] further to which the double jeopardy clause protects individuals from being put in jeopardy twice for the same offence, so, where there are two sovereigns, there are two laws and consequently two offences.

However, signs of policy change are emerging in the USA. On 9 May 2018, (then) Deputy Attorney-General Rod J Rosenstein directly addressed the problem of disproportionate enforcement and repeated punishments by multiple national and/or foreign authorities, enacting a new DOJ policy on 'Coordination of Corporate Resolution Penalties in Parallel and/or Joint Investigations and Proceedings Arising from the Same Misconduct',[135] which was then included in the US Justice Manual (known before 2018 as the US Attorneys' Manual). The aim was to encourage DOJ attorneys to coordinate, where possible, both within the DOJ (where multiple components are investigating the same corporation) and with other federal, state, local and foreign investigating authorities, 'to avoid the unnecessary imposition of duplicative fines, penalties, and/or forfeiture against the company' and to achieve 'an equitable result'.[136]

Moreover, the DOJ 'should also endeavor, as appropriate, to coordinate with and consider the amount of fines, penalties, and/or forfeiture paid to other … enforcement authorities that are seeking to resolve a case with a company for the same misconduct'.[137] The factors that the DOJ should consider in promoting coordination between DOJ components and with a different agency or a foreign government are 'the egregiousness of a company's misconduct; statutory mandates regarding penalties, fines, and/or forfeitures; the risk of unwarranted delay in achieving a final resolution; and the adequacy and timeliness of a company's disclosures and its cooperation with the Department'. In brief, the new policy intends to avoid the DOJ disproportionately enforcing laws.[138] To this end, the basic idea is that an offset or credit mechanism, in addition to multi-jurisdictional co-operation, can secure an adequate and proportionate level of deterrence.[139] Even before the issue

[134] US Supreme Court, *Gamble v US* No 17-646, 587 US (2019). On this case, see AJ Colangelo, '*Gamble*, Dual Sovereignty, and Due Process' [2019] *Cato Supreme Court Review* 189; J Hörnle, *Internet Jurisdiction: Law and Practice* (Oxford, Oxford University Press, 2021) 111.

[135] Deputy A-G, US Department of Justice, 'Letter to Heads of Department Components on Policy on Coordination of Corporate Resolution Penalties' (*Justice*, 9 May 2018) www.justice.gov/opa/speech/file/1061186/download.

[136] US Department of Justice, *US Justice Manual* (Washington, US DOJ, 2018) 1-12.100: 'Coordination of Corporate Resolution Penalties in Parallel and/or Joint Investigations and Proceedings Arising from the Same Misconduct'.

[137] ibid.

[138] ibid.

[139] See S Oded, 'Multi-Jurisdictional Anti-Corruption Enforcement: Time for a Global Approach' (2020) 28 *Journal of Law and Policy* 510, esp 531ff.

of the new policy, the DOJ, in several deferred prosecution agreements (DPAs),[140] agreed to take into account previous fines paid by the company involved to other foreign authorities in connection with parallel enforcement actions for the same wrongdoing.

This change of perspective is one of the causes underlying a recent impressive phenomenon, namely the emergence of *multi-jurisdictional settlement agreements*. One of the most significant examples of coordinated resolution and global settlement is the trilateral agreement between France, the UK and the US that involved the Dutch–French multinational Airbus, accused of participation in the setting up of a multi-year and massive bribery scheme for trade in civil and military aircraft by paying bribes in China and other countries and concealing those bribes. On 31 January 2020, the company reached a judicial agreement (*convention judiciaire d'intérêt public*) with the French Parquet National Financier (PNF) and agreed to pay a fine of €2.1 billion, in parallel with DPAs with US and UK authorities, for a total of €3.6 billion.[141] It is also noteworthy that in the *Airbus* case the investigations were conducted by a joint prosecution team set up between the French PNF and the English Serious Fraud Office and in parallel with the US DOJ and the Attorney General for the District of Columbia. These agencies also agreed on the French Anti-Corruption Agency's monitorship, since Airbus is subject to mandatory compliance under the Loi Sapin II.[142]

This evolution demonstrates two truths: only multilateralism and co-operation can ensure an effective fight against transnational corporate crimes like foreign corruption; with their ability to set and enforce rules with an extensive jurisdictional reach, the most powerful countries can apply pressure on other states to enact similar laws and avoid jurisdictional conflicts by coordinating and distributing prosecution and/or penalties.

VI. Conclusions

Addressing jurisdictional issues is crucial to effectively combating corporate crime in the context of a globalised world. But the 'jurisdictional problem' is exacerbated by the fragmentation of production into global corporate groups and

[140] eg US Department of Justice, 'Keppel Offshore & Marine Ltd and US Based Subsidiary Agree to Pay $422 Million in Global Penalties to Resolve Foreign Bribery Case' (*Justice*, 22 December 2017) www.justice.gov/opa/pr/keppel-offshore-marine-ltd-and-us-based-subsidiary-agree-pay-422-million-global-penalties (DPAs with Telia Company AB and Keppel Offshore and Marine Ltd). From 2016 up to 2020, the 'DOJ has coordinated resolutions with foreign authorities in more than 10 cases, and SEC has coordinated resolutions with foreign authorities in at least five': Criminal Division, US Department of Justice (n 60) 71 and fn 382.

[141] Airbus, 'Airbus Reaches Agreements with French, UK and US Authorities' (31 January 2020) www.airbus.com/newsroom/press-releases/en/2020/01/airbus-reaches-agreements-with-french-uk-and-us-authorities.html.

[142] B Hock, 'Policing Corporate Bribery: Negotiated Settlements and Bundling' (2021) 31 *Policing and Society* 950.

supply chains that increase the risk of business crime and human rights violations, and reduce the possibilities for effective enforcement by nation states.

Expanded forms of extraterritorial jurisdiction based on the active personality principle or protective principle, or a combination of both, along with the extension of the territoriality principle as a ground for state jurisdiction, are currently deemed essential tools in furtherance of an effective fight against cross-border economic crime. However, dissimilar rules at the national level create an unlevel playing field and could disadvantage companies that come from the country adopting the most severe jurisdictional regulations.

Moreover, the current aggressive state jurisdictional expansionism entails the risk of multiple enforcement actions and 'carbon copy' prosecutions by several authorities against multinational corporations for the same misconduct. Therefore, greater attention should also be paid to the rights of corporations under prosecution, including transnational *ne bis in idem*.

There is probably a need for a new global multilateral agreement specifically devoted to the issues of conflicts of jurisdiction, in order to secure a satisfactory level of predictability and legal certainty for individuals and corporations potentially subjected to multiple state prosecutions, and to establish a clear hierarchy between different jurisdictional claims. At the very least, human rights instruments and relevant transnational crime conventions, as in the EU area, should expressly recognise a transnational *ne bis in idem* principle.

Meanwhile, co-operation and coordination between national authorities appear to be an essential practice, on one hand, to decrease enforcement costs and support an effective response against corporate crime, and, on the other hand, to avoid duplicative enforcement or at least a 'piling on' effect, namely a disproportionate level of deterrence due to multiple penalties imposed for the *idem factum* in different countries.

In conclusion, the fight against offences committed by multinational enterprises should seek to avoid situations both of impunity and of over-criminalisation, namely the danger that the legitimate *use* of effective and dissuasive sanctions might turn into *abuse*.

5

Extraterritorial Criminal Jurisdiction in International Law: Time for an Empirical Examination

MATTHEW GARROD*

I. Introduction

The rules of international law on extraterritorial prescriptive jurisdiction, on the basis of which a state has the authority to criminalise conduct beyond its borders, have long been unclear and unsettled.[1] Given that jurisdiction remains of critical importance to minimising what would otherwise be 'all rancour and chaos' among the nearly 200 sovereign states which make up the international community, one would expect scholars, courts and important bodies within the UN system to have devoted extensive attention to developing extraterritorial jurisdiction, including the way in which states actually use it in their legal practice.[2] But that is not the case.[3] Moreover, such attention as it does receive tends to involve a fairly ritualised account of what are believed to be the standard 'bases' of jurisdiction due to an overreliance on secondary data sources and the associated predominance of

* The author would like to give special thanks to Lindsay Farmer, Julia Hörnle and Micheál Ó Floinn for valuable feedback. The author would also like to thank Nicholas Burgess for his useful comments. The usual disclaimer applies.

[1] eg *The Case of the SS Lotus (France v Turkey)* PCIJ Rep Series A No 10 (1927).

[2] R Higgins, 'International Law and the Avoidance, Containment and Resolution of Disputes' (1991) 230 *Collected Courses of the Hague Academy of International Law* 89.

[3] The International Law Commission (ILC) decided to include 'Jurisdiction with regard to crimes committed outside national territory' on its provisional list of topics for codification at its first session in 1949, *Yearbook of the International Law Commission 1949*. However, it would be almost 60 years before the ILC's Secretariat suggested that the Commission take up the topic of 'Extraterritorial jurisdiction', *Yearbook of the International Law Commission 2006*, Vol II, Annex V, para 3. There is no indication that the ILC will take it up any time soon. The International Court of Justice has declined to decide issues relating to universal jurisdiction in international law: *Arrest Warrant of 11 April 2000 (Democratic Republic of the Congo v Belgium)* [2002] ICJ Rep 3.

the literature review method.[4] The origins of these bases of jurisdiction can be traced back to the one secondary data source relied upon more than any other, namely the Harvard Law School's 'Draft Convention on Jurisdiction with Respect to Crime' (Harvard Draft), which was concluded in 1935. The Harvard Draft identified four 'general principles' of extraterritorial jurisdiction based on 'nationality', 'protection', 'universality' and 'passive personality'.[5]

In the absence of a multilateral treaty laying down general rules governing extraterritorial jurisdiction in the decades since 1935, these 'general principles' have come to represent the dominant paradigm, or what will be referred to in this chapter as the 'orthodox account' of jurisdiction in international law.[6] It is virtually impossible to find a modern scholar that does not treat the Harvard Draft's principles as the prism through which state practice is assessed, rules of customary international law are identified, and multilateral treaties with criminal law provisions are interpreted.[7] Few books or articles have attempted to provide an empirical examination of these principles based on state practice and none are comprehensive in scope,[8] while there has long been a tendency to 'advocate' the expansion of certain principles beyond the scope recognised by states.[9] Thus, much of the literature about jurisdiction proceeds by assertion rather than by proof of state practice.[10]

This study provides the empirical examination of extraterritorial jurisdiction in state practice that has been noticeably lacking since the Harvard Draft.[11] The data consists of an original worldwide survey of three main sources: (i) domestic legislation of 105 states that are representative of major legal traditions of the world;[12] (ii) 62 criminal trials that proceeded to completion in domestic courts involving at least one allegation of crimes against international law (war crimes,

[4] Scholarly writings are a subsidiary means for the determination of rules of customary international law, but they are to be treated with caution: M Wood and O Sender, 'Extraterritorial Jurisdiction and the Limits of Customary International Law' in A Parrish and C Ryngaert (eds), *Research Handbook on Extraterritoriality in International Law* (Cheltenham, Edward Elgar, forthcoming) ch 2.

[5] ED Dickinson, 'Jurisdiction with Respect to Crime' (1935) 29 (suppl 1) *American Journal of International Law* 435, 445 (Harvard Draft).

[6] Gallant refers to this account as the 'standard model' of criminal jurisdiction: KS Gallant, *International Criminal Jurisdiction: Whose Law Must We Obey?* (Oxford, Oxford University Press, 2022) ch 3.

[7] The Harvard Draft principles have even been applied in cyberspace, eg N Tsagourias, 'The Legal Status of Cyberspace: Sovereignty Redux?' in N Tsagourias and R Buchan (eds), *Research Handbook on International Law and Cyberspace* (Cheltenham, Edward Elgar, 2021) ch 1.

[8] For the most comprehensive studies of extraterritorial jurisdiction in state practice in the decades since the Harvard Draft, see Gallant (n 6); American Law Institute, *Restatement of the Law Fourth: The Foreign Relations Law of the United States* (Philadelphia, American Law Institute, 2018).

[9] *US v Yousef* 327 F3d 56, 99 (2d Cir 2003); *Arrest Warrant* (n 3) Joint Separate Opinion by Judges Higgins, Kooijmans and Buergenthal [44]; Higgins (n 2) 96.

[10] Despite the lack of empirical data concerning state practice, these principles have received extensive philosophical and theoretical treatment and critique, eg A Chehtman, *The Philosophical Foundations of Extraterritorial Punishment* (Oxford, Oxford University Press, 2010).

[11] The discussion is limited to the substantive law of prescriptive jurisdiction regarding crimes committed by non-nationals beyond the state's territory.

[12] See Appendix 1 for the list of states included in this survey. The review of domestic legislation may not always cover every legislative provision addressing extraterritorial jurisdiction in each of the 105 countries covered, but what has been included is sufficient to reflect general domestic approaches and interpretations of the Harvard Draft principles.

genocide, crimes against humanity and torture) during the period since the *Eichmann* trial in 1961 to 2017;[13] and (iii) the creation of extraterritorial jurisdiction in 42 treaties adopted since 1945 and the corresponding preparatory works.[14] In-depth insight on extraterritorial jurisdiction is gained by drawing upon semi-structured interviews with officials at the Home Office, the Foreign and Commonwealth Office and the Crown Prosecution Service who have experience in the formulation and operation of the law in the UK,[15] as well as this author's work as a consultee for the Law Commission of England and Wales.[16] Additionally, practical insight on the drafting and amendment of domestic laws with extraterritorial application, including as part of the implementation of treaties, is also gained from this author's experience as an independent expert at the UN, a role that includes the provision of technical assistance to states.[17]

From the foregoing, this study aims to provide a clearer and more accurate understanding of extraterritorial jurisdiction in international law and how states use it in practice. The findings suggest that extraterritorial jurisdiction is expanding, with states increasingly taking what could be described as an 'extraterritorial turn' in the move towards grounds of jurisdiction other than territoriality. Even states that traditionally adhered to a 'territorial' approach to jurisdiction, such as the UK and the USA, have emerged among the most aggressive states globally in the unilateral assertion of criminal law beyond national borders.[18] Additionally, these findings potentially challenge the orthodox account in at least two fundamental respects.

The first finding, as observed by the UK Supreme Court in 2013 without deciding on the issue, 'raises a point of some importance' regarding the approach of international law to the criminalisation of actions by one state if they are

[13] District Court of Israel 40/61, *Attorney General v Eichmann*, 36 ILR 28. Completed trials are tabulated in Appendix 2. For the purpose of this study, a 'completed trial' is defined as a prosecution that has been adjudicated with a formal verdict after a trial. The individual defendant was the unit of analysis. This means that if a trial was held against two defendants, two trials were counted for analysis – one per defendant.

[14] The list of treaties is presented in Appendix 3. While the title to Appendix 3 refers to the creation of extraterritorial jurisdiction in treaty law, states have differing views of whether and the extent to which the treaties listed in numbers 3–7 and 13 in Appendix 3 permit or mandate extraterritorial jurisdiction (or otherwise do not prohibit extraterritorial jurisdiction as a matter of international law) over the relevant substantive offences. For an examination of treaties creating extraterritorial jurisdiction predating 1945, see further M Garrod, 'The Expansion of Treaty-Based Extraterritorial Criminal Jurisdiction' in Parrish and Ryngaert (n 4) ch 15.

[15] In this regard, seven interviews were conducted with officials. The interviews were conducted between May and August 2017 as part of a project in collaboration with the British Institute of International and Comparative Law entitled 'Extraterritorial Criminal Jurisdiction in a Changing Global World'. Each interview lasted an average of one hour. During the interview, the interviewer took detailed notes. The content of the interviews was subsequently analysed using the software NVivo, focusing on both specific aspects peculiar to each interview and shared key themes that emerged from the whole sample of interviews.

[16] This author was a consultee for the Law Commission's *Thirteenth Programme of Law Reform* (Law Com No 377, 2017), in respect of extraterritorial jurisdiction in England and Wales. This topic was included in the Law Commission's shortlist of potential law reform projects.

[17] The views expressed in this chapter do not necessarily reflect those of the UN.

[18] eg C Doyle, 'Extraterritorial Application of American Criminal Law' (Congressional Research Service, 2016). As a permanent member of the UN Security Council, the UK has played an active role in the adoption of resolutions relating to extraterritorial jurisdiction.

carried out in another state.[19] According to the orthodox account, state power to criminalise such conduct is generally conditioned and delimited on the existence of the Harvard Draft's permissive principles.[20] Any assertion of extraterritorial jurisdiction by a state, if it is to be lawful under international law, must be based on at least one of these principles.[21] In contrast to the orthodox account, it remains inconclusive (and may be overstated) the extent to which states generally condition their authority and justify making and applying criminal law based on the Harvard Draft's principles, including in the context of treaty-making.[22]

The second potential challenge is that it is difficult to determine from state practice the extent to which such practice is consistent with the Harvard Draft's principles, the contents and boundaries of which are malleable and subject to unilateral interpretations. States assert five main categories of prescriptive jurisdiction over non-nationals for offences committed beyond the state's territory, each of which provides a connection, either at the time of the commission of the alleged crime or at the time criminal proceedings are initiated, with the state asserting jurisdiction: (i) subsequent residency or subsequent nationality of the accused; (ii) crimes directed at or posing a potential threat to the state or to a broad and undefined category of state interests; (iii) crimes directed at or in relation to persons, irrespective of nationality, who represent the state or perform state functions; (iv) crimes directed at or in relation to the state's nationals and residents (including legal entities); and (v) the performance of obligations in treaties to which the state is a party, in particular treaties imposing obligations to extradite or prosecute alleged offenders present in their territory.[23] In all categories, there is considerable variation; and, as will be shown, it is not infrequent that legislation employs widely worded language, without defining the connection between the subject matter and the state asserting jurisdiction, and hence is open to multiple interpretations.[24] At first sight, these categories of jurisdiction may simply appear

[19] *R v Gul* [2013] UKSC 64 [58].

[20] In line with the orthodox account, Gallant (n 6) ch 3 contends that these principles are part of customary international law.

[21] For discussion of alternative approaches of international law to extraterritorial jurisdiction, see C Ryngaert, *Jurisdiction in International Law* 2nd edn (Oxford, Oxford University Press, 2015) ch 2.

[22] For example, domestic legislation across the world makes no reference to the Harvard Draft's principles considered in this study, with four exceptions: Criminal Code, Art 7(a) (Albania); Criminal Code, s 7 (Czech Republic); Penal Code, Arts 8–10 (El Salvador); Penal Code, Subsection Two (Iraq). The extent to which national law-making bodies may recognise or even place reliance upon one or more of these principles, and the weight placed upon them, requires further research. In the exercise of jurisdiction, domestic courts generally do not place reliance on these principles (discussed at s IV below). Some domestic courts are even of the opinion that states may assert extraterritorial jurisdiction as they see fit unless it is explicitly prohibited in international law, eg Supreme Court of Norway, Judgment, Case No 20-024314STR-HRET [2], [28], [46]; *R v Gul* [2012] 3 All ER 83 [48]–[49]. In the context of treaty-making, the preparatory works show the lack of common intention to codify the Harvard Draft's principles; see further Garrod, 'The Expansion' (n 14).

[23] eg Convention for the Suppression of Unlawful Seizure of Aircraft (The Hague, 16 December 1970) 860 UNTS 105, Arts 4(2), 7.

[24] In addition to these five general categories of jurisdiction, some states assert extraterritorial jurisdiction by 'representation' of the territorial state in which the crime was committed. Such jurisdiction,

to represent modern formations of the Harvard Draft's principles. However, this study shows some significant differences between them, and that these categories are not easily understood within the Harvard Draft orthodox framing.

The findings of this study, by providing a new perspective, reinforce concerns as to the necessity of rethinking extraterritorial jurisdiction.[25] If the role of international law is to regulate and place limits on the geographical reach of state power, and thus minimise jurisdictional tension,[26] then law-making and reform bodies, policymakers, law enforcement and courts need a normative framework by which to guide their practice while, at the same time, maintaining the 'wide measure of discretion' that states have sought to retain since the period of the League of Nations.[27] The existing normative framework, based as it is on the Harvard Draft, not only lacks 'precisely defined rules' and is subject to elements of conceptual confusion,[28] but is also, to borrow the words of one domestic court, discussed under 'a shroud of empirical uncertainty'.[29] In this regard, this study provides the relevant empirical insights needed to begin to clarify, and more accurately understand, what states actually do and the potential limits of legislative jurisdiction in international law, while contributing to the discourse on the subject and future legislative and policy-oriented initiatives that need to take into account state practice.

Following this introduction, the remainder of this chapter presents the empirical findings on extraterritorial jurisdiction. This discussion takes places against the backdrop of a critical analysis of the Harvard Draft's principles of 'protection' (section II), 'passive personality' (section III) and 'universality' (section IV), as these principles represent the existing normative framework used in scholarship and by UN bodies for assessing the legality of jurisdictional assertions over non-nationals abroad.[30] Section V offers some brief concluding observations.

II. The Principle of 'Protective' Jurisdiction

All but one state included in the survey of legislation assert extraterritorial jurisdiction, to varying degrees, over crimes committed by non-nationals

which overlaps, to a certain degree, with territorial and extradition or prosecution jurisdiction, usually requires the territorial presence of the presumed offender and is subject to double criminality and the impossibility of extradition for reasons unrelated to the nature of the crime; eg Criminal Code, s 65 (Austria); Penal Code, Art 16(6) (Colombia); Penal Code, s 8 (Finland); Criminal Code, s 7 (Germany); Criminal Code, Art 8c (Netherlands).

[25] eg D Bethlehem, 'The End of Geography: The Changing Nature of the International System and the Challenge to International Law' (2014) 25 *European Journal of International Law* 9, 22.

[26] Ryngaert (n 21) 29–30; Harvard Draft (n 5) 439, 444, 446.

[27] *Lotus* (n 1) 19.

[28] *R (on the application of KBR, Inc) v Director of the Serious Fraud Office* [2021] UKSC 2 [25].

[29] *US v Al-Imam* 73 F Supp 3d 247, 257 (DDC 2019).

[30] eg Criminal accountability of UN officials and experts on mission: www.un.org/en/ga/sixth/gov_comments/criminal_accountability.shtml.

directed at or posing a potential threat to the state or to an indeterminate range of state interests.[31] Legislative practice might be explained as an exercise of the Harvard Draft's 'protective' principle.[32] This section will show, however, that state practice differs, in important respects, from the protective principle as conceptualised and portrayed in the orthodox account.

In contrast to the orthodox account, states do not confine jurisdiction to the protection of a small number of 'fundamental' or 'vital' interests of the state.[33] In this regard, it seems inaccurate to suggest – as do Simma and Müller – that interests must be 'so vital for a state's existence' as to justify reliance on the protective principle.[34] Moreover, proof that actual harm to state interests occurred is not required, while state interests are not confined exclusively within the state's borders, thus undermining the claim in scholarship that protective jurisdiction is (or should be) limited to conduct that is directed at or intended to cause an 'effect' in the state's territory.[35]

Generally, states have shown themselves to be sensitive to the identification of the 'interests' that require the protection of the criminal law, and employ wide and ambiguous wording in this regard.[36] Representative examples include the Turkish Penal Code, which applies to offences deemed to be 'to the detriment of Turkey, a Turkish citizen or a Turkish legal personality'.[37] The Criminal Law of the People's Republic of China is applicable to 'crimes against the PRC state or against its citizens'.[38] The Russian Criminal Code applies 'if the crimes run counter to the interests of the Russian Federation or a citizen of the Russian Federation or a stateless person permanently residing in the Russian Federation'.[39] In view of wider state practice, it seems inaccurate to suggest, as one author does, that the Russian Criminal Code represents an 'extreme expansion' of the protective

[31] Penal Code, ss 4, 5 (Botswana).

[32] Harvard Draft (n 5) 445, 543–61.

[33] Gallant (n 6) chs 6 and 7.II; C Staker, 'Jurisdiction' in M Evans (ed), *International Law* (Oxford, Oxford University Press, 2018) 301–02; I Cameron, *The Protective Principle of International Criminal Jurisdiction* (Aldershot, Dartmouth, 1994) 2–3, ch 8; Council of Europe, European Committee on Crime Problems, 'Extraterritorial Criminal Jurisdiction', reprinted in (1992) 3 *Criminal Law Forum* 441, 451.

[34] B Simma and A Müller, 'Exercise and Limits of Jurisdiction' in J Crawford and M Koskenniemi (eds), *The Cambridge Companion to International Law* (Cambridge, Cambridge University Press, 2012) 144. The same claim is made by K Ambos, *Treatise on International Criminal Law* (Oxford, Oxford University Press, 2016) 221; Council of Europe (n 33) 467.

[35] eg American Law Institute, *Restatement of the Law Third: The Foreign Relations Law of the United States* (Philadelphia, American Law Institute, 1986) § 402, comment (f); M Akehurst, 'Jurisdiction in International Law' (1972–73) 46 *British Yearbook of International Law* 145, 159.

[36] See also 'Report of the Task Force on Extraterritorial Jurisdiction' (International Bar Association, 2008) 149–50, finding that over half of the 27 states included in its survey assert jurisdiction in respect of any crime deemed to have been committed against the state's 'general, fundamental or economic interests'.

[37] Criminal Code, Art 12.

[38] Criminal Law, Art 8.

[39] Criminal Code, Art 12.

principle because the state's 'interests' (including the interests of the state's nationals) are beyond the Harvard Draft's traditional and narrow conception.[40]

The domestic legislation of some states is so widely worded that, on its face, it looks like an assertion of universal jurisdiction. However, appearances can be deceptive. For instance, the UK asserts extraterritorial jurisdiction, among the broadest in the world, over a range of offences, including those relating to terrorism and anything done 'for the benefit' of a proscribed terrorist organisation.[41] The relevant legislation does not identify the interests that require the protection of the criminal law or even require proof that an offence has any connection at all to the UK; or that the alleged offender, after the commission of the offence, is present in the territory of the UK. While some scholars interpret the UK's assertion of jurisdiction over these and other offences as 'universal jurisdiction' and claim that English criminal law does not utilise protective jurisdiction,[42] parliamentary debates during legislative drafting and empirical data in the form of semi-structured interviews with senior officials suggest that the UK has taken 'wide' extraterritorial jurisdiction for the protection of the UK's undefined interests, including those of British nationals and legal entities abroad.[43]

Of the states that are willing to define at least some of the 'interests' that require the protection of the criminal law, several such interests that may be discerned include the state's sovereignty; 'internal' and 'external' security; independence; constitution; governmental functions and the functions of public officials; economic interests and currency; official documentation; flag, emblems, coats of arms and national anthem; international reputation and status; property (owned, leased or used); diplomatic personnel and consular staff, including their premises, residences and transportation; members of the monarchy and their family members, the president, head of state, government representatives and public officials; armed forces, military facilities, equipment, property and defence capability; registered vessels and aircraft; and the environment. Some of these interests, such as security, sovereignty, independence, property located abroad, and diplomatic personnel and premises, have the support of wider state practice, as evidenced through their inclusion in grounds of extraterritorial jurisdiction created in various treaties.[44] That said, the state interests expressly included in the jurisdictional

[40] Gallant (n 6) ch 6.III.D.

[41] eg Terrorism Act 2000, s 1; Terrorism Act 2006, s 17; Criminal Justice Act 1988, s 134; Geneva Conventions Act 1957, s 1. See also *R (on the application of KBR, Inc) v Director of the Serious Fraud Office* (n 28), which concerned whether the widely worded language in section 2(3) of the Criminal Justice Act 1987 had extraterritorial effect.

[42] eg American Law Institute, *Restatement Fourth* (n 8) § 413, 213–14; M Hirst, 'Country Report "England and Wales"' in M Böse, F Meyer and A Schneider (eds), *Conflicts of Jurisdiction in Criminal Matters in the European Union, vol I: National Reports and Comparative Analysis* (Baden-Baden, Nomos, 2013) 46; M Hirst, *Jurisdiction and the Ambit of the Criminal Law* (Oxford, Oxford University Press, 2003) ch 5.

[43] Interviews 2 (Home Office), 5 (Foreign and Commonwealth Office), 6 (Crown Prosecution Service); HC Deb 3 November 2005, vol 451, cols 1049–50.

[44] See Appendix 3.

provisions of treaties are not intended to be exhaustive, which is necessary to obtain agreement during the treaty-making process.[45] Some of the commonly accepted interests in domestic legislation are also very malleable and subject to unilateral interpretations.[46] In this regard, a recent example is the formal warning issued by the Hong Kong Police Force's National Security Department that the chief executive of a UK-based human rights non-governmental organisation may be prosecuted for the offence of 'collusion with foreign or external elements to endanger national security',[47] which is described by the British Foreign Secretary as 'unjustifiable action'.[48] On the other hand, some interests may not be widely shared by states, such as crimes committed against the 'patrimony' or 'public faith' of the state;[49] the violation of trade secrets;[50] 'damage' to the 'health of the population' or the 'environment';[51] crimes against 'public health' and 'morals';[52] and crimes against the 'social order'.[53]

Another way in which state practice differs from the protective principle as conceptualised in the orthodox account is that states assert jurisdiction over a wide range of crimes against domestic law, as opposed to a limited and relatively uniform category of generally recognised crimes.[54] Additionally, since World War I, and particularly after World War II, states have asserted jurisdiction over crimes against international law (war crimes, crimes against peace, genocide and crimes against humanity) committed in relation to the state's nationals or interests, although there are variations in the approach to legislative drafting.[55] It is beyond

[45] For example, during the negotiation of extraterritorial jurisdiction in the United Nations Convention against Transnational Organized Crime 2000, 2225 UNTS 209, China and France proposed the inclusion of jurisdiction over crimes committed against the state, which would reflect jurisdiction in their respective Criminal Codes. Other delegations took the view that the concept of an 'offence committed against a state' was ambiguous and in any case would be covered by the ground of jurisdiction included in what is now Art 15(6), which provides that 'Without prejudice to norms of general international law, this Convention does not exclude the exercise of any criminal jurisdiction established by a state Party in accordance with its domestic law'; UNODC, '*Travaux Préparatoires* of the Negotiations for the Elaboration of the United Nations Convention against Transnational Organised Crime and the Protocols thereto' (2006) 129, 133.

[46] eg *US v Reumayr* 530 F Supp 2d 1210, 1221 (DNM 2008) (the government has a national security interest in private property).

[47] Law of the People's Republic of China on Safeguarding National Security in the Hong Kong Special Administrative Region 2020, Art 38.

[48] Hong Kong Watch, 'Hong Kong Watch co-founder and CEO Benedict Rogers threatened under National Security Law' (14 March 2022).

[49] Criminal Code, Art 7 (Brazil).

[50] Criminal Code, s 5(7) (Germany); Criminal Code, § 64(1)(4) (Liechtenstein).

[51] Penal Code, s 9 (Estonia).

[52] Criminal Code, Art 17 (Ethiopia).

[53] Penal Code, Art 16 (Colombia). See also Law on Combating Crimes of Terrorism and its Financing, Art 3 (Saudi Arabia), which applies to crimes that aim to 'undermine the interests of the Kingdom, its economy or national or societal security'.

[54] eg American Law Institute, *Restatement Fourth* (n 8) § 412, 209.

[55] See further, eg M Garrod, 'The Development of Protective Principle Jurisdiction over War Crimes and the Hollow Concept of Universality' (2012) 12 *International Criminal Law Review* 763. For more recent examples of legislative practice with explicit reference to the state's nationals or interests, see Criminal Code, s 64(1)(4c) (Austria); Code of Criminal Procedure, Art 10(1)*bis* (Belgium); Code of Crimes against International Law 2002, Arts 1, 3; Code of Criminal Procedure, s 153f (Germany); International Crimes Act, s 8 (Kenya); Criminal Code, s 64(1)(4a) (Liechtenstein); International

the scope of this study to elaborate the substantive crimes over which extraterritorial jurisdiction has been asserted. In some states, such as Australia, Canada, Japan, Kenya, India, New Zealand, Nigeria, Qatar, Saudi Arabia, Spain, South Africa, the UK and the USA, jurisdiction is asserted over specified (albeit often vaguely defined) offences.[56] Conversely, other states, such as Austria, Belgium, China, Denmark, Finland, France, Germany, Greece, Israel, Russia, South Korea, Sweden, Switzerland, the Netherlands and Turkey, assert jurisdiction over a broader range of offences or even every type of crime (subject to a minimum level of punishment).[57]

State practice suggests that each state has the right to define which of its own interests need to be protected through criminal law and the range of crimes that may be committed against the state. International law places few limitations on states in this regard. As discussed above, China, Russia and Turkey (among many others) have legislation asserting wide jurisdiction, often in the same provision, over crimes in relation to state interests and their nationals and residents (natural and legal persons).[58] The criminalisation of conduct in relation to the state's nationals and residents as potential victims, however, raises the question of whether such jurisdiction should be conceptualised and justified in international law as a principle of 'passive personality'.

III. The Principle of 'Passive Personality' Jurisdiction

States are, with increasing frequency, asserting extraterritorial jurisdiction over crimes committed in relation to their nationals and residents (natural and legal persons), and persons representing the state or performing state functions. Such legislation is claimed in scholarship embracing the orthodox account as growing evidence of the Harvard Draft's passive personality principle.[59] However, the interpretation of legislative practice as underpinned by this principle encounters two potential problems.

Crimes Act 2003, s 2 (Netherlands); Act on Punishment of Crimes under Jurisdiction of the International Criminal Court 2007, Art 3 (South Korea); 18 USC § 2441(b) (USA). Some states assert extraterritorial jurisdiction over serious crimes committed in relation to nationals, including crimes against international law, eg Penal Code, s 113-7 (France); International Criminal Court Act 2011, s 4 (Mauritius); Code of Criminal Procedure, Art 642(1) (Niger); Criminal Code, Art 5 (Netherlands); Code of Criminal Procedure, Art 669 (Senegal); International Criminal Court Act 2010, s 18 (Uganda). The domestic legislation of most states, however, asserts wide extraterritorial jurisdiction over crimes against international law, capable of covering crimes committed in relation to the state's nationals or interests without explicit reference to them, to comply with obligations in international treaties (discussed at s IV below).

[56] eg Unlawful Activities (Prevention) Amendment Act 2012 (India); Penal Code, Arts 4–5 (Indonesia); Criminal Code, ss 7–8 (Thailand); Penal Code, Arts 2–4 (Japan); Penal Code, s 3 (Singapore).

[57] Criminal Code, s 8(1) (Denmark); Penal Code, s 3 (Finland); Criminal Code, s 7 (Germany); Criminal Code, Arts 7–8 (Greece); Criminal Code, Art 4 (Switzerland).

[58] Criminal Code, s 64(1)(4c) (Austria); Criminal Code, Art 6 (South Korea).

[59] eg Ryngaert (n 21) 111; Council of Europe (n 33) 450.

The prior and more fundamental problem is that the origins and evolution of the passive personality principle in international law appear to be based on scholarly assertion and an element of conceptual confusion. The source of that confusion stems from the Harvard Draft itself. Since the nineteenth century, the national legislation of many states has asserted wide extraterritorial jurisdiction, often in the same legislative provision, over non-nationals for crimes committed against the state and against its nationals.[60] However, the Harvard Draft's authors conceptualised jurisdiction based on the 'nationality or national character of the person injured' by an offence as a principle of 'passive personality', which was to be distinguished from crimes directed against the state, ultimately in order to prevent its inclusion in the Harvard Draft.[61] The conceptualisation of passive personality jurisdiction has had a lasting influence on subsequent scholarship.

Some 50 years after the conclusion of the Harvard Draft, the influential Third Restatement – described by one court as 'a kind of treatise or commentary'[62] – embraced the Harvard Draft's principles and claimed that passive personality is 'increasingly accepted as applied to terrorist and other organised attacks on a state's nationals by reason of their nationality, or to assassination of a state's diplomatic representatives or other officials'.[63] The Third Restatement offered no convincing authority that passive personality jurisdiction exists in respect of terrorist acts, still less as a rule of customary international law. The single example of legislation referred to by the Third Restatement as showing passive personality jurisdiction does not in fact do so.[64] When US courts began to apply this legislation to the conduct of non-nationals, the District Court for the Southern District of New York remarked that, so far as international law is concerned, criminalising conspiracy to kill US nationals abroad is justified based on the protective principle, because Congress expressly intended this provision to have a 'protective function' and the legislation is 'clearly designed to protect a vital United States interest'.[65] Therefore, it would appear that, to a considerable degree, scholarship may have confused the alleged evolution of the passive personality principle with the protective principle. The significance of this finding is twofold. First, some scholars have advanced a philosophical argument against the passive personality principle, while at the same time accepting the protective principle as a 'normative principle' that is generally accepted under international law.[66] Such arguments are difficult to sustain, given the conflation between these principles. Second, the passive personality principle is increasingly portrayed in scholarship as a rule of customary international law, but this claim may be debatable in view of state practice.

[60] See also Gallant (n 6) chs 6.III.D, 7.II; Cameron (n 33) 35–38; Harvard Draft (n 5) 445, 579.
[61] Harvard Draft (n 5) 445.
[62] *Yousef* (n 9) 99.
[63] American Law Institute, *Restatement Third* (n 35) § 403, comment (g).
[64] 18 USC s 2332(a)–(e) (1986).
[65] *US v Bin Laden* 92 F Supp 2d 189, 221–22 (SDNY 2000).
[66] eg Chehtman (n 10) 67–68, 71–75.

In this regard, the second potential problem with the passive personality principle is the extent of current state practice in support of it. The recent Fourth Restatement claims to restate the customary international law rules on prescriptive jurisdiction, and in so doing declares that custom now permits jurisdiction based on passive personality.[67] The criticism here is twofold. The first concerns the Fourth Restatement's failure to apply with sufficient rigour the well-accepted test for custom requiring general state practice and *opinio juris*, given that it relies upon the domestic legislation of only 19 states.[68] The second problem concerns the interpretation of this relatively small sample of practice, absent evidence of *opinio juris*. The reporters on jurisdiction remarked that legislation increasingly asserts the passive personality principle, particularly with respect to terrorist offences.[69] In this regard, the Fourth Restatement restates, without question, the same principles of jurisdiction as the Third Restatement and, perhaps with some inevitability, automatically categorises these examples of legislation as evidence of passive personality when many of them are not. As a representative example, the Fourth Restatement refers to the Norwegian Penal Code, which provides that the criminal law shall be applicable to acts 'directed against a person holding a Norwegian public office'.[70] Evidently, this provision is focused entirely on the status of the victim as a public official. Likewise, US courts have held that statutes criminalising, among other activities, murder, kidnapping and assault of any officer, employee or representative of the US, including any member of the uniformed services, is intended to 'protect vital United States interests',[71] and that such offences 'directly harm' the US government.[72] Yet, the Fourth Restatement refers to these statutes as evidence of passive personality.[73]

The findings of the present study suggest that at least 89 states assert jurisdiction that potentially could be conceptualised as passive personality. Additionally, most national laws contain a general jurisdictional provision giving effect to treaties to which the state is a party, which is sufficiently broad to capture certain treaty crimes committed abroad against the state's nationals (natural or legal persons), even though the relevant domestic legal provisions may not explicitly refer to the state's nationals as victims.[74] With this more general category of jurisdiction in mind, all of the states included in this study are capable of asserting extraterritorial jurisdiction covering at least some crimes directed at the state's nationals. Legislative practice is diverse, while there exist variations in requirements regarding

[67] American Law Institute, *Restatement Fourth* (n 8) §§ 407, 411.
[68] ibid § 411, 207–08.
[69] American Law Institute, *Restatement of the Law Fourth: The Foreign Relations Law of the United States: Jurisdiction: Tentative Draft No 2* (Philadelphia, American Law Institute, 2016) 62.
[70] General Civil Penal Code 1902, para 12. The Fourth Restatement overlooks that this version of the Norwegian Penal Code is outdated see Penal Code, Act 28 of 2005, s 5 (Norway).
[71] *Bin Laden* (n 65) 202.
[72] *US v Al-Imam* 73 F Supp 3d 247, 263–64 (DDC 2019); *US v Bout* 731 F3d 233 (2nd Cir 2013); *US v Al Kassar* 582 F Supp 2d 488, 497 (SDNY 2008).
[73] American Law Institute, *Restatement Fourth* (n 8) § 402, 158–59.
[74] See further s IV below.

the crimes that are subject to a minimum level of punishment, dual criminality and the unwillingness or inability of the territorial state to exercise jurisdiction over the alleged conduct. Often, the exercise of jurisdiction is conditional on authorisation by a senior prosecutor or a governmental or state official, and states appear to have wide prosecutorial discretion in this regard.[75] Such discretion serves as an important filter in the exercise of jurisdiction and enables diplomacy with and comity between concerned states.

Legislative practice may, for analytical purposes, be divided into the protection of two general subcategories of persons as potential victims of crime abroad: (i) the state's nationals and residents (natural and legal persons); and (ii) persons who have the status of a state representative or who perform state functions, irrespective of nationality (eg public officials, agents and employees, diplomatic representatives, consular staff and military forces). There is also wide extra-territorial jurisdiction, in the same general provision, for crimes committed against both the state's 'interests' and nationals.[76] This last category is similar to legislative practice in the nineteenth century, before the Harvard Draft drew a conceptual and legal distinction between the protective and passive personality principles. The legislation of some states falls into more than one subcategory.[77] Additionally, the subcategories overlap. For instance, state 'interests' in the third subcategory is sufficiently broad to encompass the protection of potential victims in the second.

As the passive personality and protective principles have been subject to conceptual confusion since the Harvard Draft, it remains unclear, absent *opinio juris*, the extent to which states would generally justify legislative practice, as a matter of international law, based on either one of these principles, a combination of them, or even a single broad theory of protective and passive personality jurisdiction.[78] As shown in section II, state interests are sufficiently broad and malleable to include nationals. At least some of the states included in this study regard the protection of nationals (including victims who acquire nationality after the alleged crime) as a legitimate state interest, while for others there may

[75] eg Code of Criminal Procedure, Arts 10, 12*bis* (Belgium); Criminal Code, Art 7 (Brazil); Criminal Code, s 7 (Canada); Criminal Code, s 12 (Denmark); Penal Code, s 6 (Finland); Penal Code, s 113–8 (France); Criminal Code, s 3 (Hungary); Criminal Code, s 5(7) and Criminal Procedure Act, s 65 (Norway); Organic Law on the Judiciary, Art 23(6) (Spain); Criminal Code, s 8 (Sweden); Terrorism Act 2000, s 63E and Terrorism Act 2006, s 19 (UK).

[76] The 27 states in this subcategory include: Criminal Code, Art 12(2) (Azerbaijan); Criminal Code, Art 9 (Bosnia and Herzegovina); Criminal Code, Art 8 (China); Penal Code, Art 16(5) (Colombia); Criminal Code, Art 14(3) (Croatia); Criminal Code, Art 6 (Iceland); Penal Code, Art 8 (Iran); Penal Law, s 13 (Israel); Criminal Code, Art 10 (Italy); Criminal Code, Art 19 (Lebanon); Penal Code, s 4 (Malaysia); Penal Code, Art 10 (Romania); Criminal Code, Art 12 (Russia); Criminal Code, s 8 (Thailand); Penal Code, Art 4 (Venezuela); Criminal Code, Art 6(2) (Vietnam).

[77] eg Art 5 of the Dutch Criminal Code, amended in 2014, provides for jurisdiction, in the same general provision, over any crime committed 'against Dutch nationals, Dutch government officials, Dutch vehicles, and Dutch vessels', on the condition that the crime is punishable by at least eight years of imprisonment and is also a crime in the territorial state.

[78] eg *Yousef* (n 9) 96–97, justifying jurisdiction based on the protective and passive personality principles; *Attorney General v Adolf Eichmann* Criminal Appeal 336/61, 36 ILR 28, justifying jurisdiction partly based on protective, passive personality and universal principles.

be an intention to limit the exercise of jurisdiction to cases where certain state interests, such as sovereignty, security or governmental functions, are involved.[79] In criminal proceedings in which domestic courts have been called upon to exercise extraterritorial jurisdiction, serious crimes committed against the state's nationals abroad (eg genocide, torture, acts of terrorism and sex trafficking) have been found to provide a legitimate connection with state interests in the justification of jurisdiction.[80] Domestic courts have also extended jurisdiction over crimes committed in relation to the state's nationals when, in the same factual circumstances, non-nationals were included among the victims.[81] The extension of extraterritorial jurisdiction to victims that include non-nationals may be based on state interests underlying the alleged conduct rather than the nationality of the victims.

Some insight into *opinio juris* may be gleaned from the creation of optional grounds of extraterritorial jurisdiction in the context of treaty-making. This study examined 26 treaties adopted to combat certain methods of violence committed in relation to the state's nationals, some of which have wide state participation, which has contributed to the expansion of legislative practice in recent years.[82] The preparatory works of these treaties show that the protection of nationals and residents is a legitimate interest of the state and that attacks against such persons may implicate other state interests. Contrary to the orthodox account, states may not necessarily regard jurisdiction over crimes directed at nationals as falling within the principle of passive personality, and there is certainly a lack of a common intention to codify or restate this principle in treaty law. For instance, during the Ad Hoc Committee's consideration of jurisdiction as part of the drafting of the 1979 International Convention against the Taking of Hostages, France proposed an amendment to the draft convention that would add a new subparagraph obliging each state party to establish extraterritorial jurisdiction over an offence defined as hostage-taking when 'The victims of which, namely the hostages, are nationals of that State'.[83] During the debate of this proposal, France

[79] The same point was made by Higgins (n 2) 104; FA Mann, 'The Doctrine of Jurisdiction in International Law' (1964) 111 *Collected Courses of the Hague Academy of International Law* 1, 94.

[80] eg *US v Baston* 818 F3d 651, 670 (11th Cir 2016); Supreme Court of Spain, Criminal Division, Case No 798/2007 (1 October 2007); Supreme Court of Spain, Criminal Division, Case No 1362/2004 (15 November 2004) (finding that Spanish courts have jurisdiction to hear crimes of genocide, terrorism and torture because there is a 'national interest in relation to the crimes subject to accusation insofar as it includes victims of Spanish nationality'); *Yousef* (n 9) 96–97; Supreme Court of Spain, Criminal Division, Case No 327/2003 (25 February 2003); *Bin Laden* (n 65) 221–22; *Eichmann* (District Court) (n 13) [33]–[34].

[81] eg *US v Alexanda Amon Kotey and El Shafee Elsheikh* Criminal No 1:20-Cr-239, Indictment (ED Va 2020); *Yousef* (n 9) 97–111; *Bin Laden* (n 65) 201–02; Spanish National Court, Criminal Division, Nos 19/97 (4 November 1998) and 1/98 (5 November 1998). The District Court of the Hague has exercised jurisdiction over four non-national defendants for the murder of 298 people on board flight MH17, 93 of whom were non-Dutch citizens on board of fight MH17: Netherlands Public Prosecution Service, 'MH17 Plane Crash', www.prosecutionservice.nl/topics/mh17-plane-crash/prosecution-and-trial.

[82] The 26 treaties, detailed in Appendix 3, are identified with a star symbol.

[83] Report of the Ad Hoc Committee on the Drafting of an International Convention against the Taking of Hostages, UN Doc A/33/39 and Corr 1 (4 May 1978) 41; Report of the Ad Hoc Committee on the Drafting of an International Convention against the Taking of Hostages, UN Doc A/32/39 (22 September 1977), Annex II.

justified the inclusion of this ground of jurisdiction on the basis that 'it would not be normal for a State not to establish its jurisdiction when its nationals were direct victims of the hostage-taking', while other delegations were of the opinion that states have a strong interest in protecting their nationals at least against certain types of serious crimes, such as the taking of hostages.[84] France referred to this ground of jurisdiction as 'passive personal jurisdiction', without providing any explanation of the meaning of this term or its legal basis in international law.[85] While the text of the French proposal was eventually included in the convention as an optional ground of jurisdiction which may be established if a state 'considers it appropriate',[86] none of the other delegations referred to jurisdiction as passive personality or expressed views as to the validity of passive personality, or accepted that the convention would codify this principle. This ground of jurisdiction in the International Convention against the Taking of Hostages was subsequently replicated in many other treaties.[87]

In the final analysis, state practice in the form of legislation and judicial pronouncements and in the context of treaty-making suggests that the protection of nationals is a legitimate state interest for the purpose of jurisdiction in international law. It would go too far, however, to automatically construe such jurisdiction as the Harvard Draft's passive personality principle. States have yet to express general opinion and agreement on the matter. In view of state practice, it seems inaccurate to suggest that jurisdiction in relation to nationals as potential victims is one that many states have consistently objected to and consistently refused to use at all,[88] or that such jurisdiction is the most contested in contemporary international law.[89]

[84] For the debate, see UN Doc A/33/39 (n 83) 38–45. Germany proposed the adoption of a convention because it regarded certain crimes such as hostage-taking as implicating state sovereignty and independence: Letter dated 28 September 1976 from the Vice-Chancellor and Minister for Foreign Affairs of the Federal Republic of Germany to the Secretary-General, UN Doc A/31/242 (1976). During the negotiation of the Convention for the Suppression of Unlawful Acts against the Safety of Civil Aviation (Montreal, 23 September 1971) 974 UNTS 177, the delegate of Israel proposed the explicit inclusion of a category of jurisdiction covering an offence 'committed by or against a national or permanent resident of such State'. The delegate of France 'had no difficulty' accepting this proposal, while the delegate of Switzerland observed that many states provided in their criminal codes for jurisdiction for the protection of a national of a state and that this was acceptable under international law. However, the delegate of Israel's proposal was rejected by a vote of 28 to 2, with 12 abstentions. International Civil Aviation Organization, *International Conference on Air Law, Montreal, September 1971, vol I: Minutes* (UN Doc 9081-LC/170-1) 56–57.

[85] UN Doc A/33/39 (n 83) 41.

[86] Report of the Ad Hoc Committee on the Drafting of an International Convention against the Taking of Hostages, UN Doc A/34/39 (20 March 1979) 12.

[87] eg International Convention for the Suppression of Nuclear Terrorism (New York, 13 April 2005) 2445 UNTS 89, Art 9(2)(a); UN Convention Against Corruption (New York, 31 October 2003) 2349 UNTS 41 Art 42(2)(a); International Convention for the Suppression of the Financing of Terrorism (New York, 9 December 1999) 2178 UNTS 197, Art 7(2)(a); International Convention for the Suppression of Terrorist Bombings (New York, 15 December 1997) 2149 UNTS 256, Art 6(2)(a).

[88] Gallant (n 6) ch 7.I.

[89] Chehtman (n 10) 67.

IV. The Principle of 'Universal' Jurisdiction

All the states included in the survey of national legislation assert jurisdiction over non-nationals for crimes committed outside their territory in order to implement treaty regimes to which the state is a party. These treaties establish a variety of mandatory and optional grounds of extraterritorial jurisdiction ranging in content and scope and requiring proof of different connections between a state party and the facts in question.[90] One particular ground of mandatory extraterritorial jurisdiction, which has been included in 33 treaties, is what this author has termed elsewhere as 'extradition or prosecution jurisdiction'.[91] This ground is specifically intended to give effect to the obligation upon state parties to extradite or prosecute individuals found in their territory for certain offences regardless of the nationality of the offender or the location of the crime.[92] In consequence, extradition or prosecution jurisdiction is the most far-reaching, requiring proof only of the presence of the alleged offender in the territory of a state party as the connection to conduct beyond its borders.

On the basis of domestic legislation which implements treaties, two rather extraordinary empirical claims have been made in the scholarship: first, that legislative practice is based on the principle of universal jurisdiction, which provides sufficient evidence for a rule of customary international law regarding a variety of crimes;[93] and second, that between the *Eichmann* trial in 1961 and 2017 there has been a significant growth in the number of completed universal jurisdiction trials concerning allegations of crimes against humanity, genocide, war crimes and torture.[94] While there is a lack of agreement among states on the definition and purpose of universal jurisdiction under international law, and the crimes for which this principle might be applicable,[95] it is usually defined in scholarship as jurisdiction 'based solely on the nature of the crime', absent any other jurisdictional connection recognised in international law between the state and either the actor, the victim or the crime.[96] As the suppression of such crimes is of concern to every state, international law permits each state to criminalise conduct by non-nationals beyond its territory in the absence of any connection with the facts over which jurisdiction is asserted. States asserting universal jurisdiction act, without fear or

[90] Appendix 3.

[91] For examples of treaties creating extradition or prosecution jurisdiction, see the treaties in bold listed in Appendix 3. See further Garrod, 'The Expansion' (n 14).

[92] eg Unlawful Seizure of Aircraft Convention (n 23) Art 4(2).

[93] eg Gallant (n 6) ch 8.IV; Ryngaert (n 21) 111; Council of Europe (n 33) 450.

[94] M Langer and M Eason, 'The Quiet Expansion of Universal Jurisdiction' (2019) 30 *European Journal of International Law* 779, identifying 61 'universal jurisdiction' trials; D Hovell, 'The Authority of Universal Jurisdiction' (2018) 29 *European Journal of International Law* 427, identifying 52 'universal jurisdiction' trials.

[95] The Secretary-General's annual reports and the notes submitted by states on the topic of universal jurisdiction are available under Agenda Item 84 for each session of the Sixth Committee.

[96] S Macedo (ed), *The Princeton Principles on Universal Jurisdiction* (Princeton, Princeton University Program in Law and Public Affairs, 2001); Gallant (n 6) ch 8.

favour, in the capacity of protecting the fundamental values of the international community. Both empirical claims regarding universal jurisdiction encounter potential problems as a matter of international law and in the interpretation of state practice.

The prior and more fundamental problem with these empirical claims is international law as a source of authority for universal jurisdiction. The alleged origins and evolution of universal jurisdiction in international law are underpinned by three interrelated myths. Influenced by the Harvard Draft's principle of 'universality' in respect of piracy on the high seas,[97] the first of these myths is that, for centuries, universal jurisdiction has existed as a clear rule of customary international law in respect of piracy based on the 'heinous' nature of the crime. The second myth is that universal jurisdiction under customary international law expanded at the end of World War II from its historical origins over piracy to include, by analogy and based on the gravity of the conduct concerned, crimes against international law (crimes against peace, war crimes, genocide and crimes against humanity), committed within the territory of sovereign states. Third, and underpinned by these twin myths, universal jurisdiction under customary international law has been codified or restated in numerous treaties establishing the obligation upon state parties to extradite or prosecute individuals found in their territory.[98] All three myths have been extensively examined in historical context (and debunked) elsewhere.[99] The focus here, however, is the obligation to extradite or prosecute alleged offenders under treaty law, as most scholars embracing the orthodox account regard such treaties as the source for 'modern' universal jurisdiction in international law, partly in recognition that the alleged historical underpinnings of universal jurisdiction place it on 'rickety and potentially ruinous foundations', and partly because proof of customary international law is inconclusive.[100]

There never has developed an established and generally accepted terminology for 'extradition or prosecution jurisdiction', including during the negotiation of treaty regimes, and it looks very similar to universal jurisdiction.[101] The relevant

[97] Harvard Draft (n 5) 445, 563.

[98] For an influential proponent of these myths, see K Randall, 'Universal Jurisdiction under International Law' (1987–88) 66 *Texas Law Review* 785.

[99] eg M Garrod, 'Unravelling the Confused Relationship between Treaty Obligations to Extradite or Prosecute and "Universal Jurisdiction" in the Light of the *Habré Case*' (2018) 59 *Harvard International Law Journal* 125; L Reydams, 'In-Depth Analysis: The Application of Universal Jurisdiction in the Fight against Impunity' (European Parliament, 2016).

[100] Hovell (n 94) 433, 437.

[101] The preparatory works of several treaties show that some delegations referred to extradition or prosecution jurisdiction as 'universal jurisdiction' or as 'quasi-universal jurisdiction'. However, the meaning of 'universal jurisdiction' in the treaty context and the extent to which it is permitted by international law was not subjected to debate. There is no evidence from the preparatory works to suggest that delegations intended to codify or recognise the principle of universal jurisdiction, let alone as an established rule of customary international law. One would expect to see such evidence, given the great care taken when formulating the treaty provisions on jurisdiction. See further International

provisions and corresponding preparatory works of treaties that codify the obligation to extradite or prosecute alleged offenders, and the implementation of such treaties in subsequent state practice, demonstrate that the nature and purpose of extradition or prosecution jurisdiction should be distinguished from universal jurisdiction.[102] Extradition or prosecution jurisdiction in most treaties explicitly obligates each state party to establish wide extraterritorial jurisdiction to cover cases where an alleged offender is 'present in its territory' and who has not been extradited to 'any of the States mentioned' in the treaty text.[103] In the preparatory works, the states 'mentioned [in] paragraph 1' were recognised as having 'primary compulsory jurisdiction' because they are 'directly affected' by the relevant criminal conduct and thus have the 'greatest interest' to prosecute. Conversely, extradition or prosecution jurisdiction, which was sometimes termed 'jurisdiction of the State in which the offender was found', was regarded as 'subsidiary jurisdiction' for states 'less directly concerned', the establishment of which is necessary if extradition is refused or legally impossible.[104] As the number of states with 'primary' jurisdiction is carefully limited in each treaty regime based on the strength of the connection with the treaty crime,[105] the scope of extradition or prosecution jurisdiction is limited to cases that would be covered by these more narrow grounds of primary jurisdiction. It follows that the obligation to establish and exercise extradition or prosecution jurisdiction is one that is owed exclusively to the directly affected states mentioned in the treaty text. Mills arguably goes too far in the claim that extradition or prosecution jurisdiction (termed 'universal jurisdiction') may in some circumstances be owed not only to other states, but also to private parties through human rights law, in particular, the right of access to justice, which necessitates rethinking jurisdiction in international law.[106] Hovell builds on this idea and goes

Civil Aviation Organization, *International Conference of Air Law, The Hague, December 1970, vol I: Minutes* (Doc 8979-LC/165-1) 10 (USA), 59, 75 (Switzerland), 76 (Zambia), 77 (Congo); International Civil Aviation Organization, *International Conference on Air Law, Montreal* (n 84) 14 (Denmark), 21 (France), 57 (Austria), 162 (Canada, USA), 193 (Spain).

[102] Garrod, 'The Expansion' (n 14); Garrod, 'Unravelling' (n 99) 152–80; C Kreß, 'Universal Jurisdiction over International Crimes and the Institut de Droit international' (2006) 4 *Journal of International Criminal Justice* 561, 567–68.

[103] The most common version of the extradite or prosecute obligation, known as the 'Hague formula', was first articulated in the Unlawful Seizure of Aircraft Convention (n 23), and subsequently served as the model for most other treaties.

[104] International Civil Aviation Organization, *International Conference of Air Law, The Hague* (n 101), 67–87; UN Doc A/33/39 (n 83), 39 (Netherlands), 42 (Germany), 42–43 (USA), 44 (Algeria), 48 (UK).

[105] For example, the preparatory works of the Convention against the Taking of Hostages show that one problem during negotiations regarding extraterritorial jurisdiction was a proposal to widen primary jurisdiction under Art 5, to allow member states of an international organisation subject to demands by hostage takers to assert jurisdiction. This proposal was not adopted because if the UN was subjected to demands by a hostage taker, virtually every state party to the treaty would have jurisdiction over the offence: UN Doc A/33/39 (ibid) 38–39 (Netherlands), 39 (UK), 42 (Germany), 43 (Sweden), 45 (Nigeria).

[106] A Mills, 'Rethinking Jurisdiction in International Law' (2014) 84 *British Yearbook of International Law* 187. See further ECtHR, *Hussein and Others v Belgium*, Request No 45187/12, Judgment 16 March 2021 (the introduction by the Belgian legislator of criteria requiring connecting factors with Belgium in the assertion of extraterritorial jurisdiction and the decision of Belgian courts to

further still in claiming that 'modern universal jurisdiction' is best understood as being based on an individual's right of access to justice. Hovell interprets treaties establishing extradition or prosecution jurisdiction as 'recognising' universal jurisdiction, by claiming that when courts exercise such jurisdiction the question as to whether the state of nationality or the state in whose territory the alleged offence occurred is a party to the relevant treaty does not appear to be a material question.[107] However, neither of the two cases Hovell refers to in support of this claim represents an example of a court exercising jurisdiction in a criminal trial, still less universal jurisdiction.

The second problem with the empirical claims regarding universal jurisdiction is the absence of a careful analysis of state practice and *opinio juris*. As a representative example, the Fourth Restatement's reporters on jurisdiction question whether treaties provide evidence of universal jurisdiction and instead claim that legislation which implements treaties provides 'direct evidence of state practice on universal jurisdiction'.[108] Based on the legislation of 17 states, and absent evidence of *opinio juris*, customary international law is declared to permit universal jurisdiction for genocide, war crimes, crimes against humanity, torture, acts of terrorism and piracy.[109] The same criticism concerning the treatment of the passive personality principle applies, here with equal force. Moreover, legislation is interpreted as providing for universal jurisdiction when in fact it may not. As a representative example, the Fourth Restatement claims that the UK has adopted universal jurisdiction in respect of several offences relating to torture and terrorism.[110] As discussed in section II, however, the UK's approach to legislative drafting, when incorporating treaties into the law of the UK, is to adopt wider wording than required by treaty law, as opposed to the assertion of universal jurisdiction, for the protection of the UK's undefined interests. The establishment of such wide jurisdiction in domestic law, 'even where there is no apparent link to the United Kingdom', 'does not necessarily mean that [the UK] considers that these offences attract universal jurisdiction as a matter of international law'.[111] The UK has exercised such jurisdiction in completed trials relating to international crimes consistent with extradition or prosecution jurisdiction in corresponding treaty law.[112]

decline to exercise extraterritorial jurisdiction to hear and determine criminal proceedings relating to alleged genocide, absent any connection to Belgium, thus limiting the right to access a court does not violate the human right to a fair trial under Art 6 ECHR); Supreme Court of Norway, Judgment, Case No 20-024314STR-HRET [41] (the rules of international law on jurisdiction are not 'meant to protect individuals against injustice committed by governments, but rules limiting a state's exercise of its power in order to protect the sovereignty of other states').

[107] Hovell (n 94) 431–32.

[108] American Law Institute, *Restatement Fourth* (n 8) § 413, 213.

[109] ibid §§ 407, 413.

[110] ibid § 413, 213.

[111] 'Permanent Mission of the United Kingdom of Great Britain and Norther Ireland to the UN: Note No 337/19' (2019) www.un.org/en/ga/sixth/74/universal_jurisdiction/unitedkingdom_e.pdf.

[112] For completed trials, see Appendix 2.

In addition to the UK, at least 55 states have legislation containing wide and general jurisdictional provisions extending the criminal law to acts committed by non-nationals abroad pursuant to treaties to which the state is a party. Two such states, namely Belgium and Spain, have in recent years enacted legal reforms explicitly limiting extraterritorial jurisdiction consistent with treaty law.[113] In the words of the Belgian House of Representatives Justice Committee, such reform was necessary because the law, as it previously existed, was resulting in 'abusive' and 'sometimes absurd' exercises of jurisdiction by Belgian judges.[114] The state whose widely worded legislation perhaps comes the closest to universal jurisdiction (on paper), and therefore is relied upon by the Fourth Restatement, is Germany's 2002 Code of Crimes against International Law (CCAIL), domesticating the Rome Statute of the International Criminal Court (ICC).[115] On its face, the CCAIL, by virtue of Article 1, applies to war crimes, genocide and crimes against humanity 'even when the offence was committed abroad and bears no relation to Germany'. However, the German legislature has stated that it does not intend to be a 'world police officer'.[116] The CCAIL's broad scope of application is to ensure that Germany is able to meet its obligations under the Rome Statute and thus be in a position to prosecute crimes in the event that transfer of an accused to the ICC or extradition to an ICC state party with a stronger connection to a treaty offence proves impossible. The CCAIL must also be interpreted alongside the procedural limitations and wide discretion the Federal Code of Criminal Procedure bestows on the federal prosecutor (a high-level official who belongs to the executive branch of the government) in respect of its extraterritorial application. The federal prosecutor has legal authorisation to 'dispense with prosecuting an offence' and refrain from exercising jurisdiction if no concrete connection to Germany exists, for example, when neither the victim nor the perpetrator is a German citizen or the accused is not resident in Germany.[117] Clearly, the CCAIL, when read alongside broad prosecutorial discretion, which is surely relevant in reviewing state practice holistically, is not intended to apply universal jurisdiction. In its own observations of the CCAIL, the Permanent Mission of Germany to the UN has similarly acknowledged that the 'general applicability of German criminal law does not automatically legitimise universal prosecution, especially when the suspect is not a German and the crime was not committed against a German national'.[118] Germany has exercised

[113] Code of Criminal Procedure, Art 12*bis* (Belgium); Organic Law on the Judiciary, Art 23 (Spain).

[114] House of Representatives, Report of the Justice Committee, Extraordinary Session 2003, Doc 51-0103/003 (explaining that the Code of Criminal Procedure, Art 12*bis* asserts jurisdiction 'without going beyond' rules of jurisdiction in treaties and is intended to allow Belgium to meet its treaty obligations to extradite or prosecute alleged offenders).

[115] Rome Statute of the International Criminal Court (Rome, 17 July 1998) 2187 UNTS 3.

[116] M Neuner, 'German Preliminary Examinations of International Crimes' in M Bergsmo and C Stahn (eds), *Quality Control in Preliminary Examination* (Brussels, Torkel Opsahl Academic EPublisher, 2018) 131.

[117] CCAIL, Art 3.

[118] 'Permanent Mission of Germany to the UN: Note No 140/2019' (22 March 2019), www.un.org/en/ga/sixth/74/universal_jurisdiction/germany_e.pdf.

the CCAIL in criminal trials when there exists a strong connection to Germany, including when alleged crimes were committed by German residents in Germany's territory.[119]

To test the accuracy of the empirical claim that universal jurisdiction trials have been expanding since 1961, this study surveyed 62 trials that proceeded to completion in 16 states in the period between 1961 and 2017.[120] These trials were identified for analysis because they involved at least one allegation of a war crime, genocide, crimes against humanity or torture, all of which, according to the orthodox account, are universal jurisdiction crimes under international law. Additionally, many of the same trials are included in scholarship as evidence of universal jurisdiction.[121]

The findings of this survey reveal that universal jurisdiction has not been exercised in completed trials and there is not a single case where universal jurisdiction was unambiguously the basis for a court holding that it had competence under international law. The interpretation of these trials as 'universal jurisdiction' is perhaps a poor interpretation of otherwise good data. In all 62 trials, the relevant states brought trials to completion based on national legislation giving effect to their obligations pursuant to one or more of seven treaty regimes, all of which stop short of establishing universal jurisdiction.[122] Additionally, in at least 53 trials the prosecuting state had a connection with either the alleged offence or offender. The most common connection, present in 48 trials, was based on the nationality or residence of the alleged offender, including persons who acquired nationality or residence after the commission of the offence charged.[123] International law (including treaty law) gives states wide discretion to determine who is a 'national' or a 'resident' for the purpose of jurisdiction,[124] and legislative practice is varied in this regard.[125] At least 14 states that have brought trials to completion (and at least a further ten states included in this study) explicitly interpret 'nationality' broadly for the purpose of granting domestic courts extraterritorial jurisdiction regardless of where in the world an alleged offence occurred, including when the accused subsequently acquires nationality, citizenship or residency.[126] The legislation of

[119] Higher Regional Court of Stuttgart, Case No 5-3 StE 6/10 (28 September 2015); Federal Court of Justice, Case No 3 StR 236/17 (20 December 2018). See further Appendix 2.

[120] See Appendix 2. These 62 trials build upon the database of 34 completed trials originally produced by this author in 2018: Garrod, 'Unravelling' (n 99) 169–72.

[121] eg Langer and Eason (n 94); Hovell (n 94).

[122] See Appendix 2.

[123] eg Higher Regional Court of Frankfurt, Case No 5-3 StE 4/10-4-3/10 (18 February 2014); District Court of Oslo, Case No 08-018985MED-OTIR/08 (2 December 2008).

[124] See further Garrod, 'The Expansion' (n 14).

[125] For example, the International Criminal Court Act 2001, s 67A(1), as amended, grants UK courts with jurisdiction where the individual in question has become 'resident subsequent to the commission of the offence' and the concept of residence includes at least 10 different categories of individual.

[126] Australia, Belgium, Canada, Denmark, Finland, France, Germany, Israel, the Netherlands, Norway, Spain, Sweden, Switzerland and the UK. Other states asserting subsequent nationality or subsequent residence jurisdiction include: Algeria (Code of Criminal Procedure, Art 584); Bahrain (Criminal Code, Art 8); Estonia (Penal Code, s 7); Greece (Criminal Code, Art 6); Indonesia (Penal Code, Art 5); Iraq (Penal Code, Art 10); Lebanon (Penal Code, Art 20); Liechtenstein (Criminal Code, s 64(1)(10)); Niger (Code of Criminal Procedure, Art 642); Serbia (Criminal Code, Art 8).

the remaining 81 states examined by this study are potentially capable of being applicable to persons who subsequently acquire nationality or residence. Indeed, of these 81 states, the legislation of 56 of them contains a wide and general jurisdictional provision extending the criminal law to acts committed by non-nationals abroad pursuant to treaties to which the state is a party. There is certainly no explicit requirement that an alleged offender must be a national or resident at the time of the prohibited conduct. In a widely cited article, O'Keefe claims that a state may exercise jurisdiction under the nationality principle only over a person who was its national or resident 'at the time' the prohibited conduct occurred, or else it will violate the principle *nullum crimen sine lege* and cannot be considered a valid exercise of jurisdiction in the eyes of international law.[127] While O'Keefe's view may be correct as a matter of human rights law, it is not one that is reflected in the international rules on jurisdiction or in state practice, the legality of which has not been subject to protest by other states despite ample opportunity.

In only one of the 62 trials (*Eichmann*) did a domestic court place partial reliance on the Harvard Draft's principle of universality in combination with protection and passive personality, which were treated as rules of customary international law, in addition to treaties which were interpreted as permitting or at least not prohibiting extraterritorial jurisdiction, in an effort to show that Israel's Nazi and Nazi Collaborators (Punishment) Law conformed with international law.[128] While the *Eichmann* trial is frequently claimed in scholarship embracing the orthodox account as a major precedent for universal jurisdiction under customary international law, there are no examples of cases that have actually followed it. In any event, Israel's legislation does not prescribe universal jurisdiction and the *Eichmann* trial is not an example of universal jurisdiction.[129] Israel's distinct interest in the case is one that Israel's courts regarded as 'very obvious' and which 'needs no explanation'.[130] Moreover, it has been overlooked time and again that the remarks in that case regarding the Harvard Draft's principles were obiter dicta. The District Court ultimately 'followed' the judgment of the Permanent Court of International Justice in the 1927 *Lotus* case, which famously held that states have the right to assert prescriptive jurisdiction as they see fit unless prohibited by international law.[131]

[127] eg R O'Keefe, 'Universal Jurisdiction: Clarifying the Basic Concept' (2004) 2 *Journal of International Criminal Justice* 735, 742–44.

[128] *Eichmann* (District Court) (n 13) [16]–[39]. The Spanish National Court in the *Scilingo* judgment relied on so-called 'universal jurisdiction', which at the time existed solely in Spanish domestic law, for the prosecution of alleged crimes against humanity. As the National Court failed to demonstrate the existence of universal jurisdiction in international law and as crimes against humanity were not included in Spanish domestic law until several decades after the alleged prohibited conduct occurred, the Supreme Court subsequently decided not to endorse the view of the National Court regarding universal jurisdiction: National Court of Spain, Criminal Division, Case No 16/2005 (19 April 2005); Supreme Court of Spain, Criminal Division, Case No 798/2007 (1 October 2007).

[129] See further Garrod, 'Unravelling' (n 99) 180–82.

[130] *Eichmann* (District Court) (n 13) [33]–[34].

[131] *Lotus* (n 1) 19. The Supreme Court stated that 'we fully agree with every word said' by the District Court on the subject of jurisdiction, *Eichmann* (Criminal Appeal) (n 78) [12].

In sum, only in 56 of the states surveyed does legislation create widely worded jurisdiction which, on its face, establishes 'universal jurisdiction'. In contrast to the orthodox account, however, such jurisdiction is intended to implement treaty obligations, in particular extradition or prosecution jurisdiction, rather than assert universal jurisdiction. This finding is corroborated by completed trials involving allegations of international crimes, showing that the exercise of jurisdiction is far from universal, while domestic courts are yet to place reliance on universal jurisdiction as a claim to authority under international law. While some states refer to jurisdiction in domestic law as 'universal jurisdiction', that is quite separate from general state acceptance of universal jurisdiction for the same crimes, and whether universal jurisdiction exists for such crimes as a matter of international law.

V. Conclusion

Using the largest and most diverse sample of state practice collected to date, this study moves beyond the literature review method that has dominated research on jurisdiction thus far. In so doing, it offers new and compelling evidence that the ways in which states assert extraterritorial criminal jurisdiction, why they do it, and what is and what is not permissible in international law are distorted by the long-standing and dominant paradigm on jurisdiction, underpinned by the Harvard Draft's principles. The study has found that states assert five main categories of jurisdiction (subject to varying degrees and qualifications), all of which are difficult to reconcile with the Harvard Draft's principles. Based on these categories of jurisdiction, states protect a wide range of important 'interests', some of which are not articulated and defined in legislation, as well as their nationals and residents (legal and natural persons), representatives and employees. Additionally, states assert jurisdiction over non-nationals, both as alleged offenders and victims, who acquire nationality or residence after the time of the prohibited conduct, as well as persons who are present in the territory of the state regardless of where in the world the prohibited conduct occurred pursuant to treaty obligations. The categories of jurisdiction identified and examined here prioritise the rights and interests of states rather than the rights of individuals or of the international community as a whole under international human rights law.

There is insufficient evidence that states generally condition their authority to criminalise the activities of non-nationals carried out beyond the state's territory based on the Harvard Draft's principles, or that these principles have been codified or recognised in treaty law. The Harvard Draft's principles not only fail to provide a clear normative framework, but are conceptually confused and do not reflect international law. The harm of thinking about and understanding jurisdiction according to these principles is that it can result in problematic policy decisions and abusive assertions of jurisdiction by states. Moreover, the principles have engendered a fragmented approach to jurisdiction, whereby the 'protective' and 'passive personality' principles are confined to a limited number of crimes against domestic law, whereas 'universal' jurisdiction is reserved for crimes against international law. This study thus raises urgent questions about the role of the criminal law and the extent of its application extraterritorially, as well as providing new empirical backing for rethinking jurisdiction in international law and moving beyond the Harvard Draft's principles.

6

Human Rights as Penal Drivers across the World

MATTIA PINTO*

I. Introduction

Human rights became the dominant moral language of international politics in the late 1970s.[1] Since then, appeals to human rights have also increasingly been used to expand penal power across borders and jurisdictions. This penal expansion has a material component, with the creation of international criminal tribunals, the institution of criminal proceedings against perpetrators of human rights abuses and the inclusion of new human rights-based offences. The use of human rights to trigger the application of criminal law also occurs at the symbolic level of discourses and representations. In particular, the assumptions that effective human rights protection requires criminal accountability and that impunity is a cause of human rights violations have become ingrained in the human rights movement's thinking and practice.[2]

A number of scholars have noted this embrace of penality[3] by human rights – what Karen Engle calls the 'turn to criminal law in human rights'.[4] Most commentators, accepting this trend as uncontroversial, have advocated the deployment of penal means to enforce human rights.[5] Recently, however, growing

* I am very grateful for the extensive comments of Micheál Ó Floinn, Lindsay Farmer, Peter Ramsay and Matthew Garrod on early versions of this chapter.

[1] Here, I follow Samuel Moyn's genealogy of the contemporary human rights movement. See S Moyn, *The Last Utopia: Human Rights in History* (Cambridge, MA, Harvard University Press, 2010).

[2] K Engle, Z Miller and DM Davis, 'Introduction' in K Engle, Z Miller and DM Davis (eds), *Anti-Impunity and the Human Rights Agenda* (Cambridge, Cambridge University Press, 2016) 1.

[3] In this chapter, I use *penality* to refer to the entire penal sphere, including its laws, sanctions, institutions, practices, discourses and representations. See, eg D Garland, *Punishment and Welfare: A History of Penal Strategies* (Aldershot, Gower, 1985) x; D Garland, 'Penality and the Penal State' (2013) 51 *Criminology* 475, 476.

[4] K Engle, 'Anti-Impunity and the Turn to Criminal Law in Human Rights' (2015) 100 *Cornell Law Review* 1069; K Engle, 'A Genealogy of the Criminal Turn in Human Rights' in Engle et al, *Anti-Impunity* (n 2).

[5] See, eg N Roht-Arriaza, 'State Responsibility to Investigate and Prosecute Grave Human Rights Violations in International Law' (1990) 78 *California Law Review* 449; DF Orentlicher, 'Settling Accounts: The Duty to Prosecute Human Rights Violations of a Prior Regime' (1991) 100 *Yale Law*

attention has also been devoted to the limits and implications of this development, with some scholars questioning the pursuit of human rights protection through criminalisation and punishment.[6] Yet, beyond the specific case of universal jurisdiction,[7] there is little analysis of how human rights, by acting as a driving force of penal power around the world, have had an impact on the normative content and exercise of criminal jurisdiction.[8] Aiming to fill this gap, this chapter both chronicles and critiques how human rights have contributed to *penal extraterritoriality*. The term 'penal extraterritoriality' is used here to refer both to the jurisdiction by a state over conduct occurring outside its normal territorial boundaries and to what is generally termed international jurisdiction, normally claimed by international criminal tribunals.[9]

The discussion in this chapter is divided as follows. Section II explores the historical emergence and evolution of some trends of human rights-led penal extraterritoriality:[10] (i) universal jurisdiction; (ii) passive or active personality jurisdiction; (iii) international and hybrid criminal jurisdiction; and (iv) the quasi-criminal jurisdiction of human rights bodies. Section III argues that not only do human rights contribute to fostering penal extraterritoriality, but they also entail the discursive construction of distinctly *global* forms of crime and justice.[11]

Journal 2537; H Kim and K Sikkink, 'Explaining the Deterrence Effect of Human Rights Prosecutions for Transitional Countries' (2010) 54 *International Studies Quarterly* 939; K Sikkink, *The Justice Cascade: How Human Rights Prosecutions Are Changing World Politics* (New York, WW Norton, 2011); A Neier, *The International Human Rights Movement: A History* (Princeton, Princeton University Press, 2012).

[6] See, eg F Tulkens, 'The Paradoxical Relationship between Criminal Law and Human Rights' (2011) 9 *Journal of International Criminal Justice* 577; L Lazarus, 'Positive Obligations and Criminal Justice: Duties to Protect or Coerce?' in L Zedner and JV Roberts (eds), *Principles and Values in Criminal Law and Criminal Justice* (Oxford, Oxford University Press, 2012); Engle, 'Anti-Impunity' (n 4); Engle et al, *Anti-Impunity* (n 2); M Pinto, 'Awakening the Leviathan through Human Rights Law – How Human Rights Bodies Trigger the Application of Criminal Law' (2018) 34 *Utrecht Journal of International and European Law* 161; M Pinto, 'Historical Trends of Human Rights Gone Criminal' (2020) 42 *Human Rights Quarterly* 729; H Hannum, *Rescuing Human Rights: A Radically Moderate Approach* (Cambridge, Cambridge University Press, 2019).

[7] There is a large scholarship on universal jurisdiction and human rights. See, eg L Reydams, *Universal Jurisdiction: International and Municipal Legal Perspectives* (Oxford, Oxford University Press, 2004); K Roth, 'The Case for Universal Jurisdiction' (2001) 80 *Foreign Affairs* 150; M Langer, 'Universal Jurisdiction Is Not Disappearing: The Shift from "Global Enforcer" to "No Safe Haven" Universal Jurisdiction' (2015) 13 *Journal of International Criminal Justice* 245; MT Kamminga, 'Lessons Learned from the Exercise of Universal Jurisdiction in Respect of Gross Human Rights Offenses' (2001) 23 *Human Rights Quarterly* 940.

[8] But see F Mégret, '"Do Not Do Abroad What You Would Not Do at Home?": An Exploration of the Rationales for Extraterritorial Criminal Jurisdiction over a State's Nationals' (2019) 57 *Canadian Yearbook of International Law* 1, 32–40, whose analysis is limited to active national jurisdiction; A Huneeus, 'International Criminal Law by Other Means: The Quasi-Criminal Jurisdiction of the Human Rights Courts' (2013) 7 *American Journal of International Law* 1, who focuses on the 'quasi-criminal' jurisdiction of human rights bodies.

[9] For a similar use of extraterritoriality, see A Chehtman, *The Philosophical Foundations of Extraterritorial Punishment* (Oxford, Oxford University Press, 2010) ch 5.

[10] This section is a shorter, re-elaborated, version of Pinto, 'Historical Trends' (n 6).

[11] See also N McMillan, 'Imagining the International: The Constitution of the International as a Site of Crime, Justice and Community' (2016) 25 *Social and Legal Studies* 163.

Within this discursive schema, criminal jurisdiction is primarily decentralised or extraterritorial rather than territorial. Section IV highlights the adverse implications of a global penality which is normatively grounded in human rights rather than on a political order. This foundation runs the risk of casting an aura of inevitability around the operation of criminal law – thus precluding alternative, non-punitive responses to human rights violations. Another risk is that human rights, rather than moderating state penal policies, end up justifying the dissemination and expansion of punitive responses around the globe. Ultimately, the chapter shows that a global, human rights-driven penality does not necessarily increase the level of human rights protection, but rather it might become an instrument used by certain powerful countries to act coercively outside their territorial boundaries.

II. Trends of Human Rights-Led Penal Extraterritoriality

A. Universal Jurisdiction

In the 1970s, tens of thousands of political refugees from the authoritarian regimes in Eastern and Southern Europe and in South America arrived in Western Europe and North America.[12] The accounts of the treatments experienced by these exiles made it increasingly clear that domestic law provisions were unable to deal with systematic human rights abuses, especially when they constituted a means of maintaining and stabilising a totalitarian regime. Absent an international criminal court and in the face of the protests of international organisations and foreign governments, the solution was sought in the concept of universal jurisdiction.[13] Universal jurisdiction refers to the authority of a state to exercise its criminal jurisdiction over crimes regardless of the place of commission or any

[12] T Kelly, *This Side of Silence: Human Rights, Torture, and the Recognition of Cruelty* (Philadelphia, University of Pennsylvania Press, 2013) 8.

[13] Universal jurisdiction had been used until then for crimes with a cross-border component or crimes harmful to the international order, not for human rights violations. There is a critical literature suggesting that even today the foundations and the development of universal jurisdiction are not connected with human rights. See, eg E Kontorovich, 'The Piracy Analogy: Modern Universal Jurisdiction's Hollow Foundation' (2004) 45 *Harvard International Law Journal* 183; L Reydams, 'The Rise and Fall of Universal Jurisdiction' in WA Schabas and N Bernaz (eds), *Routledge Handbook of International Criminal Law* (Abingdon, Routledge, 2011); M Garrod, 'The Protective Principle of Jurisdiction over War Crimes and the Hollow Concept of Universality' (2012) 12 *International Criminal Law Review* 763; M Garrod, 'Piracy, the Protection of Vital State Interests and the False Foundations of Universal Jurisdiction in International Law' (2014) 25 *Diplomacy and Statecraft* 195; D Hovell, 'The Authority of Universal Jurisdiction' (2018) 29 *European Journal of International Law* 427. Although this chapter argues that universal jurisdiction has increasingly been used in relation to human rights violations, my discussion is not concerned with questions regarding what the foundations of universal jurisdiction are or should be, nor does it dispute its use in connection with many other factors.

link to nationality.[14] Efforts to set out state obligations to prosecute human rights violations in the absence of links between the crime and the prosecuting state might even be dated back to the four Geneva Conventions, adopted in 1949.[15] However, the Geneva Conventions were not intended as human rights treaties: their penal provisions apply only to war crimes committed within the context of an armed conflict, and not to human rights abuses more generally.

If we focus only on those treaties that are considered and labelled as human rights conventions (including, but not limited to, the core international human rights instruments), the first obligation to exercise universal jurisdiction over human rights breaches can be found in the 1973 International Convention on the Suppression and Punishment of the Crime of Apartheid.[16] Articles 4 and 5 oblige states parties to prosecute non-nationals and non-residents for the crime of apartheid committed abroad, where the accused is physically within the jurisdiction of a state party. However, it appears that this convention was adopted more for political reasons (ie to stigmatise South Africa) than to create a legal framework for the prosecution of perpetrators, and, in fact, the universal jurisdiction provisions in this convention have never been used.[17] It was the Convention against Torture and Other Cruel, Inhuman or Degrading Treatment or Punishment (Torture Convention), adopted in 1984, that marked the turn to universal jurisdiction as a means of addressing human rights violations in practice.[18] Pursuant to Articles 5–7, states parties must submit any case involving acts of torture to their competent authorities for the purpose of prosecution, without any regard for the place of commission of the acts, if suspects are in their territory and are not extradited. These provisions lay down the legal principle of *aut dedere aut judicare* (a duty to extradite or prosecute), the purpose of which is

[14] Chehtman, *The Philosophical Foundations* (n 9) 115–16. In this chapter, I use the term *universal jurisdiction* in relation to the jurisdictional provisions in a number of treaties that appear to incentivise jurisdiction over crimes once a suspect comes within the jurisdiction of the state, regardless of eg where the crimes were committed or the residence or nationality of the suspect. For different approaches, see nn 16 and 19.

[15] Geneva Convention for the Amelioration of the Condition of the Wounded and Sick in Armed Forces in the Field (Geneva, 12 August 1949) 75 UNTS 31, Art 49; Geneva Convention for the Amelioration of the Condition of Wounded, Sick and Shipwrecked Members of Armed Forces at Sea (Geneva, 12 August 1949) 75 UNTS 85, Art 50; Geneva Convention Relative to the Treatment of Prisoners of War (Geneva, 12 August 1949) 75 UNTS 135, Art 129; Geneva Convention Relative to the Protection of Civilian Persons in Time of War (Geneva, 12 August 1949) 75 UNTS 297, Art 146.

[16] International Convention on the Suppression and Punishment of the Crime of Apartheid (New York, 30 November 1973) 1015 UNTS 243. Some scholars contend that the jurisdictional provisions in this treaty form a *treaty-based jurisdiction* that is distinct from universal jurisdiction *sensu stricto*. See, eg M Garrod, 'Unraveling the Confused Relationship between Treaty Obligations to Extradite or Prosecute and "Universal Jurisdiction" in the Light of the *Habré* Case' (2018) 59 *Harvard International Law Journal* 125.

[17] C Edelenbos, 'Human Rights Violations: A Duty to Prosecute?' (1994) 7 *Leiden Journal of International Law* 5, 7: 'No state has ever tried a South African citizen for involvement in the crime of apartheid.'

[18] (New York, 10 December 1984) 1465 UNTS 85; M Nowak, M Birk and G Monina, 'Introduction' in M Nowak, M Birk and G Monina (eds), *The United Nations Convention against Torture and Its Optional Protocol: A Commentary*, 2nd edn (Oxford, Oxford University Press, 2019) 3–4.

to ensure that no safe haven from criminal prosecution is granted to perpetrators of torture.[19]

The Torture Convention thus represents a crucial moment in the promotion of penal extraterritoriality for the purpose of human rights protection.[20] The principle of *aut dedere aut judicare* had previously been deployed almost exclusively outside the human rights framework. The Swedish government, which proposed it, used as a model the so-called 'Hague formula', contained in Article 7 of the 1970 Convention for the Suppression of Unlawful Seizure of Aircraft.[21] Until the Torture Convention, the Hague formula had been used only in a number of anti-terrorism conventions.[22] The transposition of this formulation into a human rights treaty seemed unusual at the time. As Malcolm Evans has noted, many states that had no difficulty in accepting jurisdictional and extradition obligations in the context of

[19] MC Bassiouni and EM Wise, *Aut Dedere Aut Judicare: The Duty to Extradite or Prosecute in International Law* (Dordrecht, Martinus Nijhoff, 1995). Although the Torture Convention is generally interpreted as establishing universal jurisdiction, some authors have argued that the principle of *aut dedere aut judicare* should be distinguished from the universality principle. See C Ryngaert, *Jurisdiction in International Law*, 2nd edn (Oxford, Oxford University Press, 2015) 124: 'if States premise their jurisdiction solely on the territorial presence of the perpetrator in accordance with their *aut dedere aut judicare* obligations, they do not in fact exercise universal jurisdiction'. The principle of *aut dedere aut judicare* can also be used for the reciprocal protection of parallel state interests rather than the protection of fundamental values of the international community and has therefore been referred as providing 'representative universal jurisdiction' (C Kreß, 'Universal Jurisdiction over International Crimes and the *Institut de Droit international*' (2006) 4 *International Journal of Criminal Justice* 561, 567) or 'co-operative limited universality' (Reydams, *Universal Jurisdiction* (n 7) 28). Compare, however, the iteration of the *aut dedere aut judicare* principle in instruments such as the UN Convention against Transnational Organized Crime (New York, 15 November 2000) 2225 UNTS 209. Art 15(3) obliges states parties to adopt jurisdictional measures in order to implement the corresponding *aut dedere aut judicare* obligation in Art 16(10). However, Art 15(4) also incentivises wider jurisdictional measures in any case where an individual is present in a state's territory, is alleged to have committed offences covered by the Convention and the state does not extradite the individual. There is no corresponding *aut dedere aut judicare* obligation expressly tied to this jurisdictional provision (unlike Art 15(3)), so Art 15(4) looks much more like it is encouraging a form of universal jurisdiction over the crimes covered by the Convention. For a recent state interpretation of these provisions, see *In the Matter of Criminal Proceedings against Youssef Tartoussi*, Final appeal judgment, No 19672/2020, ILDC 3171 (IT 2020), 17 June 2020, where the Italian Supreme Court of Cassation found that Art 15(4) was not self-executing. See generally M Garrod, 'Extraterritorial Criminal Jurisdiction in International Law: Time for an Empirical Examination', ch 5 in the present volume.

[20] MD Evans, 'The Criminalisation of Torture as a Part of the Human Right Framework' [2014] *CRIMEN: Casopis za Krivicne Nauke* 136, 137.

[21] Convention for the Suppression of Unlawful Seizure of Aircraft (The Hague, 16 December 1970) 860 UNTS 105, Art 7 stipulates: 'The Contracting State in the territory of which the alleged offender is found shall, if it does not extradite him, be obliged without exception whatsoever and whether or not the offence was committed in its territory, to submit the case to its competent authorities for the purpose of prosecution.' See JH Burgers and H Danelius, *The United Nations Convention against Torture: A Handbook on the Convention against Torture and Other Cruel, Inhuman, or Degrading Treatment or Punishment* (Dordrecht, Martinus Nijhoff, 1988) 35.

[22] Convention for the Suppression of Unlawful Seizure of Aircraft (n 21); Convention for the Suppression of Unlawful Acts against the Safety of Civil Aviation (Montreal, 23 September 1971) 974 UNTS 177; Convention on the Prevention and Punishment of Crimes against Internationally Protected Persons, Including Diplomatic Agents (New York, 14 December 1973) 1035 UNTS 167; International Convention against the Taking of Hostages (New York, 17 December 1979) 1316 UNTS 205.

anti-terrorist conventions nevertheless did not accept them easily in a convention that they perceived to be about human rights.[23] States' initial resistance to penal extraterritoriality for torture is probably related to the fact that previous, anti-terrorism, conventions addressed crimes with transborder elements (eg hijacking aeroplanes), while the Torture Convention concerns an offence that is ordinarily committed intrastate.[24] In other words, the Torture Convention sought to elevate torture to an *international* crime for which universal jurisdiction exists (like war crimes and piracy) by relying on the heinous nature of the practice rather than the necessary presence of international or transnational elements.[25] Since the Torture Convention, several other treaties have sought to make prosecution of gross human rights violations legally obligatory.[26] While many of them do not contain provisions for universal jurisdiction,[27] some do. These include the Inter-American Convention to Prevent and Punish Torture (1985),[28] the Inter-American Convention on Forced Disappearance of Persons (1994),[29] the Optional Protocol to the Convention on the Rights of the Child on the Sale of Children, Child Prostitution and Child Pornography (2000)[30] and the International Convention for the Protection of All Persons from Enforced Disappearances (2006).[31]

All these treaties *oblige* states parties to assert universal jurisdiction if they do not extradite suspects who are present in their territory. Yet it is also generally agreed that international customary law *allows* the use of universal jurisdiction with regard to crimes considered particularly heinous by the international community, such as crimes against humanity and genocide.[32] The commitment to protect human rights plays a key role in the extraterritorial prosecution of such crimes. Although national legislation enabling universal jurisdiction for atrocity crimes is technically not the result of human rights law, it is undisputed that it serves to some extent a human rights cause.[33] An example is the adoption of universal jurisdiction provisions as part of the domestic implementation of the Rome Statute of the International Criminal Court (ICC).[34] The ICC states parties

[23] Evans (n 20) 137.

[24] Roht-Arriaza, 'State Responsibility' (n 5) 465.

[25] ibid 466. For a critique, see Garrod, 'Unraveling the Confused Relationship' (n 16).

[26] Roht-Arriaza, 'State Responsibility' (n 5) 499.

[27] See n 19 for the argument that the principle of *aut dedere aut judicare* should be distinguished from the universality principle.

[28] Inter-American Convention to Prevent and Punish Torture (Cartagena de Indias, 12 September 1985) OASTS 67, Art 12.

[29] Inter-American Convention on Forced Disappearance of Persons (Belem do Para, 9 September 1994) OASTS 60, Art 4.

[30] Optional Protocol to the Convention on the Rights of the Child on the Sale of Children, Child Prostitution and Child Pornography (New York, 25 May 2000) 2171 UNTS 227, Art 4.

[31] International Convention for the Protection of All Persons from Enforced Disappearances (New York, 20 December 2006) 2716 UNTS 3, Art 9.

[32] Chehtman, *The Philosophical Foundations* (n 9) 117–18.

[33] A Clapham, 'Human Rights and International Criminal Law' in WA Schabas (ed), *The Cambridge Companion to International Criminal Law* (Cambridge, Cambridge University Press, 2016).

[34] Rome Statute of the International Criminal Court (Rome, 17 July 1998) 2187 UNTS 3.

are encouraged to adopt universal jurisdiction statutes to facilitate co-operation with the Court in the struggle to hold human rights violators accountable.[35]

In practice, the use of universal jurisdiction for human rights abuses remained a dead letter until the late 1990s. Foreign human rights prosecutions were legally possible, but few believed that they were politically possible.[36] However, with the turn of the century, individual criminal accountability by reference to human rights gained momentum and several states began prosecutions against foreign perpetrators for wrongdoings committed abroad.[37] The general perception was that a 'new age of accountability' was replacing an 'old era of impunity'.[38] One event in particular that has been described as a trigger moment was the arrest of Chilean general and dictator Augusto Pinochet in London on a Spanish extradition warrant for torture and other human rights violations.[39] For Noemi Roht-Arriaza, this event represented the most significant move towards a global fight for accountability, whereby leaders who committed gross abuses could no longer escape from prosecution and punishment for their actions.[40] The Pinochet case gave practical effect to the Torture Convention and revitalised universal jurisdiction for human rights abuses.

In the early 2000s, human rights obligations were often invoked in the prosecution of various high-ranking politicians allegedly responsible for mass abuses. Belgium and Spain, in particular, were at the forefront of this trend, with their domestic law providing for the unconditional application of universal jurisdiction (no link with the prosecuting country was required). Yet, a series of diplomatic incidents led the two countries to amend their laws in 2003 (Belgium) and in 2009 and 2014 (Spain).[41] Despite criticism and claims that it was doomed to disappear,[42] universal jurisdiction today appears to be a common jurisdictional

[35] See M Langer, 'The Archipelago and the Wheel: The Universal Jurisdiction and the International Criminal Court Regimes' in M Minow, CC True-Frost and A Whiting (eds), *The First Global Prosecutor: Promise and Constraints* (Ann Arbor, University of Michigan Press, 2015) 224, which mentions Loi 2010-930 du 9 août 2010 portant adaptation du droit pénal à l'institution de la Cour pénale internationale, 10 August 2010, Art 8 (France); Völkerstrafgesetzbuch, 26 June 2002, s 1 (Germany).

[36] K Sikkink, 'The Age of Accountability: The Global Rise of Individual Criminal Accountability' in F Lessa and LA Payne (eds), *Amnesty in the Age of Human Rights Accountability: Comparative and International Perspectives* (Cambridge, Cambridge University Press, 2012) 36.

[37] This trend has been described as a 'justice cascade' in Sikkink, *The Justice Cascade* (n 5) and as 'a revolution in accountability' in CL Sriram, 'Revolutions in Accountability: New Approaches to Past Abuses' (2003) 19 *American University International Law Review* 301.

[38] Ban Ki-moon, 'At ICC Review Conference, Ban Declares End to "Era of Impunity"' (*UN News*, 31 May 2010) www.news.un.org/en/story/2010/05/340252.

[39] Sikkink, 'The Age of Accountability' (n 36) 37.

[40] N Roht-Arriaza, *The Pinochet Effect: Transnational Justice in the Age of Human Rights* (Philadelphia, University of Pennsylvania Press, 2005).

[41] Complaints against high-ranking politicians (eg Ariel Sharon, George HW Bush and Jiang Zemin) led to direct pressure from powerful states to repeal the laws. See, eg I de la Rasilla del Moral, 'The Swan Song of Universal Jurisdiction in Spain' (2009) 9 *International Criminal Law Review* 777; S Lefranc, 'A Tale of Many Jurisdictions: How Universal Jurisdiction Is Creating a Transnational Judicial Space' (2021) 48 *Journal of Law and Society* 573, 575.

[42] Reydams, 'The Rise and Fall' (n 13); H Kissinger, 'The Pitfalls of Universal Jurisdiction: Risking Judicial Tyranny' (2001) 80 *Foreign Affairs* 86.

basis for prosecuting human rights abuses to prevent impunity for human rights abuses – especially if committed by mid-level perpetrators.[43] As a jurisdictional claim, the exercise of universal jurisdiction entails a *claim to authority*. Yet, universal jurisdiction itself increasingly *claims authority* and gains legitimacy by relying on human rights and by being presented as a mechanism through which victims of serious human rights violations can have access to justice.[44] A recent study reports that universal jurisdiction has been endorsed by 109 states and that the number of prosecutions is growing, with 18 prosecuting countries and about 60 cases in 2020.[45] While state policies play a decisive role in the selection of the cases (eg Germany prioritises trials against Syrians; France and Belgium prioritise crimes committed in their former colonies), it appears that there has been a diversification of both the prosecuting countries and the countries where the crimes were committed.[46]

B. Passive and Active Personality Jurisdiction

Human rights are also at the basis of other claims of extraterritorial criminal jurisdiction, including those based on the principles of passive and active personality. Both of these grounds of extraterritorial jurisdiction appear to be expanding, although their underlying normative justifications remain uncertain and contested by many commentators.[47]

Passive personality refers to the jurisdiction over an act committed abroad where the victim is a national of the prosecuting state. Foreign trials through passive personality have been conducted since the 1990s for human rights violations occurring in Latin America, for example.[48] Several activists, unable to have investigations launched in their own countries, have strategically pressured prosecutors in Spain, Italy and France to start criminal proceedings domestically,

[43] M Langer and M Eason, 'The Quiet Expansion of Universal Jurisdiction' (2019) 30 *European Journal of International Law* 779.

[44] Similarly, Hovell (n 13).

[45] Lefranc (n 41) 576; see also Langer and Eason (n 43). Both Lefranc's and Langer and Eason's studies rely on a broad notion of universal jurisdiction. By adopting a narrower understanding of the universality principle, other studies have disputed the widespread application of universal jurisdiction. See L Reydams, 'The Application of Universal Jurisdiction in the Fight against Impunity' (European Parliament, 2016) papers.ssrn.com/sol3/papers.cfm?abstract_id=2929013; M Garrod, 'The Emergence of "Universal Jurisdiction" in Response to Somali Piracy: An Empirically Informed Critique of International Law's "Paradigmatic" Universal Jurisdiction Crime' (2019) 18 *Chinese Journal of International Law* 551.

[46] Lefranc (n 41) 576.

[47] Chehtman, *The Philosophical Foundations* (n 9) 59–71; D Ireland-Piper, 'Extraterritorial Criminal Jurisdiction: Does the Long Arm of the Law Undermine the Rule of Law?' (2012) 13 *Melbourne Journal of International Law* 1, 12–13; Garrod, 'Extraterritorial Criminal Jurisdiction' (n 19).

[48] K Sikkink and CB Walling, 'The Impact of Human Rights Trials in Latin America' (2007) 44 *Journal of Peace Research* 427.

with the aim of addressing human rights violations which occurred in Argentina, Chile or Uruguay against citizens with Spanish, Italian or French passports.[49] For instance, in 2021, the Italian Court of Cassation confirmed sentences of life imprisonment for 14 high-ranking officials from the Southern Cone for the torture and murder of several Italian citizens in the 1970s and 1980s during the so-called 'Operation Condor'.[50] Cases that are described in the press or even by some governments as involving universal jurisdiction are sometimes based on passive personality, because they involve nationals of the state undertaking the prosecution as the victims of the alleged crimes.[51] Significantly, passive personality appears to provide the basis of many criminal proceedings involving senior African officials before European courts.[52] In 2005, for example, Belgium relied on passive personality when it started criminal proceedings against former Chad president Hissène Habré.[53] Similarly, the French arrest warrant issued in 2006 in respect of nine Rwandan officials, allegedly involved in the plane attack that killed former Rwandan President Habyarimana, was based on a complaint filed by the daughter of the French co-pilot.[54] Passive personality was also central in Spain's decision, in 2008, to charge 40 members of the Rwanda Defence Forces in connection to the killing and disappearance of Spanish nationals in Rwanda during the 1990s.[55]

Active personality, on the other hand, is the exercise of criminal jurisdiction by states over their nationals for crimes committed abroad. This form of extraterritorial jurisdiction is not much discussed in human rights and international criminal law literature.[56] Yet states, when it comes to serious human rights violations, seem more likely to rely on the nationality of the alleged offender than to invoke universal jurisdiction.[57] According to Frédéric Mégret, when it comes to the gravest international crimes, 'active nationality jurisdiction does more work, in the background, than the aesthetically striking, but practically exceptional,

[49] F Lessa, 'Operation Condor on Trial: Justice for Transnational Human Rights Crimes in South America' (2019) 51 *Journal of Latin American Studies* 409, 435.

[50] J César, 'Processo Condor: condannati all'ergastolo 14 ex militari sudamericani' (*Osservatorio Diritti*, 14 July 2021) www.osservatoriodiritti.it/2021/07/14/processo-condor-roma-italia-operazione-condor.

[51] Amnesty International, 'Ending Impunity: Developing and Implementing a Global Action Plan Using Universal Jurisdiction' (London, Amnesty International Publications, 2009) 26, www.amnesty.org/en/wp-content/uploads/2021/07/ior530052009en.pdf.

[52] L Arimatsu, 'Universal Jurisdiction for International Crimes: Africa's Hope for Justice?' (Royal Institute of International Affairs, 2010) Chatham House Briefing Paper 2010/01, 8, www.chathamhouse.org/sites/default/files/public/Research/International%20Law/bp0410arimatsu.pdf.

[53] ibid. Hissène Habré was eventually tried and convicted by the Extraordinary African Chambers.

[54] Arimatsu (n 52) 8. The arrest warrant was lifted in 2009. See H Holland, 'Rwanda Says France Drops Kabuye Arrest Warrant' (*Reuters*, 1 April 2009) www.reuters.com/article/ozatp-rwanda-france-kabuye-20090401-idAFJOE53001S20090401.

[55] Arimatsu (n 52) 8. The case was then dismissed in 2015. See 'Spain Dismisses Rwanda War Crimes Case against 40 Officials' (*BBC News*, 8 October 2015) www.bbc.co.uk/news/world-africa-34477883.

[56] Mégret, 'Do Not Do Abroad' (n 8).

[57] ibid 4.

principle of universal jurisdiction'.[58] All the treaties containing *aut dedere aut judicare* provisions in fact also enable states parties to establish their jurisdiction when the defendant is one of their nationals.[59] In addition, a number of scholars believe that when universal jurisdiction is not available (eg for violations of the right to life), there is a self-standing human rights obligation to assert active personality jurisdiction, even absent a specific treaty provision to that effect.[60] With the rise of prosecutorial obligations under human rights law,[61] the assumption is that if a state does not investigate violations which have occurred in its territory, other states which are involved through their nationals are encouraged – if not mandated – to conduct the prosecutions themselves.

An example of the growing importance of the active nationality principle as an instrument to ensure that national borders are not barriers to human rights-driven prosecutions is the Irish Criminal Law (Extraterritorial Jurisdiction) Act 2019.[62] While the primary purpose of this Act was to enable the ratification of the Council of Europe's Istanbul Convention on Preventing and Combating Violence against Women and Domestic Violence, its measures go well beyond the requirements of the treaty.[63] The Act, which is explicitly motivated by human rights considerations,[64] extends the extraterritorial jurisdiction of a range of offences in Ireland regardless of whether they entail violence against women or domestic violence.[65] Significantly, it confers jurisdiction over conduct occurring outside the state by reference to the Irish citizenship or ordinary residence in Ireland of the alleged offender.[66]

C. International(ised) Jurisdiction

Human rights have also contributed to the institution of new forms of criminal jurisdiction which can be described as 'deterritorialised'[67] because they do not

[58] ibid 38.

[59] See, eg Torture Convention, Art 5(1)(b); Optional Protocol to the Convention on the Rights of the Child on the Sale of Children, Child Prostitution and Child Pornography (n 30) Art 4(2)(a); International Convention for the Protection of All Persons from Enforced Disappearances (n 31) Art 9(1)(b).

[60] Mégret, 'Do Not Do Abroad' (n 8) 33.

[61] Declaration of Basic Principles of Justice for Victims of Crime and Abuse of Power, UNGA Res 40/34 (29 November 1985).

[62] Criminal Law (Extraterritorial Jurisdiction) Act 2019 (Ireland).

[63] Council of Europe Convention on Preventing and Combating Violence against Women and Domestic Violence (Istanbul, 11 May 2011) (European Treaty Series No 210).

[64] The Istanbul Convention is reproduced in full in the Schedule of the Act, with all its references to the European Convention of Human Rights, the case law of the European Court of Human Rights and the human rights of women and girls.

[65] For a critical comment, see A Shieber, 'Irish Extraterritorial Jurisdiction' (*Criminal Justice Notes*, 2 April 2019) www.blogs.kent.ac.uk/criminaljusticenotes/2019/04/02/irish-extraterritorial-jurisdiction/.

[66] Criminal Law (Extraterritorial Jurisdiction) Act 2019 (Ireland), s 3.

[67] For the use of the term *deterritorialised*, see J Cockayne, 'On the Cosmopolitanization of Criminal Jurisdiction' (2005) 3 *Journal of International Criminal Justice* 514, 515.

involve a sovereign state exercising its penal powers over conduct which occurred within its territory. One example is the creation of international criminal tribunals. The history of these tribunals is often narrated as a triumphant story of human rights protection. However, international criminal justice has not always been concerned with human rights. The Nuremberg Trials, for instance, were primarily focused on aggression, while the Holocaust and other atrocities remained marginal.[68] It was only in the 1990s that international criminal adjudication was reinvented as part of the human rights project and shifted its attention to accountability for human rights violations.[69]

In 1993, the atrocities that occurred in the Balkans prompted the United Nations Security Council (UNSC) to establish the International Criminal Tribunal for the former Yugoslavia (ICTY).[70] The following year, the UNSC created the International Criminal Tribunals for Rwanda (ICTR) as a response to the genocide and other atrocities which occurred in the country.[71] Albeit primarily violations of the Geneva and Genocide Conventions, the mass atrocities committed in the Balkans and Central-East Africa were also read in terms of human rights violations due to their universal moral repugnance. Until their functions were transferred to the International Residual Mechanism for Criminal Tribunals between 2015 and 2017, the ICTY and ICTR exercised direct criminal jurisdiction over the international crimes committed in the former Yugoslavia and Rwanda.[72] They had legal authority to open and conduct prosecutions from abroad, regardless of the consent of the state with territorial jurisdiction. These ad hoc tribunals had both concurrent jurisdiction and primacy over national courts.[73] If they claimed a case, national courts had to relinquish jurisdiction in their favour. The national justice systems still had to assist the international tribunals by identifying, apprehending and surrendering suspects, by collecting documents and by taking testimony.[74]

The institutionalisation of the ad hoc tribunals led to the creation of a permanent international criminal court. The Rome Statute was eventually adopted in 1998 and entered into force in 2002. The ICC was applauded as 'a gift of hope to future generations, and a giant step forward in the march towards universal human rights and the rule of law'.[75] Since then, the Court has been presented as the

[68] S Moyn, 'From Aggression to Atrocity: Rethinking the History of International Criminal Law' in KJ Heller et al (eds), *The Oxford Handbook of International Criminal Law* (Oxford, Oxford University Press, 2020).

[69] ibid; F Mégret, 'International Criminal Justice as a Peace Project' (2018) 29 *European Journal of International Law* 835.

[70] UNSC Res 827 (25 May 1993).

[71] UNSC Res 955 (8 November 1994).

[72] Huneeus (n 8) 28.

[73] Updated Statute of the International Criminal Tribunal for the Former Yugoslavia (September 2009), Art 9; Statute of the International Criminal Tribunal for Rwanda (31 January 2010), Art 8.

[74] Huneeus (n 8) 28.

[75] K Annan, 'Secretary-General Says Establishment of International Criminal Court Is Gift of Hope to Future Generations' (*UN Meetings Coverage and Press Releases*, 20 July 1998) Press Release SG/SM/6643 L/2891, www.un.org/press/en/1998/19980720.sgsm6643.html.

cornerstone of a broad human rights agenda, namely the 'fight against impunity'.[76] The connection between human rights and international criminal law is rarely contested. Academics, practitioners and non-governmental organisations (NGOs) overwhelmingly agree that human rights are sources and *raisons d'être* of international criminal justice.[77] The ICC appears to fulfil a dual human rights mandate. It promotes fair trial and high standards of detention as models for national systems and it employs the preventive, retributive and expressive functions of criminal sentences to promote human rights standards.[78]

So far, 123 states have ratified the Rome Statute and accepted the jurisdiction of the ICC over war crimes, crimes against humanity and genocide committed in their territory or by their nationals.[79] Moreover, the ICC can have jurisdiction over an offence irrespective of where it was committed or of the nationality link in the case of a referral by the UNSC acting under chapter VII of the UN Charter.[80] However, the fight to end impunity is not limited to prosecution in international fora. International criminal law purports to pervade the domestic level by encouraging national prosecution and the implementation of criminal law mechanisms against serious human rights violations. For this reason, the jurisdiction of the ICC is based on the principle of complementarity.[81] The Court has jurisdiction over international crimes when states are 'unwilling or unable genuinely to carry out the investigation or prosecution'.[82] While national justice systems have priority (as long as they prosecute), it is the ICC that makes the determination of whether national prosecutions are adequate.[83] In this way, states are induced to undertake effective criminal investigations and trials if they want to avoid the intervention of the ICC (positive complementarity).[84] Complementarity appears to encourage 'heterogeneity in terms of the number of institutions adjudicating international crimes, but homogeneity in terms of the process they follow and the punishment they mete out'.[85]

[76] R Roth and F Tulkens, 'Introduction' (2011) 9 *Journal of International Criminal Justice* 571, 571.

[77] K Lohne, 'NGOs for International Justice – Criminal or Victims' Justice?' in A Follesdal and G Ulfstein (eds), *The Judicialization of International Law: A Mixed Blessing?* (Oxford, Oxford University Press, 2018) 127; T Meron, *The Making of International Criminal Justice: The View from the Bench: Selected Speeches* (Oxford, Oxford University Press, 2011) ch 17.

[78] There is a large debate on the purposes and objectives of international criminal law. See, eg MA Drumbl, *Atrocity, Punishment, and International Law* (Cambridge, Cambridge University Press, 2007).

[79] Rome Statute, Art 12. In addition, 44 states have so far accepted the jurisdiction of the ICC over the crime of aggression.

[80] ibid Art 13.

[81] ibid Art 1; C Stahn and MM El Zeidy, *The International Criminal Court and Complementarity: From Theory to Practice* (Cambridge, Cambridge University Press, 2011).

[82] Rome Statute, Art 17.

[83] ibid.

[84] International Criminal Court Assembly of States Parties, 'Report of the Bureau on Stocktaking: Complementarity. Taking Stock of the Principle of Complementarity: Bridging the Impunity Gap' (18 March 2010) ICC-ASP/8/51, para 16.

[85] Drumbl (n 78) 143.

In general, the creation of international or deterritorialised forms of criminal jurisdiction is to be seen as an attempt to lift the obligations to punish human rights violations out of the politics and injustice associated with the national sphere.[86] International bodies are supposed to provide a neutral and apolitical response to chaotic local politics.[87] They administer criminal justice in external settings (eg in The Hague) and in a supposedly impartial manner, through universal rules and procedures.[88] They are also opposed to domestic political powers, which are seen as incapable of managing complex social problems, including the protection of human rights.[89] The assumption of the inadequacy of domestic justice has long remained unchallenged, especially throughout the 1990s.[90] However, in more recent years, critiques and limitations of trials on the international stage have fostered the creation of tribunals that exercise a hybrid criminal jurisdiction, by integrating both domestic and international structures.[91] Hybrid and internationalised institutions include the Sierra Leone Special Court; the Extraordinary Chambers in the Courts of Cambodia; the Special Crimes Panels in Kosovo, followed by the Kosovo Specialist Chambers and Specialist Prosecutor's Office; the Special Panels and Serious Crimes Unit in East Timor; the Special Tribunal for Lebanon; the War Crimes Chamber in Bosnia and Herzegovina; the Special Court in the Central African Republic; and the Extraordinary African Chamber.[92] While each of these tribunals is uniquely structured, they are all staffed by both domestic and international actors, and use domestic and international resources to prosecute international crimes. Generally, these institutions have primacy over national courts. Yet the territorial state retains some of its jurisdiction, by participating in the prosecutions as an equal partner.[93]

D. The Quasi-criminal Jurisdiction of Human Rights Bodies

During the last three decades, the Inter-American Court of Human Rights (IACtHR), the European Court of Human Rights (ECtHR), the UN Human Rights Committee (UNHRC) and other human rights bodies have interpreted their mandates to monitor compliance with international conventions as to enable the imposition of obligations on states in criminal matters.[94] These institutions

[86] McMillan, 'Imagining the International' (n 11) 166.
[87] Engle et al, *Anti-Impunity* (n 2) 5–6.
[88] Z Miller, 'Anti-Impunity Politics in Post-Genocide Rwanda' in ibid 150–51.
[89] ibid 159–62.
[90] C Stahn, *A Critical Introduction to International Criminal Law* (Cambridge, Cambridge University Press, 2019) 164–65.
[91] F Mégret, 'In Defense of Hybridity: Towards a Representational Theory of International Criminal Justice' (2005) 38 *Cornell International Law Journal* 725.
[92] Stahn (n 90) 197–210.
[93] Huneeus (n 8) 30.
[94] Pinto, 'Awakening the Leviathan' (n 6); A Seibert-Fohr, *Prosecuting Serious Human Rights Violations* (Oxford, Oxford University Press, 2009).

increasingly rely upon human rights law to supervise national prosecutions: they order states to ensure criminal accountability at the domestic level and to co-operate with other states in transnational criminal investigations, in a process that Alexandra Huneeus has named the 'quasi-criminal jurisdiction' of human rights bodies.[95] These bodies are not criminal courts and cannot find individual responsibility. Nevertheless, they influence how national justice systems exercise criminal jurisdiction over serious human rights violations and intervene when states appear unable or unwilling to act as required. While criminal jurisdiction is formally exercised in accordance with the territorial principle, national trials are triggered, guided and closely monitored from *above*. In this sense, not only do human rights bodies impact states' exercise of criminal jurisdiction, but they themselves take on a partially internationalised criminal jurisdiction.

First, human rights bodies impose obligations on states to criminalise serious human rights violations. The ECtHR, for instance, has developed a significant body of case law in this matter.[96] The seminal case is *X and Y v Netherlands*.[97] Here, the European judges held that the 'effective deterrence [that] is indispensable' to protect sexual integrity 'can be achieved only by criminal-law provisions'.[98] Following this decision, the state duty to criminalise human rights abuses has been reiterated in the sphere of sexual life,[99] but also with respect to the right to life,[100] for cases of torture and other ill-treatment,[101] for other offences against the person,[102] as well as for forced labour and human trafficking.[103] The IACtHR has also had an influence on the enactment of criminal legislation. In *Goiburú et al v Paraguay*, the Inter-American Court stated that the duty to protect the right to life, human treatment and personal liberty includes an obligation to criminalise serious violations of those rights.[104] Through their case law on criminalisation, human rights bodies require states to exercise prescriptive criminal jurisdiction, that is, to legislate in respect of persons and conduct within their territory. Strictly speaking, this jurisdiction remains territorial, but it is influenced by the decisions of an international human rights institution. These human rights-driven obligations to criminalise have had an impact insofar as states have been encouraged to introduce new offences in their domestic legal systems. In Italy, following an

[95] Huneeus (n 8).

[96] L Lavrysen and N Mavronicola (eds), *Coercive Human Rights: Positive Duties to Mobilise the Criminal Law under the ECHR* (Oxford, Hart Publishing, 2020); K Kamber, *Prosecuting Human Rights Offences: Rethinking the Sword Function of Human Rights Law* (Leiden, Brill, 2017); S Malby, *Criminal Theory and International Human Rights Law* (Abingdon, Routledge, 2020).

[97] *X and Y v Netherlands* [1985] App No 8978/80 (ECtHR).

[98] ibid 27.

[99] *MC v Bulgaria* [2003] App No 39272/98 (ECtHR) [150].

[100] *Kiliç v Turkey* [2000] App No 22492/93 (ECtHR) [62].

[101] *MC v Bulgaria* (n 99) [174].

[102] *KU v Finland* [2008] App No 2872/02 (ECtHR) [46].

[103] *Rantsev v Cyprus and Russia* [2010] App No 25965/04 (ECtHR) [285].

[104] *Goiburú et al v Paraguay* [2006] Series C No 153 (IACtHR) [84].

ECtHR decision, Parliament approved a Bill which introduced the crime of torture as a distinct offence in the Italian Criminal Code.[105] In the UK, ECtHR case law on state obligations to criminalise labour exploitation had an important role in the adoption of the Modern Slavery Act 2015 and related efforts to increase prosecution and conviction rates for human trafficking.[106]

Second, human rights bodies impose obligations on states to investigate, prosecute and, if appropriate, punish serious human rights violations. In the context of the Organisation of American States (OAS), *Velàsquez Rodríguez v Honduras* is not only the first IACtHR decision in a contentious case but also the leading case on the Court's invocation of criminal accountability.[107] The IACtHR found that states have a dual duty, namely to refrain from violations, but also to prevent, investigate and punish them, regardless of whether state authorities are directly involved in the abuse.[108] Yet the OAS institution did not order Honduras to adopt criminal sanctions as a remedy and acknowledged that 'The objective of international human rights law is not to punish those individuals who are guilty of violations'.[109] However, the authority of this statement did not last long. In the mid-1990s, the Inter-American Court started ordering states to effectively prosecute and punish individual perpetrators.[110] Today, the IACtHR case law refers to the failure to initiate criminal investigations and deploy criminal sanctions as a violation of human rights per se. In cases of torture and enforced disappearance, the duty to punish has even attained the status of *jus cogens*.[111]

The ECtHR also orders states to enforce their criminal law through 'thorough and effective investigation capable of leading to the identification and punishment of those responsible'.[112] In addition, the Council of Europe's Committee of Ministers, which is charged with monitoring that states comply with ECtHR rulings, has frequently declared that successful prosecution of individual cases is a prerequisite to a finding of compliance.[113] The UNHRC, for its part, has developed similar case law concerning the duty to institute criminal proceedings for the defence of human rights, including for arbitrary killing, enforced disappearance, torture and ill-treatment, sexual and domestic violence and human trafficking.[114] The UN Committee Against Torture is another human rights body which has consistently ordered states to investigate and punish acts of torture and

[105] D Carolei, 'Cestaro v. Italy: The European Court of Human Rights on the Duty to Criminalise Torture and Italy's Structural Problem' (2017) 17 *International Criminal Law Review* 567.

[106] M Pinto, 'Sowing a "Culture of Conviction": What Shall Domestic Criminal Justice Systems Reap from Coercive Human Rights?' in Lavrysen and Mavronicola (n 96).

[107] *Velásquez Rodríguez v Honduras* [1988] Series C No 4 (IACtHR).

[108] ibid [166].

[109] ibid [134].

[110] *Caballero-Delgado and Santana v Colombia* [1995] Series C No 22 (IACtHR) [72(5)].

[111] *Goiburú* (n 104).

[112] *Kaya v Turkey* [1998] App Nos 158/1996/777/978 (ECtHR) [107].

[113] Huneeus (n 8) 24–25.

[114] *General Comment No 31* [2004] CCPR/C/21/Rev1/Add13 (UN Human Rights Committee) [18].

ill-treatment.[115] Finally, it is worth noting the ongoing efforts to imbue the African Court on Human and Peoples' Rights with a fully fledged criminal jurisdiction through the Malabo Protocol.[116]

Insofar as human rights bodies mandate investigations, prosecutions and criminal sanctions, they also require states to exercise enforcement jurisdiction, which refers to the capacity of a state to enforce compliance with its laws or punishment for breach. Again, criminal jurisdiction remains territorial, although it is triggered and guided by an international body. Pursuant to human rights bodies' decisions, states have started new criminal investigations and prosecutions, overturned amnesties and created new institutions to facilitate criminal accountability.[117] In *Simón, Julio Héctor y Otros*, for instance, the Argentinian Supreme Court relied on the IACtHR case law to exclude the application of amnesty, statutory limitations and the principle of non-retroactivity.[118]

Third, the ECtHR has recently developed a duty on states to co-operate in the context of transnational criminal investigations of human rights violations. In *Güzelyurtlu and Others v Cyprus and Turkey*, Turkey was found in violation of the right to life due to its failure to co-operate with Cyprus and, in particular, for not providing a reasoned reply to the extradition requests submitted by Cypriot authorities.[119] The case concerned the investigation into the murder of three people which occurred in Cyprus when the main suspects had fled to the Turkish Republic of Northern Cyprus (TRNC). The European judges did not specify which jurisdiction would have been most appropriate for a criminal trial. However, while the Court held that Cyprus could refuse to waive its criminal jurisdiction in favour of TRNC, it found that Turkey had not complied with its obligation to co-operate – which would seem to support the principle of *aut dedere aut judicare*.[120] The ECtHR applied the same reasoning in *Romeo Castaño v Belgium*, where a murder suspect had fled from Spain to Belgium.[121] In that case, Belgian authorities were found to have violated the right to life as they failed to co-operate with their Spanish counterparts, who had sought to prosecute the suspect in Spain.[122]

[115] *Communication No 353/2008 (decision on Ukraine)* [2011] UN Doc CAT/C/47/D/353/2008 (UN Committee against Torture).

[116] S Nimigan, 'The Malabo Protocol, the ICC, and the Idea of "Regional Complementarity"' (2019) 17 *Journal of International Criminal Justice* 1005.

[117] Huneeus (n 8) 2; BD Tittemore, 'Ending Impunity in the Americas: The Role of the Inter-American Human Rights System in Advancing Accountability for Serious Crimes under International Law' (2005) 12 *Southwestern Journal of Law and Trade in The Americas* 429, 449–60.

[118] *Simón, Julio Héctor y Otros* [2005] Supreme Court of Argentina 17.768, S1767XXXVIII.

[119] *Güzelyurtlu and Others v Cyprus and Turkey* [2019] App No 36925/07 [ECtHR (GC)].

[120] S Malby, 'Deciding the Criminal Forum – Can the ECHR Contribute?' (presentation at the WG Hart Legal Workshop, 26–28 April 2021; unpublished paper on file with the author).

[121] *Romeo Castaño v Belgium* [2019] App No 8351/17 [ECtHR].

[122] For a critical comment, see M Pinto, 'Romeo Castaño: "Meticulously Elaborated Interpretations" for the Sake of Prosecution' (*Strasbourg Observers*, 10 September 2019) www.strasbourgobservers.com/2019/09/10/romeo-castano-meticulously-elaborated-interpretations-for-the-sake-of-prosecution/.

Finally, it is worth mentioning that, besides through the impositions of state obligations in criminal matters, human rights bodies have impacted or may impact criminal jurisdiction in a number of other ways. An example is through the right to a fair trial. In the context of transnational criminal cases involving cross-border co-operation, case law on the right to a fair trial may be expected to influence the choice of the criminal forum, especially when such a choice may affect the principle of equality of arms or the procedural and evidential fairness of the proceedings.[123] Another example concerns the principle of *ne bis in idem* (the right not to be tried or punished twice). By preventing a defendant from being tried more than once for the same criminal conduct in different states, case law on this principle could have a role in supporting the settling of conflicts of criminal jurisdiction. However, current interpretations of the *ne bis in idem* principle by both the ECtHR and the UNHRC prevent a person from being tried and punished again only by courts of the same state, and thus do not preclude a second prosecution and punishment for the same conduct in another state.[124] As a result, the case law on the *ne bis in idem* principle of these two human rights bodies may somehow offer a green light to extraterritorial trials (or, at least, fail to shine a red light), despite previous prosecutions of the same offences in other states.[125]

III. The Creation of Global Crime and Justice

Outside the case of universal jurisdiction, human rights are seldom mentioned as one of the reasons behind the growth of extraterritorial criminal jurisdiction in recent years. In fact, penal extraterritoriality is sometimes treated as a potential threat to human rights (especially defendants' rights) rather than one of their

[123] See Malby (n 120). Malby argues that the ECtHR is yet to develop a clear jurisprudence around the right to fair trial capable of influencing the choice of criminal forum.

[124] *Krombach v France* [2018] App No 67521/14 [ECtHR (dec)]; *General Comment No 32* [2007] CCPR/C/GC/32 (UN Human Rights Committee) [57]. See Malby (n 120). However, the *ne bis in idem* principle operates between states in the context of the European Union (Convention implementing the Schengen Agreement of 14 June 1985 [2000] OJ L239/19, Art 54; Charter of Fundamental Rights of the European Union [2000] OJ C364/1, Art 50). On the other hand, US law condones re-prosecutions under the dual sovereignty theory. See, eg AJ Colangelo, 'Double Jeopardy and Multiple Sovereigns: A Jurisdictional Theory' (2009) 86 *Washington University Law Review* 769; AJ Colangelo, '*Gamble*, Dual Sovereignty, and Due Process' (2019) *Cato Supreme Court Review* 189 (discussing the Supreme Court case of *Gamble*).

[125] For a critique of some of the case law of the ECtHR (and the Court of Justice of the European Union) on the principle of *ne bis in idem* in relation to issues of criminal jurisdiction, see M Ó Floinn, 'The Concept of Idem in the European Courts: Extricating the Inextricable Link in European Double Jeopardy Law' (2017) 24 *Columbian Journal of European Law* 75, 100–01: '[The principle of *ne bis in idem*] arbitrarily operates on a first-come first-served basis in the context of multijurisdictional offending, which may prevent prosecutions of individuals by states that have stronger normative claims.' See also G Lasagni and S Mirandola, 'The European ne bis in idem at the Crossroads of Administrative and Criminal Law' (2019) 2 *Eurocrim* 126.

by-products.[126] However, in the last few decades, human rights have not only made criminal law one of the main instruments for their promotion but have also allowed it to move across and beyond borders and have shaped how criminal jurisdiction is exercised to address human rights abuses. The use of human rights to trigger the application of criminal law transcends territorial boundaries because of potential detachments between the sites where proceedings are held, the nationality of the victims and offenders, and the location of the wrongdoings. It also transcends territorial boundaries because of the widespread belief that the universal conception of human rights mandates global justice – generally translated as the need for criminal accountability regardless of the context, implications and practicability.[127]

Since the 1970s, the rise of human rights has led to the emergence of a supposedly global sensibility for certain values deemed universal – in terms of their nature (as concerning every human being) and prescribed recognition (their being non-negotiable). In the most serious cases, conduct that infringes these values has been read in terms of legally proscribed crime rather than simply injustices and wrongdoings.[128] However, this is not ordinary crime: given the universality of the breached values, crime against human rights is discursively produced as *global* crime. Unlike transnational organised crime or cybercrime, for example, where it is the conduct that is supposedly of global reach, here it is the norm that is of global concern.[129] Yet, rather than being conceived as a product of human rights sensibilities and institutions, global crime is seen to pre-exist the former and authorise the existence of the latter.[130] The story goes that human rights violations were left unaddressed for centuries because they hid behind the shield of state sovereignty.[131] They were the most serious crimes but were not punished as no system of justice to prosecute them existed. This system – the story continues – was first created in 1945, then halted, but resumed in the early 1990s. Since then, the international community has managed to penetrate 'that powerful and historically impervious fortress – state sovereignty – to reach out to all those who live within the fortress'.[132]

Insofar as human rights abuses are framed as global crime, the most appropriate response to advance the human rights regime appears to be a system of global criminal justice – albeit still dependent to a very large extent on the coercive

[126] See, eg Ireland-Piper (n 47).

[127] LA Payne, 'The Justice Paradox?' in TC Halliday and G Shaffer (eds), *Transnational Legal Orders* (Cambridge, Cambridge University Press, 2015) 440–41.

[128] McMillan, 'Imagining the International' (n 11) 165.

[129] N McMillan, *Imagining the International: Crime, Justice, and the Promise of Community* (Stanford, Stanford University Press, 2020) 2.

[130] Similarly, in the context of international criminal law, McMillan, 'Imagining the International' (n 11) 168.

[131] A Cassese, 'Reflections on International Criminal Justice' (2011) 9 *Journal of International Criminal Justice* 271, 272.

[132] ibid 273.

and legal machinery of (some) states – rather than large-scale redistribution or a profound transformation of society.[133] Criminal law and legal processes that can penetrate the borders and the boundaries of territorial sovereignty are positioned as best able to defend human rights values wherever and whenever they are threatened. This has led to the de facto creation of a decentralised system of global criminal justice.[134] As seen in section II, it comprises national courts exercising universal jurisdiction and passive or active personality jurisdiction; ad hoc international and hybrid tribunals; a permanent international court; and human rights bodies which order states to undertake criminal prosecutions. Altogether, these institutions – and the individuals, NGOs and trans-governmental networks that push them to act – promote a global norm of criminal accountability for human rights violations.[135] This system is not completely settled. As Leigh Payne has observed, 'Although the duty to prosecute gross violations of human rights seems to be a clear mandate in international law, its application soon reveals its ambiguity'.[136] Trials for human rights violations are held at the national and supranational levels; yet most perpetrators do not face prosecution. Nonetheless, the fact that impunity for human rights abuses is still widespread around the world seems to be related to deficiency in effectiveness or power politics and less to an (open) rejection of the underlying norms and values.

The creation of a global system of crime and justice has not simply facilitated penal extraterritoriality. It is arguably affecting the normative foundations of criminal jurisdiction, albeit mainly for those crimes which are serious human rights violations.[137] Conventionally, criminal jurisdiction emanates from sovereign statehood. On the one hand, each state has a monopoly over the legitimate use of violence on its territory[138] and is prima facie prevented from intervening in matters that are essentially under another state's sovereignty.[139] On the other hand, international law envisages that states may prosecute conduct occurring outside their territorial boundaries in certain exceptional circumstances.[140] The conventional

[133] R Meister, *After Evil: A Politics of Human Rights* (New York, Columbia University Press, 2011) 1. See also McMillan, *Imagining the International* (n 129).

[134] J Savelsberg, 'The Anti-Impunity Transnational Legal Order for Human Rights: Formation, Institutionalization, Consequences, and the Case of Darfur' in G Shaffer and E Aaronson (eds), *Transnational Legal Ordering of Criminal Justice* (Cambridge, Cambridge University Press, 2020) 208.

[135] On global governance through a complex web of 'government networks' comprising, for example, police investigators, financial regulators, judges and legislators, see AM Slaughter, *A New World Order* (Princeton, Princeton University Press, 2005). On the internationalisation of crime control beyond the case of human rights prosecutions and international criminal law, see P Andreas and E Nadelmann, *Policing the Globe: Criminalization and Crime Control in International Relations* (Oxford, Oxford University Press, 2008).

[136] Payne (n 127) 446.

[137] See also Mégret, 'Do Not Do Abroad' (n 8) 39–40.

[138] M Weber, 'Politics as a Vocation' in HH Gerth and CW Mills (eds), *From Max Weber: Essays in Sociology* (London, Routledge, 1948) 78.

[139] AL Parrish, 'The Effects Test: Extraterritoriality's Fifth Business' (2008) 61 *Vanderbilt Law Review* 1455, 1463–64.

[140] See A Chehtman, 'The Presumption against Extraterritorial Criminal Jurisdiction', ch 1 in the present volume; Garrod, 'Extraterritorial Criminal Jurisdiction' (n 19).

perspective may appear overturned when it comes to the global system of crime and justice founded on human rights values. Rather than resting on sovereignty, the right to punish – and the related right to assert jurisdiction – may be said to derive from the global commitment to protect 'universal, indivisible and interculturally recognised human rights'.[141] This commitment, in turn, enables states to exercise penal functions to uphold and defend universal values not only on their territory but also abroad. It also gives normative legitimacy to international courts and tribunals to adjudicate in place of national courts.[142] In the words of Mégret, here 'international law comes first and, looking downward as it were, mandates that the criminal law be used for … the protection of basic human rights'.[143]

In a context where the principle of sovereignty is subordinated to that of humanity and human rights,[144] territorial jurisdiction may no longer be the rule and extraterritorial jurisdiction the exception. Rather, all states can be seen as having the same right to exercise jurisdiction over serious human rights abuses. They merely stand as proxies enforcing universal values on behalf of the international community.[145] If priority is given to the territorial state or otherwise, it is due to practical, rather than normative, considerations. For instance, proximity to crime may be an important factor for having domestic prosecutions, while the presence of the accused in another state or political pressures at the national level may be crucial in triggering the intervention of foreign or international courts.

IV. The Risks of a Value-Based Extraterritorial Penality

The expansion of extraterritorial jurisdiction in the last few decades has not been without controversy. Several commentators have argued that penal extraterritoriality has to be heavily restricted as it may lead to diplomatic tensions;[146] it

[141] K Ambos, 'Punishment without a Sovereign? The *Ius Puniendi* Issue of International Criminal Law: A First Contribution towards a Consistent Theory of International Criminal Law' (2013) 33 *OJLS* 293, 308.

[142] LDA Corrias and GM Gordon, 'Judging in the Name of Humanity: International Criminal Tribunals and the Representation of a Global Public' (2015) 13 *Journal of International Criminal Justice* 97.

[143] Mégret, 'Do Not Do Abroad' (n 8) 40.

[144] S Adelman, 'Cosmopolitan Sovereignty' in C Bailliet and K Franko (eds), *Cosmopolitan Justice and Its Discontents* (Abingdon, Routledge, 2011) 11.

[145] Cockayne (n 67) 520; S Graf, *The Humanity of Universal Crime: Inclusion, Inequality, and Intervention in International Political Thought* (Oxford, Oxford University Press, 2021) 3; McMillan, *Imagining the International* (n 129) 31. Roger Cotterrell argues that references to an 'international community' remain for the most part purely rhetorical because it is not grounded in any sociological inquiry about what 'community' might mean and what kind of existence it might have: see R Cotterrell, 'The Concept of Crime and Transnational Networks of Community' in V Mitsilegas, P Alldridge and L Cheliotis (eds), *Globalisation, Criminal Law and Criminal Justice: Theoretical, Comparative and Transnational Perspectives* (Oxford, Hart Publishing, 2015) 17.

[146] JA Zerk, 'Extraterritorial Jurisdiction: Lessons for the Business and Human Rights Sphere from Six Regulatory Areas' (2010) Corporate Social Responsibility Initiative Working Paper No 59, 1, 12.

is often normatively unjustified;[147] and it runs the risk of undermining procedural fairness for defendants.[148] With regard to extraterritorial prosecutions of human rights violations, realist scholars in international relations have criticised universal jurisdiction for interfering with transitions to democracy and peace,[149] or impinging upon other states' sovereignty.[150] Given the number of proceedings involving African leaders, some African governments have also argued that universal jurisdiction is a form of neocolonialism.[151] The same criticism has also been directed towards international criminal adjudication and, in particular, the ICC.[152] Yet the large majority of international organisations, NGOs, practitioners and commentators working in the area of human rights strongly favour assertions of penal extraterritoriality as an effective means of responding to human rights violations. They have become accustomed to requiring penal action for human rights abuses without interrogating what is involved in this process. While a global, human rights-driven penality may appear as the 'the most civilized response' to human rights violations,[153] it is nonetheless important to critically reflect on the risks it may entail.

In political theory, criminalisation and punishment are among the most salient manifestations of state authority.[154] Criminal law contributes to one of the ultimate aims of the state, that is, the provision of security and order.[155] Accordingly, the questions of what, when and how much a state should criminalise and punish primarily invite political answers related to how a state has to fulfil its security obligations. The boundaries of crime and the form of sanctions vary in different states according to their underlying political order. However, this construction staggers when criminalisation and punishment are made global endeavours. In the absence of a *world* state, the operation of global penality cannot rest on a political order. Rather, normative order is created by appeal to universal human rights values. Global, human rights-driven penality is grounded on a value-based order, which appears as universally recognised by, and adaptable to, all political contexts.[156] Here, resort to criminal law is no longer a political *decision* but a moral

[147] Chehtman, *The Philosophical Foundations* (n 9) 59.

[148] Ireland-Piper (n 47); M Farbiarz, 'Accuracy and Adjudication: The Promise of Extraterritorial Due Process' (2016) 116 *Columbia Law Review* 625, 627.

[149] J Snyder and L Vinjamuri, 'Trials and Errors: Principle and Pragmatism in Strategies of International Justice' (2004) 28 *International Security* 5.

[150] Kissinger (n 42).

[151] CC Jalloh, 'Universal Jurisdiction, Universal Prescription? A Preliminary Assessment of the African Union Perspective on Universal Jurisdiction' (2010) 21 *Criminal Law Forum* 1.

[152] KM Clarke, *Fictions of Justice: The International Criminal Court and the Challenge of Legal Pluralism in Sub-Saharan Africa* (Cambridge, Cambridge University Press, 2009).

[153] Cassese (n 131) 271.

[154] L Zedner, 'Penal Subversions: When Is a Punishment Not Punishment, Who Decides and on What Grounds?' (2016) 20 *Theoretical Criminology* 3, 10.

[155] See, eg T Hobbes, *Leviathan* (Oxford, Oxford University Press, 1996); C Beccaria, *Dei Delitti e Delle Pene* (Milan, Mursia, 1973); L Farmer, *Making the Modern Criminal Law: Criminalization and Civil Order* (Oxford, Oxford University Press, 2016).

[156] Ambos (n 141) 309.

obligation. It is not dependent upon the choices of a political community; rather, it springs spontaneously and boundlessly from universal moral values. The more sorts of behaviours come to be regarded as gross violations of human rights with the passage of time, the more criminal law grows and expands on the global stage. The fact, for instance, that business corruption and environmental damage have increasingly been considered human rights violations seems to have encouraged efforts to punish them on an extraterritorial basis.[157] Examples are the attempts to make 'ecocide' a crime subjected to international adjudication[158] or the efforts to extend the model of the UK Bribery Act 2010, which applies extraterritorially, to other business-related human rights abuses.[159]

Ironically, human rights-driven developments risk undermining sovereign protections based on the rule of law. In fact, a value-based global penality lacks the checks and balances of the democratic process that are present when criminal law is grounded in a political order.[160] Its foundation on human rights would in theory require that penal power be exercised *humanely* and in line with international human rights standards.[161] Yet the theory is one thing; how international and domestic courts operate in practice is another matter. The danger, far from being hypothetical, is that they may embrace illiberal criminal doctrine to ensure the punishment of human rights violations at all costs.[162] Even if due process standards were consistently observed, the reins of this value-based penality would remain very much loosened. As a moral obligation, the prosecution of the gravest human rights abuses is required in every circumstance.[163] This means that amnesties, pardons or statutes of limitations are unacceptable if they cover genocide, war crimes, crimes against humanity (including disappearances) or torture.[164] Any approach that would even imply a laxity towards the responsibility of human rights violators is rejected as it would question the seriousness of

[157] Similarly, Mégret, 'Do Not Do Abroad' (n 8) 35.

[158] See P Higgins, D Short and N South, 'Protecting the Planet: A Proposal for a Law of Ecocide' (2013) 59 *Crime, Law and Social Change* 251; 'Making Ecocide a Crime' (*Stop Ecocide International*) www.stopecocide.earth/making-ecocide-a-crime.

[159] Joint Committee on Human Rights, *Human Rights and Business 2017: Promoting Responsibility and Ensuring Accountability (sixth report)* (2016–17, HL 153, HC 443); D McMullan, 'Briefing: Is the UK Living Up to Its Business & Human Rights Commitments' (Business and Human Rights Resource Centre, 2015) www.media.business-humanrights.org/media/documents/files/UK_Briefing_-_FINAL.pdf: 'Given that the government has already seen the merit in pursuing criminal sanctions for bribery abroad (and given how closely related bribery & human rights abuses often are), there would appear to be a clear opportunity to extend this model to human rights abuses.'

[160] Similarly, in relation to the ICC, K Lohne, *Advocates of Humanity: Human Rights NGOs in International Criminal Justice* (Oxford, Oxford University Press, 2019) 12.

[161] K Lohne, 'Penal Welfarism "Gone Global"? Comparing International Criminal Justice to *The Culture of Control*' (2021) 23 *Punishment and Society* 3, 11.

[162] D Robinson, 'The Identity Crisis of Criminal Law' (2008) 21 *Leiden Journal of International Law* 925; GP Fletcher and JD Ohlin, 'Reclaiming Fundamental Principles of Criminal Law in the Darfur Case' (2005) 3 *Journal of International Criminal Justice* 539; Pinto, 'Awakening the Leviathan' (n 6); Pinto 'Sowing a "Culture of Conviction"' (n 106).

[163] M Jackson, 'Amnesties in Strasbourg' (2018) 38 *OJLS* 451.

[164] JE Méndez, 'Foreword' in Lessa and Payne (n 36) xxiii.

the wrong committed and jeopardise the universality of the values breached.[165] However, this assumption prevents important countervailing interests from being taken into account, even where they may militate against criminal prosecutions.[166] These may include political stability and peace, economic justice, reconciliation, the uncovering of historical truth and institutional reform.[167] The political community where human rights violations have occurred is also deprived of the opportunity to decide for itself how to deal with situations of serious wrongdoings – perhaps pursuing unconventional avenues to justice. For instance, in 1995, South Africa established a Truth and Reconciliation Commission (TRC), whose purpose was, amongst others, to grant amnesty and waive criminal and civil liability for those who disclosed their wrongdoings during the apartheid period, if associated with a political objective.[168] Yet, the South African TRC experience is no longer regarded as a legitimate model of justice. According to Juan Méndez, today the South African-style 'conditional amnesty' would be unacceptable if it covered the gravest human rights abuses.[169]

In addition, criminal law, albeit grounded in human rights in normative terms, never loses its penal character, notably its reliance on police control and incarceration, as well as its potential to be enforced disproportionately and arbitrarily.[170] While criminal prescription and adjudication can become global and extraterritorial, criminal enforcement is always very much rooted in the state system.[171] Both international and national courts rely on states' police forces to identify and arrest alleged perpetrators of human rights abuses. If their trials conclude with a guilty verdict, they need states' prisons where those convicted and sentenced can be sent.[172] The context of police brutality, harsh prison conditions and mass incarceration across many regions of the world would be expected to advise reflexivity and caution in invocations of global penality. However, the human rights discourse tends to move these concerns into the shadows. When justified in human rights terms, prosecutions and trials are generally portrayed as humanitarian, rather than punitive, endeavours.[173] In other words, human rights run the risk of conferring

[165] Similarly, D Celermajer, *The Prevention of Torture: An Ecological Approach* (Cambridge, Cambridge University Press, 2018) 13.

[166] CS Nino, 'The Duty to Punish Past Abuses of Human Rights Put into Context: The Case of Argentina' (1991) 100 *Yale Law Journal* 2619; J Zalaquett, 'Confronting Human Rights Violations Committed by Former Governments: Principles Applicable and Political Constraints' in Aspen Institute (ed), *State Crimes: Punishment or Pardon* (Queenstown, Aspen Institute, 1989).

[167] Jackson (n 163) 17.

[168] Promotion of National Unity and Reconciliation Act 1995, Art 3(1)(b) (SA).

[169] Méndez, 'Foreword' (n 164) xxiii.

[170] Similarly, McMillan, *Imagining the International* (n 129) 35.

[171] K Lohne, 'Penal Humanitarianism beyond the Nation State: An Analysis of International Criminal Justice' (2020) 24 *Theoretical Criminology* 145, 154.

[172] K Grady, 'Towards a Carceral Geography of International Law' in S Chalmers and S Pahuja (eds), *Routledge Handbook of International Law and the Humanities* (Abingdon, Routledge, 2021) 360.

[173] Similarly, in the context of international criminal law, McMillan, *Imagining the International* (n 129) 31.

legitimacy to punitiveness by covering it up with a moral gloss. Punitiveness led by human rights arrives in a progressive and enlightened guise, and is thus readily welcomed into the system, raising only minor criticism. While human rights actors have generally condemned overreliance on criminal justice led by populist rhetoric, such an expansion is instead demanded when criminal law is used in the name of human rights. The same individuals who criticise harsh conditions of imprisonment and overcriminalisation in the context of 'tough-on-crime' policies gladly accept extensive penal control to stop human rights violations around the world.

In so doing – and this is what is more concerning – human rights become a key vehicle both for the transnationalisation of punitive projects and for lending some states the opportunity to expand their coercive power beyond their borders.[174] Recent criminological contributions have shown how penal power already travels across national borders and geographic regions, especially from the Global North to the Global South.[175] Western intervention into southern countries' penal sectors is justified on humanitarian grounds and usually takes the form of 'penal aid' aimed at state-building efforts and migration control.[176] Penal extraterritoriality in the name of human rights may be seen as another example of this trend – a trend towards 'the expansion of sovereign power over familiar, racialized, subjects and places', with the aim of 'reasserting control, or at the very least, reimagining it, in places where' Western states once ruled.[177] Far from promoting social justice in every region of the world, human rights-led penal extraterritoriality ultimately risks perpetuating unequal global power structures.

V. Conclusion

Human rights are a driving force of penal extraterritoriality. They are at the basis of the growing importance of universal jurisdiction, whose purpose is to ensure that perpetrators of the most serious human rights abuses do not escape justice, and of the increased reliance on the passive and active personality principles. Human rights considerations have also underpinned the institution of new forms of jurisdiction which are, in one sense or another, deterritorialised or internationalised. One example is the creation of international criminal tribunals, which, since the

[174] Similarly, in relation to crimes against humanity, Graf (n 145) 3; in the context of the ICC, Lohne, *Advocates of Humanity* (n 160) ch 7.

[175] M Bosworth, 'Penal Humanitarianism? Sovereign Power in an Era of Mass Migration' (2017) 20 *New Criminal Law Review* 39; Lohne, 'Penal Humanitarianism beyond the Nation State' (n 171); EM Stambøl, 'Neo-Colonial Penality? Travelling Penal Power and Contingent Sovereignty' (2021) 23 *Punishment and Society* 536.

[176] K Brisson-Boivin and D O'Connor, 'The Rule of Law, Security-Development and Penal Aid: The Case of Detention in Haiti' (2013) 15 *Punishment and Society* 515; Bosworth (n 175).

[177] Bosworth (n 175) 15.

early 1990s, have exercised direct or complementary criminal jurisdiction when state justice systems have failed to prosecute international crimes committed on their territory. Another example is the 'quasi-criminal jurisdiction' of human rights bodies, which have begun to order and supervise national prosecutions when states are unable or unwilling to act.

While several explanations have been provided for the increased importance of extraterritorial criminal jurisdiction in recent years,[178] there is still scarce attention to the role of human rights in fostering this trend. Yet not only have they affected the issue of jurisdiction in several ways, but they have done so without this development being accompanied by adequate reflection on its normative foundations and potential adverse implications. Human rights do not merely foster penal extraterritoriality; they discursively produce the idea of *global* crime – namely crime against human rights values – which naturally requires a decentralised system of *global* justice to address it. In this context, criminal jurisdiction no longer appears to emanate from national sovereignty, but from the values of the international community. Hence, the focus shifts from territorial to extraterritorial jurisdiction.

However, a global, human rights-driven penality is not necessarily more benign and less problematic. Penality – whatever its source of legitimacy and jurisdictional reach – ultimately remains the exercise of the state's coercive power. Yet, when penality operates extraterritorially in the name of human rights, it may run free of the legal and political constraints that are present when jurisdiction is primarily territorial. It may also become a tool for expanding the coercive power of states – in particular, of certain states – beyond their borders that is readily welcomed into the system, raising only minor criticism.

[178] See, eg Ireland-Piper (n 47) 6, which mentions the internationalisation of institutions, finance and criminal activity due to globalisation.

PART II

Enforcement Jurisdiction

7

Enforcement Jurisdiction in A-territorial Spaces: Addressing Crime on the High Seas and in Cyberspace

CEDRIC RYNGAERT

I. Introduction

This contribution addresses jurisdictional shifts in criminal law enforcement in 'a-territorial' spaces. An a-territorial space is defined here as a space which is neither fully territorial, like a land area that could be cartographically mapped,[1] nor fully non-territorial, like outer space. A-territorial spaces have both extraterritorial and territorial characteristics. Their spatiality exceeds territorial boundaries, but also has territorial anchor points. Two a-territorial spaces stand out in this respect: the oceans and cyberspace. Oceans are globally interconnected bodies of water which are nevertheless enclosed by land and are ploughed by vessels registered in state territories. Cyberspace is a globally interconnected, technology-powered, digital space which is nevertheless connected to state territories through cables, servers and computers.[2]

[1] On the origins of cartographically mapped territory, over which states went on to exercise territorial sovereignty, see J Branch, *The Cartographic State: Maps, Territory, and the Origins of Sovereignty* (Cambridge, Cambridge University Press, 2014). On how we are accustomed to conceive of jurisdiction as territorial, see RT Ford, 'Law's Territory (A History of Jurisdiction)' (1999) 97 *Michigan Law Review* 843. See also Mireille Hildebrandt, 'Text-Driven Jurisdiction in Cyberspace', ch 2 in the present volume.

[2] I do not claim that the oceans and cyberspace are exactly the same in terms of jurisdiction and spatiality. Mireille Hildebrandt is correct when stating 'The boundaries of the high seas were determined by those of the land; there was no overlap. The boundaries of territory in the era of cyberspace are, however, liquid': M Hildebrandt, 'Extraterritorial Jurisdiction to Enforce in Cyberspace? Bodin, Schmitt, Grotius in Cyberspace' (2013) 63 *University of Toronto Law Journal* 196, 222. The high seas and cyberspace are certainly subject to different jurisdictional regimes. However, my point is that problems of enforcement jurisdiction beset both spaces precisely because of their a-territorial characteristics, namely the 'un-territoriality' of data and the location of the high seas beyond national (quasi-territorial) jurisdiction. On the un-territoriality of data, see in particular J Daskal, 'The Un-Territoriality of Data' (2015) 125 *Yale Law Journal* 326: 'The ease and speed with which data travels across borders, the seemingly arbitrary paths it takes, and the physical disconnect between where data is stored and where it is accessed critically test [the] foundational premises [of territoriality].' While it may possibly

The partly extraterritorial nature of a-territorial spaces may complicate the 'constitutional' allocation of state sovereignty and jurisdiction by the international community,[3] which largely revolves around physical territory. That said, these spaces' territorial moorings allow for remarkable forms of jurisdictional 'territorialisation'. As far as the oceans are concerned, following the adage 'the land dominates the sea',[4] coastal states exercise functional jurisdiction over maritime areas adjacent to their territory, namely the territorial sea, the contiguous zone, the exclusive economic zone and the continental shelf.[5] In addition, port states make use of territorial offences to address vessels' extraterritorial conduct which affects the global commons.[6] As far as cyberspace is concerned, states routinely base the assumption of prescriptive (also called 'legislative') criminal jurisdiction over cyber offences on the constituent elements or territorial ubiquity doctrines. This means that, when determining the geographical reach of their state's legislation, prosecutors and courts ascertain the territorial location of certain elements of a crime, with a view to – at least formally – exercising territorial jurisdiction.[7]

However, territorialisation only takes states so far. Especially as regards enforcement jurisdiction, which pertains to 'the authority of a state to exercise its power to compel compliance with the law' it has prescribed,[8] options to territorialise the extraterritorial are decidedly limited. According to the *Lotus* dictum of the Permanent Court of International Justice (PCIJ), enforcement jurisdiction 'cannot be exercised by a State outside its territory except by virtue of a permissive rule derived from international custom or from a convention'.[9] On the high seas, an area beyond national jurisdiction, a limited permissive rule has crystallised that allows the vessel's flag state – and only the flag state – to exercise enforcement jurisdiction.[10] International agreements may also allow states to exercise limited

go too far to characterise the data that travel through cyberspace as fully non-territorial, cyberspace is undoubtedly a place or space 'in between'.

[3] On the role of sovereignty in modern constitutional and international legal theory, see, eg B Fassbender, 'Sovereignty and Constitutionalism in International Law' in N Walker (ed), *Sovereignty in Transition* (Oxford, Hart Publishing, 2003) 115–44.

[4] *North Sea Continental Shelf (Federal Republic of Germany v Denmark)* (Merits) [1969] ICJ Rep 3 [96].

[5] *Maritime Delimitation in the Area between Greenland and Jan Mayen (Denmark v Norway)* (Merits) [1993] ICJ Rep 38 [80].

[6] S Kopela, 'Port State Jurisdiction, Extraterritoriality and the Protection of Global Commons' (2016) 47 *Ocean Development and International Law* 89.

[7] For an overview of German and English case law on prescriptive criminal jurisdiction exercised on the basis of the constituent elements approach, see J Hörnle, *Internet Jurisdiction: Law and Practice* (Oxford, Oxford University Press, 2021) ch 5. On territorialisation by the USA, see D Brown, 'Extraterritorial Ambit through Offence Definitions, Technology and Economic Power', ch 3 in the present volume.

[8] American Law Institute, *Restatement of the Law Fourth: The Foreign Relations Law of the United States* (Philadelphia, American Law Institute, 2018) § 401(c).

[9] *The Case of the SS Lotus (France v Turkey)* PCIJ Rep Series A No 10 [18]–[19].

[10] United Nations Convention on the Law of the Sea (Montego Bay, 10 December 1982) 1833 UNTS 3 (UNCLOS), Art 92(1).

forms of enforcement jurisdiction, such as arrests, on other states' territory.[11] But as a general matter, unlike with respect to prescriptive jurisdiction, there is in principle no opportunity to rely on a 'constituent elements approach' in the law of enforcement jurisdiction. This means that states are not allowed to enforce their laws extraterritorially via constructed territorial 'hooks': as soon as one state's official enters another state's territory purporting to exercise enforcement power therein without the latter's consent, international law is violated.[12]

The prohibition of extraterritorial enforcement jurisdiction may stifle all manner of criminal investigations and prosecutions, even ones that are primarily territorial, but in respect of which evidence may be located abroad. It is not uncommon these days that criminal evidence is located outside the prosecuting state's territory, namely in the form of data on servers or other devices. In principle, the prosecuting state will have to obtain the sought data from the state of establishment of the relevant service provider or from the state where the data are stored on a server, but that state may not always be co-operative, and mutual legal assistance procedures may prove too cumbersome. Moreover, the location of the data may be uncertain ('loss of location'). The end result may then be a situation of impunity. The risk of impunity also follows from the limited legal opportunities to exercise enforcement jurisdiction on the high seas. On the high seas, flag states have exclusive enforcement jurisdiction, but they do not and cannot always discharge their enforcement responsibilities. The oceans are vast expanses of water; vessels may fly no flag at all (stateless vessels); and flag states may have limited resources or lack willingness to adequately monitor their vessels.

This explains why some states have decided to 'go it alone' and have exercised extraterritorial enforcement jurisdiction in apparent excess of what international law currently authorises. On the high seas, law enforcement authorities of states other than the flag state have taken enforcement action to tackle the smuggling of migrants and drugs.[13] In cyberspace, they have ordered Internet Service Providers (ISPs) to produce data stored abroad, and have even accessed such data directly via governmental hacking techniques without obtaining the consent of the state of data location.[14]

Conspicuously, when justifying their enforcement action in jurisdictional terms, states appear to rely on the principles of *prescriptive* rather than *enforcement* jurisdiction. For instance, they draw on the constituent elements approach from the law of prescriptive jurisdiction to justify their exercise of enforcement

[11] eg Commission, 'Proposal for a Council Recommendation on Operational Police Cooperation' COM (2021) 780 final, s 2.1(b)(iii), authorising officers from the competent law enforcement authority of one Member State conducting cross-border hot pursuits into another Member State's territory to, inter alia, 'stop, arrest or provisionally detain a suspect, including through means of coercion and physical force, pending the arrival of officers of the competent authorities of the Member State in whose territory the hot pursuit took place'.

[12] M Akehurst, 'Jurisdiction in International Law' (1972–73) 46 *British Yearbook of International Law* 145.

[13] This is explained further in s II.

[14] This is explained further in s III.

jurisdiction. This is understandable to the extent that prescriptive principles are more malleable. Under the *Lotus* dictum, extraterritorial enforcement jurisdiction is prohibited plain and simple (absent consent). But extraterritorial prescriptive jurisdiction is allowed in the case of a genuine connection, which includes partial territorial conduct or effects; the nationality of the perpetrator or victim; or the gravity of the crime.[15] My key claim in this chapter is that permissive principles of prescriptive jurisdiction offer the resources for more expansive assertions of extraterritorial enforcement jurisdiction aimed at tackling transnational crime. This jurisdictional shift is blurring the traditional distinction between the international law of prescriptive and enforcement jurisdiction.

This shift is inchoate, however, as only a limited number of states are explicitly pushing for change. Therefore, we find ourselves in a situation of 'a-legality', which, in the words of legal philosopher Hans Lindahl, 'denotes behaviour that calls into question the distinction itself between legality and illegality as drawn by a legal order in a given situation'.[16] This is 'the experience of *estrangement*: what participating actors cannot simply understand as (il)legal' (emphasis added) – which, however, also intimates the possibilities of another legal order.[17] The situation of a-legality regarding extraterritorial enforcement jurisdiction may subsist for some time, as it is presently unclear whether this novel legal order will truly materialise, and in particular around what jurisdictional norms the wider international community will coalesce.

This chapter examines the (alleged) shift in criminal law enforcement practices as regards smuggling on the high seas (section II) and in cyberspace (section III). Section IV concludes. The emphasis lies on the international legal norms that states, including their courts, cite as legal authority for their enforcement practices. The first claim is that states rely, at least in part, on permissive principles of prescriptive jurisdiction to justify their assertions of enforcement jurisdiction. In so doing, they collapse the distinction between both types of jurisdiction. The second claim is that the attendant expansion of extraterritorial enforcement jurisdiction may be justified under carefully defined circumstances.

II. Prescription Informing Enforcement: Smuggling on the High Seas

There are only limited options for states to exercise extraterritorial enforcement over crimes committed on the high seas. Article 92(1) of the UN Convention on the Law of the Sea (UNCLOS) provides that ships sailing under the flag of a state

[15] American Law Institute, *Restatement Fourth* (n 8) § 407.

[16] H Lindahl, *Fault Lines of Globalization: Legal Order and the Politics of A-Legality* (Oxford, Oxford University Press, 2013) 30–31.

[17] ibid 37–38.

'shall be subject to its exclusive jurisdiction on the high seas'.[18] On an exceptional basis, non-flag states can also exercise enforcement jurisdiction on the high seas, on the basis of Article 105 UNCLOS; UN Security Council (UNSC) resolutions adopted under chapter VII of the UN Charter; or ship-boarding agreements. Article 105 UNCLOS allows 'every State', on the high seas, to 'seize a pirate ship or aircraft, or a ship or aircraft taken by piracy and under the control of pirates, and arrest the persons and seize the property on board', ie to exercise enforcement jurisdiction over such ships.[19] Relevant UNSC resolutions allow UN Member States to interdict vessels falling foul of maritime embargoes, which includes the exercise of enforcement jurisdiction.[20] Such embargoes typically concern arms deliveries, eg to Somalia or Libya,[21] and are enforced by national and multinational naval operations.[22] Ship-boarding agreements are agreements in which the flag state authorises the requesting state to exercise particular forms of extraterritorial enforcement jurisdiction over the former's vessels.[23]

All in all, however, options for non-flag state enforcement jurisdiction remain limited. This has led some states to exercise enforcement jurisdiction over crimes on the high seas outside the aforementioned conventional legal framework, in particular over the smuggling of migrants and of internationally controlled drugs. Also, illegal, unreported or unsustainable fishing has been mentioned as a crime

[18] It is widely understood that this exclusivity pertains to enforcement jurisdiction: AN Honniball, 'The Exclusive Jurisdiction of Flag States: A Limitation on Pro-active Port States?' (2016) 31 *International Journal of Marine and Coastal Law* 499. However, the International Tribunal for the Law of the Sea (ITLOS) recently held that it also extends to prescriptive criminal jurisdiction: *MV 'Norstar' (Panama v Italy)* (Judgment of 10 April 2019) ITLOS Reports 2019, 25, [224]–[225]. The judgment was accompanied, however, by a strongly worded dissenting opinion signed by seven judges, who submitted at [19] that 'nothing in the text of the Convention, in its *travaux préparatoires*, in other international treaties, in customary international law, or in the practice of States suggests that article 87 and its corollary article 92 [UNCLOS] altogether excludes the right of non-flag States to exercise their prescriptive criminal jurisdiction with respect to activities on the high seas'. Whether the view of ITLOS adequately reflects international law remains to be seen. International arbitral tribunals may well take a different view.

[19] It is not fully clear whether such authority exists in relation to the maritime slave trade. UNCLOS, Art 110 only provides for the right to visit vessels engaging in the slave trade, but UNCLOS, Art 99 provides that 'Any slave taking refuge on board any ship, whatever its flag, shall *ipso facto* be free'. It has been argued that any state has the authority to detain the ship, but that 'jurisdiction to prosecute is not as well settled'; indeed, UNCLOS, Art 99 cites the responsibilities of the flag state in this respect: see R McLaughlin, 'Authorizations for Maritime Law Enforcement Operations' (2016) 98 *International Review of the Red Cross* 465, 484.

[20] M Frostad, 'United Nations Authorized Embargos and Maritime Interdiction: A Special Focus on Somalia' in G Andreone (ed), *The Future of the Law of the Sea* (Cham, Springer Nature, 2017) 213, 230, submitting that, where individuals 'have been acting in violation of a UNSC-authorized embargo, it might seem proper to use any valid criminal option available'.

[21] UNSC Res 2182 (24 October 2014) UN Doc S/RES/2182; UNSC Res 2292 (14 June 2016) UN Doc S/RES/2292.

[22] In March 2020, the EU launched a new naval mission ('Irini') to police the arms embargo against Libya, replacing Operation Sophia. See J Barigazzi, 'EU Launches Naval Mission to Police Libya Arms Embargo' (*Politico*, 26 March 2020) www.politico.eu/article/eu-launches-naval-mission-to-police-libya-arms-embargo/, explaining that 'Irini will have a tighter geographic scope and other features to reduce the risk of it acting as a "pull-factor" for migrants'.

[23] See United Nations Convention against Illicit Traffic in Narcotic Drugs and Psychotropic Substances (Vienna, 20 December 1988) 1582 UNTS 95, Art 17, also discussed below.

that should be amenable to more far-reaching enforcement, although practice is still lacking.[24]

In order to justify their enforcement measures with regard to smuggling, it appears that states have recourse to the customary international law principles of *prescriptive* jurisdiction, which offer more options for the exercise of extraterritorial jurisdiction. In so doing, states can break down the barriers between the law of prescriptive and enforcement jurisdiction.

In sub-section A below, I discuss relevant European practice regarding migrant smuggling, whereas in sub-section B, I discuss US practice regarding drug smuggling. In sub-section C, I address the international lawfulness of more liberal law enforcement practices on the high seas.

A. Migrant Smuggling: The European Experience

Europe is confronted with large-scale migrant smuggling at sea, especially in the Mediterranean.[25] To address smuggling practices, the Council of the EU stated in a Common Position that EU Member States participating in an EU naval operation in the Mediterranean (EUNAVFOR MED Operation Sophia, now Irini) may, on the high seas, interdict vessels suspected of smuggling migrants 'where the vessel is without nationality, and may take appropriate measures against the vessel, persons and cargo'.[26] Such 'appropriate measures' could well consist of the arrest or detention of vessels and persons or the confiscation of cargo, as the case may be. The legal basis for this extraterritorial enforcement jurisdiction is not clear, however.

Prima facie, the legal basis for such action is UN Security Council Resolution 2240 (2015), which has been renewed multiple times. This resolution authorises states to seize vessels confirmed as being used for migrant smuggling or human

[24] The most far-reaching form of extraterritorial enforcement over international, unreported and unregulated (IUU) fishing is that members of regional fisheries management organisations or arrangements can allow each other to board and inspect fishing vessels flying their flag: Agreement for the Implementation of the Provisions of the United Nations Convention on the Law of the Sea Relating to the Conservation and Management of Straddling Fish Stocks and Highly Migratory Fish Stocks (New York, 4 August 1995) 2167 UNTS 3, Art 21. More expansive enforcement could, however, be contemplated, as IUU fishing may be considered a serious offence. On criminalisation of IUU fishing, see A Stefanus, 'Fishing for Solutions: Criminalisation of IUU Fishing through Suppression Conventions at Global and Regional Levels' (PhD thesis, Utrecht University, 2021). For an argument in favour of extraterritorial enforcement authority of stateless vessels engaged in IUU fishing, see DM Warner-Kramer and K Canty, 'Stateless Fishing Vessels: The Current International Regime and a New Approach' (2000) 5 *Ocean and Coastal Law Journal* 227.

[25] For data on migrant smuggling, see Global Migration Data Analysis Centre, 'Smuggling of Migrants' (International Organization for Migration, 6 May 2021) www.migrationdataportal.org/themes/smuggling-migrants.

[26] Council Decision (CFSP) 2015/778 of 18 May 2015 on a European Union Military Operation in the Southern Central Mediterranean (EUNAVFOR MED) [2015] OJ L122/31, para 7. For a discussion, see M Gestri, 'EUNAVFOR MED: Fighting Migrant Smuggling under UN Security Council Resolution 2240 (2015)' (2016) 25 *Italian Yearbook of International Law* 21.

trafficking from Libya, and allows them to take 'further action with regard to such vessels', including disposal.[27] Rob McLaughlin has argued that the resolution permits maritime law enforcement agencies 'to assert sufficient jurisdiction over [these vessels] in order to take follow-on action'.[28] On closer inspection, however, the resolution does not explicitly provide for arrest and detention of *persons*, only the *inspection* of stateless vessels,[29] and provides that further action 'will be taken in accordance with applicable international law with due consideration of the interests of any third parties who have acted in good faith'.[30]

The applicable international law to which reference was made in Resolution 2240 is arguably UNCLOS and the Migrant Smuggling Protocol, which is a Protocol to the UN Convention on Transnational Crime.[31] These treaties do not allow for extraterritorial enforcement jurisdiction on the high seas with respect to migrant smuggling. Regarding stateless vessels, Article 110 UNCLOS provides that foreign warships only have the right to *visit* (board).[32] Article 8(7) of the Migrant Smuggling Protocol creates some more room for manoeuvre, providing that:

> A State Party that has reasonable grounds to suspect that a vessel is engaged in the smuggling of migrants by sea and is without nationality or may be assimilated to a vessel without nationality may [not only] board and search the vessel [but also shall], [i]f evidence confirming the suspicion is found … take appropriate measures in accordance with relevant domestic and international law.

It is the term 'appropriate measures' which was cited in the above-mentioned EU Common Position. In addition, in the 2014 *Hani* case (so far the only relevant court case), the Italian Court of Cassation based Italy's enforcement jurisdiction over migrant smuggling on the Migrant Smuggling Protocol.[33] However, as

[27] UNSC Res 2240 (9 October 2015) UN Doc S/RES/2240, para 8.

[28] McLaughlin (n 19) 483.

[29] UNSC Res 2240, para 5. In respect of 'further action', paras 7–8 only refer to flag states (requiring that 'Member States and regional organisations make good faith efforts to obtain the consent of the vessel's flag State prior to using the authority').

[30] ibid para 8. For a similar critical reading of UNSC Res 2240, see TAC Coventry, 'Appropriate Measures at Sea: Extraterritorial Enforcement Jurisdiction over Stateless Migrant Smuggling Vessels' (2019) 7 *Maritime Safety and Security Law Journal* 27; E Papastavridis, 'EUNAVFOR *Operation Sophia* and the International Law of the Sea' (2016) 2 *Maritime Safety and Security Law Journal* 69.

[31] Protocol against the Smuggling of Migrants by Land, Sea and Air, supplementing the Convention against Transnational Organized Crime (New York, 15 November 2000) 2241 UNTS 480.

[32] UNCLOS, Art 29 defines a warship as 'a ship belonging to the armed forces of a State bearing the external marks distinguishing such ships of its nationality, under the command of an officer duly commissioned by the government of the state and whose name appears in the appropriate'. Civilian maritime law enforcement vessels are not warships. However, it is not excluded that a state's coast guard uses military vessels or warships for enforcement purposes. For China, see S Sakamoto, 'China's New Coast Guard Law and Implications for Maritime Security in the East and South China Seas' (*Lawfare Blog*, 16 February 2021) www.lawfareblog.com/chinas-new-coast-guard-law-and-implications-maritime-security-east-and-south-china-seas.

[33] *In the Matter of Criminal Proceedings against Hani*, Final appeal judgment, No 36052/2014 ILDC 2412 (IT 2014), 20 August 2014, para 2 (basing enforcement jurisdiction inter alia on 'the right to visit ships without nationality on the high seas provided for by Articles 110(1)(d) and 91 of the UNCLOS', as well as 'Articles 7 and 8(2) of the Supplementing Protocol against the Smuggling of Migrants, which

Thea Coventry argued, inter alia on the basis of a close analysis of the *travaux préparatoires* of the Protocol, it is doubtful whether the term 'appropriate measures' was actually meant to include far-reaching powers of enforcement jurisdiction, such as arrest, on the high seas.[34]

In the absence of a legal basis in treaty law, enforcement jurisdiction over migrant smuggling on the high seas can only be justified on the basis of customary international law.[35] It is conspicuous in this respect that the Italian Court in *Hani* apparently doubted the existence of a treaty basis for extraterritorial enforcement jurisdiction over migrant smuggling, and instead resorted additionally to the customary principles of prescriptive jurisdiction in order to justify enforcement. The Court held that 'According to international law, state jurisdiction entails the authority to adopt coercive measures pursuant to a state's national law unless these were in violation of universally recognised fundamental principles'.[36] This clearly echoes the PCIJ's dictum on the legality of prescriptive jurisdiction in the *Lotus* case.[37] Elsewhere in the *Hani* judgment, cues can be found regarding the relevant

entitled states to intercept and take appropriate measures against vessels whenever there were reasonable grounds to suspect that they were engaging in the smuggling of migrants by sea, regardless of whether they flew the flag of another state or whether they were ships without nationality'). *Hani* pertained to the arrest by Italian law enforcement authorities of the Egyptian captain of a stateless vessel smuggling migrants on the high seas, and the captain's subsequent trial in Italy.

[34] Coventry (n 30) 17–19. The Protocol does not further define 'appropriate measures' and the Protocol's parent convention, the UN Convention on Transnational Organized Crime (UNTOC), pointedly does not explicitly provide for jurisdiction over stateless vessels arrested on the high seas (UNTOC, Art 15 *a contrario*). Papastavridis, 'EUNAVFOR' (n 30) 70 is of the view that the diversion of the suspected smugglers to the ports of Italy was lawful under UNSC Res 2240, that enforcement jurisdiction was only exercised in Italian ports and that the relevant issue is only one of prescriptive jurisdiction. According to Papastavridis, prescriptive jurisdiction could arguably be exercised on the basis of UNTOC, Art 16(10) in conjunction with UNTOC, Art 15(3). UNTOC, Art 16(10) provides that 'A State Party in whose territory an alleged offender is found, if it does not extradite such person in respect of an offence to which this article applies solely on the ground that he or she is one of its nationals, shall, at the request of the State Party seeking extradition, be obliged to submit the case without undue delay to its competent authorities for the purpose of prosecution'. UNTOC, Art 15(3) provides that 'For the purposes of article 16, paragraph 10, of this Convention, each State Party shall adopt such measures as may be necessary to establish its jurisdiction over the offences covered by this Convention when the alleged offender is present in its territory and it does not extradite such person solely on the ground that he or she is one of its nationals'. However, it is unlikely that these clauses are relevant, as the presumed offender is unlikely to have Italian nationality. UNTOC, Art 15(4) provides that 'Each State Party may also adopt such measures as may be necessary to establish its jurisdiction over the offences covered by this Convention when the alleged offender is present in its territory and it does not extradite him or her', irrespective of his nationality, but the Italian Court of Cassation decided in 2020 that this provision is not self-executing: *In the Matter of Criminal Proceedings against Youssef Tartoussi*, Final appeal judgment, No 19672/2020, ILDC 3171 (IT 2020), 17 June 2020. Regardless, UNSC Res 2240 only provides explicit authority for diversion of vessels. The better view is arguably that the smugglers were already arrested and detained on the high seas and not just in Italian ports. Accordingly, they were subject to extraterritorial enforcement jurisdiction.

[35] Note that UNTOC, Art 15(6) does not exclude more far-reaching jurisdictional assertions, provided such jurisdiction is in keeping with customary international law.

[36] *Hani* (n 33) 5.

[37] *Lotus* (n 9) [19]; M Bo, 'Case Analysis: *In the Matter of Criminal Proceedings against Hani*, Final appeal judgment, No 36052/2014 ILDC 2412 (IT 2014), 20 August 2014' (ORIL, 25 September 2015) para A10: 'it should be noted that the concept of jurisdiction in Anglo-Saxon systems embraces

principles of prescriptive jurisdiction that the Court envisaged. When pointing out that 'by disembarking migrants onto ill-suited vessels, migrants' lives were put into serious danger',[38] the Court hinted at the exercise of universal jurisdiction, which tends to be justified on the basis of the gravity of the crime rather than on any link with the prosecuting state.[39] And when drawing attention to the 'circumstance that would require the intervention on the part of the nearest coastal state, ie Italy',[40] the Court may have nodded to the protective principle.[41]

The universality and protective principles are principles belonging to the law of prescriptive jurisdiction. Whether reliance on these principles in the context of enforcement jurisdiction regarding migrant smuggling on the high seas is legally convincing is a different question, which will be addressed in section IIC. But the point made here is that, from a legal perspective, the EU and at least one Italian court appear to ground the legality of assertions of enforcement jurisdiction on principles drawn from the law of prescriptive jurisdiction. From a policy perspective, such enforcement appears to be based on the urgent political imperative, nurtured by sustained popular pressure, for Europe to 'do something' about the thousands of irregular migrants dying each year when crossing the Mediterranean.[42]

B. Drug Smuggling: The US Experience

A similar extension of extraterritorial enforcement jurisdiction takes place in the context of drug smuggling. This is particularly the case in the USA, which, acting under the Maritime Drug Law Enforcement Act (MDLEA) and the Drug Trafficking Vessel Interdiction Act, exercises both enforcement and prescriptive jurisdiction over stateless vessels involved in drug smuggling on the high seas off the US coast, as well as over foreign-flagged vessels insofar as flag state consent has been secured.[43] The USA commits considerable resources to such operations.[44]

legislative, adjudicatory, and enforcement jurisdiction … The Court's reference to the concept of jurisdiction in international law, while discussing the legality of the coercive measures against Hani, arguably evidenced the questionable legal basis of enforcement measures against stateless ships suspected of being engaged in migrants' smuggling.'

[38] *Hani* (n 33) 2.

[39] Princeton Project on Universal Jurisdiction, *The Princeton Principles on Universal Jurisdiction* (S Macedo ed, Princeton, Princeton University Press, 2001): Principle 1.1 states that 'universal jurisdiction is criminal jurisdiction based solely on the nature of the crime, without regard to where the crime was committed, the nationality of the alleged or convicted perpetrator, the nationality of the victim, or any other connection to the state exercising such jurisdiction'.

[40] *Hani* (n 33) 2.

[41] Coventry was of the view that the Court's position was based on either the universality or protective principle. See Coventry (n 30) 27–28. However, in all fairness, the judgment itself does not explicitly posit that migrant smuggling on the high seas threatens the security of Italy.

[42] F Alagna, 'From Sophia to Irini: EU Mediterranean Policies and the Urgency of "Doing Something"' (2020) 32 *Istituto Affari Internazionali*.

[43] Respectively 46 USC §§ 70501–07 and Pub L 122 Stat 4296. See further Brown (n 7).

[44] See M Spetalnick and P Stewart, 'Trump Doubles U.S. Military Assets in Caribbean, Bolstering Drug Fight after Maduro Indictment' (*Reuters*, 1 April 2020).

Just as with migrant smuggling, there is no clear treaty basis for extraterritorial enforcement jurisdiction over stateless vessels involved in drug smuggling on the high seas. As already stated, under Article 110 UNCLOS, foreign warships only have the right to visit (board) stateless vessels, not to exercise enforcement jurisdiction.[45] Relevant treaties only require states to 'co-operate' in the suppression of illicit traffic in narcotic drugs, without providing for extraterritorial enforcement or prescriptive jurisdiction.[46] Ship-boarding agreements between the flag state and the enforcing state may provide for additional enforcement powers. For instance, Article 17(4) of the 1988 UN Convention against Illicit Traffic in Narcotic Drugs and Psychotropic Substances provides that:

> In accordance with … treaties in force between them or in accordance with any agreement or arrangement otherwise reached between those Parties, the flag State may authorize the requesting State to, *inter alia*:
>
> (a) board the vessel;
> (b) search the vessel;
> (c) if evidence of involvement in illicit traffic is found, take appropriate action with respect to the vessel, persons and cargo on board.

Such 'appropriate action' may include powers of arrest, but such powers should certainly not be presumed.[47]

In the absence of unambiguous treaty authorisation to take extraterritorial enforcement action, courts and commentators have resorted to the customary principles of prescriptive jurisdiction to ascertain the legality not only of US prescriptive jurisdiction, but also of US extraterritorial enforcement jurisdiction.[48] Various US courts have defended the wide jurisdictional scope of the MDLEA, in terms of both prescription and enforcement, on the ground that drug trafficking aboard vessels on the high seas threatens US security, thereby resorting to the protective principle.[49] Other courts have relied on universality, citing the universal criminalisation of drug smuggling.[50] Some commentators have justified assertions

[45] ED Papastavridis, 'Crimes at Sea: A Law of the Sea Perspective' in ED Papastavridis and KN Trapp (eds), *Crimes at Sea* (Hague Academy of International Law, Leiden, Brill Nijhoff, 2014) 30: 'any State may exercise the right of visit on these vessels, but not to assert also jurisdiction'.

[46] UNCLOS, Art 108; UN Convention against Illicit Traffic in Narcotic Drugs and Psychotropic Substances (n 23) Art 17.

[47] See notably *Georgiev*, Final appeal judgment, No 13596/2019, ILDC 3009 (IT 2019), 28 March 2019, H4: 'The Dutch judicial authorities had not authorized the Italian *Guardia di Finanza* to take personal enforcement measures against the crew members [suspected of drug smuggling]. The authorization was limited to allowing the Italian authorities to board and inspect the ship.'

[48] Courts and commentators also engage at length with the constitutionality of extraterritorial enforcement and prescription. In particular, US courts have held that the MDLEA is validly based on the US Congress's authority to define and punish felonies on the high seas and offences against the law of nations: see Art I, s 8, cl 10 for the relevant clause in the US Constitution. For relevant case law, see, eg *United States v Ledesma Cuesta*, 347 F.3d 527, 532 (3d Cir 2003).

[49] See *United States v Cardales* 168 F.3d 548, 553 (1st Cir 1999); *United States v Sinisterra* No 06-15824, 2007 WL 1695698, *3 (11th Cir 2007).

[50] *United States v Salcedo-Ibarra* 2009 WL 1953399 (MD Fla 6 July 2009).

under the MDLEA on the basis of a combined application of the protective and universality principles.[51] Others simply cite a vessel's status as stateless, which would arguably subject it to the jurisdiction of all states,[52] even if this is internationally contested.[53] These arguments in favour of a wide jurisdictional scope have been met with some resistance in the USA itself, for that matter. Some US courts require demonstration of a more specific nexus between the offence and the USA.[54] Also, commentators have been pushing back against broad interpretations of the protective and universality principles.[55]

Regardless of the merits of this US discussion, what is striking at this point is (i) that the arguments made by proponents as well as detractors are couched in terms of principles of prescriptive jurisdiction and (ii) that these arguments are used to make sense not just of US prescriptive jurisdiction, but also of US enforcement jurisdiction on the high seas. The implication is that the doctrinal distinction between enforcement and prescriptive jurisdiction collapses. Absent conventional authorisation, the exercise of enforcement jurisdiction tends to be justified by principles drawn from the law of prescriptive jurisdiction. The debate appears to be limited to the exact conditions of application of these principles. Is there a real security threat? Is drug smuggling a universal jurisdiction crime? Similar reasoning can be found in the context of cybercrime enforcement, which I will address in section III.

C. The International Lawfulness of Liberal Law Enforcement on the High Seas

European and US legal practice regarding smuggling, of both migrants and drugs, demonstrates that principles of prescriptive jurisdiction are being transposed to the realm of enforcement jurisdiction. From a utilitarian law enforcement

[51] AJ Casavant, 'In Defense of the U.S. Maritime Drug Law Enforcement Act: A Justification for the Law's Extraterritorial Reach' (2017) 8 *Harvard National Security Journal* 191, 224–25.

[52] AHA Soons, 'Law Enforcement in the Ocean' (2004) 3 *WMU Journal of Maritime Affairs* 3, 13; *United States v Caicedo*, 47 F.3d 370, 372 (9th Cir 1995). Colangelo, focusing on notice to defendants (ie due process), does not consider it 'arbitrary or fundamentally unfair' to exercise extraterritorial – in fact, universal – jurisdiction over stateless vessels: AJ Colangelo, 'What Is Extraterritorial Jurisdiction?' (2014) 99 *Cornell Law Review* 1303, 1328. In case of flag state consent, Colangelo sees no sovereignty problems, but mentions potential fair notice concerns on the ground that the individual defendant may not have expected US law to apply: AJ Colangelo, 'Spatial Legality' (2015) 107 *Northwestern University Law Review* 69, 109.

[53] A Bennett, 'That Sinking Feeling: Stateless Ships, Universal Jurisdiction, and the Drug Trafficking Vessel Interdiction Act' (2012) 74 *Yale Journal of International Law* 443, 461; McLaughlin (n 19) 486.

[54] For an overview, see C Doyle, 'Extraterritorial Application of American Criminal Law' (Congressional Research Service, 31 October 2016). See also *United States v Angulo-Hernandez* 576 F.3d 59, 61 (1st Cir 2009) (Torruella J dissenting from denial of *en banc* review).

[55] SM Chaissan, '"Minimum Contacts" Abroad: Using the International Shoe Test to Restrict the Extraterritorial Exercise of United States Jurisdiction under the Maritime Drug Law Enforcement Act' (2007) 38 *University of Miami Inter-American Law Review* 641, 665; N Bialostozky, 'Extraterritoriality

perspective, this transposition is understandable, as the law of prescriptive jurisdiction is more permissive than the law of enforcement jurisdiction: as soon as some jurisdictional nexus (in particular security) is present, maritime law enforcement authorities could arrest and seize stateless vessels, as well as persons and cargo on board.[56] Some would even go as far as to state that enforcement jurisdiction could be exercised over stateless vessels without any jurisdictional nexus, ie a form of universal jurisdiction.[57]

Thea Coventry has understandably questioned whether the state practice underpinning these 'liberal' views on enforcement jurisdiction is sufficiently uniform to buttress a customary international law norm.[58] Indeed, it is mostly European states and the USA which, for reasons of capacity and political willingness, engage in extraterritorial law enforcement operations regarding offences of smuggling. The concern is that reliance on their sole practice may lead to 'hegemonic modification of custom'.[59]

At the same time, it is of particular relevance that the sort of enforcement jurisdiction discussed in this section has not led to substantial international protest. Still, this is hardly surprising, as in the case of jurisdiction over stateless vessels there is no (flag) state to protest in the first place, whereas in the case of jurisdiction over foreign-flagged vessels, as exercised by the USA under the MDLEA, any foreign state protest has been pre-empted by the USA securing flag state consent via bilateral ship-boarding arrangements.

The danger of hegemonic modification of custom should certainly be acknowledged. However, it should not be overstated. As I have argued elsewhere in the context of prescriptive jurisdiction, a unilateral jurisdictional assertion is far less intrusive if it gives effect to shared international norms,[60] in particular norms that have been laid down in widely ratified treaties, such as the Migrant Smuggling Protocol or the Drug Trafficking Convention. What prima facie looks like unilateralism may then, on closer inspection, just be the enforcement of a multilaterally shared norm. Precisely because of international agreement on the need to suppress smuggling, states may be granted some leeway in the interpretation of the scope of their jurisdictional powers.[61] And precisely by exercising their jurisdiction,

and National Security: Protective Jurisdiction as a Circumstance Precluding Wrongfulness' (2014) 52 *Columbia Journal of Transnational Law* 618, 660; E Kontorovich, 'Beyond the Article I Horizon: Congress's Enumerated Powers and Universal Jurisdiction over Drug Crimes' (2009) 93 *Minnesota Law Review* 1191.

[56] D Guilfoyle, 'The High Seas' in DR Rothwell et al (eds), *The Oxford Handbook of the Law of the Sea* (Oxford, Oxford University Press, 2015) 218.

[57] ibid.

[58] Coventry (n 30) 28.

[59] ibid.

[60] C Ryngaert, *Selfless Intervention: The Exercise of Prescriptive Jurisdiction in the Common Interest* (Oxford, Oxford University Press, 2020).

[61] Put differently, underlying substantive norms of international law may impact the scope of jurisdictional principles. See also Casavant (n 51) 224–25; *cf United States v Pizzarusso* 388 F.2d 8, 10 (2d Cir 1968).

they contribute to the effectiveness of the multilateral regime. Maggie Gardner has usefully defined this phenomenon as 'channelled unilateralism'.[62] Admittedly, only more powerful states may in practice exercise jurisdiction, but as Gardner has observed, 'given the multilateral framework, the powerful state need not be a hegemon. In fact, channelled unilateralism should work well in a multipolar world as a tool for sharing the burden of building transnational criminal law regimes.'[63] Indeed, without first movers exploring the outer boundaries of their jurisdiction, international norms may remain under-enforced, and transnational criminal law conventions may remain ineffective.[64]

Ultimately, extraterritorial enforcement jurisdiction over smuggling on the high seas appears to be reasonable if a number of conditions are met: (i) the status of a vessel as stateless; (ii) the existence of a connecting factor drawn from the law of prescriptive jurisdiction (notably security); as well as (iii) the fact that smuggling is criminalised by widely ratified transnational criminal law conventions.

III. Enforcement Jurisdiction in Cyberspace

A relaxation of the prohibition of extraterritorial enforcement jurisdiction, under the influence of the principles of prescriptive jurisdiction, can also be witnessed with respect to another 'a-territorial' space: cyberspace. The issue is whether law enforcement authorities gathering evidence in a criminal investigation can access data that may be held abroad on a server or other form of computer device. In principle, these agencies will have to rely on mutual legal assistance treaties to obtain access. However, these multilateral processes are often seen as too cumbersome.[65] Instead, authorities may be tempted to make use of direct or indirect means of unilaterally accessing such data. They may either remotely access a device abroad, eg via governmental 'hacking' of a computer, or they may order an intermediary, such as an ISP, to produce the data stored abroad. There is an ongoing discussion, fuelled by court decisions and regulatory changes, especially in Europe and the USA,[66] as to whether such techniques are in keeping with

[62] As Maggie Gardner has observed, such a treaty 'changes the conversation: some options now look more legal': M Gardner, 'Channeling Unilateralism' (2015) 56 *Harvard International Law Journal* 297, 301.

[63] ibid 346.

[64] Gardner also gives the example of the enforcement of anti-bribery treaties: ibid 325–32.

[65] Hörnle, *Internet Jurisdiction* (n 7) 158.

[66] US Clarifying Lawful Overseas Use of Data (CLOUD) Act, Pub L 115-141, 132 Stat 348; Commission, 'Proposal for a Regulation of the European Parliament and of the Council on European Production and Preservation Orders for Electronic Evidence in Criminal Matters' COM (2018) 225 final; Commission, 'Proposal for a Directive of the European Parliament and of the Council Laying Down Harmonised Rules on the Appointment of Legal Representatives for the Purpose of Gathering Evidence in Criminal Proceedings' COM (2018) 226 final. For an overview of relevant evolutions in the USA, the EU and Australia, see J Daskal, 'Privacy and Security across Borders' (2019) 128 *Yale Law Journal Forum* 1029.

international law, in particular the law of enforcement jurisdiction. Jurisdictional conservatives may be of the view that the *Lotus*-based prohibition of enforcement jurisdiction amounts to a total bar on states unilaterally accessing data stored abroad.[67] However, most voices are more nuanced and see windows in international law for such practices.[68] It is striking in this respect that these voices frame such windows, at least in part, by the law of prescriptive jurisdiction. This is obviously no surprise, since, as mentioned above, the permissive principles of prescriptive jurisdiction provide more leeway for extraterritorial action. The upshot, however, is a conflation of prescriptive and enforcement jurisdiction, with the latter being justified by recourse to principles traditionally governing the former.

This conflation is understandable to the extent that the – at times coincidental – territorial location of digital data on a particular server, without any other substantial link with the territorial state, cannot reasonably be considered as determinative of enforcement jurisdiction. These issues are brought into even starker relief in case of loss of location, where any territorial grounding may be only fleeting, or inexistent in the case of floating data centres. As long as mutual legal assistance procedures remain unsatisfactory, states may have to be granted some limited authority to secure evidence abroad, with a view to effectively combating transnational (cyber)crime. Such authority can be derived from connecting factors drawn from the law of prescriptive jurisdiction.

In sub-section A below, I argue that, at least as far as production orders are concerned, the conflation of prescription and enforcement has its roots in an older US practice of extraterritorial discovery orders in civil matters. In sub-section B, I outline how states and their courts rely on permissive principles of prescriptive jurisdiction to justify expansive practices of extraterritorial enforcement jurisdiction. In sub-section C, I explain how they resort to the same law of prescriptive jurisdiction to limit overbroad assertions of enforcement jurisdiction. Ultimately, what is key is that extraterritorial enforcement jurisdiction is exercised *reasonably*, with respect for foreign states' interests and fundamental rights.

[67] See M Zoetekouw, 'Internationaalrechtelijke aspecten van het wetsvoorstel Computercriminaliteit III' (2017) 1 *Tijdschrift voor Internetrecht* 30. Zoetekouw only discusses extraterritorial network searches, however.

[68] See J Kleijssen and P Perri, 'Cybercrime, Evidence and Territoriality: Issues and Options' in M Kuijer and W Werner (eds), *Netherlands Yearbook of International Law 2016: The Changing Nature of Territoriality in International Law* (The Hague, Asser Press, 2017) 147–73; J Daskal, 'Transnational Government Hacking' (2020) 10 *Journal of National Security Law and Policy* 677, 700. See also English court decisions upholding the admissibility of evidence in England acquired in the EncroChat operation, in which French police, through servers based in France, had sent an implant to all EncroChat devices in the world under cover of an apparent update, which caused the device to transmit to the French police all the data held on it: *R (C) v DPP* [2020] EWHC Admin 2967 [46], [50] (the court dismissing the defendant's argument that 'There was no operative lawful authority for the extraterritorial interference with the UK-located handsets by French authorities'); *A v R* [2021] EWCA Crim 128 [79] (concluding that 'the EncroChat material was stored by or in a telecommunications system when it was intercepted', and hence was admissible before English courts under English law).

A. Extraterritorial Discovery as Indirect Enforcement Jurisdiction

The discussion of states' authority to access data held abroad is not entirely new. In fact, the discussion predates the Internet era. Especially in the 1970s and 1980s, US courts regularly ordered defendants over whom they had personal jurisdiction to produce documents held abroad under threat of subpoena, eg in matters of anti-trust or securities fraud.[69] Such 'civil discovery' is not so different from ordering an ISP over whom a state has personal jurisdiction to produce a customer's digital data (eg email content) held abroad.[70]

It was never fully clarified how, conceptually speaking, such orders could be justified under the law of jurisdiction.[71] Some courts have considered them to be instances of territorial jurisdiction.[72] The Norwegian Supreme Court, for example, held in the *Tidal* case, which concerned Norwegian law enforcement authorities downloading 'source codes' from a server in the USA during a search in Norway, that 'it is clear that Norwegian authorities have enforcement jurisdiction over the Norwegian company and its employees present in this country', and that 'On these grounds, Norwegian authorities may order the company and these persons to provide the information necessary for Norwegian authorities to access the data'.[73] Other courts, in contrast, have considered such orders to be extraterritorial in nature, and thus off-limits. Most notably, the UK Supreme Court, in *R (KBR) v SFO*, relying on the presumption against extraterritoriality, ruled that the UK Parliament had not intended to give the UK Serious Fraud Office the extraterritorial power to compel a non-UK person to produce documents held outside the UK, and that it was immaterial that there was a 'sufficient connection' between that person and the UK.[74]

Arguably, FA Mann's characterisation of discovery orders as amounting to indirect extraterritorial enforcement jurisdiction is most convincing.[75] After all,

[69] See *United States v Bank of Nova Scotia I* 619 F.2d 1384 (11th Cir 1982); *SEC v Banca della Svizzera Italiana* 92 FRD 111 (SDNY 1981).

[70] C Ryngaert, 'Conflicts of Jurisdiction over Orders to Produce Documents Located Abroad: Reappraising "Conflict of International Jurisdiction: Ordering the Production of Documents in Violation of the Law of the Situs" (Ivo Onkelinx 1971-I)' [2015] *Revue belge de droit international* 423.

[71] C Ryngaert, *Jurisdiction in International Law*, 2nd edn (Oxford, Oxford University Press, 2015) ch 3.7. Tellingly, the commentary to the American Law Institute, *Restatement of the Law Third: The Foreign Relations Law of the United States* (Philadelphia, American Law Institute, 1987) § 442 limited itself to blandly stating that discovery 'is an exercise of jurisdiction'.

[72] See one of the earlier discovery cases in the USA: *Adidas Canada v SS Seatrain Bennington* F Supp 1984 WL 423, 2 (SDNY 1984). Relevant practice is not limited to US courts. In the context of banking supervision, see also, eg Dutch Case 16/113 *DNB v MTE*, ECLI:NL:CBB:2018:2, para 5.2.

[73] *Tidal Music AS v Public Prosecution Authority* HR-2019-610-A (Case no 19-010640STR-HRET), 28 March 2019, para 68. Accordingly, the judge could not 'see that the search will affect another state to an extent that it constitutes a violation of the principle of sovereignty' (para 71).

[74] *R (KBR, Inc) v Director of the Serious Fraud Office* [2021] UKSC 2, overturning an earlier decision of the High Court.

[75] See FA Mann, *The Doctrine of International Jurisdiction Revisited after Twenty Years* (The Hague, Martinus Nijhoff, 1985) 49.

the documents or data to which the orders ultimately relate are located outside the territory of the issuing state. Conceiving of transnational discovery orders as indirectly extraterritorial does not itself shed much light on their validity, however. To determine validity, a contextual analysis will always be called for. For instance, law enforcement agencies ordering access from employees coupled with actual searches by police officers (ie the *Tidal* scenario) may be more controversial than the classic discovery orders that are served on a parent company for execution by employees of a foreign subsidiary, where the relevant documents are located.

For our purposes, it is conspicuous, in any event, that courts in favour of 'extraterritorial' discovery have tended to tie its legality to the legality of the jurisdictional assertion over the underlying subject matter.[76] Put differently, enforcement is considered as parasitic on prescription. In addition, principles belonging to the realm of prescriptive jurisdiction, especially jurisdictional reasonableness (which requires balancing the different interests involved), have been relied on to justify or mitigate the extraterritorial scope of discovery orders.[77]

B. Prescriptive Principles Supporting Expansive Enforcement Jurisdiction

The collapse of a clear jurisprudential distinction between enforcement and prescription in the field of extraterritorial discovery orders has now materialised in the field of cyberspace as well. Sure enough, courts and commentators may simply deny that orders for the production of data held abroad are captured by the *Lotus* prohibition of enforcement jurisdiction, as law enforcement agents do not set foot on foreign territory to obtain these data.[78] However, realising that such a crude argument is unlikely to sway opponents, recourse is often had to an additional device drawn from the law of prescriptive jurisdiction. This is typically done in an implicit manner, ie there is no formal reliance on prescriptive jurisdiction. However, the tactic is undeniable.

[76] See, eg the UK's brief as amicus curiae in *Rio Tinto Zinc Corportation and Others v Westinghouse Electric Corporation* [1978] AC 547, 589–95; G Marston, 'United Kingdom Materials on International Law 1979' (1979) 50 *British Yearbook of International Law* 283, 355; *SEC v Banca della Svizzera Italiana* 92 FRD 111 (SDNY 1981); M Böse, *An Assessment of the Commission's Proposal on Electronic Evidence* (Brussels, European Parliament, 2018) 31.

[77] Many US extraterritorial discovery decisions were based on balancing the interests of the USA, the foreign country and the private litigants involved. See, eg H Buxbaum, 'Assessing Sovereign Interests in Cross-Border Discovery Disputes: Lessons from *Aérospatiale*' (2003) 38 *Texas International Law Journal* 87; A Lowenfeld, *International Litigation and the Quest for Reasonableness* (Oxford, Clarendon Press, 1996) 9. Reasonableness was famously codified in American Law Institute, *Restatement Third* (n 71) § 403, which governed the exercise of prescriptive jurisdiction.

[78] OS Kerr and SD Murphy, 'Government Hacking to Light the Dark Web: What Risks to International Relations and International Law?' (2017) 70 *Stanford Law Review Online* 58, 66.

Take, for instance, the Belgian Supreme Court judgment in *Yahoo! Inc v Belgium*,[79] which pertained to a Belgian public prosecutor's effort to obtain subscriber information held by US-based ISP Yahoo. After making the predictable argument that production orders do not 'require Belgian police officers or magistrates, nor [any] persons acting on their behalf to be physically outside the jurisdiction',[80] the Court added that Belgian law applied to 'any operator or service provider that actively directs [its] economic activity to consumers in Belgium',[81] as a result of which Belgium could order Yahoo to disclose data to Belgian law enforcement authorities. This is a 'targeting' approach that appears to be a combination of the *territorial effects doctrine* and *the passive personality principle*,[82] both of which belong to the law of prescriptive jurisdiction. Thus, the Court's argument appears to be that Belgian law enforcement agents can exercise enforcement jurisdiction as soon as an ISP's activities affect Belgian territory and/or individuals in Belgium. Similar arguments were made in a subsequent case in which Belgian law enforcement agencies had ordered Luxembourg-based Skype to disclose the content of communications linked to a Skype account: such an order was valid, in part, because Skype was '[target]ing Belgian consumers on the Belgian economic market'.[83]

Another example is section 39(2B) of the Singapore Code of Criminal Procedure, which provides that 'where the police officer or authorised person knows that the computer mentioned in that subsection is located outside Singapore, or does not know whether that computer is located in or outside Singapore, the police officer or authorised person' may exercise enforcement powers if 'the owner of that computer consents to the exercise of those powers'. This clause appears to draw on the personality principle of the law of prescriptive jurisdiction, insofar as it allows transnational searches where the owner of the data or the computer consents and it elevates this personal consent over a foreign

[79] *Yahoo! Inc v Belgium* Hof van Cassatie (Supreme Court of Belgium, 1 December 2015), No P.13.2082.N, translated in J Vandendreissche, 'Case Translation: Belgium' (2016) 13 *Digital Evidence and Electronic Signature Law Review* 156.

[80] ibid [6].

[81] ibid [8].

[82] The effects doctrine originates in US antitrust law. See *United States v Alcoa* 148 F.2d 416 (2d Cir 1945). A state can exercise passive personality jurisdiction over offences of which its victims are nationals. On the combined application of both principles in the context of extraterritorial data privacy law, see C Ryngaert and M Taylor, 'The GDPR as *Global* Data Protection Regulation' (2020) 114 *American Journal of International Law Unbound* 5. In the field of data, 'targeting', as a variation on effects, was famously espoused by the European Court of Justice in Case C-131/12 *Google Spain SL and Google Inc v Agencia Española de Protección de Datos (AEPD) and Mario Costeja González* ECLI:EU:C:2014:317, [2014] 3 CMLR 50. This case concerned the exercise of prescriptive jurisdiction by Spain over US-based Google, in the context of the right to erasure (delisting requests). See also DJB Svantesson, 'Extraterritoriality and Targeting in EU Data Privacy Law: The Weak Spot Undermining the Regulation' (2015) 5 *International Data Privacy Law* 226.

[83] *Public Prosecutor v Skype*, Tribunal de Première Instance (Tribunal of First Instance, 27 October 2016) No. ME20.F1.105151-12, paras 1.2–1.5; confirmed by Court of Appeal Antwerp, 15 November 2017, Case No 2016/CO/1006.

state's sovereign interest not to have extraterritorial enforcement take place on its territory.[84] A similar rule is, for that matter, stated in Article 32 of the Cybercrime Convention, which provides that

> [a] Party may, without the authorisation of another Party … access or receive, through a computer system in its territory, stored computer data located in another Party, if the Party obtains the lawful and voluntary consent of the person who has the lawful authority to disclose the data to the Party through that computer system.[85]

Enforcement jurisdiction piggybacking on permissive principles of prescriptive jurisdiction also appears to be the US approach under Rule 41 of the US Federal Rules of Criminal Procedure, which provides that

> a magistrate judge with authority in any district where activities related to a crime may have occurred has authority to issue a warrant to use remote access to search electronic storage media and to seize or copy electronically stored information located within or outside that district [including outside the US] if … the district where the media or information is located has been concealed through technological means.[86]

Under this Rule, as soon as there is prescriptive territorial jurisdiction ('authority in any district where activities related to a crime may have occurred'), the relevant judge may issue a warrant to unilaterally seize data regardless of location. Admittedly, the Department of Justice (DOJ) takes the view that 'should the media searched prove to be outside the United States, a warrant would have no extraterritorial effect'.[87] However, in case of loss of knowledge of actual location, in practice, such a warrant may have exactly this effect, to the extent that it eventually turns out that the searched computer *is* located on the territory of another state.[88] Accordingly, also in relation to data stored extraterritorially, under US Rule 41, enforcement appears to be parasitic on prescription.

The literature has also defended this parasitism. For instance, Marianne Hirsch Ballin, frustrated by narrow interpretations of the *Lotus* principle, has proposed drawing inspiration from the law of prescriptive jurisdiction when determining the legality of extraterritorial network searches (ie direct access of automated

[84] I thank Micheál Ó Floinn for pointing this out to me.

[85] Budapest Convention on Cybercrime (European Treaty Series No 185). See also Cybercrime Convention Committee, 'T-CY Guidance Note #3: Transborder Access to Data (Article 32)' (Council of Europe, 2014).

[86] US Federal Rules of Criminal Procedure (2016), r 41(B)(6).

[87] Letter from Mythili Raman, Acting Assistant Attorney General, US Department of Justice, to Reena Raggi, Chair, Advisory Committee on the Criminal Rules (18 September 2013) 5.

[88] M Rauschecker, 'Rule 41 Amendments Provide for a Drastic Expansion of Government Authority to Conduct Computer Searches and Should Not Have Been Adopted by the Supreme Court' (2017) 76 *Maryland Law Review* 1085, 1100. The DOJ does not discount this possibility, but requires that reasonable efforts be used 'to identify whether the computer to be searched is located inside or outside the United States'; the DOJ goes on to state that 'If there is reason to believe that the computer is in a specific foreign country, prosecutors should consult with the Office of International Affairs about appropriate coordination with foreign law enforcement partners as well as potential diplomatic and sovereignty issues before performing a remote search': DOJ, *Justice Manual*, para 9-13.525.

networks, eg by means of hacking techniques).[89] In this context, she referred to the *travaux préparatoires* of new Dutch legislation regarding such searches, in which the Dutch government implied that extraterritorial investigations could be carried out in respect of suspects abroad who had presumably committed criminal acts in the Netherlands.[90] Again, in this reasoning, the legality of enforcement jurisdiction is simply a function of the legality of prescriptive jurisdiction over the underlying offence: as soon as a law enforcement agency can establish its prescriptive jurisdiction over an offence, it automatically has the power to order the disclosure of information which it deems relevant to investigate the offence and prosecute the offender, and/or perform extraterritorial searches.

C. Prescriptive Principles Limiting Expansive Enforcement Jurisdiction

It bears notice that, if enforcement is parasitic on prescription, the scope of production orders and network searches may dramatically expand, as prescriptive jurisdiction can often be established relatively easily, especially in respect of activities in cyberspace which have connections with multiple states.[91] Such parasitism ultimately appears to be based, as de Hert et al have argued, on arguments of law enforcement utilitarianism, with little attention being paid to the interests of foreign states or individuals.[92]

If enforcement simply follows prescription, jurisdictional overreach may loom large. This realisation has, in turn, led to a quest to limit the scope of enforcement jurisdiction, ie to restrict a state's unilateral access to foreign-based evidence. Strikingly, again, recourse has been had to long-standing limiting principles of prescriptive jurisdiction, this time to circumscribe the reach of enforcement jurisdiction. Thus, the principles have been suggested to limit a state's extraterritorial access to those data which belong to its own citizens and residents, or at least to persons with a nationality other than the state of data location.[93] This is an application of the personality principle. Other voices have advocated a limitation to evidence which supports investigations 'into (almost) universally penalised

[89] MFH Hirsch Ballin, 'De rol van grenzen bij opsporing: grenzeloze inzet van opsporingsbevoegdheden?' ['The Role of Boundaries in Investigation: Boundless Exercise of Investigatory Powers?'] [2018] *Ars Aequi* 462, 466.

[90] Ibid, citing Wet Computercriminaliteit III [Act on Cybercrime III], *Kamerstukken II* 2015/16, 34372, 3, 49–50.

[91] For a critique of the overbroad assertions of jurisdiction to which the application of the permissive principles of prescriptive jurisdiction can give rise, see DJB Svantesson, *Solving the Internet Jurisdiction Puzzle* (Oxford, Oxford University Press, 2017).

[92] P de Hert et al, 'Legal Arguments Used in Courts Regarding Territoriality and Cross-Border Production Orders: From Yahoo Belgium to Microsoft Ireland' (2018) 9 *New Journal of European Criminal Law* 326, 352.

[93] See J Daskal, 'Borders and Bits' (2018) 71 *Vanderbilt Law Review* 179, 229. See also US Cloud Act, 18 USC § 2523(b)(4)(A).

serious crimes, such as child pornography'.[94] This echoes the universality principle. The Law Commission of England and Wales takes the more general position that extraterritorial searches are permissible as long as 'a sufficient or substantial connection [exists] between certain subject-matter (persons or property) and their own jurisdiction'.[95] This is a nod to the genuine connection requirement, which is, according to the Fourth Restatement of the US Foreign Relations Law, the basic principle of prescriptive jurisdiction.[96] The literature has also suggested the application of a case-by-case interest-balancing test, with a view to ascertaining whether a state has a sufficiently strong connection to, or sovereign interest in, accessing extraterritorial evidence.[97] This is akin to an application of the principle of jurisdictional reasonableness.

Reasonableness also undergirds the legitimacy of search warrants under Rule 41 of the US Federal Rules of Criminal Procedure. In fact, the position of the US Department of Justice is that the very 'existence of the warrant would support the reasonableness of the search'.[98] The animating idea here is that the intervention of a judge, who ascertains whether law enforcement agencies have sufficiently demonstrated probable cause that evidence of a crime will be found, suffices to guarantee the reasonableness of search warrants. However, it is doubtful whether mere judicial intervention, without any additional limitations and protections, can ensure the reasonableness of extraterritorial enforcement jurisdiction.[99]

The takeaway point is that principles of prescriptive jurisdiction, such as territoriality, personality, universality, genuine connection and reasonableness, have come to draw the contours of permissible enforcement jurisdiction in cyberspace. This appears to collapse the doctrinal distinction between the prescription and enforcement regimes. On the one hand, this collapse has been facilitated by doubts over the exact jurisdictional categorisation of production orders: do such orders amount to assertions of (extraterritorial) enforcement jurisdiction or just prescriptive jurisdiction? On the other hand, even if such orders do amount to enforcement jurisdiction, it has dawned on many law-applying agencies and observers that a rigid application of the *Lotus* enforcement prohibition fails to address serious threats posed by and in cyberspace. In that context, it is only logical to reach for more liberal principles of prescriptive jurisdiction, which allow for limited forms of extraterritoriality. In the end, only a jurisdictional purist would

[94] B Koops and M Goodwin, 'Cyberspace, the Cloud, and Cross-Border Criminal Investigation: The Limits and Possibilities of International Law' (Tilburg University, 2015) Tilburg Law School Research Paper No 5/2016, 6. See also Kerr and Murphy (n 78).

[95] *Search Warrants* (Law Com No 396, 2020), para 16.79.

[96] American Law Institute, *Restatement Fourth* (n 8) § 407.

[97] PS Berman, 'Legal Jurisdiction and the Deterritorialization of Data' (2018) 71 *Vanderbilt Law Review En Banc* 11, 28.

[98] Letter from Mythili Raman to Reena Raggi (n 87) 5.

[99] On possible challenges to warrants by non-resident aliens, see R Bercovitz, 'Law Enforcement Hacking: Defining Jurisdiction' (2021) 121 *Columbia Law Review* 1251.

lament the dissolution of the boundaries between prescriptive and enforcement jurisdiction. A realist should admit that, because of technological evolutions, the law of jurisdiction may have to, and should, evolve too.[100] In fact, the checks and balances offered by the law of prescriptive jurisdiction, which comprises first-order permissions (territoriality, nationality, universality) and second-order limitations (connection, reasonableness), may be well suited for a tailored delimitation of enforcement jurisdiction in cyberspace.

What jurisdictional principles, whether or not borrowed from the law of prescriptive jurisdiction, do or should govern enforcement jurisdiction in cyberspace is an ongoing question.[101] However, for purposes of legitimacy and predictability, it is key that an international consensus coalesces around such principles.[102] These principles could be laid down in a treaty. In this respect, on 17 November 2021, a Second Additional Protocol to the Budapest Convention on Cybercrime on enhanced co-operation and disclosure of electronic evidence was approved by the Committee of Ministers of the Council of Europe, which allows states parties to directly order the production of subscriber and domain name registration information – but not traffic or content data – held by ISPs on the territory of other states, thereby bypassing the latter's authorities.[103]

Treaties in this field are unlikely to attract very widespread ratification, however. For instance, the Budapest Convention has only been ratified by 68 states.[104] It is not clear how many states will ratify its Second Additional Protocol.[105] Moreover, if such treaties are ratified, their vague language and the possibility of opt-outs may fail to provide the hoped-for legal certainty. For instance, the Second Additional

[100] PS Berman and J Daskal, 'Legal Challenges of Data Dominance: *Yahoo! v. LICRA* and *Microsoft – Ireland* Cases' in HM Watt et al (eds), *Global Private International Law: Adjudication without Frontiers* (Cheltenham, Edward Elgar, 2019) 403.

[101] For a discussion on the applicable international law governing governmental hacking techniques, see, eg A Ghappour, 'Searching Places Unknown: Law Enforcement Jurisdiction on the Dark Web' (2017) 69 *Stanford Law Review* 1075 (arguing that such techniques may violate international law); against Kerr and Murphy (n 78) (arguing that these techniques do not violate customary international law, in particular because no international protest has arisen).

[102] See also Daskal, 'Privacy and Security' (n 66).

[103] Second Additional Protocol, Arts 6–7. These provisions update the Budapest Convention's provisions on extraterritorial data access, which have been considered insufficient. For a discussion, see JB Maillart, 'The Limits of Subjective Territorial Jurisdiction in the Context of Cybercrime' [2018] *ERA Forum* 375, 380–83. Prima facie, the Budapest Convention on Cybercrime, Art 18(1)(b) appears to provide the legal basis for extraterritorial production orders, ie orders to produce data stored by an ISP abroad, where it provides that 'Each Party shall adopt such legislative and other measures as may be necessary to empower its competent authorities to order … a service provider offering its services in the territory of the Party to submit subscriber information relating to such services in that service provider's possession or control'. For an interpretation in favour of extraterritoriality, see Cybercrime Convention Committee, 'T-CY Guidance Note #10: Production Orders for Subscriber Information (Article 18 Budapest Convention)' (Council of Europe, 2017). However, this provision fails to explicitly provide for extraterritorial application.

[104] See Council of Europe, 'Chart of Signatures and Ratifications of Treaty 185', www.coe.int/en/web/conventions/full-list/-/conventions/treaty/185/signatures.

[105] The Protocol opened for signature on 12 May 2022. 41 states have signed the Protocol (as of June 2023) but only one (Serbia) has so far ratified it.

Protocol gives considerable discretion to states parties in implementing production orders, insofar as they shall adopt such legislative and other measures 'as may be necessary'; may impose additional conditions on production orders; and may even reserve the right not to apply the relevant provision of the Protocol.[106] Clearly, account had to be taken of states parties' various sensitivities and diverging legal approaches.

As an alternative to multilateral treaties, principles may develop organically through unwritten customary international law, via a process of action, reaction and acquiescence. Customary international law has the advantage of flexibility, which is a key asset in the fast-changing field of regulating cyberspace. It is not clear whether customary international law on extraterritorial enforcement jurisdiction has already crystallised. The Supreme Court of Norway thought not.[107]

Most likely is that relevant principles on cross-border access to data, especially regarding extraterritorial production orders, will be enshrined in bilateral agreements. Agreements are already in place between the USA and the UK[108] and the USA and Australia,[109] and an agreement between the USA and the EU may be adopted in the near future.[110] These agreements appear to draw on principles of prescriptive jurisdiction to justify or limit enforcement jurisdiction. Take, for example, the US–Australia agreement. Nationality acts as a shield in that Australian authorities could not target US citizens, regardless of location.[111] In contrast, nationality acts as a legitimating jurisdictional link to the extent that, for example, the data of a person located in the Netherlands could be ordered by Australian law enforcement from a US service provider, possibly without notifying the authorities in the Netherlands.[112] It is arguable that enforcement jurisdiction in this scenario will likely be justified on the basis of prescriptive territorial jurisdiction, namely on the ground that a crime was committed in

[106] Second Additional Protocol, Art 7(9)(a).

[107] *Tidal* (n 73) para 58, observing that 'no custom under international law exists in this area'.

[108] Agreement on Access to Electronic Data for the Purpose of Countering Serious Crime (UK–US) (3 October 2019).

[109] Agreement on Access to Electronic Data for the Purpose of Countering Serious Crime (Australia–US) (15 December 2021).

[110] On 25 September 2019, formal negotiations started on an EU–US agreement 'to facilitate access to electronic evidence in criminal investigations'. See US Department of Justice, 'Joint US–EU Statement on Electronic Evidence Sharing Negotiations' (*Justice*, 26 September 2019) www.justice.gov/opa/pr/joint-us-eu-statement-electronic-evidence-sharing-negotiations.

[111] US–Australia Agreement, Art 4(3): 'Orders subject to this Agreement shall not intentionally target a Receiving-Party Person.'

[112] US–Australia Agreement, Art 5(1): 'In cases where an Order subject to this Agreement is issued for data in respect of an individual who is reasonably believed to be located outside the territory of and is not a national, citizen, or a lawful permanent resident of the Issuing Party, the Issuing Party's Designated Authority shall notify the appropriate authorities in the third country where the person is located, except in cases where the Issuing Party considers that it would be detrimental to operational or national security, or impede the conduct of an investigation, or imperil human rights'; in conjunction with Art 1(6): 'Covered Person means a person who, upon application of the procedures required by Article 7.1, is reasonably believed not to be a Receiving-Party Person at the time the Agreement is invoked for an Order pursuant to Article 5'.

Australia by the Dutch person.[113] This last scenario – which may be quite controversial – also points to the need to pay heed not only to sovereign interests, but also to the fundamental rights of data subjects. In this respect, the proposal for a European Production Order has also been criticised for being concerned only with the interests of the state issuing the order and of the state where the ISP is located, and not with the rights of the accused or data subject.[114]

IV. Concluding Observations

In a-territorial spaces like the high seas and cyberspace, international (treaty) law offers only limited opportunities to exercise extraterritorial enforcement jurisdiction with respect to crime. On the high seas, only flag states can in principle exercise such jurisdiction, with limited exceptions for crimes of piracy and breaches of UNSC-imposed maritime embargoes. In cyberspace, in keeping with the principle that enforcement jurisdiction cannot be exercised extraterritorially, only the state in which the relevant data is stored (on a server or device) can access such data.

Some states have considered this state of affairs to be unsatisfactory, as it may create impunity for criminal activity. On that basis, they have been pushing for a relaxation of the limitations of extraterritorial enforcement jurisdiction. They have exercised enforcement jurisdiction on the high seas over stateless vessels involved in drugs or human smuggling. Furthermore, they have ordered ISPs to produce data under their control, regardless of location. It is striking that these states justify these assertions by drawing on permissive principles of prescriptive jurisdiction, such as territoriality, personality, security and universality. In so doing, they blur the distinction between prescriptive and enforcement jurisdiction.

It is not yet fully clear how these practices should be understood from an international law perspective. Multilateral treaties do not explicitly authorise them, although some bilateral agreements are in place or are being developed. Customary international law may potentially provide authority, but relevant practice is largely limited to Western states, even if foreign governmental protest has been negligible. The scope of authorisation is closely related to the exact boundary conditions governing the exercise of extraterritorial enforcement jurisdiction. What substantive and procedural safeguards apply to extraterritorial data production orders? What crimes are covered by an authorisation to exercise extraterritorial enforcement jurisdiction over stateless vessels on the high seas?

[113] I thank Micheál Ó Floinn for pointing this out to me.

[114] Hörnle, *Internet Jurisdiction* (n 7) 219. The latter person may be located in a third state and may have limited remedies at his disposal. See EPO Proposal, Art 17, providing that the data subject must bring legal review in the issuing state rather than the state of his domicile. See further J Hörnle, 'What Triggers the Extraterritorial Application of Fundamental Rights? From Effective Control over Territory to State Act Theory in Cross-Border Surveillance', ch 9 in the present volume.

From a normative perspective, states' law enforcement utilitarianism should be taken seriously in this discussion. Indeed, a strict interpretation of the prohibition of extraterritorial enforcement jurisdiction may beget impunity. At the same time, unconditionally allowing such jurisdiction is not defensible either, as this may be at loggerheads with foreign state sovereignty and may breach individual rights.

8

Fitbit Health Data, Apple's Geodata and Google Searches: Cross-Border Law Enforcement and the Territoriality Principle

UTA KOHL*

I. Introduction

Statecraft in the digital age is not business as usual. Whereas processes of law-making have been relatively undisturbed by online activity and novel technologies, traditional law enforcement has encountered obstacles and opportunities in equal measure in the hyper-networked, data-driven digital era which have triggered seismic shifts in their approaches. A primary obstacle to law enforcement lies in the intensification of transnational activities. The internationalisation of routine social and commercial activities of citizens, consumers and enterprise or the deliberate evasion of local criminal laws challenges law enforcement processes that traditionally could assume the presence of local users as well as local providers (such as media companies or the retail sector, including entertainment, banking, transport, delivery and accommodation) that acted as choke points through which national legal normativity could be channelled, and whose help could be enlisted at the investigative stage of law enforcement. There are attempts to replicate some of this channelling through the co-option of global platforms as national gatekeepers – adjudicators and enforcers – of illegal or harmful online content, as in the case of the German Network Enforcement Law (2017), the EU Digital Services Act (2022) or the UK Online Safety Bill 2022.[1] The German Network Enforcement

* I am grateful for Micheál Ó Floinn's feedback and patience.

[1] Gesetz zur Verbesserung der Rechtsdurchsetzung in Sozialen Netzwerken (1 September 2017) BGBl I S 3352; Regulation (EU) 2022/2065 of the European Parliament and of the Council on a single market for digital services and amending Directive 2000/31/EC (Digital Services Act) [2022] OJ L277/1; Ireland's Online Safety and Media Regulation Bill (21 February 2022); UK's Online Safety Bill 2022 (11 May 2022); France's Law Reinforcing Respect of the Principles of the Republic Loi No 2021–1109 (24 August 2021), Art 42.

Law signals in its title that what is at stake are not the substantive rules of existing legal regimes, but rather how to make them stick online. The EU Digital Services Act is also concerned with the enforcement of existing content prohibitions online by imposing due diligence duties on platforms and their supervision through national authorities.[2] Yet, these efforts barely touch on the opportunities global communication networks have created for criminals, from terrorism and drug dealing to human trafficking and online child abuse.[3]

A related transnational enforcement problematic lies in the heightened fluidity of data across digital networks as an important law enforcement resource, in contrast to the greater stability of analogue information in space and time. The fluidity of digital data and its non-exclusivity have given rise to fierce competition over its control by platforms, users and governments which has expressed itself on multiple fronts: the fallout after the Snowden revelations of the wholesale surveillance of European personal data by US security agencies with the aid of online platforms;[4] the rise of data retention and localisation laws;[5] the ongoing controversy about the transfer of EU personal data to US servers as litigated in *Schrems I* (2015)[6] and *Schrems II* (2020);[7] or the more localised litigation over the access by law enforcement agencies to data on foreign shores. In the high-profile case of *Microsoft Corp v United States* (2016),[8] Microsoft sought to show its commitment to user privacy by resisting a US search warrant – concerning the content of an email account of a suspect (the nationality of whom was unknown[9]) in a federal drug trafficking investigation – on the basis that the email content was stored on its Irish servers and was thus arguably outside the legitimate reach of search warrants under US law.[10] For the initial judge granting the warrant and

[2] See Digital Services Act, Art 1 on its subject matter and scope; Recital 68 creates room for a Code of Conduct to govern otherwise harmful content.

[3] For some of these areas, heightened obligations have been created within wider regulatory regimes (eg UK Online Safety Bill), whilst others have been subject to *lex specialis* (eg Regulation (EU) 2021/784 of the European Parliament and of the Council on addressing the dissemination of terrorist content online [2021] OJ L172/79).

[4] CC Miller, 'Tech Companies Concede to Surveillance Program' *New York Times* (New York, 7 June 2013) www.nytimes.com/2013/06/08/technology/tech-companies-bristling-concede-to-government-surveillance-efforts.html.

[5] A Chander and UP Lê, 'Data Nationalism' (2015) 64 *Emory Law Journal* 677.

[6] C-362/14 *Maximillian Schrems v Data Protection Commissioner* ECLI:EU:C:2015:650.

[7] C-311/18 *Data Protection Commissioner v Facebook Ireland Ltd and Maximillian Schrems* ECLI:EU:C:2020:559 (*Schrems II*).

[8] *Microsoft Corp v United States* 829 F3d 197 (2d Cir 2016); *In re Warrant to Search a Certain Email Account Controlled and Maintained by Microsoft Corp* 15 F Supp 3d 466 (SDNY 2014); discussed in Editorial, 'Microsoft Corp v United States: Second Circuit Holds that the Government Cannot Compel an Internet Service Provider to Produce Information Stored Overseas' (2016) 130 *Harvard Law Review* 769.

[9] *Microsoft Corp* (n 8) 230. See also P De Hert and J Thumfart, 'The Microsoft Ireland Case, The Cloud Act and the Cyberspace Sovereignty Trilemma: Post-Territorial Technologies and Companies Question Regulatory State Monopolies' in W Hötzendorfer, C Tschohl and F Kummer (eds), *International Trends in Legal Informatics: Festschrift for Erich Schweighofer* (Bern, Weblaw, 2020) 373 (on the attempt by companies, here Microsoft, to reposition themselves in respect of their uses' data after the Snowden revelations).

[10] Under the Stored Communications Act 1986: 18 USC §§ 2701–12.

the first court of appeal, a warrant requiring access to data was not comparable to normal physical search and seizure warrants for transnational purposes, as US law enforcement did not have to set a foot in Ireland. Microsoft itself could comply with the order from its US headquarters. The information stored in Ireland could be had in the USA at the push of a button on US territory. It would seem wasteful not to press that button, as the Clarifying Lawful Use of Data Act (2018) (the CLOUD Act)[11] now explicitly permits – with parallel developments occurring elsewhere at national,[12] regional[13] or international level.[14] In short, the increased fluidity of data has made it far more accessible to public agencies from anywhere in the world with multiple overlapping competence claims. Given the geopolitical value of personal and population data, states have sought to maximise their own access to such data, through cross-border data requests as well as data localisation laws,[15] whilst trying to resist and block, if possible, other states' access to their population's data sets.[16]

On the domestic front, the rich sets of personal data on individual and group behaviours continuously extracted from network interactions present a gold mine for law enforcement. National enforcement agencies now routinely tap into the corporate reservoirs of personal data[17] – often with outcome-determinative results reminiscent of DNA evidence, but with broader evidential utility. In 2018, a prosecution in Germany secured a rape and murder conviction based on the data from the accused's iPhone's health app (added to iPhones from 2014), which had 'recorded a portion of his activity as "climbing stairs", which authorities were able to correlate with the time he would have dragged his victim down the river

[11] 18 USC § 2713. See J Hörnle, *Internet Jurisdiction: Law and Practice* (Oxford, Oxford University Press, 2021) 57f. For a critical response to the extraterritoriality of the CLOUD Act by the European Data Protection Board and Supervisor, see 'EDPB–EDPS Joint Response on the US Cloud Act' (OUT2019–0007, 10 July 2019) edps.europa.eu/sites/default/files/publication/19-07-10_edpb_edps_cloudact_coverletter_en.pdf.

[12] See, eg the UK Investigatory Powers Act 2016, s 261(10), which defines 'telecommunications operator' as any 'person who offers or provides a telecommunications service to persons in the United Kingdom' (eg Internet-based services such as web-based email, messaging applications and cloud-based services). Such operators are subject to interception warrants (s 43), orders for communication data (s 66) and 'bulk acquisition warrants' (s 170), as well as 'technical capability notices' (s 253).

[13] See, eg Commission, 'Proposal for a Regulation of the European Parliament and of the Council on European Production and Preservation Orders for Electronic Evidence in Criminal Matters' COM (2018) 225 final.

[14] See, eg Second Additional Protocol to the Convention on Cybercrime on enhanced co-operation and disclosure of electronic evidence (Strasbourg, 12 May 2022) (European Treaty Series No 224), where Arts 6 and 7 allow for access to narrow categories of data from service providers outside their territories (domain name registration information and subscriber data respectively).

[15] See Chander and Lê (n 5).

[16] Hong Yanqing, '"Game of Laws": Cross-Border Data Access for Law Enforcement Purposes' (Yale Law School, 2018) law.yale.edu/sites/default/files/area/center/china/document/game_of_laws-7.pdf. For EU blocking initiatives, see L Hornkohl, 'The Extraterritorial Application of Statutes and Regulations in EU Law' (2022) Max Planck Institute Luxembourg Research Paper No 2022(1), www.mpi.lu/research/working-paper-series/2022/wp-2022-1/.

[17] For the pervasiveness of access requests, see, eg Google, 'Transparency Report: Global Requests for User Information', transparencyreport.google.com/user-data/overview?hl=en_GB.

embankment, and then climbed back up'.[18] In the same year, a pharmacist in the UK was convicted for the murder of his wife based on the data trail he had left behind – his online searches about strangulation and the effects of insulin, and the geo- and health data of his and his wife's mobiles:

> In the minutes that followed Jessica's death, Patel's phone monitored frantic activity, racing around the house as he staged the burglary and running up and down the stairs. Jessica's health app remained still until after her death when it recorded a movement of 14 paces as her husband took the iPhone from her body and deposited it outside to make it look as though the 'burglar' had dropped it as he left.[19]

Meanwhile, genealogy websites, like 23andme or ancestry.com, with databases of millions of DNA profiles, have been forced to open their data collections to police searches,[20] thus supplementing existing limited police DNA databases. This routine access by law enforcement to privately generated and administered personal data sets spanning data trails from the wide spectrum of network interactions is decisive at the ex post sanction stage, but also creates opportunities for controlling populations.[21] It certainly has significant ripple effects on behaviours in anticipation of law enforcement – modulating individual choices either to circumvent detection or, more subtly, into compliance. Shortly after the US Supreme Court overturned the long-standing precedent of *Roe v Wade*[22] on a woman's right to abortion, women across the USA deleted period-tracking apps from their phones because data from the app could be subpoenaed in a prosecution for an illegal abortion.[23] Apart from the profound privacy concerns this raises, it also means that the benefits of the app for family planning and early detection of health issues are foregone.

Taking it a step further, governmental agencies and courts have been early adopters of machine-learning algorithms to complement or even replace human

[18] S Cole, 'Apple Health Data Is Being Used as Evidence in a Rape and Murder Investigation' (*Vice*, 11 January 2018) www.vice.com/en/article/43q7qq/apple-health-data-is-being-used-as-evidence-in-a-rape-and-murder-investigation-germany; A Dernback, 'Urteil im Freiburger Mordprozess erwartet: "Es war doch nur eine Frau" – der Fall Hussein K' *Der Tagesspiegel* (22 March 2018) www.tagesspiegel.de/gesellschaft/panorama/es-war-doch-nur-eine-frau-der-fall-hussein-k-3936826.html.

[19] N Parveen, 'Pharmacist Jailed for Murdering Wife to Start New Life with Boyfriend' *The Guardian* (5 December 2018) www.theguardian.com/uk-news/2018/dec/05/uk-pharmacist-mitesh-patel-jailed-for-30-years-wife-jessica-murder-premeditated. See also 'Greece Killing: Husband Confesses to Caroline Crouch Death' (*BBC News*, 18 June 2021) www.bbc.co.uk/news/world-europe-57523469.

[20] N Ram, 'A Judge Said Police Can Search the DNA of 1 Million Americans Without Their Consent. What's Next?' (*Science*, 7 November 2019) www.science.org/content/article/judge-said-police-can-search-dna-millions-americans-without-their-consent-what-s-next.

[21] J Dong, 'A Chinese City May Have Used a Covid App to Block Protesters, Drawing an Outcry' *New York Times* (New York, 16 June 2022) www.nytimes.com/2022/06/16/business/china-code-protesters.html.

[22] *Roe v Wade* 410 US 113 (1973), overturned in *Dobbs v Jackson Women's Health Organization* 597 US __ (2022).

[23] F Garamvolgyi, 'Why US Women Are Deleting Their Period Tracking Apps' *The Guardian* (28 June 2022) www.theguardian.com/world/2022/jun/28/why-us-woman-are-deleting-their-period-tracking-apps.

decision-making in many regulatory spheres, including in criminal justice and immigration, social security and child welfare contexts.[24] In the US case of *State of Wisconsin v Loomis* (2016),[25] the Wisconsin Supreme Court upheld the denial of parole and consequential six-year prison term for a drive-by shooting based, in part, on the 'Correctional Offender Management Profiling for Alternative Sanctions' black-box algorithm (COMPAS), which had classified Loomis as high risk to the community – when neither the sentencing court nor Loomis had any insight into the actual workings of COMPAS to contest its accuracy and scientific validity. As the algorithm was 'only' used to corroborate the judge's opinion, and as Loomis had known the personal information that fed it, it did not matter exactly how the result was arrived at. This is consistent with the relatively blind use of corporate self-learning algorithms by public bodies more generally. The UK Justice and Home Affair Committee concluded in its report *Technology Rules?* (2022)[26] that:

> [T]he market itself is worryingly opaque … public bodies often do not know much about the systems they are buying and will be implementing, due to the seller's insistence on commercial confidentiality – despite the fact that many of these systems will be harvesting, and relying on, data from the general public.[27]

This chapter offers reflections on these shifts towards data-driven, corporatised and globalised statecraft with a focus on cross-border data access through the lens of public international law. The discussion situates cross-border law enforcement activities within the territoriality principle under customary international law and argues that prescriptive and enforcement jurisdiction under international law are not alternatives that match onto legislative activities and law enforcement actions at the domestic level. Rather they apply cumulatively to the exercise of any state authority. By implication, as long as extraterritorial claims (prescriptive jurisdiction) are – as an exercise of state authority – made or actioned within the state territory (enforcement jurisdiction), no objections on the ground of a violation of territorial sovereignty could be raised. So extraterritorial data requests made or performed in the territory of the requesting state are wholly unexceptional. Even insofar as they *are* a factual interference in the territory of another state, the preoccupation of enforcement jurisdiction with prohibiting displays of state functions in another state means that it is rarely engaged by data interventions.

[24] See, eg L Dencik et al, 'The "Golden View": Data-Driven Governance in the Scoring Society' (2019) 8 *Internet Policy Review* 1; L Dencik et al, *Data Justice* (London, SAGE, 2022).

[25] *Loomis v Wisconsin* 881 NW 2d 749 (Wis 2016).

[26] Justice and Home Affairs Committee, *Technology Rules? The Advent of New Technologies in the Justice System* (HL 2021–22, 180).

[27] ibid 4.

II. Cross-Border Data Access: Strict and Elastic Territoriality

Intuitively, the problematic of law enforcement's cross-border data access appears to fall within the ambit of enforcement jurisdiction under international law – and not simply because of their common reference to 'enforcement'. The coercive means uniquely at the disposal of the state seem to justify the strict territorial limits of enforcement jurisdiction, and thereby protect each state's territorial sovereignty from the extraterritorial coercive reach of other states. This would chime with Max Weber's classic political conception of the state, according to which the 'monopoly of legitimate physical force' is what distinguishes it 'from all other historical forms of domination'.[28] Whilst, for Weber, physical force was 'neither the only nor the normal instrument of state acting and … only the last resort when other means have failed',[29] it was nonetheless the defining feature of the state over and beyond its administrative and legal order as its bureaucratic foundation. By territorially restricting the coercive force of one state, the monopoly of legitimate physical force of other states can be maintained.

Although, in international law, the idea of a state's 'monopoly' is mirrored in references to 'exclusivity', this exclusivity is not explicitly linked to coercion or the use of force. Max Huber framed sovereignty in the relation between states thus: 'Independence in regard to a portion of the globe is the right to exercise therein, to the exclusivity of any other States, *the functions of a State*' (emphasis added).[30] By the same token, centralised coercion or legitimate physical force is not singled out as decisive to the definition of statehood in international law. After all, an institution that is in the final analysis reducible to physical force, even if legitimate, sits uncomfortably with the idea of law or the rule by law, which imports both the notion of reason or rationality as an alternative to physical force and the idea of obedience flowing from the status of the command as a legal one.[31] In international law, physical force goes at best towards 'effective government' as the constitutive element of a state for the purposes of recognition. James Crawford observed that '[t]he requirement that a putative State have an effective government might be regarded as central to its claim for statehood',[32] and this entails '*the actual exercise*

[28] A Anter, 'The Modern State and its Monopoly on Violence' in E Hanke and S Whimster (eds), *The Oxford Handbook of Max Weber* (Oxford, Oxford University Press, 2019) 227, 229.

[29] ibid.

[30] *Island of Palmas (Netherlands v US)* (1928) 2 RIAA 828, 838.

[31] For a critique of the normative necessity of coercion to law, see H Oberdiek, 'The Role of Sanctions and Coercion in Understanding Law and Legal Systems' (1976) 21 *American Journal of Jurisprudence* 71; HLA Hart, *The Concept of Law*, 3rd edn (Oxford, Oxford University Press, 2012) 193: '"Sanctions" are … required not as a normal motive for obedience, but as a *guarantee* that those who would voluntarily obey shall not be sacrificed to those who would not. To obey, without this, would be to risk going to the wall … [W]hat reason demands is *voluntary* cooperation in a *coercive* system.'

[32] J Crawford, 'The Criteria for Statehood in International Law' (1976) 48 *British Yearbook of International Law* 93, 116; see also 114: 'The only requirement is that the State must consist of a certain coherent territory effectively governed.'

of authority, and the right or title to exercise that authority' (emphasis added).[33] So, although 'effective government' encompasses the spectrum of governmental powers, governmental authority must be 'strong enough to assert themselves throughout the territories of the State',[34] which suggests after all some coercion or force. Still, 'effective government' is also neither framed as nor reduced to a state's coercive powers, but wedded to the broader notion of the state being an effective normative institution as reflected in the exercise of its authority:[35] 'to be a State, an entity must possess a government or a system of government in general control of its territory, to the exclusion of other entities not claiming through or under it'.[36]

Even the classic statement by the Permanent Court of International Justice in *Lotus* (1927)[37] on 'enforcement jurisdiction' (although not identified as such) is framed in terms wider than coerciveness:

> the first and foremost restriction imposed by international law upon a State is that – failing the existence of a permissive rule to the contrary – it may not *exercise its power in any form* in the territory of another State. In this sense jurisdiction is certainly territorial (emphasis added).[38]

The Permanent Court remained silent on what it meant by a state 'exercising its power *in any form*' in the territory of another state, but distinguished it from a state's prescriptive jurisdiction in relation to which the Court allowed for wide extraterritorial claims of authority:

> It does not, however, follow that international law prohibits a State from exercising jurisdiction in its own territory, in respect of any case which relates to acts which have taken place abroad … Such a view would only be tenable if international law contained a general prohibition to States to extend the application of their laws and the jurisdiction of their courts to persons, property and acts outside their territory … But this is certainly not the case under international law as it stands at present. Far from laying down a general prohibition to the effect that States may not extend the application of their laws and the jurisdiction of their courts to persons, property and acts outside their territory, it leaves them in this respect a wide measure of discretion … every State remains free to adopt the principles which it regards as best and most suitable.[39]

[33] ibid 117.

[34] J Crawford, *The Creation of States in International Law*, 2nd edn (Oxford, Oxford University Press, 2007) 58, citing the *Aaland Islands Case* (1920) League of Nations Official Journal Spec Supp 3.

[35] *Island of Palmas* (n 30) 839: 'Just as before the rise of international law, boundaries of lands were necessarily determined by the fact that the power of a State was exercised within them, so too, under the reign of international law, the fact of peaceful and continuous display is still one of the most important considerations in establishing boundaries between States.'

[36] Crawford, *The Creation* (n 34) 59. Note, as a matter of political reality, 'In global comparison, the Weberian state is rather the exception than the rule of political organization. Only 16 percent of the world population live under the conditions of modern statehood, while nearly three quarters live in areas of low statehood and 10 percent live in completely state-free and disordered territories': Anter (n 28) 234.

[37] *The Case of the SS Lotus (France v Turkey)* PCIJ Rep Series A No 10, [2], [18].

[38] ibid [18].

[39] ibid [19].

It seems that, for the court, the touchstone for the territorial extent of jurisdiction lay in *where* the state exercised its authority, rather than *what* state function was performed, or its coercive or non-coercive nature under domestic law. So, if the state exercises its authority within its territory (by making a demand or claim or order), its jurisdiction is wide and can have extraterritorial effects on overseas subjects or objects. Meanwhile, a state cannot exercise or perform its functions outside its territory no matter what form it takes. This still begs the question of when exactly the state ought to be taken to have acted within its territory and when outside it – as reflected in Lord Justice Leggatt's sentiment in *Jimenez v The First Tier Tribunal (Tax Chamber)* (2019)[40] that 'Delineating the precise boundary between prescriptive (or legislative) and enforcement jurisdiction in international law is far from straightforward'.[41]

Although both prescriptive and enforcement jurisdiction use territory as their touchstone concept, their differences in use reflect the dual character of territory, and implicitly comment on the essential nature of each type of jurisdiction. On the one hand, territory signifies not land per se, but a state's authority, dominion or control over a physical portion of the globe.[42] Buxbaum stated that '"[t]erritoriality" and "extraterritoriality"... are claims of authority, or of resistance to that authority, that are made by particular actors with particular substantive interests to promote'.[43] As a legal construct denoting control over land, territory or territoriality has elasticity which is fully present in the territoriality principle as understood by prescriptive jurisdiction. This idea of territory easily accommodates transnationality by allowing wide extraterritorial claims of authority. Territory-as-control shows that the idea of states as self-contained parcels is an abstraction of a far messier reality to which it applies, however imperfectly. On the other hand, territory also refers to the physical underlay 'without which the State entity could neither come into being nor survive'.[44] On this meaning, territory 'constitutes the tangible framework for the manifestation of power',[45] and this physical framework has none of the elasticity implicit in territory-as-control, but offers a solid, stable and tangible background for the physical performance of state authority and for delimiting it, as constituted in the concept of enforcement jurisdiction. Thus, enforcement jurisdiction is performance-orientated and locates this performance within a physical space. The examples typically given of such performed activities

[40] *R (On the Application of Jimenez) v First Tier Tribunal (Tax Chamber)* [2019] EWCA Civ 51.

[41] ibid [53].

[42] Note the distinction between 'territory' and 'dominion' in, eg G Crabb, *English Synonyms Explained* (London, George Routledge & Sons, 1880) 613: 'Both these terms respect a portion of country under a particular government; but the word Territory brings to our minds the land which is included; Dominion conveys to our minds the power which is exercised.'

[43] H Buxbaum, 'Territory, Territoriality, and the Resolution of Jurisdictional Conflict' (2009) 57 *American Journal of Comparative Law* 631, 635.

[44] ST Bernardez, 'Territorial Sovereignty' in RL Bindschedler et al (eds), *Encyclopedia of Public International Law*, Installment 10 (Amsterdam, Elsevier, 1987) 487.

[45] MN Shaw, 'Territory in International Law' (1982) 13 *Netherlands Yearbook of International Law* 61, 62.

are coercive in nature, but this is not necessarily so. Typically, FA Mann referred to a state not being allowed to 'send police officers into a foreign State to arrest the criminal and carry him across the frontier'.[46] Lombois expressed the difference between prescriptive jurisdiction and enforcement jurisdiction along coercive/non-coercive lines:

> The law may very well decide to cast its shadow beyond its borders; the judge may well have a voice so loud that, speaking in his house, his condemnations are heard outside; the reach of the police officer is only as long as his arm … he is a constable only at home.[47]

Meanwhile, for Michael Akehurst, the forbidden acts were public rather than coercive 'act[s] by one State in the territory of another',[48] as, for example: officials collecting taxes in the territory of another state; sitting as a judge or recruiting soldiers in another state (neither of which is obviously coercive); inspecting ships in a foreign port for the purpose of enforcing its own quarantine regulations; the seizure of individuals or property in the territory of another state; the entry of armed forces into the territory of another state; or the intrusion of military aircrafts into foreign air space.[49]

Akehurst's example of adjudication illustrates the difference between prescriptive and enforcement jurisdiction nicely. When a judge adjudicates, it attracts both prescriptive and enforcement jurisdiction cumulatively: her claim of authority vis-à-vis an extraterritorial subject or event falls within prescriptive jurisdiction as a legal demand. Meanwhile, the location from which she adjudicates is delimited by enforcement jurisdiction, ie she can only sit as a judge in the territory of the state that appointed her. So, prescriptive and enforcement jurisdiction are simultaneously applicable: the former looks to the claim of authority made by a public actor and the latter to the location of the adjudicative performance; or, put as a two-stage test: did the performance of state authority occur within the territory and, if so, was the claim or demand supported by a territorial (or other) connection?[50]

The focus on the location of the performance of the state function as an initial trigger for the delimitation of its authority has found itself at odds with the ghostliness of data.[51] For sure, data on global computer networks exists in time and

[46] FA Mann, 'The Doctrine of Jurisdiction Revisited after Twenty Years' (1984) 186 *Recueil des Cours* 9, 37.

[47] C Lombois, *Droit Penal International*, 2nd edn (Paris, Daloz, 1979) 536, cited in P Trudel, 'Jurisdiction over the Internet: A Canadian Perspective' (1998) 32 *The International Lawyer* 1027, 1047.

[48] M Akehurst, 'Jurisdiction in International Law' (1972–73) 46 *British Yearbook of International Law* 145.

[49] ibid 145–49.

[50] *cf* J Crawford, *Brownlie's Principles of Public International Law*, 9th edn (Oxford, Oxford University Press, 2019) 456 and fn 2, where the author groups adjudication under enforcement on the basis that adjudication 'actualises' a prescription which is correct through a domestic law lens but misconstrues the preoccupation of enforcement jurisdiction under international law.

[51] J Daskal, 'Law Enforcement Access to Data Across Borders: The Evolving Security and Rights Issues' (2016) 8 *Journal of National Security Law and Policy* 473.

space, but its high fluidity and easy replicability means that it can be extracted effortlessly from remote locations. States have responded to the global presence of this enormous fluid resource in two complementary ways. First, they have framed cross-border data requests, wherever possible, not as state acts (or as acts by a private actor as the state's agent) performed in the territory of another state, but as regulatory claims made by the state authority within its jurisdiction against local or overseas actors *subject to their jurisdiction*. Second, they have also by and large refused to treat data interventions in the territory of another state as violations of sovereignty,[52] as is consistent with the preoccupation of enforcement jurisdiction with displays of foreign state authority. These two avenues and their effects will now be discussed in turn.

III. Prescriptive Jurisdiction: Cross-Border Data Claims and the Presumption against Extraterritoriality

Many states have made expansive unilateral claims over extraterritorial data by treating such access as regulatory *demands* made within their territory rather than as *actions* performed outside it, and thereby eschewed enforcement jurisdiction and its strict territoriality. In common law jurisdictions, the issue of extraterritorial data access by government agencies has been located within, and framed by, judicial and academic discussion on the 'presumption against extraterritoriality'. The presumption imposes a territorial framing on statutory law, including law on the investigatory powers of governmental agencies – bar evidence of a contrary legislative intent. Although the presumption as a domestic tool of statutory interpretation is ostensibly designed to promote extraterritorial restraint in transborder interactions, the argument below is that by invoking the presumption, courts have in fact constructed extraterritorial data access squarely and solely as a matter of legislative intent and 'claim jurisdiction' as such opened it up to the elastic territoriality of prescriptive jurisdiction.

A. Overseas Data

A high-profile and much-publicised case on the territorial restrictions, if any, on cross-border data access is *Microsoft v US* (2016),[53] in which the lower courts had

[52] UNGA, 'Official Compendium of Voluntary National Contributions on the Subject of How International Law Applies to the Use of Information and Communications Technologies by States Submitted by Participating Government Experts in the Group of Governmental Experts on Advancing Responsible State Behaviour in Cyberspace in the Context of International Security Established Pursuant to General Assembly Resolution 73/266' (13 July 2021) UN Doc A/76/136 (Official Compendium).

[53] See n 8 above.

held that content data retrieved by Microsoft in the USA from its Irish servers pursuant to a search warrant did not trigger any extraterritoriality as it neither 'involve[d] the deployment of American law enforcement personnel abroad ... [nor required] the physical presence of service providers' employees at the location where data are stored'.[54] Consequently, 'there is no question of international law, but solely of the purport of the municipal law which establishes the duty of the citizen in relation to his own government'.[55] On appeal, however, the Second Circuit Court held that the warrant did have an extraterritorial dimension.[56] So it appeared to take the location of the data in Ireland seriously. Yet, in fact, it based its decision on the presumption against extraterritoriality, which, it said, had not been rebutted in the Stored Communications Act 1986. Thus, the hindrance lay not in any potential violation of international law, but in the failure of the domestic legislature to clearly signal the extraterritorial reach of the statute. The presumption against extraterritoriality is a tool of statutory interpretation that implicitly recognises territoriality under international law as an overarching principle; this, however, does not turn it into a derivative rule or requirement under international law.[57] As the presumption is rebuttable by the domestic legislature, it necessarily assumes that extraterritoriality can be claimed without violating international law. For this reason alone, it is self-contradictory to assert that but for the presumption international law would be violated.[58] It would amount to a proposition that international law can only be breached in exceptional circumstances and when the domestic legislature has given the green light. Furthermore, whether rebutted or not, the presumption applies to demands made in legislation and thus falls within prescriptive jurisdiction, which under international law is permissive (even if not going as far as *Lotus* suggests).[59] Meanwhile, enforcement jurisdiction, which *is* restrictive, would not be breached by a statute per se, but would look to the location of public acts that may flow from it. By the same token, if the strict limitations of enforcement jurisdiction were breached under international law, then the existence of a domestic statute permitting the violating act could hardly neutralise the violation at the international level. Whilst the presumption is

[54] *In re Warrant to Search a Certain E-Mail Account* (n 8) 475.

[55] ibid 476 (2014), citing *Blackmer v US* 284 US 421, 437 (1932).

[56] *Microsoft Corp* (n 8): 'his narrative affords inadequate weight to the facts that the data is stored in Dublin, that Microsoft will necessarily interact with the Dublin datacenter in order to retrieve the information for the government's benefit, and that the data lies within the jurisdiction of a foreign sovereign'.

[57] A Mills, 'Rethinking Jurisdiction in International Law' (2014) 84 *British Yearbook of International Law* 187, 226, commenting in the context of the Alien Tort Statute on the domestic nature of the presumption.

[58] There are frequent statements to that effect, eg *R (on the application of KBR, Inc) v Director of the Serious Fraud Office* [2021] UKSC 2 [24]: 'The presumption reflects, in part, the requirements of international law that one State should not by the claim or exercise of jurisdiction infringe the sovereignty of another State in breach of rules of international law.'

[59] On the anomaly of the *Lotus* ruling in terms of the hierarchy of international law as binding on states, see Mills (n 57) 190–94.

more persuasively couched as an instrument of non-binding comity or courtesy,[60] comity is, on the ground, a fickle predictor of jurisdictional restraint in the name of transnational co-operation. Indeed, the presumption has frequently – in the name of comity – been used in a protectionist rather than co-operative way. In cases like *F Hoffmann-La Roche Ltd v Empagran* (2004) or *Morrisons v National Australia Bank Ltd* (2010),[61] it helped to shield US companies from accountability for their wrongdoing abroad by making the location of their victim within or outside the jurisdiction the touchstone of accountability. At the same time, in the USA, the presumption is expressly subject to the 'domestic effects' exception, according to which US law applies as a matter of course to acts or actors outside the territory where they cause harm within the territory, regardless of whether the law in the place of the originating act is or is not permissive.[62] In these scenarios, the presumption has shown itself to be highly attuned to domestic interests rather than as a device to protect the interests of other states.

In *Microsoft v US*, the decision of the Second Circuit Court served as an invitation to the legislature to expand the territorial remit of warrants, which Congress promptly did through the CLOUD Act in 2018, thereby settling the contested nature of these warrants – whether as a device executed by a law enforcement agency abroad or as a (local) demand by law enforcement directed at private actors in respect of overseas data – firmly in favour of the latter. The District Court had already gone down that route when it stated that, in contrast to a normal warrant, '[a warrant under the Stored Communications Act] is executed by a service provider rather than a government law enforcement agent, and … does not require the presence of an agent during its execution'.[63] The presumption thus functioned as a tool to shift the issue of extraterritoriality from the courts to the legislature, and acted as no more than a (temporary) territorial restraint on the executive, whilst awaiting legislative permission to the contrary. The judgment implies that although the retrieval of information by Microsoft from its Irish servers involved extraterritoriality (as explicitly acknowledged), no illegal interference with the territory of Ireland would occur under international law. Data is both there and not there, alive and dead, a bit like Schrödinger's cat. The ease of its transferability and the relative happenstance of its location make arguments based on the significance of its particular location rather artificial. For the same reason, the location of the server has never been decisive for prescriptive jurisdiction where states have

[60] See, eg WS Dodge, 'The New Presumption against Extraterritoriality' (2020) 3 *Harvard Law Review* 1582; JR Paul, 'Comity in International Law' (1991) 32 *Harvard International Law Journal* 1; *Hilton v Guyot* 159 US 113, 164 (1895).

[61] *F Hoffmann-La Roche Ltd v Empagran SA* 124 S Ct 2359 (2004); *Morrisons v National Australia Bank Ltd* 130 S Ct 2869 (2010); for a discussion on the presumption, see U Kohl, 'Territoriality and Globalization' in S Allen et al (eds), *The Oxford Handbook of Jurisdiction in International Law* (Oxford, Oxford University Press, 2019).

[62] *Pakootas v Teck Cominco Metals Ltd* 452 F 3d 1066, 1077 (9th Cir 2006), following *Steele v Bulova Watch Co* 344 US 280 (1952).

[63] *Microsoft Corp* (n 8) 214.

looked to more stable criteria as a basis for competence. Similarly, it is not artificial to focus on the location of Microsoft in the USA and its consequential subjection to US law as a basis for the retrieval. Yet, that cannot erase the fact that Ireland's sovereignty was, however marginally, implicated by the ordered retrieval of data from servers on its territory.

B. Overseas Platforms

Other states have followed suit and taken the same approach to cross-border data access, albeit with more expansive repercussions. Under the CLOUD Act, a service provider already 'subject to the jurisdiction of the United States'[64] can be required to produce data 'that is in its custody, control, or possession'.[65] Thus, the critical jurisdictional foundation for data production orders or search warrants is that the provider is subject to US jurisdiction. As most of the large platforms are based in the USA, the Act has de facto been applied to local companies, but this is a fortuitous outcome rather than a matter of jurisdictional restraint. Indeed, in *Microsoft v US*, the data was held in data centres which were at least partially operated by its subsidiaries, which were less obviously subject to the jurisdiction of the USA.[66] Nevertheless, the case was quickly resolved after the passing of the CLOUD Act, presumably on the basis that the parent company subject to the jurisdiction of the USA was considered in control of any data held within the corporate group, conveniently glossing over the separate personality of each company within the group.[67] Other states have also extended the reach of their data production orders or search warrants to platforms subject to their jurisdiction, and this has caught platforms not physically based in their territory. Typically, in *Yahoo! Inc v Belgium* (2015),[68] and as followed in *Public Prosecutor v Skype* (2016),[69] the Belgian Supreme Court upheld the order against Yahoo to disclose the identity of one of its subscribers in a criminal prosecution for fraud on the basis that Yahoo had a commercial presence in Belgium, albeit no physical presence, and was thus answerable to Belgian courts and subject to Belgian laws.[70] So, the Belgian courts effectively treated the order against Yahoo – not unlike the US Second Circuit Court treated the warrant against Microsoft – as a matter of

[64] The CLOUD Act § 2(2). See also US Department of Justice, *Promoting Public Safety, Privacy, and the Rule of law Around the World: The Purpose and Impact of the CLOUD Act* (White Paper, April 2019) 3. For a critique of its extraterritorial remit, see Hornkohl (n 16) 30.

[65] CLOUD Act § 2(2).

[66] *Microsoft Corp* (n 8) 202.

[67] Discussed in *R (On the Application of KBR Inc) v The Director of the Serious Fraud Office* [2018] EWHC 2368 [60]ff.

[68] *Yahoo! Inc v Belgium* Hof van Cassatie (Supreme Court of Belgium, 1 December 2015), No P.13.2082.N, translated in J Vandendreissche, 'Case Translation: Belgium' (2016) 13 *Digital Evidence and Electronic Signature Law Review* 156; for the earlier decision, see *Yahoo! Inc v Belgium* AR P.11.1906.N/2 (Supreme Court, 4 September 2012).

[69] *Public Prosecutor v Skype*, Tribunal de Première Instance (Tribunal of First Instance, 27 October 2016) No. ME20.F1.105151-12.

[70] *Yahoo* (2016) (n 68) [6].

prescriptive jurisdiction, whereby it made a regulatory claim within its territory addressing a party outside it but subject to its jurisdiction, rather than actioning that claim in the territory of another state.

Fundamentally, the same questions were also addressed by the UK Supreme Court decision in *KBR, Inc v Director of the Serious Fraud Office* (2021),[71] which did not involve data or platforms and so provides an opportunity for reflecting on what might be so different about the digital network context. The Supreme Court was asked to deliberate on the territorial reach of disclosure orders under the Criminal Justice Act 1987, section 2(3) and whether it would permit such order against KBR – a US parent company which did not carry on business in the UK (in contrast to the facts in *Yahoo! Inc v Belgium* and *Public Prosecutor v Skype*) – in the context of a bribery investigation of its UK subsidiaries. Much like the US court in *Microsoft v US*, the court used the presumption against exterritoriality to arrive at a narrow territorial construction of the statute and by implication invited Parliament to widen the power's territorial ambit.[72] Presumably if or when Parliament does so, it will require some territorial link upon which production orders against parties outside the UK may be based. The earlier reasoning by the Divisional Court in the same case[73] – as overruled by the Supreme Court – pointed to a possible justifying link: the disclosure orders could be directed to 'foreign companies in respect of documents held outside the jurisdiction when there is a *sufficient connection* between the company and the jurisdiction' (emphasis added).[74] Such connection could have been established in the case, given that the investigations concerned payments and contracts by KBR's local subsidiaries which had 'required the approval of KBR Inc and were paid by KBR Inc through its US based treasury function'.[75] The activities of the US parent company were thus central to the activities of the local subsidiaries under investigation. Still, the 'sufficient connection' had to be implied into the statute and is undoubtedly open-ended, so the Supreme Court arguably rightly rejected it – both for its uncertainty and as illegitimate judicial law-making.[76]

Here lies a crucial difference with most online constellations. Overseas platforms almost invariably conduct business in the jurisdiction whether or not they are physically present there (as in *Yahoo! Inc v Belgium* or *Public Prosecutor v Skype*),[77] and as such fall under the standard head of jurisdiction of 'carrying on business in the jurisdiction', which is often used as a justifying link in regulatory

[71] *KBR* (2021) (n 58).

[72] ibid para 65: 'there is no basis for the implication of such a limitation and any attempt to do so would exceed the appropriate bounds of interpretation and usurp the function of Parliament'.

[73] *KBR* (2018) (n 67).

[74] ibid [71].

[75] ibid [72].

[76] *KBR* (2021) (n 58) [65]. But *cf* the Investigatory Powers Act 2016, s 261 in relation to orders against the parent of a local subsidiary.

[77] See nn 68 and 69 above.

contexts in order to extend local criminal or regulatory law to foreign operators.[78] In the Internet context, a well-known example is Article 3(2) of the General Data Protection Regulation (GDPR), which extends the GDPR's territorial ambit to overseas controllers who offer services in the EU, with their compliance being backed by administrative criminal sanctions.[79] The fact that in these contexts states make coercive claims backed by criminal sanctions against such overseas online providers is entirely unproblematic as a matter of prescriptive jurisdiction; and given that there is no physical performance of state authority in the territory of another state, they do not offend the limits of enforcement jurisdiction.[80] Indeed, considering that international law on jurisdiction is barely, if at all, concerned with civil laws and disputes, prescriptive jurisdiction is primarily concerned with extending coercive substantive and procedural laws backed by criminal sanctions extraterritorially.[81] Such wide claims are essential to protect the local law space from being undermined by outside providers who offer their goods and their services within the jurisdiction without a presence. Broadly, the same holds true for disclosure or data protection orders, whether framed as a warrant or otherwise. The fact that here domestic law enforcement agencies make the demands does not bring them into conflict with enforcement jurisdiction, given that they are made on local territory (discussed below), as illustrated by various examples. An example of a treaty-based disclosure order against a provider who is commercially present in the requesting state's territory but formally and physically absent is Article 18 of the Cybercrime Convention:

> A Party shall adopt such legislative and other measures as may be necessary to empower its competent authorities to order: … *a service provider offering its services in the territory* of the Party to submit subscriber information relating to such services in that service provider's possession or control. (emphasis added)[82]

Although Article 18 orders are limited to subscriber data and so are severely circumscribed in scope, the provision is fully consistent with the standard

[78] For examples in the UK, see the Financial Service and Markets Act 2000, ss 418 and 419; the Modern Slavery Act 2015, s 54; or the Bribery Act 2010, s 7(5).

[79] See Regulation (EU) 2016/679 of the European Parliament and of the Council on the protection of natural persons with regard to the processing of personal data and on the free movement of such data, and repealing Directive 95/46/EC (General Data Protection Regulation) [2016] OJ L119/1, Arts 83 and 84.

[80] *cf* the statement in *KBR* (2021) (n 58) [24]: 'The presumption reflects, in part, the requirements of international law that one State should not by the claim or exercise of jurisdiction infringe the sovereignty of another State in breach of rules of international law. Thus, for example, legislation requiring conduct in a foreign State which would be in breach of the laws of that State or otherwise inconsistent with the sovereign right of that State to regulate activities within its territory may well be a breach of international law.' Concurrent regulatory claims by different states over the same activities is a very common phenomenon in respect of global service providers.

[81] See, eg Akehurst (n 48) 170ff; *cf* Crawford, *Brownlie's Principles* (n 50) 471.

[82] Budapest Convention on Cybercrime (European Treaty Series No 185), Art 18(1)(b). For more expansive domestic law provisions, see, eg the UK Investigatory Powers Act 2016, ss 66 and 261(10) (above n 12).

application of prescriptive jurisdiction based on 'services being offered in the territory'. Furthermore, just because states are unwilling to go beyond subscriber data does not signal that customary international law forbids more expansive demands, but rather indicates that states are unwilling to enter into reciprocal treaty-based arrangements on more sensitive data, such as content data.[83]

By implication, given that a territorial nexus between the requesting state and the platform (in the form of a commercial presence) is generally present in the online context, states have used data production orders as a convenient alternative to the complementary regime of requests under mutual legal assistance treaties (MLATs). For the latter, no jurisdictional link with the provider is required; yet they are otherwise more cumbersome and uncertain, as they involve oversight by the requested state.[84] This has shifted extraterritorial data access away from states (as a bilateral affair between two states) to demands made by state authorities directly against online platforms – albeit with resistance from their home states in the form of blocking statutes, particularly where those requests go over and beyond the mutually agreed type of data, eg subscriber data.[85]

The presumption against extraterritoriality has offered at best a temporary bulwark to this development, which speaks to an intensification of globalisation where even routine activity is mediated by global network providers that can deliver their services without physical presence in the territory and extract valuable personal data locally without it being stored there. If anything, the presumption has accommodated this expanded factual extraterritoriality by prompting legislatures to match it through 'rebuttal', that is, opting for an extended investigatory reach of the statute. Certainly, constructing investigatory orders essentially as claims made at home with an extraterritorial effect (either in terms of the data or the provider) rather than as the actioning of such claims by a private agent on behalf of law enforcement agencies in the territory of another state has the effect of circumventing the performance-oriented territoriality of enforcement jurisdiction.

[83] Cybercrime Convention, Arts 32 and 39(3): 'Nothing in this Convention shall affect other rights, restrictions, obligations and responsibilities of a Party.'

[84] *KBR* (2018) (n 67) [85]–[96]: 'even where there is an available MLA regime, there may be good practical reasons for the Director preferring to proceed by way of s.2(3) notices. Such reasons, which … include delay, the risk of a request being ignored and the burden on the requested state of dealing with a request when direct recourse to the holder of the requested material would be simpler.' The Crime (Overseas Production Orders) Act 2019, s 4(8), which allows for overseas production orders against a person with no connection to the UK, falls within MLATs.

[85] For prominent blocking statutes forbidding a local person from complying with a foreign data production order outside formally agreed channels, see eg GDPR, Art 48, which forbids disclosures based on court order 'of a third country requiring a controller … to transfer or disclose personal data … [and which will only be] recognised or enforceable in any manner if based on an international agreement, such as a mutual legal assistance treaty, in force between the requesting third country and the Union or a Member State'; or 18 USC § 2702, which prohibits the disclosure of customer communication or records, other than 'to a foreign government pursuant to an order from a foreign government that is subject to an executive agreement'.

C. Drivers behind De Facto Data Exceptionalism

There has been some academic and governmental opposition to this de facto data and platform exceptionalism.[86] Opponents to extraterritorial data requests argue that data ought to be treated like its analogue counterparts, for which formal processes as laid down in MLATs facilitate the exchange, however cumbersome and unreliable. As shown above, this argument is only partially sound insofar as it is the extension of existing rules to data and platforms which has caused the shift in the transnational investigatory landscape rather than any special rules or dispensations applicable to data or platforms. Still, given the significant novel effects of these requests outside of MLATs, there is some validity to the argument for the technological neutrality of the law, that like matters ought to be treated alike regardless of the medium. By the same token, however, expansive cross-border investigatory powers often do no more than maintain the status quo for law enforcement, especially vis-à-vis information previously held locally, such as data from phones or computer systems, and which now, after migrating into the Cloud, may be held anywhere.[87] The Divisional Court in *KBR v SFO* (2018) rightly observed that '[i]t is scarcely credible that a UK company could resist an otherwise lawful s.2(3) notice on the ground that the documents in question were held on a server out[side] of the jurisdiction'.[88] Equally, there is no reason, in principle, why a non-UK provider of services in the UK should be treated any differently to a UK provider of the same services. In light of this functional equivalence of the provider and the data, and recalling that 'effective government' is a constitutive element of statehood, it may be argued that international law is not merely permissive vis-à-vis expansive territorial data claims, but in fact expects them. Not accessing such data would undermine the governing capacity of states in their territories. As a matter of law, when a platform is already subject to a state's prescriptive jurisdiction (based on its commercial presence in the jurisdiction), it is but a small change of register to add data requests to the repertoire of existing regulatory expectations.

Letting cross-border data demands slip the net of MLATs frees domestic law enforcement authority from some of its territorial shackles. As the global resource of digital data escapes the control of governmental gatekeepers, states seeking access to such data are empowered. Yet the safeguards built into MLATs are also foregone. For example, in the UK, mutual legal assistance is designed as a safeguard against oppressive foreign state authority and is thus predicated on dual criminality (ie relatively compatible legal standards), and may also be denied on grounds of 'politically motivated prosecutions', public order, state security, double jeopardy or the reasonable belief that 'the request has been made for the

[86] eg AK Woods, 'Against Data Exceptionalism' (2016) 68 *Stanford Law Review* 729.
[87] Daskal (n 51) 457.
[88] *KBR* (2018) (n 67) [64].

purpose of investigating, prosecuting or punishing a person on account of his/her race, gender, sexual orientation, religion, nationality, ethnic origin or political opinions'.[89] Here, governmental gatekeeping of locally held information explicitly fulfils a protective function by preventing information from being released and used in ways contrary to fundamental rights and local public values. Such protection, however, also assumed a correlation between locally held information and the presence of the data subject or object in the territory. As such correlation may or may not exist in the online context, the incentive and legitimacy for governmental gatekeeping may have weakened.

IV. Enforcement Jurisdiction: Display of State Authority and Invisible Data Intrusions

Even in the absence of a jurisdictional basis for cross-border data demands against overseas platforms, enforcement jurisdiction and its strict territoriality is, for reasons explained below, still unlikely to be engaged by extraterritorial data interventions in the vast majority of cases. Whilst numerous national legal initiatives have been launched to strengthen a state's territorial sovereignty and integrity, public international law, in particular customary international law, has proven peculiarly resistant to absorbing twenty-first-century statecraft within its field of vision.

A. Enforcement Jurisdiction is not Concerned with Coerciveness Per Se

As discussed above, international law does not draw the distinction between prescriptive and enforcement jurisdiction along coercive/non-coercive lines as understood domestically. In that sense, there is at best a weak or coincidental match between the three arms of government (legislative, adjudicative, executive) at domestical level and prescriptive and enforcement jurisdiction in international law, despite various academic statements to the contrary.[90]

What may be considered coercive in domestic law is not a particular preoccupation for international law in the context of enforcement jurisdiction or territorial sovereignty. Indeed, as coercive cross-border data production orders backed by criminal penalties are widely considered to be within the permissive

[89] Home Office, 'Request for Mutual Legal Assistance in Criminal Matters: Guidelines for Authorities outside the United Kingdom' (Home Office, March 2022) 20.

[90] Including by this author in U Kohl, *Jurisdiction and the Internet: Regulatory Competence over Online Activity* (Cambridge, Cambridge University Press, 2007) 16–18. See also Mills (n 57) 194–95.

remit of prescriptive jurisdiction, the international community signals that these orders do not violate the strict territoriality of enforcement jurisdiction, regardless of their coercive status domestically. Furthermore, it may be argued that all legal obligations, whether civil or criminal law, are coercive. Even civil law occurs with the backing of coercive state powers, which emerge on an escalating scale: they are there in their embryonic form in a mere legal obligation, which transforms into a more compelling force when at issue in trial before a court, and are imbued with the full force of public power at the point when a bailiff recovers a judgment debt. By the same token, much of the coercive force of a legal command flows from its status as law, so much so that even a mere prescription has an inherently coercive nature.

At the domestic level, however, the steps taken by a state to enforce a law, or impose sanctions for non-compliance, tend be considered 'coercive' properly so called. The warrant authorised in the Stored Communications Act and at stake in *Microsoft v US* was a coercive criminal procedure, albeit with some disagreement about its precise nature.[91] Nevertheless, on any domestic construction, these warrants would be considered 'coercive' insofar as they were integral to enforcing the domestic law through government agencies. Equally, the criminal procedure invoked in *Yahoo! Inc v Belgium* was coercive insofar as it allowed the public prosecutor 'when investigating crimes or misdemeanors … to request the cooperation of the operator of an electronic communications network …; the refusal to communicate the required information is punished with a fine'.[92] As the Belgian Supreme Court acknowledged, '[t]his sanction is intended to enforce the co-operation obligation of the operators and providers and qualifies the provisions of article 46*bis*, § 2, of the Code of Criminal Procedure as a coercive measure in nature'.[93] In these cases, the platforms challenged the extraterritoriality of the investigatory orders because they felt coerced to co-operate with law enforcement agencies. Yet, from the perspective of international law, neither the governmental agency's involvement or coercive intention nor its actual coercive effect on (local or overseas) platforms brought the demand into conflict with the territorial limits of enforcement jurisdiction.

B. Enforcement Jurisdiction is Preoccupied with the Display of State Authority

The reason for this lies in the fact that enforcement jurisdiction under international law is preoccupied with the visible physical performance of a state function in the territory of another state. The physical execution of an extraterritorial search warrant would fall within the ambit of enforcement jurisdiction under

[91] See n 63 above and accompanying text.
[92] *Yahoo! Inc v Belgium* (n 68) [2]–[3].
[93] ibid [3].

international law if a government agent performed it in another state's territory. In *Microsoft v US*, the warrant involved no physical searches in Ireland:

> It is obtained like a search warrant when an application is made to a neutral magistrate who issues the order only upon a showing of probable cause. On the other hand, it is executed like a subpoena in that *it is served on the provider in possession of the information and does not involve government agents entering the premises of the provider to search its servers and seize the e-mail account in question*. (emphasis added)[94]

Even if the government agent had searched Microsoft's premises in the USA and had accessed data there from its Irish servers,[95] it is unlikely to have engaged enforcement jurisdiction. By the same token, the Belgian court stressed that its data production order against Yahoo was legitimate because

> [it was designed to] obtain identification data following a criminal offence that falls within the scope of the investigation authority of the Belgian criminal jurisdiction. *This measure does not require Belgian police officers or magistrates, nor by persons acting on their behalf to be physically outside the jurisdiction*. Nor does this measure require the performance of any physical act abroad. This is therefore a coercive measure with a limited scope, the implementation of which requires no intervention outside the Belgian territory. (emphasis added)[96]

Similarly, for Justice Leggat in *Jimenez v The First Tier Tribunal (Tax Chamber)*, the performative aspect of law enforcement was critical in deciding whether or not international law took an interest, and that performative aspect was *not* fulfilled by sending a letter overseas through the post. '[S]ending a notice by post to a person in a foreign state requiring him to produce information that is reasonably required for the purpose of checking his tax position in the UK'[97] would not violate the strict limits of enforcement jurisdiction or state sovereignty, given that it 'does not involve the performance of any official act within the territory of another state – as would, for example, sending an officer of Revenue and Customs to enter the person's business premises in a foreign state and inspect business documents'.[98]

What emerges from these opinions is that enforcement jurisdiction is not engaged simply by a physical intrusion (a letter does not count), but requires a visible intervention, and one that involves a human actor in some official capacity (although a private actor may act as an agent for the state).[99] It is the physical display, or the open performance or manifestation of authority, by one state in the

[94] *In re Warrant to Search a Certain Email Account* (n 8) 466.

[95] Notably in the case, the warrant, although served on Microsoft, used boilerplate language and was addressed to 'any authorised law enforcement officer' and commanded the recipient to search 'the premises known and described as the email account'.

[96] *Yahoo* (2016) (n 68) [6].

[97] *Jimenez* (n 40) [53].

[98] ibid.

[99] Akehurst (n 48) 147: 'it makes no difference whether a State employs its own officials to make inquiries or whether it hires private detectives, accountants, etc. the act is illegal regardless of the status of the State's agent'.

territory of another state which matters to states, and which finds expression in customary international law. Arbitrator Max Huber's well-known dicta in *Island of Palmas Case* (1928) is directly on point:

> an element which is essential for the constitution of sovereignty should not be lacking in its continuation … practice, as well as doctrine, recognizes … that the continuous and peaceful *display* of territorial sovereignty … is as good as a title' (emphasis added).[100]

He then stated it once more: 'Territorial sovereignty … involves the *exclusive* right to *display* the activities of a State' (emphasis added).[101] So, the strict territoriality of enforcement jurisdiction protects each state's right – and obligation – to display its exclusive dominion, or monopoly of state authority, in its territory. In other words, international law in this context is not focused on the protection of a state's actual dominion, but the appearance of it – although undoubtedly originally on the assumption that actual and apparent dominion match. For Max Huber, the recognition of abstract rights, taken for granted in domestic law, functioned poorly within the horizontal framework of international law, which thus required the manifestation of state authority – in perpetuity:

> Although municipal law, thanks to its complete judicial system, is able to recognize abstract rights of property as existing apart from any material display of them, it has none the less limited their effect by the principles of prescription and the protection of possession. International law, the structure of which is not based on any super-State organisation, cannot be presumed to reduce a right such as territorial sovereignty, with which almost all international relations are bound up, to the category of an abstract right, without concrete manifestations.[102]

So, states remain under continuing pressure to be *visibly* in charge in their territories, which goes hand in hand with an intolerance of any competing displays of the authority by other states in their territory. For that reason, enforcement jurisdiction is at least as much of a burden on the interfered with state as a restraint on the interfering state. Protesting against a foreign state's data intervention would implicitly also be an admission by the protesting state that its authority has been compromised.[103]

Foregrounding visible manifestations of another's state authority as a trigger for a violation of territorial sovereignty against Huber's background explanation is instructive on a number of levels. First, it contextualises why customary international law remains so wedded to a physical conception of sovereignty that seems archaic and more befitting earlier, more overtly physical ages from which international law and the concept of statehood emerged, as opposed to

[100] *Island of Palmas* (n 30) 839.
[101] ibid.
[102] ibid.
[103] There may be some parallels with the behaviour of corporations in response to cyber interventions. See, eg E Amir, S Levi and T Livne, 'Do Firms Underreport Information on Cyber-Attacks? Evidence from Capital Markets' (2018) 23 *Review of Accounting Studies* 1177.

twenty-first-century digitised statecraft. Second, it explains the relative lack of condemnation – as a matter of international law – by the community of states of extraterritorial data demands and other digital interventions despite their far greater capacity to disrupt and undermine *actual* state authority than any isolated activity of a foreign officer on display. Data interventions are invisible, and as such are not an immediate threat to manifestations of territorial sovereignty. By extension, the threshold for violating the non-intervention principle is rarely treated as being met in cyber contexts.[104] In fact, states are incentivised to downplay the effects of any foreign data interference as a violation of their territorial sovereignty, particularly in light of the relative difficulty of policing data borders and thus preventing intrusions.[105] New Zealand's government commented that the a-territorial nature of cyberspace 'make[s] it difficult for states to prevent malicious cyber activity being conducted from or routed through their territory'.[106] In the 2021 SolarWinds incident,[107] Russia's Foreign Intelligence Service managed to hack into the computer networks of nine US federal agencies and 100 private sector companies, which gave it 'the ability to spy on or potentially disrupt more than 16,000 computer systems worldwide'.[108] Whilst the USA and its allies, including Australia, Canada, the EU and the UK, 'condemned Russia's behavior as malicious, destabilizing, or malign',[109] they did not frame their disapproval as a violation of international law. For a cyber activity to amount to a *use of force*, that is, an armed attack, it must have 'physical consequences … [akin to] the kind of damage that dropping a bomb or firing a missile would [have]'.[110] Whilst interventions that fall short of physical force may still violate the *non-intervention rule*,[111] they have to be 'coercive' – forcing another state's hand in a matter of its *domaine reserve*, which includes 'choice[s] of a political, economic, social, and cultural system, and the formulation of foreign policy'.[112] Cyber interferences

[104] MN Schmitt and L Vihul (eds), *Tallinn Manual 2.0 on the International Law Applicable to Cyber Operations*, 2nd edn (Cambridge, Cambridge University Press, 2017) 17–20, discussed in K Eichensehr, 'Not Illegal: The SolarWinds Incident and International Law' [2022] *European Journal of International Law* 9, papers.ssrn.com/sol3/papers.cfm?abstract_id=4178258.

[105] For blocking statutes, see n 85 above.

[106] New Zealand Foreign Affairs and Trade, 'The Application of International Law to State Activity in Cyberspace' (DPMC, 1 December 2020) para 13, dpmc.govt.nz/publications/application-international-law-state-activity-cyberspace.

[107] Eichensehr (n 104).

[108] ibid 3–4.

[109] ibid 4.

[110] UNGA (n 52) 137 (USA).

[111] The Charter of the United Nations (San Francisco, 26 June 1945), Art 2(4) provides, 'All Members shall refrain in their international relations from the threat or use of force against the territorial integrity or political independence of any State'.

[112] *Case Concerning Military and Paramilitary Activities in and against Nicaragua (Nicaragua v United States)* [1986] ICJ Rep 14 [205]. In the absence of physical force, it is necessary to establish a coercive intervention: 'The principle of non-intervention involves the right of every sovereign State to conduct its affairs without outside interference': (1) it must 'bear on matters in which each State is permitted … to decide freely', including 'the choice of a political, economic, social and cultural system, and the

with 'national democratic processes such as elections, or military, security or critical infrastructure systems' arguably satisfy that requirement,[113] but a mere cross-border data production order is unlikely to do so. Where the non-intervention principle has been invoked to demand jurisdictional restraint, the overreach in question – often in respect of prescriptive jurisdiction rather than enforcement – threatened significant (economic) interferences.[114] Below the threshold of the non-intervention rule, there is disagreement on whether a violation of sovereignty as a stand-alone principle is possible,[115] but even amongst those states who accept it, it is widely agreed that 'negligible physical effects and functional impairments'[116] or '*de minimis* effects'[117] do not amount to a violation. In short, the international community, with some exceptions,[118] does not appear to view cross-border data flows (even if compelled by a public agency) as *in and of themselves* triggering a violation of international law. With this as a background, it becomes clear why Ireland's territorial sovereignty was not considered to be sufficiently engaged in *Microsoft v US*.[119] Having said that, for Michael Akehurst, protest by an interfered with state – such as Ireland – was an indication of the extraterritorial overreach.[120]

Third, foregrounding manifestations of state authority on another state's territory over real but bodiless interferences also means that international law below the high threshold of the non-intervention principle tolerates a vast amount of transborder interventions and movements of a benign and belligerent nature,

formulation of foreign policy'; and (2) it must involve 'coercion in regard to such choices, which must remain free ones' (see [202]–[205]). The threshold of the principle of non-intervention is too high to catch most cross-border data interventions. See N Tasgourias, 'Electoral Cyber Interference, Self-Determination and the Principle of Non-Intervention in Cyberspace' in D Broeders and B van den Berg (eds), *Governing Cyberspace: Behavior, Power and Diplomacy* (London, Rowman & Littlefield, 2020).

[113] UNGA (n 52) 25 (Germany).

[114] DJ Gerber, 'The Extraterritorial Application of German Antitrust Laws' (1983) 77 *American Journal of International Law* 756, 772ff.

[115] UNGA (n 52) 139 (USA): 'a State's remote cyber operations involving computers or other networked devices located on another State's territory do not constitute a per se violation of international law.'

[116] ibid 33 (Germany); see also 88 (Switzerland), commenting that 'the threshold for a breach of the non-intervention principle is significantly higher than that for a violation of state sovereignty'.

[117] ibid 139 (USA).

[118] eg ibid 18 (Brazil): 'State sovereignty is … applicable as a standalone rule, including to the use of ICTs by States … Interceptions of telecommunications, for instance, whether or not they are considered to have crossed the threshold of an intervention in the internal affairs of another State, would nevertheless be considered an internationally wrongful act because they violate state sovereignty. Similarly, cyber operations against information systems located in another State's territory or causing extraterritorial effects might also constitute a breach of sovereignty.'

[119] Ireland's amicus curiae brief in *Microsoft Corp* (n 8) (23 December 2014) blogs.microsoft.com/wp-content/uploads/sites/149/2014/09/Ireland-AmicusBrief.pdf, in which the Irish government noted that the Irish Supreme Court in *Walsh v National Irish Bank* [2013] 1 ESC 2 held that it could 'order the disclosure by an Irish corporation of information in its possession, notwithstanding that the information is physically located in another jurisdiction'.

[120] Akehurst (n 48) 169–70.

without seeking to discipline them, and leaves it to domestic laws and agencies to do so. By extension, the idea of territorial sovereignty, or *exclusive* territorial control, is illusory insofar as extraterritorial performances of state authority are discounted in international law as long as they do not involve foreign government personnel entering the state. As long ago as 1987, Bernardez commented that whilst the territory as a physical underlay

> helps guarantee the State's independence and security … it must be admitted that in recent decades the material function of territory has in particular instances, and especially as seen from outside, been affected by the impact of such new phenomena as fast communications, sophisticated weaponry and integrated economic regions.[121]

As this was well before data on global computer networks became a key resource for the exercise of state authority, it cannot but be concluded that the material function of territory as a basis of independence and security has further diminished. Moreover, as customary international law on enforcement jurisdiction only captures physical 'surface' interventions, it has – as it stands – little to contribute to interstate relations in the context of contemporary digitised statecraft.

C. Domestic Control Over Data

None of this is to suggest that states are disinterested in controlling as much data as possible – both to and from their territories. Quite the reverse. The widespread emergence of data localisation laws,[122] blocking statutes[123] and expansive statutory powers on cross-border data access[124] speaks to its mission-critical role for internal and external security, as well as to the geopolitical competitiveness of states over 'their' data.[125] Arguably, it is precisely because access to data is operationally and strategically so vital that is has been kept below the threshold of international law. This means that states – especially those dominating the information environment – are free to adopt legal positions favourable to their own domestic interests, however unco-operative and duplicitous. For example, the USA simultaneously claims access to data outside its territory (even from those only marginally connected with its jurisdiction) and seeks to block equivalent access by other states except where there exists a bilateral agreement.[126] In contrast, an internationally

[121] Bernardez, 'Territorial Sovereignty' (n 44) 487–88.

[122] Chander and Lê (n 5).

[123] See n 85 above; Hornkohl (n 16).

[124] See n 12 above.

[125] See, eg 18 USC § 2523 Executive agreements on access to data by foreign governments under the CLOUD Act; § 2523(b)(2) and (3) makes the minimisation of data on US persons by the foreign government a precondition for entering into an agreement with foreign governments to facilitate their access to data held by US platforms. On EU protectiveness of their residents' data, see *Schrems II* (n 7), followed by the Trans-Atlantic Data Privacy Framework (EU–US) (Brussels, March 2022).

[126] See n 85 above.

agreed legal position on cross-border data access directly from platforms would necessarily embody a more principled stance that invested all states, on a formal basis, with the same rights and obligations, and would thereby reflect a degree of reciprocity and global solidarity: a clearly prohibitive rule would make data access attempts outside MLATs illegal, whilst a clearly permissive rule would make blocking attempts suspect.

An early example of a principled international law stance – albeit one of limited scope – is Article 32 of the Cybercrime Convention, which allows a state party, in the absence of a jurisdictional foundation,[127] to access 'without the authorisation of another Party' either (i) 'publicly available (open source) stored computer data, regardless of where the data is located geographically', or (ii) 'computer data located in another Party … [with] the lawful and voluntary consent of the person who has the lawful authority to disclose the data'. Article 32 was understood as 'an exception to the principle of territoriality … [that] permits unilateral transborder access without the need for mutual assistance under limited circumstances'.[128] Its relatively ready acceptability at the time suggests that it likely codified existing state practice, and so effectively legalised a state practice in a legal no man's land; unsupported by international law, but also not violating it. Again, the fact that Article 32 is limited in scope does not mean unilateral cross-border access of data is otherwise prohibited; as the Explanatory Report stated, 'other situations are neither authorised, nor precluded'.[129]

Two decades later, the Second Additional Protocol to the Convention on Cybercrime (2021)[130] has delivered a slightly expanded reciprocal regime over and beyond MLATs. Article 7 permits a state party to request 'subscriber information' directly from a service provider in another state (without a jurisdictional foundation), accompanied by a reciprocal duty on the requested state to facilitate such disclosures.[131] This co-operative permissiveness is limited to subscriber data (it does not cover traffic or content data),[132] and even then the requested state may choose to supervise disclosures through involvement of a public agency.[133] Beyond the relatively narrow category of subscriber data, data demands remain largely within the confines of traditional MLAT regimes, or

[127] *cf* the Cybercrime Convention, Art 18 on data production orders directed at service providers, which requires that the service provider is subject to the requesting state's jurisdiction.

[128] Cybercrime Convention Committee, 'T-CY Guidance Note #3: Transborder Access to Data (Article 32)' (Council of Europe, 2014) 2.

[129] Explanatory Report to the Convention on Cybercrime (23 November 2001) [293]. See also n 83 above on the Cybercrime Convention, Art 39(3).

[130] Second Additional Protocol (n 14).

[131] Art 7 of the Second Additional Protocol applies when Art 18 of the Cybercrime Convention cannot be invoked due to a lack of a jurisdictional connection.

[132] Note subscriber and traffic data is covered in Art 8, which provides for an expediated mutual assistance regime between the public authorities of two states.

[133] Second Additional Protocol (n 14) Art 7(2)(b).

their newer, expediated versions.[134] The reluctance to move away from MLATs in favour of states accessing data directly from platforms may be read as an attempt to preserve the safeguards built into MLATs, and so constitutes some resistance to the surrender of data oversight to platforms as its new global gatekeepers. However, as shown above, in most cases, extraterritorial data requests draw on a jurisdictional foundation and thereby fall outside the purview of the formal processes of MLATs.

V. Conclusion: Territoriality's Untold Stories

Territoriality under customary international law emerges from the above account as an uncomfortably strained construct of a bygone age in which the boundedness of physical space *actually* constrained communities and meaningfully served as a platform for the display of state authority *actually* held. Still, at first sight, territoriality appears to have accommodated twenty-first-century, data-driven, corporatised, globalised statecraft: it allows for expansive claims of authority against local or overseas platforms (prescriptive jurisdiction) made within its territory (enforcement jurisdiction) and downplays the resultant extraterritorial interferences in another state's territory as falling short of a violation of territorial sovereignty. Thus, it accommodates what needs to be done from a state-centric perspective: it allows for the regulation of global platforms which have profound effects on domestic, social, economic and political spheres, and gives access to their data reservoirs as indispensable for domestic law enforcement. Yet, in this facilitation also lies its shortfall. Territoriality becomes virtually bereft of restrictive or disciplining effects on modern statecraft – other than at the very outer physical or coercive boundaries. Enforcement jurisdiction, at first glance, promises real bite by seemingly forbidding the exercise of state authority in the territory of another state as 'the first and foremost restriction' imposed by international law. Yet, states have been reluctant to move away from their preoccupation with the physical display of authority by another state in their territories and to account for the pervasive reality of digital interventions. Overall, the paradoxical effect is that as the interconnectedness between states in the exercise of their authority – mediated through platforms – has dramatically increased, the role played by the overarching legal framework appears to have diminished. Bilateral agreements (eg those falling under the CLOUD Act) and multilateral conventions (eg the Cybercrime Convention) fill some of the lacuna beyond the familiar grounds of the cumbersome MLATs.

The thinness of territoriality as an ordering principle for the exercise of state authority in digital society has causes (and effects) going over and beyond its

[134] eg Second Additional Protocol Arts 8–10 seek to expediate mutual assistance in respect of electronic evidence.

physical orientation. As the construct of territory or territoriality under international law is deeply state-centric, it can account neither for the role played by global platforms in the creation of alternative public spaces that map only imperfectly and under pressure onto state territories nor for their centrality to regulatory processes, as carriers and implementers of regulatory messages and controllers of large sets of personal data. In these roles and processes, platforms are not simply passive actors answerable to state authority. On the data front, they exercise significant discretion on how to comply with the request: 'discretion in how critically they evaluate the legality of requests, in slowing down the process by insisting on proceduralism, and in minimizing their capacity to respond to legal requests by implementing encryption'.[135] They thereby have a systemic impact on the effectiveness of the exercise of governmental authority. Yet, public international law has no way of 'seeing' these global platforms other than as domestic private actors subject to state authority. In positivist legal terms, this is correct; yet, from a critical legal perspective, this view is profoundly reductionist insofar as the co-dependencies of states on global platforms for their exercise of authority cannot be seen, understood or critiqued. The structural blindness of territoriality to significant actors with substantial quasi-authority outside the state paradigm means that its explicatory power of the normative ordering in contemporary global network society is limited and thin, which makes it ultimately uninteresting.

Along the same lines, the state-centric nature of territoriality also means that individuals are recognised only indirectly in their role as subjects of the state and subject to its authority, which is oddly out of tune with their elevation as ends in themselves in and through international human rights law. In the above account, the fact that the contested data is *personal* data and frequently of a highly sensitive nature does not figure prominently in the data narratives on territorial sovereignty. For sure, individual interests in personal data, as recently championed by platforms,[136] tend to form the background to domestic litigation. So the substantive driver behind the debate on the extraterritorial reach of warrants under the Stored Communications Act in *Microsoft v US* were privacy concerns: does the constitutional privacy protection that attaches to warrants under the Fourth Amendment, as implemented through the Act, extend to personal data of non-US citizens stored outside US territory? However, fundamental rights protection is, in essence, also understood through the state paradigm, or, as the Second Circuit Court in *Microsoft v US* observed:

> As the term is used in the Constitution, a warrant is traditionally moored to privacy concepts applied within the territory of the United States: 'What we know of the history of the drafting of the Fourth Amendment … suggests that its purpose was to restrict

[135] Editorial, 'Cooperation or Resistance?: The Role of Tech Companies in Government Surveillance' (2018) 131 *Harvard Law Review* 1722, 1723.

[136] ibid.

> searches and seizures which might be conducted by the United States in domestic matters.'[137]

Still, although territoriality supplies the content and boundaries for fundamental rights protection, there are also signs that fundamental rights protection delimits territoriality. For example, the 'executive agreements' under the CLOUD Act are made conditional on the domestic law of the foreign government affording 'robust substantive and procedural protections for privacy and civil liberties', demonstrating 'respect for the rule of law and principles of nondiscrimination' and adherence 'to applicable international human rights obligations', including fair trial rights and prohibitions on arbitrary arrest and detention.[138] Effectively, the heightened global integration of national law enforcement activities also creates a push towards a convergence of human rights standards, as dictated by the states that dominate the dataverse.

[137] *Microsoft Corp* (n 8) 212.
[138] 18 USC § 2523(b).

9

What Triggers the Extraterritorial Application of Fundamental Rights? From Effective Control Over Territory to State Act Theory in Cross-Border Surveillance

JULIA HÖRNLE

I. Introduction

This chapter discusses possible answers to the question of whether a state's constitutional or international human rights[1] guarantees apply beyond that state's borders, and if so, what the conditions are for the extraterritorial application of fundamental rights in the context of bulk surveillance.[2] To this end, the chapter examines recent jurisprudence in this area from the European Court of Human Rights (ECtHR) and the German Constitutional Court (GCC). 'Extraterritoriality' here means that the individuals whose fundamental rights are engaged by the surveillance of a state are located outside the territory of that state.[3] Extraterritoriality of human rights is a fundamentally important question in the twenty-first century,[4] given the increasing threats emanating from modern technology.

[1] For the purposes of this chapter, I have used the following terminology: 'constitutional rights' refer to fundamental rights in national constitutions; 'human rights' refer to fundamental rights in international conventions; and 'fundamental rights' refers to both.

[2] This chapter will not discuss different types of investigative techniques – therefore terminology such as 'surveillance' and 'interception' are loosely used to denote the collection of communications data, encompassing both content and metadata, the collection of data which is stored and in transit, and targeted and untargeted investigations.

[3] M Milanovic, *Extraterritorial Application of Human Rights Treaties: Law, Principles, and Policy* (Oxford, Oxford University Press, 2011) 8.

[4] See also R Wilde, 'Human Rights beyond Borders at the World Court: The Significance of the International Court of Justice's Jurisprudence on the Extraterritorial Application of International Human Rights Law Treaties' (2013) 12 *Chinese Journal of International Law* 639, 673.

One reason behind the increasing need for both the extraterritorial surveillance of foreigners and co-operation between intelligence agencies is that crime and national security threats frequently originate abroad. The key question is how this need can be reconciled with the cross-border protection of fundamental rights.[5] Another reason for extraterritorial action and international co-operation is that the relevant intelligence and criminal evidence is located in the 'cloud'.[6] This necessitates law enforcement authorities gaining access to data in the cloud; installing cloud intercept capabilities with foreign communication providers; or engaging in international investigatory co-operation.[7] New instruments have emerged enabling the cross-border exercise of investigative powers, be it through mutual legal assistance or direct access by law enforcement and intelligence agencies to data controlled by foreign communication service providers or stored on foreign computers. While these powers have been widely (and controversially) discussed in the literature[8] (so will not be discussed here), less attention has been given to the question of jurisdiction in respect of the application of fundamental rights in the criminal justice and intelligence arena.[9]

It is all the more astonishing that in Germany until 2016, and in other countries even now, the area of communications data interception for the purposes of intelligence surveillance[10] was not regulated, as if the rule of law could not reach into the field of intelligence and data sharing.[11] This has been a bone of contention with human rights advocates for some time.[12] Therefore, it is a victory that the German Constitutional Court has acknowledged that the rule of law (and the German Constitution) reigns supreme in the murky waters of intergovernmental intelligence surveillance co-operation.

In the jurisprudence of the ECtHR, the question of the extraterritorial application of rights has only directly arisen in the context of military operations on foreign territory, or in the context of extradition and death row cases.[13]

[5] M Rojszczak, 'Extraterritorial Bulk Surveillance after the German BND Act Judgment' (2021) 17 *European Constitutional Law Review* 1, 2.

[6] See further J Hörnle, *Internet Jurisdiction: Law and Practice* (Oxford, Oxford University Press, 2021) ch 6.

[7] W Schluckebier, 'Sicherheitsgewährleistung' in J-H Dietrich et al (eds), *Reform der Nachrichtendienste zwischen Vergesetzlichung und Internationisierung* (Tübingen, Mohr Siebeck, 2019) 6.

[8] Hörnle (n 6); DJB Svantesson, 'Law Enforcement Cross-Border Access to Data' (22 November 2016) papers.ssrn.com/sol3/papers.cfm?abstract_id=2874238; AM Osula, 'Mutual Legal Assistance and Other Mechanisms for Accessing Extraterritorially Located Data' (2015) 9 *Masaryk University Journal of Law and Technology* 43; AM Osula, 'Transborder Access and Territorial Sovereignty' (2015) 31 *Computer Law and Security Review* 719.

[9] S Gless, 'Bird's-Eye View and Worm's-Eye View: Towards a Defendant-Based Approach in Transnational Criminal Law' (2015) 6 *Transnational Legal Theory* 117; Hörnle (n 6) ch 7.

[10] As opposed to law enforcement.

[11] A Lubin, 'We Only Spy on Foreigners: The Myth of a Universal Right to Privacy and the Practice of Foreign Mass Surveillance' (2018) 18 *Chicago Journal of International Law* 513.

[12] ibid 516.

[13] *Soering v United Kingdom* (A/161) (1989) 11 EHRR 439, albeit that these death row cases are not really extraterritorial, as the decision to extradite is made within the territory of the extraditing state in the knowledge of the effects in the requesting state. See also B Rainey, E Wicks and C Ovey, *Jacobs,*

However, as we will see, the Court has applied Article 8 of the European Convention on Human Rights (ECHR) to international data sharing and cross-border data flows in the context of criminal investigations and intelligence co-operation.

The novelty of these issues is best illustrated by the following three scenarios. In the first scenario, a group of states (such as the Five Eyes alliance[14]) exchange intelligence information on third-party nationals, who are located outside their respective territories, which has been gained through bulk surveillance of Internet communications. This operation raises the question of whether the state carrying out the surveillance and the states sharing the information are bound by the fundamental rights contained in their respective constitutions (or the applicable international human rights treaties to which they are a party).

In the second scenario, if law enforcement authorities in State A, with mutual legal assistance from State B, obtain disclosure of data from a social media account (such as subscriber and content data) controlled in State B in order to assist State A's criminal investigation and prosecution of Person C, a national of State C, do the fundamental rights protections in State A, B and/or C apply?

In the third scenario, if the USA builds an intercept capability into a direct messaging service operated in the UK, based on the Executive Agreement between the USA and the UK, does this facility have to comply with privacy standards in the UK and/or the USA?

The gap in fundamental rights protection in cross-border data flows for intelligence and law enforcement purposes can be overcome through bifurcation, namely by: (i) the acting state extending the territorial scope of rights protection under its national constitutional law; and (ii) achieving protection through the notion of state responsibility for human rights obligations under international treaties, such as the ECHR or the International Covenant on Civil and Political Rights (ICCPR). The argument made in this chapter is that rights protection under both limbs should not be limited to territory, but should attach to the specific state act which is interfering with fundamental rights. I call this 'state act theory'. It is the act of a state which triggers its constitutional fundamental rights protections and its responsibility under the human rights treaties it has ratified. For international co-operation, which involves data transfers or other forms of data sharing, the state transferring the data has a responsibility to ensure that the recipient state guarantees the application of a minimum fundamental rights framework.[15]

The contribution of this chapter is a discussion of whether fundamental rights laid down in national constitutions and human rights treaties apply

White and Ovey: The European Convention on Human Rights, 6th edn (Oxford, Oxford University Press, 2014) 90.

[14] The Five Eyes alliance is a co-operation between the foreign intelligence services of the USA, Canada, the UK, Australia and New Zealand which has its origins in the Second World War and the Cold War.

[15] Schluckebier (n 7) 13–14.

extraterritorially in the context of cross-border data flows for intelligence or law enforcement purposes.

It does this by first examining the case law of the ECtHR (section II), then moving on to recent jurisprudence by the GCC[16] (section III). By way of comparison, it then analyses the extraterritorial application of fundamental rights in the USA in section IV. Section V examines whether digital constitutionalism would help to overcome the limitations of extraterritoriality and state responsibility. This examination leads to a formulation of a new 'state act theory' derived from the GCC's latest jurisprudence. This is an idealistic vision; we are not yet at a point where such a state act theory is becoming customary international law, but the case law discussed in this chapter calls for setting out this vision. Section V then returns to the examples mentioned above to illustrate the limited application of fundamental rights to cross-border interception, and discusses the operation of the US–UK Executive Agreement in this respect. This contrasts sharply with the notion of digital constitutionalism and the GCC's state act theory, and shows that there is no universal recognition of the protection of fundamental rights.

II. State Responsibility and the ECHR: The Jurisprudence of the ECtHR

A. State Responsibility and Jurisdiction

State responsibility is the pivotal concept in this area. Under international law, if a state, through its officials, carries out an act which is a breach of its international law obligations (such as a human rights obligation), that state is liable to make reparations (such as paying compensation).[17] Article 1 of the International Law Commission Articles on State Responsibility (ILC Articles) states that 'Every internationally wrongful act of a State entails the international responsibility of that State'.[18] This raises the question of whether this responsibility is owed to an individual or a state. Who the responsibility is owed to depends on the nature of the obligation under international law. Article 33(1) states that the obligation can be owed to another state or to the international community at large, or, as would be the case for international human rights obligations under the ECHR and as acknowledged in Article 33(2), the obligation may create a right for individuals.[19]

[16] Bundesverfassungsgericht (BVerfG).

[17] MN Shaw, *International Law*, 9th edn (Cambridge, Cambridge University Press, 2021) 677.

[18] International Law Commission, 'Responsibility of States for Internationally Wrongful Acts' (2001) Yearbook of the ILC vol II, pt 2 (ILC Articles) legal.un.org/ilc/texts/instruments/english/draft_articles/9_6_2001.pdf.

[19] 'This part is without prejudice to any right, arising from the international responsibility of a State, which may accrue directly to any person or entity other than a State.'

For state responsibility to be triggered under international law, there must be a wrongful act. Regarding infringement of human rights obligations, this must be part of international law, such as an obligation under the ECHR. Therefore, there is a distinction between a state's constitutional rights obligation under that state's domestic, constitutional law and a state's human rights obligations under international law. The ambit of constitutional fundamental rights is governed by national law, whereas the extent of the international human rights obligations is governed by international law, including the principles of state responsibility. Article 2 of the ILC Articles elaborates further on the 'internationally wrongful act' and defines it as 'an action or omission' which is '(a) is attributable to the State under international law and (b) constitutes a breach of an international obligation of the State'.[20] Article 3 makes it clear that 'The characterization of an act of a State as internationally wrongful is governed by international law. Such characterization is not affected by the characterization of the same act as lawful by internal law.'[21]

The question of how state responsibility relates to jurisdiction has not been fully answered, and much confusion persists.[22] Jurisdiction and state responsibility are closely aligned: in the modern (post-World War II) sphere of international human rights, jurisdiction is the first step towards state responsibility.[23] Therefore, the concept of jurisdiction is important for understanding state responsibility. Jurisdiction is conceived of as authority and legitimate control over territory. But it is increasingly also understood as control over persons.[24] As we will see below, this tendency is also apparent from the jurisprudence of the ECtHR.

The concept of jurisdiction is related to the concept of state responsibility, as it decides when an act can be attributed to a particular state. In other words, there first has to be an assessment of whether wrongful conduct can be attributed to a state as an act of state (for example as opposed to an act of a private person or the act of another state). Secondly, state responsibility can only arise if there is an element of control, which leads to state responsibility in respect of that wrongful act.[25]

Attribution is one of the requirements for state responsibility, and therefore the key question is whether and how extraterritorial acts of a state can be attributed to a state. A state may incur responsibility where officials of that state cause injury to a national in another state, even outside the context of war and foreign incursion.[26] Article 4 of the ILC Articles makes it clear that responsibility is triggered by any

[20] ILC Articles (n 18).

[21] ibid.

[22] A Sari, 'Untangling Extra-Territorial Jurisdiction from International Responsibility in *Jaloud v Netherlands*: Old Problem, New Solutions?' (2014) 53 *Military Law and the Law of War Review* 287.

[23] G Noll, 'Theorizing Jurisdiction' in A Orford and F Hoffmann (eds), *The Oxford Handbook of the Theory of International Law* (Oxford, Oxford University Press, 2016) 605. See also Hörnle (n 6) 3.

[24] Milanovic (n 3) 119; Hörnle (n 6) 3.

[25] Sari (n 22) 289–90. Sari argues that the ECtHR in *Jaloud* insufficiently examined the question of control (in terms of the responsibility for the acts of the Dutch military forces).

[26] Shaw (n 17) 684.

act of a state organ, whatever its position and whether it carries out executive, legislative or judicial functions,[27] even if the act is ultra vires, exceeding the power or jurisdiction of the particular state organ.[28] State responsibility is largely based on the level of control a state has over the wrongful act.[29] This is also largely the approach the ECtHR has taken in its recent jurisprudence.

B. Jurisprudence of the ECtHR in Cases of Extraterritorial Military Operations

Most of the jurisprudence on the extraterritorial application of the ECHR concerns military interventions and extrajudicial killing (primarily engaging Articles 2 and 3 ECHR), a very different subject matter to the extraterritorial surveillance of communications (primarily engaging Article 8). However, the ECtHR's rulings on jurisdiction and state responsibility in the former cases can be directly applied to the latter cases, and the Court has in fact referred to its case law on military interventions (*Al Skeini*) in the context of its case law on international surveillance (*Big Brother Watch*).

The question whether a state's responsibilities under a treaty apply outside its territory is a question of interpreting the ambit of the treaty itself, and the Law of Treaties does not predefine the territorial or extraterritorial application of a treaty.[30]

Article 1 of the ECHR renders the ambit of the Convention congruent with the jurisdiction of the contracting state: 'The High Contracting Parties shall secure to *everyone within their jurisdiction* the rights and freedoms defined in … this Convention' (emphasis added). Article 1 means that establishing the jurisdiction of a contracting party is a prerequisite to state responsibility.[31] This raises the question of whether the ECHR applies to a state's actions *outside that state's territory*. Or, put another way, it raises the question of whether jurisdiction is limited to acting on that state's territory, or more precisely territory under its control.[32] The concept of jurisdiction therefore has two sides: one is delineating the power and authority of the state to act, and the other is the state's responsibility to comply with its constitutional or international human rights obligations. Article 1 expresses the principle that, for the purposes of the ECHR, these two sides are congruent.

The difficulties of interpretation arise from the well-established principle under international law that agents of a state do not have competence to act outside the territory of that state,[33] and that they therefore do not so act, bar in

[27] ILC Articles (n 18).
[28] ibid Art 7.
[29] Shaw (n 17) 687.
[30] Milanovic (n 3) 2.
[31] Rainey et al (n 13) 89.
[32] As held in *Banković v Belgium (Admissibility)* App No 52207/99 (2007) 44 EHRR SE5.
[33] As a manifestation of the principle of non-interference.

exceptional circumstances such as armed conflict. This principle is challenged by the ample opportunity enabled by the Internet to remotely access and process data. Therefore, at least to some extent, remote access by law enforcement and intelligence services to computer data is a relatively new challenge to the territoriality principle.[34]

Extraterritoriality can arise from agents of a state physically acting outside that state's borders, and in fact the ECtHR has primarily considered the extraterritoriality of the ECHR in the context of occupations and armed conflicts. But, of course, extraterritoriality may additionally arise where state agents, such as law enforcement or intelligence agencies, act *physically* but remotely within their own state's borders, and directly impact on the rights of foreign citizens resident or domiciled abroad, for example through interception and surveillance activities.

This section first examines the ECtHR's long-standing case law on extraterritorial jurisdiction in the context of armed conflict and military interventions, and then considers the ECtHR's application of Article 8 to foreign intelligence. The case law has been described as

> problematic, suffering from rampant casuistry and conceptual chaos. It is a jurisprudence of (at times quite unprincipled) compromise, caused mostly by the Court's understandable desire to avoid the merits of legally and politically extremely difficult cases by relying on the preliminary issue of extraterritorial application.[35]

The first landmark case on the extraterritorial application of ECHR rights was *Loizidou v Turkey*.[36] The Court held that Turkey may be responsible under the Convention for alleged breaches in Cyprus, because the contracting parties to the ECHR can be responsible outside of their own territory in several situations: (i) when 'the extradition or expulsion of a person by a Contracting Party may give rise to an issue under Article 3' (prohibition of torture); (ii) when a contracting party's authorities act in a manner that produces 'effects outside their own territory'; and (iii) when a contracting party 'as a consequence of military action – whether lawful or unlawful – exercises effective control of an area outside its national territory'.[37] Remote data access and data sharing for law enforcement or intelligence purposes do not fall under any of these categories, since the state action here does not merely produce effects outside the territory of the state, but, arguably, the contracting state actually acts simultaneously on both its own territory, through the interception or surveillance measures it takes, and on the foreign territory, by accessing, transferring or processing data. Hence, the exercise of surveillance powers falls under a separate, possibly a fourth, category.[38]

[34] See further Hörnle (n 6).

[35] Milanovic (n 3) 4.

[36] *Loizidou v Turkey* App No 15318/89 (1997) 23 EHRR 513.

[37] ibid judgment (preliminary objections) [62].

[38] See also M Löffelmann, 'Die Ausland-Ausland Fernmeldeaufklärung' in Dietrich et al (n 7) 39, who argues that surveillance of foreign data subjects is a territorial act with foreign impact, not purely extraterritorial.

Loizidou concerned a claimant in Cyprus claiming infringement of her rights to access a property in the Turkish-occupied northern part of Cyprus, and the question was whether Turkey had jurisdiction because of its military occupation. The ECtHR held that the control did not need to be legitimate control under international law but, rather, overall, effective control over territory.[39] It is a factual rather than a legal determination.[40]

The ECtHR controversially repurposed this 'overall, effective control' test in the *Banković* admissibility decision.[41] The case was brought against the 17 contracting NATO states involved in the 1999 aerial bombing of a TV station in Serbia by the families of the deceased victims. The ECtHR held that the case was inadmissible because the victims did not fall within the jurisdiction of the states in question, so the ECHR did not apply. The Court found that the NATO states lacked effective control over the area because they did not have troops on the ground. The Court in effect limited the 'effective control' test to situations where contracting parties occupy the territory in question through a military presence or through the consent of the government of the territory, so that the contracting party exercises 'public powers' that would normally be exercised by the government of the territory.[42]

The ECtHR rejected the applicants' argument that the states controlled the military equipment used to carry out the airstrike as a 'cause and effect' concept of jurisdiction that would have meant that a contracting state is liable whenever they control state action taking place outside their territory, holding that this is insufficient for jurisdiction.[43]

The ECtHR revisited the extraterritorial application of the ECHR in the *Al-Skeini* case.[44] In that case, the relatives of six Iraqi nationals alleged that their relatives were within the jurisdiction of the UK when they were killed and that there had been no effective investigation into their deaths, violating the UK's responsibilities under Article 2.

The Court reiterated its previous case law that the ECHR applies primarily within the territory of the contracting parties, as well as when a contracting party exercises effective control over an area outside of its territory.[45] Interestingly for our purposes, however, the Court revisited its doctrine on state responsibilities under the ECHR where the state's acts impact individuals outside of the territory, departing from its previous holding in *Banković*. The ECtHR reiterated that contracting parties are responsible under the ECHR when they either act or do so in such a way as to produce effects outside of their territory, but 'only in

[39] *Loizidou* (n 36) judgment (merits) [56].
[40] Milanovic (n 3) 26–28.
[41] *Banković* (n 32).
[42] ibid [71].
[43] ibid [75].
[44] *Al-Skeini v United Kingdom* App No 55721/07 (2011) 53 EHRR 18.
[45] ibid [131]–[132], [138]–[140].

exceptional cases'.[46] The Court then listed these exceptional cases, which included acts of diplomats; situations in which the contracting party 'exercises all or some of the public powers normally to be exercised by' the government of the territory; and circumstances involving custodial detention of an individual by the contracting party.[47] The Court then departed from *Banković* and concluded:

> [W]henever the State, through its agents, *exercises control and authority over an individual*, and thus jurisdiction, the State is under an obligation under Article 1 to secure to that individual the rights and freedoms … of the Convention that are relevant to the situation of that individual. In this sense, therefore, the Convention rights can be 'divided and tailored'. (emphasis added)[48]

The ECtHR ultimately found that the six Iraqi nationals were within the jurisdiction of the UK for purposes of the Convention because the UK, together with the USA, had assumed public powers that would normally be exercised by the Iraqi government. These powers included the maintenance of security in the territory, including security operations in the area in question. Therefore, UK authorities 'exercised authority and control over individuals killed', which established state responsibility under the ECHR.[49] Thus, the ECtHR made important statements in this judgment affirming state responsibility based on state agent authority, even though this was linked to control over territory. *Al-Skeini* affirms the validity of state responsibility based on state agent authority and control, not dissimilar to the reasoning of the GCC in a case concerning the German foreign intelligence service, the Bundesnachrichtendienst (the *BND* case) (although in international cases, jurisdiction additionally needs to be shown). Likewise, in *Jaloud*, in the context of a multinational security operation in Iraq, the Netherlands was responsible for not sufficiently investigating the killing of an Iraqi national at a checkpoint, based on the notion that the Netherlands had full command of its contingent[50] and was asserting authority and control over persons passing through that checkpoint.[51]

In *Issa*,[52] a case concerning Turkish incursions into northern Iraq, the ECtHR referred, with approval, to pronouncements of the UN Human Rights Committee[53] and the Inter-American Commission on Human Rights[54] to the effect that if a person on foreign territory is under the authority and control of the non-territorial state, then that state has effective control for the purposes of jurisdiction.

[46] ibid [131].
[47] ibid [133]–[136].
[48] ibid [137].
[49] ibid [149].
[50] *Jaloud v Netherlands* App No 47708/08 (2015) 60 EHRR 29 [143].
[51] ibid [152].
[52] *Issa v Turkey* App No 31821/96 (2005) 41 EHRR 27 [71].
[53] *Lopez Burgos v Uruguay* App No 52/1979 [12.3]; *Celiberti de Casariego v Uruguay* Comm No 56/1979 [10.3].
[54] *Coard v United States* (29 September 1999) Report No 109/99, Case No 10.951 [37], [39], [41], [43].

The *Al-Skeini*, *Jaloud* and *Issa* jurisprudence replaces the 'effective control' over territory test with an *effective control over persons* test.[55] Where jurisdiction is based on effective control over persons, the non-territorial state, which does not fully control the territory, cannot be required to guarantee the full range of fundamental rights guaranteed in the Convention.[56] It can, however, be obliged to guarantee the rights relevant to the particular situation which gives it authority and control over the person; so, for example, in the case of military detention, it must guarantee the right to life and the prohibition of torture, or in the case of surveillance operations, the qualified right to privacy in Article 8 ECHR.

These rulings indicate that the extraterritorial responsibility of contracting states may be engaged where they have a degree of control over a person as a consequence of the exercise of state authority, and where the exercise of state authority engages only a particular right under the ECHR, such as Article 8. The principle that state responsibility is based on state agent authority and control must be tempered by the ECtHR's language that the ECHR extends extraterritorially 'only in exceptional cases'.[57] This raises the question whether surveillance and interception fall under the category of exceptional cases.

Another such exceptional case was *Carter v Russia*,[58] where the widow of the former Russian FSB agent Alexander Litvinenko brought a claim against Russia in connection with her husband's murder with the radioactive isotope polonium-210.[59] Russia argued that, since Litvinenko was poisoned in London, the case was outside the ambit of the ECHR because the events had occurred outside Russian jurisdiction and the exception to the jurisdictional principle in *Al Skeini* (physical control over a person) did not apply.[60] The applicant argued that 'the application of fatal force by a State agent was sufficient' for jurisdiction, as otherwise assassinations by a state outside that state's territory would not be governed by that state's international human rights responsibilities, leading to the wrong incentives.[61] The ECtHR held that the two main elements of extraterritorial jurisdiction of a contracting state required to trigger state responsibility under the Convention are: (i) the effective control by the state over an area outside its territory (spatial concept of jurisdiction); and (ii) state agent authority and control over individuals (personal concept of jurisdiction).[62] The Court agreed with the applicant that the use of force by a state's agents operating outside its territory may

[55] Rainey et al (n 13) 93.
[56] ibid 94.
[57] ibid [131].
[58] *Carter v Russia* App No 20914/07 (2022) 74 EHRR 12.
[59] The Court took into account the reported results of the UK Inquiry: Home Office, *The Litvinenko Inquiry: Report into the Death of Alexander Litvinenko* (January 2016, HC 695) assets.publishing.service.gov.uk/government/uploads/system/uploads/attachment_data/file/493860/The-Litvinenko-Inquiry-H-C-695-web.pdf.
[60] *Carter* (n 58) [112].
[61] ibid [114].
[62] ibid [125].

bring the individual under the control of that state's authorities, and this alone was sufficient for jurisdiction under Article 1 and was one of the exceptions to territorial jurisdiction established in *Al Skeini*. The Court expressly stated that extraterritorial jurisdiction does not depend on control over physical premises or territory, but that the exercise of physical power and control over a person is sufficient,[63] whether or not the exercise of power is lawful.[64] Citing *Jaloud*, the Court held that if a contracting state, through its agents, exercises physical power over a person, it is obliged to guarantee that person those human rights under the ECHR which are applicable to the specific situation.[65] Therefore, the Court held that arbitrary extraterritorial killings through state agents were indeed a breach of Russia's Article 2 obligations.

C. Jurisprudence of the ECtHR on State Responsibility and Extraterritorial Surveillance

While extraterritorial spying on communications may not be as drastic and serious a secret service operation as extraterritorial unlawful assassination, the ECtHR has confirmed that Convention rights can be 'divided and tailored' in the sense that for extraterritorial state action to be within the ambit of a state's ECHR obligations it is not necessary that the state has complete control over the person.[66] Control emanating from state action may be limited in the sense that only some of the rights under the ECHR may be applicable. The control over a person in surveillance and interception cases would be control over a person's personal data, such as content and communications data, thus engaging Article 8.

The ECtHR Grand Chamber decisions in *Centrum för Rättvisa v Sweden*[67] and *Big Brother Watch v the UK*[68] concerned the compatibility of bulk surveillance measures and foreign intelligence sharing with the ECHR,[69] and follow 2018 decisions by the Third Section[70] and First Section[71] of the ECtHR, respectively. In these 2018 cases, the ECtHR had no difficulties applying Convention standards to the surveillance measures that impacted foreign persons on foreign territory. These decisions were then used by the GCC as authority for the view that contracting states should respect human rights under international law beyond

[63] ibid [126].
[64] ibid [127].
[65] ibid [126].
[66] ibid.
[67] *Centrum för Rättvisa v Sweden* App No 35252/08 (Grand Chamber) Judgment, 25 May 2021.
[68] *Big Brother Watch and others v The United Kingdom* App nos 58170/13, 62322/14 and 24960/15 (Grand Chamber) Judgment, 25 May 2021.
[69] Under the Foreign Intelligence Act, s 1(1) (Sweden) and the Regulation of Investigatory Powers Act 2016, s 8(4) (RIPA) (now superseded by the Investigatory Powers Act 2016) (UK).
[70] *Centrum för Rättvisa v Sweden* App No 35252/08 (Third Section) Judgment, 19 June 2018.
[71] *Big Brother Watch v The United Kingdom* App No 58170/13 (First Section) Judgment, 13 September 2018.

national borders.[72] Like the Third and First Sections, the Grand Chamber did not explicitly examine the extraterritoriality issue, as this was not raised by the parties.[73] The Grand Chamber did not analyse questions relating to the extraterritoriality of the interception or the transmission of data to foreign states, or those relating to jurisdiction which arose from the fact that some of the data related to persons not present or domiciled in the UK. However, in both cases, the Court quite clearly applied Article 8 to the interception of the communications data of individuals who were outside the jurisdiction, expressly acknowledging that bulk interception was used for the very purposes of obtaining the data of individuals outside the territory.[74] Therefore, the Grand Chamber clearly applied Article 8 to foreign communications, implicitly assuming that the UK had jurisdiction. The Court held that one aspect in which bulk surveillance was different from targeted intervention was that bulk surveillance is frequently used for the surveillance of international communications, by which the Court meant the monitoring of communications of 'persons outside the State's territorial jurisdiction', who could not be monitored in other ways (such as traditional means of interception).[75] The extraterritorial nature of the surveillance was precisely one of the factors why the Court considered established safeguards to be insufficient.

After its comparative analysis, the Court in *Centrum* observed that at least seven contracting states, namely Finland, France, Germany, the Netherlands, Sweden, Switzerland and the UK, operate official and legalised[76] bulk interception of foreign communications.[77] It held that bulk interception of communications as such was permissible as it fell into the margin of appreciation by states in order to face evolving security and crime prevention interests.[78] The Court opined that extraterritorial bulk interception may be legitimate and necessary

> in view of the proliferation of threats that States currently face from networks of international actors, using the Internet both for communication and as a tool, and the existence of sophisticated technology which would enable these actors to avoid detection.[79]

As regards foreign intelligence sharing, and in particular the receipt of intelligence from the foreign intelligence services of a non-contracting state (here, the USA), the ECtHR[80] held in *Big Brother Watch* that the receiving contracting state (such as the UK in respect of data received from the USA) was not responsible for potential breaches of human rights in the surveillance activities of the foreign, executing

[72] Note that the Court's discussion of the ECtHR jurisprudence in BVerfGE 54, 152–31, 19 May 2020, 1 BvR 2835/17 (*BND* case) is the second point set out under the heading at [93].

[73] *Big Brother Watch* (n 68) [272].

[74] See, eg *Centrum för Rättvisa* (n 67) [258]–[259]; *Big Brother Watch* (n 68) [345], [358].

[75] *Centrum för Rättvisa* (n 67) [258], [261]; *Big Brother Watch* (n 68) [344].

[76] Presumably this implies that other states carry out unofficial, informal interception regimes, but this was not discussed by the Court.

[77] *Centrum för Rättvisa* (n 67) [131].

[78] ibid [261]; *Big Brother Watch* (n 68) [347].

[79] *Centrum för Rättvisa* (n 67) [254]; *Big Brother Watch* (n 68) [340].

[80] Both the Chamber and Grand Chamber: *Big Brother Watch* (n 68) [420], [495].

state, as these activities occurred outside its jurisdiction.[81] It thereby did not follow the submission of the International Commission of Jurists, who argued that the US–UK foreign intelligence co-operation was a composite, joint act triggering the responsibility of both states under Article 15 of the ILC Articles, or a case of aiding and abetting under Article 16.[82] Responsibility was only triggered if the receiving state exercised authority or control over the foreign intelligence service or directly collaborated with it.[83]

It is logical that a state is only responsible for acts it can control or directly participates in. Thus, if agents of State A carry out tasks in State B under the direct control and supervision of the authorities in State B, the responsible state is State B. This is also in accordance with the ILC Articles, which provide in Article 6 that:

> The conduct of an organ placed at the disposal of a State by another State shall be considered an act of the former State under international law if the organ is acting in the exercise of elements of the governmental authority of the State at whose disposal it is placed.[84]

Additionally, Article 8 provides that:

> The conduct of a person or group of persons shall be considered an act of a State under international law if the person or group of persons is in fact acting on the instructions of, or under the direction or control of, that State in carrying out the conduct.

Following the argument made in the *Big Brother Watch* judgment, state responsibility and jurisdiction depend on the degree of authority (for example through domestic enabling legislation) and control over the surveillance activities. It is interesting that the ECtHR does not base its argument on control over territory, but on control over the intelligence service and control over the data processing, referring to *Al-Skeini* in this regard. Thus, by implication, state responsibility over surveillance activities is based on authority and control over the activity. The intercepting state is responsible for the activities required to obtain the data and the receiving state is responsible for the initial request and subsequent processing, use and storage of the data.[85] The Grand Chamber held in *Big Brother Watch* that the same safeguards which are required for domestic interception and surveillance are applicable to data received from foreign states.[86]

Moreover, the ECtHR, like the GCC, held that where a contracting state transfers intercepted data to a foreign (non-contracting) state, the contracting state must ensure minimum guarantees in respect of that exchange. This means that the exporting state must ensure that the recipient state has adequate safeguards for the use, storage and destruction of the data, and such transfers must be subject to

[81] ibid [495].
[82] ibid [320], [493].
[83] ibid [495], quoting *Al-Skeini* (n 44).
[84] ILC Articles (n 18).
[85] *Big Brother Watch* (n 68) [496].
[86] ibid [498].

independent supervision.[87] Therefore, the guarantees apply both to the *receipt* and the *onward transfer* of data.

The ECtHR did not make a distinction as to whether this data relates to domestic or foreign domiciled persons. Implicitly, this means that the human rights guarantees and safeguards apply to both categories of persons, ie those subject to extraterritorial and territorial surveillance. Thus, jurisdiction in respect of surveillance activities is not limited to territory. Interestingly, however, the Court expressly found that the receiving state has the same responsibilities regarding human rights in processing the data, whether it obtains the data through sharing data with a foreign government or whether it obtains the data through directly accessing a foreign database.[88]

Therefore, the ECtHR jurisprudence can be summarised in two principles: firstly, human rights apply extraterritorially, provided that the surveillance can be attributed to the state as a state act, and that the state has control over the surveillance activities; and secondly, in cases of data transfer and international co-operation, each state is responsible for its own activities, but states also have an obligation to ensure that the other state has a minimum level of human rights guarantees and safeguards in its legal framework.

III. The Jurisprudence of the GCC

A. Context

The question of jurisdiction has been relevant in two recent decisions of the GCC which led the Court to examine whether it was permissible under the German Constitution (GC)[89] to share law enforcement (the Bundeskriminalamt (*BKA*) case) and intelligence data (the *BND* case) with foreign authorities in the context of international co-operation, and the extent to which GC rights and data protection law apply to such data sharing. The earlier *BKA* case of 20 April 2016[90] concerned the compatibility of the new powers given to the Federal Criminal Police in the BKA Act to take measures to prevent, investigate and prosecute international terrorism, which included questions about the scope of international co-operation. The *BKA* case addressed questions of the applicability of German data protection and GC rights standards to the processing of data by foreign law enforcement authorities in international terrorism cases after data has been shared. This was significantly built on by the *BND* case of 19 May 2020,[91] which examined the

[87] ibid [362].
[88] ibid [497]–[499].
[89] Grundgesetz (literally 'Foundation Law').
[90] Decision of the GCC of 20 April 2016 1 BvR 966/09 – 1 BvR 1140/09; BVerfGE 141, 220 (*BKA* case).
[91] *BND* case (n 72).

procedural safeguards for data sharing between German and foreign intelligence services and the extraterritorial applicability of the fundamental rights standards laid down in the GC to non-Germans.

The background to the *BND* case is that after Edward Snowden's revelations about the US National Security Agency's (NSA) Internet surveillance programmes in 2013, questions were asked about the co-operation of the BND with the NSA and the Five Eyes alliance.[92] In particular, the publication of the links between the tapping of fibre optic cables owned by Deutsche Telekom, the operations of the BND branch in Bad Aibling (a former NSA station), and Operation Eikonal, a BND–NSA collaboration, caused a stir in German politics. The German Parliament had appointed a Select Committee to examine the German implications of the NSA activities, which reported in 2017.[93] All these activities raised troubling questions about German sovereignty over questions of security and privacy, as well as the tension between the necessity of international co-operation and the extraterritorial protection of constitutional rights. A judicial review of the legislation enabling these practices was raised by a number of foreign journalists, and this led to the GCC's decision in the *BND* case.[94]

At the centre of the German controversy lies the nature of bulk, mass surveillance which has the purpose of fishing out those communications which are of significance to intelligence. For this purpose, intelligence services access both communication pipes and communication networks, for example, through the use of search terms (selectors) followed by the use of data-mining analysis. These selectors focus on types of content or traffic data. Bulk surveillance is a type of strategic and systematic surveillance unconnected to specific events or a reasonable suspicion, and includes data retention for up to six months. Its purpose is to gain information about security threats or simply new intelligence insights which are relevant to foreign or domestic policy-making of the German government. However, a large part of these activities pursue foreign intelligence co-operation with other services (NSA and Five Eyes), including implementing selectors determined by foreign intelligence services and transmitting large quantities of unfiltered, unstructured raw data.[95]

Recent years have seen significant changes in the national and international operation of intelligence services: firstly, an increase in legalisation and procedural rules; and secondly, both a strengthening of safeguards and a significant extension of powers of surveillance, as well as international co-operation and interdependency of agencies for national security.[96]

[92] Rojszczak (n 5) 15.

[93] 'Beschlussempfehlung und Bericht des 1 Untersuchungsausschusses gemäß Artikel 44 des Grundgesetzes' (Deutscher Bundestag, 23 June 2017) Doc No 18/12850, dip21.bundestag.de/dip21/btd/18/128/1812850.pdf.

[94] 'Worldwide Mass Surveillance by Germany's Intelligence Service Declared Unconstitutional in Landmark Ruling on Press Freedom in the Digital Age' (*Reporters Without Borders*, 19 May 2020) rsf.org/en/worldwide-mass-surveillance-germany-s-intelligence-service-declared-unconstitutional-landmark.

[95] 'Beschlussempfehlung und Bericht' (n 93).

[96] Löffelmann (n 38) 34.

B. The *BND* Case of the German Constitutional Court of 2020

Given this context, the GCC decided in May 2020[97] that surveillance activities directed at or affecting foreigners on foreign territory *are* subject to the constitutional guarantees in Article 10(1) (secrecy of communications) and Article 5(1), 2nd sentence (freedom of the press) of the GC, as well as informational self-determination and the integrity of IT systems.[98] It also held that the mandatory requirement[99] to cite the constitutional rights engaged by a specific piece of legislation – in this case, the legislation containing the interception powers – had not been complied with. Therefore, this legislation (the so-called BND Act 2016), which empowered the German intelligence services to carry out Internet surveillance activities, was unconstitutional. The BND Act 2016 was the first piece of legislation which put the activities of the German foreign intelligence services on a statutory footing. It has since been revised by the BND Act 2021, passed by the German Parliament in March 2021 to comply with the decision.[100]

While the GCC held that the German enabling legislation was unconstitutional, the Court accepted that foreign intelligence and surveillance activities and co-operation with other states can be carried out in accordance with the GC, provided proper compliance tests and safeguards are introduced, which the decision sets out in detail. The first key holding of the Court is a structured analysis of these compliance tests and safeguards. The second key holding in the case affirms the extraterritorial reach of fundamental rights in the GC: the constitutional rights protections apply to foreigners in other countries. The fundamental rights protections in the GC apply against interference by any German authorities, including all activities of the German security services. Neither the nature of these activities nor their extraterritoriality makes them exempt.

C. Extraterritoriality and Safeguarding Fundamental Rights in Foreign Intelligence *Sharing*

Sharing of intelligence data must be authorised through specific provisions in the legislation and subjected to its own proportionality analysis.[101] As mentioned in the introduction, the GCC had already decided[102] on the sharing of law enforcement data with foreign, non-EU countries governed by the Act on the Federal Police Authority (the BKA Act 2008), which extended the powers of the German

[97] *BND* case (n 72).
[98] BVerfGE NJW 2008, 822.
[99] German Constitution, Art 19(1).
[100] https://www.bundestag.de/dokumente/textarchiv/2021/kw12-de-nachrichtendienst-830120.
[101] *BND* case (n 72) [227]–[228].
[102] See *BKA* case (n 90).

Federal Police Authority (the BKA) in 2009 for the prevention, investigation and prosecution of serious crime (especially terrorism). These two GCC decisions have established important standards for fundamental rights safeguards under the GC for data sharing in respect of intelligence data (the *BND* case) and law enforcement data (the *BKA* case).[103]

First of all, German agents must ensure that foreign services observe the rule of law, data protection and fundamental rights standards in further processing the data after sharing.[104] It is primarily the duty of the German authorities to assess the general fundamental rights situation in the receiving states.[105] If there are concerns, the German agents must request sufficient guarantees from the receiving states.[106] They must consider the risks in the countries concerned and assess the risk relating to specific persons, and this includes separate assessments as regards persons whose data is confidential and protected, such as journalists' sources and lawyer–client communications. These evaluations must be documented.[107]

While the fundamental rights compliance of data processing after the data has been shared with a foreign government is primarily the obligation of that foreign government,[108] the GCC made clear that such sharing must not take place unless the foreign government has adequate safeguards in place. If no such safeguards are in place, the sharing must not take place. As a minimum, the GCC stipulated four conditions: (i) the receiving state must guarantee basic data protection safeguards; (ii) it must use the data in a fundamental rights-compliant manner; (iii) it must reassure the German authorities that it complies with fundamental rights standards; and (iv) it must give sufficient information to the German authorities to show such compliance.[109] Data protection standards in the receiving state need not be the same as in Germany; they must merely be 'adequate'.[110] This requires, as

[103] In the *BKA* decision, the GCC found the BKA Act void as non-compliant with the GCC. It was replaced on 1 June 2017 by the 'Gesetz zur Neustrukturierung des BKA Gesetzes'.

[104] *BND* case (n 72) [233]–[237].

[105] In the USA, the Cloud Act envisages executive agreements allowing qualifying governments to access communications data from US service providers. The Cloud Act provides that only governments that respect fundamental rights, have adequate privacy protections, fair trial rights, prohibition of arbitrary detention and torture, a procedural framework for digital investigations with appropriate safeguards, the minimum powers outlined in the Cybercrime Convention and respect the rule of law may enter into such an executive agreement. This qualifying status must be certified by the US Attorney General with the concurrence of the Secretary of State: 18 USC § 2523(b).

[106] Under EU law, Directive 2016/680 of the European Parliament and of the Council on the protection of natural persons with regard to the processing of personal data by competent authorities for the purposes of the prevention, investigation, detection or prosecution of criminal offences or the execution of criminal penalties, and on the free movement of such data [2016] OJ L119/89 applies to data processing by law enforcement authorities, including data sharing. EU law does not apply to foreign intelligence services: Consolidated Version of the Treaty of the European Union [2016] OJ C202/1, Art 4(2).

[107] *BND* case (n 72) [240]–[241]; *BKA* case (n 90) [339].

[108] *BND* case (n 72) [233]; *BKA* case (n 90) [326].

[109] *BND* case (n 72) [234].

[110] The German word is 'angemessen' – this is similar to the logic in the ECJ *Schrems I* decision, where the Court held that the third country had to ensure 'a level of protection of fundamental rights and freedoms that is essentially equivalent': Case C-311/18 *Data Protection Commissioner v Facebook Ireland Ltd and Maximillian Schrems* ECLI:EU:C:2020:559 [105].

a minimum, purpose limitation, limited data retention, a duty to delete data, data security and limited distribution; and these standards must be prescribed by law and be reflected in actual legal practice in the foreign, recipient states.[111]

The legislation must make clear that Germany must not lend a willing hand to fundamental rights abuses in other states which do not respect the rule of law and which may use the data for political persecution or for inhumane or humiliating treatment or punishment.[112] This obligation can also be backed up by international law. Article 16 of the ILC Articles provides for state responsibility, in respect of State A aiding and abetting the commission of an internationally wrongful act by State B. State A is internationally responsible if it aided in knowledge of the circumstances of the wrongful act and the act would be internationally wrongful if committed by State A. This only applies if State A is subject to the same international human rights obligations as State B (for example having ratified the same treaty).[113] However, one of the limitations of the ILC Articles is that it is not clear what amounts to the same obligation – in the example of Germany co-operating with the USA, Germany is deriving its obligations from the GC and the ECHR, which do not contain the same obligations as the US Constitution.[114]

Where there is a risk that the receiving state uses the intelligence data for operative purposes, the BND must ask the foreign service for a guarantee that it will not transmit the data to law enforcement unless it obtains the express permission of the German authorities.[115]

The GCC acknowledged the need for sharing data,[116] but discussed three problematic practices in respect of intelligence data: (i) the so-called 'circle exchange'; (ii) data sharing where the selectors are determined by the foreign service (the NSA); and (iii) unstructured bulk data.

The 'circle exchange' of data is contrary to the GC.[117] Since intelligence services are not allowed, or in any case are restricted under national law, to carry out mass surveillance against their own populations, a 'circle exchange' would enable them to spy on each other's population and then exchange the data. So, for example, a 'circle exchange' between the USA and Germany would be that the NSA spies on Germans and the BND spies on US citizens, and the intelligence agencies exchange their respective intelligence information accordingly, thus avoiding any national law restrictions on spying on their own citizens.[118] The Court pointed out that co-operation is necessary and permitted by the GC, but that it must be subjected

[111] *BND* case (n 72) [236]; *BKA* case (n 90) [334]–[335].
[112] *BND* case (n 72) [237]; *BKA* case (n 90) [336]–[337].
[113] ILC Articles (n 18).
[114] Albeit that both parties have ratified the ICCPR.
[115] *BND* case (n 72) [242].
[116] ibid [245]–[246]; *BKA* case (n 90) [102], [325].
[117] *BND* case (n 72) [248].
[118] See the explanation in P Beuth, 'Ein neues Teil im Überwachungspuzzle? Hinweis auf den angeblichen Ringtausch von Geheimdiensten' *Die Zeit* (26 June 2014) www.zeit.de/digital/datenschutz/2014-06/bnd-datenweiterleitung-nsa-seit-2004/komplettansicht.

to clear rules in the legislation and co-operation framework agreements, which provide, inter alia, that data of the collecting state's own nationals must be filtered out, either before or after sharing.[119]

Regarding selectors chosen by foreign intelligence services, the BND must maintain effective control of these search terms and the automated data transmission, and must obtain fundamental rights guarantees in respect of the surveilled persons.[120] This means that the BND is responsible for checking the foreign-provided selectors and must remove those which may affect vulnerable individuals, such as dissidents or whistleblowers, and which may affect confidential and privileged communications, such as journalists' sources and lawyer–client or doctor–patient communications, and that these checking processes might require a quasi-judicial decision.[121] It is not entirely clear what the GCC means here when it uses the phrase 'quasi-judicial decision',[122] but it is clear that this assessment of selectors cannot be completely automated and requires suitably qualified human judgement.[123]

Unstructured, unfiltered bulk data sharing with foreign intelligence services, to enable the retention and analysis of data according to their own capabilities, is only permissible in very restricted circumstances. There must be a specific and concrete threat based on previous intelligence on the preparation of a terrorist attack or cyberattack, or the smuggling of weapons along a particular route.[124] The receiving states must not store such unstructured, unfiltered bulk data for longer than six months.[125]

D. The Extraterritorial Application of Fundamental Rights in the GC

The *BND* case answered a question that had not been definitively considered by prior case law: 'if and to what extent citizens of other states can invoke the fundamental rights of the GC to challenge measures of the German State impacting in other countries?'[126] The two relevant provisions in the GC are Articles 1(2) and (3). The conception of human rights as being universal is indicated by the wording of Article 1(2) GC: 'the German Nation recognises human rights to be inviolable and inalienable rights as the foundation of every human community, peace and justice *in the world*' (emphasis added).

[119] *BND* case (n 72) [253].
[120] ibid [255]–[256], [322]–[323].
[121] ibid [256]–[257].
[122] 'Gerichtsähnliche Vorabkontrolle'.
[123] *BND* case (n 72) [258].
[124] ibid [263].
[125] ibid [264].
[126] ibid [61].

Article 1(3) explicitly provides that the fundamental rights set out in the GC bind legislative organs, the executive and the judiciary as directly applicable law. Since Article 1(3) ties the applicability of constitutional rights to all acts of the three branches of the German state, it has been argued that the only viable interpretation of the GC is that the fundamental rights apply to all state acts, even extraterritorially.[127]

However, German scholars have also argued the opposite. For example, it has been argued that the authority of the state must be limited to the territory of the state and that this includes constitutional norms. The GC drafters had no intention of extending the application of the GC beyond the territory of Germany.[128] Another argument made against the application of Article 10 of the GC to foreign intelligence has been the difference in the wording of Articles 1(2) and (3). While the international provision in Article 1(2) uses the term 'human rights', Article 1(3) refers to 'fundamental rights' in the GC. State responsibility in respect of human rights stems from international (including treaty-based) obligations; by contrast, constitutional rights refer to state obligations arising from the national constitution (such as the GC). Thus, the argument goes that while Germany may be *universally* bound by its international human rights obligations, the constitutional rights protections are limited to the state's territory.[129]

However, the GCC did not follow these lines of argument and based its decision on the language of the GC, as well as the purpose of the GC and current economic and political circumstances (such as globalisation and the need for international co-operation). The GCC stressed that the purpose of the GC was to guard against unreasonable interference with fundamental rights by the state against anyone: the aim is to provide comprehensive constitutional rights protection and to place the individual at the centre of constitutional law. The GCC concluded that fundamental rights ought to provide protection whenever and wherever the German state acts, as such acts create a need for protection against state authority – irrespective of where and towards whom the state does act.[130]

The ruling is highly significant, as this is the first time that the GCC has actually decided the matter. The Court found nothing in the text or the legislative history of the GC that would suggest constitutional rights protection should end at the national border or be limited to German territory. Constitutional rights protection is therefore not limited to effective control over territory, or even effective control over an individual, nor is it dependent on jurisdiction.[131]

[127] B Schiffbauer, 'Die Würde des Rechtsstaates ist unantastbar' (*JuWissBlog*, 19 May 2020) No 75/2020, www.juwiss.de/75-2020/.

[128] Löffelmann (n 38) 35–36.

[129] eg: the distinction between GC, Art 10 (secrecy of communications) and ECHR, Art 8 (privacy); Löffelmann (n 38) 36–37.

[130] *BND* case (n 72) [89].

[131] Rojszczak (n 5) 17.

The ruling is not only important in the context of GC law, it is also highly significant for customary international law and international digital constitutionalism. It is a recognition that increasingly states will have to co-operate in matters of national security and crime prevention, and that to hold otherwise would lead to a lacuna as regards the protection of fundamental rights. In this connection, the GCC emphasised that this interpretation of the GC is in line with Germany's 'place in the international community as a partner that abides by the rule of law', as indicated in Article 1(2) GC.[132] The Court held that the rule of law requires the universality of fundamental rights.[133] It found that globalisation and the expanding scope of German state action beyond its territory require a corresponding extension of fundamental rights protection, referring to the obligations of state actors under international law.[134]

This explanation by the GCC is reminiscent of the doctrine of comity: the need for international data flows and co-operation requires that states offer to extend their protection beyond their border. Not only did the Court find that there is no territorial limitation, but it also held that there is no limit on the type of sovereign powers to which fundamental rights should be applied.[135] According to the Court, the applicability of fundamental rights extends to any activity where the state has control over the rights of a person. In particular, it explicitly held that the fundamental rights protections cover all state authority, not just in use of armed force scenarios.[136] The Court stated that the authority of the state is 'bound comprehensively and universally by the fundamental rights, irrespective of the specific functions, the types of actions or the respective object of the exercise of state functions'.[137] The Court did, however, clearly note that its holding only binds German state authority to fundamental rights protection, thus ensuring that the universal extension of rights is consistent with the international law principle of non-intervention in the affairs of other states.[138] Thus, the Court found no conflict with the law of other states. GC rights protection is based on the act of the state which asserts its authority – it is bound to that specific act. The GCC briefly reviewed the ECtHR's case law on the scope of the ECHR and found that the ECHR jurisprudence does not preclude the applicability of GC rights abroad.[139]

In conclusion, there is a clear contrast between the scope of the ECHR, which bases its applicability on effective control over territory or effective control over an individual, and the scope of the GC's application, which applies to every official state act of Germany, based on the 'absolute inviolability' of human dignity under Article 1(1) GC, which is universal. Germany is unilaterally committed to

[132] *BND* case (n 72) [89].
[133] ibid [93]–[96].
[134] ibid [96]–[97].
[135] ibid [88].
[136] ibid [90]–[91].
[137] ibid [91].
[138] ibid [101], [110]–[111].
[139] ibid [97].

extending its constitutional fundamental rights extraterritorially. This is not the same as saying that Germany is protecting foreigners abroad from fundamental rights violations, thereby interfering with the sovereignty of other states, since the GC rights guarantee only applies to German state acts.

The safeguards enumerated in the German *BND* case, and its earlier *BKA* case, will influence digital constitutionalism in the EU and, possibly, beyond.

IV. The US Position and the ICCPR

A. Extraterritorial Application of the US Constitutional Rights?

States conceive the scope of protection of fundamental rights differently according to their own constitutional tradition. By contrast to the German position, the US Constitution guarantees citizens' rights, but the US Constitution as such does not restrict the power of US state authorities in general.[140] The US Constitution does not grant a fundamental right of privacy to foreigners not on US territory and does not protect against unreasonable searches of property situated outside the USA.[141] The US Constitution has no extraterritorial effect except with respect to US citizens.[142] Therefore, the starting point of the US position is that US authorities such as the NSA are not fettered by the Fourth Amendment when conducting extraterritorial surveillance of foreigners and that the US Constitution has limited application in this area. Rojszczak recognises essentially three reasons for this, namely: the extensive use of surveillance of foreigners for national security purposes in the USA; the limited role of international human rights treaties to which the USA is a part; and the narrow formulation of the right to privacy in the Fourth Amendment, which essentially only protects against unreasonable searches.[143]

A small gloss is added to this starting point by the cases in which detainees in Guantanamo Bay applied for a writ of *habeas corpus*, and the US Supreme Court ultimately held that the detainees have the right to challenge their extra-legal detention in the US courts on the basis that, while Guantanamo Bay was de jure Cuban territory, the USA had sufficient jurisdiction on its naval base for the US Constitution to apply.[144] This jurisprudence does not change the principle that the US Constitution does not apply outside US jurisdiction, but it recognises that the USA can have (some) jurisdiction outside its territorial borders. The Supreme

[140] *US v Verdugo-Urquidez* 494 US 259; 110 S Ct 1056, 1060–66 (1990).
[141] ibid; *US v Gorshkov* US Dist, WD Washington, 23 May 2001, unreported, 2001 WL 1024026.
[142] *US v Pink* 315 US 203, 62 S Ct 552 (1942).
[143] Rojszczak (n 5) 6–7.
[144] Culminating in *Boumediene v Bush* 553 US 723; 128 S Ct 2229 (2008).

Court held that even when the USA acted outside its borders, its powers were not absolute and unlimited, but were subject to such restrictions as expressed in its Constitution.[145] The US Supreme Court also emphasised that Guantanamo Bay was not a transient possession of the USA, as it had been within the constant jurisdiction of the USA for many years, which means that the decision has limited significance to places where US control is only temporary.[146]

B. The ICCPR and its Extraterritorial Application?

Moreover, as pointed out by Milanovic,[147] the USA has argued that its human rights obligations under international law[148] do not apply outside its territory. For example, it argued that these rights are inapplicable to the 'unlawful enemy combatants' it detained on its base in Guantanamo Bay in Cuba or during its military engagement in Iraq and Afghanistan, and that only the law of armed conflict applies to these operations.[149] The UN Human Rights Committee has robustly pushed back against this notion, including in the context of extraterritorial killings by unmanned drones, arguing that the law of armed conflict, international humanitarian law and international human rights law apply.[150]

The ambit of state responsibility under the ICCPR is contained in Article 2(1): 'Each State Party to the present Covenant undertakes to respect and to ensure to all individuals within its territory *and* subject to its jurisdiction the rights recognized in the present Covenant' (emphasis added).

The International Court of Justice, in its Advisory Opinion on the *Wall*,[151] considered that the ICCPR applies 'in respect of acts done by a State in the exercise of its jurisdiction outside its own territory'. Likewise, the UN Human Rights Committee has opined that these two conditions should be read as alternatives,

[145] ibid 765–66.
[146] ibid 768–69.
[147] Milanovic (n 3) 1.
[148] The US ratified the ICCPR in 1992, but it has become a state party to only a few of the UN treaties.
[149] John Bellinger (Head of Delegation, Department of State, US Government) argued that the UN Convention against Torture and Other Cruel, Inhuman or Degrading Punishment (New York, 10 December 1984) 1465 UNTS 85 (ratified by the US on 21 October 1994) did not apply as the law on armed conflict was the *lex specialis* overriding the standards set in the Convention. See UN Committee against Torture, 'Committee Against Torture Begins Review of Report of the United States (OHCHR, 5 May 2006) www.ohchr.org/en/press-releases/2009/10/committee-against-torture-begins-review-report-united-states. See also M Waxman, 'Opening Statement by Matthew Waxman on the Report Concerning the International Covenant on Civil and Political Rights' (Geneva, UN Human Rights Committee, 17 July 2006) 2001-2009.state.gov/g/drl/rls/70392.htm, stating that the International Covenant on Civil and Political Rights does not apply outside a state's territory.
[150] UN Human Rights Council, 'Use of Armed Drones for Targeted Killings: Report of the Special Rapporteur on Extrajudicial, Summary or Arbitrary Executions' (15 August 2020) UN Doc A/HRC/44/38, 10ff.
[151] UNGA, 'Advisory Opinion of the International Court of Justice on the Legal Consequences of the Construction of a Wall in the Occupied Palestinian Territory' (13 July 2004) UN Doc A/ES-10/273, paras 104–10 (Wall Opinion).

ie the ICCPR applies if the individual whose rights have been affected is in the territory of the state or if the state exercises jurisdiction over the individual. Only one of these conditions need be fulfilled. The UN Human Rights Committee has stated that the rights need to be granted to persons who 'find themselves in the territory *or* subject to the jurisdiction of the State Party' (emphasis added).[152] Milanovic agrees with this disjunctive interpretation, arguing that the text could be interpreted either conjunctively or disjunctively,[153] but that the objective of universal application and the purpose of the ICCPR require the disjunctive interpretation.[154]

The disjunctive interpretation, however, would mean that a state has to ensure that human rights are granted to individuals within its territory over which it does not have de jure jurisdiction, for example persons in a foreign embassy or a leased military base. This interpretation might trigger Cuba's international state responsibility for the US operations at Guantanamo Bay.[155] In the context of foreign intelligence operations, this might trigger State A's responsibility vis-à-vis persons in State A for surveillance and interception operations by State B, or for State B accessing personal data from a foreign service provider concerning persons resident in State A. Milanovic makes the important distinction[156] between negative and positive human rights obligations: negative obligations imply that the state should refrain from performing an act which might violate human rights, whereas a positive obligation requires an active guarantee to ensure that individuals enjoy rights, including against third parties (such as the press or foreign states, under Article 8 ECHR). Alternative one, namely the obligation to protect persons subject to a state's jurisdiction, is related to the negative obligation not to infringe rights, whereas Alternative two – protection of persons in the territory – relates to an active duty to guarantee rights against third parties.

V. An (Idealistic) Vision: Extraterritoriality and Human Rights – Digital Constitutionalism as the Future Answer?

As we have seen, the ambit of the two human rights treaties examined in this chapter, the ECHR[157] and the ICCPR,[158] was worded to be confined to a state's

[152] This clearly contradicts the USA's understanding of Art 2(1). See UN Human Rights Committee, 'General Comment No 31: The Nature of the General Legal Obligation Imposed on States Parties to the Covenant' (26 May 2004) UN Doc CCPR/C/21/Rev 1/Add 13, para 10.
[153] This has also been pointed out by the ICJ in the Wall Opinion (n 151) para 108.
[154] Milanovic (n 3) 223–27.
[155] Cuba has signed, but not ratified, the ICCPR, and has ratified the UN Convention against Torture.
[156] Milanovic (n 3) 18.
[157] s IIB above.
[158] s IVB above.

jurisdiction. This has led to interpretational difficulties concerning the application of international human rights obligations to extraterritorial state acts. The latest jurisprudence of the ECtHR has clarified that jurisdiction is not limited to territorial jurisdiction or control over territory, but instead focuses on the assertion of jurisdiction over persons. This includes, within the scope of application of the ECHR, extraterritorial state acts. In the context of constitutional rights, the GCC has gone even further by extending the fundamental rights of the GC to all foreigners where their rights are infringed by acts of the German state. As I have speculated above, there is a chance that other constitutional courts in Continental Europe might be influenced by this extraterritorial extension of fundamental rights to acts of the state. While the USA has consistently and emphatically emphasised that it limits its fundamental rights obligations (both under treaty law and the US Constitution) to its territory, in the jurisprudence on the *habeas corpus* of Guantanamo Bay detainees, the US Supreme Court widened the notion of US territory to this naval base over which Cuba has de jure sovereignty but the USA has de facto control (and has had for a number of years). This means that even the USA has recognised that in specific, very limited circumstances fundamental rights might apply outside its national territory and that its extraterritorial state acts can lead to state responsibility.

What is clear from all these developments is an increasing acceptance by the courts that extraterritorial jurisdiction is increasingly asserted by states and that therefore there is a concomitant need to recognise the extraterritoriality of fundamental rights obligations.

This is all the more important in view of the digital technologies of our age involving cross-border data flows, the cross-border interception and surveillance of foreigners' Internet data for the purposes of law enforcement and intelligence, and the cross-border mining of the data of foreigners, but also other digital technologies such as remotely targeted drones and (in the near future) weapons systems controlled by artificial intelligence. Arguably, these digital technologies require a new approach to the protection of fundamental rights across borders. This approach can be described by two elements: the 'state act theory', as developed by the GCC, and the concept of digital constitutionalism.

Traditionally, the notion of governments bounded by constitutional rules was firmly associated with territory.[159] However, data is not territorial; it clearly transcends national borders. This 'unterritoriality of data'[160] requires that states act beyond national borders, and therefore the notion of constitutionalism demands that governments should be bound by their own constitutional rules, including

[159] G De Gregorio and R Radu, 'Digital Constitutionalism in the New Era of Internet Governance' (2022) 30 *International Journal of Law and Information Technology* 68, 79–84.

[160] J Daskal, 'The Un-Territoriality of Data' (2015) 125 *Yale Law Journal* 326; L Floridi, 'The Fight for Digital Sovereignty: What It Is, and Why It Matters, Especially for the EU' (2020) 33 *Philosophy and Technology* 369, 372.

fundamental rights, even when they are acting with effect outside their national borders.[161] As the US Supreme Court has opined in *Boumediene*:[162]

> The Constitution grants Congress and the President the power to acquire, dispose of, and govern territory, not the power to decide when and where its terms apply. Even when the United States acts outside its borders, its powers are not 'absolute and unlimited' but are subject 'to such restrictions as are expressed in the Constitution'.[163]

While the USA limits this limitation of powers by the US Constitution to territory over which the USA has de facto control, the GCC has gone much further by attaching fundamental constitutional rights protection to every act of state. This 'state act theory', arising under national constitutional law, means that as soon as an act can be attributed to the German government, it should be compliant with the GCC's proportionality analysis, need for safeguards, etc. The avantgarde approach pioneered by the GCC means that there are no extra-legal spaces for government action and that the rule of law applies even where the German state acts outside any territory it controls, such as accessing data in the cloud or co-operating with foreign communication service providers.

However, this raises interesting questions where the German state has de jure control over an activity but is *politically* bound to follow decisions made by another entity or another state. It is not entirely clear how power politics will fit into intelligence co-operation in the future. One example of this would be its co-operation with the NSA over the collection of Internet data.[164] The GCC, in its carefully calibrated decision, acknowledged the need for international co-operation and the reciprocity of data exchanges,[165] and accepted to some extent practices such as selectors mandated by the foreign partner and the transfer of unfiltered, unstructured bulk communications data,[166] but it restricted these practices and imposed limitations, as well as prohibiting practices such as 'circle exchanges'.[167] It remains to be seen how realistic the imposition of these limitations is, given that some of these practices are the product of political negotiation with powerful partners. Given contemporary challenges to national security, the need for data exchanges with friendly foreign countries and the rise in power of states such as China and Russia, which do not respect individual fundamental rights, this may be an idealistic (rather than realistic) vision.

The (limited) operation of state act theory and international digital constitutionalism can be illustrated by the three examples mentioned in section I above. In the first scenario, a group of states exchange intelligence information on third-party nationals outside their respective territories which was gained by

[161] De Gregorio and Radu (n 159) 79–84.
[162] *Boumediene v Bush* 553 US 723, 765; 128 S Ct 2229 (2008).
[163] Quoting *Murphy v Ramsey* 114 US 15, 44, 5 S Ct 747, 29 L Ed 47 (1885).
[164] See the discussion in s IIIA above.
[165] You only get if you give ….
[166] See the discussion in s IIID above.
[167] ibid.

intercepting Internet communications. Germany would only be able to take part in this exchange to the extent that the GC (and the ECHR) allows, which requires the application of safeguards, including ex post facto review and supervision, and a degree of transparency. Other states which have ratified the ECHR would be similarly bound. By contrast, the USA would not apply its constitutional standards or the provisions of the ICCPR, but may be prepared to filter out data concerning Germans in its co-operation with Germany on a reciprocal basis (ie with Germany filtering out data about US persons).

In the second scenario, State A, under mutual legal assistance from State B, obtains disclosure of data from a social media account (such as subscriber and content data) controlled in State B in order to assist State A's criminal investigation and prosecution of Person C, a national of State C. In this example, both State A and State B are acting extraterritorially in respect of State C; if they are contracting states to the ECHR, they are bound by the safeguards mandated by Article 8. State B collects and transfers the data to State A, which processes the data as part of its criminal investigation and prosecution, so that the actions of both State A and State B potentially engage Article 8. The ECHR applies extraterritorially to these acts because they involve control over one aspect of Person C's fundamental rights, namely data privacy, which, following the jurisprudence of the ECtHR, would be sufficient to trigger state responsibility.[168] If either State A or State B were to follow the 'state action' doctrine, their national constitutional rights would overlay the ECHR protection. Since State C is not acting in this scenario, the fundamental rights guaranteed in State C are not relevant. Either State A or State B might refuse to co-operate if it assessed that the fundamental rights situation in the other state were so deficient that non-co-operation would be justified.[169]

Finally, in the third scenario, the USA directly builds an intercept capability for live content data on a direct messaging or teleconferencing service[170] operated in the UK, based on the Executive Agreement between the USA and the UK.[171] In this scenario, US constitutional protections do not apply extraterritorially and the UK would have no control over the intercept capability,[172] meaning the UK would have no obligations under the ECHR to guarantee Article 8 safeguards for such interceptions. The Agreement is limited to targeted interceptions – it does not cover bulk, mass surveillance methods. It is limited to the purposes of prevention,

[168] See the discussion in s IIB above.

[169] But this also depends on the exceptions and derogations in the mutual assistance agreement in force between the states.

[170] The Agreement on Access to Electronic Data for the Purpose of Countering Serious Crime (UK–US) (3 October 2019) (UK–US Agreement), Art 1(3) and (11) covers both live and stored communications and content and communications data.

[171] ibid.

[172] Orders are issued directly to the UK communications service provider, and the Issuing Authority (in the USA) would make the arrangements for secret transmission without UK involvement: ibid Arts 5(5) and 6(2).

detection, investigation or prosecution of 'serious' crime.[173] Furthermore, the USA would not be allowed to target the data of UK residents,[174] but it could target its own residents or citizens (who benefit from Fourth Amendment protections) and foreign entities of third-party states (who do not benefit).[175] The Agreement creates elaborate obligations on the UK to minimise the risk that it collaterally obtains the data of US persons[176] or that it subsequently discloses such data to US authorities,[177] but no such obligations exist reciprocally for the USA.[178] The Agreement also does not contain enforceable rights for individuals affected by its provisions:

> This Agreement is intended to facilitate the ability of the Parties to obtain electronic data. The provisions of this Agreement shall not give rise to a right or remedy on the part of any private person, including to obtain, suppress or exclude any evidence, or to impede the execution of Legal Process.[179]

The UK–US Agreement is a permitting regime – it effectively switches off any domestic law of the states parties which would have prohibited the domestic communications provider from disclosing data to the foreign government in order to comply with the privacy and data protection obligations of its domestic state (ie a blocking statute, such as the US Stored Communications Act or the applicable UK data protection laws, such as Part 3 of the Data Protection Act 2018). Its purpose is to allow communications providers' compliance with foreign orders without infringing domestic data privacy laws.[180] While this helps communication providers to avoid conflicts of law, it is disastrous news from a fundamental rights perspective, as it switches off domestic laws which have been designed to provide for data privacy rights without providing adequate protections to the persons whose data is being disclosed. While the UK–US Agreement itself does *not* provide for any data privacy protections (such as purpose limitation, maximum data retention periods, or data deletion obligations), it does contain a clause

[173] ibid Art 4(1). 'Serious crime' is defined in Art 1(14) as an offence with a maximum sentence of imprisonment for three years or more – this is not in fact a high threshold, nor is there a need for showing probable cause.

[174] Or, more precisely, any UK government or state entity, an unincorporated association, a corporation located or registered in the UK, or any other person located in the UK, see Art 1(12).

[175] In terms of fundamental rights protection, the arrangement is only extraterritorial in respect of these third state persons.

[176] UK–US Agreement (n 170) Art 7(2)–(5).

[177] Which is there to avoid the UK asking for data of US persons from US communications providers and then subsequently disclosing that data to US authorities, thereby undermining US safeguards protecting US persons under the Fourth Amendment. However, this protection is not only one-sided (ie not applying to the UK), but it also has a number of exceptions: data that 'relates to significant harm, or the threat thereof, to the United States or US Persons, including crimes involving national security such as terrorism, significant violent crime, child exploitation, transnational organized crime, or significant financial fraud': ibid Art 7(5). Thus, limited circle exchanges are allowed.

[178] Other than a general 'good faith, reasonable efforts' that the account is not held by a UK person: ibid Art 4(1).

[179] ibid Art 3(4).

[180] ibid Art 3(1).

which prohibits both states from using interception orders to infringe freedom of speech, as well as an anti-discrimination clause.[181] The Agreement expressly states that the data obtained will be treated in accordance with the recipient state's domestic law,[182] but is silent about the fact that foreigners have no data privacy rights under US law. Furthermore, the party which has received the data may not pass the data on to a third government or international organisation unless the recipient state decides to publish the data, in which case it can be treated as non-confidential and passed on to third parties.[183] The only material protection in respect of the use of the data is that the USA may not use the data received in connection with a criminal prosecution which leads to the death penalty without permission from the UK.[184] Article 9, entitled 'privacy and data protection safeguards', does *not* contain any safeguards other than vague references to the EU–US Umbrella Agreement,[185] which provides no meaningful data privacy standards and no clear authorisation or oversight regime,[186] and the Judicial Redress Act 2015, which provides very limited rights of redress for data privacy infringements.[187] Thus, by signing the Executive Agreement, the UK has effectively contracted out of its data protection obligations for the purpose of targeted, direct access requests by US authorities. Arguably, agreeing to this Executive Agreement and implementing it into domestic UK law could be seen as a breach of Article 8 ECHR on the part of the UK, as it will disapply human rights protection from individuals whose data is sought extraterritorially by the USA through direct access requests to UK communications service providers. Thus, in the last example, the UK would not be responsible for the infringement of the ECHR by the specific intercept capability built on UK territory by the USA (over which the UK has jurisdiction, but no control). However, the UK may be responsible for its decision to contract out of its data privacy protections for all US direct access orders to UK communication providers generally, as this gives carte blanche to US authorities in respect of the data of foreigners.

The contrast between the notion of digital constitutionalism and the German state act theory, on the one hand, and the implementation of US direct access to

[181] ibid Art 4(2): 'Orders subject to this Agreement may not be used to infringe freedom of speech or for disadvantaging persons based on their race, sex, sexual orientation, religion, ethnic origin, or political opinions.'

[182] ibid Art 8(1).

[183] ibid Art 8(2).

[184] ibid Art 8(4)(a); the UK may not use the data in such a manner that would raise freedom of speech concerns in the USA, eg the prosecution of hate speech: Art 8(4)(b).

[185] Agreement between the United States of America and the European Union on the protection of personal information relating to the prevention, investigation, detection and prosecution of criminal offences [2016] OJ L336, which no longer applies to the UK, as the UK withdrew from the EU on 31 January 2020. It is very doubtful whether this vague reference to an agreement which does not apply in the relationship between the UK and the USA does anything to incorporate data privacy standards into the direct access framework of this Agreement.

[186] See further my analysis in Hörnle (n 6) s 4.4.

[187] On both the EU–US Umbrella Agreement and the Judicial Redress Act 2015, see ibid.

UK service providers in the UK–US Agreement on the other could not be sharper, as the whole purpose of the UK–US Agreement is to switch off fundamental rights protections in the UK in respect of UK service providers without any safeguards (other than the non-imposition of the death penalty).

The UK–US Agreement is an example of how power politics in international relations can defeat digital constitutionalism and fundamental rights protection. The USA's refusal to extend data privacy rights to foreigners on foreign territory should be a barrier to international co-operation, but the USA's territorial control over many of the US service providers who hold the data of foreigners in Silicon Valley means that it has political power over data. And the USA has leveraged this power to extract data from the UK in return. It can only be hoped that the UK–US Agreement is one day successfully challenged before the ECtHR.

10

Enforcement Jurisdiction and CLOUD Act Agreements: Clarity or Confusion?

TIM COCHRANE

I. Introduction

This chapter considers how new direct access CLOUD Act agreements interact with enforcement jurisdiction in public international law.[1] CLOUD Act agreements – promoted by the USA and issued under its 2018 Clarifying Lawful Overseas Use of Data Act (CLOUD Act)[2] – are the most developed of a new generation of 'direct access' mechanisms emerging around the globe, intended to speed up law enforcement's ability to obtain data for criminal investigations from service providers operating in other jurisdictions. Although CLOUD Act agreements are primarily promoted by their member states based on their claimed *private* international law benefit – reducing conflicts of law otherwise faced by service providers – this chapter argues that these agreements may provide an additional significant benefit at *public* international law: as well as reducing conflicts, such mechanisms may allow states to actively expand their enforcement jurisdiction extraterritorially against service providers previously beyond their reach altogether. The extent to which such expanded jurisdiction is achievable in practice merits further research into both international law and domestic US and UK law.

Following this introductory section, section II provides background context. It details the CLOUD Act and the first agreement signed pursuant to it, between

[1] The chapter comprises updated extracts of analysis originally published as T Cochrane, 'Hiding in the Eye of the Storm Cloud: How CLOUD Act Agreements Expand US Extraterritorial Investigatory Powers' (2021) 32 *Duke Journal of Comparative and International Law* 153. The author would like to thank the journal and the individuals who provided comments to that article, as well as Micheál Ó Floinn for additional comments on this chapter. The usual disclaimers apply.

[2] Clarifying Lawful Overseas Use of Data (CLOUD) Act, Pub L 115-141, 132 Stat 1213 (codified in scattered sections of 18 USC).

the USA and the UK in October 2019 (the US–UK Agreement)[3] – the key example of this chapter. It also articulates the main claimed benefit of CLOUD Act agreements by states: the reduction of conflicts of law for service providers – a private international law benefit.

Section III considers the interaction between CLOUD Act agreements and public international law. It first discusses conceptions of jurisdiction at international law, focusing on enforcement jurisdiction. It then explains that CLOUD Act agreements appear to enable signatory states to extend their international jurisdiction by enforcing their own laws extraterritorially against overseas service providers through the lifting of the international law prohibition against extraterritorial enforcement jurisdiction. It finally raises various unanswered questions arising from this analysis. Ultimately, while the extension of enforcement jurisdiction is a material public international law benefit in theory, the extent to which such expanded jurisdiction is realisable in practice turns on evolving legal issues at both international and domestic law.

This chapter's analysis is necessarily tentative, as this new generation of direct access mechanisms are only very recently beginning to enter into force. After some delays, the US–UK Agreement entered into force in October 2022.[4] It is expected to be shortly followed by a materially similar agreement signed between the USA and Australia in December 2021[5] – this is the only other CLOUD Act agreement concluded to date, although negotiations with Canada are ongoing.[6] The implementing statutes passed by the UK and Australia to enable their CLOUD Act agreements with the USA also contemplate additional data-sharing agreements

[3] Agreement on Access to Electronic Data for the Purpose of Countering Serious Crime (UK–US) (3 October 2019) (US–UK Agreement).

[4] US Department of Justice, 'Landmark US–UK Data Access Agreement Enters into Force' (*Justice*, 3 October 2022) www.justice.gov/opa/pr/landmark-us-uk-data-access-agreement-enters-force.

[5] Agreement between the Government of the United States of America and the Government of Australia on Access to Electronic Data for the Purpose of Countering Serious Crime (US–AU) (15 December 2021) (US–AU CLOUD Act Agreement). See US Department of Justice, 'United States and Australia Enter CLOUD Act Agreement to Facilitate Investigations of Serious Crime' (*Justice*, 15 December 2021) www.justice.gov/opa/pr/united-states-and-australia-enter-cloud-act-agreement-facilitate-investigations-serious-crime. Australia 'anticipated that the Australia–US CLOUD Act agreement w[ould] be operational by the end of 2022': Australian Department of Home Affairs, 'Australia–US CLOUD Act Agreement' (*Home Affairs*, 25 January 2022) www.homeaffairs.gov.au/about-us/our-portfolios/national-security/lawful-access-telecommunications/australia-united-states-cloud-act-agreement. However, although the US–AU CLOUD Act Agreement has passed the applicable negative resolution process within US Congress, it is currently under review by the Australian Parliament. As the US–AU Agreement was recently approved by Australia's Joint Standing Committee on Treaties, binding treaty action by Australia is likely in early 2023. See Australian Parliament Joint Standing Committee on Treaties, *Agreement between the Government of Australia and the Government of the United States of America on Access to Electronic Data for the Purpose of Countering Serious Crime* (December 2022) Report 204, 49.

[6] US Department of Justice, 'United States and Canada Welcome Negotiations of a CLOUD Act Agreement' (*Justice*, 22 March 2022) www.justice.gov/opa/pr/united-states-and-canada-welcome-negotiations-cloud-act-agreement.

with other states.[7] The other main direct access mechanisms are an EU 'e-Evidence' proposal and the Second Additional Protocol to the Convention on Cybercrime[8] – a convention commonly referred to as the Budapest Convention.[9] The EU's e-Evidence proposal is still under discussion,[10] while the Second Additional Protocol was only signed in mid-2022 and is awaiting ratification by five Member States before it comes into force.[11]

This chapter engages with contested and ambiguous legal concepts. Where applicable, it considers how these terms are understood both at international law as well as within US and UK law – it assumes these domestic legal systems can inform our evolving understanding of these concepts,[12] not least because the USA and UK are the first two signatory states to implement direct access mechanisms,[13] and the US–UK Agreement itself primarily operates through each state's domestic law.[14] For example, international law itself can be imperfectly sub-divided into 'private' and 'public' realms.[15] Private international law, also known as 'conflict of laws', 'resolv[es] controversies between private persons … primarily in domestic litigation, arising out of situations having a relationship to more than one state'.[16]

[7] For the UK, see Crime (Overseas Production Orders) Act 2019 (COPOA 2019), ss 1(2), (5), 4(2); Investigatory Powers Act 2016, s 52. For Australia, see Telecommunications Legislation Amendment (International Production Orders) Act 2021, sch 1, para 3. See also T Cochrane, 'Law Enforcement Cross-Border Data Sharing: A CLOUD Act Agreement for Aotearoa New Zealand?' [2021] *New Zealand Law Review* 401.

[8] Commission, 'Proposal for a Regulation of the European Parliament and of the Council on European Production and Preservation Orders for Electronic Evidence in Criminal Matters' COM (2018) 225 final; Second Additional Protocol to the Convention on Cybercrime on enhanced co-operation and disclosure of electronic evidence (Strasbourg, 12 May 2022) (European Treaty Series No 224).

[9] See generally Convention on Cybercrime (Budapest, 23 November 2001) (European Treaty Series No 185).

[10] See Council, 'Regulation on European Production and Preservation Orders for Electronic Evidence in Criminal Matters' Procedure 2018/0108/COD; 'Directive Laying Down Harmonised Rules on the Appointment of Legal Representatives for the Purpose of Gathering Evidence in Criminal Proceedings' Procedure 2018/0107/COD.

[11] See Second Additional Protocol (n 8) Art 16; Council of Europe, 'Chart of Signatures and Ratifications of Treaty 224' (17 August 2022) www.coe.int/en/web/conventions/full-list?module=signatures-by-treaty&treatynum=224.

[12] A Nollkaemper, *National Courts and the International Rule of Law* (Oxford, Oxford University Press, 2011) 8, 264.

[13] ibid 271–72. See generally Vienna Convention on the Law of the Treaties (Vienna, 23 May 1969) 1155 UNTS 331 (VCLT), Art 31(3)(b).

[14] See text to nn 40–41 below.

[15] American Law Institute, *Restatement of the Law Third: The Foreign Relations Law of the United States* (Philadelphia, American Law Institute, 1987) § 101; J Crawford, *Brownlie's Principles of Public International Law*, 9th edn (Oxford, Oxford University Press, 2019) 458. These two fields may, however, overlap and inform each other in practice. See generally A Mills, *The Confluence of Public and Private International Law: Justice, Pluralism and Subsidiarity in the International Constitutional Ordering of Private Law* (Cambridge, Cambridge University Press, 2009) ch 6; U Kohl, *Jurisdiction and the Internet* (Cambridge, Cambridge University Press, 2009) 232–40.

[16] American Law Institute, *Restatement Third* (n 15) § 101. See also Crawford (n 15) 458; Mills, *The Confluence* (n 15) 1–2.

Public international law, also known simply as 'international law', regulates 'the conduct of states and international organizations'.[17] Although this chapter focuses on the impact of CLOUD Act agreements at public international law, it also briefly considers their private international benefit in section IIC, as this is the main benefit claimed by CLOUD Act agreement signatories.

Fundamental to this chapter's analysis is 'jurisdiction', which this chapter primarily explores in relation to public international law.[18] In that context – and, indeed, within domestic US and UK law[19] – the term is contextual and often confusing, comprising various overlapping and challenged aspects, as outlined below in section IIIA.[20] A linked concept is 'extraterritoriality': while this term is used throughout this chapter to refer generally to 'situations where a state's exercise of jurisdiction somehow extends beyond its territory',[21] what amounts to an 'extraterritorial' (as opposed to territorial) exercise of international jurisdiction, particularly in an online or other digital context, is debated[22] – it has also long been true that 'Americans and Europeans [including the UK] understand extraterritoriality to mean different things' under their domestic laws.[23]

Finally, this chapter also focuses on 'service providers', referring to entities that provide digital communication or related storage services to the public.[24] It uses the (related) term 'foreign service providers' relatively – again, imperfectly – to refer to service providers who are predominantly operating beyond the jurisdiction of a requesting state (which may have some or no connection with that requesting state).

[17] American Law Institute, *Restatement Third* (n 15) § 101. See also Crawford (n 15) 3–11.

[18] See s IIIA below. See also Mills, *The Confluence* (n 15) 228: 'In public international law, the term "jurisdiction" is used in a much broader sense than in private international law.'

[19] See *Anisminic Ltd v Foreign Compensation Comm* [1968] 2 QB 862, 889 (HOL) (Diplock LJ); *United States v LA Tucker Truck Lines Inc* 344 US 33, 39 (1952) (Frankfurter J dissenting). See, eg *R (Privacy International) v Investigatory Powers Tribunal* [2019] UKSC 22; *United States v Rodgers* 466 US 475, 479–80 (1984). But see also American Law Institute, *Restatement of the Law Fourth: The Foreign Relations Law of the United States* (Philadelphia, American Law Institute, 2018) § 401 comment a, noting that, while 'Domestic and international law on jurisdiction influence each other, [they] are distinct bodies of law'.

[20] *R (Smith) v Oxfordshire Assistance Deputy Coroner* [2010] UKSC 29 [237] (Lord Collins); American Law Institute, *Restatement Fourth* (n 19) § 401. See also Kohl (n 15) 16–18; eg *R (KBR, Inc) v Director of the Serious Fraud Office* [2021] UKSC 2 [24]–[25] (*KBR (SC)*); *R (Jimenez) v First Tier Tribunal (Tax Chamber)* [2019] EWCA Civ 51 [53]; *FTC v Compagnie De Saint-Gobain-Pont-a-Mousson* 636 F.2d 1300, 1318 (DC Cir 1980). See also n 15 above; J Hörnle, *Internet Jurisdiction: Law and Practice* (Oxford, Oxford University Press, 2021) 5, suggesting jurisdiction in this context should be divided into 'four distinct and specialist areas of law'.

[21] Following RJ Currie, 'Cross-Border Evidence Gathering in Transnational Criminal Investigation: Is the Microsoft Ireland Case the Next Frontier?' (2016) 53 *Canadian Yearbook of International Law* 63, 69. See also Hörnle (n 20) 21–22, further detailing extraterritoriality.

[22] See nn 133–36 below and accompanying text.

[23] See R Michaels, 'Two Paradigms of Jurisdiction' (2006) 27 *Michigan Journal of International Law* 1003, 1058–61. See also text to nn 33–34 below, discussing the US position.

[24] See, eg US–UK Agreement, Art 1(7).

II. The CLOUD Act, the US–UK Agreement and Private International Law

A. The CLOUD Act

This discussion begins with the CLOUD Act, described by its US Senate sponsor 'as a tremendously important bill that will help to solve the problems that have arisen in recent years with cross-border law enforcement requests'.[25] This legislation, enacted in March 2018, 'accomplished two things'.[26] First – the focus of most commentary – it added 18 USC § 2713 to the US Stored Communications Act (SCA).[27] The SCA 'creates a set of Fourth Amendment-like privacy protections by statute' for stored data held by US service providers.[28] It limits the bases by which such providers may voluntarily disclose users' data and regulates the methods by which the US government may compel disclosure.[29] The SCA's new § 2713, implemented through the CLOUD Act, now requires service providers subject to US jurisdiction to disclose data pursuant to SCA requests 'within such provider's possession, custody, or control, regardless of' the data's location.[30] This addition famously mooted the then-pending US Supreme Court *Microsoft Ireland* litigation.[31] Whether § 2713 simply 'restor[ed] the widely accepted and long-standing understanding of US law', as the USA claims,[32] or actively expanded the SCA's reach extraterritorially is debated.[33] In any event, § 2713 confirmed Congress's intention to provide the SCA broad extraterritorial scope over data.[34]

[25] 164 Cong Rec S596 (daily edn, 5 February 2018) (statement of Senator Orrin Hatch). For further details on the background to the CLOUD Act and the US–UK Agreement, see T Cochrane, 'Digital Privacy Rights and CLOUD Act Agreements' (2021) 47 *Brooklyn International Law Journal* 1, 17–24.

[26] RW Downing, 'Prospects for Transatlantic Cooperation on the Transfer of Electronic Evidence to Promote Public Safety' (Academy for European Law Conference, London, 5 April 2019) www.justice.gov/opa/speech/deputy-assistant-attorney-general-richard-w-downing-delivers-remarks-academy-european-law.

[27] CLOUD Act, § 103(a)(1), 18 USC § 2713. See generally Stored Communications Act, 18 USC §§ 2701-13 (as amended by the CLOUD Act).

[28] OS Kerr, 'A User's Guide to the Stored Communications Act, and a Legislator's Guide to Amending It' (2004) 72 *George Washington Law Review* 1208, 1212.

[29] ibid 1212–13. See 18 USC §§ 2701–13. See, eg *United States v Warshak* 631 F.3d 266, 288 (6th Cir 2011); *In re Search of Information Associated with Four Redacted Gmail Accounts* 371 F Supp 3d 843, 844–46 (D Or 2018).

[30] CLOUD Act, § 103(a)(1), 18 USC § 2713.

[31] See generally *In re Warrant to Search a Certain E-Mail Account Controlled and Maintained by Microsoft Corp* 829 F.3d 197 (2d Cir 2016); *United States v Microsoft Corp* 138 S Ct 356 (2017), vacated as moot, 138 S Ct 1186 (2018).

[32] US Department of Justice, *Promoting Public Safety, Privacy, and the Rule of Law Around the World: The Purpose and Impact of the CLOUD Act* (White Paper, April 2019) (US White Paper) 7.

[33] See, eg R Vatanparast, 'Data Governance and the Elasticity of Sovereignty' (2020) 46 *Brooklyn Journal of International Law* 1, 27 ('The CLOUD Act expanded the territorial reach of the SCA'); *cf* P Swire and J Daskal, 'Frequently Asked Questions about the US CLOUD Act' (*Cross-Border Data Forum*, 16 April 2019) www.crossborderdataforum.org/frequently-asked-questions-about-the-u-s-cloud-act/ ('[T]he US CLOUD Act did not expand the territorial reach of US law, under [Department of Justice's] unchanging view and, in the view of the authors, the most likely prior reading of the law').

As its second accomplishment – the focus of this chapter – the CLOUD Act allows the USA to enter into bilateral executive agreements with foreign states to facilitate law enforcement data sharing through a new statutory mechanism codified at 18 USC § 2523.[35] CLOUD Act agreements arise in part from dissatisfaction by law enforcement about the effectiveness of the main existing method that law enforcement has to obtain overseas data from foreign service providers: mutual legal assistance (MLA).[36] Access to data through MLA often takes months or even years,[37] in part because an MLA request from one country must normally be reviewed by, and executed under the law of, the state in which the data and/or service provider is based.[38] Direct access mechanisms claim to 'reduce this time period considerably',[39] by allowing their members to use their own local law to compel data from foreign service providers operating in other member states.[40] As the USA has explained, 'the framework envisaged by the CLOUD Act [is] that each nation would use its own law to access data'.[41]

Various ex ante safeguards and other restrictions apply to CLOUD Act agreements.[42] Before such an agreement comes into force, for example, the US Attorney General must certify to Congress that the co-signatory state provides sufficient protection for human rights and similar standards in their law.[43]

[34] *cf* the position prior to 18 USC § 2713 in the Second Circuit: *In re Warrant* (n 31) 222. See also Hörnle (n 20) 200.

[35] CLOUD Act, § 105(a), 18 USC § 2523.

[36] See generally N Boister, *Introduction to Transnational Criminal Law* (Oxford, Oxford University Press, 2018) 311–22; US Department of Justice, *Justice Manual* (2020) paras 9-13.500 to 9-13.525; Home Office, 'Request for Mutual Legal Assistance in Criminal Matters: Guidelines for Authorities outside of the United Kingdom' (March 2022) (MLA Guidelines). For discussion as to why MLA is typically required in this context, see Cochrane, 'Digital Privacy Rights' (n 25) 11–13.

[37] Home Office, *Explanatory Memorandum to the Agreement between the Government of the United Kingdom of Great Britain and Northern Ireland and the Government of the United States of America on Access to Electronic Data for the Purpose of Countering Serious Crime* (Cm 178, 2019) (UK Explanatory Memorandum) para 2; US White Paper (n 32) 1, 10. See also RA Clarke et al, 'Liberty and Security in a Changing World: Report and Recommendations of The President's Review Group on Intelligence and Communications Technologies' (12 December 2013) 226–27, expressing concerns with MLA and recommending reforms.

[38] See Boister (n 36) 311.

[39] US Department of Justice, 'US and UK Sign Landmark Cross-Border Data Access Agreement to Combat Criminals and Terrorists Online' (*Justice*, 3 October 2019) www.justice.gov/opa/pr/us-and-uk-signlandmark-cross-border-data-access-agreement-combat-criminals-and-terrorists (Data Access Agreement Press Release).

[40] See US White Paper (n 32) 11. See also RW Downing, 'What the US CLOUD Act Does and Does Not Do' (5th German–American Data Protection Day, Munich, 16 May 2019) www.justice.gov/opa/speech/deputy-assistant-attorney-general-richard-w-downing-delivers-remarks-5th-german-american (Downing, Germany Speech), noting that 'the CLOUD Act permits each party to apply its own requirements for compulsory orders in accordance with the rule of law'.

[41] US White Paper (n 32) 11.

[42] See Cochrane, 'Digital Privacy Rights' (n 25) 23–24, elaborating on these protections.

[43] CLOUD Act, § 105(a), 18 USC § 2523(b)(1). See, eg the certification issued in respect of the US–UK Agreement: US Attorney General, 'Explanation of Each Consideration in Determining that the Agreement Satisfies the Requirements of 18 USC § 2523(b)' (December 2019).

The effectiveness of these provisions for the protections of rights in practice, however, remains to be seen.[44] In any event, crucially, CLOUD Act agreements – like MLA[45] – are reciprocal.[46] Each state must 'afford reciprocal rights of data access' to the other.[47] This new CLOUD Act agreement mechanism has been summarised as follows:[48]

> Countries that sign executive agreements with the US no longer need to go through the [MLA] process to request communications content from US-based providers; rather they can, pursuant to a long list of substantive and procedural safeguards directly request the data from US-based providers, so long as they are seeking the data of foreigners located outside the United States. Conversely, those governments must commit to ensuring that US law enforcement can directly request communications content from their local providers – also enabling the United States to bypass the otherwise applicable [MLA] process.

B. The US–UK Agreement

The USA and the UK signed the US–UK Agreement in October 2019.[49] Announcing it, (then) US Attorney General William Barr stated that 'This agreement will enhance the ability of the United States and the United Kingdom to fight serious crime … by allowing more efficient and effective access to data needed for quick-moving investigations'.[50] In contrast to the months or years it can take to obtain data through MLA, the UK estimates that the entire data collection process under this new mechanism should take 'in the order of 60 days and perhaps less'.[51]

The express terms of the US–UK Agreement purport to allow each state to directly enforce its own legal orders for preservation, disclosure and interception of electronic communications against service providers in the other jurisdiction.[52] It achieves this through a 'core obligation': each state agrees to remove all 'blocking statutes' – meaning in this context any 'conflicting legal obligations' that

[44] See Cochrane, *Digital Privacy Rights* (n 25) 73–76; Hörnle (n 20) 211–15.

[45] Boister (n 36) 311; Home Office, 'MLA Guidelines' (n 36) 8.

[46] CLOUD Act, § 105(a), 18 USC §2523(b)(4)(I); eg US–UK Agreement, Art 2(3)(b). See Data Access Agreement Press Release (n 39); S Raman, 'Remarks to the Center for Strategic and International Studies' (*Justice*, 24 May 2018) www.justice.gov/opa/speech/associate-deputy-attorney-general-sujit-raman-delivers-remarks-center-strategic-and. See also Hörnle (n 20) 214.

[47] CLOUD Act, § 105(a), 18 USC §2523(b)(4)(I).

[48] J Daskal and P Swire, 'A Possible US–EU Agreement on Law Enforcement Access to Data?' (*Just Security*, 21 May 2018) www.justsecurity.org/56527/eu-agreement-law-enforcement-access-data/.

[49] US–UK Agreement, p 17.

[50] Data Access Agreement Press Release (n 39).

[51] Home Office, 'Impact Assessment: Police, Crime, Sentencing and Courts Bill' (30 June 2021) HO0383, 7.

[52] US–UK Agreement, Arts 1(10)–(11), 2(1), 3(1)–(2), 6(1), 10(1)–(2) and 10(6).

'prevent disclosure'[53] – in their domestic law that may otherwise prevent service providers from lawfully responding to requests from law enforcement.[54] The SCA ordinarily functions as such a blocking statute, normally prohibiting US service providers from disclosing electronic communications content other than to US law enforcement.[55] The UK Investigatory Powers Act 2016 and other UK legislation operate similarly.[56] As a result, foreign law enforcement seeking data held by service providers subject to US or UK law – eg US law enforcement seeking data from UK providers and vice versa – typically need to use MLA.[57]

The US–UK Agreement was subject to negative resolution periods in the UK Parliament and US Congress, although these periods both expired without objection.[58] Since 8 July 2020, the countries have therefore been free to implement the agreement through an exchange of diplomatic notes.[59] Although the responsible UK minister announced in September 2020 that implementation was expected by the end of that year,[60] that was delayed, apparently due to data protection concerns and 'practical issues' with the UK's domestic legal framework for issuing requests.[61] On 21 July 2022, however, the USA and UK announced that the US–UK Agreement would be brought into force on 3 October 2022 – three years to the day after it was signed.[62]

[53] See US White Paper (n 32) 3, 10–11; UK Explanatory Memorandum (n 37) para 8. See generally H Buxbaum, 'Assessing Sovereignty Interests in Cross-Border Discovery Disputes: Lessons from *Aérospatiale*' (2003) 38 *Texas International Law Journal* 87, 95–98, discussing blocking statutes.

[54] US White Paper (n 32) 4; UK Explanatory Memorandum (n 37) paras 7–8; Data Access Agreement Press Release (n 39); HL Deb 20 November 2018, vol 794, cols 139–40.

[55] 18 USC §§ 2701–02. See SP Mulligan, 'Cross-Border Data Sharing under the CLOUD Act' (Congressional Research Service, 2018) R45173, 11, referring to the overarching legislation containing the SCA and the Wiretap Act, the Electronic Communications Privacy Act, 18 USC § 2501 et seq, as a blocking statute.

[56] Investigatory Powers Act 2016, ss 3, 11; HL Deb 20 November 2018, vol 794, cols 139–40. See, eg Computer Misuse Act 1990. See also Law Commission, *Search Warrants* (Law Com No 396, 2020) para 18.40.

[57] UK Explanatory Memorandum (n 37) para 2; US White Paper (n 32) 3, 10–11.

[58] See P Greaves and P Swire, 'New Developments for the UK and Australian Executive Agreements with the US under the CLOUD Act' (*Cross-Border Data Forum*, 19 July 2020) www.crossborderdataforum.org/new-developments-for-the-u-k-and-australian-executive-agreements-with-the-u-s-under-the-cloud-act-2/; UK Parliament, 'Agreement, done at Washington on 3rd October 2019, between the Government of the United Kingdom of Great Britain and Northern Ireland and the United States of America on Access to Electronic Data for the Purpose of Countering Serious Crime' api.parliament.uk/view/treaty/bjKV1oDq. See generally CLOUD Act, § 105(a), 18 USC §2523(b)(4)(I).

[59] US–UK Agreement, Art 16. See Greaves and Swire (n 58).

[60] See Draft Investigatory Powers (Communications Data) (Relevant Public Authorities and Designated Senior Officers) Regulations 2020, 10 September 2020, col 4.

[61] For data protection concerns, see Commission, 'Commission Implementing Decision of 28 June 2021 pursuant to Regulation (EU) 2016/679 of the European Parliament and of the Council on the Adequate Protection of Personal Data by the United Kingdom' C(2021) 4800 final, para 155. For practical issues, see Home Office, 'Impact Assessment' (n 51) 7.

[62] US Department of Justice, 'Joint Statement by the United States and the United Kingdom on Data Access Agreement' (*Justice*, 21 July 2022) www.justice.gov/opa/pr/joint-statement-united-states-and-united-kingdom-data-access-agreement; US–UK Agreement, p 10.

C. CLOUD Act Agreements and Private International Law

CLOUD Act Agreements have been promoted by the USA (and the UK) based on their private international law benefit.[63] Indeed, the USA's position is that: 'The only legal effect of a CLOUD [Act] agreement is to eliminate the legal conflict for qualifying orders'[64] – a position critiqued in this chapter in section III below. It is, however, appropriate to first outline the claimed private international law benefit of CLOUD Act agreements, given they are being promoted on this basis. As a US representative explained:[65]

> [W]e live in a world of conflicting cross-currents – the simultaneous need to reach out for data stored abroad and concern about limiting the ability of others to reach in. And these contradictory pressures create a global landscape rife with potential conflicts of law. The global technology companies that hold electronic evidence are frequently subject to more than one country's laws. All too often, one country may order them to disclose data needed for an investigation, while another country's laws may 'block' disclosure of that same data. It is a constant push and pull.

'The US Congress enacted the CLOUD Act as a way [to] reduce [these] conflicts of law', the USA has remarked.[66] As others have noted, the broad extraterritorial scope of the CLOUD Act's first accomplishment, the new 18 USC § 2713,[67] in fact risks precisely the opposite, ie intensifying conflicts.[68] This chapter, however, focuses on the CLOUD Act's second achievement – its new bilateral agreements mechanism. Such agreements, in contrast, do offer scope to reduce conflicts; under them, 'Both countries … agree to eliminate the conflicts of law so that [they] can more efficiently obtain the information needed to protect their citizens'.[69] CLOUD Act agreements create an international law obligation on their signatory states

[63] US White Paper (n 32) 1, 3–5, 9 and 11–14. See UK Explanatory Memorandum (n 37) 5–6. See generally Data Access Agreement Press Release (n 39), noting that the US–UK Agreement 'will dramatically speed up investigations by removing legal barriers'.

[64] US White Paper (n 32) 5. For elaboration, see Cochrane, 'Hiding' (n 1) 165–67.

[65] Downing, Germany Speech (n 40). See also D Anderson, *A Question of Trust: Report of the Investigatory Powers Review* (London, HM Government, 2015) 204, cautioning that 'service providers operating internationally … do not see it as their role to resolve the conflicts of jurisdiction that arise … But the reality is that providers are at the centre of resolving those conflicts on a daily basis'.

[66] Downing, Germany Speech (n 40), in which CLOUD Act agreements were also referred to as 'a Respite from Conflicts'; J Daskal, 'Privacy and Security across Borders' (2018–19) 132 *Yale Law Journal Forum* 1029, 1036 fn 25, stating that 'the whole point of becoming a qualifying foreign government' by obtaining a CLOUD Act agreement is 'to minimize legal conflict'.

[67] See text to nn 27–34 above.

[68] eg KS Gallant, *International Criminal Jurisdiction: Whose Law Must We Obey?* (Oxford, Oxford University Press, 2022) 330; Hörnle (n 20) 197; S Allen, 'Enforcing Criminal Jurisdiction in the Clouds and International Law's Enduring Commitment to Territoriality' in S Allen et al (eds), *The Oxford Handbook of Jurisdiction in International Law* (Oxford, Oxford University Press, 2019) 381, 404–09. See also Cochrane, 'Digital Privacy Rights' (n 25) 18, quoting J Daskal, 'Law Enforcement Access to Data across Borders: The Evolving Security and Rights Issues' (2016) 8 *Journal of National Security Law and Policy* 473, 477–78.

[69] Downing, Germany Speech (n 40).

to lift any blocking statutes in their domestic law that would otherwise prohibit service providers subject to that law from complying with a data request from law enforcement of the counter-party state.[70]

I have detailed elsewhere how the USA and UK have attempted to implement this international law obligation within their domestic laws.[71] Essentially, although the SCA contains blocking provisions that normally prevent US providers from providing communications content directly to UK law enforcement, these will fall away once the UK requests such data through the US–UK Agreement given the new immunity provisions each state has legislated.[72] UK law enforcement may then freely issue requests under their own law for such data to US service providers, and US service providers need not worry that responding may breach the SCA. The intention is that 'The only law governing the disclosure would be the law of the country issuing the order'.[73] As a result, providers will apparently be immunised almost entirely under US law for responding to such requests. Precisely the same reciprocal scenario arises: UK providers responding to US law enforcement requests will be similarly immunised from liability arising under UK law when doing so. While such immunity provisions cannot override potential constitutional or other human rights liability for states or responding service providers, these currently appear to have limited scope in this context.[74]

III. The Prohibition against Extraterritorial Enforcement Jurisdiction, CLOUD Act Agreements and Unanswered Questions

A. Public International Law Jurisdiction and the Prohibition against Extraterritorial Enforcement Jurisdiction

CLOUD Act agreements allow their members to expand jurisdiction internationally by lifting what is known as the prohibition against extraterritorial enforcement jurisdiction at international law. International law jurisdiction can be divided into several categories, including jurisdiction to prescribe, ie 'to make law applicable to persons, property or conduct', and jurisdiction to enforce, ie 'to exercise … power

[70] See, eg US–UK Agreement, Arts 3(1) and 10(1).

[71] Cochrane, 'Hiding' (n 1) 170–75.

[72] See nn 55–56 above and accompanying text.

[73] Downing, Germany Speech (n 40). See also E Norris and MJ Cohen, 'How US Authorities Obtain Foreign Evidence in Cross-Border Investigations' in Law Business Research Ltd, *Americas: Investigations Review 2021* (London, Global Investigations Review, 2020) 25, noting that 'Because the CLOUD Act removes US legal prohibitions on disclosing electronic information in response to [UK]-issued legal process, a [UK] reviewing court would not need to engage in a conflict of laws analysis'.

[74] See Cochrane, 'Hiding' (n 1) 171 fn 107 and 175 fn 126.

to compel compliance with law'.[75] These categories, however, remain debated.[76] Traditionally, enforcement jurisdiction is typically engaged when state authorities, including law enforcement, use compulsion to exercise legal functions, including to gather admissible evidence.[77] Conversely, enforcement jurisdiction is (therefore) not engaged by law enforcement acts that are not backed by the possibility of sanction.[78] US and UK courts recognise the continued force of this prohibition,[79] although there are growing debates there and elsewhere as to whether and how it should apply to cross-border data flows, as discussed below.[80]

International law is often permissive concerning extraterritorial prescriptive jurisdiction.[81] In contrast, 'Enforcement jurisdiction is strictly territorially bounded':[82] what is known as 'the prohibition against extraterritorial enforcement jurisdiction' normally prohibits states from exercising enforcement jurisdiction in the territory of a foreign sovereign.[83] This prohibition would traditionally prohibit US or UK law enforcement from seeking to compel a foreign service provider not operating in their territory to disclose data under international law, as two seminal cases – one in the USA and one in the UK – from the 1980s bear out. In 1980, the DC Circuit Court of Appeals rejected an attempt by the Federal Trade Commission 'to serve its investigatory subpoenas directly upon citizens of other

[75] American Law Institute, *Restatement Fourth* (n 19) § 401 and pt IV, ch 3; Crawford (n 15) 440; *Smith* (n 20) [24]–[43] (Lord Mance); *FTC* (n 20) 1315–17.

[76] See, eg American Law Institute, *Restatement Fourth* (n 19) § 401, listing jurisdiction to adjudicate, ie 'to apply law to persons or things', as a third intermediary category. The late Judge Crawford considered this an instance of enforcement jurisdiction, although he conceded that at least aspects 'may be better seen as a manifestation of prescriptive jurisdiction': Crawford (n 15) 440 fn 3. See A Mills, 'Rethinking Jurisdiction in International Law' (2014) 84 *British Yearbook of International Law* 187, 194–95 (summarising differing views). See also, eg DJB Svantesson, *Solving the Internet Jurisdiction Puzzle* (Oxford, Oxford University Press, 2017) 225, rejecting 'the convention of categorising jurisdiction as being prescriptive, adjudicative, or enforcement jurisdiction'.

[77] American Law Institute, *Restatement Fourth* (n 19) pt IV, ch 3, introductory note and § 432 comment a; *Jimenez* (n 20) [45]; Boister (n 36) 311.

[78] See, eg *Jimenez* (n 20) [51]–[57]. See also *KBR (SC)* (n 20) [58]–[59]. See generally *Commodity Futures Trading Commission v Nahas* 738 F.2d 487, 494 n 14 (DC Cir 1984): 'The distinction between service of compulsory process and service of notice is critical under principles of international law due to the difference in judicial enforcement power that accompanies each.'

[79] eg *Usoyan v Republic of Turkey* 6 F.4th 31, 39 (DC Cir 2021), citing American Law Institute, *Restatement Fourth* (n 19) § 432 comment b; *Perry v Serious Organised Crime Agency* [2012] UKSC 35 [94]. See also Kohl (n 15) 200, referring to this prohibition generally as a 'fundamental, universally accepted principle'; *cf KBR (SC)* (n 20) [50]–[51], following *Perry* but noting uncertainties.

[80] See text to nn 133–36 below.

[81] American Law Institute, *Restatement Fourth* (n 19) §§ 401 comment b, 407 comment c, 422 note 1. See Currie (n 21) 70; Crawford (n 15) 462; C Ryngaert, *Jurisdiction in International Law*, 2nd edn (Oxford, Oxford University Press, 2015) 29–30; Kohl (n 15) 16.

[82] Currie (n 21) 70; FA Mann, *Further Studies in International Law* (Oxford, Clarendon Press, 1990) 32.

[83] See *The Case of the SS Lotus (France v Turkey)* PCIJ Rep Series A No 10 [18]–[19]; *Island of Palmas Arbitration (US v Netherlands)* (1928) 2 RIAA 829, 838–40; *Corfu Channel (UK v Albania)* [1949] ICJ Rep 4 34–35; M Akehurst, 'Jurisdiction in International Law' (1972–73) 46 *British Yearbook of International Law* 145, 146–48. See generally Mills, 'Rethinking' (n 76) 195: 'The territorial character of enforcement jurisdiction is well established.'

countries by registered mail', holding that 'the *act of service itself* constitutes an act of American sovereign power within the area of the foreign country's territorial sovereignty'.[84] The court held that enforcing such subpoenas – an act still recognised as requiring enforcement jurisdiction by US courts[85] – 'would clearly extend American enforcement jurisdiction beyond the limits of its prescriptive jurisdiction' under its empowering statute, and would '[violate] a fundamental principle of international law'.[86] Five years later, Hoffmann J (as he then was), in the Chancery Division of the High Court of England and Wales, rejected a similar attempt to serve a subpoena on an American bank not party to the underlying proceedings.[87] He noted that subpoenas, requiring the production of documents backed by the threat of sanction, are 'an exercise of sovereign authority'; as such, unilaterally requiring compliance by a foreign (US) non-party with a subpoena would be 'an infringement of the sovereignty of the United States'.[88]

B. CLOUD Act Agreements Lift the Prohibition against Extraterritorial Enforcement Jurisdiction

The US–UK Agreement will allow the above 1980s authorities on enforcement jurisdiction to be distinguished, expanding the ability for its members to assert extraterritorial jurisdiction over foreign service providers at the level of public international law. This is because the prohibition against extraterritorial enforcement jurisdiction applies only to *unilateral* acts; where the foreign state of the territory concerned consents, no jurisdictional issue arises in respect of that foreign state under international law.[89] Foreign state consent may be provided

[84] *FTC* (n 20) 1304.

[85] ibid 1316. See, eg *In re Search of Info. Associated with [redacted]@gmail.com* No 16-MJ-00757, 2017 WL 3445634, *14 (DDC, 31 July, 2017): 'The SCA warrant was merely an exercise of this Court's enforcement jurisdiction'. See also American Law Institute, *Restatement Fourth* (n 19) § 432 reporters' note 1, referring to 'executing an order for the production of documents' as an act 'constituting jurisdiction to enforce'. But see also C Ryngaert, 'Conflicts of Jurisdiction over Orders to Produce Documents Located Abroad' (2015) 48 *Revue Belge de droit international* 423, 424–27, discussing potentially conflicting US case law.

[86] *FTC* (n 20) 1318. See also, eg *In re Silver Wheaton Corp Sec Litig* No 215CV5146CASJEMX, 2018 WL 11394848, *4 (CD Cal 2 August 2018).

[87] *Mackinnon v Donaldson, Lufkin & Jenrette Security Corp* [1986] Ch 482, 493–95. See *SAS Institute Inc v World Programming Ltd* [2020] EWCA (Civ) 599 [68]–[70], leave to appeal granted but subsequently withdrawn by consent, suggesting *Mackinnon* describes enforcement jurisdiction. See generally Crawford (n 15) 462.

[88] *Mackinnon* (n 87) 494.

[89] American Law Institute, *Restatement Fourth* (n 19) § 401 comment b; Crawford (n 15) 462. See also C McLachlan, *Foreign Relations Law* (Cambridge, Cambridge University Press, 2016) 424. See generally *Compania Naviera Vascongado v Steamship 'Cristina' and Persons Claiming and Interest Therein* [1938] AC 485 (HOL) 496–97; *Schooner Exch v McFadden* 11 US 116, 136 (1812).

through an international treaty – like the US–UK Agreement[90] – or informally.[91] Through the US–UK Agreement, the USA and the UK have prima facie provided sufficient consent to permit law enforcement from the other state to expand enforcement jurisdiction in international law over service providers operating in their jurisdiction, through the lifting of 'blocking statutes' that otherwise purport to make this unlawful under US or UK law.[92] As other aspects of international law jurisdiction are generally permissive – in practice, the prohibition against extraterritorial enforcement jurisdiction is the primary hurdle[93] – this is a potentially significant, arguably 'sovereignty-enhancing', benefit.[94] However, an act may be lawful at international law but unlawful under domestic law.[95] It is therefore necessary to turn to domestic law to determine whether this benefit is realisable in practice.

The UK appears well placed to reap this benefit – indeed, it expressly asserts the ability to do so, saying that the US–UK Agreement will enable its law enforcement to compel data from providers previously 'beyond the reach of existing domestic court orders' that could only be reached through MLA.[96] New UK legislation enacted specifically for the US–UK Agreement, the Crime Overseas Production Orders Act 2019 (COPOA), permits court orders compelling stored data from foreign service providers operating in the USA under threat of contempt of

[90] See T Christakis and K Propp, 'The Legal Nature of the UK–US CLOUD Agreement' (*Cross-Border Data Forum*, 20 April 2020) www.crossborderdataforum.org/the-legal-nature-of-the-uk-us-cloud-agreement/, concluding that CLOUD Act agreements are 'binding international agreement[s]' under international law, citing VCLT, Art 2(1)(a).

[91] American Law Institute, *Restatement Fourth* (n 19) § 442 reporters' note 3; Crawford (n 15) 462. See PL Bellia, 'Chasing Bits Across Borders' [2001] *University of Chicago Legal Forum* 35, 80, suggesting that 'a state can simply give the searching state permission to examine data located within its territory'; eg *Reid v Covert* 354 US 1, 15 (1957); *Casdagli v Casdagli* [1919] AC 145 (HOL) 156.

[92] Text to nn 52–57 above.

[93] See n 81 above. It is theoretically possible that a state may be able to establish enforcement jurisdiction but not, for example, prescriptive jurisdiction. *cf* Mann (n 82) 19: 'The mere existence of legislative jurisdiction is insufficient to justify the State to exercise enforcement jurisdiction in another State's territory.' See also, eg Gallant (n 68) 532. However, this appears unlikely to arise in practice here, ie where law enforcement are seeking to obtain data for criminal investigations into breaches of serious crime, including terrorism. See US–UK Agreement, Arts 1(5) and (14) and 2(1).

[94] HL Buxbaum, 'Transnational Regulatory Litigation' (2006) 46 *Virginia Journal of International Law* 252, 308, arguing in the regulatory context that, 'if one theorizes sovereignty as status within the international community', then 'bilateral cooperation instruments' can be described as 'sovereignty-enhancing'; *cf* New Zealand Law Commission and Ministry of Justice, *Review of the Search and Surveillance Act 2012: Issues Paper* (NZLC IP40, November 2016) para 6.127: 'A [CLOUD Act] agreement would … involve sacrificing a degree of sovereignty'. See also Kohl (n 15) 26–27, 201, offering additional analysis.

[95] See, eg *FTC* (n 20) 1315, recognising that 'some exercises of jurisdiction to which international law does not object may violate the Constitution or laws of the United States'; *cf* Hörnle (n 20) 81–82: 'National rules can be coextensive with public international law, but they must not contradict the principles under public international law, as this is likely to infringe the sovereignty of another state.'

[96] Explanatory Notes to COPOA 2019, paras 1–4. See COPOA 2019, ss 1(2), 1(4)–(5), 4(2), providing for these powers.

court,[97] even where these providers have no UK presence whatsoever.[98] Jennifer Daskal has described this as 'a broad assertion of authority', but one 'premised on consent', as requests must be channelled through the US–UK Agreement (or any future similar arrangements with other foreign states).[99] Domestic UK law does not appear on its face to constrain meaningfully the UK from making ample use of the US–UK Agreement in this way. At UK law, two aspects of jurisdiction will normally be required in this context: 'personal jurisdiction, ie who can be brought before the court, [and] subject matter jurisdiction, ie to what extent the court can claim to regulate the conduct of those persons'.[100]

Personal jurisdiction appears straightforward. In the UK, personal jurisdiction is apparently satisfied through service of process,[101] including when courts are asked to determine whether they can exercise personal jurisdiction over overseas parties.[102] Orders to service providers compelling data for criminal investigations may generally require analysis through a civil procedure rather than a criminal lens.[103] However, the relatively onerous service requirements for civil proceedings in the UK are said to be 'irrelevant' here, as the Administrative Court found in the recent *KBR* litigation when assessing related criminal investigation information-gathering powers – comments left undisturbed on appeal by the Supreme Court.[104] Indeed, COPOA imposes discrete service requirements, which 'have been drafted to allow for flexibility',[105] permitting overseas service in a wide range of scenarios,

[97] Criminal Procedure Rules 2020, SI 2020/759 (CrimPR), r 47.71.

[98] COPOA 2019, ss 4(2), (8)(a), permitting orders against persons operating or based in a territory outside the UK where that territorial sovereign is party to a 'designated international co-operation agreement' with the UK, 'whether or not the person also creates, processes, communicates or stores data by electronic means in the United Kingdom'. See R Junck et al, 'What Recent US and UK Reforms to Information Sharing Mean for Cross-Border Investigations' (*Global Investigations Review*, 18 July 2019) globalinvestigationsreview.com/what-recent-us-and-uk-reforms-information-sharing-mean-cross-border-investigations.

[99] J Daskal, 'Transnational Government Hacking' (2020) 10 *Journal of National Security Law and Policy* 677, 695. See COPOA 2019, ss 1(2), 1(5), 4(2).

[100] *Société Eram Shipping Co v Cie Internationale de Navigation* [2003] UKHL 30 [22]–[23], quoting *Mackinnon* (n 87) 493; *SAS* (n 87) [68]–[71]. See, eg *Lucasfilm Ltd v Ainsworth* [2009] EWCA Civ 1328 [99], reversed on other grounds, [2011] UKSC 39.

[101] *Mackinnon* (n 87) 493. See *Stichting Shell Pensioenfonds v Kyrs* [2014] UKPC 41 [27]; eg *Lucasfilm Ltd* (n 100) [99]. See generally L Collins et al (eds), *Dicey, Morris & Collins: The Conflict of Laws*, 16th edn (London, Sweet & Maxwell, 2022) para 11-004.

[102] See, eg *Re Liddell's Settlement Trusts* [1936] Ch 365 (CA) 374 (Romer LJ): 'The moment a person is properly served … that person, so far as the jurisdiction of this Court is concerned, is precisely in the same position as a person who is in this country.' This case concerned persons ordinarily resident in the UK but has been applied more broadly, including to foreign service providers: eg, *Re J (A Child)* [2013] EWHC 2694 (Fam) [54].

[103] See Ryngaert, 'Conflicts of Jurisdiction' (n 85) 431: 'the principles of cross-border discovery are now also being applied, by analogy, to search warrants in the criminal law'. See also Cochrane, 'Hiding' (n 1) 194 and fn 242, detailing US law to this effect.

[104] *R (KBR, Inc) v Director of the Serious Fraud Office* [2018] EWHC 2368 (Admin) (*KBR (HC)*) [99](i). See *KBR (SC)* (n 20) [26]. For further on *KBR*, see T Cochrane, 'The Presumption against Extraterritoriality, Mutual Legal Assistance, and the Future of Law Enforcement Cross-Border Evidence Collection' (2022) 85 *MLR* 526.

[105] HL Deb 10 September 2018, vol 792, col 196GC, where it was also stated that 'If a person is located outside the UK and the other conditions for granting a [COPOA 2019] production order are fulfilled, a production order can be served'.

including electronically.[106] It therefore appears that this service requirement can be readily established in practice.[107]

In contrast, subject matter jurisdiction will often be more difficult. Speaking generally, personal jurisdiction concerns whether a party can be subject to the jurisdiction of UK courts in principle; conversely, subject matter jurisdiction generally considers whether the subject matter of the applicable (statutory or other) powers a UK court is asked to exercise properly extend to that party in the circumstances.[108] 'Whether a court has subject matter jurisdiction is a question of the construction of the relevant statute.'[109] Questions of subject matter jurisdiction often arise when UK courts are asked to consider whether statutory or other powers extend extraterritorially.[110] Indeed, it is firmly settled under UK law that the extraterritorial scope (if any) of a statute 'is a matter of subject matter jurisdiction'.[111] A statute's extraterritorial subject matter may be express or implied.[112] Where, however, the legislature has 'provided expressly for [a statute's] extraterritorial application', as the US Congress did with the CLOUD Act and the UK Parliament has with COPOA,[113] UK courts will give effect to that intent – even if it is inconsistent with international law.[114] UK courts normally apply a 'presumption against extraterritoriality', limiting a statute's extraterritoriality to avoid infringing the sovereignty of foreign states and due to broader comity concerns.[115] The House of Lords has held that 'Where, however, Parliament incorporates into domestic legislation an international [agreement] which necessarily gives to that domestic legislation extraterritorial effect in the broadest sense an entirely different situation arises'.[116] Then, 'the basis for the presumption no longer

[106] COPOA 2019, ss 9, 14; Explanatory Notes to COPOA 2019, para 52; CrimPR, r 47.68(4); US–UK Agreement, Arts 5(5) and 10(2). See also COPOA 2019, s 14(4)(d)(i), further permitting overseas service 'in accordance with arrangements made … by the Secretary of State'; US–UK Agreement, Arts 6(2) and 10(6).

[107] It is, however, possible that more onerous requirements, beyond merely proving service, will ultimately be required to establish personal jurisdiction over overseas service providers facing COPOA 2019 requests, as discussed at s IIIC below.

[108] See, eg *SAS* (n 87) [69]–[79]. See generally *Société Eram* (n 100) [75] (Lord Hobhouse), noting that 'the possible question of subject matter jurisdiction is always important'.

[109] *Jetivia SA v Bilta Ltd* [2015] UKSC 23 [212].

[110] *Masri v Consolidated Contractors Intl Co* [2008] EWCA Civ 303 [30].

[111] *KBR (HC)* (n 104) [72](i), affirmed on this point *KBR (SC)* (n 20) [59]. See *Bilta (UK) Ltd v Nazir (No 2)* [2015] UKSC 23 [212] (Lords Toulson and Hodge); *Masri* (n 110) [30]. See generally *Jetivia* (n 109) [212].

[112] *KBR (SC)* (n 20) [28]–[29]; D Feldman, D Bailey and L Norbury, *Bennion, Bailey, and Norbury on Statutory Interpretation*, 8th edn (London, LexisNexis Butterworths, 2020) para 6.10.

[113] See *KBR (HC)* (n 104) [61].

[114] See, eg *Assange v Swedish Prosecution Authority* [2012] UKSC 22 [265]. See generally *R (Miller) v Secretary of State for Exiting the European Union* [2017] UKSC 5 [56], [167], [244], affirming parliamentary sovereignty and the UK's dualist approach to international law.

[115] *KBR (SC)* (n 20) [27]–[32]. See *Masri* (n 110) [38]–[39]; *Société Eram* (n 100) [67]; *Mackinnon* (n 87) 494. See also *KBR (SC)* [28]: 'The more exorbitant the jurisdiction, the more is likely to be required of the statutory provisions in order to rebut the presumption against extra-territorial effect'; Cochrane, 'The Presumption' (n 104) 529–30, further detailing this presumption.

[116] *Holmes v Bangladesh Biman Corp* [1989] 1 AC 1112 (HOL) 1148 (Lord Jauncey) and 1132–38, in which Lord Griffiths and Lord Bridges arrive at the same conclusion pronounced by Lord Jauncey.

exists'.[117] Here, similarly, there is no need to limit extraterritorial jurisdiction to avoid infringing US sovereignty, given the US–UK Agreement evidences the USA's consent for such extraterritoriality.[118] As these jurisdictional requirements are met, the UK therefore appears to have significant scope to use the US–UK Agreement to expand its jurisdiction over foreign service providers.

I have set out the equivalent US law position elsewhere;[119] space permits only a summary here. Essentially, while US law mandates facially similar rules – as well as the same presumption against extraterritoriality – the relative significance of subject-matter jurisdiction and personal jurisdiction are inverse there. In other words, subject-matter jurisdiction is typically straightforward but personal jurisdiction is not. In interstate contexts, personal jurisdiction is traditionally strictly constrained by the Fourteenth Amendment to the US Constitution and it is commonly believed that similar limitations apply in international contexts under the Fifth Amendment.[120] Specifically, under the Fifth Amendment's Due Process Clause, personal jurisdiction over non-resident persons is thought to arise only where, first, that party has 'certain minimum contacts' with the forum in which the court sits and, secondly, where asserting jurisdiction over them would be 'reasonable' in the circumstances.[121] The USA appears to suggest that it is unable to make use of the second benefit of CLOUD Act agreements – expanding enforcement jurisdiction – due to the Fifth Amendment's Due Process Clause, which it refers to as a 'strict test' limiting its ability to compel data from foreign service providers.[122] I argue elsewhere, however, that this claim should be doubted for several reasons,[123] touched on below.

C. Unanswered Questions

While direct access mechanisms appear to provide a significant public international law benefit – allowing states to expand enforcement jurisdiction over foreign service providers – the extent to which such expanded jurisdiction is realisable in practice by any given state turns on several further unsettled questions. Ultimately, bold assertions of wide extraterritorial jurisdiction pursuant to direct access mechanisms – of which the UK's COPOA statute is the clearest example – may be

[117] ibid 1148. See also *Gorbachev v Guriev* [2022] EWCA Civ 1270 [53]: 'the principle of territoriality is concerned with the *illegitimate* usurpation of authority over foreign nationals'.

[118] *Holmes* (n 116) 1137–38: 'In such circumstances our domestic legislation is not an interference with the sovereignty of other countries but the recognition of their wish that we should alter our law to accord with the common will.'

[119] Cochrane, 'Hiding' (n 1) 192–204.

[120] See, eg Downing, Germany Speech (n 40). See also *Livnat v Palestinian Authority* 851 F.3d 45, 55 (DC Cir 2017), reaching this conclusion.

[121] *Bristol-Myers Squibb Co v Superior Court of California*, 137 S Ct 1773, 1785–86 (2017).

[122] See text to n 64 above. For elaboration, see Cochrane, 'Hiding' (n 1) 164–69.

[123] Cochrane, 'Hiding' (n 1) 194–204.

incompatible with, or need to be read down to accord with, both public international law as well as any given state's own domestic law. This final sub-section introduces three related areas worthy of further research.

Looking first to public international law, it is arguable whether the prohibition against extraterritorial enforcement jurisdiction should be applied in the binary manner that the above analysis assumes. As discussed, CLOUD Act agreements appear to lift the prohibition against extraterritorial enforcement jurisdiction vis-à-vis the other signatory state. Whether a state has sufficient 'consent' to extend their enforcement jurisdiction to obtain data from foreign service providers may, however, be a multifactorial rather than binary question.[124] Indeed, 'overlapping or conflicting claims' are entirely possible under the principles of public international law.[125] The 'un-territorial' nature of electronic data renders it particularly vulnerable to such overlapping sovereignty claims.[126] As such, the fact that UK law enforcement has the consent of the USA to serve an extraterritorial request for data on service providers based in the USA may merely be necessary but not sufficient at international law; other (non-consenting) states may have legitimate sovereignty claims over that provider and/or the requested data.[127] Consider, for example, that UK law enforcement is expected to direct the bulk of its US–UK Agreement requests to global service providers.[128] Such providers operate in multiple jurisdictions, often in circumstances subjecting them to data protection regimes like the EU General Data Protection Regulation (GDPR).[129] Data protected by the GDPR, such as the Facebook messages of a French national, may well need to be processed by Facebook to comply with a request by, for example, US law enforcement under the US–UK Agreement. This may be deliberate – the US–UK Agreement contemplates that its signatories may target third-country persons[130] – or simply inadvertent, when UK law enforcement seeks, for example,

[124] See, eg A Lubin, 'The Prohibition on Extraterritorial Enforcement Jurisdiction in the Datasphere' in A Parrish and C Ryngaert (eds), *Research Handbook on Extraterritoriality in International Law* (Cheltenham, Edward Elgar, forthcoming) ch 20.

[125] Mills, *The Confluence* (n 15) 236.

[126] AS Obendiek, 'What Are We Actually Talking About? Conceptualizing Data as a Governable Object in Overlapping Jurisdictions' (2022) 66 *International Studies Quarterly* sqab080; eg *United Company Rusal PLC v HSBC Bank PLC* [2011] EWHC 404 (QB) [104]. See also Allen (n 68) 387 and fn 21, noting that the un-territoriality of data may make it difficult for law enforcement seeking overseas data to verify 'which state to approach for the purposes of securing its consent in order to render their extraterritorial actions lawful'. See generally J Daskal, 'The Un-Territoriality of Data' (2015) 125 *Yale Law Journal* 326.

[127] See Lubin (n 124) 15.

[128] See, eg HC Deb 30 January 2019, vol 653, cols 859–60: 'This legislation [COPOA 2019] is about the data predominantly held by Facebook and Google and everything else.'

[129] Regulation 2016/679 of the European Parliament and of the Council of 27 April 2016 on the protection of natural persons with regard to the processing of personal data and on the free movement of such data, and repealing Directive 95/46/EC (General Data Protection Regulation) [2016] OJ L119/1. See, eg R Bala et al, 'Magic Quadrant for Cloud Infrastructure and Platform Services' (Gartner, 1 September 2020), noting that major service providers operating in the USA have data centres in the UK and Europe.

[130] US–UK Agreement, Art 5(10).

Facebook messages of a UK national communicating with a French national. In such a scenario, while the USA's implementation of the US–UK Agreement may remove the blocking effect of US laws, service providers may nonetheless remain subject to foreign laws that prevent disclosure, such as the GDPR under EU law.[131] I have suggested elsewhere that this conflict requires agreement between the USA and the EU in order to be resolved.[132]

More generally, the extent to which the prohibition against extraterritorial enforcement jurisdiction should even be considered applicable in online and other digital contexts is an evolving issue. Some scholars suggest that the prohibition remains in force and applicable within the digital sphere.[133] Others have, however, doubted whether compelling overseas data in such contexts engages this prohibition.[134] The Law Commission of England and Wales has notably recently claimed that 'Strict adherence to the *Lotus*-based principle of enforcement jurisdiction is neither possible nor desirable when electronic data is sought'.[135] Reflecting a similar view, Dan J Svantesson has suggested that a new, more permissive category of 'investigatory jurisdiction' permitting extraterritorial data gathering should be recognised, based on an overall reasonableness assessment.[136] While it is beyond the scope of this chapter to opine on this issue, it is pressing and worthy of further elucidation.

Further analysis of equivalent domestic law jurisdictional limits is also appropriate. In particular, the extent to which domestic law – including notably constitutional (including human rights) law – constrains the ability of states to meaningfully extend enforcement jurisdiction extraterritorially should be further examined. I have previously suggested that, despite the broad jurisdictional assertion COPOA comprises, a UK court may ultimately 'read down' its subject matter to avoid infringing foreign nations' sovereignty or for related comity concerns.[137] This is most likely to occur where compliance with a UK COPOA order would require the responding service provider to breach foreign law[138] – UK courts have, however, previously dismissed claimed fears that foreign law would be breached absent evidence of 'a real risk of an adverse sanction'.[139] It also remains debatable

[131] See Cochrane, 'Hiding' (n 1) 176–80, detailing the interaction between the GDPR and the US–UK Agreement.

[132] ibid 180.

[133] eg Currie (n 21) 93–94. See also Crawford (n 15) 462–64; Boister (n 36) 329–31.

[134] See, eg Gallant (n 68) 170–71, 331; Hörnle (n 20) 5. See also Ryngaert, *Jurisdiction* (n 81) 81–82. The Court of Appeal has also recently indicated that data held on UK servers on behalf of overseas persons can be subject to the jurisdiction of UK courts as 'the principle of territoriality has little or no application' in that context: *Gorbachev* (n 117) [84].

[135] Law Commission (n 56), para 16.87.

[136] Svantesson (n 76) 165–67. See also Hörnle (n 20) 7. Other scholars have similarly recommended a 'reasonableness' test, eg Ryngaert, *Jurisdiction* (n 81) ch 5.

[137] See *KBR (SC)* (n 20) [24]–[25].

[138] *Bank Mellat v HM Treasury* [2019] EWCA Civ 499 [63](iii); *Masri* (n 110) [47].

[139] *Palladian Partners LP v Republic of Argentina* [2022] EWHC 2059 (Comm) [9]; eg *Owners of the Motor Vessel 'Gravity Highway' v Owners of the Motor Vessel 'Maritime Maisie'* [2020] EWHC 1697 (Comm) [50]–[52]. See generally *Bank Mellat* (n 138) [63](i).

whether a UK court would interpret COPOA as properly permitting orders to be issued to US service providers with no UK connections whatsoever; most, but not all, of COPOA's service methods assume overseas providers have at least some UK operations.[140] In other contexts, UK courts have read down apparently unlimited extraterritorial jurisdiction over foreign persons by requiring that such persons have a 'sufficient connection' to the UK.[141] Such an interpretation may also be appropriate to give effect to the recipient service providers' own 'due process' rights under Article 6(1) of the European Convention on Human Rights.[142] Although historically this right appears to have had little impact in this context,[143] it is an area suitable for further research.

As outlined above, the equivalent US law due process rights are, in contrast, assumed to constrain meaningfully US extraterritorial jurisdiction.[144] I have, however, argued elsewhere that the extent to which the Fifth Amendment Due Process Clause genuinely limits the ability of US courts to issue extraterritorial orders under the US–UK Agreement[145] – or even applies at all[146] – is debatable, given developing US jurisprudence. This is an unsettled and evolving area of law: the scope of the Fifth Amendment's Due Process Clause protections has recently been addressed by the Fifth Circuit,[147] and will shortly be considered by the Second Circuit.[148] The US government has notably opined in the Second Circuit litigation that 'the Fifth Amendment allows a more expansive assertion of personal jurisdiction than the Fourteenth Amendment'[149] – undermining the widely held belief that these two provisions impose similar constraints, and potentially giving

[140] See n 106 above; Explanatory Notes to COPOA 2019, para 52: 'Where a person has no principal office in the UK, documents can also be served at any place in the UK where that person carries on business or conducts business activities.'

[141] eg *Masri* (n 110) [36].

[142] Convention for the Protection of Human Rights and Fundamental Freedoms (Rome, 4 November 1950) 213 UNTS 221 (ECHR), Art 6(1), relevantly providing that 'In the determination of his civil rights and obligations … everyone is entitled to a fair and public hearing within a reasonable time by an independent and impartial tribunal established by law'. See also Mills, *The Confluence* (n 15) 268, discussing 'the emergence of international minimum standards of due process and procedural fairness' in public international law.

[143] R Michaels, 'Jurisdiction: Foundations' in J Basedow et al (eds), *Elgar Encyclopedia of Private International Law* (Cheltenham, Edward Elgar, 2017) J.2. See Mills, *The Confluence* (n 15) 269. The European Court of Human Rights has found violations of due process under the ECHR, Art 6(1), where national courts 'hav[e] overstepped the limits of [their] jurisdiction'; eg *Sokurenko and Strygun v Ukraine* App No 29458/04 (ECtHR, 20 July 2006) [24]–[28]. However, it appears that the extent of such jurisdiction is treated purely as a matter of domestic law, leaving states free to assert broad extraterritorial authority. See generally *Sokurenko and Strygun* [116].

[144] See text to n 122 above.

[145] Cochrane, 'Hiding' (n 1) 194–201.

[146] ibid 201–04.

[147] *Douglass v Nippon Yusen Kabushiki Kaisha* 46 F.4th 226 (5th Cir 2022), petition for cert filed (USA, 14 December 2022) (No 22A386).

[148] *Fuld v Palestine Liberation Organization* 578 F Supp 3d 577 (SDNY 2022), appeal filed, No 22-496(CON) (2nd Cir, 8 March 2022).

[149] Brief for Intervenor-Appellant at 19, *Fuld v Palestine Liberation Organization*, No 22-496(CON), 2022 WL 2399673, *19 (2d Cir, 27 June 2022).

scope for broader extraterritorial assertions of jurisdiction by US law enforcement. Again, further analysis of this area of US constitutional law is warranted.

IV. Conclusion

CLOUD Act agreements, alongside other direct access mechanisms, appear to offer their member states the ability to expand enforcement jurisdiction in public international law against foreign service providers previously beyond the reach of law enforcement. This is a potentially significant benefit, sitting alongside the much-touted private international law benefit of these new mechanisms, and may well incentivise states accordingly. States considering CLOUD Act or similar agreements should, however, bear in mind that they are reciprocal:[150] while one state's law enforcement may be able to extend enforcement jurisdiction over service providers operating in other signatory states, they must agree to provide the same benefit to the law enforcement of the counter-party state. In this regard, as Julia Hörnle articulates, CLOUD Act agreements effect both an extension and a 'mutual cessation of sovereignty'.[151] As I have set out elsewhere, the impact of such cessation of sovereignty requires careful consideration by states.[152]

This chapter also hopes to spur further research, including into the unanswered questions outlined above by both international and constitutional legal scholars. The introduction of direct access mechanisms appears to challenge our traditional understandings of jurisdiction at public international law – already under threat in the digital era – and may ultimately have similar impacts on related constitutional laws within signatory states, including notably due process rights. The potential impact of CLOUD Act agreements and similar proposals on these laws is a fruitful area of study. Until then, states should take seriously the reciprocity of these mechanisms and the many uncertain areas of law with which they interact and proceed with such mechanisms – if at all – with caution.

[150] See text to nn 46–47 above.
[151] Hörnle (n 20) 212.
[152] Cochrane, 'Hiding' (n 1) 209–10.

11

Law Enforcement Access to Encrypted Data across Borders

JESSICA SHURSON*

I. Introduction

New encryption technologies have created problems for law enforcement access to digital evidence. Technologies such as sophisticated device encryption and default end-to-end encryption for communications inhibit access to data by both criminal actors and the law enforcement authorities (LEAs) who seek to protect society from those actors. While LEAs will have the legal authority to access data from electronic communications, they may lack the technical ability to do so. To address this 'going dark' problem, some states have proposed allowing LEAs to have 'exceptional access' to encrypted data – that is, third-party access to data that would otherwise be unreadable due to encryption. Critics argue that any exceptional access will both undermine privacy and risk being used by criminal actors for nefarious purposes. This chapter does not seek to settle this debate,[1] but rather considers how LEA orders requiring exceptional access capabilities may work in practice, in light of new mechanisms for LEA access to cross-border data based on mutual trust.[2]

* For comments on earlier drafts of this chapter, I am grateful to Ian Walden, Julia Hörnle, David Thaw, Neil Brown, Bernard Keenan, Tim Cochrane, and the participants of the Cybersecurity Law and Policy Scholars Conference in March 2021 and the WG Hart Workshop in April 2021. Of course, any errors remain my own.

[1] For more on this debate, see I Walden, '"The Sky Is Falling!" – Responses to the "Going Dark" Problem' (2018) 34 *Computer Law and Security Review* 901, 905; G Corn and D Brenner-Beck, '"Going Dark": Encryption, Privacy, Liberty, and Security in the "Golden Age of Surveillance"' in D Gray and S Henderson (eds), *The Cambridge Handbook of Surveillance Law* (Cambridge, Cambridge University Press, 2017); E Manpearl, 'The International Front of the Going Dark Debate' (2018) 22 *Virginia Journal of Law and Technology* 158.

[2] While there can be some overlap between intelligence and criminal investigations, especially in the context of terrorism, this chapter is limited in its scope to criminal investigations. For more on exceptional access mechanisms for intelligence operations, see Manpearl (n 1), regarding UK national security notices.

This chapter uses the term 'mutual trust' to refer to new co-operative reforms for LEA data access that allow an LEA in one state (the 'requesting state') to send production orders for data directly to a service provider in another state (the 'receiving state'). Professor Walden refers to these agreements as mutual trust agreements because the receiving state trusts the requesting state to send a request for data directly to service providers in the receiving state, without case-by-case mediation by the authorities in the receiving state.[3] In this way, the term 'mutual trust' is used generically and does not necessarily refer to the concept of mutual trust in the EU unless explicitly stated. This mutual trust is usually based on similar criminal procedure and human rights protections in both the requesting and receiving states.

The US CLOUD Act[4] is the first law to set up a framework for mutual trust agreements, and the UK was the first country to enter into a bilateral executive agreement with the USA under this framework. The UK–US Agreement on Access to Electronic Data for the Purpose of Countering Serious Crime (UK–US Agreement) allows UK LEAs to send interception and production orders, authorised under UK law, directly to the US service providers for communications and content data.[5] Without such an agreement, US communications service providers (CSPs) are usually blocked from intercepting or disclosing the content of communications directly to UK law enforcement by the US Electronic Communications Privacy Act (ECPA).[6] The ECPA prohibits CSPs from disclosing content data unless the disclosure is required by a warrant issued by a US court.[7] Under the new UK–US Agreement, the USA trusts the UK to send orders directly to US-based CSPs, thus removing the effect of the blocking provisions of the ECPA.

This new mutual trust model for LEA access to data across borders is a response to the current unsuitability of old legal mechanisms for access to cross-border evidence – namely, mutual legal assistance treaties (MLATs). The MLAT procedures are lengthy, often rely on formal communications channels, with multiple officials involved, and often require LEAs to meet the criminal procedural requirements of the foreign state where the evidence is located or controlled.[8] Criminal investigations increasingly rely on digital evidence due to the proliferation of

[3] I Walden, 'Accessing Data in the Cloud: The Long Arm of the Law Enforcement Agent' in C Millard (ed), *Cloud Computing Law*, 2nd edn (Oxford, Oxford University Press, 2021) 451.

[4] The Clarifying Lawful Overseas Use of Data Act (CLOUD Act) amended the relevant portions of the Electronic Communications Privacy Act: 18 USC § 2523 (added by Pub L 115-141, div V, § 105(a)).

[5] Agreement on Access to Electronic Data for the Purpose of Countering Serious Crime (UK–US) (3 October 2019).

[6] Electronic Communications Privacy Act, 18 USC § 2702.

[7] ibid § 2703. Service providers are blocked from providing content data by the ECPA without a US warrant, or after the changes made by the CLOUD Act, pursuant to a CLOUD Act executive agreement. Service providers have never been blocked by the ECPA from providing non-content data to foreign LEAs, meaning these providers can and often do provide subscriber information and metadata (otherwise known as traffic data) to foreign LEAs voluntarily.

[8] J Hörnle, *Internet Jurisdiction: Law and Practice* (Oxford, Oxford University Press, 2021) 155–57.

Internet and cloud-based communications technologies. The US MLAT system, in particular, has become overwhelmed by requests and has been unable to keep pace with increasing demand because of the market dominance of US CSPs.[9] As a result, the UK sought negotiations for a more efficient procedure to obtain data from US CSPs.[10] The result of these negotiations was the second part of the US CLOUD Act, which introduced the executive agreement framework.[11]

The CLOUD Act agreements only govern the preservation, interception, disclosure and production of data by CSPs. The CLOUD Act is silent as to the implementation of any capabilities required to facilitate such interception, with the exception of one provision. The CLOUD Act specifies that the executive agreements 'shall not create any obligation that providers be capable of decrypting data or limitation that prevents providers from decrypting data'.[12] Thus, the Act has been called 'neutral' on the issue of encryption by the US Department of Justice, as well as by scholars and commentators.[13] This chapter considers the effect of this purported 'neutrality' on orders known as 'technical capability notices' (TCNs) under UK and Australian law. LEAs may issue TCNs to require CSPs to implement a variety of capabilities to facilitate interception of communications, including capabilities that will give LEAs exceptional access to encrypted data. These TCNs are extraterritorial in scope, meaning authorities in the UK and Australia may serve these notices on US CSPs pursuant to their domestic law.

With the move to mutual trust agreements, the question of extraterritorial TCNs takes on new relevance. For example, if the USA is not playing an active role in mediating the disclosure of data by its US-based CSPs due to this new mutual trust paradigm, then is the door opened to extraterritorial TCNs already authorised

[9] A 2018 European Commission study showed that 55% of all criminal investigations in Member States required cross-border digital evidence. In addition, MLAT requests directed to the US Department of Justice increased tenfold between 2008 and 2018, exacerbating an already slow process further. See Commission, 'Impact Assessment: *Accompanying the Document*: Proposal for a Regulation of the European Parliament and of the Council on European Production and Preservation Orders for Electronic Evidence in Criminal Matters; and; Proposal for a Directive of the European Parliament and of the Council Laying Down Harmonised Rules on the Appointment of Legal Representatives for the Purpose of Gathering Evidence in Criminal Proceedings' SWD (2018) 118 final, 14 and 25.

[10] A Travis, 'Secret Report Urges Treaty Forcing US Web Firms' Cooperation in Data Sharing' *The Guardian* (2 June 2015) www.theguardian.com/world/2015/jun/02/web-firms-data-sharing-secret-treaty; D Anderson, *A Question of Trust: Report of the Investigatory Powers Review* (London, HM Government, 2015) 209.

[11] The first part of the CLOUD Act only clarified the territorial reach of US warrants for data: 18 USC § 2713.

[12] 18 USC § 2523(b)(3).

[13] US Department of Justice, 'Promoting Public Safety, Privacy, and the Rule of Law around the World: The Purpose and Impact of the CLOUD Act' (White Paper, April 2019) (US White Paper). See also H Abraha, 'Regulating Law Enforcement Access to Electronic Evidence across Borders: The United States Approach' (2020) 29 *Information and Communications Technology Law* 324, 342; N Swire, 'Applying the CLOUD Act to the UK–US Bilateral Data Access Agreement' (*Lawfare*, 28 October 2019) www.lawfareblog.com/applying-cloud-act-us-uk-bilateral-data-access-agreement; T Christakis, '21 Thoughts and Questions about the UK–US CLOUD Act Agreement' (*European Law Blog*, 17 October 2019) europeanlawblog.eu/2019/10/17/21-thoughts-and-questions-about-the-uk-us-cloud-act-agreement-and-an-explanation-of-how-it-works-with-charts/.

by the law of the foreign state? The development of the UK–US Agreement and the substantially similar Australia–US Agreement has led to confusion concerning whether these notices may be served on US CSPs pursuant to these bilateral agreements. This question has been dismissed by some commentators, who point to the decryption-neutrality provision of the CLOUD Act,[14] but commentators have also argued that these TCN regimes 'violate' the neutrality provision.[15]

This chapter examines the implications of these new CLOUD Act agreements on the extraterritoriality of TCNs in UK and Australian law as a case study to consider a broader question: how are states' efforts to access encrypted data across borders impacted by the emerging paradigm of mutual trust agreements? Should these agreements, which extend extraterritorial jurisdiction for production and interception orders, address the appropriate jurisdictional reach of TCNs as well?

These questions are even more relevant in the context of encryption because there are often global cybersecurity implications when decryption capabilities are implemented.[16] In other words, if one country requests a CSP to remove or weaken encryption for one user on a communications platform, that can affect the security of all users on that platform. And many of these communications technologies are used globally. Thus, a technical capability that affects encryption is not necessarily limited to one state's territory, but rather, may be extraterritorial in scope.

The chapter proceeds as follows. Following this introduction, section II provides a brief introduction to encryption and the historical use of interception capabilities, which sets up the discussion of UK and Australian law on technical capability notices in section III. Whilst there is some ambiguity in the UK and Australian statutes, the laws in both states can be read to authorise orders to overseas CSPs to either bypass or remove encryption. Given the extraterritorial reach of TCNs, section IV then considers how these TCNs may interact with CLOUD Act agreements and concludes that the decryption-neutrality provision of the CLOUD Act has no effect on TCNs. While there is no enforcement mechanism for TCNs pursuant to US law, the orders would be enforceable pursuant to UK and Australian law, placing TCNs in the same position vis-à-vis US law as interception and production orders under the CLOUD Act agreements. Section V concludes the chapter.

This case study shows that it is essential to consider how the disclosure of data across borders may interact with requirements for LEA exceptional access

[14] J Daskal and P Swire, 'The UK–US CLOUD Act Agreement Is Finally Here, Containing New Safeguards' (*Lawfare*, 8 October 2019) www.lawfareblog.com/uk-us-cloud-act-agreement-finally-here-containing-new-safeguards.

[15] P Swire, 'Telecommunications Legislation Amendment (International Production Orders) Bill 2020: Submission 11' (submission to the Parliamentary Joint Committee on Intelligence and Security, Parliament of Australia, 2020) www.aph.gov.au/Parliamentary_Business/Committees/Joint/Intelligence_and_Security/IPOBill2020/Submissions.

[16] OS Kerr and B Schneier, 'Encryption Workarounds' (2018) 106 *Georgetown Law Journal* 989, 995–96. See also A Rozenshtein, 'Wicked Crypto' (2018) 9 *UC Irvine Law Review* 1181, 1185; H Abelson et al, 'Keys under Doormats: Mandating Insecurity by Requiring Government Access to All Data and Communications' (2015) 1 *Journal of Cybersecurity* 69.

to decrypted data to ensure a fair balancing of interests in these agreements.[17] This consideration is even more necessary because data disclosure agreements based on mutual trust are becoming a common paradigm for reform of cross-border data access systems. The USA is negotiating an agreement with the EU,[18] the EU is debating its own e-Evidence proposals for a new mutual trust framework within the EU,[19] and a Second Additional Protocol to the Budapest Convention on Cybercrime has incorporated mutual trust principles for the disclosure of subscriber information data and domain name information.[20] States may believe they can leave encryption out of the negotiations by adopting neutrality provisions, but what may result from this position should be examined. This chapter concludes that orders requiring CSPs to implement *capabilities* for the interception and disclosure of digital evidence are inextricably linked to interception and production orders, and thus should be considered in the ongoing debate over the appropriate jurisdictional reach of investigatory powers. This is especially the case for CLOUD Act agreements for data sharing because the CLOUD Act's 'encryption neutrality' provision raises the issue of encryption without further clarification for US-based CSPs on how they should respond to foreign TCNs.

II. A Brief Introduction to Encryption and Interception Capabilities

Encryption encodes information to make it unreadable to anyone except the intended parties to the communication. Modern cryptography uses common and widely known algorithms to secure data with encryption 'keys'.[21] The algorithm transforms plaintext into 'cyphertext', which can be turned back into plaintext through the use of the key.[22] CSPs have built encryption into their applications,

[17] Andrew Woods argues that privacy issues relating to law enforcement access to data – including both jurisdictional and technological barriers – should be negotiated collectively, rather than serially, to allow for a fair balance of interests: AK Woods, 'Encryption Substitutes' (2017) Hoover Working Group on National Security, Technology, and Law, Aegis Series Paper No 1705, www.scribd.com/document/354096059/Encryption-Substitutes#download.

[18] US Department of Justice, 'Joint US–EU Statement on Electronic Evidence Sharing Negotiations' (*Justice*, 26 September 2019) www.justice.gov/opa/pr/joint-us-eu-statement-electronic-evidence-sharing-negotiations. See also T Christakis and F Terpan, 'EU–US Negotiations on Law Enforcement Access to Data: Divergences, Challenges and EU Law Procedures and Options' (2021) 11 *International Data Privacy Law* 81.

[19] Commission, 'Proposal for a Regulation of the European Parliament and of the Council on European Production and Preservation Orders for Electronic Evidence in Criminal Matters' COM (2018) 225 final.

[20] Second Additional Protocol to the Budapest Convention on Cybercrime on enhanced co-operation and disclosure of electronic evidence (Strasbourg, 12 May 2022) (European Treaty Series No 224), Arts 6–7.

[21] Kerr and Schneier (n 16) 993.

[22] D Clark, *Designing an Internet* (Cambridge, MA, MIT Press, 2018) 195.

which handles the secure key exchange for users to efficiently encrypt and decrypt communications.[23]

Encryption can be used to protect communications between users of messaging apps or email, to facilitate e-commerce and secure web traffic, and to secure devices such as phones and computers.[24] Many messaging platforms use a type of encryption known as 'end-to-end encryption'. This type of encryption means CSPs do not hold any encryption keys. Rather, the keys are generated and stored on the devices of the end users – the sender and recipient of the message.[25] This type of encryption usually means that no one except the end users will be able to read the plaintext of communications, including LEAs who may possess a valid warrant or production order for this data. This is a classic situation cited by LEAs to support their argument that their investigations are 'going dark' due to encryption.[26] Despite the popular conception that end-to-end encryption guarantees secure communications, there are ways that LEAs can gain access to the plaintext of the end-to-end encrypted messages.

Rather than requiring CSPs to decrypt communications, LEAs can require CSPs to implement other capabilities by altering security protocols other than the encryption itself. One such proposed capability is known as the ghost user protocol. The UK's Government Communications Headquarters (GCHQ) has suggested that messaging services can add surreptitious participants to communications, otherwise known as 'ghost users'.[27] End-to-end encrypted messaging services like Signal, Whatsapp and Zoom could potentially add an LEA 'ghost user' by modifying a security protocol that authenticates the users on a group chat without notifying the other parties to the messages.[28] Essentially, messages sent between Alice and Bob become messages sent between Alice, Bob and the invisible LEA agent. Alice and Bob do not see the LEA agent present as an end user of the messages, but the LEA agent can read all of Alice and Bob's messages.

[23] Rozenshtein (n 16) 1185.

[24] Kerr and Schneier (n 16) 990. Encryption used to protect data stored locally on a user's computer generally implicates different laws on compelled decryption that are targeted at users, rather than CSPs, and thus is outside the scope of this paper. For more on this, see S Mason, A Gillespie and J Shurson, 'Encrypted Data' in S Mason and D Seng (eds), *Electronic Evidence and Electronic Signatures*, 5th edn (London, University of London Press, 2021).

[25] JL Zittrain et al, 'Don't Panic: Making Progress on the Going Dark Debate' (Berkman Center for Internet and Society at Harvard University, 2016) 4–5, cyber.harvard.edu/pubrelease/dont-panic/Dont_Panic_Making_Progress_on_Going_Dark_Debate.pdf.

[26] J Comey, 'Going Dark: Are Technology, Privacy, and Public Safety on a Collision Course?' (Federal Bureau of Investigation, 16 October 2014) www.fbi.gov/news/speeches/going-dark-are-technology-privacy-and-public-safety-on-a-collision-course; A Rudd, 'We Don't Want to Ban Encryption, but Our Inability to See what Terrorists are Plotting Undermines Our Secruity' *The Telegraph* (31 July 2017) www.telegraph.co.uk/news/2017/07/31/dont-want-ban-encryption-inability-see-terrorists-plotting-online/.

[27] I Levy and C Robinson, 'Principles for a More Informed Exceptional Access Debate' (*Lawfare*, 29 November 2018) www.lawfareblog.com/principles-more-informed-exceptional-access-debate; M Green, 'On Ghost Users and Messaging Backdoors' (*Cryptography Engineering Blog*, 17 December 2018) blog.cryptographyengineering.com/2018/12/17/on-ghost-users-and-messaging-backdoors/.

[28] B Keenan, 'State Access to Encrypted Data in the United Kingdom: The "Transparent" Approach' (2020) 49 *Common Law World Review* 223, 232–33.

This exceptional access mechanism[29] maintains the encryption of messages in transmission, but allows LEAs to gain access to the encryption keys as one of the end users.

Additionally, rather than requiring decryption, LEAs may require CSPs to implement capabilities that grant LEAs 'exceptional access' to encrypted data by accessing the data at points where it is already readable as plaintext. One such method involves CSPs sending targeted code updates to specific mobile devices that would enable LEAs to surreptitiously view the data on the phone where data is stored in plaintext.[30] In other words, the CSP delivers code to an individual device that allows the LEA to gain access to the device remotely – this is sometimes referred to as an LEA 'hacking' technique.[31] This capability does not require decryption per se, but instead bypasses encryption by altering different security protocols that protect the plaintext data.[32]

Computer scientists would distinguish between 'decryption' (in the technical sense of using a key to decrypt data into a readable form) and bypassing encryption through the modification of other security protocols (such as the example just discussed). This distinction could be important when one considers the language of the CLOUD Act, which refers only to 'decryption'. However, legal commentary on this 'decryption-neutral' provision tends to generalise it as a reference to removing or bypassing 'encryption'.[33] And it is doubtful that the legislature intended such a technically precise distinction. Because this chapter intends to discuss the powers that affect encryption more generally, it will consider the 'decryption' neutrality language in the CLOUD Act to refer to any attempt to remove or bypass encryption protections.[34]

Any exceptional access measure, whether compelled decryption or other encryption workarounds, are 'dual use' technologies.[35] They can be used to grant

[29] Often commentators refer to exceptional access mechanisms as 'backdoors', but there is no uniform definition of this term.

[30] Encryption Working Group, 'Moving the Encryption Policy Conversation Forward' (Carnegie Endowment for International Peace, 2019) 11 carnegieendowment.org/files/EWG__Encryption_Policy.pdf.

[31] For more on LEA hacking, see R Bercovitz, 'Law Enforcement Hacking: Defining Jurisdiction' (2021) 121 *Columbia Law Review* 1251; J Daskal, 'Transnational Government Hacking' (2019) 10 *Journal of National Security Law and Policy* 677; S Hennessey, 'Lawful Hacking and the Case for a Strategic Approach to "Going Dark"' (*Brookings*, 7 October 2016) www.brookings.edu/research/lawful-hacking-and-the-case-for-a-strategic-approach-to-going-dark/; SM Bellovin et al, 'Lawful Hacking: Using Existing Vulnerabilities for Wiretapping on the Internet' (2014) 12 *Northwestern Journal of Technology and Intellectual Property* 1.

[32] For other encryption workarounds that LEAs may use without the assistance of CSPs, see Kerr and Schneier (n 16). In addition, for an example of other methods available to LEAs, see US Department of Justice, Southern District of California, 'FBI's Encrypted Phone Platform Infiltrated Hundreds of Criminal Syndicates; Result is Massive Worldwide Takedown' (8 June 2021) https://www.justice.gov/usao-sdca/pr/fbi-s-encrypted-phone-platform-infiltrated-hundreds-criminal-syndicates-result-massive (last accessed 8 June 2022).

[33] Daskal and Swire (n 14): 'these agreements are agnostic as to the requirements with respect to encryption and decryption'.

[34] Hopefully the computer scientists will forgive this generalisation.

[35] Kerr and Schneier (n 16) 995.

access to LEAs or any other third party. Just as criminals may use encryption to hide their criminality and LEAs use encryption workarounds to discover that criminality, good faith actors use encryption to safeguard their data and criminals may use encryption workarounds to compromise that data. While the extent of the systemic weaknesses introduced by encryption workarounds or decryption orders may vary, there are cybersecurity implications for everyone when these capabilities are introduced.[36]

Nonetheless, states are increasingly seeking powers that will allow LEAs to access encrypted data in a readable form.[37] Many of these powers are not necessarily 'new', but are merely an extension of historical provisions governing interception capabilities.[38] States have long required telecommunications carriers to provide LEAs with the capability to intercept communications through technical capability notices.[39] Intercept capabilities generally are required by most jurisdictions, but they differ in scope and may not always include decryption.[40] The Cybercrime Convention also requires parties to adopt measures that require CSPs to intercept communications on behalf of law enforcement, but it is silent on decryption.[41]

These historical laws requiring interception capabilities are now being extended to Internet-facilitated and cloud CSPs. This is the case in both the UK and Australia. The next section will give a brief overview of TCN provisions in UK and Australian law relating to exceptional access to encrypted data.

[36] ibid 995–96. See also Rozenshtein (n 16) 1185; Abelson et al (n 16).

[37] For example, in May 2022, the European Commission proposed a new regulation for combating child sexual abuse that would require CSPs to scan messages and content for child sexual abuse materials: Commission, 'Proposal for a Regulation of the European Parliament of the Council Laying Down Rules to Prevent and Combat Child Sexual Abuse' COM (2022) 209 final. This would necessitate exceptional access to content otherwise encrypted through end-to-end encryption. See J Brodkin, '"War upon End-to-End Encryption": EU Wants Big Tech to Scan Private Messages' (*Ars Technica*, 11 May 2022) arstechnica.com/tech-policy/2022/05/war-upon-end-to-end-encryption-eu-wants-big-tech-to-scan-private-messages/. The UK Online Safety HC Bill (2021–22) [4] may impose on CSPs a duty to moderate harmful content on their platforms. While the Online Safety Bill does not ban end-to-end encryption, it appears that CSPs could not fulfil the duties imposed by the Bill without removing or weakening their encryption protocols. C Voge and R Wilton, 'Internet Impact Brief: End-to-End Encryption under the UK's Draft Online Safety Bill' (*Internet Society*, January 2022) www.internetsociety.org/wp-content/uploads/2022/01/IIB_Encryption_UK_Online_Safety_Bill_EN-1.pdf. UK policymakers have suggested that the Online Safety Bill would only require selective 'exceptional access' measures for LEAs.

[38] Walden, 'The Sky is Falling' (n 1) 905 notes that exceptional access, in the form of 'backdoors', is 'precisely what intercept legislation applicable to telecommunications operators has been requiring, going back to the days when telecommunications operators were state monopolies'.

[39] I Walden, *Computer Crimes and Digital Investigations*, 2nd edn (Oxford, Oxford University Press, 2016) 241.

[40] ibid 241–42; for a discussion of intercept capabilities regarding decryption in the Five Eyes countries, see M Mann, A Daly and A Molnar, 'Regulatory Arbitrage and Transnational Surveillance: Australia's Extraterritorial Assistance to Access Encrypted Communications' (2020) 9(3) *Internet Policy Review*.

[41] Budapest Convention on Cybercrime (European Treaty Series No 185), Arts 20–21. The intercept capabilities required of service providers are limited to existing capabilities and do not require them to build in new capabilities: Explanatory Report to the Convention on Cybercrime (23 November 2001), [221].

III. Technical Capability Notices

A. The UK

The Investigatory Powers Act 2016 (IPA) provides that the Secretary of State may serve a TCN on a telecommunications operator when such a notice is 'necessary for securing that the operator has the capability to provide any assistance which the operator may be required to provide in relation to any relevant authorisation'.[42] In other words, the UK authorities will require a telecommunications operator to implement the capability necessary to comply with future demands for data under the law. 'Telecommunications operator' is broadly defined as an operator who offers or provides access to a system that facilitates the transmission of communications by electronic means, to persons in the UK.[43] This definition encompasses nearly every provider of Internet, communications and cloud computing services and systems used by persons in the UK.

The IPA itself only sets out the broad authorisation of TCNs. The specifics of what capabilities may be required are set out further in regulations and a Code of Practice.[44] IPA, section 253(5) sets out obligations that may be specified in the regulations. These obligations concern numerous capabilities, most of which are not related at all to encryption. Importantly for our purposes, the IPA includes within the obligations those 'relating to the removal by a relevant operator of electronic protection applied by or on behalf of that operator to any communications or data'.[45]

The Regulations indicate that a TCN may require a CSP to remove 'electronic protection' – which likely includes encryption – and to disclose the data 'in intelligible form', in other words, in plaintext.[46] These provisions could be interpreted to include the encryption workarounds described in the previous section.

[42] IPA, s 253(1). The relevant authorisations include interception and examination warrants under pt 2, authorisations for communications data under pt 3, equipment interference warrants under pt 5 and bulk warrants under pt 6. There is also a transitional provision in place that specifies that the 'relevant authorisation' for the purposes of technical capability notices include warrants under the Regulation of Investigatory Powers Act 2000, pt 1, c 1, and warrants under the Intelligence Services Act 1994, s 5. These provisions are in place until parts of the IPA come into full force at a date that is yet to be determined. See IPA (Commencement No 4 and Transitional and Saving Provisions) Regulations 2018, SI 2018/341, reg 6.

[43] This is a paraphrased definition of the very detailed, numerous and interlocking definitions in the IPA, s 261. For the specific definitions of terms used in my paraphrased definition, see IPA, ss 261(10) ('telecommunications operator'), 261(11) ('telecommunications service') and 261(13) ('telecommunication system').

[44] IPA, ss 253(3) and 241. The Home Office, *Interception of Communications: Code of Practice* (London, HM Government, 2018) (Code of Practice) is advisory only.

[45] IPA, s 253(5)(c).

[46] The Investigatory Powers (Technical Capability) Regulations 2018, SI 2018/353, reg 3(2) and sch 1, para 8. See also Walden, *Computer Crimes* (n 39) 231.

There is a debate about whether a TCN can require a CSP to remove or decrypt end-to-end encryption.[47] But for the purposes of this chapter, it is assumed that a TCN may require either the decryption or redesign of systems that enable end-to-end encrypted messages.[48] Other types of encryption and systems security may also be affected, and CSPs may be required to consult with the government before building any future end-to-end encrypted communications systems.[49]

The Act specifies that 'a technical capability notice may be given to persons outside the United Kingdom (and may require things to be done, or not to be done, outside the United Kingdom)',[50] and the service of process can be sent to a person overseas by electronic means.[51] The Code of Practice further elaborates that the Secretary of State should consider 'any requirements or restrictions under the law of [a foreign] country that may arise when the operator complies' with the notice.[52] This implies, at least, that if there were a foreign blocking statute in effect, the TCN may not be issued or enforced.

According to the IPA, the TCN is enforceable against a person either inside or outside the UK 'by civil proceedings by the Secretary of State for an injunction, or for specific performance of a statutory duty under the Court of Session Act 1988' (which includes potential fines or imprisonment for noncompliance), or 'for any other appropriate relief'.[53] Of course, the potential for enforcement will depend on the position of the overseas CSP in relation to the territory of the UK – that is, whether the CSP has offices, personnel or assets within the jurisdiction.[54]

[47] A CSP can only be required to remove electronic protection that it applies or is applied on its behalf. When this limitation is read in light of the 'technical feasibility' factor, then a TCN may not require the removal of end-to-end encryption where these protections are 'applied, or controlled, by subscribers or users'. See I Walden, 'Communications Privacy' in I Walden (ed), *Telecommunications Law and Regulation*, 5th edn (Oxford, Oxford University Press, 2018) 660 and fn 75. Although there may still be some uncertainty with how far this design claim can act as a defence for CSPs, Walden has stated that the IPA's use of the phrase 'where reasonably practicable' would strengthen the possibility of a design defence in the UK: Walden, 'The Sky is Falling' (n 1) 904. But as another commentator has noted, 'if the software on my device encrypts my data, is it working on my behalf or on behalf of the software vendor and service provider? Both interpretations are defensible': P Le Riche, 'The Investigatory Powers Bill – It's Time to Take a Closer Look' (*Graham Cluley*, 22 March 2016) grahamcluley.com/investigatory-powers-closer-look/. See also B Acharya et al, 'Deciphering the European Encryption Debate: United Kingdom' (New America Open Technology Institute, 2017) na-production.s3.amazonaws.com/documents/Transatlantic_Encryption_UK__Final.pdf.

[48] This chapter assumes that it is likely that the government could argue that the CSP has ultimate control over encryption, even end-to-end encryption, and thus it is technically feasible for them to remove the encryption protocol.

[49] Code of Practice, para 8.33.

[50] IPA, s 253(8).

[51] ibid s 255(6).

[52] Code of Practice, para 8.13.

[53] IPA, s 255(10); Code of Practice, para 8.22. Interestingly, a technical capability notice is only enforceable against a person outside of the UK if it relates to a warrant pursuant to pt 2 or 6 or an authorisation under pt 3. Thus, notices requiring capabilities for compliance with equipment interference warrants under pt 5 are not enforceable against a person outside of the UK even though they can be served extraterritorially, meaning targeted code updates to a person's computer may not be a capability that could be imposed on an overseas CSP.

[54] Walden, 'Accessing Data' (n 3) 435.

If a US-based CSP does not have assets within the UK, there would be no direct enforcement mechanism against a US-based CSP that simply refused to comply with the TCN.[55] The UK could attempt to use an indirect enforcement mechanism, such as blocking access to the service, but this may be unlikely in the case of large US-based CSPs.

In practice, it will be difficult to know whether TCNs have been successfully enforced extraterritorially, in part because parties are barred from disclosing their very existence.[56] The Code of Practice specifies that this gag order is in place so as not to jeopardise investigations or harm a CSP's commercial interests.[57] A CSP may petition the Secretary of State to lift this gag order, but there is no guidance in the law as to when or how that might take place.[58]

It may be possible to detect changes made pursuant to a TCN through a careful reading of a CSP's service policy. For example, reddit used a so-called 'warrant canary' in its 2014 transparency report, which stated: 'As of January 29, 2015, reddit has never received a [US] National Security Letter, an order under the [US] Foreign Intelligence Surveillance Act, or any other classified request for user information.'[59] That statement was missing from reddit's 2015 transparency report, indicating that it had received some type of request for user information that it could not disclose. Canaries are controversial, however, and reddit's CEO later stated that he had been advised not to comment on the omission; although cryptically he added, 'Even with the canaries, we're treading a fine line', presumably referring to the non-disclosure requirements of US law on national security letters.[60] In addition, these canaries may be illegal under IPA, section 255 if they are considered to disclose the existence or contents of a notice. Nonetheless, looking for warrant canaries, or similar changes to CSP's encryption policy disclosures, may offer some clues. At the time of writing, the terms of service of WhatsApp, iMessage and Signal all state that messages are end-to-end encrypted.[61]

[55] A US court certainly would not enforce the UK TCN, injunction or related judgment for noncompliance. It is a long-accepted principle of international law, UK common law and US law that one state will not enforce the public laws of another state. In the USA, the 1962 Uniform Foreign-Money Judgments Recognition Act and the 2005 Uniform Foreign-Country Money Judgments Act exclude judgments for fines and penalties. See American Law Institute, *Restatement of the Law Fourth: The Foreign Relations Law of the United States* (Philadelphia, American Law Institute, 2018) § 489. See also American Law Institute, *Restatement of the Law Second: Conflict of Laws* (Philadelphia, American Law Institute, 1971) § 89; L Collins (ed), *Dicey, Morris and Collins: The Conflict of Laws*, 14th edn (London, Sweet & Maxwell, 2006).

[56] IPA, s 255(8).

[57] Code of Practice, para 8.23.

[58] ibid.

[59] 'Transparency Report 2014' (*reddit*, 2014) www.reddit.com/wiki/transparency/2014/.

[60] K Zetter, 'Reddit Hints – Without Saying Anything – That It Got a National Security Letter' (*Wired*, 31 March 2016) www.wired.com/2016/03/reddit-warrant-canary-hints-it-got-a-national-security-letter/. For more on national security letters under US law, see H Bloch-Wehba, 'Process without Procedure: National Security Letters and First Amendment Rights' (2016) 49 *Suffolk University Law Review* 367.

[61] 'WhatsApp Security' (*WhatsApp.com*) www.whatsapp.com/security/?lang=en; 'IMessage and FaceTime & Privacy' (*Apple Support*) support.apple.com/en-gb/HT209110; 'Signal Messenger: Speak Freely' (*Signal Messenger*) signal.org/en/index.html.

B. Australia

In 2017, the Australian Parliament passed the Telecommunications and Other Legislation Amendment (Assistance and Access) Act 2018 (TOLA), which amended the Telecommunications Act 1997 to require more extensive co-operation from service providers in granting LEAs access to communications.[62] Prior to the amendments introduced by TOLA, the Telecommunications Act had required domestic CSPs to assist law enforcement as 'reasonably necessary'.[63] TOLA broadened the scope of the act to CSPs beyond the domestic carriers and broadened the scope of the required assistance.

The Telecommunications Act applies to 'designated communications providers', which includes a person or an entity that provides electronic services with end users in Australia, as well as a person or entity that supplies software, components and equipment on behalf of telecommunications networks in Australia.[64] This broad definition is similar to that used by the UK in that it includes overseas CSPs that offer services, hardware or software in Australia.

The Australian scheme is more complex than the UK's and sets out three types of notices that may be served on CSPs: technical assistance requests (TARs), technical assistance notices (TANs) and technical capability notices (TCNs).[65] TARs are requests made to CSPs for voluntary assistance, while TANs accompany warrants to require the use of already-implemented capabilities;[66] thus, neither are the focus of this chapter.

A TCN requires that a CSP be 'capable of giving listed help' to the relevant agency.[67] Like the UK, a TCN requires the implementation of capabilities for future use. Similarly, TCNs do not replace warrants or other legal authorisations that would otherwise be required under Australian law for the disclosure of data.[68] These notices are separate instruments that complement a legal authorisation for disclosure under existing law.[69]

TCNs are issued by or on behalf of a security or law enforcement authority to a CSP, compelling assistance to do a 'listed act or thing'.[70] Importantly, the first listed act – 'removing one or more forms of electronic protection that are or were applied by, or on behalf of, the provider' – can only be required by a TAN or voluntary

[62] Revised Explanatory Memorandum to the Telecommunications and Other Legislation Amendment (Assistance and Access) Bill 2018, paras 2–6.

[63] Telecommunications Act 1997 (as amended by TOLA), s 313. See also Revised Explanatory Memorandum (ibid) [10].

[64] Telecommunications Act 1997, s 317C.

[65] ibid s 317C.

[66] ibid s 317L.

[67] ibid s 317T.

[68] ibid s 317ZH.

[69] ibid s 317ZH(1). See also Revised Explanatory Memorandum (n 62) [11], [32], [36].

[70] Telecommunications Act 1997, s 317E.

request, not by a TCN.[71] In other words, Australian law can only compel a CSP to remove electronic protection if the CSP is already capable of such an action. Thus, unlike the UK, it appears an Australian TCN cannot require end-to-end encrypted messaging services to redesign their systems to remove the encryption.

Even though TCNs cannot require removal of encryption, a TCN may nonetheless facilitate encryption workarounds authorised under three other listed capabilities. A TCN could be used to require that the disclosure of data pursuant to a warrant or authorisation be in a particular format, such as plaintext.[72] Likewise, a TCN may require a provider to build a capability necessary to facilitate giving effect to a warrant to access certain equipment, devices, services or software.[73] In addition, a TCN may require a different act or thing as required by the Home Affairs Minister, which is defined as 'listed help'.[74] Thus, at any time, it appears that the Home Affairs Minister could require nearly any type of capability, possibly including an encryption workaround such as the ghost protocol, but excluding the removal of encryption or another protection.

Ultimately, it is difficult to determine the extent to which Australian TCNs may bypass encryption.[75] Much like the UK IPA, the Australian law is vague. As Apple warned in its submission to the Parliamentary Joint Committee on Intelligence and Security (PJCIS), 'the bill grants extraordinarily broad and vague powers that, the government may argue, allow them to force companies to build tools that ultimately weaken the security of their products or create significant cybersecurity risks more broadly'.[76] These capabilities are consistent with the government's rhetoric surrounding the TOLA Bill, which was expressly drafted and enacted as a response to encryption.[77]

Like the UK, it will be difficult to determine whether TCNs are used to bypass or remove encryption protections because CSPs are prohibited from disclosing the nature of the notices and what 'listed act or thing' they require the CSP to implement or exploit.[78] The Act authorises CSPs to publish transparency reports

[71] ibid s 317T(4)(c)(i).

[72] ibid s 317E(1)(d).

[73] ibid s 317E(1)(da) and (e).

[74] ibid s 317T(4).

[75] The Act contains various safeguards, which may also impact an assessment of the extent to which a TCN can be used to require CSPs to bypass encryption. See ibid ss 317P, 317RA, 317V, 317ZAA and 317ZG(1). It is outside the scope of this chapter to include an in-depth analysis of how these safeguards may impact the issuance of a TCN that affects encryption. However, a determination of how these safeguards are met is made by a member of the executive branch, making it more likely that the decision favours LEA interests. See ibid ss 317TAAA, 317L and 317LA.

[76] Apple, Inc, 'Review of the Telecommunications and Other Legislation Amendment (Assistance and Access) Bill 2018: Submission 53' (submission to the PJCIS, Parliament of Australia, 2018) 3, www.aph.gov.au/Parliamentary_Business/Committees/Joint/Intelligence_and_Security/TelcoAmendmentBill2018/Submissions.

[77] Revised Explanatory Memorandum (n 62) [1]–[6].

[78] Telecommunications Act 1997, s 317ZF.

disclosing the number of notices that they receive in a given period; however, the type of capability required by the TCN will remain classified.

The Act specifies that TCNs may apply 'within and outside Australia'.[79] In other words, the notices can apply extraterritorially to CSPs that may be 'offshore'.[80] Given the broad definition of covered providers in the law, nearly any CSP operating anywhere will be subject to these notice provisions. The Act states that a notice can be served extraterritorially by sending it through the post or to an 'electronic address'.[81] Enforcement is another matter.

CSPs may assert as a defence that compliance with the action required by the notice would require the CSP to take an action in a foreign country that would violate the law of that foreign country.[82] There is no defence, however, if the action was taken by the CSP *in Australia* and would violate the law of a foreign country. There is no further elaboration in the law on what it means to 'take action'. For example, if a US-based CSP is required to send malicious code from a computer in the USA to a user's device in Australia, is the action in the USA or in Australia? If a US-based CSP is required to add a ghost user to a group message from a computer in the USA but the messaging was between users in Australia through network infrastructure there, is the action in the USA or Australia?

CSPs that do not comply with a TCN are subject to civil penalties of up to 10 million AUD. As with the UK, the direct enforcement of a TCN depends on the establishment of the CSP within the territory of Australia.[83] Nonetheless, given the severe civil penalties for non-compliance, and the market incentives, CSPs may have good reasons to comply.[84]

IV. Extraterritoriality of TCNs in Light of the CLOUD Act

A. The Agreements

Article 3 of the UK–US Agreement specifies that each party should ensure its domestic law does not prohibit its CSPs from responding to orders from the other

[79] ibid s 317ZH(2). See also Revised Explanatory Memorandum (n 62) [37].

[80] Revised Explanatory Memorandum (n 62) [37].

[81] Telecommunications Act 1997, s 317ZL. See also Revised Explanatory Memorandum (n 63) [693]–[697].

[82] Telecommunications Act 1997, s 317ZB(5).

[83] Text to nn 53–55 above.

[84] This point is illustrated further by the actions of Google and Facebook in 2021 with regard to a new Australian law requiring platforms to pay media companies when hosting news content on their platforms. Google and Facebook have negotiated with publishers in Australia to comply with the new law (although Facebook did briefly refuse to comply, negotiations resolved the matter within a few days): S Morrison, 'Why Facebook Banned (and Then Unbanned) News in Australia' (*Vox*, 25 February 2021) www.vox.com/recode/22287971/australia-facebook-news-ban-google-money.

party relating to 'the preservation, authentication, disclosure, and production of electronic data'.[85] There is no mention in the Agreement of orders that would require CSPs to implement capabilities to facilitate the preservation, authentication, disclosure or production of data. In other words, the Agreement is silent as to TCNs. This is consistent with the scope of the CLOUD Act, which is also limited to the preservation, interception, disclosure and production of data. Thus, TCNs fall outside the scope of the CLOUD Act agreement between the UK and USA, and, as such, the Agreement has no impact on whether the UK may serve TCNs on US-based CSPs.

Nonetheless, there was confusion on this point when the agreement was signed. On the same day that the UK–US Agreement was signed, the UK Home Secretary Priti Patel, the US Attorney General William Barr and the Australian Minister for Home Affairs Peter Dutton signed an open letter to Facebook asking it to abandon its plans to introduce end-to-end encryption across its messaging services.[86] Perhaps due to the timing of these two announcements, *The Times* erroneously reported that the UK–US Agreement would force US service providers 'to disclose encrypted messages' to UK authorities.[87] This was inaccurate, but nonetheless caused a stir before it could be corrected.

In addressing this confusion, Professors Jennifer Daskal and Peter Swire argued that the CLOUD Act was agnostic on encryption, but also observed:

> There is, nonetheless, a possibility that the UK government could use its separate statutory authority to demand decryption, in the same investigation that the UK seeks an order under the agreement. The major service providers have strongly objected to the UK decryption authority. If such a decryption order were to occur, the provider presumably would object to the order and would have the objection process in the agreement as a new mechanism for doing so.[88]

But would the objection process in the new UK–US Agreement address such an objection? The UK–US Agreement provides a complaint mechanism for CSPs who believe that a UK production order, made pursuant to the Agreement, may violate the Agreement or US law (or in the case of UK service providers, if they believe that a US production order violates the Agreement or UK law). The CSP makes a complaint to the 'designated authority' of their home country. In the above scenario, where a TCN essentially 'accompanies' a production order authorised under the Agreement, the UK could not invoke the Agreement in support of the TCN itself, as TCNs do not fall under any provision of the Agreement. Only the production order would be made pursuant to the Agreement. If, however,

[85] UK–US Agreement, Art 3(1).

[86] Open Letter from Priti Patel, William P Barr, Kevin K McAleenan and Peter Dutton to Mark Zukerberg (4 October 2019) www.justice.gov/opa/press-release/file/1207081/download.

[87] S Swinford, 'Police Can Access Suspects' Social Media Messages in Deal with US' *The Times* (London, 28 September 2019) 4.

[88] Daskal and Swire (n 14).

for the sake of argument, the UK authorities did purport to serve a TCN on a US-based CSP pursuant to the Agreement, then the Agreement's objection process would be a suitable mechanism to resolve such a dispute. But would the objection process address an objection if the TCN does not purport to be issued pursuant to the Agreement?

The designated authority is only concerned with orders made pursuant to the Agreement and the CLOUD Act, which, as stated above, is limited to the preservation, authentication, disclosure and production of data. Therefore, such a TCN would not fall within the purview of the designated authority because it does not fall under any provision of the Agreement. Further, to my knowledge, there is no blocking provision concerning technical capability notices in US law that CSPs could argue a UK order violates, nor is there any blocking provision in the UK–US Agreement.[89] Thus, the CSP could not raise a conflicting foreign law as a defence under UK law.[90]

The UK Home Office press release on the agreement said 'The agreement does not change anything about the way companies can use encryption and does not stop companies from encrypting data'.[91] This is, of course, correct. The agreement does not have any direct effect on encryption – the Agreement is completely silent on the matter.

The Australia–US Agreement is identical to the UK–US Agreement in that Article 3 provides: 'Each Party undertakes to ensure that its domestic laws relating to the *preservation, authentication, disclosure, and production of electronic data* permit Covered Providers to comply with Legal Process' (emphasis added) under the agreement.[92] Likewise, there are no provisions implicating TCNs or any capability that a service provider may be required to implement in order to comply with an order under the agreement. Thus, as with the UK–US Agreement, the Australia–US Agreement is silent on TCNs.

To make necessary changes to Australian law for the facilitation of such an agreement, the Telecommunications Legislation Amendment (International Production Orders) Act 2021 (IPO Act) was passed on 24 June 2021.[93] The IPO

[89] A CSP may attempt to argue that the UK's extraterritorial service of the TCN is illegal as a matter of international law. However, although controversial, enforcement jurisdiction based on effects or targeting is becoming more common. This chapter lacks the space to consider this argument in full. For more on states relying on principles of prescriptive jurisdiction, like effects and targeting, to exercise enforcement jurisdiction extraterritorially, see C Ryngaert, 'Enforcement Jurisdiction in A-territorial Spaces: Addressing Crime on the High Seas and in Cyberspace', ch 7 in the present volume. See also T Schultz, 'Carving Up the Internet: Jurisdiction, Legal Orders, and the Private/Public International Law Interface' (2008) 19 *European Journal of International Law* 799.

[90] Text to n 52 above.

[91] Home Office and P Patel, 'News Story: UK and US Sign Landmark Data Access Agreement' (*Gov.uk*, 4 October 2019) www.gov.uk/government/news/uk-and-us-sign-landmark-data-access-agreement. This statement was possibly included due to the confusion regarding *The Times* reporting to the contrary: *cf* Swinford (n 87).

[92] Agreement on Access to Electronic Data for the Purpose of Countering Serious Crime (Australia–US) (15 December 2021) (Australia–US Agreement), Art 3(1).

[93] Telecommunications Legislation Amendment (International Production Orders) Act 2021.

Act amended the Telecommunications (Interception and Access) Act 1979 to create an 'international production order' that may be served extraterritorially on a CSP in connection with a 'designated international agreement', such as the Australia–US Agreement.[94] When the IPO Bill was being considered, critics raised concerns that an IPO could be accompanied by TCNs, with some asserting that there was a conflict between Australian law and the decryption-neutrality provision of the US CLOUD Act.[95]

In his submission to the PJCIS on the IPO Bill, Professor Swire made this argument:

> If the Bill becomes law, and an executive agreement exists, then the Australian government would be able to seek the content of communications directly from a [CSP] under an IPO. The Australian government would also have available the Assistance and Access Bill. Together, the Australian government could then claim it can require mandatory technical assistance from a [CSP].[96]

This is true. But it was also the case with the UK, which had already entered into a CLOUD Act agreement with the USA, making it difficult to conclude that Australian law would impermissibly conflict with the CLOUD Act's decryption-neutrality provision.

Professor Swire's submission goes further and states that the ability of the Australian government to require a TCN 'would be *due to* the executive agreement. The result would appear to be creating an "obligation that providers be capable of decrypting data"'.[97] The submission that the 'ability to claim such assistance would be *due to* the executive agreement' is incorrect. Both Australian and UK law already authorise TCNs pursuant to domestic law. Australia and the UK can claim such assistance due to the domestic laws in those countries.

Likewise, the Australian or UK production order, which may accompany a TCN, also only has legal effect due to the domestic laws in Australia and the UK.[98] The only difference a CLOUD Act executive agreement makes is to remove the effect of the ECPA blocking provision, thus allowing the US-based CSPs to comply with the accompanying production order. There is no blocking provision in US law on TCNs; therefore, a US-based CSP may comply with a TCN.

Neither the UK–US Agreement nor the Australia–US Agreement 'violates' the decryption-neutrality provision in the CLOUD Act because neither Agreement provides for TCNs. Both the UK and Australian law on TCNs only authorise TCNs pursuant to domestic law. If a TCN requiring decryption under UK or Australian

[94] Telecommunications (Interception and Access) Act 1979, sch 1.

[95] See, eg Google, 'Telecommunications Legislation Amendment (International Production Orders) Bill 2020: Submission 21' (submission to the PJCIS, Parliament of Australia, 30 April 2020) www.aph.gov.au/Parliamentary_Business/Committees/Joint/Intelligence_and_Security/IPOBill2020/Submissions; Swire, 'Submission 11' (n 15).

[96] Swire, 'Submission 11' (n 15).

[97] ibid.

[98] Australia–US Agreement, Art 3(2); UK–US Agreement, Art 3(2).

law purported to have the force of US law *pursuant to* the CLOUD Act or a CLOUD Act executive agreement, then it would be a violation. But neither UK nor Australian law purports to make these notices enforceable pursuant to US law, and such a claim would be nonsensical.

Although somewhat tenuous, there may be an argument that these CLOUD Act agreements now preclude an attempt by US CSPs to resist the enforcement of TCNs by attempting to raise an ECPA defence for the disclosure of the underlying data. CSPs may have been able to claim that the ECPA prohibited them from disclosing any content data made available as a result of the assistance required by the notices, and thus complying with a notice would be pointless. This could especially be the case with a TCN requiring decryption because encryption usually protects the content of communications. But the ultimate success of this argument is doubtful, given that TCNs are distinct legal instruments to warrants or production orders. TCNs require different actions on the part of service providers and may be executed independently of production orders. Further, the UK or Australia could use an MLAT to eventually obtain the content data made available as a result of the capability.

During negotiations for CLOUD Act agreements in both cases, commentators suggested that the TCN provisions of UK and Australian law would harm the ability of the UK and Australia, respectively, to reach CLOUD Act agreements with the USA due to the neutrality provision.[99] That was clearly not the case. This brings us to the question: is the CLOUD Act, and therefore the US position on decryption, actually 'neutral'?

B. Neutrality as Tolerance

Ultimately, the CLOUD Act and the agreements do not have any *direct* effect on TCNs. But nonetheless, the USA entered into these agreements, which paves the way for UK and Australian authorities' unfettered access to data held by US-based CSPs, knowing full well that UK and Australian law provided for extraterritorial TCNs. While not explicit acquiescence, the USA is seemingly tolerating extraterritorial TCNs.

This is not unprecedented. Prior to passing the CLOUD Act, the USA tolerated *some* foreign extraterritorial production orders. The ECPA does not block non-US LEAs from requesting the production of subscriber information, traffic

[99] See G Nojeim and C Galvagna, 'UK Investigatory Powers Bill Imperils Public Safety by Undermining Data Sharing with the US' (Center for Democracy and Technology, 6 September 2016) cdt.org/insights/uk-investigatory-powers-bill-imperils-public-safety-by-undermining-data-sharing-with-the-us/; P Greaves and P Swire, 'New Developments for the UK and Australian Executive Agreements with the US under the CLOUD Act' (*Cross-Border Data Forum*, 19 July 2020) www.crossborderdataforum.org/new-developments-for-the-u-k-and-australian-executive-agreements-with-the-u-s-under-the-cloud-act-2/.

data or other non-content data from US-based CSPs.[100] The ECPA permits CSPs to comply with foreign requests for these types of data voluntarily. In other words, the foreign production orders were not mandatory pursuant to US law, but neither did US law prohibit the CSP from disclosing these types of data.

The 'decryption-neutral' provision in the CLOUD Act means a UK or Australian TCN is similarly situated vis-à-vis US law: neither mandatory, nor prohibited. But this position is not neutral, as this voluntary regime for subscriber information and non-content data shows. Now, the USA could be seen to permit foreign states to serve these extraterritorial orders on US-based CSPs, shifting the onus to the CSP to determine whether to comply. As the Department of Justice White Paper on the CLOUD Act states, 'This neutrality allows for the encryption issue to be discussed separately among governments, companies, and other stakeholders'.[101]

The purpose of the CLOUD Act and accompanying bilateral agreements is to remove the effect of the ECPA blocking provision for foreign LEA production orders for content data. Thus, production orders for content data are now also in this paradigm vis-à-vis US law: neither mandatory, nor prohibited.[102] CSPs may voluntarily comply with these orders pursuant to US law. But just because US law considers these orders voluntary does not mean that the domestic law of the UK and Australia consider compliance voluntary. These production orders are *mandatory* pursuant to the domestic law of the UK and Australia.

UK and Australian TCNs that require decryption are also in this position: potentially permitted yet voluntary according to US law; mandatory under UK or Australian domestic law. The CLOUD Act does not require CSPs to comply with such an order, but neither does it block these TCNs. Thus, similarly to orders for subscriber information or metadata under the ECPA, US law seems to allow UK or Australian authorities to send a TCN requiring decryption to a US-based CSP. The CSP is left to assess the risks – to both security and commerce – with non-compliance.

Interestingly, the decryption-neutrality provision of the CLOUD Act was not in the initial Department of Justice proposal to Congress in 2016,[103] nor was it in the text of the bill on which hearings were held in May of 2017 before the Senate Judiciary Committee.[104] It does appear, however, in the final version of the CLOUD Act, which was attached to the end of the omnibus budget bill and passed in 2018.[105] Therefore, there is no legislative history providing the reasons for, or the ramifications of, the inclusion of this provision.

[100] See n 7 above.
[101] See US White Paper (n 13) 6.
[102] Walden, 'Accessing Data' (n 3) 460 and fn 124.
[103] US Department of Justice, 'Legislation to Permit the Secure and Privacy-Protective Exchange of Electronic Data for the Purposes of Combatting Serious Crime Including Terrorism' (15 July 2016) 1 www.documentcloud.org/documents/2994379–2016-7-15-US-UK-Biden-With-%20Enclosures.html#document/p1.
[104] See CLOUD Bill S2383 (115th Congress, 2d Session) www.congress.gov/115/bills/s2383/BILLS-115s2383is.pdf.
[105] Consolidated Appropriations Act, HR 1625, Pub L 115-141 (2018).

It appears that the US Congress chose to dodge the question of encryption when drafting the CLOUD Act. This is understandable when a satisfactory resolution to the encryption debate regarding LEA access seems nearly impossible. Rather than remaining silent on the issue, the decryption-neutrality provision was included in the CLOUD Act, in effect highlighting the absence of any consideration of the appropriate jurisdictional reach of investigatory powers that compel CSPs to implement interception capabilities. But by drafting 'neutrality' into the agreement, the CLOUD Act at least seems to tolerate orders that require decryption.

This conclusion is supported by the fact that Congress knew the first partner for an executive agreement would be the UK, whose laws provide for both decryption and other methods of bypassing encryption. This cuts against any argument that the US Congress has been particularly committed to encryption in the past.[106] A blocking provision for these TCNs could have been included in the CLOUD Act.[107] Instead, in terms of the legal obligations of US-based CSPs, UK and Australian TCNs and production orders are now in a similar position vis-à-vis US law by virtue of these agreements.

A US-based CSP that is extraterritorially served with a TCN may view the enforceability of that instrument differently to a production order issued pursuant to a CLOUD Act agreement. Obviously, the USA has entered into certain CLOUD Act agreements and US law now expressly permits US-based CSPs to comply with production orders pursuant to such agreements. The lack of a blocking statute for a TCN does not rise to the level of express permittance. Nonetheless, the US-based CSP is not mandated to comply with either order by virtue of domestic US law, and the CSP may decide whether to comply or risk sanctions in the non-US issuing state.

The purportedly 'neutral' position taken by the USA on matters of encryption in negotiating new bilateral agreements does then make some sense if considered from a cost perspective. In removing the effect of the blocking provision of the ECPA for the production of content data, the agreements avoid the conflicts of laws that were potentially costly for US-based service providers. By including the decryption 'neutrality' provision, the US Congress made clear that the CLOUD Act and resulting agreements would not create another conflict of laws by blocking decryption orders. In other words, this provision prevents US-based CSPs from getting caught in a costly conflict of laws situation, in which compliance with the laws of one state (issuing the TCN) would directly result in the violation of the laws of a second state (containing a blocking provision). In essence, this passes off the necessary governance of a collective action problem to private corporations. It is then up to CSPs to decide whether to comply with some states' efforts to weaken encryption.

[106] See Swire, 'Submission 11' (n 15). See also n 109 below and text to n 109.

[107] C Galvagna, 'The Necessity of Human Rights Legal Protections in Mutual Legal Assistance Treaty Reform' (2019) 9(2) *Notre Dame Journal of International and Comparative Law* 57, 70: the CLOUD Act 'wastes an opportunity to prohibit [encryption backdoors] outright'.

V. Conclusion

One might be left wondering, if it has no effect on encryption, what is the purpose of the decryption-neutral provision in the CLOUD Act? It was a late addition. It was made after concerns had been raised that these agreements may sneak in encryption backdoors. But it says the Act 'shall not create any obligation … or … a limitation'. If one seeks to read between the lines here, it almost seems that the intention of the provision is to communicate the message: 'this Act has nothing to say on encryption, but because you may be worried, and we want to avoid controversy, we promise that we will not use these agreements to sneak in back door requirements; but we also are not limiting our partners from requiring an implementation of backdoor capabilities'.[108]

This position seems to benefit both the USA and its allies. The UK and Australia can serve TCNs that affect encryption on US CSPs, and the USA effectively avoids any political responsibility, while US law enforcement may indirectly benefit from the same orders. The US tolerance of foreign decryption orders may also signal the beginning of a broader change in encryption policy in the USA, with similar capabilities being introduced in proposed legislation before Congress.[109]

The USA could have made the choice to block decryption orders from its foreign partners, but it did not do so. As the Department of Justice White Paper makes clear, the CLOUD Act does not 'prevent countries from addressing decryption requirements in their own domestic laws',[110] and the USA knew at the time of the CLOUD Act that the potential decryption requirements in UK law (the TCN provisions in the IPA) were extraterritorial in scope. In effect, the USA is tolerating decryption orders without being transparent about this position.

What this case study shows is that future mutual trust agreements on the production of content data should clearly state a position on the jurisdictional reach of TCNs. This is especially true when states enter into agreements with states that have laws allowing for extraterritorial TCNs, like the UK and Australia. The CLOUD Act agreements examined in this chapter show that the result of the attempt of the USA to be 'neutral' on decryption orders merely results in tolerating the extraterritorial reach of these orders.

[108] During the negotiations on the CLOUD Bill in the US Congress, civil liberty advocates criticised the Bill on the ground that foreign governments could attach decryption orders to data production orders if the ECPA blocking provision was lifted. See S Bradford Franklin, 'Left Out of the Party on Cloud Nine: A Response to Jennifer Daskal' (*Just Security*, 13 February 2018) www.justsecurity.org/52189/left-party-cloud-nine/.

[109] Members of Congress introduced two new bills that would provide for decryption orders in 2020. See Law Access to Encrypted Data Bill S4051 (116th Congress, 2d Session) www.congress.gov/bill/116th-congress/senate-bill/4051/text; Eliminating Abusive and Rampant Neglect of Interactive Technologies Bill S3398 (116th Congress, 2d Session) www.congress.gov/bill/116th-congress/senate-bill/3398/text.

[110] See US White Paper (n 13) 18.

The possible exercise of jurisdiction by the UK and Australia in serving a TCN on a US-based CSP has been called 'extraterritorial' throughout this chapter because it may have an extraterritorial effect. But it is important to note that this extension of jurisdiction is based on a targeting or effects doctrine of jurisdiction, such that it may actually be deemed a *territorial* exercise of jurisdiction.[111] Enforcement may be trickier, but these CSPs do business in the UK and Australia, and likely want to continue doing so. Some US CSPs have radically changed their encryption models to stay in certain markets (eg China),[112] and it is not farfetched to consider that they would make similar concessions to the UK and Australia. Privacy is a great marketing tool, but making a profit from services is what keeps CSPs in business.

As countries enter into these mutual trust agreements, borders lose their prominence. Arguably, this reflects the realities of the globalisation of communications and is a necessary step to enabling criminal procedure mechanisms to keep pace with the resulting globalisation of evidence. But as these communications technologies are global in scope, so too does the security of the communications technologies become a global concern. Disclosure orders crossing borders for specific data in specific cases is a very different consideration to the type of exceptional access mechanisms that could give LEAs, and possibly cybercriminals, access to vast amounts of data. This is a collective action problem and requires collective solutions – ideally in the form of multilateral treaties.[113]

Currently, the ideal candidate for multilateral co-operation on decryption capabilities is the Cybercrime Convention, which does not cover TCNs. While the Convention requires parties to adopt measures that require CSPs to intercept communications on behalf of LEAs, those capabilities are limited to existing capabilities and do not require CSPs to build in new capabilities.[114] Furthermore, the Convention is silent on decryption.

The likelihood of broad agreement on encryption among the states parties to the Cybercrime Convention, however, is limited. The Second Protocol to the Convention, recently opened for signatures, shows that multilateral co-operation based on mutual trust is still limited to subscriber data and domain name registry information.[115] The mutual trust is not broad enough to cover traffic data or

[111] See Ryngaert (n 89). Ryngaert shows that states use permissive principles of prescriptive jurisdiction, such as partial territorial conduct or effects, to justify 'expansive assertions of extraterritorial enforcement jurisdiction aimed at tackling transnational crime' (s I). See also Schultz (n 89).

[112] T McKay, 'Apple Moves Chinese iCloud Encryption Keys to China, Worrying Privacy Advocates' (*Gizmodo*, 25 February 2018) gizmodo.com/apple-moves-chinese-icloud-encryption-keys-to-china-wo-1823312628.

[113] A Guzman, *How International Law Works: A Rational Choice Theory* (New York, Oxford University Press, 2008) 64: 'multilateral agreements allow states to overcome collective action problems that bilateral agreements cannot adequately address'.

[114] Cybercrime Convention, Arts 20–21; Explanatory Report to the Convention on Cybercrime (23 November 2001) [221].

[115] Second Additional Protocol (n 20) Arts 6–7. The Second Additional Protocol also contains provisions for expedited access to traffic data through mutual legal assistance measures. However, only subscriber information is available through mutual trust measures allowing direct cooperation with CSPs (Art 8).

content data. This narrow application of mutual trust for obtaining certain types of data across borders makes sense, given the risks involved in allowing broad and unmitigated access to more privacy-invasive traffic and content data. It seems unlikely, then, that broad agreement on the jurisdictional reach of decryption capabilities, arguably even more privacy-invasive, would be possible. Likewise, states like the UK and Australia are unlikely to agree to limit the reach of their own capabilities that are already a part of domestic law.

This chapter has shown that attempting to leave the debate about exceptional access capabilities, and interception capabilities generally, outside these mutual trust frameworks is problematic. As mutual trust mechanisms normalise the extraterritorial jurisdictional reach of investigatory powers, and as states increasingly exercise these powers unilaterally,[116] it becomes more important for states to consider the jurisdictional reach of exceptional access capabilities, and interception capabilities generally, when making these agreements. Otherwise, these states abdicate their responsibilities to CSPs and place their trust in private corporations to solve the problems that arise when the decryption orders of one state may collectively affect global cybersecurity.

[116] Ryngaert (n 89).

12

Unexplained Wealth Orders against Politically Exposed Persons as a Response to Jurisdictional Limitations: Problems and Potential

ÁINE CLANCY

I. Introduction

There is nothing new in public officials misappropriating the contents of state coffers and concealing the proceeds offshore.[1] Examples abound of senior public officials abusing their powers by stealing the resources of the countries in which they hold office ('states of origin') and moving those assets abroad to 'receiving states' while the populaces of the former live in poverty.[2] Notwithstanding the apparent crystallisation of individual accountability for kleptocracy into an international law norm,[3] modern kleptocrats are continuing to transform their state institutions and develop their polities in ways which allow them to loot their state resources systemically, whilst simultaneously protecting themselves and their families from criminal accountability.[4]

The strict territorial limits of enforcement jurisdiction can serve the cause of corrupt foreign senior public officials, their families and their associates (collectively, 'politically exposed persons', or PEPs) seeking to evade accountability for

[1] See R Kroeze, A Vitória and G Geltner (eds), *Anti-Corruption in History: From Antiquity to the Modern Era* (Oxford, Oxford University Press, 2018).

[2] See JC Sharman, *The Despot's Guide to Wealth Management: On the International Campaign against Grand Corruption* (Ithaca, NY, Cornell University Press, 2017); R Ivory, *Corruption, Asset Recovery and the Protection of Property in Public International Law: The Human Rights of Bad Guys* (Cambridge, Cambridge University Press, 2014) 38–55.

[3] See HJ Kim and JC Sharman, 'Accounts and Accountability: Corruption, Human Rights, and Individual Accountability Norms' (2014) 68 *International Organisation* 418.

[4] A Cooley, J Heathershaw and JC Sharman, 'The Rise of Kleptocracy: Laundering Cash, Whitewashing Reputations' (2011) 29 *Journal of Democracy* 39, 40–42.

grand corruption offences.[5,6] Where a state of origin opts not to pursue criminal charges against a corrupt PEP, whether because of institutional capture, institutional incapacity or insufficiency of evidence, the relevant offenders will avoid criminal law consequences in that state.[7] Receiving states that wish to prosecute a corrupt PEP for grand corruption offences substantially committed in a state of origin may struggle in many cases to establish a sufficiently strong territorial link on which to base an assertion of jurisdiction over those offences. Even where such states *can* establish a territorial nexus allowing them in principle to prosecute offences linked to kleptocracy as a matter of public international law,[8] such crimes are rarely prosecuted in practice owing to the evidential challenges inherent in prosecuting offences substantially committed abroad, or because geopolitical considerations operate to prevent those prosecutions.[9] Nowhere is this more evident than in the UK. Even though the London property market is apparently viewed as a popular destination in which to launder the proceeds of kleptocracy,[10] to date, very few foreign PEPs have been prosecuted in the UK for extraterritorial theft, handling of stolen goods or fraud offences linked to acts of grand corruption.[11]

This chapter investigates whether a civil investigative tool recently introduced in the UK, the unexplained wealth order (UWO), has the potential to transcend the enforcement challenges and jurisdictional limitations faced by receiving states

[5] In this chapter, 'PEPs' is as defined in the UK's Proceeds of Crime Act 2002 (POCA), s 362B(7). A PEP is 'an individual who is, or has been, entrusted with prominent public functions by an international organisation or by a State other than the United Kingdom or another EEA State', and any such individual's family members, close associates or anyone 'otherwise connected' with such an individual.

[6] The terms 'grand corruption' and 'kleptocracy' are used interchangeably in this chapter. There are no treaty-based definitions of 'corruption', 'official corruption', 'kleptocracy' or 'grand corruption'. On definitional problems in anti-corruption treaties, see J Wouters, C Ryngaert and AS Cloots, 'The International Legal Framework against Corruption: Achievements and Challenges' (2013) 14 *Melbourne Journal of International Law* 205, 235–39. In this chapter, 'grand corruption' is understood in the sense of the definition developed by Transparency International (TI) and tacitly endorsed by the United Nations: grand corruption means the commission of any of the offences in the Convention against Corruption (New York, 31 October 2003) 2349 UNTS 41 (UNCAC), Arts 15–25 as part of a scheme that: (i) involves a high level public official; and (ii) results in or is intended to result in a gross misappropriation of public funds or resources, or gross violations of the human rights of a substantial part of the population or of a vulnerable group. See TI, 'Submission to the 8th UNCAC CoSP Grand Corruption as a Major Obstacle to Achievement of the Sustainable Development Goals' (12 December 2019) CAC/COSP/2019/NGO/1.

[7] This is not uncommon. For numerous examples, see T Daniel and J Maton, 'Is the UNCAC an Effective Deterrent to Grand Corruption?' in J Horder and P Alldridge (eds), *Modern Bribery Law: Comparative Perspectives* (Cambridge, Cambridge University Press, 2013) 316–22.

[8] On the concepts of subjective territoriality and objective territoriality, see C Ryngaert, *Jurisdiction in International Law*, 2nd edn (Oxford, Oxford University Press, 2015) 77–80.

[9] See A Chehtman, 'Strategic Approaches to Extraterritorial Jurisdiction in Latin America' in A Parrish and C Ryngaert (eds), *Research Handbook on Extraterritoriality in International Law* (Cheltenham, Edward Elgar, forthcoming) ch 11.

[10] See, eg TI UK and Thomson Reuters, 'London Property: A Top Destination for Money Launderers' (2 December 2016) www.transparency.org.uk/foreign-ownership-london-property-shrouded-secrecy.

[11] One exception is a former governor of Delta State in Nigeria, James Ibori, pleading guilty in England in 2012 to, inter alia, conspiracy to defraud.

in responding to overseas grand corruption. Where 'unexplained wealth' held by a foreign PEP is located within the UK, the UWO enables UK enforcement authorities to civilly recover and repatriate those assets to a country of origin without a criminal conviction first being handed down in any jurisdiction.[12] The UWO's availability holds potential as a means of tackling kleptocratic impunity because it presents a way of providing at least a quasi-criminal justice response to kleptocracy in circumstances where assets are moved to a receiving state where recovery using the measure is publicised.[13] Consequently, even if a corrupt senior public official evades prosecution in a state of origin and a prosecution is not possible in a receiving state, corrupt PEPs may nevertheless face criminal (or at least quasi-criminal) repercussions for their wrongdoing.

This chapter argues that where civil recovery is made against the assets of PEPs using UWOs, the process and the punitive consequences are such that the process can be interpreted as a quasi-criminal measure; it inhabits a liminal space falling short of a formal criminal prosecution, but can constitute a criminal sanction in effect. This is because, through its aspersive character, it publicly delivers a form of retributive justice akin to individual criminal accountability rather than merely providing a value-neutral form of dispute resolution more typical of civil procedural responses to misconduct.

However, the jurisdictional implications of using a quasi-criminal measure in this way raise some concerns. UWOs involve receiving states' courts indirectly determining that PEPs have benefited from crimes committed in states of origin. Where asset recoveries ensue following the issue of UWOs, enforcement authorities' concerted publicising of those recoveries in support of their crime deterrence objectives,[14] coupled with a receiving state's court's determination of a respondent's benefit from criminality, risks straying into the realm of criminal law enforcement in circumstances where there may be no jurisdictional nexus with the underlying criminal conduct. In addition, receiving states' courts implicitly determining that the laws of the state of origin have been broken, and sanctioning PEPs for that breach, may violate the rule against enforcing foreign penal law known as the 'public law taboo'.[15]

Including this introduction, this chapter is structured in seven sections. The next section provides more detail on the applicable jurisdictional principles and the obstacles to taking enforcement action against grand corruption offences

[12] Where there is a concern that returned assets will be accessible by the same corrupt public officials who misappropriated them in the first place, receiving states can instead arrange for the assets to be returned indirectly to the state of origin via non-governmental organisations (NGOs) and/or administered by special foundations established for the benefit of that state's citizenry. See PJ Davis, 'To Return the Funds at All: Global Anticorruption, Forfeiture, and Legal Frameworks for Asset Return' (2016) 47 *University of Memphis Law Review* 291. Depending on the repatriation model used, such asset administration could be viewed as a form of neocolonialism.

[13] For a detailed description of UWOs and their operation, see s III below.

[14] See nn 66–69 below and accompanying text.

[15] ibid.

from outside the territory in which those offences are committed. Section III describes UWOs and the conditions necessary for their use. In order to develop an argument later that civil recovery may fall foul of some jurisdictional principles, section IV briefly sketches out some key interpretations of the meaning and function of criminal punishment. In section V, the idea that civil recovery orders resulting from UWOs can be conceptualised as a form of quasi-criminal penal measure is examined. Section VI considers the implications of this idea in the context of enforcement jurisdiction in public international law. Finally, section VII concludes that, notwithstanding some concerns arising in terms of jurisdiction, civil recovery through UWOs represents a potentially useful means of tackling kleptocratic impunity where the proceeds are held in receiving states. UWOs are available against two categories of respondents:[16] PEPs and persons suspected of involvement with serious crime (or those connected to such persons).[17] The focus in this chapter is on UWOs against PEPs because the frequently interstate nature of grand corruption crimes presents an interesting lens through which to assess the implications of civil recovery using UWOs from a jurisdictional perspective.

II. Grand Corruption and Limitations on Territorial Enforcement

In the *Lotus* decision, in distinguishing between prescriptive jurisdiction and enforcement jurisdiction, the Permanent Court of International Justice made it clear that 'the first and foremost restriction imposed by international law upon a State is that – failing the existence of a permissive rule to the contrary – it may not exercise its power in any form in the territory of another State'.[18]

The prohibition on extraterritorial enforcement of jurisdiction absent any rule to the contrary established in the *Lotus* case is grounded in the principle of sovereign equality of states, the related principles of mutual respect between states for their respective territorial integrities and non-intervention by states in the internal affairs of other states.[19] The imperative of states respecting each other's sovereign prerogatives to have exclusive authority over their territories means that no state may engage 'in public acts on the territory of another State without the latter's permission'.[20] To do so would constitute a violation of the latter's sovereignty, in

[16] POCA, s 362B(4)(b).

[17] In this context, a 'person' is defined as including both natural persons and incorporated bodies. See Interpretation Act 1978, sch 1. The Economic Crime (Transparency and Enforcement) Act 2022 (the 2022 Act), s 45 has expanded the category of those answerable to UWOs to include 'responsible officers' (as defined in the 2022 Act, s 25) of UWO respondents who are not individuals.

[18] *The case of the SS Lotus (France v Turkey)* PCIJ Rep Series A No 10 [18].

[19] See ST Bernardez, 'Territorial Sovereignty', in RL Bindschedler et al (eds), *Encyclopedia of Public International Law*, Installment 10 (Amsterdam, Elsevier, 1987), 487; *cf* Charter of the United Nations and Statute of the International Court of Justice (San Francisco, 26 June 1945); A Moiseienko and S Hufnagel, 'Targeted Sanctions, Crimes and State Sovereignty' (2015) 6 *New Journal of European Criminal Law* 351, fn 23.

[20] Bernardez (n 19).

breach of international law.[21] Consequently, where a corrupt PEP commits grand corruption offences exclusively in a state of origin and subsequently moves the proceeds to a receiving state, and where the state of origin declines to exercise enforcement jurisdiction for any reason, the PEP may be unlikely to face criminal prosecution or punishment in any state for the offence.

A corollary of the rule against extraterritorial enforcement in international law is a rule which mediates the use of domestic public laws outside the territory where they were created, known as the 'public law taboo'. The taboo forms part of what William Dodge describes as 'the structural rules of transnational law'.[22] It prohibits, inter alia, the application and enforcement of one state's criminal laws and civil 'penal' laws of a public nature by another state. It is historically rooted in the territorial nature of criminal law,[23] and is a rule recognised in particular in common law jurisdictions.[24] The taboo is tactically helpful as a means of avoiding 'the potential for embarrassment and straining of relations between States' because it allows states to point to a neutral reason for refusing to enforce potentially problematic judgments or laws of foreign courts.[25] However, it also means that an individual cannot be punished by state authorities in one state relying on another state's criminal laws for a crime committed on the territory of the latter.

In considering the prohibition on extraterritorial enforcement, Alejandro Chehtman provides an explanation for why imposing punishment in a state other than the state where a crime was committed should be avoided by reference to an account of sovereignty based on the collective interests of the inhabitants of the territorial state. Drawing on Wesley Hohfeld's classical analysis of legal rights,[26] Chehtman suggests that collectives of individuals within states are jointly owed collective claim-rights to prosperity and self-worth, which contribute to the (morally valuable) well-being of those individuals.[27] This collective claim-right of a state's inhabitants to self-worth imposes a duty on the state to protect that claim-right. This, in turn, provides a normative justification for a state's claim-rights to sovereignty: most notably, in Chehtman's analysis, a claim-right to territorial integrity, allowing that state to ensure the physical security of the collective; and a claim-right to self-government which accounts for the state's political sovereign

[21] H Steinberger, 'Sovereignty', in RL Bindschedler et al (eds), *Encyclopedia of Public International Law*, Installment 10 (Amsterdam, Elsevier, 1987), 397, 413.

[22] WS Dodge, 'Breaking the Public Law Taboo' (2002) 43 *Harvard International Law Journal* 161, 162.

[23] Dodge (ibid) 193, 206–08 notes that criminal cooperation treaties allowing for mutual legal assistance are one example of the erosion by treaty of certain aspects of the taboo in international law. James Crawford cites the Convention on Mutual Assistance in Criminal Matters between the Member States of the European Union [2000] OJ C197/3 as an example: J Crawford, *Brownlie's Principles of Public International Law*, 9th edn (Oxford, Oxford University Press, 2019) 464. Notably, the UNCAC includes a treaty-made exception to the taboo in an asset-recovery context. Art 54(1)(a) requires receiving states to take action to give effect to confiscation orders made by a court of a state of origin.

[24] Crawford, *Brownlie's Principles* (n 23) 465.

[25] See U Kohl, *Jurisdiction and the Internet* (Cambridge, Cambridge University Press, 2007) 220.

[26] W Hohfeld, *Fundamental Legal Conceptions* (New Haven, CT, Yale University Press, 1919).

[27] A Chehtman, *The Philosophical Foundations of Extraterritorial Punishment* (Oxford, Oxford University Press, 2010) 27.

power to criminalise and punish certain acts to ensure the well-being of the collective. These claim-rights, Chehtman argues, mean that a territorial state holds a prima facie immunity from other states extraterritorially applying their criminal laws on its territory.[28] Where a state purports to punish extraterritorially, he suggests it is against these claim-rights of the territorial state that the enforcement power must be justified.[29] In the context of a state suffering the effects of recent kleptocracy, having the prima facie power to punish in respect of acts occurring on its territory may serve, on Chehtman's account, to ensure the public good of having a system of criminal rules in force, and as an important component of building the self-respect and autonomy of the state's populace as a sovereign collective.[30]

The territorial limits of enforcement jurisdiction can facilitate corrupt PEPs in a couple of ways. First, if a state of origin does not pursue a prosecution against its senior public officials for alleged crimes of kleptocracy, and assuming no other jurisdictional nexus is available from which other states might prosecute the underlying conduct, it is unlikely that those PEPs will face prosecution anywhere. There is no means under international law of compelling a state of origin to prosecute in such cases. The United Nations Convention against Corruption (UNCAC) requires all states parties to criminalise 'embezzlement, misappropriation or other diversion by a public official for his or her benefit'.[31] However, as general a rule, even if international law instruments mandate the creation of jurisdictional bases, they do not mandate their exercise.

Second, the transnational nature of modern kleptocracy means that it is possible that more than one state may be entitled to assert jurisdiction over misconduct. However, even if a state other than a state of origin *can* legitimately claim a form of prescriptive jurisdiction on the basis of a territorial nexus with the relevant offence, law enforcement agencies cannot lawfully engage in investigations within another state territory – a form of enforcement jurisdiction – without the latter's consent.[32] Evidential challenges, including the high burdens of proof necessary to secure criminal convictions and the difficulties involved in accessing evidence and witnesses abroad, mean that criminal prosecutions in states other than a state of origin are unlikely to ensue without a state of origin's co-operation. It is open to receiving states to seek the assistance of states of origin in gathering admissible evidence and in serving witness summonses through mutual legal assistance (MLA) processes (also known as judicial co-operation). However, this is

[28] ibid 24–28.

[29] ibid.

[30] Noting that the state as a political authority claiming 'supreme law-making and enforcement authority over certain territory' constitutes one of the key propositions within the classical doctrine of state sovereignty: ibid 20.

[31] UNCAC, Art 17.

[32] See N Boister, *An Introduction to Transnational Criminal Law*, 2nd edn (Oxford, Oxford University Press, 2018) 281, where he discusses this principle being emphasised both in the *Lotus* decision and subsequently in the Convention against Transnational Organised Crime (New York, 15 November 2000) 2225 UNTS 209, Art 4.

dependent on pre-existing bilateral or multilateral MLA agreements, and success in engaging with kleptocracies through this route may not always be possible even where these do exist. Such co-operation processes are based around reciprocity – there is no general international customary law obligation on states to grant judicial co-operation to other states.[33] To the extent, therefore, that a state of origin opts against consenting to and assisting with a receiving state's investigation, the state of origin's corrupt PEPs will likely avoid a satisfactory criminal prosecution and/or having criminal punishment and accountability imposed upon them in any jurisdiction.

In any event, it is not a foregone conclusion that receiving states will be in a position to assert a jurisdictional claim over foreign criminal conduct. Outside of circumstances where there is a recognised extraterritorial basis for prosecution (eg the nationality principle),[34] the most obvious route to claiming jurisdiction will be on the basis of objective territoriality and the identification of a territorial nexus with the offence.[35] Objective territoriality allows a state to assert jurisdiction where any essential constituent element of an offence is consummated on its territory, notwithstanding that the offence was commenced outside that territory.[36] It has been described as a principle of public international law which is 'generally accepted and widely applied'.[37] In many cases, however, misappropriated resources may have been washed through and/or held for significant periods in numerous jurisdictions before eventually being used to acquire assets in a receiving state,

[33] Boister (n 32) ch 18.

[34] Such expansive forms of jurisdiction are increasing under UK law. See, eg Bribery Act 2010, s 12, which allows the UK to prosecute bribery offences committed overseas by, inter alia, UK residents and citizens.

[35] In England, the Criminal Justice Act 1993 (CJA), s 2 specifically contemplates exercises of jurisdiction in relation to offences such as fraud and theft which have extraterritorial dimensions, provided that at least one constituent element (or 'relevant event') of the offence occurs in England, with 'relevant event' defined as 'any act or omission or other event (including any result of one or more acts or omissions) proof of which is required for conviction of the offence'. Therefore, if there is evidence that a corrupt PEP committed even part of a theft or fraud in England (eg where a theft involves moving the stolen assets to England as part of the appropriation of property), this is a sufficient territorial nexus to constitute an offence under English law. *cf* J Hörnle, *Internet Jurisdiction: Law and Practice* (Oxford, Oxford University Press, 2021) ch 5. For a recent judicial discussion of the territorial ambit of criminal jurisdiction in England and Wales, see the Court of Appeal's decision in *R v Pogmore* [2017] EWCA Crim 925. Beyond the CJA offences, the English courts have recently become significantly less conservative in assuming jurisdiction, endorsing the 'substantial measures' test in accepting jurisdiction for criminal offences. Where a substantial measure of the criminality has occurred within England, this allows the English courts to 'accept jurisdiction unless it can be argued that another country is better placed to assume jurisdiction according to the principles of international comity'. See Hörnle (idem) 139, citing the Court of Appeal's decision in *R v Sheppard and Whittle* [2010] 1 WLR 2779 by way of illustration. For convenience and brevity, all references in this chapter to the criminal laws and the courts of England and Wales are to 'English' laws and courts respectively.

[36] See Harvard Research in International Law, 'Draft Convention on Jurisdiction with Respect to Crime: Article 3. Territorial Jurisdiction' (1935) 29(Suppl) *American Journal of International Law* 480, 488. Again, note the apparent expansion of objective territoriality observed by the English courts referenced in n 35.

[37] Crawford, *Brownlie's Principles* (n 23) 442. See also the examples in n 35 above.

or an offence may have been committed exclusively in a state of origin. In either of those circumstances (depending on how relevant offences are defined in the former case), territoriality as a basis for jurisdiction cannot necessarily be relied upon, rendering the establishment of territorial jurisdiction in the receiving state difficult or impossible.

For completeness, it is worth noting that claims to state and diplomatic immunity can constitute further sovereignty-based obstacles to ensuring that corrupt PEPs are held accountable for grand corruption outside of the stolen assets' states of origin.[38] Wariness around offending the integrity of other states' leaders can also play a role in receiving states' inaction in addressing the proceeds of corruption being held on their territories. Following the Arab Spring, for example, action was swiftly taken by, inter alia, Canada,[39] Switzerland,[40] the UK,[41] the European Union[42] and the USA[43] to recover and repatriate assets which had been openly and suspiciously held in those countries by individuals linked to notoriously corrupt regimes. Where the relevant despots remained in office, however, similar recovery action was notably absent.[44] Such inaction might be attributed to the principle that sovereign states do not intervene in the internal or foreign affairs of other states,[45] and/or to related immunity principles.[46] Where a receiving state takes anti-corruption asset recovery action against the property of another state's politically powerful officials, such actions may raise concerns that they constitute

[38] Personal immunity from foreign criminal jurisdiction for leaders, heads of state and foreign ministers comes from the principle that states may not sit in judgement of other states. The scope of state and diplomatic immunities is, however, somewhat limited, applying only for the duration of a relevant official's term or posting. Claims of functional immunity (*ratione materiae*) are unlikely to succeed because the immunity extends only to acts undertaken on behalf of the state. It is difficult to see such claims succeeding in the context of corrupt acts against a state. On state and diplomatic immunity, see R O'Keefe, *International Criminal Law* (Oxford, Oxford University Press, 2015) ch 10.

[39] See B Crawford, 'The Freezing Assets of Corrupt Officials Act: A Critical Analysis' (2015) 56 *Canadian Business Law Journal* 407.

[40] See G Pavlidis 'Asset Recovery: A Swiss Leap Forward?' (2017) 20 *Journal of Money Laundering Control* 150, 153–54.

[41] Secretary of State for Foreign and Commonwealth Affairs, *British Foreign Policy and the 'Arab Spring'* (Cm 8436, 2012).

[42] eg Council Regulation (EU) No 101/2011 concerning restrictive measures directed against certain persons, entities and bodies in view of the situation in Tunisia [2011] OJ L31/1.

[43] Exec Order No 13566 of 25 February 2011 Blocking Property and Prohibiting Certain Transactions Related to Libya 76 FR 11315.

[44] Even in the context of the recent Russian invasion of Ukraine, for example, whilst sanctions against, inter alia, senior Russian politicians and oligarchs were swiftly imposed pursuant to the 2022 Act, Pt 3 in the UK, no permanent recovery of any assets is reported as having occurred as of the date of writing (January 2023). The effect of the sanctions is merely to freeze assets (to prevent sanctioned parties from dealing in the assets) on an interim basis (with the result that enforcement authorities have intervened in some cases to prevent the dissipation of some non-real estate assets). There remains scope for the sanctions to be lifted. Where assets are the subject of asset recovery orders, by contrast, the assets are permanently seized.

[45] See M Jamnejad and M Wood, 'The Principle of Non-Intervention' (2009) 22 *Leiden Journal of International Law* 345, 372.

[46] ibid 364–66.

an exercise of extraterritorial enforcement jurisdiction in contravention of public international law. Thus, corrupt PEPs are well placed to benefit from the territorial limitations of enforcement jurisdiction. The next section considers UWOs, and how they may operate to address the impunity generated through these territorial enforcement restrictions.

III. Unexplained Wealth Orders

This section will explain why UWOs were introduced; how they work in practice; their status as a civil measure; their usefulness in circumventing territorial enforcement limitations and holding corrupt PEPs to account; and why they might be regarded as 'quasi-criminal' measures.

The introduction of UWOs against PEPs was underpinned by concerns around kleptocrats laundering the proceeds of grand corruption in the UK.[47] There has been much media and civil society interest in the London property market's status as a location for corrupt foreign PEPs to conceal their illicitly acquired wealth.[48] Historically, very little enforcement action of any kind was taken in respect of the proceeds of foreign corruption in the UK because of, inter alia, the investigative challenges discussed in the previous section. UWOs against PEPs were designed to address 'the concern about those involved in corruption overseas, laundering the proceeds of crime in the UK; and the fact that it may be difficult for law enforcement agencies to satisfy the evidential standard at the outset of an investigation'.[49] In applying for orders, enforcement authorities need not demonstrate a link between the assets which are the subject of a UWO and criminality of any type.[50] Instead, to obtain UWOs, enforcement authorities must simply satisfy the High Court to a civil standard that (i) a PEP or someone suspected of involvement with serious crime (or anyone connected with such a person)[51] holds the property identified in the application for the order; (ii) the property is worth at least £50,000;

[47] Explanatory Notes to the Financial Crimes Act 2017, para 13.

[48] See, eg TI UK and Thomson Reuters (n 10); S Goodrich (ed), *Faulty Towers: Understanding the Impact of Overseas Corruption on the London Property Market* (London, TI UK, 2017).

[49] Home Office, 'Impact Assessment: Criminal Finances Act – Unexplained Wealth Orders' (20 June 2017) IA No HO0282, para 14.

[50] Save for where a presumption of 'recoverable property' is raised pursuant to a UWO against a PEP, the position in civil recovery is that unexplained wealth cannot without more raise a presumption that property is recoverable. See *R (on the application of the Director of the Assets Recovery Agency) v Green* [2005] EWHC 3168 (Admin). For UWOs against the category of eligible respondents other than PEPs (individuals suspected of benefiting from serious crime or their family members or connected persons), the court must be satisfied that there are 'reasonable grounds for suspecting' that the respondent or a person connected to the respondent is or has been involved in serious crime: POCA, s 362B(4)(b).

[51] If a 'connected person' to someone who holds or has held prominent public functions or to someone who is reasonably suspected of involvement in a serious crime is not a natural person, then a 'responsible officer' of that entity can be required to respond to a UWO: see n 17 above.

and (iii) there are reasonable grounds for suspecting that the 'known sources of the respondent's lawfully obtained income' would have been insufficient to acquire the property or that the property was acquired through unlawful conduct (collectively, the statutory tests).[52] Provided that each criterion is fulfilled to the Court's satisfaction, it may issue a UWO.

UWOs require respondents to provide explanations of how they were able to acquire named assets specified in the orders, and to produce supporting documents showing the assets' provenance within the time frames set out in the orders.[53] Placing the onus on respondents to establish that their assets are *not* the proceeds of crime overcomes some of the evidentiary difficulties usually faced by enforcement authorities in investigating transnational crimes. If a PEP cannot explain how they were able to acquire a property, or does not respond within the directed time frame (or at all), a rebuttable presumption is raised that the relevant property constitutes 'recoverable property'[54] 'obtained through unlawful conduct'.[55] Where a presumption of 'recoverable property' is raised and unrebutted, an enforcement authority can apply to the High Court for civil recovery of property the subject of a UWO, and if the High Court is satisfied on the balance of probabilities that this property constitutes 'recoverable property', the Court must make a civil recovery order (CRO) in respect of the asset.[56] In this way, corrupt PEPs are permanently deprived of their misbegotten gains without a criminal conviction being first required in any jurisdiction using a form of non-conviction-based asset recovery.[57]

The UK's Parliament clearly intended for UWOs to have extraterritorial effect. The legislation expressly provides that respondents who are overseas may be made answerable to orders.[58] Criminal sanctions are not threatened against UWO respondents who are outside the jurisdiction for failure to comply with UWOs,[59] but instead a presumption of 'recoverable property' is raised. Based on domestic case law on the extraterritorial effect of investigative orders to date, only *criminal* sanctions for failure to comply with investigative orders attract the opprobrium of the UK courts for breaching international law.[60] As UWOs do not purport to

[52] POCA, s 362B.

[53] ibid s 362A. Enforcement authorities typically seek interim freezing orders at the same time that they apply for UWOs.

[54] ibid s 362C(2).

[55] ibid s 274.

[56] ibid s 266.

[57] For more on non-conviction-based asset recovery, and civil recovery processes generally, see J Hendry and C King, 'How Far Is Too Far? Theorising Non-Conviction-Based Asset Forfeiture' (2015) 11 *International Journal of Law in Context* 398.

[58] POCA, s 362A(2) provides that 'An application for an order must … specify the person whom the enforcement authority thinks holds the property ("the respondent") (and the person specified may include a person outside the United Kingdom)'.

[59] Presumably in recognition of the non-enforceability of POCA disclosure orders served outside of the jurisdiction as established in *Serious Organised Crime Agency v Perry* [2012] UKSC 35, [2013] 1 AC 182.

[60] See A Davidson, 'Extraterritoriality and Statutory Interpretation: The Increasing Reach of Investigative Powers' (2020) 1 *Public Law* 1, 3–4.

impose direct positive obligations on respondents in other territories with threats of criminal sanction for non-compliance,[61] it might be argued that their introduction was uncontroversial as a form of extraterritorial legislative jurisdiction.

Initial UWO applications from enforcement authorities to the High Court are typically made ex parte to prevent forewarned respondents from dissipating assets. They are held in private unless the judge hearing the application directs otherwise.[62] This is 'to protect the integrity of the [relevant enforcement authority's] investigation to which the UWO relates, as well as to protect the rights of the respondent to the UWO'.[63] The aspersive aspect of UWOs is something that was discussed in Parliament when the legislative provisions establishing UWOs were debated: 'We need to be careful that [PEPs] … are sufficiently protected from the making of an application that could trash their reputation and … leaves him or her exposed to the allegations made against them'.[64] Even after initial ex parte applications are made and orders issued, UWO respondent details are often subject to ongoing reporting restrictions (including anonymity orders) until either (i) civil recovery orders are issued or (ii) UWOs are challenged. In UWO cases heard so far, at that point, reporting restrictions have generally been lifted.[65] To the extent that a PEP complies punctually with an order and can show that their assets are of legitimate provenance, their details are unlikely to ever be publicised.

Where respondents challenge UWOs, judges must navigate between either (potentially) unfairly besmirching the reputation of the respondents in making the proceedings public or diminishing the deterrence impact sought by the enforcement authorities by imposing reporting restrictions and holding the hearings in private.[66] In both UWO cases dealing with PEPs to date, *Baker* and *Hajiyeva*,[67] subsequent challenges to the orders were not only held publicly, but were very heavily publicised in the media, which was permitted to report, inter alia, on

[61] See the decision of Lord Phillips in *Perry* (n 59) [94].

[62] CPR Practice Direction 11.1.

[63] Per Murray J in *National Crime Agency v Hussain* [2020] EWHC 432 (Admin); [2020] 1 WLR 2145 [17].

[64] HC Deb 25 October 2016, vol 616, col 207 (Edward Garnier QC MP).

[65] In *Hussain* (n 63), for example, the existence of the UWO ceased to be confidential having been superseded by a property-freezing order at a public hearing. In *Hajiyeva v National Crime Agency* [2020] EWCA Civ 108, [2020] 4 All ER 147, the respondent, in appealing her UWOs unsuccessfully, sought for anonymity orders to remain in place on the basis that attendant publicity would damage her and her husband's rights pursuant to Convention for the Protection of Human Rights and Fundamental Freedoms (Rome, 4 November 1950) (ECHR), Arts 3 and 8. See *National Crime Agency v Mrs A (Ruling on Anonymity)* [2018] EWHC 2603 (Admin).

[66] National Crime Agency (NCA), 'Civil Financial Investigations and Associated Publicity' (18 February 2021) para 5, www.nationalcrimeagency.gov.uk/who-we-are/publications/.

[67] *National Crime Agency v Baker* [2020] EWHC 822 (Admin), [2020] Crim LR 976; *Hajiyeva* (n 65). In *Baker*, the UWOs were ultimately overturned because the applications submitted by the National Crime Agency for the orders were found to have been made on a flawed basis. As of the date of writing (January 2023), there have been only four UWO investigations involving nine UWOs: A Shalchi, 'Unexplained Wealth Orders' (14 April 2022) HC Research Briefing CBP 9098. In addition to the two PEP cases, two cases have involved UWOs taken under the 'suspicion of involvement with serious crime' limb: see n 50 above.

the identities of the parties. Where the High Court issues civil recovery orders following presumptions of 'unlawful property' being raised pursuant to UWOs, it is enforcement authority policy to 'Publicise civil investigations to the maximum possible extent … [and] [i]nform the media (as we do in criminal cases) and relevant NGOs of upcoming civil investigation events such as open court hearings'.[68] This policy is informed by, among other things, enforcement authority belief that publicising civil investigation orders supports 'reducing crime by helping to deter future criminal activity'.[69] To be clear, for reasons discussed in the next section, it is only when assets are actually recovered through civil recovery orders and publicised that the impact of the measure might be said to take on the complexion of quasi-criminal punishment.

Court adjudications on UWOs and civil recovery orders are made by the civil rather than the criminal courts. CROs are based on findings made on the balance of probabilities that the property that is the subject of an order was 'obtained through unlawful conduct'.[70] To obtain UWOs, enforcement authorities must satisfy the High Court on the balance of probabilities that the statutory tests have been met. CROs are *in rem* measures, so it is the relevant assets specified in an order that are ostensibly legally tainted with an association of criminality.[71] No adjudication is formally made on the guilt or innocence of the respondent.[72] Civil recovery is regarded in theory as a restitutionary measure. On the account of some commentators, it is used as a tool to avoid unjust enrichment, rather than as a form of sanction.[73]

Arguments that non-conviction-based recovery proceedings (of which civil recovery proceedings are an example) substantively comprise an exercise of criminal jurisdiction, and that civil recovery constitutes a form of criminal punishment, have been considered and rejected by both the English courts and the European Court of Human Rights.[74] However, a court finding that a PEP holds 'recoverable property', coupled with the publicity of the sort accompanying each of the *Baker* and *Hajiyeva* decisions and the fact that details of the impugned misconduct allegedly resulting in a UWO respondent holding 'recoverable property' are included in

[68] NCA (n 66).

[69] ibid.

[70] POCA, s 304(1).

[71] J Hendry and C King 'Expediency, Legitimacy, and the Rule of Law: A Systems Perspective on Civil/Criminal Procedural Hybrids' (2017) 11 *Criminal Law and Philosophy* 733.

[72] P Alldridge, *Money Laundering Law: Forfeiture, Confiscation, Civil Recovery, Criminal Laundering and Taxation of the Proceeds of Crime* (Oxford, Hart Publishing, 2003) 232–33.

[73] See J Vogel, 'The Legal Construction that Property Can Do Harm' in JP Rui and U Sieber (eds), *Non-Conviction-Based Confiscation in Europe: Possibilities and Limitations on Rules Enabling Confiscation without a Criminal Conviction* (Berlin, Duncker & Humblot, 2015) 225, 236.

[74] Most recently in *Gogitidze and others v Georgia* App No 36862/05 (2016) 62 EHRR 14, a case involving civil recovery from a corrupt PEP in a UWO-type context. The decision has been described as an attempt by the EctHR to 'put forward a more comprehensive vision concerning non-conviction-based confiscation regimes': M Simonato, 'Confiscation and Fundamental Rights across Criminal and Non-Criminal Domains' (2017) 18 *ERA Forum* 365, 366.

UWO applications, ensures that UWO-related civil recoveries convey a distinctly censorial message.

As discussed in section II, the likelihood of kleptocrats committing grand corruption offences being subjected to such punishment by sympathetic states of origin is low. To ensure that corrupt PEPs are individually held to account, UWOs allow receiving states to make creative use of ostensibly restitutionary or remedial measures which do not prima facie breach the prohibition on extraterritorial enforcement but which encompass the two elements traditionally regarded as essential to criminal punishment (discussed in the next section). It is in this regard that civil recovery through UWOs holds such potential as a quasi-criminal measure and as a means of ensuring that corrupt PEPs face censorial accountability. The next two sections develop this suggestion, showing how civil recovery using UWOs imposes punishment more akin to retribution than restitution and discussing how the process is quasi-criminal rather than a value-neutral civil procedure.

IV. What is Criminal Punishment?

In contemporary criminal justice theory, the meaning and purpose of punishment is contested, but there is some consensus that two of its fundamental elements are those of censure and of sanction or 'hard treatment'.[75] Hart notes that 'the judgment of community condemnation'[76] accompanying findings of criminal guilt is the only sanction which is peculiar to the criminal law. He argues that the societal censure derived from a conviction is what distinguishes criminal sanctions from civil ones. He suggests that the censorious element explains why even those who receive suspended sentences are to be regarded as having been punished by the criminal law.[77] Expanding his argument, Hart notes that in the civil sphere, damages are available for tortious and contractual disputes. He further notes that the 'insane', aliens and recalcitrant witnesses are still imprisoned, and debtors used to be. He argues that in each of those cases, the absence of societal condemnation is the 'vital difference' between a criminal and civil sanction. Others similarly emphasise the symbolic significance unique to the imposition of punishment as against non-punitive sanctions. Joel Feinberg, for example, distinguishes between 'theoretical hard treatment' such as tax bills or parking fines, which serve primarily to regulate activities, and measures bearing a 'punitive intent', which communicate that particular conduct is forbidden.[78] Andrew von Hirsch describes such

[75] L Zedner, 'Penal Subversions: When Is a Punishment Not Punishment, Who Decides, and on What Grounds?' (2016) 2 *Theoretical Criminology* 3, 6.

[76] HM Hart, 'The Aims of the Criminal Law' (1958) 23 *Law and Contemporary Problems* 401, 404.

[77] ibid 405.

[78] J Feinberg, 'The Expressive Function of Punishment' (1965) 49 *The Monist* 397, 405.

non-punitive penalties as 'morally neutral sanctions'. The difference between these regulatory sanctions and criminal punishment, he suggests, is that, for the former, *blame* is not apportioned for conduct and the offender is not treated as a moral agent.[79]

Examining the communicative component of punishment for crimes further, its purpose is not limited solely to symbolic public condemnation. Feinberg lists a number of important corollary outcomes of punishment addressed not to the offender, but to the public at large. First, he identifies punishment as an opportunity for 'authoritative disavowal' of particular types of behaviour: 'It tells the world that [an offender] had no right to do what he did, that he was on his own in doing it, that his government does not condone that sort of thing.'[80] Second, he explains that it performs a 'symbolic non-acquiescence', where a state's imposition of punishment equates to it 'going on the record' to testify on behalf of the people it represents as to their recognition that certain types of behaviour are wrong and harmful.[81] Third, Feinberg points to the communicative aspect as performing a vindication of the law: that the law's enforcement upholds the persuasive character of the law rather than the law's existence operating as an empty rhetorical device in condemning certain actions. Finally, he points to the availability of state censure as a way in which others can be informally absolved of suspicion, for example 'When something scandalous has occurred and it is clear that the offender must be one of a small number of suspects'.[82] Viewed through the lens of Feinberg's analysis, imposing criminal punishment or even quasi-criminal punishment is a potent means of expressing a state's abhorrence of particular behaviours and of communicating opprobrium for certain acts.

With regard to the 'sanction' element of punishment, there is similarly some consensus that for a measure to be truly punitive it must involve some 'hard treatment' such as imprisonment or penal fines to be endured by an offender.[83] The justification for hard treatment varies amongst theorists, with von Hirsh arguing that while censure appeals to the offender as a moral agent, hard treatment constitutes a prudential reason supplemental to censure's normative expression of wrongdoing for abstaining from certain behaviours.[84] Alternatively, Feinberg posits that hard treatment injects an essentially reprobative element into punishment.[85] Duff suggests that hard treatment functions, inter alia, as a kind of secular penance that can provide a vehicle of moral persuasion to an otherwise unrepentant offender to

[79] A von Hirsch, *Censure and Sanctions* (Oxford, Clarendon Press, 1993) 11.
[80] Feinberg (n 78) 401.
[81] ibid 402.
[82] ibid 403–04.
[83] ibid 400.
[84] von Hirsh (n 79) 13.
[85] He argues that without hard treatment, it is possible to conceive of ritualistic condemnation and 'of inflictions and deprivations which, because of different symbolic conventions, have no reprobative force': Feinberg (n 78) 400.

express remorse, or to a repentant offender to reinforce their penance as a means of restoring his or her bonds with the community.[86] Whilst penal theorists are willing to contemplate that certain types of hard treatment are through symbolic convention capable of expressing society's condemnation for misconduct, there is relatively limited appetite amongst the leading communicative penal theorists to countenance the idea that censure by itself may constitute hard treatment. Duff and Garland argue, for example, that if criminal punishment were merely communicative, then punishment could simply be imposed by way of a formal statement of condemnation at the end of a trial.[87] This inversion of Hart's example of a suspended sentence without public condemnation would likely be a similarly unsatisfactory outcome for many in terms of retribution and deterrence.

When viewing civil recovery through UWOs which are publicised, Duff and Garland's suggestion that condemnation alone is intrinsically incapable of including an element of hard treatment might be criticised as insufficiently attuned to context. It assumes that all individuals will bear the impact of condemnation equally, and/or that the level of condemnation will be uniform. However, if the formal condemnation were to occur in respect of a public individual whose livelihood is founded on a perception of ostensible integrity, and such condemnation is widely publicised (noting that all UWOs involving PEPs to date *have* been widely publicised), the punitive impact would be different from, say, that imposed on an unremarkable petty criminal whose offence is unlikely to make the news. In this way, civil recovery using UWOs against PEPs may cross the line from a civil restitutionary or remedial process to a de facto retributive process. It cannot strictly be said to be a criminal punishment: not only is it not a formal conviction from a criminal court, but the sanction involved lacks the longer-term administrative and societal hallmarks of criminal punishment like a criminal record. Even so, because of its clearly condemnatory tenor, the publicity surrounding UWOs arguably transforms civil recovery using the measure from a civil remedy to a form of quasi-criminal punishment.

V. Civil Recovery through UWOs as a Punitive Quasi-criminal Measure

Although it is, in theory, not necessary to establish a link with criminality in order to obtain UWOs against PEPs, in practice, both enforcement authorities and the courts review and inquire into criminal conduct as part of the process. As they base their investigations and decisions respectively on those reviews and inquiries, and because the civil recovery through UWOs can result in PEPs being publicly

[86] A Duff, 'Penal Communications: Recent Work in the Philosophy of Punishment' (1996) 20 *Crime and Justice* 1, 56.

[87] A Duff and D Garland, *A Reader on Punishment* (Oxford, Oxford University Press, 1994) 71.

censured and having their assets seized for their association with that misconduct, the process and punishment might be regarded as an enforcement of quasi-criminal jurisdiction.[88]

Moiseienko and Hufnagel observe that in imposing targeted sanctions, states are responding to forms of alleged wrongdoing that are usually treated as criminal offences in domestic legal systems. They argue that such action might be perceived as a de facto exercise of enforcement jurisdiction.[89] They reason that even though targeted sanctions do not involve punishment following a formal adjudication of guilt, the sanctioning state might be suggested as achieving 'punishment objectives by other, formally non-criminal methods'.[90] This is because that state (i) publicly accuses an individual of wrongdoing (albeit outside its territory)[91] and (ii) imposes punitive restrictive measures such as asset-freezing against the accused individual, even though it may have no competence to formally prosecute the individual under traditionally recognised bases of jurisdiction in public international law.[92] They suggest that in such circumstances 'the state applying the sanction is arguably assuming competence to punish the underlying criminal conduct',[93] and that those actions 'resemble criminal trials in their symbolic impact'.[94] In other words, they suggest that the hard treatment wrought by the sanctions, coupled with the public condemnation which the sanctions symbolise, meets the criteria typical of criminal punishment outlined in the previous section. Targeted sanctions can be relatively straightforwardly categorised as an example of executive (enforcement) jurisdiction because they involve the direct implementation of law by the state.

The symbolic condemnatory heft might be regarded as even greater where publicised civil recovery through UWOs is used. The form of public international law jurisdiction this process comprises is open to debate. The granting of UWOs and CROs involves the High Court formally adjudicating on whether property the subject of a UWO represents the proceeds of crime. On the face of it, this represents a form of judicial or adjudicative jurisdiction. However, it is difficult to distinguish between the distinct limits of judicial jurisdiction, enforcement jurisdiction and legislative jurisdiction, which overlap with each other, particularly where the distinction 'is not universally accepted as reflecting international law'.[95]

[88] For more on quasi-criminal jurisdiction generally, see A Huneeus, 'International Criminal Law by Other Means: The Quasi-Criminal Jurisdiction of the Human Rights Courts' (2013) 107 *American Journal of International Law* 1.

[89] Moiseienko and Hufnagel (n 19).

[90] ibid 360.

[91] Either unilaterally, as part of a regional organisation, or at the behest of the UN Security Council. The legislative framework for sanctions in the UK is the Sanctions and Anti-Money Laundering Act 2018, which was recently amended by the 2022 Act to expedite the making of sanctions regulations in response to the Russian invasion of Ukraine.

[92] On the bases of jurisdiction under public international law, see generally Crawford, *Brownlie's Principles* (n 23) ch 21.

[93] Moiseienko and Hufnagel (n 19) 353.

[94] ibid 361.

[95] A Mills, 'Rethinking Jurisdiction in International Law' (2014) 84 *British Yearbook of International Law* 187, 195.

Alex Mills suggests that the exercise of adjudicative jurisdiction can, depending on the circumstances, additionally be characterised as:

> [E]ither prescriptive (if the judge is participating in law-making, including through interpretation of the scope of application of the law or development of a common law system) or enforcement (if the judge is ordering the seizure of a person or assets).[96]

Notwithstanding targeted sanctions and UWO/CRO processes each involving an arm of the state intervening to prevent property holders from dealing with assets, as UWOs and CROs are issued based on an exercise of adjudicative and enforcement jurisdiction rather than merely on the making of a political judgement,[97] they are perhaps a more credible and formal means of censuring misconduct than targeted sanctions, albeit the censure is imposed in a less direct way.

Although it is an *in rem* procedure, publicised civil recovery pursuant to UWOs bears hallmarks of criminal process from the perspective both of respondents and enforcing states. Antony Duff suggests that when enforcement authorities accuse someone of a crime, the impact is so aspersive as to transform an ordinary member of society into 'someone who simply cannot be trusted', and someone who is no longer entitled to what he terms the 'civic presumption of innocence'.[98] Respondents to UWOs are subject to similar reproach – they similarly become subject to investigation by state enforcement powers, and must either assume financial and procedural burdens to protest their innocence (or technically, their property's 'innocence') or have their properties seized by the state and have that seizure publicised as a means of criminal deterrence.

There are numerous features of UWO/CRO proceedings which are typically only found in criminal proceedings. These include, but are not limited to, the availability to the state of investigative powers typically confined to criminal proceedings; the objective of meting out punishment (rather than restitution or compensation to the wronged party) and to 'deprive criminals' of the proceeds of crime;[99] and the weightier societal condemnation implicit in a criminal conviction.[100] While categorised as a civil mechanism, UWOs against PEPs involve a claim of suspicion of criminality (or at the very least, of benefiting from criminality) by a state body against the official of another jurisdiction (or their family members or close associates). Unlike typical 'civil' interactions between a state and an individual, UWOs

[96] ibid.

[97] On the differences between 'legislative', 'judicial' and 'executive' jurisdiction, see M Akehurst, 'Jurisdiction in International Law' (1972–73) 46 *British Yearbook of International Law* 145; *cf* Mills (n 95).

[98] A Duff, 'Who Must Presume Whom to Be Innocent of What' (2013) 42 *Netherlands Journal of Legal Philosophy* 170, 184.

[99] Home Office (n 49): 'The primary objective of UWOs is to deprive criminals from benefiting from the proceeds of unlawful activities.'

[100] C King, 'Using Civil Processes in Pursuit of Criminal Law Objectives: A Case Study of Non-Conviction-Based Asset Forfeiture' (2012) 16 *International Journal of Evidence and Proof* 337, 338–39.

and civil recovery proceedings more generally involve adversarial court proceedings. Applicants are criminal law enforcement bodies who use their expertise in investigating crimes to build applications against potential respondents. Asset holders can be deprived (using civil recovery powers) of the suspected proceeds of crime, thereby theoretically deterring other potential corrupt actors.[101]

Where CROs are made further to UWOs, the media typically uses language impugning the reputation of the PEP respondent. Orders are often referred to in news reports as 'McMafia orders', suggesting the respondents' criminal culpability,[102] even if a UWO is subsequently found to have been made on a flawed basis.[103] Each of the two PEP UWO investigations to date were the subject of such coverage.[104] It therefore exhibits characteristics more typical of criminal, rather than civil, procedure and bolsters a public perception that respondents are being held accountable for benefiting from crime, albeit without the symbolically important vindication for respondents available through a confirmation of innocence provided to criminal defendants where a prosecution fails.[105]

It might be argued that some individuals who are the subject of state claims of criminality in criminal investigations similarly do not have the opportunity to benefit from symbolically beneficial acquittals, yet still endure widely publicised claims of their suspected criminality. Such individuals may also suffer from a punitive taint of criminality. One important difference between those cases and UWO-centred publicity is that the law recognises that for the former, putative suspects are entitled to seek recourse by way of damages for injury to reputation from those who disseminate stigmatising information (whether well founded or not) prior to a charge or a finding of guilt being made.[106] It is unclear whether,

[101] The deterrence impact of asset recovery in the UK is contested because, inter alia, there is limited empirical evidence of it. See Y Chistyakova, D Wall and S Bonino, 'The Back-Door Governance of Crime: Confiscating Criminal Assets in the UK' (2021) 27 *European Journal on Criminal Policy and Research* 495.

[102] Misha Glenny's investigative account of transnational organised crimes committed by elites across Europe, Asia and the Americas is titled *McMafia: A Journey through the Global Criminal Underworld* (New York, Knopf Books, 2008). UWOs first became available to enforcement authorities in January 2018, a period coinciding with the BBC airing an eponymous TV drama series drawing on the book's themes. Given the types of proceeds targeted by UWOs, 'McMafia orders' became a convenient sobriquet for the orders.

[103] See n 109 below.

[104] See n 67 above. The headline for the following article, which discussed each of those cases, is one representative example: S O'Neill, '£1.5m Legal Bill Forces Rethink over McMafia Wealth Orders' *The Times* (London, 13 July 2020) 8.

[105] L Campbell, 'Criminal Labels, the European Convention on Human Rights and the Presumption of Innocence' (2013) 76 *Modern Law Review* 681.

[106] A recent prominent example of this is Sir Cliff Richard's successful action against the BBC: *Richard v British Broadcasting Corporation and another* [2018] EWHC 1837 (Ch) [248] (Mann J): 'As a general rule it is understandable and justifiable (and reasonable) that a suspect would not wish others to know of the investigation because of the stigma attached.' The Supreme Court has subsequently held that, in general, a person under a criminal investigation has, prior to being charged, a reasonable expectation of privacy in respect of information relating to that investigation: *Bloomberg LP v ZXC* [2022] UKSC 5. It has not extended this principle to civil investigations.

for PEPs who have had their property recovered and have exhausted an appeals regime against UWOs and/or subsequent civil recovery orders, the same principles would apply because they have been neither charged nor convicted. There is a possibility that a court may order an enforcement authority not to publicise the fact of a civil recovery or to impose reporting restrictions. This, however, would be contrary to current enforcement authority policy,[107] and has not happened so far for UWOs against PEPs. In such instances, the quasi-criminal impact of the measure would be radically diminished (and consequently, less likely to raise the jurisdictional problems identified in section VI below). If a court were to make an anonymity ruling on a civil recovery against a PEP, the decision would likely face significant opposition from enforcement authorities and from media outlets who have to date stridently and successfully argued in favour of open justice principles in making the details of PEP-related UWOs known.[108]

There are two final general observations to be made on the quasi-criminal nature of civil recovery using UWOs. First, the exercise of quasi-criminal adjudication powers by the High Court raises concerns because its mandate is expanded to adjudication on criminal matters without it having any apparent capacity or authority for that mandate. Moreover, those adjudications are based on lower burdens of proof and evidentiary standards than are required in criminal contexts. Second, one potentially positive outcome of the process is that once a corrupt PEP is exposed as holding the proceeds of corruption in the UK, the accompanying publicity may trigger (or at least exert pressure to adopt) more concerted enforcement action in respect of the alleged underlying corruption in the relevant territorial state.[109]

VI. The Significance of Using UWOs for Civil Recovery in the Context of Jurisdiction

Where a presumption is raised through a UWO that property is 'recoverable property' and the High Court subsequently makes an order of civil recovery against that property, it is confirming that, in its view, on the balance of probabilities, the property was 'obtained through unlawful conduct'. Section 241 of the POCA provides that 'unlawful conduct' is conduct which 'occurs in a country or territory outside the United Kingdom and is unlawful under the criminal law applying in

[107] See text to nn 66–68.

[108] See, eg *Mrs A* (n 65). On open justice, see J Jaconelli, *Open Justice: A Critique of the Public Trial* (Oxford, Oxford University Press, 2002).

[109] A beneficial owner of the properties which were the subject of the litigation in *Baker* (n 67) was dismissed as leader of the Kazakh senate one month after the High Court's confirmation of the discharge of the UWOs applicable to her London property. Analysts attributed the dismissal to the publicity generated by the case: M Bennets, 'Heir to Kazakh Leadership Sacked after Property Row' *The Times* (London, 5 May 2020) 29.

that country or territory', or if it occurs in a part of the UK, it is unlawful under the criminal law of that part. In other words, the POCA apparently constitutes a form of prescriptive jurisdiction over crimes committed abroad, and the UWO provisions thereunder are clearly intended to have extraterritorial effect.[110] However, the legislation is framed in a way that is, by itself, unlikely to cause much consternation from an international law perspective, because the powers created only impact upon UK property, and the legislation has as its main purpose protecting the UK's economy from being flooded with 'dirty money' from abroad.[111] As UWOs are directed against UK property holders, even if those respondents are abroad, this likely satisfies the 'close connection' limitation imposed by international law on legislative jurisdiction in circumstances where that legislation has extraterritorial effect.[112] Nevertheless, assuming civil recovery pursuant to UWOs constitutes a form of quasi-criminal punishment imposed in response to conduct which occurred abroad 'and is unlawful under the criminal law applying in [a state of origin]', this potentially has jurisdictional implications.

First, when the High Court decides that property is the product of conduct 'unlawful under the criminal law' of another state and therefore should be subject to a CRO, it is not purporting to rule on the guilt or innocence of any party, nor is it applying the criminal laws of another jurisdiction. No prior criminal conviction is necessary in any jurisdiction for a CRO to be made.[113] It is, however, stating that, on the balance of probabilities, (i) acts contrary to the criminal laws of that other state have occurred in that state and (ii) the proceeds of those acts are, or are represented by, assets in the UK.[114] On one (admittedly liberal) interpretation of the 'public law taboo', this risks falling foul of the taboo.

The public law taboo has been heavily criticised by commentators, not least because it leaves a 'vast area of law … in respect of which States are left entirely to their own devices',[115] and this is clear where kleptocracy is concerned. Where a state of origin fails to address those crimes, the public law taboo may frustrate the attempts of other states to take action where the proceeds of grand corruption are held on their territories. Uta Kohl notes how the taboo leaves non-territorial states with a choice of 'imperfect' unilateral measures to be adopted within their own borders. Civil recovery through UWOs is a good example of such a measure.[116] Where a state of origin will not or cannot investigate kleptocracy, civil recovery powers allow UK courts to assess UK property beneficially owned by particular PEPs as representing the proceeds of criminal acts committed in the state of origin and in contravention of the criminal laws of that state.

[110] See n 58 above.
[111] Shalchi (n 67).
[112] On which, see FA Mann, *The Doctrine of International Jurisdiction Revisited after Twenty Years*, Recueil des cours vol 186 (The Hague, Martinus Nijhoff, 1984) ch 2.
[113] POCA, ss 305 and 306.
[114] P Alldridge, 'Proceeds of Crime Law Since 2003 – Two Key Areas' [2004] *Criminal Law Review* 170.
[115] Kohl (n 25) 220–21.
[116] ibid.

As the focus of civil recovery powers is on the criminal provenance of the property and the circumstances in which it is held rather than on any alleged acts of the owner, this allows the courts to elide substantive questions on who may have committed what crimes, and where. However, the upshot of issuing a CRO against a foreign PEP is that a court has concluded (albeit not expressly) that the criminal laws of the PEP's state of origin have been breached. It is highly unlikely that a breach of the taboo will ever be claimed in practice where civil recovery is involved: it typically arises where courts *refuse* to enforce or apply foreign public laws.[117] It is, however, an interesting theoretical jurisdictional problem potentially arising through the exercise of a court's adjudicative powers.

Second, on one view, imposing civil recovery measures against PEPs using UWOs is not formally an exercise of extraterritorial enforcement jurisdiction because the receiving state is not exercising 'its power in any form in the territory of another state'.[118] Moreover, as an *in rem* mechanism, where a court issues a CRO in respect of a UK-based property, it is the property's criminal provenance rather than the guilt of the property holder on which the court is ruling. Strictly speaking, therefore, any enforcement action is confined within the borders of the UK. However, on an alternative view, the use of UWOs, when coupled with publicised CROs, arguably represents an exorbitant extraterritorial exercise of both adjudicative *and* enforcement jurisdiction. The impact of the adverse publicity accompanying the process, together with the punitive effect of the orders themselves, on respondents who are abroad goes beyond any of the civil sanctions for failure to respond to investigations hitherto determined by the UK courts as not amounting to an exercise of enforcement jurisdiction in another state.[119] It might be argued that the process's impact is sufficiently punitive in effect to be akin to a de facto criminal conviction in character. If this suggestion is accepted, then it follows that it is open for a UK court to find, as it did where criminal sanctions were threatened against individuals abroad for failure to respond to disclosure orders, that UWOs imposed on PEPs abroad potentially constitute a breach of international law.[120]

A further observation is necessary. In the recent Supreme Court decision of *R (on the application of KBR, Inc) v Director of the Serious Fraud Office*, Lord Lloyd-Jones distinguished between powers directly exercisable by, for example, the Director of the Serious Fraud Office (an example of executive jurisdiction) and powers conferred by a court.[121] He seemed to suggest that, in practice, the

[117] Dodge (n 22).

[118] See text to nn 18, 60 and 61 above.

[119] See, eg the decision in *R (Jimenez) v First Tier Tribunal (Tax Chamber)* [2019] EWCA Civ 51, [2019] 1 WLR 2956 [54] (Leggatt LJ): 'a state is not entitled to enforce its penal, revenue or other public laws in a foreign country. But that does not prevent the state from taking measures to enforce a financial penalty against assets of the debtor situated within its own territorial jurisdiction or against the debtor personally if he enters its territory.'

[120] See, eg *Perry* (n 59) [94] (Lord Phillips).

[121] *R (on the application of KBR, Inc) v Director of the Serious Fraud Office* [2021] UKSC 2, [2022] AC 519 [65].

exercise of adjudicative jurisdiction by the latter (in issuing UWOs and/or CROs, for example) would typically involve the court additionally exercising its legislative jurisdiction powers to interpret the laws in a way that would safeguard against such excessive exercise.[122] James Crawford suggests that the UK's view is that a state:

> [A]cts in excess of its own jurisdiction when its measures purport to regulate acts which are done outside its territorial jurisdiction by persons who are not its own nationals and which have no, or no substantial, effect within its territorial jurisdiction.[123]

An English court issuing UWOs and CROs which, when publicised, de facto if not de jure go beyond morally neutral civil sanctions may be an example of excessive enforcement jurisdiction in circumstances where no territorial or extraterritorial nexus with the underlying offences or conduct exists, although it is difficult to make a clear case for this, given that the immediate impact of the measures are on UK-based property. The UK can rely on some constructive ambiguity in the international law of jurisdiction on this because it can argue that, even where it holds no basis on which to assert enforcement jurisdiction over foreign criminal conduct, by using UWOs/CROs it is merely using a form of adjudicative jurisdiction to regulate property ownership in its own territory rather than regulating acts outside its territory. This is the basis on which the UWO legislation is perhaps unproblematic as a form of legislative jurisdiction.[124] However, as acts of criminality outside the English courts' adjudicative and enforcement jurisdiction form part of the basis on which that regulation was created,[125] this argument is not altogether convincing. It remains to be seen whether English courts will limit any such excess in practice, as envisaged by Lord Lloyd-Jones.

Finally, even though civil recovery using UWOs can arguably constitute an excessive exercise of adjudicative and enforcement jurisdiction, the process might be said to be justifiable in the context of kleptocracy, given the gravity of the humanitarian and human rights implications involved.[126] In the ongoing skirmishes between sovereigntists and internationalists in the debate on loosened constraints on territoriality,[127] appeals should be made to the interests of the populaces of states in the grip of corrupt regimes as a limited basis for potential extraterritorial enforcement where kleptocracy is concerned. The realities of globalisation and the relative ease and speed with which assets can be stolen from the coffers of states of origin only to arrive, often through multi-jurisdictional and circuitous routes,

[122] ibid.
[123] Crawford, *Brownlie's Principles* (n 23) 463, citing E Lauterpacht (ed), *British Practice in International Law* (London, British Institute of International and Comparative Law, 1964) 153.
[124] See n 112 and accompanying text.
[125] See n 49 and accompanying text.
[126] Sharman (n 2); Ivory (n 2).
[127] AL Parrish, 'Reclaiming International Law from Extraterritoriality' (2009) 93 *Minnesota Law Review* 815.

to receiving states create strong arguments in favour of less rigorous adherence to strict territorial enforcement principles where grand corruption is concerned.

Alejandro Chehtman has suggested that the prima facie immunity held by territorial states against extraterritorial enforcement might be overridden 'on the basis of some fundamental interest of the individuals' of those states.[128] In the case of states of origin whose governing regimes hold permissive attitudes to grand corruption, those regimes' failures to enforce anti-corruption laws domestically could be viewed as negating claims to that immunity, because the immunity is abused at the expense of the well-being of their populaces. Where a state's governing administration no longer functions in favour of (and in fact undermines) the well-being of its populace, the immunity is perhaps implicitly forfeited at what Chehtman describes as the 'bar of justice'.[129] The use by extraterritorial bodies, in limited circumstances, of quasi-criminal measures in addressing misconduct linked to grand corruption is therefore potentially justifiable. However, the fact that the forum for determining whether a sovereign state's claim-rights against extraterritorial punishment should be forfeited (at least insofar as it applies to confiscation of the UK-based proceeds of the relevant misconduct – something that is an implicit effect of the issuing of UWOs and CROs against foreign PEPs) is the court of another state[130] is undoubtedly controversial and potentially of concern to jurisdictional purists.

In his contribution to this volume, Ryngaert notes that there is a dawning realisation that the strict limits of the *Lotus* enforcement prohibition fail to address serious threats posed in cyberspace in light of their global implications.[131] He notes that in an investigative context, there is perhaps an emerging case for relaxing principles of extraterritorial enforcement jurisdiction in carefully defined circumstances in order to avoid impunity.[132] Parallel arguments might be made in the context of investigating kleptocratic misconduct.

VII. Conclusion

This chapter has suggested that UWOs, in circumstances where they result in CROs being made and their use is publicised, are quasi-criminal in purpose, process and punitive impact. It has considered whether the process is capable of breaching

[128] Chehtman, *The Philosophical Foundations* (n 27) 28.

[129] ibid 10.

[130] To be clear, a state of origin's claim-right to punish crimes committed on its territory will be impacted upon only to the extent that the state of origin wished to include confiscation of the UK-based assets representing the proceeds of an offender's crime which are already the subject of UK CROs as a component of the offender's punishment.

[131] C Ryngaert, 'Enforcement Jurisdiction in A-territorial Spaces: Addressing Crime on the High Seas and in Cyberspace', ch 7 in the present volume.

[132] ibid 186–87.

international law, given its extraterritorial legislative reach, and given the potential for excessive adjudicative and enforcement jurisdiction to be exercised in applying the measures. It is not possible to make a clear argument that the process can or will breach international law, but its quasi-criminal nature raises interesting and potentially contentious jurisdictional questions.

Even if publicised civil recovery against corrupt PEPs using UWOs generates jurisdictional concern and potentially allows the High Court to make determinations impacting on international *political* matters, the process is a potentially useful means of tackling impunity by circumventing territorial enforcement limitations which can stymie the investigation of kleptocrats. Normative imperatives of ensuring that the populaces of states of origin are aided in having individuals who stole from them being held to individual criminal (or at least, quasi-criminal) account provide a justification for their use, at least in principle. Civil recovery using UWOs as a quasi-criminal response to kleptocracy, comprising both a 'hard treatment' element and a condemnatory element typical of criminal punishment, is one means of achieving individual accountability. To allay risks that the process may generate in terms of jurisdiction, there is scope for the reform of, or further guidance on the correct operation of, the regime. Reforms might include, for example, amending the relevant laws to expressly provide that any use of the process must factor in comity implications, or requiring broader application of reporting restrictions so that claims to the quasi-criminal impact of the measure are weakened. These are questions for another day. This chapter has also suggested that there are sufficient jurisdictional concerns with the operation of the UWO regime to take these questions seriously if the process is to become a defensible means of tackling kleptocratic impunity.

Appendices to Chapter 5

APPENDIX 1

List of States whose Domestic Legislation Concerning Extraterritorial Jurisdiction is Examined

Afghanistan

Penal Code (1976; revised 2017), Arts 1, 2, 16, 20, 22, 23, 24, 26
Law on Combatting Terrorist Offences (2008), Art 4
Law on Combatting the Financing of Terrorism (2015), Art 5

Albania

Criminal Code (1995; as amended through 2015), Arts 6–8

Algeria

Penal Code (as of 2010), Art 3; also, part I, bk II
Code of Criminal Procedure (as of 2007), Arts 581–91

Andorra

Penal Code (2005), preliminary title, Art 8

Angola

Penal Code (2020), Arts 4–5

Argentina

Penal Code (1984; as amended through 2018), Arts 1–4

Law 26.200 for the Implementation of the Rome Statute, approved by Law No 25390 and ratified on 16 January 2001, of the International Criminal Court (2007), Arts 1–4

Armenia

Criminal Code (2003; as amended through 2018), Arts 14–15

Australia

Criminal Code Act (1995; as amended through 2021), ss 11.5, 14, 14.1, 15.1–15.4, 16.1–16.4, 71.16, 72.4, 72.31, 73.4, 73.12, 80.4, 82.11, 91.7, 91.10, 91.14, 92.6, 92A.2, 102.9, 103.3, 115.1–115.9, 117.2, 123.3, 135.5, 137.3, 139.3, 142.3, 145.6, 147.3, 148.3, 268.117, 270.3A, 270.9, 271.10, 271.11, 273B.2, 274.2, 274.5, 300.3, 372.4, 376.5, 380.5, 390.7, 400.15, 471.9, 471.14, 471.30, 475.2
War Crimes Amendment Act (1988)

Austria

Penal Code (1974; as amended through 2014), Arts 64–65

Azerbaijan

Criminal Code (2000; as amended through 2015), Art 12

Bahrain

Criminal Code (1976; as amended through 2019), Arts 5–9

Bangladesh

Penal Code (1860; as amended through 2020), ss 3, 4, 108A
Anti-Terrorism Act (2013), s 1
Torture and Custodial Death (Prevention) Act (2013)
Prevention and Suppression of Human Trafficking Act (2012), s 5
Anti-Terrorism Act (2009), s 5
Anti-Terrorism Ordinance (2008), s 5

Belarus

Criminal Code (1999; as amended through 2022), Arts 5–6

Belgium

Penal Code (1867; as amended through 2021), Arts 3, 4
Code of Criminal Procedure (1878; as amended through 2022), preliminary title, chap 2, Arts 6–10, 10*bis*, 10*ter*, 10*quater*, 11, 12, 12*bis*, 13, 14

Bolivia

Penal Code (1972; as amended through 2003), Art 1

Bosnia and Herzegovina

Criminal Code (2003; as amended through 2018), Arts 12–13
Code of Criminal Procedure (2003; as amended through 2018), Art 210

Botswana

Penal Code (1964; as amended through 2010), ss 4, 5, 34–59
Defence Force Act (2018), ss 3, 44
Anti-Human Trafficking Act (2014), s 30
Geneva Conventions Act (1970), s 3

Brazil

Penal Code (1940; as amended through 2018), Arts 6–7

Bulgaria

Penal Code (1968; as amended through 2017), Arts 3–6

Burkina Faso

Penal Code (2018), Arts 113-1–113-2

Cameroon

Penal Code (2016), ss 7–12

Canada

Criminal Code (1985; as amended through 2022), ss 6, 7, 46, 465, 477.1, 477.2
Crimes against Humanity and War Crimes Act (2000; as amended through 2019), ss 6, 8

Chad

Penal Code (2017), Arts 6–11
Law on the Suppression of Acts of Terrorism in the Republic of Chad (2020), Art 32

China

Criminal Law of the People's Republic of China (1979; as amended through 2015), Arts 6–12
Law of the People's Republic of China on Safeguarding National Security in the Hong Kong Special
Administrative Region (2020), Art 38

Colombia

Penal Code (2000), Arts 14–16

Costa Rica

Criminal Code (1970; as amended through 2010), Arts 2, 5, 6, 7, 20

Croatia

Criminal Code (2011; as amended through 2019), Arts 9–18

Cyprus

Criminal Code (1959; as amended through 2006), s 5
Combating Terrorism Act (2010), s 4

Czech Republic

Criminal Code (2009; as amended through 2011), Arts 17–20, 20a

Denmark

Criminal Code (1930; as amended through 2020), ss 6–12

Ecuador

Penal Code (1971), Art 5
Organic Integral Criminal Code (2014), Arts 14–16

Egypt

Penal Code (1937; as amended through 2009), Arts 1, 2, 3, 206
Anti-Terrorism Law (2015), Art 4

El Salvador

Penal Code (1997; as amended through 2010), Arts 8–12
Special Law Against Acts of Terrorism (2006), Art 2

Estonia

Criminal Code (2001; as amended through 2017), ss 6–11

Ethiopia

Criminal Code (2004; as amended through 2009), Arts 11–15, 17–19, 25
Prevention and Suppression of Terrorism Crimes Proclamation (2020), Art 3

Finland

Criminal Code (1889; as amended through 2021), ss 1–8, 10, 11, 12, 15

France

Penal Code (as of 2022), Arts 113, 113-1–113-14
Code of Criminal Procedure (as of 2022), Arts 628-1, 689, 689-1–689-14, 693, 697-3, 704-1, 705, 706-17, 706-75, 706-107, 706-176

Georgia

Criminal Code (1999), Arts 4, 5

Germany

Criminal Code (1975; as amended through 2019), ss 5, 6, 7, 9, 14, 17
Code of Criminal Procedure (1987, as amended through 2019), s 153
Code of Crimes against International Law (2002), s 1

Ghana

Criminal Code (1960; as amended through 2003), ss 20, 24
Geneva Conventions Act (2009)
Anti-Terrorism Act (2008), s 5
Courts Act (1993), s 56
State Secrets Act (1962), s 12
Ghana Independence Act (1957), s 3

Greece

Criminal Code (2019), Arts 5–8, 16

Guatemala

Penal Code (1973), Arts 5, 6, 20

Guyana

Criminal Law (Offenses) Act (1894; as amended through 2012), ss 4, 5
Sexual Offences Act (2010), s 35
Anti-Money Laundering and Countering the Financing of Terrorism Act (2009), s 7
Hijacking and Piracy Act (2008), s 15

Hungary

Criminal Code (1978, as amended through 2012), ss 3, 4

Iceland

Criminal Code (1940; as amended through 2018), Arts 4–7

India

Penal Code (1860, as amended through 2011), ss 2–4, 108A
Unlawful Activities Prevention Act (1967; as amended through 2019), ss 15, 17
Suppression of Unlawful Acts Against Safety of Maritime Navigation and Fixed Platforms on Continental Shelf Act (2002), s 3
Tokyo Convention Act (1975), s 6
Geneva Convention Act (1960), s 4

Indonesia

Penal Code (1982, as amended through 1999), Arts 4–7, 9, 479j, 479l, 479m, 479n, 479o
Law Concerning Electronic Information and Transaction (2008), Art 2

Iran

Penal Code (1991; as amended through 2012), Arts 1–12

Iraq

Penal Code (1969; as amended through 2012), Arts 6, 9, 10, 13
Anti-Terrorism Law (2005), s 1

Ireland

Criminal Law (Extraterritorial Jurisdiction) Act (2019), s 3
International Criminal Court Act (2006), 12
Criminal Justice (Terrorist Offences) Act (2005), s 6
Criminal Justice (United Nations Convention Against Torture) Act (2000), s 2
Geneva Conventions (Amendment) Act (1998), s 3

Israel

Penal Code (1977; as amended through 2006), ss 1, 7, 13–15
The Counter-Terrorism Law (2016), ss 10, 41
Nazi and Nazi Collaborators (Punishment) Law (1950), s 1

Italy

Penal Code (1930; as amended through 2014), Arts 4, 6, 7, 8, 9, 10

Japan

Criminal Code (1907; as amended through 2017), Arts 1–8

Kenya

Penal Code (1930; revised 2014), ss 5, 6, 40–43, 391, 393, 394
The Computer Misuse and Cybercrimes Act (2018), s 66
Counter-Trafficking in Persons Act (2012), s 25
Prevention of Terrorism Act (2012), s 38
International Crimes Act (2008; revised 2012), ss 6, 8, 18
The Geneva Conventions Act (1968), s 3

Kazakhstan

Criminal Code (1999; as amended through 2019), Arts 7–9

Latvia

Criminal Code (1998; as amended through 2022), ss 2–4
Law on the Prevention of Money Laundering and Terrorism Financing (2008; as amended through 2019), s 5

Lebanon

Penal Code (1956; as amended through 2015), Arts 15–26

Liechtenstein

Criminal Code (1987; as amended through 2021), ss 61–67

Lithuania

Criminal Code (2000; as amended through 2017), Arts 4–9

Luxembourg

Criminal Code (as amended through 2021), Arts 3, 4
Code of Criminal Procedure (1808; as amended through 2016), Arts 4-1–7-5

Malaysia

Penal Code (1936; as amended through 2017), ss 2–4, 108A; also chaps VI, VIA and VIB
Malaysia Extra-territorial Offences Act (1976; as amended through 2008), s 2
Courts of Judicature Act (1964; as amended through 2014), s 22

Malta

Criminal Code (1854; as amended through 2023), Art 5

Mauritius

Courts Act (1945; as amended through 2020), s 134
International Criminal Court Act (2012), s 4
The Combating of Trafficking in Persons Act (2009), s 15
Merchant Shipping Act (2007), s 218
Biological and Toxin Weapons Convention Act (2004), s 8
Convention for the Suppression of the Financing of Terrorism Act (2003), s 7
The Computer Misuse and Cybercrime Act (2003), s 19
Prevention of Terrorism Act (2002), s 30
Dangerous Drugs Act (2000), s 29
Civil Aviation (Hijacking and other Offences) Act (1985; as amended through 2007), s 7A

Mexico

Penal Code (1931; as amended through 2013), Arts 2–5

Moldova

Criminal Code (2002; as amended through 2009), Art 11
Code of Criminal Procedure (2003; as amended through 2009), Arts 4, 5

Monaco

Code of Criminal Procedure (1963; as amended through 2023), Arts 5, 6, 6-1, 6-1-1, 6-2, 7, 8, 8-1, 9

Montenegro

Criminal Code (2003; as amended through 2012), Arts 134–37

Netherlands

Criminal Code (1881; as amended through 2023), Arts 2–8, 51
International Crimes Act (2003), Arts 2–8

New Zealand

Crimes Act (1961; as amended through 2021), ss 5–10
Counter-Terrorism Legislation Act (2021), ss 17–20
Terrorism Suppression Act (2002), ss 5, 5A
International Crimes and International Criminal Court Act (2000), s 8

Niger

Law No 2003-025 amending Law No 61-27 establishing the Penal Code (2003), Art 208.8
Code of Criminal Procedure (1961; as amended through 2004), Arts 642–49
Order No 2010-86 on Combating Trafficking in Persons (2010), Art 33

Nigeria

Criminal Code Act (1916; as amended through 2016), ss 8, 12, 12A, 13, 14, 37
Terrorism (Prevention and Prohibition) Act (2022), s 76
Cybercrime Act (2015), s 33
Terrorism (Prevention) Act (2011), s 32

Norway

Penal Code (2005; entered into force 2015; as amended through 2020), ss 4–8
General Civil Penal Code (1902; repealed 2015), s 12

Pakistan

Penal Code (1860; as amended through 2012), ss 4, 108A
Prevention of Electronic Crimes Act (2016), s 1
Protection of Pakistan Act (2014), s 2

Philippines

The Revised Penal Code of the Philippines (1930; as amended through 2012), Art 2
Anti-Terrorism Act (2020), s 4
Cybercrime Prevention Act (2012), s 21
Expanded Anti-Trafficking in Persons Act (2012), s 23
The Terrorism Financing and Prevention Act (2012), s 19

Poland

Penal Code (1997; as amended through 2012), Arts 5, 6, 109–14, 117–39, 166–67
Act on Anti-Terrorist Activities and on the Amendments to Other Acts (2016), Art 18

Portugal

Penal Code (1982; as amended through 2015), Arts 4–7

Qatar

Penal Code (2004; as amended through 2014), Arts 10, 13–18
Law on Combatting Money Laundering and Terrorism Financing (2019), Art 3
Law on Combatting Trafficking in Human Beings (2011), Arts 1, 15

Republic of South Korea

Criminal Code (1998; as amended 2013), Arts 2–6, 225–30, 238, 287–92, 294, 296
Act on Counter Terrorism for the Protection of Citizens and Public Security (2018), Art 19
Act on Prohibition Against the Financing of Terrorism and Proliferation of Weapons of Mass Destruction (2014; as amended 2016), Art 3
Act on Punishment of Crimes under Jurisdiction of the International Criminal Court (2007; as amended 2011), Art 3

Romania

Penal Code (2009; as amended through 2017), Arts 8–12

Russia

Criminal Code (1996; as amended through 2012), Arts 11–14
Code of Criminal Procedure (2001; as amended through 2012), Arts 2, 3

Rwanda

Law Relating to the Criminal Procedure (2019), Arts 154–59
Law Determining Offences and Penalties in General (2018), Arts 9–15
Law Relating to the Prevention, Suppression and Punishment of Trafficking in Persons and Exploitation of Others (2018), Art 2
Organic Law on the Organization of Prosecution for Offences Constituting the Crime of Genocide or Crimes Against Humanity Committed since 1 October 1990 (1996), Art 1

Saudi Arabia

Law of Combating Terrorist Crimes and its Financing (2017), Art 3
Anti-Trafficking in Persons Law (2009), Art 4

Senegal

Code of Criminal Procedure (1965; as amended through 2016), Arts 664–77
Act No 2018-03 on Combating Money-Laundering and the Financing of Terrorism (2018), Art 130
Act No 2007-05 amending the Criminal Procedure Code on the implementation of the Treaty of Rome establishing the International Criminal Court (2007), Art 2
Act No 2007-02 amending the Penal Code (2007), Art 2

Serbia

Penal Code (2005; as amended through 2019), Arts 5–10

Sierra Leone

Constitution (1991; as amended through 2013), s 40
Criminal Procedure Act (1963)

The Cybercrime Act (2020), s 12
Geneva Conventions Act (2012), s 2
The Anti-Money Laundering and Combating of Financing of Terrorism Act (2012)

Singapore

Penal Code (1871; as amended through 2020), ss 2–4, 108A, 108B
Misuse of Drugs Act (1973; as amended through 2020), s 13
Organized Crime Act (2015), ss 2, 6–14, 48
Terrorism (Suppression of Financing) Act (2002; as amended through 2021), ss 2, 34

Slovakia

Penal Code (2005; as amended through 2018), ss 3–7

Slovenia

Penal Code (2012; as amended through 2017), Arts 4, 10–14

South Africa

The Protection of Constitutional Democracy Against Terrorist and Related Activities Amendment Act (2022), s 1
Cybercrimes Act (2020), s 24
Prevention and Combatting of Trafficking in Persons Act (2013), s 12
Civil Aviation Act (2009), s 142
The Protection of Constitutional Democracy Against Terrorist and Related Activities Act (2004), s 15
Implementation of the Rome Statute of the International Criminal Court Act (2002), ss 4, 5
Prevention and Combatting of Corrupt Practices Act (2003), s 35
Prevention of Organised Crime Act (1998), s 1
Regulation of Foreign Military Assistance Act (1998), s 9
South Africa Citizens in Antarctica Act (1962), s 2

Spain

Organic Law on the Power of the Judiciary (1985; as amended through 2016), Arts 21–23

Sri Lanka

Penal Code (1885; as amended through 2021), s 2
Computer Crime Act (2007), s 2
Convention against Torture and other Cruel, Inhuman or Degrading Treatment or Punishment Act (1994; as amended through 2021), s 4
Geneva Conventions Act (2006), s 4
Convention on Preventing and Combating Trafficking in Women and Children for Prostitution Act (2005), s 3
Suppression of Terrorist Bombing Act (1999), s 3
Prevention of Terrorism (Temporary Provisions) Act (1979; as amended through 1988)

Sweden

Criminal Code (1962; as amended through 2014), chap 2, ss 1–5, 7
Act on Criminal Responsibility for Public Provocation, Recruitment and Training concerning Terrorist Offences and other Particularly Serous Crime (2010; as amended through 2016), s 9
Act on Criminal Responsibility for Terrorist Offences (2003)

Switzerland

Penal Code (1937; as amended through 2012), Arts 3–8
Military Penal Code (1927; as amended through 2007), Art 10

Tanzania

Penal Code (1945; as amended through 2022), ss 6, 7, 40, 41, 384
Prevention and Combatting of Corruption Act (2007), s 2
Prevention of Terrorism Act (2002), s 2

Trinidad and Tobago

Anti-Terrorism Act (2005; as amended through 2014), ss 2, 3, 25
Computer Misuse Act (2000), s 12

Thailand

Penal Code (1956; as amended 2003), ss 4–11
Anti-Human Trafficking Act (2008), s 11
Computer Crime Act (2007), s 17
Act on Measures for the Suppression of Offenders in an Offence Relating to Narcotics (1991), s 5

Turkey

Criminal Code (2004; as amended through 2016), Arts 8, 11–13, 19

Turkmenistan

Criminal Code (1997; as amended through 2013), Arts 7–9

Uganda

Penal Code (1950; as amended through 2014), ss 4, 5, 23–28, 317, 390, 391
Computer Misuse Act (2010), s 30
Prevention of Trafficking in Persons Act (2009), s 19
Anti-Terrorism Act (2002), s 4
The Geneva Conventions Act (1964), s 2

Ukraine

Criminal Code (2001; as amended through 2020), Arts 6–10

UK

Domestic Abuse Act (2021), s 72
Counter Terrorism and Border Security Act (2019), s 6
The Serious Crime Act (2015), s 81
Bribery Act (2010), s 12
Terrorism Act (2006, as amended through 2022), s 17
Antiterrorism, Crime and Security Act (2001, as amended through 2022), ss 44, 51, 113, 113A, 113B
International Criminal Court Act (2001, as amended through 2022), ss 52, 59, 67, 67A, 67B

Terrorism Act (2000, as amended through 2022), ss 1, 59, 62–63, 63A–63E
War Crimes Act (1991), s 1
Aviation and Maritime Security Act (1990), s 1
Criminal Justice Act (1988), s 134
Aviation Security Act (1982), ss 1–2, 5
Taking of Hostages (1982), s 1
Suppression of Terrorism Act (1978), s 4
Geneva Conventions Act (1957; as amended through 2009), s 1

USA

15 USC ss 1, 6A, 8
18 USC ss 7, 32, 37, 38, 43, 111, 112, 113, 175, 175c, 228, 229, 351, 470, 831, 924c, 1030, 1091, 1111–1114, 1116, 1117, 1201, 1203, 1448, 1583, 1584, 1589, 1590, 1591, 1596, 1651, 1961, 1962, 2280, 2281, 2283, 2285, 2290, 2291, 2331, 2332, 2332a, 2332b, 2332f, 2332g, 2332h, 2339B, 2339C, 2339D, 2340A, 2423, 2441, 2442(c)(3), 2703, 2713, 2772, 2773, 2775, 2280, 2281, 3261, 46501(b), 46502, 46504, 46506
25 USC s 1301
46 USC ss 70501–07
49 USC ss 46502(b)(2)(C), 46506
50 USC ss 4801(13), 4811, 4842, 4843

Venezuela

Penal Code (1998; as amended through 2005), Arts 4, 6
Special Law Against Computer Crimes (2001), Art 3

Vietnam

Penal Code (1985; as amended through 2015), Arts 5, 6

Zimbabwe

Criminal Law (Codification and Reform) Act (2004; as amended through 2012), s 5
Trafficking in Persons Act (2014), s 7
Geneva Conventions Act (1981; as amended through 2001), s 3

APPENDIX 2

Table Containing Trials Involving One or More Core International Crimes that Proceeded through to a Verdict between 1961 and December 2017

Year	Prosecuting state	Number and nationality of the accused at the time the alleged offence was committed	Prosecuting state's territorial, personal or interest connection at the time of criminal proceedings	International law basis for jurisdiction	Exercise of jurisdiction permissive or mandatory	Possibility of extradition to a state or international criminal tribunal
1961	Israel District Court of Jerusalem, Case No 40/61, *Attorney General v Eichmann*, Judgment 11 December 1961 Supreme Court of Israel, Case No 336/61, *Attorney General v Adolf Eichmann*, Judgment 29 May 1962	Nazi (1)	The accused had committed alleged crimes against the state's nationals and 'assault' against the state's 'existence'	World War II Treaties / Genocide Convention	Permissive	No
1988	Israel District Court of Jerusalem, Case No 373/86, *State of Israel v John (Ivan) Demjanjuk*, Judgment 25 April 1988	Nazi (1)	The accused had committed alleged crimes against the state's nationals and 'assault' against the state's 'existence'	World War II Treaties / Genocide Convention	Permissive	No

(continued)

Appendix 2 ***(Continued)***

Year	Prosecuting state	Number and nationality of the accused at the time the alleged offence was committed	Prosecuting state's territorial, personal or interest connection at the time of criminal proceedings	International law basis for jurisdiction	Exercise of jurisdiction permissive or mandatory	Possibility of extradition to a state or international criminal tribunal
1990	Canada Ontario Court of Appeal, Case No 574/90, *R v Finta* (1992), 53 OAC 1 (CA), Judgment 29 April 1992 Supreme Court of Canada, *R v Finta* [1994] 1 SCR 701, Judgment 24 March 1994	Nazi (1)	The accused had belonged to a former enemy and the alleged crimes occurred in Nazi occupied territory during World War II between 1939 and 1945. Additionally, the accused had subsequently acquired citizenship in Canada	World War II Treaties. Additionally, jurisdiction was based on the domestic law of Canada	Permissive	No
1993	Australia Supreme Court of South Australia, *Polyukhovich*, Judgment 18 May 1993, unreported High Court of Australia, *Polyukhovich v Commonwealth* [1991] HCA 32, Decision 14 August 1991	Nazi (1)	The accused had belonged to a former enemy and the alleged crimes occurred in Nazi occupied territory during World War II between 1939 and 1945. Additionally, the accused had subsequently acquired citizenship in Australia	World War II Treaties. Additionally, jurisdiction was based on the domestic law of Australia	Permissive	No
1994	Denmark Eastern Division of the Danish High Court, Case No S-3396-94, *Prosecution v Refik Sarić*, Judgment 25 November 1994	FY (1)	The accused had subsequently acquired residence in Denmark	Geneva Conventions	Mandatory	No

1995	Austria					
	District Court of Slazburg, *Public Prosecutor v Duško Cvjetković*, Judgment 31 May 1995, unreported Supreme Court of Austria, Case No 15Os 99/94, *Duško Cvjetković*, Judgment 13 July 1994	FY (1)	The accused had subsequently acquired residence in Austria	Genocide Convention. Additionally, jurisdiction was based on the principle of representation in the domestic law of Austria	Permissive	No
1997	Germany					
	Higher Regional Court of Bavaria, Case No 3 St 20/96, *Public Prosecutor v Novislav Djajić*, Judgment 23 May 1997	FY (1)	The accused had subsequently acquired permanent residence in Germany	Geneva Conventions	Mandatory	No
	Higher Regional Court of Düsseldorf, Case No IV-26/96 2 StE 8/96, *Nikolai Jorgić*, Judgment 26 September 1997 Federal Supreme Court, Case No 3 StR 215/98, *Nikolai Jorgić*, Judgment 30 April 1999 Federal Constitutional Court, Case No 2 BvR 1290/99, *Nikolai Jorgić*, Judgment 12 December 2000	FY (1)	The accused had permanently resided in Germany for more than 20 years prior to the commission of the alleged crimes	Genocide Convention. Additionally, jurisdiction was based on the principle of representation in the domestic law of Germany	Mandatory	No
	Switzerland					
	Lausanne Military Tribunal, Division I, *Gabrez*, Judgment 18 April 1997 Military Court of Cassation, *Gabrez*, Judgment 5 September 1997	FY (1)	The accused had subsequently acquired residence in Switzerland	Geneva Conventions / Additional Protocols I and II	Mandatory	No

(continued)

Appendix 2 ***(Continued)***

Year	Prosecuting state	Number and nationality of the accused at the time the alleged offence was committed	Prosecuting state's territorial, personal or interest connection at the time of criminal proceedings	International law basis for jurisdiction	Exercise of jurisdiction permissive or mandatory	Possibility of extradition to a state or international criminal tribunal
1999	Germany					
	Higher Regional Court of Dusseldorf, Case No IV 9/97 2 StE 6/97, *Maksim Sokolović*, Judgment 29 November 1999 Federal Supreme Court, Case No 3 StR 372/00, *Maksim Sokolović*, Judgment 21 February 2001	FY (1)	The accused was a permanent resident in Germany prior to the commission of the alleged crimes	Geneva Conventions	Mandatory	No
	Higher Regional Court of Bavaria, Case No 6 St 1/99, *Kjuradj Kusljić*, Judgment 15 December 1999 Federal Supreme Court, Case No 3 StR 244/00, *Kjuradj Kusljić*, Judgment 21 February 2001	FY (1)	The accused had resided in Germany for 20 years prior to the commission of the alleged crimes and received a German pension	Geneva Conventions	Mandatory	No
	Switzerland					
	Lausanne Military Tribunal, Division II, *Niyonteze*, Judgment 30 April 1999 Geneva Military Appeals Tribunal, *Niyonteze*, Judgment 26 May 2000 Military Court of Cassation, *Niyonteze*, Judgment 27 April 2001	Rwanda (1)	The accused had subsequently acquired citizenship in Switzerland	Geneva Conventions / Additional Protocol II	Mandatory	No

	UK Central Criminal Court of England and Wales, *R v Sawoniuk*, Judgment 1 April 1999, unreported Court of Appeal, Case No 1999/02465/X4, *R v Sawoniuk* [2000] EWCA Crim 9, Judgment 10 February 2000 ECtHR, *Sawoniuk v UK*, Application No 63716/00, Judgment 29 May 2001	Nazi (1)	The accused had belonged to a former enemy and the alleged crimes occurred in Nazi occupied territory during World War II between 1939 and 1945. Additionally, the accused had subsequently acquired citizenship in the UK	World War II Treaties. Additionally, jurisdiction was based on the domestic law of England and Wales	Permissive	No
2001	Belgium Assize Court of Brussels, *Public Prosecutor v Alphonse Higaniro, Vincent Ntezimana, Consolata Mukangango and Julienne Mukabutera*, Judgment 8 June 2001 (transcript of record on file with author)	Rwanda (4)	The accused had resided in Belgium prior to the commission of the alleged crimes. The alleged crimes involved the murder of Belgian nationals and 10 Belgian peacekeepers who were members of the UN Assistance Mission for Rwanda	Geneva Conventions / Additional Protocol II	Mandatory	No
2004	Netherlands District Court of Rotterdam, Case No AO7178, *Prosecutor v Nzapali*, Judgment 7 April 2004	Democratic Republic of the Congo (1)	The accused had subsequently acquired residence in the Netherlands	Convention against Torture	Mandatory	No
2005	Belgium Court of Assizes of the Administrative District of Brussels-Capital, *Étienne Nzabonimana* and *Samuel Ndashyikirwa*, Judgment 29 June 2005 (transcript of record on file with author)	Rwanda (2)	The accused had subsequently acquired residence in Belgium	Geneva Conventions / Additional Protocol II	Mandatory	No

(continued)

Appendix 2 ***(Continued)***

Year	Prosecuting state	Number and nationality of the accused at the time the alleged offence was committed	Prosecuting state's territorial, personal or interest connection at the time of criminal proceedings	International law basis for jurisdiction	Exercise of jurisdiction permissive or mandatory	Possibility of extradition to a state or international criminal tribunal
	France					
	Montpellier Court of Appeal, *Fédération Internationale des Ligues des Droits de l'Homme* et al *v Ould Dah*, Judgment 25 May 2001	Mauritania (1)	The alleged victims had subsequently acquired residence in France and the accused was present in France	Convention Against Torture	Mandatory	No
	Court of Cassation, Criminal Division, Case No 02-85379, *Ely Ould Dah*, Judgment 23 October 2002					
	Assize Court of Gard, Case Nos 70/05 and 71/05, *Ely Ould Dah*, Judgment 1 July 2005					
	ECtHR, *Ould Dah v France*, Application No 13113/03, Judgment 17 March 2009					
	Netherlands					
	District Court of the Hague, Case No 09/751005-04, *Public Prosecutor v Hesam* and *Jalalzoy*, Judgment 14 October 2005	Afghanistan (2)	The accused had subsequently acquired residence in the Netherlands	Geneva Conventions / Additional Protocol II	Mandatory	No

	Hague Court of Appeal, Case Nos 09-751004-04 and 09-750006-05, *Hesam* and *Jalalzoy*, Judgment 29 January 2007 Supreme Court of the Netherlands, Case Nos 07/10063 and 07/10064, *Hesam* and *Jalalazoy*, Judgment 8 July 2008					
	Spain National Court of Spain, Case No 16/2005, *Scilingo*, Judgment 19 April 2005 Supreme Court of Spain, Case No 798/2007, *Scilingo*, Judgment 1 October 2007	Argentina (1)	Spanish nationals were included among the victims of the alleged crimes	Genocide Convention	Mandatory	No
	UK Central Criminal Court of England and Wales, Case No T2203 7676, *R v Zardad*, Judgment 18 July 2005, unreported Court of Appeal, Case No 200505339/D3, *R v Zardad* [2007] EWCA Crim 279, Judgment 7 February 2007	Afghanistan (1)	The accused had subsequently acquired residence in the UK	Convention Against Torture	Mandatory	No
2007	Belgium Court of Assizes of the Administrative District of Brussels-Capital, *Bernard Ntuyahaga*, Judgment 5 July 2007 (transcript of record on file with author)	Rwanda (1)	The accused had resided in Belgium prior to the commission of the alleged crimes. The alleged crimes involved the murder of Belgian nationals and 10 Belgian peacekeepers who were members of the UN Assistance Mission for Rwanda	Geneva Conventions / Additional Protocol II	Mandatory	No

(continued)

Appendix 2 *(Continued)*

Year	Prosecuting state	Number and nationality of the accused at the time the alleged offence was committed	Prosecuting state's territorial, personal or interest connection at the time of criminal proceedings	International law basis for jurisdiction	Exercise of jurisdiction permissive or mandatory	Possibility of extradition to a state or international criminal tribunal
	Netherlands District Court of the Hague, Case No 09/750001-06, *Public Prosecutor v Abdullah*, Judgment 25 June 2007 Hague Court of Appeal, Case No 22-004581-07.a, *Abdullah*, Judgment 16 July 2009	Afghanistan (1)	The accused had subsequently acquired residence in the Netherlands	Geneva Conventions / Additional Protocol II	Mandatory	No
2008	France Court of Assizes of Bas-Rhin, Case No CA 08/36, *Khaled Ben Saïd*, Judgment 15 December 2008 Court of Assizes of the Meurthe-et-Moselle, Case No 73/2010, *Khaled Ben Saïd*, Judgment 24 September 2010	Tunisia (1)	The victim had subsequently acquired citizenship in France	Convention Against Torture	Mandatory	No
	Norway District Court of Oslo, Case No 08-018985MED-OTIR/08, *Public Prosecuting Authority v Mirsad Repak*, Judgment 2 December 2008 Supreme Court of Norway, Case No 2010/934, *Mirsad Repak*, Judgment 3 December 2010	Rwanda (1)	The accused had subsequently acquired citizenship in Norway	Geneva Conventions	Mandatory	No

2009	Belgium					
	Court of Assizes of the Administrative District of Brussels-Capital, *Ephrem Nkezabera*, Judgment 1 December 2009 (transcript of record on file with author)	Rwanda (1)	The accused had subsequently acquired residence in Belgium	Geneva Conventions / Additional Protocol II	Mandatory	No
	Canada					
	Superior Court, Criminal Division, *R v Désiré Munyaneza* 2009 QCCS 2201, Judgment 22 May 2009	Rwanda (1)	The accused had subsequently acquired residence in Canada	International Criminal Court Statute. Canada's domestic legislation implementing this treaty applies jurisdiction temporally to offences committed before the treaty was adopted and the legislation came into force	Mandatory	No
	Netherlands					
	District Court of the Hague, Case Nos 09/750009-06 and 09/750007-07, *Public Prosecutor v Joseph Mpambara*, Judgment 23 March 2009	Rwanda (1)	The accused had subsequently acquired residence in the Netherlands	Convention Against Torture	Mandatory	No

(continued)

Appendix 2 ***(Continued)***

Year	Prosecuting state	Number and nationality of the accused at the time the alleged offence was committed	Prosecuting state's territorial, personal or interest connection at the time of criminal proceedings	International law basis for jurisdiction	Exercise of jurisdiction permissive or mandatory	Possibility of extradition to a state or international criminal tribunal
2010	Finland District Court of Itä-Uusimaa, Case No R09/404, *Prosecutor v Francois Bazaramba*, Judgment 11 June 2010 Helsinki Court of Appeal, Case No R10/2555, *Francois Bazaramba*, Judgment 30 March 2012	Rwanda (1)	The accused had subsequently acquired residence in Finland	Genocide Convention. Additionally, jurisdiction was based on the principle of representation in the domestic law of Finland	Mandatory	No
2011	Sweden District Court of Stockholm, Case No B 382-10, *Ahmet Makitan*, Judgment 8 April 2011	FY (1)	The accused had subsequently acquired citizenship in Sweden	Geneva Conventions	Mandatory	No
2012	Sweden District Court of Stockholm, Case No B 5373-10, *Public Prosecutor v Milić Martinović* Judgment 20 January 2012 Svea Court of Appeal, Case No B 1248-12, *Milić Martinović*, Judgment 9 December 2012	FY (1)	The accused had subsequently acquired residence in Sweden	Geneva Conventions / Additional Protocol II	Mandatory	No

2013	Canada					
	Ontario Superior Court of Justice, *R v Jacques Mungwarere* 2013 ONCS 4594, Judgment 5 July 2013	Rwanda (1)	The accused had subsequently acquired citizenship in Canada	International Criminal Court Statute. Canada's domestic legislation implementing this treaty applies jurisdiction temporally to offences committed before the treaty was adopted and the legislation came into force	Mandatory	No
	Netherlands					
	District Court of the Hague, Case No 09/748004-09, *Public Prosecutor v Yvonne Basebya*, Judgment 1 March 2013	Rwanda (1)	The accused had subsequently acquired nationality in the Netherlands	Genocide Convention	Permissive	No
	Norway					
	District Court of Oslo, Case No TOSLO-2012-106377, *Public Prosecuting Authority v Sadi Bugingo*, Judgment 14 February 2013	Rwanda (1)	The accused had subsequently acquired citizenship in Norway	Genocide Convention	Mandatory	No
	Borgarting Court of Appeal, Case No LB-2013-41556, *Sadi Bugingo*, Judgment 16 January 2015					

(continued)

Appendix 2 *(Continued)*

Year	Prosecuting state	Number and nationality of the accused at the time the alleged offence was committed	Prosecuting state's territorial, personal or interest connection at the time of criminal proceedings	International law basis for jurisdiction	Exercise of jurisdiction permissive or mandatory	Possibility of extradition to a state or international criminal tribunal
	Sweden					
	District Court of Stockholm, Case No B 18271-11, *Prosecutor v Stanislas Mbanenande*, Judgment 20 June 2013 Svea Court of Appeal, Case No B 6659-13, *Stanislas Mbanenande*, Judgment 19 June 2014	Rwanda (1)	The accused had subsequently acquired citizenship in Sweden	Geneva Conventions / Additional Protocol II / Genocide Convention	Mandatory	No
2014	France					
	Assize Court of Paris, Case No 13/0033, *Public Prosecutor v Pascal Simbikangwa*, Judgment 14 March 2014 Assize Court of Appeal of Seine-Saint-Denis, Case No 51/2016, *Pascal Simbikangwa*, Judgment 3 December 2016	Rwanda (1)	The accused had subsequently acquired residence in France	International Criminal Tribunal for Rwanda Statute	Mandatory	No
	Germany					
	Higher Regional Court of Frankfurt, Case No 5-3 StE 4/10–4–3/10, *Onesphore Rwabukombe*, Judgment 18 February 2014 Higher Regional Court of Frankfurt am Main, Case No 4–3 StE 4/10–4–1/15, *Onesphore Rwabukombe*, Judgment 29 December 2015	Rwanda (1)	The accused had subsequently acquired nationality in Germany	Genocide Convention	Mandatory	No

2015	Germany					
	Higher Regional Court of Stuttgart, Case No 5-3 StE 6/10, Judgment 28 September 2015 Federal Court of Justice, Case No 3 StR 236/17, Judgment 20 December 2018	Rwanda (2)	The accused were long-term residents in Germany prior to the commission of the alleged crimes. The alleged crimes were committed in German territory	International Criminal Court Statute	Mandatory	No
	Sweden					
	District Court of Stockholm, Case No B 13656-14, *Prosecutor v Mouhannand Droubi*, Judgment 26 February 2015 District Court of Stockholm, Case No B 2639-16, *Prosecutor v Mouhannand Droubi*, Judgment 11 May 2016 (retrial) Svea Court of Appeal, Case No 4770-16, *Mouhannand Droubi*, Judgment 5 August 2016	Syria (1)	The accused had subsequently acquired permanent residence in Sweden	Geneva Conventions	Mandatory	No
2016	Austria					
	Regional Court of Linz, Judgment, 6 July 2016, unreported	FY (1)	The accused had subsequently acquired citizenship in Austria	Geneva Conventions	Mandatory	No
	Finland					
	District Court of Pirkanmaa, Case No R 16/1304, *Prosecutor v Ammar Jebbar-Salman*, Judgment, 18 March 2016	Iraq (1)	The accused had subsequently acquired residence in Finland	International Criminal Court Statute	Mandatory	No
	District Court of Kanta-Häme, Case No R 16/214, *Prosecutor v Hadi Habeeb Hilal*, Judgment 22 March 2016	Iraq (1)	The accused had subsequently acquired residence in Finland	International Criminal Court Statute	Mandatory	No

(continued)

Appendix 2 ***(Continued)***

Year	Prosecuting state	Number and nationality of the accused at the time the alleged offence was committed	Prosecuting state's territorial, personal or interest connection at the time of criminal proceedings	International law basis for jurisdiction	Exercise of jurisdiction permissive or mandatory	Possibility of extradition to a state or international criminal tribunal
	France					
	Assize Court of Paris, Case No 14/0044, *Octavien Ngenzi* and *Tito Barahira*, Judgment 6 July 2016 Assize Court of Appeal of Paris, Case No 16/066, *Octavien Ngenzi* and *Tito Barahira*, Judgment 6 July 2018	Rwanda (2)	The accused had subsequently acquired residence in France	International Criminal Tribunal for Rwanda Statute	Mandatory	No
	Senegal					
	Extraordinary African Chambers, *Minister of Public v Hissein Habré*, Judgment 30 May 2016 Appeals Chamber of the Extraordinary African Chambers, *The Prosecutor v Hissein Habré*, Decision 27 April 2017	Chad (1)	The accused had subsequently acquired residence in Senegal	Extraordinary African Chambers within the Courts of Senegal Statute	Mandatory	No
	Sweden					
	District Court of Stockholm, Case No B 12882-14, *Prosecutor v Claver Berikindi*, Judgment 16 May 2016 Svea Court of Appeal, Case No B 4951-16, *Claver Berikindi*, Judgment 15 February 2017	Rwanda (1)	The accused had subsequently acquired citizenship in Sweden	Genocide Convention / Geneva Conventions / Additional Protocol II	Mandatory	No

	Blekinge District Court, Case No B 569-16, *Prosecutor v Raed Thaer Abdulkareem*, Judgment 6 December 2016	Iraq (1)	The accused had subsequently acquired residence in Sweden	International Criminal Court Statute	Mandatory	No
	Scania and Blekinge Court of Appeal, Case No B 3187-16, *Raed Thaer Abdulkareem*, Judgment 11 April 2017					
	UK					
	Central Criminal Court of England and Wales, Case No 2013/05698, *R v Kumar Lama*, Judgment 7 September 2016	Nepal (1)	The accused had subsequently acquired residence in the UK	Convention Against Torture	Mandatory	No
2017	Austria					
	Regional Court of Innsbruck, Judgment 11 May 2017, unreported	Palestine (1)	The accused had subsequently acquired residence in Austria	Geneva Conventions	Mandatory	No
	Finland					
	District Court of Pirkanmaa, Case No 16/6930, *Prosecutor v Ahmad Shhab Hamad* and *Daham Shhab Hamad*, Judgment 24 May 2017	Iraq (2)	The accused had subsequently acquired residence in Finland	International Criminal Court Statute	Mandatory	No
	Appeal Court of Turku, Case No R 17/1229, *Ahmad Shhab Hamad* and *Daham Shhab Hamad*, Judgment 28 February 2020					

(continued)

Appendix 2 ***(Continued)***

Year	Prosecuting state	Number and nationality of the accused at the time the alleged offence was committed	Prosecuting state's territorial, personal or interest connection at the time of criminal proceedings	International law basis for jurisdiction	Exercise of jurisdiction permissive or mandatory	Possibility of extradition to a state or international criminal tribunal
	Germany					
	Higher Regional Court of Berlin, Case No (2A) 172 OJs 26/16 (3/16), *Prosecutor v Rami K*, Judgment 1 March 2017	Iraq (1)	The accused had subsequently acquired residence in Germany	International Criminal Court Statute	Mandatory	No
	Stuttgart Higher Regional Court, Case No 3 StE 5/16, *Prosecutor v Suliman Al-S*, Judgment 20 September 2017	Syria (1)	The accused had subsequently acquired residence in Germany	International Criminal Court Statute	Mandatory	No
	Netherlands					
	District Court of the Hague, Case No 09/748013-12, *Public Prosecutor v Eshetu Alemu*, Judgment 15 December 2017	Ethiopia (1)	The accused and some victims had subsequently acquired nationality in the Netherlands	Geneva Conventions / Additional Protocol II	Mandatory	No
	Sweden					
	District Court of Stockholm, Case No B 3787-16, *Prosecutor v Haisam Omar Sakhanh*, Judgment 16 February 2017	Syria (1)	The accused had subsequently acquired residence in Sweden	Geneva Conventions / Additional Protocol II	Mandatory	No

	District Court of Stockholm, Case No B 11191-17, *Prosecutor v Mohammad Abdullah*, Judgment 25 September 2017	Syria (1)	The accused had subsequently acquired permanent residence in Sweden	Geneva Conventions / Additional Protocol II	Mandatory	No
Total	17 states	62 trials				

Notes: The aim of this table is to identify (i) which states have exercised extraterritorial jurisdiction and brought trials to completion in respect of crimes against international law, the prosecution of which are supposed to be of equal concern to all states; (ii) the nationality of the accused at the time of the commission of the alleged crime; (iii) the territorial, personal or state interest connection at the time criminal proceedings were initiated; (iv) the international legal basis for the assertion of domestic jurisdiction (including, where applicable, in the opinion of national courts); (v) whether the exercise of jurisdiction was permissive or mandatory; and (vi) whether the accused could be extradited to another state or to an international criminal tribunal.

The term 'resident' in column four does not mean in all cases that a defendant resided in the territory of forum state lawfully; on the contrary, in several completed trials a defendant's asylum application was rejected but the defendant could not be extradited to the state where the alleged crime was committed or to an international criminal tribunal. The reference to the 'mandatory' exercise of jurisdiction in column six is because jurisdiction was obligatory pursuant to an applicable treaty or because a domestic court interpreted the relevant treaty regime as imposing such an obligation. For the purpose of this study, the term 'Nazi' is treated as a nationality and refers to individuals who committed crimes in Germany or territories occupied by Germany as Nazis or Nazi collaborators during the period of World War II. These individuals belonged to a 'common enemy' during the period of the war, in which the relevant prosecuting states were engaged, and subsequently acquired citizenship. The term 'former Yugoslav' (FY) is also treated as a nationality and refers to individuals who committed crimes during armed conflict in the territory of the former Socialist Federal Republic of Yugoslavia since 1 January 1991 and whose prosecution and punishment has been authorised by the UN Security Council under Chapter VII of the UN Charter. All international treaties in column five are detailed in Appendix 3. In this regard, 'World War II Treaties' in column five are numbered 1 and 2 in Appendix 3.

APPENDIX 3

List of Treaties Creating Extraterritorial Jurisdiction adopted between 1945 and 2017, in Chronological Order

Treaties creating obligatory extradition or prosecution jurisdiction, in various formulations, are in bold. The treaties identified with a star symbol enable states, either expressly in the treaty text or impliedly by means of treaty interpretation, to exercise extraterritorial jurisdiction when their nationals are the victims or the intended victims of the relevant substantive offences. Some states interpret the treaties listed in numbers 3–7 and 13 as permitting or mandating extraterritorial jurisdiction over the relevant substantive offences, even though the treaty text does not expressly refer to extraterritorial jurisdiction.

1. Charter of the International Military Tribunal at Nuremberg, annexed to Agreement for the Prosecution and Punishment of the Major War Criminals of the European Axis 1945, 82 UNTS 280
2. Law No 10 of the Control Council of Germany 1945, (1946) 3 Official Gazette Control Council for Germany 50
3. *Convention on the Prevention and Punishment of the Crime of Genocide 1948, 78 UNTS 277
4. ***Geneva Convention (I) for the Amelioration of the Condition of the Wounded and Sick in Armed Forces in the Field 1949, 75 UNTS 31**
5. ***Geneva Convention (II) for the Amelioration of the Condition of Wounded, Sick and Shipwrecked Members of Armed Forces at Sea 1949, 75 UNTS 85**
6. ***Geneva Convention (III) Relative to the Treatment of Prisoners of War 1949, 75 UNTS 135**
7. ***Geneva Convention (IV) Relative to the Protection of Civilian Persons in Time of War 1949, 75 UNTS 287**
8. *Convention on Offences and Certain Other Acts Committed on Board Aircraft 1963, 704 UNTS 219
9. **Convention for Suppression of Unlawful Seizure of Aircraft 1970, 860 UNTS 105**
10. **Convention for the Suppression of Unlawful Acts against the Safety of Civil Aviation 1971, 974 UNTS 177**

11. **OAS Convention to Prevent and Punish Acts of Terrorism Taking the Form of Crimes against Persons and Related Extortion That Are of International Significance 1971, 1438 UNTS 191**
12. ***Convention on the Prevention and Punishment of Crimes against Internationally Protected Persons, Including Diplomatic Agents 1973, 1035 UNTS 167**
13. Protocol Relating to the Protection of Victims of Non-International Armed Conflicts 1977, 1125 UNTS 609
14. ***International Convention against the Taking of Hostages 1979, 1316 UNTS 205**
15. ***Convention against Torture and Other Cruel, Inhuman or Degrading Treatment or Punishment 1984, 1465 UNTS 85**
16. **United Nations Convention against Illicit Traffic in Narcotic Drugs and Psychotropic Substances 1988, 1582 UNTS 95**
17. ***Convention for the Suppression of Unlawful Acts of Violence against the Safety of Maritime Navigation 1988, 1678 UNTS 221**
18. **Protocol for the Suppression of Unlawful Acts of Violence at Airports Serving International Civil Aviation 1988, 1589 UNTS 474**
19. ***Protocol for the Suppression of Unlawful Acts against the Safety of Fixed Platforms Located on the Continental Shelf 1988, 1678 UNTS 304**
20. ***Convention on the Safety of United Nations and Associated Personnel 1994, 2051 UNTS 363**
21. Statute of the International Criminal Tribunal for Rwanda, annexed to UNSC Res 955 (8 November 1994) UN Doc S/RES/955
22. ***International Convention for the Suppression of Terrorist Bombings 1997, 2149 UNTS 256**
23. Rome Statute of the International Criminal Court 1998, 2187 UNTS 3
24. ***International Convention for the Suppression of the Financing of Terrorism 1999, 2178 UNTS 197**
25. ***OAU Convention on the Prevention and Combating of Terrorism 1999, 2219 UNTS 208**
26. ***Optional Protocol to the Convention on the Rights of the Child on the Sale of Children, Child Prostitution and Child Pornography 2000, 2171 UNTS 227**
27. ***United Nations Convention against Transnational Organized Crime 2000, 2225 UNTS 209**
28. ***Protocol to Prevent, Suppress and Punish Trafficking in Persons, Especially Women and Children, supplementing the United Nations Convention against Transnational Organized Crime 2000, 2237 UNTS 319**
29. ***Protocol against the Smuggling of Migrants by Land, Sea and Air, supplementing the United Nations Convention against Transnational Organized Crime 2000, 2241 UNTS 507**

30. ***Protocol against the Illicit Manufacturing of and Trafficking in Firearms, Their Parts and Components and Ammunition, supplementing the United Nations Convention against Transnational Organized Crime 2001, 2326 UNTS 208**
31. ***United Nations Convention against Corruption 2003, 2349 UNTS 41**
32. **International Convention for the Suppression of Nuclear Terrorism 2005, 2445 UNTS 89**
33. ***Protocol of 2005 to the Convention for the Suppression of Unlawful Acts against the Safety of Maritime Navigation 2005, IMO Doc LEG/CONF.15/21**
34. **Protocol of 2005 to the Protocol for the Suppression of Unlawful Acts against the Safety of Fixed Platforms Located on the Continental Shelf 2005, IMO Doc LEG/CONF.15/22**
35. ***International Convention for the Protection of All Persons from Enforced Disappearance 2006, 2716 UNTS 3**
36. **Association of Southeast Asian Nations Convention on Counter-Terrorism 2007, 3200 UNTS 1**
37. ***Shanghai Cooperation Organization Convention against Terrorism 2009, 2815 UNTS 69**
38. ***Convention on the Suppression of Unlawful Acts Relating to International Civil Aviation 2010, ICAO Doc 9960**
39. ***Protocol Supplementary to the Convention for the Suppression of Unlawful Seizure of Aircraft 2010, ICAO Doc 9959**
40. Statute of the Extraordinary African Chambers within the Courts of Senegal Created to Prosecute International Crimes Committed in Chad between 7 June 1982 and 1 December 1998, annexed to Agreement on the Establishment of the Extraordinary African Chambers within the Courts of Senegal Between the Government of the Republic of Senegal and the African Union 2012
41. Protocol to Amend the Convention on Offences and Certain Other Acts Committed on Board Aircraft 2014, ICAO Doc 10034
42. **European Convention on Offences relating to Cultural Property 2017, CETS No 221**

INDEX

J

www.ingramcontent.com/pod-product-compliance
Ingram Content Group UK Ltd.
Pitfield, Milton Keynes, MK11 3LW, UK
UKHW020232290926
15470UKWH00002B/494

9 781509 954223